States and Societies

This reader is part of an integrated package of teaching materials designed for students of the Open University course D209 *The State and Society*. The opinions expressed in it are not necessarily those of the course team or of the University.

States and Societies

Edited by David Held
James Anderson
Bram Gieben
Stuart Hall
Laurence Harris
Paul Lewis
Noel Parker
Ben Turok

Martin Robertson . Oxford
in association with
The Open University

First published in 1983 by Martin Robertson &
Company Ltd, 108 Cowley Road, Oxford OX4 1JF.

British Library Cataloguing in Publication Data

States and societies.
1. State, The
I. Held, David *1947–*
320.1   JC11

ISBN 0-85520-658-6
ISBN 0-85520-695-4 pbk

Typeset by Pioneer, East Sussex
Printed and bound in Great Britain by
Billing and Sons Ltd., Worcester

Contents

Preface

The state is not a unified entity. It is a multi-dimensional phenomenon, the nature of which varies across time and space. Any attempt to understand the state must consider its spatial and temporal dimensions — the horizontal 'stretch' of the state across territory (from Empires to nation-states), the depth of state intervention in social and economic life, and the changing form of all these things over time. There have been many different kinds of state, and each type has had a different mix of institutions and relations.

In the first instance, this book focuses on the modern state — that type of state which emerged with the early development of the European state system from the sixteenth century. Secondly, it examines the modern state through both historical and contemporary lenses. We cannot know what kind of thing the modern state is unless we understand its development. Thirdly, we bring a number of distinct approaches — political, economic, philosophical and sociological — to bear on these questions.

While the focus of this book is squarely on 'the' modern state it is also on 'society'. To link two such ambiguous concepts together risks making the object of inquiry almost infinitely large. The problem is that the state is enmeshed in society; in a sense, it is constituted by society, and society in turn is shaped by the state. But the fact that 'state' and 'society' are inextricably bound together does not mean of course that we cannot for analytical purposes distinguish particular aspects for attention.

Accordingly, in the Introduction an account is offered of some of the key ideas that crop up again and again in the analysis of states. Part 1 offers extracts from a selection of the many writings that over four centuries have defined the terms of reference of debates about the state. The second part presents a series of chapters which examine the formation of modern states in a range of different types of society. The chapters in Part 3 raise questions about the representative and interventionist aspects of states, highlighting especially the significance of citizenship and the relation between 'public' and 'private' life. Part 4 brings together chapters on the relation between the state and the economy in capitalist and socialist societies; while Part 5 explores the interaction of power and legitimacy in diverse countries. The chapters in Part 6 explore the relation between states and the world economy, setting out the relations of power and dependence that exist, as well as the character of the arms race between the superpowers. Finally, in Part 7, issues are raised about future directions for the state from a variety of political perspectives. Each part has an introduction by one of the editors sketching its themes and explaining the rationale for the selection of material.

In preparing this volume we have had inevitably to shorten some articles (and indeed books!) in the interests of presenting as comprehensive a selection of materials as we could. Because the contributions are all from original articles and books, this, like any Reader, cannot be a substitute for reading the originals. We hope that the extracts stimulate enough interest to encourage readers to turn to the originals in the areas that most excite them, while giving a useful self-contained introduction to other areas. Editorial cuts are shown in two ways. If a cut is just a matter of a few words it is marked by three dots . . . ; if it involves anything more substantial it is marked by three dots in square brackets: [. . .]. Editors' comments are marked in square brackets thus: [Eds' comments], and editors' italic emphasis thus: [Eds' emphasis].

This collection of readings was prepared for an Open University course (D209), and thus is only part of an integrated package of teaching texts, television programmes, radio broadcasts and tape cassettes. However, the editors hope it will be of wide interest, not only to students in the social sciences and humanities, but also to those who have a general interest in the nature of the state. We think it is a valuable source book for anyone interested in this central area of contemporary discussion and research.

In preparing this work we have received advice from several people and taxed the patience of many more. We should like to thank the following for all their help: David Beetham, Bob Jessop, John Keane, Anthony Giddens, Joan Higgs, Yvonne Honeywell, Carol Smith, Iris Manzi, Grahame Thompson, Greg McLennan, Tony Walton, Allan Cochrane, and other members of the Open University Course Team.

The Editors

Introduction: Central Perspectives on the Modern State

DAVID HELD

The state — or apparatus of 'government' — appears to be everywhere, regulating the conditions of our lives from birth registration to death certification. Yet, the nature of the state is hard to grasp. This may seem peculiar for something so pervasive in public and private life, but it is precisely this pervasiveness which makes it difficult to understand. There is nothing more central to political and social theory than the nature of the state, and nothing more contested. It is the objective of this Introduction to set out some of the key elements of the conflict of interpretation.[1]

In modern Western political thought, the idea of the state is often linked to the notion of an impersonal and privileged legal or constitutional order with the capability of administering and controlling a given territory.[2] This notion found its earliest expression in the ancient world (especially in Rome) but it did not become a major object of concern until the early development of the European state system from the sixteenth century onwards. It was not an element of medieval political thinking. The idea of an impersonal and sovereign political order, i.e. a legally circumscribed structure of power with supreme jurisdiction over a territory, could not predominate while political rights, obligations and duties were closely tied to property rights and religious tradition. Similarly, the idea that human beings as 'individuals' or as 'a people' could be active citizens of this order — citizens of their state — and not merely dutiful subjects of a monarch or emperor could not develop under such conditions.

Specially commissioned for this volume
© The Open University 1983

The historical changes that contributed to the transformation of medieval notions of political life were immensely complicated. Struggles between monarchs and barons over the domain of rightful authority; peasant rebellions against the weight of excess taxation and social obligation; the spread of trade, commerce and market relations; the flourishing of Renaissance culture with its renewed interest in classical political ideas (including the Greek city-state and Roman law); the consolidation of national monarchies in central and southern Europe (England, France and Spain); religious strife and the challenge to the universal claims of Catholicism; the struggle between Church and State — all played a part.[3] As the grip of feudal traditions and customs was loosened, the nature and limits of political authority, law, rights and obedience emerged as a preoccupation of European political thought. Not until the end of the sixteenth century did the concept of the state become a central object of political analysis.

While the works of Niccolo Machiavelli (1469–1527) and Jean Bodin (1530–96) are of great importance in these developments, Thomas Hobbes (1588–1679) directly expressed the new concerns when he stated in *De Cive* (1642) that it was his aim 'to make a more curious search into the rights of states and duties of subjects'.[4] Until challenged by, among others, Karl Marx in the nineteenth century, the idea of the modern state came to be associated with a 'form of public power separate from both the ruler and ruled, and constituting the supreme political authority within a certain defined boundary'.[5] But the nature of that public power and its relationship to ruler and ruled were the subject of controversy and uncertainty. The following questions arose: What is the state? What should it be? What are its origins and foundations? What is the relationship between state and society? What is the most desirable form this relationship might take? What does and should the state do? Whose interest does and should the state represent? How might one characterize the relations among states?

This essay focuses on four strands or traditions of political analysis which sought to grapple with such questions: (1) *liberalism*, which became absorbed with the question of sovereignty and citizenship; (2) *liberal democracy*, which developed liberalism's concerns while focusing on the problem of establishing political accountability; (3) *Marxism*, which rejected the terms of reference of both liberalism and liberal democracy and concentrated upon class structure and the forces of political coercion; and (4), for want of a more satisfactory label, *political sociology*, which has, from Max Weber to Anglo-American pluralism and 'geopolitical' conceptions of the state, elaborated concerns with both the institutional mechanisms of the state and the system of nation-states more generally. None of these traditions of analysis, it should be stressed, forms a unity; that is to say, each is a heterogeneous body of thought encompassing interesting points of divergence. There is also some common ground, more noticeable in the work of contemporary figures, across these separate traditions. I shall attempt to indicate this briefly throughout the essay and in my concluding remarks. It is important to appreciate that, in a field in which there is as vast a range of literature as this, any selection has an arbitrary element to it. But I hope to introduce some of the central perspectives on the modern state.

A distinction is often made between normative political theory or political philosophy on the one hand, and the descriptive-explanatory theories of the social sciences on the other. The former refers to theories about the proper form of political organization and includes accounts of such notions as liberty and equality. The latter refers to attempts to characterize actual phenomena and events and is marked by a strong empirical element. The distinction, thus, is between theories which focus on what is desirable, what should or ought to be the case, and those that focus on what is the case. The political writings of people like Hobbes, Locke, and Mill are generally placed in the first camp, while those of, for instance, Weber are put in the second; Marx occupying sometimes one domain, sometimes the other, depending on the writings one examines. But it will become clear that, while this distinction should be borne in mind, it is hard to use it as a classificatory device for theories of the state. For many political philosophers see what they think the state ought to be like in the state as it is. Social scientists, on the other hand, cannot escape the problem that facts do not simply 'speak for themselves': they are, and they have to be, interpreted; and the framework we bring to the process of interpretation determines what we 'see', what we notice and register as important.

The essay begins with the thought of Hobbes which marks a point of transition between a commitment to the absolutist state and the struggle of liberalism against tyranny. It is important to be clear about the meaning of 'liberalism'.[6] While it is a highly controversial concept, and its meaning has shifted historically, I will use it here to signify the attempt to define a private sphere independent of the state and thus to redefine the state itself, i.e, the freeing of civil society — personal, family and business life — from political interference and the simultaneous delimitation of the state's authority. With the growing division between the state and civil society, a division which followed the expansion of market economies, the struggle for a range of freedoms and rights which were in principle to be universal became more acute. Gradually, liberalism became associated with the doctrine that freedom of choice should be applied to matters as diverse as marriage, religion, economic and political affairs — in fact, to everything that affected daily life.[7] Liberalism upheld the values of reason and toleration in the face of tradition and absolutism.[8] In this view, the world consists of 'free and equal' individuals with natural rights. Politics should be about the defence of the rights of these individuals — a defence which must leave them in a position to realize their own capacities. The mechanisms for regulating individuals' pursuit of their interests were to be the constitutional state, private property, the competitive market economy — and the distinctively patriarchal family. While liberalism celebrated the rights of individuals to 'life, liberty and property', it should be noted from the outset that it was generally the male property-owning individual who was the focus of so much attention; and the new freedoms were first and foremost for the men of the new middle classes or the bourgeoisie. The Western world was liberal first, and only later, after extensive conflicts, liberal democratic or democratic; that is, only later was a universal franchise won which allowed all mature adults the chance to express their judgment about the performance of those who govern them.[9] But even now, the very meanings of the terms 'liberalism' and 'democracy' remain unsettled.

Sovereignty, citizenship and the development of liberalism

Hobbes was among the first to try to grasp the nature of public power as a special kind of institution — as he put it, an 'Artificiall Man', defined by permanence and sovereignty, the authorized representative 'giving life and motion' to society and the body politic.[10] He was preoccupied, above all, with the problem of order, which resolved itself into two questions: Why is 'a great LEVIATHAN or STATE' necessary? and What form should the state take? Through a theory of human nature, sovereign authority and political obligation, he sought to prove that the state must be regarded as ultimately both absolute and legitimate, in order that the worst of evils — civil war — might be permanently averted.[11]

In so arguing, Hobbes produced a political philosophy which is a fascinating point of departure for reflection on the modern theory of the state; for it is at once a profoundly liberal and illiberal view.[12] It is liberal because Hobbes derives or explains the existence of society and the state by reference to 'free and equal' individuals, the component elements, according to him, of social life — 'men as if but even now sprung out of the earth and suddenly, like mushrooms, come to full maturity, without all kind of engagement to each other.'[13] It is liberal because Hobbes is concerned to uncover the best circumstances for human nature — understood as naturally selfish, egoistical and self-interested — to find expression. And it is liberal because it emphasizes the importance of consent in the making of a contract or bargain, not only to regulate human affairs and secure a measure of independence and choice in society, but also to legitimate, i.e. justify, such regulation. Yet Hobbes's position is also, as I shall attempt to show, profoundly illiberal: his political conclusions emphasize the necessity of a practically all-powerful state to create the laws and secure the conditions of social and political life. Hobbes remains of abiding interest today precisely because of this tension between the claims of individuality on the one hand, and the power requisite for the state to ensure 'peaceful and commodious living', on the other.[14]

In *Leviathan* (1651), Hobbes set out his argument in a highly systematic manner. Influenced by Galileo, he was concerned to build his 'civil science' upon clear principles and closely reasoned deductions. He started from a set of postulates and observations about human nature. Human beings, Hobbes contended, are moved by desires and aversions which generate a state of perpetual restlessness. Seeking always 'more intense delight', they are profoundly self-interested; a deep-rooted psychological egoism limits the possibilities for human cooperation. In order to fulfil their desires, human beings (though in different ways and degrees) seek power. And because the power gained by one 'resisteth and hindreth the power of another', conflicts of interest are inevitable: they are a fact of nature. The struggle for power, for no other reason than self-preservation and self-interest (however disguised by rationalization) defines the human condition. Hobbes thus emphasizes 'a generall inclination of all mankind, a perpetuall and restlesse desire of Power after power, that ceaseth only in Death'.[15] The idea that human beings might come to respect and trust one another, treat each other as if they could keep promises and honour contracts, seems remote indeed.

Hobbes desired to show, however, that a consistent concern with self-interest does not simply lead to an endless struggle for power.[16] In order to prove this he introduced a 'thought experiment' employing four interrelated concepts: state of nature, right of nature, law of nature and social contract. He imagined a situation in which individuals are in a state of nature — that is, a situation without a 'Common Power' or state to enforce rules and restrain behaviour — enjoying 'natural rights' to use all means to protect their lives and to do whatever they wish, against whoever they like and to 'possess, use, and enjoy all that he would, or could get'.[17] The result is a constant struggle for survival: Hobbes's famous 'Warre of every one against every one'. In this state of nature individuals discover that life is 'solitary, poore, nasty, brutish and short' and, accordingly, that to avoid harm and the risk of an early death, let alone to ensure the conditions of greater comfort, the observation of certain natural laws or rules is required.[18] The latter are things the individual ought to adhere to in dealings with others if there is sufficient ground for believing that others will do likewise.[19] Hobbes says of these laws that 'they have been contracted into one easy sum, intelligible even to the meanest capacity; and that is, *Do not that to another which thou wouldest not have done to thyself*'.[20] There is much in what he says about laws of nature that is ambiguous (above all, their relation to the 'will of God'), but these difficulties need not concern us here. For the key problem, in Hobbes's view, is: under what conditions will individuals trust each other enough to 'lay down their right to all things' so that their long-term interest in security and peace can be upheld? How can individuals make a bargain with one another when it may be, in certain circumstances, in some people's interest to break it? An agreement between people to ensure the regulation of their lives is necessary, but it seems an impossible goal.

His argument, in short, is as follows: if individuals surrender their rights by transferring them to a powerful authority which can force them to keep their promises and covenants, then an effective and legitimate private and public sphere, society and state, can be formed. Thus the social contract consists in individuals handing over their rights of self-government to a single authority — thereafter authorized to act on their behalf — on the condition that every individual does the same. A unique relation of authority results: the relation of sovereign to subject. A unique political power is created: the exercise of sovereign power or sovereignty — the authorized (hence rightful) use of power by the person or assembly established as sovereign.[21] The sovereign's subjects have an obligation and duty to obey the sovereign; for the position 'sovereign' is the product of their social contract, and 'sovereignty' is above all a quality of the position rather than of the person who occupies it. The contract is a once-and-for-all affair, creating an authority able to determine the very nature and limits of the law.

There can be no conditions placed on such authority because to do so would undermine its very *raison d'être*.

The sovereign has to have sufficient power to make agreements stick, to enforce contracts, and to ensure that the laws governing political and economic life are upheld. Power must be effective. Since, in Hobbes's view, 'men's ambitions, avarice, anger and other passions' are strong, the 'bonds of words are too weak to bridle them . . . without some fear of coercive power'.[22] In short: 'covenants, without the sword, are but words, and of no strength to secure a man at all'.[23] Beyond the sovereign state's sphere of influence there will always be the chaos of constant warfare; but within the territory controlled by the state, with 'fear of some coercive power', social order can be sustained.

It is important to stress that, in Hobbes's opinion, while sovereignty must be self-perpetuating, undivided and ultimately absolute, it is established by the authority conferred by the people.[24] The sovereign's right of command and the subjects' duty of obedience is the result of consent — the circumstances individuals would have agreed to if there had actually been a social contract. Although there is little about Hobbes's conception of the state which today we would call representative, he argues in fact that the people rule through the sovereign. The sovereign is their representative: 'A Multitude of men, are made *One* Person, when they are by one man, or one Person, Represented'.[25] Through the sovereign a plurality of voices and interests can become 'one will', and to speak of a sovereign state assumes, Hobbes held, such a unity. Hence, his position is at one with all those who argue for the importance of government by consent and reject the claims of the 'divine right of Kings' and, more generally, the authority of tradition. Yet, his conclusions run wholly counter to those who often take such an argument to imply the necessity of some kind of popular sovereignty or democratic representative government.[26] Hobbes was trying to acknowledge, and persuade his contemporaries to acknowledge, a full obligation to a sovereign state. As one commentator usefully put it:

> Hobbes was not asking his contemporaries to make a contract, but only to acknowledge the same obligation they would have had if they had made such a contract. He was speaking not to men in a state of nature, but to men in an imperfect political society, that is to say, in a society which did not guarantee security of life and commodious living (as witness its tendency to lapse into civil war). He was telling them what

they must do to establish a more nearly perfect political society, one that would be permanently free from internal disturbance.[27]

A strong secular state was offered as the most effective, appropriate and legitimate political form. The right of citizens to change their ruler(s) was, accordingly, regarded as superfluous.

The fundamental purpose of sovereignty is to ensure 'the *safety of the people*'. By 'safety' is meant not merely minimum physical preservation. The sovereign must ensure the protection of all things held in property: 'Those that are dearest to a man are his own life, and limbs; and in the next degree, (in most men) those that concern conjugall affection; and after them riches and means of living'.[28] Moreover, the sovereign must educate the people to respect all these kinds of property so that men can pursue their trades and callings, and industry and the polity can flourish. At this point Hobbes suggests certain limits to the range of the sovereign's actions: the sovereign should neither injure individuals nor the basis of their material wellbeing, and should recognize that authority can be sustained only so long as protection can be afforded to all subjects.[29]

There are a number of particularly noteworthy things about Hobbes's conception of the state. First, the state is regarded as pre-eminent in political and social life. While individuals exist prior to the formation of civilized society and to the state itself, it is the latter that provides the conditions of existence of the former. The state alters a miserable situation for human beings by changing the conditions under which they pursue their interests. The state constitutes society through the powers of command of the sovereign (set down in the legal system) and through the capacity of the sovereign to enforce the law (established by the fear of coercive power). The state does not simply record or reflect socio-economic reality, it enters into its very construction by establishing its form and codifying its forces. Second, it is the self-seeking nature of individuals' behaviour and patterns of interaction that makes the indivisible power of the state necessary. The sovereign state must be able to act decisively to counter the threat of anarchy. Hence it must be powerful and capable of acting as a single force. Third, the state, and practically all it does, can and must be considered legitimate. For the 'thought experiment', drawing on the notions of a state of nature and social contract, shows how individuals with their own divergent interests come to commit themselves to the idea that only a great Leviathan or state or 'Mortall God' can articulate and defend the 'general' or 'public' interest. The sovereign state represents 'the public' — the sum of individual interests — and thus can create the conditions for individuals to live their lives and to go about their competitive and acquisitive business peacefully. Hobbes's argument recognizes the importance of public consent (although he was not always consistent about its significance), and concludes that it is conferred by the social contract and its covenants.

Hobbes's arguments are extraordinarily impressive. The image of an all-powerful Leviathan is a remarkably contemporary one; after all, most states in the twentieth century have been run by 'Mortall Gods', people with seemingly unlimited authority backed by the armed forces. (Consider the number of dictatorships that now exist.) Moreover, the idea that individuals are merely self-interested is also a depressingly modern one. Such a conception of human beings is presupposed in the economic and political doctrines of many writers today.[30] But the impressiveness of some of Hobbes's views should not of course be confused with their acceptability. Hobbes's account, for example, of sovereignty, obligation and the duties of citizens are all contestable, as are his general doctrines about human nature. The constitutive role of the state (the degree to which the state forms society), coercive power (the degree to which such power is or must be central to political order), representation (the degree to which a sovereign authority can claim to articulate the public interest without forms of democratic accountability), and legitimacy (the degree to which states are considered just or worthy by their citizens) — all have been and still are subject to debate.

John Locke (1632–1704) raised a fundamental objection to the Hobbesian argument that individuals could only find a 'peaceful and commodious' life with one another if they were governed by the dictates of an indivisible sovereign. He said of this type of argument: 'This is to think that Men are so foolish that they take care to avoid what Mischiefs may be done them by *Pole-Cats*, or *Foxes*, but are content, nay think it Safety, to be devoured by Lions'.[31] In other words, it is hardly credible that people who do not fully trust each other would place their trust in an all-powerful ruler to look after their interests. What obstacles are there to the potential 'violence and oppression', as Locke put it, 'of this Absolute Ruler'?[32] What would make such a system of rule compelling and trustworthy?

Locke approved of the revolution and settlement of 1688, which imposed certain constitutional limits on the authority of the Crown. He rejected the notion of a great Leviathan, pre-eminent in all social spheres, an uncontested unity establishing and enforcing law according to the sovereign's will. For Locke, the state (he spoke more often of 'government') can and should be conceived as an 'instrument' for the defence of the 'life, liberty and estate' of its citizens; that is, the state's *raison d'être* is the protection of individuals' rights as laid down by God's will and as enshrined in law.[33] Society, conceived of as the sum of individuals, exists prior to the state, and the state is established to guide society. He placed a strong emphasis on the importance of government by consent — consent which could be revoked if the government and its deputies fail to sustain the 'good of the governed'. Legitimate government requires the consent of its citizens, and government can be dissolved if the trust of the people is violated. What Locke meant by 'consent' is controversial,[34] but whatever position one takes on this question the contrast between the views of Locke and Hobbes remains remarkable. Moreover, while Locke did not develop a systematic doctrine about the desirability of a mixed form of government or a division of powers within the state, he has been associated for many generations with such a view.[35] He accepted that the state should have supreme jurisdiction over its territory, but was critical of the notion of the indivisibility of state power and suggested an important alternative conception.

It is interesting that the idea of social contract and the state of nature can yield a variety of political positions. Locke, like Hobbes, saw the establishment of the political world as preceded by the existence of individuals endowed with natural rights. Locke, like Hobbes, was concerned to derive and explain the very possibility of government. Locke, like Hobbes, was concerned about what form legitimate government should take and about the conditions for security, peace and freedom. But the way in which he conceived these things was considerably different. In the important second of the *Two Treatises of Government* (which was published for the first time in 1690), Locke starts with the proposition that individuals are originally in a state of nature, a '*State of perfect Freedom* to order their Actions, and dispose of their Possessions, and Persons as they think fit, within the bounds of the Law of Nature, without asking leave, or depending upon the will of any other Man'.[36] The state of nature is a state of liberty but not 'a state of license'. Individuals are bound by duty to God and governed only by the law of nature. The law of nature (the precise meaning of which is difficult to pin down in the *Two Treatises*) specifies basic principles of morality — individuals should not take their own lives, they should try to preserve each other and should not infringe upon one another's liberty. The law can be grasped by human reason but it is the creation of God, the 'infinitely wise Maker'.[37]

Humans — in fact, Locke spoke here only of men — are free and equal because reason makes them capable of rationality, of following the law of nature. They enjoy natural rights. The right of governing one's affairs and enforcing the law of nature against transgressors is presupposed, as is the obligation to respect the rights of others. Individuals have the right to dispose of their own labour and to possess property. The right to property is a right to 'life, liberty and estate'.[38] (Locke also uses 'property' in a narrower sense to mean just the exclusive use of objects.[39])

Adherence to the law of nature, according to Locke, ensures that the state of nature is not a state of war. However, the natural rights of individuals are not always safeguarded in the state of nature for certain 'inconveniences' exist: not all individuals fully respect the rights of others; when it is left to each individual to enforce the law of nature there are too many judges and hence conflicts of interpretation about the meaning of the law; and when people are loosely organized they are vulnerable to aggression from abroad.[40] The central 'inconvenience' suffered can be summarized as the inadequate regulation of property in its broad sense, the right to 'life, liberty and estate'.[41] Property is prior to both society and the state; and the difficulty of its regulation is the critical reason which compels 'equally free men' to the establishment of both. Thus the remedy for the inconveniences of the state of nature is an agreement or contract to create, first, an independent society and, second, a political society or government.[42] The distinction between these two agreements is important, for it makes clear that authority is bestowed by individuals in society on government for the purpose of pursuing the ends of the governed; and should these ends fail to be adequately represented, the final judges are the people — the citizens of the state — who can dispense both with their deputies and, if need be, with the existing form of government itself.

In Locke's opinion, it should be stressed, the formation of the state does not signal the transfer of all subjects' rights to the state.[43] The rights of law making and enforcement (legislative and executive rights) are transferred, but the whole process is conditional upon the state adhering to its essential purpose: the preservation of 'life, liberty and estate'. Sovereign power, i.e. sovereignty, remains ultimately with the people. The legislative body enacts rules as the people's agent in accordance with the law of nature, and the executive power (to which Locke also tied the judiciary) enforces the legal system. This separation of powers was important because:

> It may be too great a temptation to humane frailty apt to grasp at Power, for the same Persons who have the Power of making Laws, to have also in their hands the power to execute them, whereby they may exempt themselves from Obedience to the Laws they make, and suit the Law, both in its making and execution, to their own private advantage, and thereby come to have a distinct interest from the rest of the community, contrary to the end of Society and Government.[44]

Thus, an absolutist state and the arbitrary use of authority are inconsistent with the integrity and ultimate ends of society. Locke believed in the desirability of a constitutional monarchy holding executive power and a parliamentary assembly holding the rights of legislation, although he did not think this was the only form government might take and his views are compatible with a variety of other conceptions of political institutions. Moreover, it is not always clear who was qualified to vote for the assembly: it sometimes appears simply as if 'the people' (minus women and slaves of both sexes!) are entitled, but it is almost certain that Locke would not have dissented from a franchise based strictly on property holding.[45]

The government rules, and its legitimacy is sustained, by the 'consent' of individuals. 'Consent' is a crucial and difficult notion in Locke's writings. It could be interpreted to suggest that only the continually active personal agreement of individuals would be sufficient to ensure a duty of obedience, i.e. to ensure a government's authority and legitimacy.[46] However, as one critic aptly put it, 'Locke took much of the sting (and interest) out of this view by his doctrine of "tacit consent", according to which individuals may be said to have consented to a government in any society subsequent to the supposed contract simply by owning property, or by "lodging only for a week", by "travelling freely on the highway" and indeed even by being "within the territories of that government".'[47] Locke seems to have thought of the active consent of individuals as having been crucial only to the initial inauguration of a legitimate state. Thereafter consent follows from majority decisions of 'the people's' representatives and from the fact of adherence or acquiescence to the legal system; for what property now is, and what protection and security people can enjoy, is specified by law.[48] The government, by virtue of the original contract and its covenants, is bound by the law of nature and, thus, bound to guarantee 'life, liberty and estate'. The price of this is a duty to obey the law, an obligation to the state, unless the law of nature is consistently violated by a series of tyrannical political actions. Should such a situation occur, rebellion to form a new government, Locke contended, might not only be unavoidable but just.

One commentator has summarized Locke's views well:

> God, the Creator, determined the ends of man, his creature . . . God gave men reason to understand their situation on earth and, above all, their duty within this situation. He gave them senses as channels through which they could apprehend this situation. Government and social order were contrivances devised for them through their own reason and sense experience to improve this situation. It was a *subordinate practical convenience*, not a focus of value in itself.[49]

The duties of the state are the maintenance of law and order at home and protection against aggression from abroad. In Locke's famous words: 'Wherever Law ends Tyranny begins'. Free from tyranny, people would enjoy the maximum scope to pursue their own privately-initiated interests. The state should be the regulator and protector of society: individuals are best able by their own efforts to satisfy their needs and develop their capacities in a process of free exchange with others.

Political activity for Locke is instrumental; it secures the framework or conditions for freedom so that the private ends of individuals might be met in civil society. The creation of a political community or government is the burden individuals have to bear to secure their ends. Thus, membership of a political community, i.e. citizenship, bestows upon the individual both responsibilities and rights, duties and powers, constraints and liberties.[50] In relation to Hobbes's ideas this was a most significant and radical view. For it helped inaugurate one of the most central tenets of European liberalism; that is, that the state exists to safeguard the rights and liberties of citizens who are ultimately the best judges of their own interests; and that accordingly the state must be restricted in scope and constrained in practice in order to ensure the maximum possible freedom of every citizen. In most respects it was Locke's rather than Hobbes's views which helped to lay the foundation for the development of liberalism and prepared the way for the tradition of popular representative government. Compared to

Hobbes, Locke's influence on the world of practical politics has been considerable.

Locke's writings seem to point in a number of directions at once. They suggest the importance of securing the rights of individuals, popular sovereignty, majority rule, a division of powers within the state, constitutional monarchy and a representative system of parliamentary government — a direct anticipation of key aspects of British government as it developed in the nineteenth and early twentieth centuries, and of central tenets of the modern representative state. But, at best, most of these ideas are only in rudimentary form and it is certain that Locke did not foresee many of the vital components of democratic representative government, for instance, competitive parties, party rule, and the maintenance of political liberties irrespective of class, sex, colour and creed.[51] It is not a condition of legitimate government or government by consent, on Locke's account, that there be regular periodic elections of a legislative assembly, let alone universal suffrage.[52] Moreover, he did not develop a detailed account of what the limits might be to state interference in people's lives and under what conditions civil disobedience is justified. He thought that political power was held 'on trust' by and for the people, but failed to specify adequately who were to count as 'the people' and under what conditions 'trust' should be bestowed. He certainly never imagined that such power might be exercised directly by the citizens themselves, i.e. in some form of direct or self-government. While Locke was unquestionably one of the first great champions of liberalism he cannot, in the end, be considered a democrat (even if we restrict the meaning of this term to support for a universal franchise), although his works clearly stimulated the development of both liberal and democratic government, what we may call liberal democracy.[53]

Power, accountability and liberal democracy

If Hobbes and Locke saw the state as a regulator and protector, it was above all because of fears about the problems and dangers individuals faced if left to their own devices. People could not live adequately without a guiding force, although Locke added that the guiding force — the trustee of the people — could not be fully trusted either: there must be limits upon legally sanctioned political power. This latter argument was taken significantly further by two of the very first advocates of liberal democracy: Jeremy Bentham (1748—1832) and James Mill (1773—1836) who, for my purposes here, can be treated together. For these two thinkers, liberal democracy was associated with a political apparatus that would ensure the accountability of the governors to the governed. Only through democratic government would there be a satisfactory means for choosing, authorizing and controlling political decisions commensurate with the public interest, i.e. the interests of the mass of individuals. As Bentham wrote: 'A democracy . . . has for its characteristic object and effect . . . securing its members against oppression and depredation at the hands of those functionaries which it employs for its defence' . . .[54] Democratic government is required to protect citizens from despotic use of political power whether it be by a monarch, the aristocracy or other groups. Bentham's and Mill's argument has been usefully referred to as the 'protective case for democracy'.[55] Only through the vote, secret ballot, competition between potential political leaders (representatives), elections, separation of powers and the liberty of the press, speech and public association could 'the interest of the community in general' be sustained.[56]

Bentham and Mill were impressed by the progress and methods of the natural sciences and were decidedly secular in their orientations. They thought of the concepts of social contract, natural rights and natural law as misleading philosophical fictions which failed to explain the real basis of the citizen's commitment and duty to the state. This basis could be uncovered by grasping the primitive and irreducible elements of actual human behaviour. The key to their understanding of human beings, and of the system of governance most suited to them, lies in the thesis that humans act to satisfy desire and avoid pain. In brief their argument is as follows: the overriding motivation of human beings is to fulfil their desires, maximize their satisfactions or utilities, and minimize their suffering; society consists of individuals seeking as much utility as they can get from whatever it is they want; individuals' interests conflict with one another for 'a grand governing law of human nature', as Hobbes thought, is to subordinate 'the persons and properties of human beings to our pleasures'.[57] Since those who govern will naturally act in the same way as the governed, government must, to avoid abuse, be directly accountable to an electorate called upon frequently to decide if their objectives have been met.

What, then, should be the government's objectives? Government must act according to the principle of utility: it must aim to ensure, by means of careful calculation, the achievement of the greatest happiness for the greatest number — the only scientifically defensible criterion, Bentham and Mill contended, of the public good. It has four subsidiary goals: 'to provide subsistence; to produce abundance; to favour equality; to maintain security'.[58] Of these four the last is by far the most critical; for without security of life and property there would be no incentive for individuals to work and generate wealth: labour would be insufficiently productive and commerce could not prosper. If the state pursues this goal (along with the others to the extent that they are compatible), it will therefore be in the citizen's self-interest to obey it.

Bentham, Mill and the Utilitarians generally provided one of the clearest justifications for the liberal democratic state which ensures the conditions necessary for individuals to pursue their interests without risk of arbitrary political interference, to participate freely in economic transactions, to exchange labour and goods on the market and to appropriate resources privately. These ideas became the basis of classical nineteenth-century 'English liberalism': the state was to have the role of the umpire or referee while individuals pursued, according to the rules of economic competition and free exchange, their own interests. Periodic elections, the abolition of the powers of the monarchy, the division of powers within the state plus the free market would lead to the maximum benefit for all citizens. The free vote and the free market were *sine qua non*. For a key presupposition was that the collective good could be properly realized in many domains of life only if individuals interacted in competitive exchanges, pursuing their utility with minimal state interference. Significantly, however, this argument had another side. Tied to the advocacy of a 'minimal' state whose scope and power was to be strictly limited, there was a strong commitment in fact to certain types of state intervention, for instance, the curtailment of the behaviour of the disobedient, whether they be individuals, groups or classes.[59] Those who challenge the security of property or the market society undermine the realization of the public good. In the name of the public good, the utilitarians advocated a new system of administrative power for 'person management'.[60] Prisons were a mark of this new age. Moreover, whenever *laissez-faire* was inadequate to ensure the best possible outcomes, state intervention was justified to re-order social relations and institutions. The enactment and enforcement of law, backed by the coercive powers of the state, and the creation of new state institutions was legitimate to the extent that it upheld the general principle of utility.

Bentham and Mill were reluctant democrats. In considering the extent of the franchise they found grounds for excluding, among others, the whole of the labouring classes and female population, despite the fact that many of their arguments seemed to point squarely in the direction of universal suffrage. Their ideas have been aptly referred to as 'the founding model of democracy for a modern industrial society'.[61] Their account of democracy establishes it as nothing but a logical requirement for the governance of a society, freed from absolute power and tradition, in which individuals have endless desires, form a body of mass consumers and are dedicated to the maximization of private gain. Democracy, accordingly, becomes a means for the enhancement of these ends — not an end in itself, for perhaps the cultivation and development of all citizens. As such it is at best a partial form of democratic theory.[62]

The 'highest and harmonious' development of individual capacities was, however, a central concern of James Mill's son, John Stuart Mill (1806—73).[63] If Bentham and James Mill were reluctant democrats but prepared to develop arguments to justify democratic institutions, John Stuart Mill was a clear advocate of democracy, preoccupied with the extent of individual liberty in all spheres of human endeavour. Liberal democratic or representative government was important for him, not just because it established boundaries for the pursuit of individual satisfaction, but because it was an important aspect of the free development of individuality: participation in political life (voting, involvement in local administration and jury service) was vital to create a direct interest in government and, consequently, a basis for an involved, informed and developing citizenry. Mill conceived of democratic politics as a prime mechanism of moral self-development.[64] He likened periodic voting to the passing of a 'verdict by a juryman' — ideally the considered outcome of a process of active deliberation about the facts of public affairs, not a mere expression of personal interest.

John Stuart Mill's absorption with the question of the autonomy of individuals and minorities is brought out most clearly in his famous and influential study, *On Liberty* (1859). The aim of this work is to elaborate and defend a principle which will establish 'the nature and limits of the power which can be legitimately exercised by society over the individual'.[65] Mill recognized that some regulation and interference in individuals' lives is necessary but sought an obstacle to arbitrary and self-interested intervention. He put the crucial point thus:

> The object . . . is to assert one very simple principle, as entitled to govern absolutely the dealings of society with the individual in the way of compulsion and control, whether the means used be physical force in the form of legal penalties or the moral coercion of public opinion. That principle is that

the sole end for which mankind are warranted, individually or collectively, in interfering with the liberty of action of any of their number is self-protection. That the only purpose for which power can be rightfully exercised over any member of a civilised community, against his will, is to prevent harm to others.[66]

Social or political interference with individual liberty may be justified only when an act (or a failure to act), whether it be intended or not, 'concerns others' and then only when it 'harms' others. The sole end of interference with liberty should be self-protection. In those activities which are merely 'self-regarding', i.e., only of concern to the individual, 'independence is, of right, absolute'; for 'over himself, over his own body and mind, the individual is sovereign'.[67]

Mill's principle is, in fact, anything but 'very simple': its meaning and implications remain controversial.[68] For instance, what exactly constitutes 'harm to others'? Does the publication of pornography cause harm? But leaving aside difficulties such as these, it should be noted that in his hands the principle generated a defence of many of the key liberties associated with liberal democratic government. The 'appropriate region of human liberty' became: first, liberty of thought, feeling, discussion and publication; second, liberty of tastes and pursuits ('framing the plan of our life to suit our own character'); and third, liberty of association or combination assuming, of course, it causes no harm to others.[69] The 'only freedom which deserves the name is that of pursuing our own good in our own way, so long as we do not attempt to deprive others of theirs or impede their efforts to obtain it'.[70] Mill contended, moreover, that the current practice of both rulers and citizens was generally opposed to his doctrine and unless a 'strong barrier of moral conviction' can be established against such bad habits, growing infringements on the liberty of citizens can be expected as the centralized bureaucratic state expands to cope with the problems of the modern age.[71]

Liberty and democracy create, according to Mill, the possibility of 'human excellence'. Liberty of thought, discussion and action are necessary conditions for the development of independence of mind and autonomous judgment; they are vital for the formation of human reason or rationality. In turn, the cultivation of reason stimulates and sustains liberty. Representative government is essential for the protection and enhancement of both liberty and reason. Without it arbitrary laws might, for instance, be created which enhance the likelihood of tyranny. Representative democracy is the most suitable mode of government for the enactment of laws consistent with the principle of liberty, as the free exchange of goods in the market place is the most appropriate way of maximizing economic liberty and economic good.[72] A system of representative democracy makes government accountable to the citizenry and creates wiser citizens capable of pursuing the public interest. It is thus both a means to develop self-identity, individuality and social difference — a pluralistic society — and an end in itself, an essential democratic order.

Given that individuals are capable of different kinds of things and only a few have developed their full capacities, would it not be appropriate if some citizens have more sway over government than others? Regrettably for the cogency of Mill's argument he thought as much and recommended a plural system of voting; all adults should have a vote but the wiser and more talented should have more votes than the ignorant and less able. Mill took occupational status as a rough guide to the allocation of votes and adjusted his conception of democracy accordingly: those with the most knowledge and skill — who happened to have most property and privilege — could not be outvoted by those with less, i.e. the working classes.[73] Mill was extremely critical of vast inequalities of income, wealth and power; he recognized that they prevented the full development of most members of the labouring classes and yet he stopped short — far short — of a commitment to political and social equality. The idea that all citizens should have equal weight in the political system remained outside his actual doctrine. Moreover, since he ultimately trusted so little in the judgment of the electorate and the elected, he defended the notion that Parliament should have only a right of veto on legislation proposed and drawn up by a non-elected commission of experts.

It was left by and large to the extensive and often violently repressed struggles of working-class and feminist activists in the nineteenth and twentieth centuries to achieve in some countries genuinely universal suffrage. This achievement was to remain fragile in countries such as Germany, Italy, Spain and was in practice denied to some groups, for instance, many Blacks in the United States before the civil rights movement in the 1950s and 1960s. Through these struggles the idea that 'citizenship rights' should apply to all adults became slowly established;[74] many of the arguments of the liberal democrats could be turned against the *status quo* to reveal the extent to which the principle and aspirations of equal political participation and equal human development remained unfulfilled. It was only with the actual achievement of full citizenship that liberal democracy took on its distinctively modern form:

> a cluster of rules . . . permitting the broadest . . . participation of the majority of citizens in political decisions, i.e. in decisions affecting the whole collectively. The rules are more or less the following: (a) all citizens who have reached legal age, without regard to race, religion, economic status, sex etc. must enjoy political rights, i.e. the right to express their own opinion through their vote and/or to elect those who express it for them; (b) the vote of all citizens must have equal weight; (c) all citizens enjoying political rights must be free to vote according to their own opinion, formed as freely as possible, i.e. in a free contest between organized political groups competing among themselves so as to aggregate demands and transform them into collective deliberations; (d) they must also be free in the sense that they must be in a position of having real alternatives, i.e. of choosing between different solutions; (e) whether for collective deliberations or for the election of representatives, the principle of numerical majority holds — even though different forms of majority rule can be established (relative, absolute, qualified), under certain circumstances established in advance; (f) no decision taken by a majority must limit minority rights, especially the right to become eventually, under normal conditions, a majority.[75]

The idea of democracy remains complex and contested. The development towards the notion of the liberal democratic state in the works of Hobbes, Locke, Bentham and the two Mills comprises a most heterogeneous body of thought. Its enormous influence, especially in the Anglo-American world, has spawned seemingly endless debates and conflicts.[76] However, the whole liberal democratic tradition stands apart from an alternative perspective: the theory of what can be called 'direct' or 'participatory' democracy which had one of its earliest exponents in Rousseau (1712—78). It is worth saying something briefly about Rousseau, not only because of the importance of his thought, but because he had, according to some writers at least, a direct influence on the development of the key counterpoint to liberal democracy — the Marxist tradition.[77]

The idea that the consent of individuals legitimates government and the state system more generally was central to both seventeenth- and eighteenth-century liberals as well as to nineteenth- and twentieth-century liberal democrats. The former regarded the social contract as the original mechanism of individual consent, while the latter focused on the ballot box as the mechanism whereby the citizen periodically conferred authority on government to enact laws and regulate economic and social life. Rousseau was dissatisfied, for reasons I can only briefly allude to, with arguments of both these types. Like Hobbes and Locke, he was concerned with the question whether there is a legitimate and secure principle of government.[78] Like Hobbes and Locke he offered an account of a state of nature and the social contract. In his classic *Social Contract* (published in 1762), he assumed that although humans were happy in the original state of nature, they were driven from it by a variety of obstacles to their preservation (individual weaknesses, common miseries, natural disasters).[79] Human beings came to realize that the development of their nature, the realization of their capacity for reason, the fullest experience of liberty, could be achieved only by a social contract which established a system of cooperation through a law-making and enforcing body. Thus there is a contract, but it is a contract which creates the possibility of *self*-regulation or *self*-government. In Hobbes's and Locke's versions of the social contract, sovereignty is transferred from the people to the state and its ruler(s) (although for Locke the surrender of the rights of self-government was a conditional affair). By contrast Rousseau was original, as one commentator aptly put it, 'in holding that no such transfer of sovereignty need or should take place: sovereignty not only originates in the people; it ought to stay there'.[80] Accordingly, not only did Rousseau find the political doctrines offered by Hobbes and Locke unacceptable, but those of the type put forward by the liberal democrats as well. In a justly famous passage he wrote:

> Sovereignty cannot be represented, for the same reason that it cannot be alienated . . . the people's deputies are not, and could not be, its representatives; they are merely its agents; and they cannot decide anything finally. Any law which the people has not ratified in person is void; it is not law at all. The English people believes itself to be free; it is gravely mistaken; it is free only during the election of Members of Parliament; as soon as the Members are elected, the people is enslaved; it is nothing.[81]

Rousseau saw individuals as ideally involved in the direct creation of the laws by which their lives are regulated. The sovereign authority is the people making the rules by which they

live. Like John Stuart Mill after him, Rousseau celebrated the
notion of an active, involved citizenry in a developing process of
government, but he interpreted this in a more radical manner:
all citizens should meet together to decide what is best for the
community and enact the appropriate laws. The governed, in
essence, should be the governors. In Rousseau's account, the idea
of self-government is posited as an end in itself; a political order
offering opportunities for participation in the arrangement of
public affairs should not just be a state, but rather the formation of
a type of society — a society in which the affairs of the state are
integrated into the affairs of ordinary citizens.[82]

The role of the citizen is the highest to which an individual can
aspire. The considered exercise of power by citizens is the only
legitimate way in which liberty can be sustained. The citizen must
both create and be bound by 'the supreme direction of the general
will' — the publically generated conception of the common good.[83]
The people are sovereign only to the extent that they participate
actively in articulating the 'general will'. It is important to
distinguish the latter from the 'will of all': it is the difference
between the sum of judgments about the common good and the
mere aggregate of personal fancies and individual desires.[84] Citizens
are only obligated to a system of laws and regulations on the
grounds of publicly reached agreement, for they can only be
genuinely obligated to a law they have prescribed for themselves
with the general good in mind.[85] Hence, Rousseau draws a critical
distinction between independence and liberty:

> Many have been the attempts to confound independence and
> liberty: two things so essentially different, that they recipro-
> cally exclude each other. When every one does what he
> pleases, he will, of course, often do things displeasing to
> others; and this is not properly called a free state. Liberty
> consists less in acting according to one's own pleasure, than
> in not being subject to the will and pleasure of other people.
> It consists also in our not subjecting the wills of other people
> to our own. Whoever is the master over others is not himself
> free, and even to reign is to obey.[86]

Liberty and equality are inextricably linked. For the social contract
'establishes equality among the citizens in that they . . . must all
enjoy the same rights'.[87]

Rousseau argued in favour of a political system in which the
legislative and executive functions are clearly demarcated. The

former belong to the people and the latter to a 'government' or 'prince'. The people form the legislative assembly and constitute the authority of the state; the 'government' or 'prince' (composed of one or more administrators or magistrates) executes the people's laws.[88] Such a 'government' is necessary on the grounds of expediency: the people require a government to coordinate public meetings, serve as a means of communication, draft laws and enforce the legal system.[89] The government is a result of an agreement among the citizenry and is legitimate only to the extent to which it fulfils 'the instructions of the general will'. Should it fail to so behave it can be revoked and changed.[90]

Rousseau's work had a significant (though ambiguous) influence on the ideas in currency during the French Revolution as well as on traditions of revolutionary thought, from Marxism to anarchism. His conception of self-government has been among the most provocative, challenging at its core some of the critical assumptions of liberal democracy, especially the notion that democracy is the name for a particular kind of state which can only be held accountable to the citizenry once in a while. But Rousseau's ideas do not represent a completely coherent system or recipe for straightforward action. He appreciated some of the problems created by large-scale, complex, densely populated societies, but did not pursue these as far as one must.[91] He too excluded all women from 'the people', i.e. the citizenry, as well as, it seems, the poor. The latter appear to be outcasts because citizenship is made conditional upon a small property qualification (land) and/or upon the absence of dependency on others.[92] Rousseau's primary concern was with what might be thought of as the future of democracy in a non-industrial, agriculturally-based community. As a vision of democracy it was and remains evocative and challenging, but it was not connected to an account of political life in an industrial capitalist society. It was left to Marx, Engels and Lenin, among others, to pursue these connections.

Class, coercion and the Marxist critique

Individuals; individuals in competition with one another; freedom of choice; politics as the arena for the maintenance of individual interests, the protection of 'life, liberty and estate'; the democratic state as the institutional mechanism for the articulation of the general or public interest (as opposed to simple private desires): all these are essential preoccupations of the liberal democratic tradition. While Marx (1818—83) and Engels (1820—95) did not deny that people had unique capacities, desires and an interest in free choice, they attacked relentlessly the idea that the starting point of the analysis of the state can be the individual, and his or her relation to the state. As Marx put it, 'man is not an abstract being squatting outside the world. Man is the human world, the state, society'.[93] Individuals only exist in interaction with and in relation to others; their nature can only be grasped as a social and historical product. It is not the single, isolated individual who is active in historical and political processes, but rather human beings who live in definite relations with others and whose nature is defined through these relations. An individual, or a social activity, or an institution (in fact, any aspect of human life) can only be properly explained in terms of its historically evolving interaction with other social phenomena — a dynamic and changing process of inextricably related elements.

The key to understanding the relations between people is, according to Marx and Engels, class structure.[94] Class divisions are not, they maintain, found in all forms of society: classes are a creation of history, and in the future will disappear. The earliest types of 'tribal' society were classless. This is because, in such types of society, there was no surplus production and no private property; production was based upon communal resources and the fruits of productive activity were distributed through the community as a whole. Class divisions arise only when a surplus is generated, such that it becomes possible for a class of non-producers to live off the productive activity of others. Those who are able to gain control of the means of production form a dominant or ruling class both economically and politically. Class relations for Marx and Engels are thus necessarily exploitative and imply divisions of interest between ruling and subordinate classes. Class divisions are, furthermore, inherently conflictual and frequently give rise to active class struggle. Such struggles form the chief mechanism or 'motor' of historical development.

With the break-up of feudalism and the expansion of market economies, the class system of modern Western capitalist societies became slowly established. The class divisions of these societies are based, above all, Marx and Engels argued, upon one dominant exploitative relationship: that between those with capital and those who only have their labouring capacity to sell. 'Capitalists' own factories and technology while wage-labourers, or 'wage-workers', are propertyless. As capitalism matures, the vast majority of the population become wage-workers, who have to sell their labour-power on the market to secure a living. Societies are capitalist to the extent that they can be characterized as dominated by a mode of production which extracts surplus from wage-workers in the form of 'surplus value' — the value generated by workers in the productive process over and above their wages, and appropriated by the owners of capital.[95] This relationship between capital and wage-labour designates, in Marx's and Engel's account, the essential social and political structure of the modern epoch.

How then can the nature of the state be understood? What is the role of the state in the context of a class society? Central to the liberal and liberal democratic traditions is the idea that the state can claim to represent the community or public interest, in contrast to individuals' private aims and concerns. But, according to Marx and Engels, the opposition between interests that are public and general, and those that are private and particular is, to a large extent, illusory.[96] The state defends the 'public' or the 'community' as if: classes did not exist; the relationship between classes was not exploitative; classes did not have fundamental differences of interest; these differences of interest did not define economic and political life. In treating everyone in the same way, according to principles which protect the freedom of individuals and defend their right to property, the state may act 'neutrally' while generating effects which are partial — sustaining the privileges of those with property. Moreover, the very claim that there is a clear distinction between the private and the public, the world of civil society and the political, is dubious. The key source of contemporary power — private ownership of the means of production — is ostensibly *depoliticized*; that is, treated as if it were not a proper subject of politics. The economy is regarded as non-political, in that the massive division between those who own and control the means of production, and those who must live by wage-labour, is regarded as the outcome of free private contracts, not a matter for the state. But by defending private property the state already has taken a side. The state, then, is not an independent structure or set of institutions above society, i.e. a 'public power' acting for 'the public'. On the contrary, it is deeply embedded in socio-economic relations and linked to particular interests.

There are at least two strands in Marx's account of the relation between classes and the state; while they are by no means explicitly distinguished by Marx himself, it is illuminating to disentangle them.[97] The first, henceforth referred to as position (1), stresses that the state generally, and bureaucratic institutions in particular, may take a variety of forms and constitute a source of power which need not be directly linked to the interests, or be under the unambiguous control of, the dominant class in the short term. By this account, the state retains a degree of power independent of this class: its institutional forms and operational dynamics cannot be inferred directly from the configuration of class forces — they are 'relatively autonomous'. The second strand, position (2), is without doubt the dominant one in his writings: the state and its bureaucracy are class instruments which emerged to coordinate a divided society in the interests of the ruling class. Position (1) is certainly a more complex and subtle vision. Both positions are elaborated below. I shall begin with position (1) for it is expressed most clearly in Marx's early writings and highlights the degree to which the second view involves a narrowing down of the terms of reference of Marx's analysis of the state.

Marx's engagement with the theoretical problems posed by state power developed from an early confrontation with Hegel (1770–1831), a central figure in German idealist philosophy and a crucial intellectual influence on his life. In the *Philosophy of Right*, Hegel portrayed the Prussian state as divided into three substantive divisions — the legislature, the executive and the crown — which together express 'universal insight and will'.[98] For him, the most important institution of the state is the bureaucracy, an organization in which particular interests are subordinated to a system of hierarchy, specialization, expertise and coordination on the one hand, and internal and external pressures for competence and impartiality on the other. According to Marx, in the *Critique of Hegel's Philosophy of Right*, Hegel failed to challenge the self-image of the state and, in particular, of the bureaucracy.[99]

The bureaucracy is the 'state's consciousness'. Marx describes the bureaucracy, by which he means the corps of state officials, as 'a particular closed society within the state', which extends its power or capacity through secrecy and mystery.[100] The individual bureaucrat is initiated into this closed society through 'a bureaucratic confession of faith' — the examination system — and the caprice of the politically dominant group. Subsequently the bureaucrat's career becomes everything, passive obedience to those in higher authority becomes a necessity and 'the state's interest becomes a particular private aim'. But the state's aims are not thereby achieved, nor is competence guaranteed.[101] For, as Marx wrote,

> The bureaucracy asserts itself to be the final end of the state . . . The aims of the state are transformed into aims of bureaus, or the aims of bureaus into the aims of the state. The bureaucracy is a circle from which no one can escape. Its hierarchy is a hierarchy of knowledge. The highest point

entrusts the understanding of the particulars to the lower echelons, whereas these, on the other hand, credit the highest with an understanding in regard to the universal [the general interest]; and thus they deceive one another.[102]

Marx's critique of Hegel involves several points, but one in particular is crucial: in the sphere of what Hegel referred to as 'the absolutely universal interest of the state proper' there is, in Marx's view, nothing but 'bureaucratic officialdom' and 'unresolved conflict'.[103] Marx's emphasis on the structure and corporate nature of bureaucracies is significant because it throws into relief the 'relative autonomy' of these organizations and foreshadows the arguments elaborated in what may be his most interesting work on the state, *The Eighteenth Brumaire of Louis Bonaparte*.

The Eighteenth Brumaire is an eloquent analysis of the rise to power between 1848 and 1852 of Louis Napoleon Bonaparte and of the way power accumulated in the hands of the executive at the expense of, in the first instance, both civil society and the political representatives of the capitalist class, the bourgeoisie. The study highlights Marx's distance from any view of the state as an 'instrument of universal insight' or 'ethical community' for he emphasized that the state apparatus is simultaneously a 'parasitic body' on civil society and an autonomous source of political action. Thus, in describing Bonaparte's regime, he wrote:

This executive power, with its enormous bureaucratic and military organization, with its ingenious state machinery, embracing wide strata, with a host of officials numbering half a million, beside an army of another half million, this appalling parasitic body . . . enmeshes the body of French society like a net and chokes all its pores.[104]

The state is portrayed as an immense set of institutions, with the capacity to shape civil society and even to curtail the bourgeoisie's capacity to control the state.[105] Marx granted the state a certain autonomy from society: political outcomes are the result of the interlock between complex coalitions and constitutional arrangements.

The analysis offered in *The Eighteenth Brumaire*, like that in the *Critique*, suggests that the agents of the state do not simply coordinate political life in the interests of the dominant class of civil society. The executive, under particular circumstances — for example, when there is a relative balance of social forces — has the capacity to promote change as well as to coordinate it. But

Marx's focus, even when discussing this idea, was essentially on the state as a conservative force. He emphasized the importance of its information network as a mechanism for surveillance, and the way in which the state's political autonomy is interlocked with its capacity to undermine social movements threatening to the *status quo*. Moreover, the repressive dimension of the state is complemented by its capacity to sustain belief in the inviolability of existing arrangements. Far then from being the basis for the articulation of the general interest, the state, Marx argued, transforms 'universal aims into another form of private interest'.

There were ultimate constraints on the initiatives Bonaparte could take, however, without throwing society into a major crisis, as there are on any legislative or executive branch of the state. For the state in a capitalist society, Marx concluded from his study of the Bonapartist regime, cannot escape its dependence upon that society and, above all, upon those who own and control the productive process. Its dependence is revealed whenever the economy is beset by crises; for economic organizations of all kinds create the material resources on which the state apparatus survives. The state's overall policies have to be compatible in the long run with the objectives of manufacturers and traders, otherwise civil society and the stability of the state itself are jeopardized. Hence, though Bonaparte usurped the political power of the bourgeoisie's representatives, he protected the 'material power' of the bourgeoisie itself — a vital source of loans and revenue. Accordingly, Bonaparte could not help but sustain the long-term economic interests of the bourgeoisie and lay the foundation for the regeneration of its direct political power in the future, whatever else he chose to do while in office.[106]

Marx attacked the claim that the distribution of property lies outside the constitution of political power. This attack is, of course, a central aspect of Marx's legacy and of what I am calling position (2). Throughout his political essays and especially in his more polemical pamphlets such as the *Communist Manifesto*, Marx (and indeed Engels) insisted on the direct dependence of the state on the economic, social and political power of the dominant class. The state is a 'superstructure' which develops on the 'foundation' of economic and social relations.[107] The state, in this formulation, serves directly the interest of the economically dominant class: the notion of the state as a site of autonomous political action is supplanted by an emphasis upon class power, an emphasis illustrated by the famous slogan of the *Communist Manifesto*: 'The executive of the modern state is but a committee for managing the common affairs of the whole bourgeoisie'. This formula does not imply that the state is dominated by the bourgeoisie as a whole: it may be independent of sections of the bourgeois class.[108] The state, nevertheless, is characterized as essentially dependent upon society and upon those who dominate the economy: 'independence' is exercised only to the extent that conflicts must be settled between different sections of capital (industrialists and financiers, for example), and between 'domestic capitalism' and pressures generated by international capitalist markets. The state maintains the overall interests of the bourgeoisie in the name of the public or general interest.

There are, then, two (often interconnected) strands in Marx's account of the relation between classes and the state: the first conceives the state with a degree of power independent of class forces; the second upholds the view that the state is merely a 'superstructure' serving the interests of the dominant class. On the basis of position (1) it is possible to think of the state as a potential arena of struggle which can become a key force for socialist change. The social democratic tradition, as developed by people like Eduard Bernstein (1850—1932), elaborated this notion: through the ballot box the heights of state power could be scaled and used against the most privileged, while one by one institutions of the state could be progressively turned against the interests of capital.[109] In contradistinction, revolutionary socialist traditions developed from position (2). Following Marx's analysis, Lenin insisted that the eradication of capitalist relations of production must be accompanied by the destruction of the capitalist state apparatus: the state, as a class instrument, had to be destroyed and direct democracy — as imagined in part by Rousseau — installed.[110]

Position (1) has been emphasized above because it is generally downplayed in the secondary literature on Marx.[111] Marx's work on the state remained incomplete. Position (1) left several important questions insufficiently explored. What is the basis of state power? How do state bureaucracies function? What precise interest do political officials develop? Position (2) is even more problematic: it postulates a capitalist-specific (or, as it has been called more recently, 'capital logic') organization of the state and takes for granted a simple causal relation between the facts of class domination and the vicissitudes of political life. But Marx's combined writings do indicate that he regards the state as central to the integration and control of class divided societies. Furthermore, his work suggests important limits to state intervention within capitalist societies. If intervention undermines the process of capital accumulation, it simultaneously undermines the material basis of the state; hence, state policies must be consistent with capitalist relations of production. Accordingly, a dominant economic class can rule without directly governing, that is, it can exert determinate political influence without even having representatives in government. This idea retains a vital place in contemporary debates among Marxists, liberal democratic theorists and others.

On the whole, Lenin (1870–1924) followed the tenets of Marx's position (2). His views are stated succinctly in *State and Revolution* (1917), where he listed his first task as the 'resuscitation of the real teaching of Marx on the state'.[112] Lenin conceived of the state as a 'machine for the oppression of one class by another'. The modern representative state was 'the instrument for the exploitation of wage-labour by capital' — 'a special repressive force'.[113] Thus, the distinguishing feature of the state, apart from its grouping of people on a territorial basis, is its dependence on force, exercised through specialized bodies such as the army, police and prison service. Many of the routine activities of the state, from taxation to legislation concerned with the protection of officials, exist essentially to ensure the survival of these repressive institutions.

The ruling classes maintain their grip on the state through alliances with government — alliances created both by government dependence on the stock exchange and by the corruption of ministers and officials. The vital business of the state takes place, not in representative assemblies, but in the state bureaucracies, where alliances can be established out of public view. Further, even democratic rights such as freedom of association, freedom of the press, or freedom of assembly, are a major benefit to the dominant classes. They can claim these institutions are 'open' while controlling them 'through ownership of the media, control over meeting places, money, and other resources'.[114]

Although *State and Revolution* reiterates what I have called Marx's position (2), Lenin made more than Marx did of one central point: the crystallization of class power within the organs of state administration. For the Lenin of *State and Revolution*, 'so long as the state exists, there is no freedom. When freedom exists, there will be no state'. Strong central control would be necessary after the Revolution, but a precondition of revolutionary success is the destruction of the 'old state machine': 'The bureaucracy and the standing army, direct products of class oppression, have to be smashed. The army would be replaced by armed workers and the bureaucrats by elected officials subject to recall'.[115] There would be 'immediate introduction of control and supervision by *all*, so that *all* may become "bureaucrats" for a time and that, therefore, nobody may be able to become a "bureaucrat"'. Officials and soldiers would be necessary but they would not become 'privileged persons divorced from the people and standing *above* the people'. Lenin never doubted that discipline was essential in political organizations, but he argued that this does not entail the creation of an elite of functionaries.[116] Following the lessons which Marx and Engels drew from the Paris Commune — lessons interpreted to some degree in the spirit of Rousseau's vision of direct democracy — Lenin maintained that the new socialist order must and could replace 'the government of persons' by 'the administration of things'.[117]

The survival of bureaucracy in the early days of post-Revolutionary Russia was frequently explained by Lenin in terms of the lingering influence of capitalism and the old regime. He continually affirmed a causal relation between forms of state organization and classes, even in his famous 'last testament' where problems concerning central administration and the bureaucratization of the party and the state were sources of great anxiety.[118] This position had dire consequences: it led, in part, to the widespread belief among Bolsheviks that, with the abolition of capitalist property relations (and the expansion of forces of production), problems of organization, control and coordination could be easily resolved.

There are many tensions in Lenin's treatment of the state and political organization. He thought that the work of the new socialist order could be conducted by workers organized in a framework of direct democracy (soviets), yet he defended the authority of the party in nearly all spheres. His argument that state bureaucracies need not entail fixed positions of power and privilege is suggestive, but it remains, especially in light of the massive problems of organization faced during and after the Revolution, a very incomplete statement. Lenin failed to examine the degree to which state organizations are influenced by diverse interests, political compromises and complex circumstances which do not merely reflect 'class antagonisms which must be reconciled from above'. To this extent his views on the state do not represent an advance on Marx's position (1).

In the last 20 years there has been a massive revival of interest in the analysis of state power among contemporary Marxist writers.[119] Marx left an ambiguous heritage, never fully reconciling his understanding of the state as an instrument of class domination with his acknowledgment that the state might also have significant political independence. Lenin's emphasis on the oppressive nature of capitalist state institutions certainly did not resolve this ambiguity; and his writings seem even less compelling after Stalin's purges and the massive growth of the Soviet state itself. Since the deaths of Marx and Engels, many Marxist writers have made contributions of decisive importance to the analysis of politics (for instance, Lukács, Korsch and Gramsci explored the many complex and subtle ways dominant classes sustain power), but not until recently has the relation between state and society been fully re-examined in Marxist circles.

Ralph Miliband provided a stimulus with the publication of *The State in Capitalist Society* in 1969.[120] Noting the increasingly central position of the state in Western societies, he sought to re-assess the relationship Marx posited between class and state on the one hand, and, on the other, to evaluate the reigning liberal democratic view of state—society relations, a view which posited the state as the referee adjudicating between competing interests in society. (This latter view involved a pluralist model of society, which I shall discuss later.) Against those who held that the state is a neutral arbiter among social interests, he argued: (a) that in contemporary Western societies there is a dominant or ruling class which owns and controls the means of production; (b) that the dominant class has close links to powerful institutions, political parties, the military, universities, the media, etc; and (c) that it has disproportionate representation at all levels of the state apparatus, especially in the 'command positions'. The capitalist class, Miliband contended, is highly cohesive and constitutes a formidable constraint on Western governments and state institutions, ensuring that they remain 'instruments for the domination of society'. However, he insisted — defending what I called Marx's position (1) — that in order to be politically effective, the state must be able to separate itself routinely from ruling-class factions. Government policy may even be directed against the short-run interest of the capitalist class. He was also quick to point out that under exceptional circumstances the state can achieve a high order of independence from class interests, for example, in national crises and war.

Nicos Poulantzas challenged Miliband's views in a debate which has received much attention.[121] In so doing, he sought to clarify further Marx's position (1). He rejected what he considered Miliband's 'subjectivist' approach — his attempt to explore the relation among classes, bureaucracy, and the state through 'inter-personal relations' (for Miliband, the social background of state officials and links between them and members of powerful institutions). Although Poulantzas exaggerated the differences between his position and Miliband's, his starting point was radically different. He did not ask: Who influences important decisions and determines policy? What is the social background of those who occupy key administrative positions? The 'class affiliation' of those in the state apparatus is not, according to Poulantzas, crucial to its 'concrete functioning'.[122] Much more important for Poulantzas are the structural components of the capitalist state which lead it to protect the long-term framework of capitalist production even if this means severe conflict with some segments of the capitalist class.

In order to grasp these structural components, it is essential, Poulantzas argued, to understand that the state is the unifying element in capitalism. More specifically, the state must function to ensure (a) the 'political organization' of the dominant classes which, because of competitive pressures and differences of immediate interest, are continually broken up into 'class fractions'; (b) the 'political disorganization' of the working classes which, because of the concentration of production, among other things, can threaten the hegemony of the dominant classes.[123] Since the dominant classes are vulnerable to fragmentation, their long-term interests require protection by the state. The state can sustain this function only if it is 'relatively autonomous' from the particular interests of diverse fractions. What is more, the state itself, Poulantzas stressed, is not a monolithic bloc; it is an arena of conflict and schism (the 'condensation of class forces').[124] The degree of autonomy actual states acquire depends on the relations among classes and class fractions and on the intensity of social struggles. Relative autonomy 'devolves' on the state 'in the power relations of the class struggle'. Thus, the centralized modern state is both a necessary result of 'the anarchic competition in civil society' and a force in the reproduction of such competition and division.[125]

Poulantzas's views have by no means met with universal approval among Marxists. Foremost amongst those who reject his perspective are Claus Offe and Jürgen Habermas, who belong to a quite different 'tradition' of Marxist thought.[126] Among their criticisms is the charge that Poulantzas (and Miliband) regard capitalist states only from a 'negative' perspective; that is to say, the state is treated only from the point of view of how far it stabilizes capitalist economic enterprise, or prevents the development of potentially revolutionary influences. This results in a peculiar de-emphasis, which Offe and Habermas seek to avoid, of the capacity of the working classes to influence the course and organization of state administration.[127] Further, Poulantzas' emphasis on the state as the 'condensation of class forces' means that his account of the state is drawn without sufficient internal definition or institutional differentiation. How institutions operate and the manner in which the relationship among élites, government officials, and parliamentarians evolves, are neglected. In contrast,

Offe and Habermas examine how the state sustains the institutional order in which capitalistic mechanisms occupy a prime place and how it mediates (expresses and changes) class antagonisms. Attention is focused on the way social conflicts and severe economic problems are 'displaced' onto the state, initiating an erosion of mass loyalty to the *status quo*, i.e. a legitimation crisis. (These ideas are set out in more detail on pp. 487—97.)

Contemporary Marxism is in a state of flux. There are now as many differences between Marxists as between liberals or liberal democrats. Moreover, the reconsideration of the classical Marxist account of the state — in part stimulated by the state's growth in Western and Eastern Europe during recent decades — has led to a reappraisal by some Marxists of the liberal democratic tradition with its emphasis on the importance of individual liberties and rights, i.e. citizenship.[128] The significance of 'citizenship rights' as a limit to the extension of state power has been more fully appreciated. At the same time, some liberal democrats have come to understand the limitations placed on political life by, among other things, massive concentrations of economic ownership and control.[129] But exactly how one reconciles some of the most important insights of these fundamentally competing traditions of thought remains an open question.

Bureaucracy, parliaments and the nation-state

The notion that the state, and bureaucratic organization in particular, constitute 'parasitic' entities is a position Marx and many other Marxists have espoused. Max Weber (1864—1920), a founder of sociology, a champion of European liberalism and of the German nation-state, contested this view. Although he drew extensively upon Marx's writings, he did so critically and nowhere more critically perhaps than with reference to the modern state. In contrast to Marx, Engels and Lenin, Weber resisted all suggestion that forms of state organization were 'parasitic' and a direct product of the activities of classes. He stressed the similarities between private and public organizations as well as their independent dynamics. Moreover, the idea that institutions of the modern state should be 'smashed' in a revolutionary process of transformation was, according to him, at best a foolhardy view.

Centralized administration may be inescapable. Weber's consideration of this issue makes his work especially important. He dismissed the feasibility of direct democracy,

... where the group grows beyond a certain size or where the administrative function becomes too difficult to be satisfactorily taken care of by anyone whom rotation, the lot, or election may happen to designate. The conditions of administration of mass structures are radically different from those obtaining in small associations resting upon neighborly or personal relationships ... The growing complexity of the administrative task and the sheer expansion of their scope increasingly result in the technical superiority of those who have had training and experience, and will thus inevitably favor the continuity of at least some of the functionaries. Hence, there always exists the probability of the rise of a special, perennial structure for administrative purposes, which of necessity means for the exercise of rule.[130]

The question of the class nature of the state is, Weber maintained, distinct from the question of whether a centralized bureaucratic administration is a necessary feature of political and social organization. It is simply misleading to conflate problems concerning the nature of administration in itself with problems concerning the control of the state apparatus.[131] In Weber's opinion, Lenin's commitment to the 'smashing' of the state was based on his failure to see these as two distinct issues.

Weber developed one of the most significant definitions of the modern state, placing emphasis upon two distinctive elements of its history: territoriality and violence. The modern state, unlike its predecessors which were troubled by constantly warring factions, has a capability of monopolizing the legitimate use of violence within a given territory; it is a nation-state in embattled relations with other nation-states rather than with armed segments of its own population. 'Of course,' Weber emphasized,

... force is certainly not the normal or only means of the state — nobody says that — but force is a means specific to the state ... the state is a relation of men dominating men [and generally — one should add — men dominating women], a relation supported by means of legitimate (i.e. considered to be legitimate) violence.[132]

The state maintains compliance or order within a given territory; in individual capitalist societies this involves crucially the defence of the order of property and the enhancement of domestic economic interests overseas, although by no means all the problems of order can be reduced to these. The state's web of agencies and institutions finds its ultimate sanction in the claim to the monopoly of coercion, and a political order is only, in the last instance, vulnerable to crises when this monopoly erodes.

However, there is a third key term in Weber's definition of the state: legitimacy. The state is based on a monopoly of physical coercion which is legitimized (that is, sustained) by a belief in the justifiability and/or legality of this monopoly. Today, Weber argued, people no longer comply with the authority claimed by the powers that be merely on the grounds, as was common once, of habit and tradition or the charisma and personal appeal of individual leaders. Rather, there is general obedience by 'virtue of "legality", by virtue of the belief in the validity of legal statute and functional "competence" based on rationally created *rules*'.[133] The legitimacy of the modern state is founded predominantly on 'legal authority', i.e, commitment to a 'code of legal regulations'.

Foremost among the state's institutions are the administrative apparatuses — a vast network of organizations run by appointed officials. Although such organizations have been essential to states at many times and places in history, 'only the Occident', on Weber's account, 'knows the state in its modern scale, with a professional administration, specialized officialdom, and law based on the concept of citizenship'. These institutions had 'beginnings in antiquity and the Orient', but there they 'were never able to develop'.[134]

The modern state is not, Weber contended, an effect of capitalism; it preceded and helped promote capitalist development.[135] Capitalism, however, provided an enormous impetus to the expansion of rational administration, that is, the type of bureaucracy founded on legal authority. Weber extended the meaning of the concept of bureaucracy: when Marx and Lenin wrote about it, they had in mind the civil service, the bureaucratic apparatus of the state, but Weber applied the concept much more broadly, as characterizing all forms of large-scale organization (the civil service, political parties, industrial enterprises, universities, etc.). In the contemporary world, he believed, private and public administration are becoming more and more bureaucratized.[136] That is to say, there is a growth of office hierarchy; administration is based upon written documents; specialist training is presupposed and candidates are appointed according to qualification; formal responsibilities demand the full working capacities of officials; officials are 'separated from ownership of the means of administration'.[137]

Under practically every imaginable circumstance, bureaucracy is, according to Weber, 'completely indispensable'.[138] The choice is only 'between bureaucracy and dilettantism in the field of administration'. Weber explained the spread of bureaucracy in the following terms:

> The decisive reason for the advance of bureaucratic organiza-
> tion has always been its purely *technical* superiority over any
> other form of organization. The fully developed bureaucratic
> apparatus compares with the non-mechanical modes of
> production. Precision, speed, unambiguity, knowledge of the
> files, continuity, discretion, unity, strict subordination, reduc-
> tion of friction and of material and personal costs — these
> are raised to the optimum point in the strictly bureaucratic
> administration, and especially in its monocratic form.[139]

As economic life becomes more complex and differentiated, bureaucratic administration becomes more essential.

While rule by officials is not inevitable, considerable power accrues to bureaucrats through their expertise, information and access to secrets. This power can become, Weber says, 'over-towering'. Politicians and political actors of all kinds can find themselves dependent on the bureaucracy. A central question — if not preoccupation — for Weber was, how can 'bureaucratic power' be checked? He was convinced that, in the absence of checks, public organization would fall prey to powerful private interests (among others, organized capitalists and major landholders) who would not have the nation-state as their prime concern; moreover, in times of national emergency, there would be ineffective leadership. Bureaucrats, unlike politicians, cannot take a passionate stand. They do not have the training — and bureaucracies are not structurally designed — for the consideration of political, alongside technical or economic, criteria. However, Weber's solution to the problem of unlimited bureaucratization was not one that depended merely on the capacity of individual politicians for innovation. Writing about Germany, he advocated a strong parliament which would create a competitive training ground for strong leadership and serve as a balance to public and private bureaucracy.[140] In so arguing, Weber was taking 'national power and prestige' as his prime concern. As one commentator aptly noted, 'Weber's enthusiasm for the representative system owed more to his conviction that national greatness depended on finding able leaders than to any concern for democratic values'.[141]

Weber's position on the relationship between social structure, bureaucracy and the state can be clarified further by examining his assessment of socialism. He believed that the abolition of private capitalism 'would simply mean that . . . the *top management* of the nationalized or socialized enterprises would become bureaucratic'.[142] Reliance upon those who control resources would be enhanced, for the abolition of the market would be the abolition of a key countervailing power to the state. The market generates change and social mobility: it is the very source of capitalist dynamism.

> State bureaucracy would rule alone if private capitalism were eliminated. The private and public bureaucracies, which now work next to, and potentially against, each other and hence check one another to a degree, would be merged into a single hierarchy. This would be similar to the situation in ancient Egypt, but it would occur in a much more rational — and hence unbreakable — form.[143]

While Weber argued that 'progress' toward the bureaucratic state is given an enormous impetus by capitalist development, he believed that this very development itself, coupled with parliamentary government and the party system, provided the best obstacle to the usurpation of state power by officials.

Weber accepted that intense class struggles have occurred in various phases of history and that the relationship between capital and wage-labour is of considerable importance in explaining many of the features of industrial capitalism. However, he dissented strongly from the view that the analysis of power could be assimilated to the analysis of classes. For Weber, classes cannot be reduced to economic relations, and they constitute in themselves only one aspect of the distribution of and struggle for power. What Weber calls 'status groups', political parties and nation-states are at least as significant.[144] The fervour created by sentiments of group solidarity, or of ethnic community, or of power prestige, or of nationalism generally, is a vital part of the creation and mobilization of political power in the modern age. But of all these the most important for Weber was the struggle between nation-states — a decisive feature of the modern world which promised to keep history open to 'human will' and the 'competition of values' in an ever more rationalized, bureaucratic world.[145]

Weber's attempt to analyse the internal workings of public (and private) organizations and his observations about trends in bureaucratization constitute a major contribution to understanding the state. His work provides a counterbalance to the Marxist and particularly Leninist emphasis on the intimate connection between state activities, forms of organization and class relations.[146] The argument that private and public administrations are similarly structured — as opposed to causally determined by class power — is important and provocative.

But Weber's analysis also has severe limits. His assumption that the development of bureaucracy leads to increased power for those at the highest levels of administration, leads him to neglect the ways in which those in subordinate positions may increase their power.[147] In modern bureaucratic systems there appear to be considerable 'openings' for those in 'formally subordinate positions to acquire or regain control over their organizational tasks' (for example, by hindering or blocking the collection of vital information for centralized decision making).[148] Bureaucracies may enhance the potential for disruption from 'below' and increase the spaces for circumventing hierarchical control. Weber did not characterize adequately internal organizational processes and their significance for developments in other political spheres. In addition, one can search his writings in vain for a satisfactory explanation of the precise character of the relation between the growing bureaucratic centralization of the state and modern capitalism.[149] In his historical account of patterns of bureaucratization in diverse societies, he did not isolate the degree to which certain bureaucratic processes may be specific to, or influenced by, capitalist development *per se*. He failed to disentangle the 'impact of cultural, economic and technological forces' on the growth of bureaucracy, and to say to what extent these were independent of capitalist development. In the end, the particular connection between the state, bureaucrat- ization and capitalism is left obscure. Further, although Weber's stress on the conflicts between nation-states captures an important aspect of the international context of states, it is also left clouded by a variety of intriguing but incomplete reflections on the nature of such states and by a dubious patriotic fervour.

Weber's writings have had an enormous influence on the development of sociology and political science in the Anglo- American world. They have stimulated a rich variety of develop- ments, two of which deserve some attention here: 'pluralism' or empirical democratic theory (which takes as a starting point Weberian ideas about the multi-dimensionality of power) and 'geopolitical' conceptions of politics (which focus on the state at the intersection of national and international conditions and pressures). While neither of these bodies of work has grown out of Weber's work alone, his writings have certainly had a notable impact on both.

A variety of pluralist theories have been expounded, but I shall focus initially on what may be regarded as the 'classical version' of pluralism developed in the writings of Laswell, Truman and Dahl, among others.[150] This version had a pervasive influence in the 1950s and 1960s. Relatively few political and social theorists would accept it in unmodified form today, though many politicians, journalists and others in the mass media still appear to do so. Dahl and his colleagues deployed Weberian ideas as part of their effort to challenge fundamental Marxian axioms about class as the central structural determinant of the state and political outcomes. In the process they totally recast the connections between state, bureau-cratic organizations and classes, and shifted the attention of political sociology and political science to those institutional arrangements designed to ensure a responsiveness by political leaders to citizens — in particular, the competition for electoral support and the activities of social groups or organized interests in relation to government.[151]

The essence of the classical pluralist position stems from the view that there are many determinants of the distribution of power other than class and, therefore, many power centres. But this idea is taken much further than Weber took it himself. In the pluralist account, power is non-hierarchically and competitively arranged. It is an inextricable part of an 'endless process of bargaining' between numerous groups representing different interests, e.g. business organizations, trade unions, parties, ethnic groups, students, prison officers, women's institutes, religious groups.[152] Clearly there are many inequalities in society (of schooling, health, income, wealth, etc.) and not all groups have equal access to equal resources. However, nearly every 'interest group' has some advantage which can be utilized in the democratic process to make an impact. Hence the determination of political decisions at either a local or national level cannot reflect a 'majestic march' of 'the public' united upon matters of basic policy — as imagined, albeit in quite different ways, by Locke, Bentham and Rousseau.[153] Political outcomes are, rather, the result of governments and, ultimately, the executive trying to mediate and adjudicate between competing demands. In this process the state becomes almost indistinguishable from the ebb and flow of bargaining, the competitive pressure of interests. Indeed, individual government departments are sometimes conceived as just another kind of interest group.

This situation is not regarded as a bad thing; for competition among social groups, in the context of the open contest for government — the rules of democratic procedure — ensures that the competition is fair and creates government by multiple groups or multiple minorities which, in turn, secures the democratic character of a regime. Dahl calls this 'polyarchy' or rule by the many or 'minorities government'.[154] It is, in his view, both a desirable state of affairs and one to which most liberal democracies approximate.

The position can be criticized on many grounds — grounds which many 'pluralists', among them Dahl, would now accept.[155] The existence of many power centres hardly guarantees that government will (a) listen to them all equally; (b) do anything other than communicate with leaders of such groups; (c) be susceptible to influence by anybody other than those in powerful positions; (d) do anything about the issues under discussion, and so on.[156] Additionally, it is patently clear that not only do many groups not have the resources to compete in the national political arena with the clout of, say, multinational corporations, but many people do not even have access to the minimum resources for political mobilization. Moreover, the very capacity of governments to act in ways that interest groups may desire is constrained, as many Marxists have argued and as 'neo-pluralists' like Charles E. Lindblom now accept. The constraints on Western governments and state institutions — constraints imposed by the requirements of private accumulation — systematically limit policy options. The system of private investment, private property, etc, creates objective exigencies which must be met if economic growth and stable development are to be sustained. If these arrangements are threatened, economic chaos quickly ensues and the legitimacy of governments can be undermined. As Lindblom put it, 'depression, inflation, or other economic disasters can bring down a government. A major function of government, therefore, is to see to it that businessmen perform their tasks'.[157] The state must follow a political agenda which is at least favourable to, i.e, biased towards, the development of the system of private enterprise and corporate power. Of course, 'neo-pluralists' retain some of the essential tenets of 'classical pluralism' including the account of the way liberal democracy generates a variety of interest groups and provides a crucial obstacle to the development of a monolithic unresponsive state.

One of the most severe deficiencies of existing theories of the state is their tendency to concentrate on, for example, group bargaining within *a* nation-state (pluralism), or on the citizen and his or her relation to *the* state (liberal democracy), or on the relation between classes, the economy and the state in *a* capitalist country albeit with imperialist ambitions (Marxism). It is important to relate 'the state' to the context of international conditions and pressures. For instance, the capitalist world was created in dependence on an international market — the 'European world economy' — which generated multiple interconnections between nation-states that were beyond the control of any one such state.[158] Weber's work has had a notable impact on the development of ideas such as these, emphasizing how the very nature of the state crystallizes at the intersection of international and national conditions and pressures.

Among social scientists who have pursued this perspective today is Theda Skocpol.[159] Her work bears the mark of Weber as well as other closely related figures, including the historian Otto Hintze (1861—1940).[160] Hintze sought to show how two phenomena, above all, condition the real organization of the state. 'These are, first, the structure of social classes, and second, the external ordering of ... states — their position relative to each other, and their overall position in the world.'[161] Struggles among social classes at home and conflicts among nations have a dramatic impact on the organization and power of states. The 'shape' of a state — its size, external configuration, military structure, ethnic composition and relations, labour composition, among other things — is deeply rooted in the history of external events and conditions.[162] The state is, as Skocpol put it, 'Janus-faced, with an intrinsically dual anchorage in class-divided socio-economic structures and an international system of states'.[163]

Skocpol rejects 'society-centred' approaches to the explanation of the state and governmental activities because their explanatory strategies involve conceiving of the state simply as an 'arena' for the struggle of groups, movements and/or classes contending for advantage, or as merely a 'functional entity' responding to the 'imperatives' or 'needs' of civil society or the capitalist economy. Either way the focus is on societal 'inputs' and 'outputs' to and from the state and the state itself *qua* specific kinds of organizations, resources and relations is blocked from view.[164] There are intrinsic limits to all theories, whether pluralist or Marxist, which adopt such approaches: they cannot provide an adequate focus on states 'as distinctive structures with their own specific histories'.[165]

If class relations as well as complex international circumstances provide the context of the state, how should the state itself be conceptualized? In Skocpol's account,

> The state properly conceived ... is a set of administrative, policing, and military organizations headed, and more or less well coordinated by, an executive authority. Any state first

and fundamentally extracts resources from society and deploys those to create and support coercive and administrative organizations . . . Of course . . . political systems . . . also may contain institutions through which social interests are represented in state policy making as well as institutions through which non-state actors are mobilised to participate in policy implementation. Nevertheless, the administrative and coercive organizations are the basis of state power . . .[166]

Such a perspective helps illuminate: the way state organizations themselves vary; how the capacities of state organizations change in relation to the organization and interest of socio-economic groups and the 'transnational' environment; how state personnel develop interests in internal security, policy formulation, and competition with other nation-states which may be at variance with the interests of other social groups or classes. It allows, Skocpol argues, the distinctiveness and histories of particular state agencies to be unpacked, thus 'bringing the state back in' to the abstract theory of the state.[167]

These reflections were developed by Skocpol in relation to the theory of revolutions, but on their own it is clear that they constitute less a theory and more a framework for analysis of the state — a useful framework, nonetheless, to the extent that it offsets some of the limitations of 'society-centred' theories.[168] At the same time, however, it may fail, as Wallerstein's work implies, to stress adequately the way the sovereignty of nation-states has been, and is ever more, compromised by the international interconnections of the world economy.[169] Further, while it is indeed important to examine the 'corporate identity' of state organizations and the interests state personnel develop, it is critical not to overstate this; for among the most valuable contributions of both Marxists and pluralists are insights into how social struggle is 'inscribed' into the organization, administration and policies of the state — the extent, for example, to which parliamentary forms themselves are the outcome of conflicts over the old powers of the monarchy, landed nobility and bourgeoisie. Moreover, the economic and electoral constraints on state activities mean that state autonomy from societal relations will almost always, at least in Western capitalist societies, be compromised, with the exception perhaps of phases of military adventure and war — although, it must be admitted, this exception begins to look ever more significant as the means of waging war become more menacing.[170]

Concluding remarks

There are many conceptual problems in surveying over four hundred years of writing on 'the modern state'. Even if writers since the late sixteenth century have taken the state to mean all the institutions and relations associated with 'government', these terms of reference have been profoundly altered. Most of the writers dealt with have taken different positions on what the state could, and indeed should, do; and in the case of figures like Bentham, Marx and Weber, it is clear that their analyses actually refer to disparate political phenomena. In concluding this essay, it may be useful to highlight some of the problems and disagreements.

Among the developments in the theory of the state since the sixteenth century, two notable innovations stand out: the concept of the state as an impersonal or 'anonymous' structure of power, and the problem of reconciling authority and liberty through a fundamentally new view of the 'rights, obligations and duties' of subjects. While Hobbes marks an intermediate point between absolutism and liberalism, liberal political theory since Locke clearly affirms the state as an impersonal (legally circumscribed) structure, and connects this idea to an institutional theory of political power, such as the division between legislatures and executives. The central problem facing liberal and liberal democratic theory concerned the relationship between the state, as an independent authority with supreme right to declare and administer law over a given territory, and the individual, with a right and interest to determine the nature and limits of the state's authority. In short, the question was: how should the 'sovereign state' be related to the 'sovereign people' who were in principle the source of its powers?

Modern liberal and liberal democratic theory has constantly sought to justify the sovereign power of the state while at the same time justifying limits upon that power. The history of this attempt since Machiavelli and Hobbes is the history of arguments to balance might and right, power and law, duties and rights. On the one hand, the state must have a monopoly of coercive power in order to provide a secure basis upon which trade, commerce and family life can prosper. On the other hand, by granting the state a regulatory and coercive capability, liberal political theorists were aware that they had accepted a force which could (and frequently did) deprive citizens of political and social freedoms.

It was the liberal democrats who provided the key institutional innovation to try to overcome this dilemma — representative democracy. The liberal concern with reason, law and freedom of choice could only be upheld properly by recognizing the political equality of mature individuals. Such equality would ensure not only a secure social environment in which people would be free to pursue their private activities and interests, but also that the state's personnel would do what was best in the general or public interest, e.g. pursue the greatest happiness of the greatest number. Thus, the democratic constitutional state, linked to the free market, resolved, the liberal democrats argued, the problems of ensuring both authority and liberty.

The struggle of liberalism against tyranny and the struggle by liberal democrats for political equality represented, according to Marx and Engels, a major step forward in the history of human emancipation. But for them the great universal ideals of 'liberty, equality and justice' could not be realized simply by the 'free' struggle for votes in the political system and by the 'free' struggle for profit in the market place. The advocates of the democratic state and the market economy present them as the only institutions under which liberty can be sustained and inequalities minimized. However, by virtue of its internal dynamics, the capitalist economy inevitably produces systematic inequality and hence massive restrictions on real freedom. While each step towards formal political equality is an advance, its liberating potential is severely curtailed by inequalities of class. As Marx wryly put it: 'Just as Christians are equal in heaven yet unequal on earth, so the individual members of a people are equal in the heaven of their political world yet unequal in the earthly existence of society'.[171]

In class societies, Marx and Engels maintained, the state cannot become the vehicle for the pursuit of the 'common good' or 'public interest'. Far from the state playing the role of emancipator, protective knight, umpire or judge in the face of disorder, the agencies of the state are enmeshed in the struggles of civil society. Marxists conceive of the state as an extension of civil society, reinforcing the social order for the enhancement of particular interests — in capitalist society, the long-run interests of the capitalist class. It is not the state, as Marx put it in his early writings, which underlies the social order, but the social order which underlies the state. Marx did not deny the desirability of liberty and equality — far from it. His argument is that political emancipation is only a step toward human emancipation, i.e. the *complete* democratization of society as well as the state. In his view, liberal democratic society fails when judged by its own principles; and to take these principles seriously is to become a socialist. 'True democracy' can only be established with the destruction of social classes and ultimately the abolition of the state itself: the state must 'wither away' leaving a system of self-government linked to collectively shared duties and work.[172]

The history of Marxism, and of socialism more generally, since Marx has been distinguished by deep conflicts about how to define appropriate political goals and about how to develop political strategy in historical conditions often quite different from those envisaged by Marx himself. A preoccupation with actually taking power shifted attention, at least in much of the work of Lenin and his followers, to questions about the role of the Party, Party organization and the nature of the transition to socialism. In the process, consideration of the problem of state power was regarded as of secondary importance to the practical exigencies of making revolution.

Weber believed that the Bolsheviks' political ambitions were premissed on a deficient understanding of the nature of the modern state and the complexity of political life. In his account, the history of the state and the history of political struggle could not in any way (even 'in the last instance') be reduced to class relations: the origins and tasks of the modern state suggested it was far more than a 'superstructure' on an economic 'base'. Moreover, even if class relations were transformed, institutions of direct democracy could not replace the state; for there would be a massive problem of coordination and regulation which would inevitably be 'resolved' by bureaucracy, and by bureaucracy alone unless other institutions were nourished to check its power. The problems posed in the liberal pursuit of a balance between might and right, power and law, are, Weber thought, inescapable elements of modernity.

Weber feared that political life in West and East would be ever more ensnared by a rationalized, bureaucratic system of administration — a 'steel-hard cage', as he wrote. Against this he championed the countervailing power of private capital, the competitive party system and strong political leadership to secure national power and prestige; all of which could prevent the domination of politics by state officials. In so arguing, the limitations of his political thought become apparent: some of the key insights and principles of both Marxist and liberal political theory seem to have been set aside. The significance of massive inequalities of political and class power are played down because of the priority of power, i.e. interstate, politics; and this priority leaves the balance between might and right in the end to the judgment of 'charismatic' political leaders locked into the competition between state and economic bureaucracies — a situation which comes perilously close to accepting that even the tenets of traditional liberalism can no longer be upheld in the modern age.

The difficulties of coming to a judgment about the modern state are compounded when one examines it in relation to the system of nation-states and the international interconnections of the world economy. The more one explores this context, the more tenuous appears the abstract idea of 'the state'. Historical and geographical variation in the relations between states, as well as in the nature of the states themselves, force us to ask whether the search for a theory of 'the state' is misplaced. Yet while we must be sensitive to the existence of 'states' and 'societies', we recognize a continuity through states in their modern guise — a peculiar mix of force and right, that constrains and shapes the lives of generations. This presence compels us to pursue seriously — and ever more urgently in the face of the global struggle for resources and the escalating capacity for mass destruction — the issues of might and right, liberty and equality, class power and domination, violence and the nation-state.

Notes and References

1. I have benefited enormously from the comments and advice of many people on earlier drafts of this essay. I would like to thank in particular: David Beetham, John Dunn, Anthony Giddens, Bram Gieben, Stuart Hall, Joel Krieger, John Keane, Paul Lewis, Noel Parker, Michelle Stanworth, John Thompson, Tony Walton and Adam Westoby.

2. See Quentin Skinner, *The Foundations of Modern Political Thought,* 2 Vols, Cambridge, Cambridge University Press, 1978. Cf. Franz Neumann, *The Democratic and the Authoritarian State,* New York, Free Press, 1964.

3. See, for example, Gianfranco Poggi, *The Development of the Modern State,* London, Hutchinson, 1978; Charles Tilly, 'Reflections on the history of European state-making', in C. Tilly (ed.) *The Formation of National States in Western Europe*, Princeton, Princeton University Press, 1975; Theda Skocpol, *States and Social Revolutions: A Comparative Analysis of France, Russia and China,* Cambridge, Cambridge University Press, 1979; Reinhard Bendix, *Kings or People*, Berkeley, University of California Press, 1980; S. I. Benn and R. S. Peters, *Social Principles and the Democratic State,* London, Allen & Unwin, 1959; and John Keane, *Public Life and Late Capitalism,* Cambridge, Cambridge University Press, 1983, Essay 6.

4. Quoted in Skinner, *The Foundations of Modern Political Thought,* Vol. 2, p. 349.

5. *Ibid*, p. 353, and see his concluding remarks on this idea, pp. 349—58.
6. See Jürgen Habermas, *Strukturwandel der Öffentlichteit*, Neuwied, Luchterhand, 1962; Carole Pateman, *The Problem of Political Obligation*, Chichester, John Wiley and Sons, 1979; and John Keane, *Public Life and Late Capitalism*.
7. See C. B. Macpherson, *The Real World of Democracy*, Oxford, Oxford University Press, Ch. 1. Cf. Anthony Giddens, *A Contemporary Critique of Historical Materialism*, London, Macmillan, 1981, Chs 8 and 9.
8. For an interesting discussion see John Dunn, *Western Political Theory in the Face of the Future*, Cambridge, Cambridge University Press, 1979, Ch. 2.
9. Macpherson, *The Real World of Democracy*, p. 6.
10. Hobbes, *Leviathan*, edited by C. B. Macpherson, Harmondsworth, Penguin, 1968, p. 81. For an interesting reflection on this idea see Kenneth Dyson, *The State Tradition in Western Europe*, Oxford, Martin Robertson, 1980, Ch. 7.
11. For a helpful introductory account see John Plamenatz, *Man and Society*, Vol. 1, London, Longman, 1963, pp. 116—54.
12. See Dunn, *Western Political Theory in the Face of the Future*, pp. 23, 42—3, 50. Cf. Quentin Skinner, 'The ideological context of Hobbes's political thought', *The Historical Journal*, IX, 3, 1966, pp. 286—317.
13. Hobbes, *De Cive* in *The English Works of Thomas Hobbes*, edited by Sir William Molesworth, London, 1839—44, Vol. 2, p. 109 and quoted in Steven Lukes, *Individualism*, New York, Harper and Row, 1973, p. 77.
14. Cf. C. B. Macpherson, 'Introduction' to Hobbes, *Leviathan*. For a fuller account see his *The Political Theory of Possessive Individualism*, Oxford, Clarendon Press, 1962.
15. Hobbes, *Leviathan*, p. 161.
16. See R. S. Peters, *Hobbes*, Harmondsworth, Penguin, 1956, Ch. 9, or his concise statement in *The Encyclopedia of Philosophy*, Vol. 4, New York, Macmillan, 1967, pp. 41—3.
17. See *Leviathan*, Part 1, Chs 13—15.
18. *Ibid*, Ch. 13.
19. See Plamenatz, *Man and Society*, Vol. 1, pp. 122—32, for a clear discussion of these ideas.
20. See *Leviathan*, Chs 14 and 15.
21. An interesting discussion of this idea of sovereignty in relation to other conceptions can be found in S. I. Benn, 'The uses of sovereignty', *Political Studies*, 3, 1955, pp. 109—22.
22. See *Leviathan*, Ch. 14.
23. *Ibid*, p. 223.
24. *Ibid*, pp. 227—8.
25. *Ibid*, p. 220.

26. Cf. R. S. Peters, *Hobbes,* Ch. 9.
27. C. B. Macpherson, 'Introduction' to Hobbes, *Leviathan*, p. 45. Cf. *Leviathan*, p. 728.
28. *Leviathan,* pp. 376, 382—3.
29. *Ibid,* Ch. 21.
30. See, for example, Milton Friedman, *Capitalism and Freedom,* Chicago, University of Chicago Press, 1962.
31. Locke, *Two Treatises of Government,* a critical edition with an 'Introduction' by Peter Laslett, Cambridge, Cambridge University Press, 1963, p. 372. See Laslett's comment in note 36 on the same page.
32. *Ibid,* p. 371.
33. See John Dunn, *The Political Thought of John Locke,* Cambridge, Cambridge University Press, 1969, Part 3.
34. Cf. Plamenatz, *Man and Society,* Ch. 6 and Dunn, 'Consent in the political theory of John Locke', in *Political Obligation in its Historical Context,* Cambridge, Cambridge University Press, 1980, pp. 29—52.
35. See Laslett, 'Introduction' to Locke, *Two Treatises of Government,* pp. 130—5.
36. Locke, *Two Treatises of Government,* p. 309.
37. *Ibid,* p. 311.
38. *Ibid,* p. 395, para. 123.
39. *Ibid,* pp. 327—44. Interesting and contrasting accounts of Locke on property can be found in Macpherson, *The Political Theory of Possessive Individualism,* Plamenatz, *Man and Society* and Dunn, *The Political Thought of John Locke.*
40. See, for example, *Two Treatises of Government,* pp. 316—17, para. 13.
41. *Ibid,* p. 308, para. 3 and pp. 395—6, para. 124.
42. *Ibid,* pp. 372—6, paras 94—7. See Laslett, 'Introduction' to this work, pp. 127—8, whose account of these agreements I have followed.
43. *Ibid,* for example, pp. 402—3, para. 135 and pp. 412—13, para. 149.
44. *Ibid,* p. 410. Cf. Plamenatz, *Man and Society,* pp. 218, 228—9.
45. Cf. Dunn, *The Political Thought of John Locke,* Ch. 10 and Julian H. Franklin, *John Locke and the Theory of Sovereignty,* Cambridge, Cambridge University Press, 1978.
46. See Plamenatz, *Man and Society,* p. 228.
47. Lukes, *Individualism*, pp. 80—1.
48. See Dunn, 'Consent in the political theory of John Locke', pp. 36—7.
49. Dunn, *Western Political Theory in the Face of the Future,* p. 39 (my emphasis).
50. Cf. Laslett, 'Introduction', pp. 134—5.
51. *Ibid,* p. 123.
52. Plamenatz, pp. 231, 251—2.

53. One must guard against exaggerating this claim. See Dunn, 'The politics of Locke in England and America in the eighteenth century', in *Political Obligation in its Historical Context*, pp. 53—77.

54. Bentham, *Constitutional Code*, Bk. 1, Ch. 9 in *The Works of Jeremy Bentham*, Vol. IX, edited by Bowring, p. 47, quoted in C. B. Macpherson, *The Life and Times of Liberal Democracy*, Oxford, Oxford University Press, 1977, p. 36.

55. See Macpherson, *The Life and Times of Liberal Democracy*, Ch. 2, which provides an account of Bentham and James Mill to which I am indebted.

56. Cf. Bentham, *Fragment on Government*, in W. Harrison (ed.), Oxford, Blackwell, 1960 and James Mill, *An Essay on Government*, Cambridge, Cambridge University Press, 1937.

57. Cf. the extracts from Bentham, *Fragment on Government*, in Part 1, 'Classical Conceptions of the State', of this volume.

58. See Bentham, *Principles of the Civil Code*, in *Works*, Vol. I.

59. See James Mill, 'Prisons and prison discipline', in *Essays on Government*, London, J. Innis, 1828, pp. 1—24.

60. Cf. Michel Foucault, *Discipline and Punish*, London, Allen Lane, 1977, Part 3, and Michael Ignatieff, *A Just Measure of Pain*, London, Macmillan, 1978, Ch. 6. I am grateful to John Keane for comments on this issue.

61. Macpherson, *The Life and Times of Liberal Democracy*, pp. 42—3.

62. Cf. Carole Pateman, *Participation and Democratic Theory*, Cambridge, Cambridge University Press, 1970, Ch. 1.

63. See John Stuart Mill, *Representative Government* in *Utilitarianism, Liberty, and Representative Government*, London, Dent and Sons, 1951 and, in particular, the extracts from this work in Part 1, 'Classical Conceptions of the State', of this volume. See also Mill, *On Liberty*, Harmondsworth, Penguin, 1982.

64. Cf. Macpherson, *The Life and Times of Liberal Democracy*, Ch. 3 and Dunn, *Western Political Theory in the Face of the Future*, pp. 51—3.

65. J. S. Mill, *On Liberty*, p. 59.

66. *Ibid*, p. 68.

67. *Ibid*, p. 69.

68. See Alan Ryan, *The Philosophy of John Stuart Mill*, London, Macmillan, 1970.

69. *On Liberty*, pp. 71—2.

70. *Ibid*, p. 72.

71. *Ibid*, Ch. 5.

72. Mill was committed to *laissez-faire* in economic policy in his early works, but he later modified his views. See Pateman, *Participation and Democratic Theory*, Ch. 2.

73. See Macpherson, *The Life and Times of Liberal Democracy*, pp. 57—64 for a discussion of the complexity of Mill's reflections on voting.

74. For a fuller account of 'citizenship rights' and some of the struggles concerning them, see the extracts by Marshall and Therborn in Part 3 of this volume.

75. Noberto Bobbio, 'Are there alternatives to representative democracy?' *Telos,* 35, Spring 1978, p. 17.

76. In Britain and the United States a variety of theories of the liberal democratic state have developed in recent times including various theories of pluralism elaborated by, among others, Schumpeter, Laswell, Truman and Dahl, and 'liberal anarchist' or 'libertarian' views expounded by, for example, Hayek and Nozick. Pluralist views are discussed later in this chapter and Nozick's work is introduced in the final Part of this volume.

77. See, for example, Lucio Colletti, *From Rousseau to Lenin,* London, New Left Books, 1972.

78. Rousseau, *The Social Contract,* Harmondsworth, Penguin, 1968, p. 49.

79. *Ibid,* p. 59.

80. Maurice Cranston, 'Introduction', *The Social Contract*, p. 30.

81. *The Social Contract*, p. 141.

82. Caution is required about the use of the term democracy in relation to Rousseau's writings. He refers to the political system under discussion as 'republicanism'. See *ibid,* pp. 114 and 82, and for a general account, Bk. 3, Chs 1—5.

83. *Ibid,* pp. 60—1.

84. *Ibid,* pp. 72—3, 75.

85. *Ibid,* p. 65. cf. p. 82.

86. '*Lettres écrites de la montagne*', 2, letter 8, in J. J. Rousseau, *Oeuvres Complètes de J. J. Rousseau,* Paris, 1911, 3, p. 227, quoted in Keane, *Public Life and Late Capitalism,* Essay 6.

87. *The Social Contract*, p. 76. cf. p. 46.

88. *Ibid,* Bk. 3, Chs 1, pp. 11—14, 18. There are additional institutional positions set out by Rousseau, for instance, that of 'the Lawgiver', which cannot be elaborated here. See *ibid,* pp. 83—8, 95—6.

89. *Ibid,* p. 102.

90. *Ibid,* pp. 136—9, 148.

91. *Ibid,* for example, Bk. 3, Ch. 4.

92. Cf. William Connolly, *Appearance and Reality,* Cambridge, Cambridge University Press, 1981, Ch. 7, for an interesting discussion.

93. Marx, *The Critique of Hegel's Philosophy of Right,* Cambridge, Cambridge University Press, 1970, p. 131 (modified translation).

94. For an overview of Marx's and Engels's account of class see Anthony Giddens and David Held (eds), *Classes, Power and Conflict,* Part 1, London, Macmillan, 1982, pp. 12—39.

95. *Ibid,* pp. 28—35.

96. See John Maguire, *Marx's Theory of Politics,* Cambridge, Cambridge University Press, 1978, Ch. 1.

97.   This discussion draws heavily on my paper with Joel Krieger, 'Theories of the state: some competing claims' in S. Bornstein *et al.* (eds) *The State in Capitalist Europe*, London, Allen & Unwin, 1983, as do some remaining parts of this chapter. However, the arguments have been modified and developed in several respects.

98.   G. W. F. Hegel, *The Philosophy of Right*, trans. T. M. Knox, Oxford, Oxford University Press, 1967. See M. Perez-Diaz, *State, Bureaucracy and Civil Society*, London, Macmillan, 1978 for a clear and helpful discussion of Marx's relation to Hegel. The view of Hegel I have briefly presented here is very much Marx's view — a view which is challengeable in many respects. Cf. Gillian Rose, *Hegel Contra Sociology*, London, Athlone, 1981, especially Ch. 7.

99.   Marx, *The Critique of Hegel's Philosophy of Right*, pp. 41—54.

100. *Ibid*, p. 46.

101. *Ibid*, pp. 48, 51.

102. *Ibid*, pp. 46—7.

103. *Ibid*, p. 54.

104. Marx, *The Eighteenth Brumaire of Louis Bonaparte*, New York, International Publishers, 1963, p. 121.

105. See Maguire, *Marx's Theory of Politics* and M. E. Spencer, 'Marx on the state,' *Theory and Society*, 7, 1—2, pp. 167—98.

106. See *The Eighteenth Brumaire of Louis Bonaparte*, pp. 118 ff.

107. See, for instance, Marx and Engels, *The Communist Manifesto*, New York, International Publishers, 1948, and Marx, 'Preface' to *A Contribution to the Critique of Political Economy*, London, Lawrence and Wishart, 1971.

108. Cf. Ralph Miliband, 'Marx and the state,' *Socialist Register, 1965*, London, Merlin Press, 1965.

109. Edüard Bernstein, *Evolutionary Socialism*, New York, Schocken Books, 1961.

110. See Lenin, *State and Revolution*, New York, International Publishers, 1971.

111. Some important exceptions are Maguire, *Marx's Theory of Politics;* Perez-Diaz, *State, Bureaucracy and Civil Society*; and Hal Draper, *Karl Marx's Theory of Revolution*, Vol. 1, New York, Monthly Review Press, 1977.

112. *State and Revolution*, p. 7. For an account which is sensitive to the complexities of the development of Lenin's thought, see Neil Harding, *Lenin's Political Thought*, 2 Vols, London, Macmillan, 1977 and 1981.

113. *State and Revolution*, p. 17.

114. *Ibid*, pp. 72—3.

115. *Ibid*, pp. 35—9.

116. Lenin was far from consistent on these matters. For a useful discussion see R. Brown *et al. Bureaucracy*, Port Melbourne, Edward Arnold, 1979, pp. 72—87.

117. *State and Revolution*, p. 16.

118. See M. Lewin, *Lenin's Last Struggle*, London, Pluto Press, 1975.

119. For surveys of this material see Bob Jessop, 'Recent theories of the capitalist state,' *Cambridge Journal of Economics,* 1, 1977, pp. 343–73, and D. A. Gold *et al,* 'Recent developments in Marxist theories of the capitalist state,' *Monthly Review,* 27, 5–6, 1975.
120. See Miliband *The State in Capitalist Society,* London, Weidenfeld & Nicolson, 1969. Cf. his 'The capitalist state — reply to Nicos Poulantzas,' in R. Blackburn (ed.) *Ideology in Social Science,* London, Fontana, 1972, and *Marxism and Politics,* Oxford, Oxford University Press, 1977.
121. See Poulantzas, 'The problem of the capitalist state,' in R. Blackburn (ed.) *Ideology in Social Science.*
122. Poulantzas, *Political Power and Social Classes,* London, New Left Books, 1973, pp. 331–40.
123. *Ibid,* pp. 287–8.
124. See Poulantzas *Classes in Contemporary Capitalism,* London, New Left Books, 1975.
125. See Poulantzas *State, Power, Socialism,* London, Verso and New Left Books, 1980, for his most interesting elaboration of these ideas.
126. For an introduction to this tradition see David Held, *Introduction to Critical Theory,* London, Hutchinson, 1980. For a brief summary of the ideas of Offe and Habermas (with relevant references) see the last chapter in Part 5 of this volume.
127. Cf. Giddens, *A Contemporary Critique of Historical Materialism,* Ch. 9, and Boris Frankel, 'The state of the state after Leninism,' *Theory and Society,* 7, 1/2, 1979.
128. See, for example, the chapters in the final Part of this volume by Poulantzas and Macpherson. Cf. Giddens, 'Class division, class conflict and citizenship rights,' in *Profiles and Critiques in Social Theory,* London, Macmillan, 1983.
129. For example, Charles E. Lindblom, *Politics and Markets,* New York, Basic Books, 1977, whose work is discussed briefly in the following section.
130. Weber, *Economy and Society,* Vol. 2, Berkeley, University of California Press, 1978, pp. 951–2.
131. See Martin Albrow, *Bureaucracy,* London, Pall Mall, 1970, pp. 37–49.
132. Weber, 'Politics as a vocation', in H. H. Gerth and C. W. Mills (eds) *From Max Weber,* New York, Oxford University Press, 1972, p. 78.
133. *Ibid,* p. 79, and see the extracts from Weber's work in Part 1, 'Classical Conceptions of the State', of this volume.
134. Weber, *General Economic History,* London, Allen & Unwin, 1923, p. 232.
135. *Economy and Society,* Vol. 2, pp. 1381 ff.
136. *Ibid,* p. 1465.
137. *Economy and Society,* Vol. 1, pp. 220–1.
138. *Ibid,* p. 223.
139. *Economy and Society,* Vol. 2, p. 973.

140. See Wolfgang J. Mommsen, *The Age of Bureaucracy,* Oxford, Basil Blackwell, 1974.
141. Albrow, *Bureaucracy,* p. 48 and see Mommsen, *ibid,* last chapter.
142. *Economy and Society,* Vol. 2, p. 1402.
143. *Ibid,* p. 143.
144. See the Weber extracts in *Classes, Power and Conflict,* edited by Giddens and Held, pp. 60—86.
145. See Guenther Roth and Wolfgang Schluchter, *Max Weber's Vision of History,* Berkeley, University of California Press, 1979.
146. Cf. Erik Olin Wright *Class, Crisis and the State,* London, New Left Books, 1978, Ch. 4.
147. Giddens, *Central Problems in Social Theory: Action, Structure and Contradiction in Social Analysis,* London, Macmillan, 1979, Ch. 4.
148. *Ibid,* pp. 147—8.
149. See Joel Krieger, *Undermining Capitalism,* Princeton, Princeton University Press, 1983, for an interesting and important discussion of Weber's concept of bureaucracy.
150. Cf, for example, D. B. Truman, *The Governmental Process,* New York, Knopf, 1951; and Robert A. Dahl, *A Preface to Democratic Theory,* Chicago, University of Chicago Press, 1956, *Polyarchy: Participation and Opposition,* New Haven, Yale University Press, 1971, and *Who Governs? Democracy and Power in an American City,* New Haven and London, Yale University Press, 1975.
151. See Pateman, *Participation and Democratic Theory,* Ch. 1.
152. See the extract from Dahl in Part 1, 'Classical Conceptions of the State', of this volume.
153. Dahl, *A Preface to Democratic Theory,* p. 146.
154. *Ibid,* p. 133.
155. See Dahl, 'Pluralism revisited,' *Comparative Politics,* 10, 1978, pp. 191—204.
156. See Jack Lively, *Democracy,* Oxford, Basil Blackwell, 1975, pp. 20—4, 54—6, 71—2, 141—5, for a discussion of these points. Cf. Steven Lukes, *Power,* London, Macmillan, 1977.
157. Lindblom, *Politics and Markets,* pp. 122—3.
158. See Immanuel Wallerstein, *The Modern World-System,* New York, Academic Press, 1974.
159. See Skocpol, *States and Revolutions.* Cf. her chapter, as well as those by Anderson and Nairn, in Part 2 of this volume.
160. *States and Revolutions,* p. 307, n.77. Cf. Otto Hintze in Felix Gilbert (ed.) *Historical Essays,* New York, Oxford University Press, 1975, Chs 4—6, 11.
161. Hintze, *Historical Essays,* p. 183.
162. For some of the theoretical background to these ideas see Dyson, *The State Tradition in Western Europe.*
163. Skocpol, *States and Revolutions,* p. 32.
164. *Ibid,* pp. 25—33.

165. See Jonathan Zeitlin, 'Shop floor bargaining and the state: a contradictory relationship', p. 24, to be published in S. Tolliday and J. Zeitlin (eds), *Shop Floor Bargaining and The State: Historical and Contemporary Perspectives* (forthcoming, 1984).

166. *States and Revolutions,* p. 29.

167. See Skocpol, 'Bringing the state back in', *Items* (SSRC) 36, 1/2, June 1982, pp. 1–8.

168. Cf. Zeitlin, 'Shop floor bargaining and the state', pp. 24–6.

169. Cf. Wallerstein, *The Modern World-System,* and 'The rise and future demise of the world capitalist system', *Comparative Studies in Society and History,* 16, 4, 1974, pp. 387–415.

170. Cf. Giddens, *A Contemporary Critique of Historical Materialism,* Ch. 10.

171. Marx, *The Critique of Hegel's Philosophy of Right,* p. 80.

172. These ideas are explored further in the final Part of this volume.

Part 1

Classic Conceptions of the State

Introduction

NOEL PARKER

The extracts in Part 1 provide a range of far-reaching and fundamental definitions of the state and its relation to society, taken from four centuries of writings on the state, on which it is possible to construct theories that can be applied to the modern state in all its diversity. We offer you this selection to give you a feel of how thinkers past and present have sought some fundamental features in the historical currents of political development they witnessed; to encourage you to enjoy their writings at greater length elsewhere; to provide you with an initial vocabulary for the fundamentals of the modern state before going on to more specific writings about it; and to help you grasp in bold terms some contrasting positions on the state. Since these are the aims of Part 1, we feel that you will not find the brevity and starkness of the authors' statements a drawback. It must, of course, be borne in mind not only that the selection of 'classic' authors is inevitably incomplete and to some extent arbitrary, but also that the passages reproduced are only a tiny fraction of their output. But compressing them in this way renders them more accessible and counterposes their ideas all the more dramatically.

While it would contradict the aims of this part to set out a summary of what the authors say, it is appropriate to indicate some themes and contrasts that run through the chronological order of the selection. Thus, in the earliest excerpts, on Machiavelli and Hobbes, we find evolved the central role of power in the state. Against the background of the instability, rivalry and war between sixteenth-century Italian states, Machiavelli conveys a hard-nosed, practical approach to power. He accepts that 'the prince' must judiciously mix a show of dignity, virtue and law for his subjects with menace and deception in his relations with them and with other states. Justifications for the behaviour of states are thus sharply distinguished from those of private citizens — in what was

59

subsequently to be called 'reason of state'. In Hobbes, the justification of state power is more thoroughly integrated into a theory of human relations and the role of the state in them. The equality between individuals which is the starting point of much modern political thinking here explains the need for state power, which is created by a once-and-for-all agreement, to save men from the miserable consequences of their unchecked passions (a continuous war 'of every man, against every man') by investing all power in a sovereign which is alone capable of enforcing the laws of nature in reality. The argument is supported by implicit reference to the recently ended English Civil War of the 1640s.

Even in one of the most modern selections, the extracts from Weber, this idea of the state's monopoly of legitimate coercive forces can still be found. But in Weber's case the grounds and practices that legitimate that monopoly are more intricate and diverse than for Hobbes, and comprehend in particular peculiarly modern features of the state, such as an extensive formal bureaucracy and the wide appeal of 'national' prestige.

While Hobbes explains and justifies state power in a society of equal individuals, three late eighteenth-century writers, Rousseau, Paine and Wollstonecraft try to incorporate two new elements into the earlier theoretical mix: some kind of citizens' power (what we today think of as democracy, though they used the word differently); and the broader effects of the state upon social and moral development. But they do this while holding fundamentally differing views of social relations. Going beyond the relative optimism of Locke, who wrote a century earlier, Paine sees human society as an arena in which amicable relations, agreed rules of behaviour and human morality develop naturally. The state, which up to then had suppressed this natural humanity, must foster and build upon it, largely by preserving natural rights and following the will of society or the nation as a whole. Wollstonecraft's work, written the year after that of Paine, sees political and social organization in similar terms of moral improvement, but demands in particular the independence and education of women. On the other hand, Rousseau (chronologically the first of the three), though just as sceptical about existing states, thought human society itself a breeding ground for inequality, dissension and oppression, to which ill-constructed state power contributed. True sovereignty had, then, to be brought into existence by the formation of the state along new lines, upon the basis of equality. Individuals, obliged to think in terms of equal subjection to the law they were enacting, would incline in their political deliberations to the good of the community as a whole.

It is clearly difficult to combine state power, equality amongst individuals and democratic sovereignty in the people. For equality appears as likely to engender internal conflict, requiring an oppressive state to reinforce itself and monopolize power, as it is likely to encourage a united democratic will. The key question seems to be whether social relations beyond the confines of state power evolve equality and consensus, or inequality and conflict. Put in more modern terms, this is the problem of how to accommodate the existence of different classes in society into a theory of the state.

There are various ways out of the dilemma. Bentham, whose extract here was written in the decade after Rousseau, but whose prolific output continued long after the death of Paine, Rousseau, and Wollstonecraft, scorned the attempt to show that the state can be founded upon any 'natural' order or voluntary consent. Rather, the purposes that the state pursues and the distribution of state power can be assessed in terms of their utility. The aim of the state is not to act for any fundamental equality or sovereignty in the people, but rather to distribute the benefits of state power and the penalties of resisting it such that individuals will judge it more advantageous to comply than disobey. Burke, attacking the 1789 Revolution in France goes further: the social order must for him be maintained with the same degree of mystique, tradition and religious practice as in the past, though the mix must be adjusted to changing conditions. On the other hand, natural rights and the democratic will, as Paine thought of them, must be decisively eschewed if the state is to benefit the members of society.

Another response to the dilemma posed by trying to combine state power, equality and democracy is to extend democracy still further, even to the extent of advocating anarchy. Thus Godwin argued, just six years after Paine, that it is fundamentally incoherent and wrong for the members of society to cede their power and responsibility to an agent such as the state. Rather, they should decide matters concerning their mutual relations for themselves in the virtual absence of any state power, via loosely organized and federated local meetings.

For Hegel, the first of our nineteenth-century writers and probably the most difficult of all to represent in an extract, the historical evolution of the state brings a solution to the conflicts between individuals by absorbing their subjective experience of their own individuality — but not in mere social tradition and mystique. The modern state, by combining culture, national identity and law, offers individuals the opportunity of willing participation in the realized form of a universal ethical truth which is the comprehensive rational order itself.

The sense of historical evolution towards a resolution of political problems is present, too, in the three mid nineteenth-century writers we have selected, Mill, Marx and Engels. They try in different ways to build progressive social and political evolution into their conceptions of democracy and the state. Mill makes the principle utility of state institutions their tendency to further a society's capacity for democracy. But he also redefines the democratic goal of people's sovereignty as 'representative' and 'equal' democracy, and the right of all to have their case argued rather than to administer the state power itself. Representative institutions have to be so constructed that all significant classes are equal in them and no viewpoint can be rejected out of hand in 'class legislation'. In advancing the cause of 'liberalism' as against 'democracy', Hayek in this century is likewise concerned with limiting the democratic use of state power — in his case via a definition of the free economic system. And the idea of pressures from social classes finds an echo, too, in the modern American writing of Dahl, for whom the power of the state can be understood as a varied assemblage of institutions negotiating demands from an even greater diversity of social groups.

Against Mill, it is also possible, of course, to argue that inequality and class differences can themselves direct the evolution of society and produce the state itself. Our other nineteenth-century theorists, Marx and Engels, argued precisely this. The thinking of the two being closely intertwined, we include excerpts from each and a joint one. In the first, Marx and Engels declare their expectation of a future transition to democracy through the development of social classes and relations of production. In the second excerpt, Engels sets out an overall conception of the state as the coercive device to contain class conflict (either by oppressing one class to the advantage of the other, propertied one, or by holding the ring between them). In the third, Marx describes class conflicts mediated in the actual political conflicts which gave rise to the relatively independent state run in France by Louis Bonaparte after 1851.

Within the Marxist tradition in the twentieth century, Lenin's writing here argues that a political framework so democratic as to resemble Godwin's anarchism is achievable once the crucial purpose of oppressive state power, the oppression of a majority class by a minority one, has been set aside via the victory and dictatorship of the proletarian majority. And Gramsci can be read as an exegesis of the varied mechanisms which operate class oppression via the state — or change, or break down. These mechanisms bring the individuals' economic behaviour into line with that required for the dominant class, though this is done at least as much by the 'neutrality' of law and the morality of civil society as by crude oppression.

As you can see, the relation of power, equality and democracy, together with their historical evolution, is one theme running through the ideas of the writers in this part. Because they pursue common questions, and indeed build upon each others' answers, it is tempting to imagine a sequence of development in which each simply developed the ideas of his predecessors. But this impression of a history of concepts of the state would, of course, be grotesquely naive. It is true that Rousseau read and extended Hobbes; Mill, Bentham; Lenin and Gramsci, Marx and Hegel; and so on. But writers on the state are enmeshed in history in other ways. They have not written merely for each other, but also in an attempt to understand or even to influence the historical currents which they experience — as Mill wrote to accommodate British nineteenth-century representative democracy to the evolution of social classes, or Lenin to set out the rationale of his own political leadership. And yet, in theorizing about the fundamental character of the state, they have also tried to generalize about its nature beyond the limits of the historical conjuncture known to them.

They must have succeeded in generalizing to some extent; for otherwise their different conceptions would not provide us with the tools they do to define some of the contemporary issues about the state and society which are the subject of later parts of this book. Contrast, for example, the views of Rousseau and of Gramsci concerning the relations of state and economy. For Rousseau, the normal drift of economic life is inimical to healthy political life, so that the state can and must confine the citizens' economic relations to terms of near equality if political life is to define the general interest. For Gramsci, the normal role of the state is to foster the social organization required for some given pattern of economic relations. Or compare the different views in this part on whether society determines the state or vice versa (Burke versus Engels) and whether individuals create the state or vice versa (Paine versus Hegel). Or, again, consider the differing criteria for a state power accepted as 'legitimate' which are offered by Hobbes, Bentham, Godwin, Burke, Hegel or Weber. Or, finally, look for the different notions of nationalism that occur in Paine or Gramsci. It is by starkly presenting fundamentally differing views of issues like this that these classic authors can provide a vocabulary for the fundamentals of the modern state.

Note *Sub-headings* — in cases where it is helpful, we have included authors' sub-headings or, occasionally, added our own.

1.1

Machiavelli: The Prince

I say that a prince should want to have a reputation for compassion rather than for cruelty: nonetheless, he should be careful that he does not make bad use of compassion. [. . .] So a prince should not worry if he incurs reproach for his cruelty so long as he keeps his subjects united and loyal. By making an example or two he will prove more compassionate than those who, being too compassionate, allow disorders which lead to murder and rapine. These nearly always harm the whole community, whereas executions ordered by a prince only affect individuals. A new prince, of all rulers, finds it impossible to avoid a reputation for cruelty, because of the abundant dangers inherent in a newly won state. Virgil, through the mouth of Dido, says:

Res dura, et regni novitas me talia cogunt
Moliri, et late fines custode tueri.[1]

Nonetheless, a prince should be slow to take action, and should watch that he does not come to be afraid of his own shadow; his behaviour should be tempered by humanity and prudence so that over-confidence does not make him rash or excessive distrust make him unbearable.

From this arises the following question: whether it is better to be loved than feared, or the reverse. The answer is that one would like to be both the one and the other; but because it is difficult to combine them, it is far better to be feared than loved if you cannot be both. One can make this generalization about men: they are ungrateful, fickle, liars, and deceivers, they shun danger and are greedy for profit; while you treat them well, they are yours. They would shed their blood for you, risk their property, their lives,

Niccolo Machiavelli (1469—1527)
Source: *The Prince,* trans. George Bull (Penguin Classics, Revised edition, 1975) pp. 95—7, 99—102. Copyright © George Bull, 1961, 1975.

their children, so long, as I said above, as danger is remote; but when you are in danger they turn against you. Any prince who has come to depend entirely on promises and has taken no other precautions ensures his own ruin; friendship which is bought with money and not with greatness and nobility of mind is paid for, but it does not last and it yields nothing. Men worry less about doing an injury to one who makes himself loved than to one who makes himself feared. The bond of love is one which men, wretched creatures that they are, break when it is to their advantage to do so; but fear is strengthened by a dread of punishment which is always effective.

The prince should nonetheless make himself feared in such a way that, if he is not loved, at least he escapes being hated. For fear is quite compatible with an absence of hatred; and the prince can always avoid hatred if he abstains from the property of his subjects and citizens and from their women. If, even so, it proves necessary to execute someone, this should be done only when there is proper justification and manifest reason for it. But above all a prince should abstain from the property of others; because men sooner forget the death of their father than the loss of their patrimony. It is always possible to find pretexts for confiscating someone's property; and a prince who starts to live by rapine always finds pretexts for seizing what belongs to others. On the other hand, pretexts for executing someone are harder to find and they are less easily sustained.

However, when a prince is campaigning with his soldiers and is in command of a large army then he need not worry about having a reputation for cruelty; because, without such a reputation, he can never keep his army united and disciplined. [. . .]

EVERYONE realizes how praiseworthy it is for a prince to honour his word and to be straightforward rather than crafty in his dealings; nonetheless contemporary experience shows that princes who have achieved great things have been those who have given their word lightly, who have known how to trick men with their cunning, and who, in the end, have overcome those abiding by honest principles.

You should understand, therefore, that there are two ways of fighting: by law or by force. The first way is natural to men, and the second to beasts. But as the first way often proves inadequate one must needs have recourse to the second. [. . .] A prudent ruler cannot, and should not, honour his word when it places him at a disadvantage and when the reasons for which he made his promise no longer exist. If all men were good, this precept would not be good; but because men are wretched creatures who would not keep their word to you, you need not keep your word to them. And a prince will never lack good excuses to colour his bad faith. [. . .] But one must know how to colour one's actions and to be a great liar and deceiver. Men are so simple, and so much creatures of circumstances, that the deceiver will always find someone ready to be deceived.

A prince, therefore, need not necessarily have all the good qualities I mentioned above, but he should certainly appear to have them. I would even go so far as to say that if he has these qualities and always behaves accordingly he will find them ruinous; if he only appears to have them they will render him service. He should appear to be compassionate, faithful to his word, guileless, and devout. And indeed he should be so. But his disposition should be such that, if he needs to be the opposite, he knows how. You must realize this: that a prince, and especially a new prince, cannot observe all those things which give men a reputation for virtue, because in order to maintain his state he is often forced to act in defiance of good faith, of charity, of kindness, of religion. And so he should have a flexible disposition, varying as fortune and circumstances dictate. As I said above, he should not deviate from what is good, if that is possible, but he should know how to do evil, if that is necessary.

A prince, then, should be very careful not to say a word which does not seem inspired by the five qualities I mentioned earlier. To those seeing and hearing him, he should appear a man of compassion, a man of good faith, a man of integrity, a kind and a religious man. And there is nothing so important as to seem to have this last quality. Men in general judge by their eyes rather than by their hands; because everyone is in a position to watch, few are in a position to come in close touch with you. Everyone sees what you appear to be, few experience what you really are. And those few dare not gainsay the many who are backed by the majesty of the state. In the actions of all men, and especially of princes, where there is no court of appeal, one judges by the result. So let a prince set about the task of conquering and maintaining his state; his methods will always be judged honourable and will be universally praised. The common people are always impressed by appearances and results. In this context, there are only common people, and there is no room for the few when the many are supported by the state. A certain contemporary ruler, whom it is better not to name, never preaches anything except peace and good faith; and he is an enemy of both one and the other, and if he had ever honoured either of them he would have lost either his standing or his state many times over.

Note

1. Translation: It is a harsh thing to do, but the very newness of my kingdom compels me to shoulder such burdens, and to set a guard on my borders [Eds].

1.2

Hobbes: Leviathan

Men by nature equal. Nature hath made men so equal, in the faculties of the body, and mind; as that though there be found one man sometimes manifestly stronger in body, or of quicker mind than another; yet when all is reckoned together, the difference between man, and man, is not so considerable, as that one man can thereupon claim to himself any benefit, to which another may not pretend, as well as he. For as to the strength of body, the weakest has strength enough to kill the strongest, either by secret machination, or by confederacy with others, that are in the same danger with himself. [. . .]

Hereby it is manifest, that during the time men live without a common power to keep them all in awe, they are in that condition which is called war; and such a war, as is of every man, against every man. For WAR, consisteth not in battle only, or the act of fighting; but in a tract of time, wherein the will to contend by battle is sufficiently known. [. . .]

Whatsoever therefore is consequent to a time of war, where every man is enemy to every man; the same is consequent to the time, wherein men live without other security, than what their own

Thomas Hobbes (1588—1679)
Source: From *Leviathan, or The Matter, Forme and Power of a Commonwealth Ecclesiastical and Civil* (1962) Fontana, pp. 141, 143—4, 173—4, 176—7. First published in 1651.

strength, and their own invention shall furnish them withal. In such condition, there is no place for industry; because the fruit thereof is uncertain: and consequently no culture of the earth; no navigation, nor use of the commodities that may be imported by sea; no commodious building; no instruments of moving, and removing, such things as require much force; no knowledge of the face of the earth; no account of time; no arts; no letters; no society; and which is worst of all, continual fear, and danger of violent death; and the life of man, solitary, poor, nasty, brutish, and short. [...]

It may peradventure be thought, there was never such a time, nor condition of war as this; and I believe it was never generally so, over all the world: but there are many places, where they live so now. For the savage people in many places of America, except the government of small families, the concord whereof dependeth on natural lust, have no government at all; and live at this day in that brutish manner, as I said before. Howsoever, it may be perceived what manner of life there would be, where there were no common power to fear, by the manner of life, which men that have formerly lived under a peaceful government, use to degenerate into, in a civil war. [...]

THE final cause, end, or design of men, who naturally love liberty, and dominion over others, in the introduction of that restraint upon themselves, in which we see them live in commonwealths, is the foresight of their own preservation, and of a more contented life thereby; that is to say, of getting themselves out from that miserable condition of war, which is necessarily consequent . . . to the natural passions of men, when there is no visible power to keep them in awe, and tie them by fear of punishment to the performance of their covenants, and observation of those laws of nature . . .

For the laws of nature, as *justice, equity, modesty, mercy,* and, in sum, *doing to others, as we would be done to,* of themselves, without the terror of some power, to cause them to be observed, are contrary to our natural passions, that carry us to partiality, pride, revenge, and the like. And covenants, without the swords, are but words, and of no strength to secure a man at all. Therefore notwithstanding the laws of nature, which every one hath then kept, when he has the will to keep them, when he can do it safely, if there be no power erected, or not great enough for our security; every man will, and may lawfully rely on his own strength and art, for caution against all other men. And in all places, where men have lived by small families, to rob and spoil one another, has been a trade, and so far from being reputed against the law of nature, that the greater spoils they gained, the greater was their honour; and men observed no other laws therein, but the laws of honour; that is, to abstain from cruelty, leaving to men their lives, and instruments of husbandry. And as small families did then; so now do cities and kingdoms which are but greater families, for their own security, enlarge their dominions, upon all pretences of danger, and fear of invasion, or assistance that may be given to invaders, and endeavour as much as they can, to subdue, or weaken their neighbours, by open force, and secret arts, for want of other caution, justly; and are remembered for it in after ages with honour.

Nor is it the joining together of a small number of men, that gives them this security; because in small numbers, small additions on the one side or the other, make the advantage of strength so great, as is sufficient to carry the victory; and therefore gives encouragement to an invasion. The multitude sufficient to confide in for our security, is not determined by any certain number, but by comparison with the enemy we fear; and is then sufficient, when the odds of the enemy is not of so visible and conspicuous moment, to determine the event of war, as to move him to attempt.
[...]

The only way to erect such a common power, as may be able to defend them from the invasion of foreigners, and the injuries of one another, and thereby to secure them in such sort, as that by their own industry, and by the fruits of the earth, they may nourish themselves and live contentedly; is, to confer all their power and strength upon one man, or upon one assembly of men, that may reduce all their wills, by plurality of voices, unto one will: which is as much as to say, to appoint one man, or assembly of men, to bear their person; and every one to own, and acknowledge himself to be author of whatsoever he that so beareth their person, shall act, or cause to be acted, in those things which concern the common peace and safety; and therein to submit their wills, every one to his will, and their judgments, to his judgment. This is more than consent, or concord; it is a real unity of them all, in one and the same person, made by covenant of every man with every man, in such manner, as if every man should say to every man, *I authorize and give up my right of governing myself, to this man, or to this assembly of men, on this condition, that thou give up thy right to him, and authorize all his actions in like manner.* This done, the multitude so united in one person, is called a COMMONWEALTH, in Latin CIVITAS. This is the generation of the great LEVIATHAN, or rather, to speak more reverently, of that *mortal god*, to which we owe under the *immortal God,* our peace and defence. [. . .] And in him consisteth the essence of the commonwealth; which, to define it, is *one person, of whose acts a great multitude, by mutual covenants one with another, have made themselves every one the author, to the end he may use the strength and means of them all, as he shall think expedient, for their peace and common defence.*

And he that carrieth this person is called SOVEREIGN, and said to have *sovereign power*; and every one besides, his SUBJECT.

The attaining to this sovereign power, is by two ways. One, by natural force; as when a man maketh his children, to submit themselves, and their children to his government, as being able to destroy them if they refuse; or by war subdueth his enemies to his will, giving them their lives on that condition. The other, is when men agree amongst themselves, to submit to some man, or assembly of men, voluntarily, on confidence to be protected by him against all others. This latter, may be called a political commonwealth, or commonwealth by *institution*; and the former, a commonwealth by *acquisition.*

1.3

Rousseau: The Social Contract

MAN was born free, and he is everywhere in chains. Those who think themselves the masters of others are indeed greater slaves than they. How did this transformation come about? I do not know. How can it be made legitimate? That question I believe I can answer. [. . .] The social order is a sacred right which serves as a basis for all other rights. And as it is not a natural right, it must be one founded on covenants. The problem is to determine what those covenants are. [. . .]

Jean-Jacques Rousseau (1712−78)
Source: From *The Social Contract* (1968) Penguin, pp. 49, 50, 59−64, 72−3, 75−6, 81, 96, 102, 131, 135. Trans. Maurice Cranston. Reprinted by permission of A. D. Peters & Co. Ltd. First published in 1762.

The social pact

I ASSUME that men reach a point where the obstacles to their preservation in a state of nature prove greater than the strength that each man has to preserve himself in that state. Beyond this point, the primitive condition cannot endure, for then the human race will perish if it does not change its mode of existence. [. . .]

'How to find a form of association which will defend the person and goods of each member with the collective force of all, and under which each individual, while uniting himself with the others, obeys no one but himself, and remains as free as before.' This is the fundamental problem to which the social contract holds the solution. [. . .]

[The] articles of association, rightly understood, are reducible to a single one, namely the total alienation by each associate of himself and all his rights to the whole community. Thus, in the first place, as every individual gives himself absolutely, the conditions are the same for all, and precisely because they are the same for all, it is in no one's interest to make the conditions onerous for others.

Secondly, since the alienation is unconditional, the union is as perfect as it could be, and no individual associate has any longer any rights to claim; for if rights were left to individuals, in the absence of any higher authority to judge between them and the public, each individual, being his own judge in some causes, would soon demand to be his own judge in all; and in this way the state of nature would be kept in being, and the association inevitably become either tyrannical or void.

Finally, since each man gives himself to all, he gives himself to no one; and since there is no associate over whom he does not gain the same rights as others gain over him, each man recovers the equivalent of everything he loses, and in the bargain he acquires more power to preserve what he has.

If, then, we eliminate from the social pact everything that is not essential to it, we find it comes down to this: 'Each one of us puts into the community his person and all his powers under the supreme direction of the general will; and as a body, we incorporate every member as an indivisible part of the whole.'

Immediately, in place of the individual person of each contracting party, this act of association creates an artificial and collective body composed of as many members as there are voters in the assembly, and by this same act that body acquires its unity, its common *ego*, its life and its will. The public person thus formed by the union of all other persons was once called the *city*, and is now known as the *republic* or the *body politic*. In its passive role it is called the *state*, when it plays an active role it is the *sovereign*; and when it is compared to others of its own kind, it is a *power*. Those who are associated in it take collectively the name of a *people*, and call themselves individually *citizens*, in so far as they share in the sovereign power, and *subjects*, in so far as they put themselves under the laws of the state. [...]

The sovereign

Now, as the sovereign is formed entirely of the individuals who compose it, it has not, nor could it have, any interest contrary to theirs; and so the sovereign has no need to give guarantees to the subjects, because it is impossible for a body to wish to hurt all of its members, and, as we shall see, it cannot hurt any particular member. The sovereign by the mere fact that it is, is always all that it ought to be. [...] Every individual as a man may have a private will contrary to, or different from, the general will that he has as a citizen. His private interest may speak with a very different voice from that of the public interest. [...]

Hence, in order that the social pact shall not be an empty formula, it is tacitly implied in the commitment — which alone can give force to all others — that whoever refuses to obey the general will shall be constrained to do so by the whole body, which means nothing other than that he shall be forced to be free; for this is the condition which, by giving each citizen to the nation, secures him against all personal dependence, it is the condition which shapes both the design and the working of the political machine, and which alone bestows justice on civil contracts — without it, such contracts would be absurd, tyrannical and liable to the grossest abuse. [...]

Whether the general will can err

The people is never corrupted, but it is often misled; and only then does it seem to will what is bad.

There is often a great difference between the will of all [what all individuals want] and the general will; the general will studies only the common interest while the will of all studies private interest, and is indeed no more than the sum of individual desires. But if we take away from these same wills, the pluses and minuses which cancel each other out, the sum of the difference is the general will. [. . .]

But if groups, sectional associations are formed at the expense of the larger association, the will of each of these groups will become general in relation to its own members and private in relation to the state; we might then say that there are no longer as many votes as there are men but only as many votes as there are groups. The differences become less numerous and yield a result less general. [. . .]

The limits of the sovereign power

How should it be that the general will is always rightful and that all men constantly wish the happiness of each but for the fact that there is no one who does not take that word 'each' to pertain to himself and in voting for all think of himself? This proves that the equality of rights and the notion of justice which it produces derive from the predilection which each man has for himself and hence from human nature as such. It also proves that the general will, to be truly what it is, must be general in its purpose as well as in its nature; that it should spring from all and apply to all; and that it loses its natural rectitude when it is directed towards any particular and circumscribed object — for in judging what is foreign to us, we have no sound principle of equity to guide us. [. . .]

Whichever way we look at it, we always return to the same conclusion: namely that the social pact establishes equality[1] among the citizens in that they all pledge themselves under the same conditions and must all enjoy the same rights. Hence by the nature of the compact, every act of sovereignty, that is, every authentic act of the general will, binds or favours all the citizens equally, so that the sovereign recognizes only the whole body of the nation and makes no distinction between any of the members who compose it. [. . .]

When the people as a whole makes rules for the people as a whole, it is dealing only with itself; and if any relationship emerges, it is between the entire body seen from one perspective and the same entire body seen from another, without any division whatever. Here the matter concerning which a rule is made is as general as the will which makes it. And *this* is the kind of act which I call a law. [. . .]

The public force thus needs its own agent to call it together and put it into action in accordance with the instructions of the general will, to serve also as a means of communication between the state and the sovereign, and in a sense to do for the public person what is done for the individual by the union of soul and body. This is the reason why the state needs a government, something often unhappily confused with the sovereign, but of which it is really only the minister.

What, then, is the government? An intermediary body established between the subjects and the sovereign for their mutual communication, a body charged with the execution of the laws and the maintenance of freedom, both civil and political. [...]

JUST as the particular will acts unceasingly against the general will, so does the government continually exert itself against the sovereign. And the more this exertion increases, the more the constitution becomes corrupt, and, as in this case there is no distinct corporate will to resist the will of the prince and so to balance it, sooner or later it is inevitable that the prince will oppress the sovereign and break the social treaty. This is the inherent and inescapable defect which, from the birth of the political body, tends relentlessly to destroy it, just as old age and death destroy the body of a man. [...]

The principle of political life dwells in the sovereign authority. The legislative power is the heart of the state, the executive power is the brain, which sets all the parts in motion. The brain may become paralyzed and the individual still live. A man can be an imbecile and survive, but as soon as his heart stops functioning, the creature is dead.

Note

1. Rousseau subsequently qualifies the notion of equality thus [Eds]: . . . as for equality, this word must not be taken to imply that degrees of power and wealth should be absolutely the same for all, but rather that power shall stop short of violence and never be exercised except by virtue of authority and law, and, where wealth is concerned, that no citizen shall be rich enough to buy another and none so poor as to be forced to sell himself; this in turn implies that the more exalted persons need moderation in goods and influence and the humbler persons moderation in avarice and covetousness.

1.4

Bentham: Fragment on Government

On the theory of an original contract

A compact . . . it was said, was made by the King and people: the terms of it were to this effect. The people, on their part, promised to the King a *general obedience*. The King, on his part, promised to *govern* the people in such a *particular* manner always, as should be *subservient* to their happiness. I insist not on the words: I undertake only for the sense; as far as an imaginary engagement, so loosely and so variously worded by those who have imagined it, is capable of any decided signification. Assuming then, as a general rule, that promises, when made, ought to be observed; and, as a point of fact, that a promise to this effect in particular had been made by the party in question, men were more ready to deem themselves qualified to judge when it was such a promise was *broken*, than to decide directly and avowedly on the delicate question, when it was that a King acted so far in *opposition* to the happiness of his people, that it were better no longer to obey him. [. . .]

But, after all, for what *reason* is it, that men *ought* to keep their promises? The moment any intelligible reason is given, it is this: that it is for the *advantage* of society they should keep them; and if they do not, that, as far as *punishment* will go, they should be *made* to keep them. It is for the advantage of the whole number that the promises of each individual should be kept: and, rather than they should not be kept, that such individuals as fail to keep them should be punished. If it be asked, how this appears? the answer is at hand: Such is the benefit to gain, and mischief to avoid, by keeping them, as much more than compensates the mischief of so much punishment as is requisite to oblige men to it. Whether the

Jeremy Bentham (1748—1832)
Source: From *Fragment on Government* (1960) Basil Blackwell, pp. 52, 54—5, 92—5, 101, 102—3. First printed in 1780 as a response to William Blackstone's *Commentaries on the Law of England* (1765—9).

dependence of *benefit* and *mischief* (that is, of *pleasure* and *pain*) upon men's conduct in this behalf, be as here stated, is a question of *fact*, to be decided, in the same manner that all other questions of fact are to be decided, by testimony, observation, and experience.

This then, and no other, being the *reason* why men should be made to keep their promises, viz, that it is for the advantage of society that they should, is a reason that may as well be given at once, why *Kings*, on the one hand, in governing, should in general keep within established Laws, and (to speak universally) abstain from all such measures as tend to the unhappiness of their subjects: and, on the other hand, why *subjects* should obey Kings as long as they so conduct themselves, and no longer; why they should obey in short *so long as the probable mischiefs of obedience are less than the probable mischiefs of resistance*: why, in a word, taking the whole body together, it is their *duty* to obey, just so long as it is their *interest*, and no longer. This being the case, what need of saying of the one, that *he* PROMISED so to *govern*; of the other, that they PROMISED so to *obey*, when the fact is otherwise? [. . .]

As to the LAW *of Nature*, if (as I trust it will appear) it be nothing but a phrase; if there be no other medium for proving any act to be an offence against it, than the mischievous tendency of such act; if there be no other medium for proving a law of the *state* to be contrary to it, than the *inexpediency* of such law, unless the bare unfounded disapprobation of any one who thinks of it be called a proof; . . . if, in a word, there be scarce any law whatever but what those who have not liked it have found, on some account or another, to be repugnant to some text of scripture; I see no remedy but that the natural tendency of such doctrine is to impel a man, by the force of conscience, to rise up in arms against any law whatever that he happens not to like. What sort of government it is that can consist with such a disposition . . . It is the principle of *utility*, accurately apprehended and steadily applied, that affords the only clue to guide a man through these straits. It is for that, if any, and for that alone to furnish a decision which neither party shall dare in *theory* to disavow. It is something to reconcile men even in theory. They are at least, *something* nearer to an effectual union, than when at variance as well in respect of theory as of practice. [. . .] It is *then,* we may say, and not till then, allowable to, if not incumbent on, every man, as well on the score of *duty* as of *interest*, to enter into measures of resistance; when, according to the best calculation he is able to make, *the probable mischiefs of resistance* (speaking with respect to the community in general) *appear less to him than the probable mischiefs of submission*. This then is to him, that is to each man in particular, the *juncture for resistance.* [...] The *field,* if one may say so, of the supreme governor's authority, though not *infinite,* must unavoidably, I think, *unless where limited by express convention,*[1] be allowed to be *indefinite.* Nor can I see any narrower, or other bounds to it, under this constitution, or under any other yet *freer* constitution, if there be one, than under the most *despotic. Before* the juncture I have been describing were arrived, resistance, even in a country like this, would come too soon: were the juncture arrived *already*, the time for resistance would be come already, under such a government even as any one should call *despotic.*

In regard to a government that is *free,* and one that is *despotic,* wherein is it then that the difference consists? [...] It is not that the power of one any more than of the other has any certain bounds to it. The distinction turns upon circumstances of a very different complexion: on the *manner* in which that whole mass of power, which, taken together, is supreme, is, in a free state, *distributed* among the several ranks of persons that are sharers in it; on the *source* from whence their titles to it are successively derived; on the frequent and easy *changes* of condition between govern*ors* and govern*ed,* whereby the interests of the one class are more or less indistinguishably blended with those of the other; on the *responsibility* of the governors; or the right which a subject has of having the reasons publicly assigned and canvassed of every act of power that is exerted over him; on the *liberty of the press*; or the security with which every man, be he of the one class or the other, may make known his complaints and remonstrances to the whole community; on the *liberty of public association*; or the security with which malcontents may communicate their sentiments, concert their plans, and practise every mode of opposition short of actual revolt, before the executive power can be legally justified in disturbing them. [...]

I cannot look upon this as a mere dispute of words. I cannot help persuading myself, that the disputes between contending parties — between the defenders of a law and the opposers of it, would stand a much better chance of being adjusted than at present, were they but explicitly and constantly referred at once to the principle of UTILITY. [...] This, we see, is a ground of controversy very different from the former. The question is now manifestly a question of conjecture concerning so many future contingent matters of fact: to solve it, both parties then are naturally directed to support their respective persuasions by the only evidence the nature of the case admits of; the evidence of such *past* matters of fact as appear to be analogous to those contingent *future* ones. [...] Men, let them but once clearly understand one another, will not be long ere they agree. It is the perplexity of ambiguous and sophistical discourse that, while it distracts and eludes the apprehension, stimulates and inflames the passions.

Note

1. This respects the case where one state, has, upon *terms*, submitted itself to the government of another: or where the governing bodies of a number of states agree to take directions in certain specified cases, from some *body* or other that is distinct from all of them: consisting of members, for instance, appointed out of each.

1.5

Burke: Reflections on the Revolution in France

The Revolution [in England in 1688] was made to preserve our *ancient*, indisputable laws and liberties and that *ancient* constitution of government which is our only security for law and liberty. If you are desirous of knowing the spirit of our constitution and the policy which predominated in that great period which has secured it to this hour, pray look for both in our histories, in our records, in our acts of parliament, and journals of parliament, and not in the sermons of the Old Jewry and the after-dinner toasts of the Revolution Society. In the former you will find other ideas and another language. Such a claim is as ill-suited to our temper and wishes as it is unsupported by any appearance of authority. The very idea of the fabrication of a new government is enough to fill

Edmund Burke (1729–97)
Source: From *Reflections on the Revolution in France* (1955) Bobbs-Merrill, pp. 35–6, 66–71. First published in 1790. The book is written in the form of a letter to a French friend provoked by an address given on 4 November 1789 by Richard Price to the Revolution Society in London.

us with disgust and horror. We[1] wished at the period of the Revolution, and do now wish, to derive all we possess as *an inheritance from our forefathers*. Upon that body and stock of inheritance we have taken care not to inoculate any scion alien to the nature of the original plant. All the reformations we have hitherto made have proceeded upon the principle of reverence to antiquity; and I hope, nay, I am persuaded, that all those which possibly may be made hereafter will be carefully formed upon analogical precedent, authority, and example. [. . .]

It is no wonder, therefore, that with these ideas of everything in their constitution and government at home, either in church or state, as illegitimate and usurped, or at best as a vain mockery, they[2] look abroad with an eager and passionate enthusiasm. Whilst they are possessed by these notions, it is vain to talk to them of the practice of their ancestors, the fundamental laws of their country, the fixed form of a constitution whose merits are confirmed by the solid test of long experience and an increasing public strength and national prosperity. They despise experience as the wisdom of unlettered men; and as for the rest, they have wrought underground a mine that will blow up, at one grand explosion, all examples of antiquity, all precedents, charters, and acts of parliament. They have 'the rights of men.' Against these there can be no prescription, against these no agreement is binding; these admit no temperament and no compromise; anything withheld from their full demand is so much of fraud and injustice. Against these their rights of men let no government look for security in the length of its continuance, or in the justice and lenity of its administration. [. . .]

Far am I from denying in theory, full as far is my heart from withholding in practice (if I were of power to give or to withhold) the *real* rights of men. In denying their false claims of right, I do not mean to injure those which are real, and are such as their pretended rights would totally destroy. If civil society be made for the advantage of man, all the advantages for which it is made become his right. It is an institution of beneficence; and law itself is only beneficence acting by a rule. Men have a right to live by that rule; they have a right to do justice, as between their fellows, whether their fellows are in public function or in ordinary occupation. They have a right to the fruits of their industry and to the means of making their industry fruitful. They have a right to the acquisitions of their parents, to the nourishment and improvement of their offspring, to instruction in life, and to consolation in death. Whatever each man can separately do, without trespassing upon others, he has a right to do for himself; and he has a right to a fair portion of all which society, with all its combinations of skill and force, can do in his favour. In this partnership all men have equal rights, but not to equal things. He that has but five shillings in the partnership has as good a right to it as he that has five hundred pounds has to his larger proportion. But he has not a right to an equal dividend in the product of the joint stock; and as to the share of power, authority, and direction which each individual ought to have in the management of the state, that I must deny to be amongst the direct original rights of man in civil society, for I have in my contemplation the civil social man, and no other. It is a thing to be settled by convention.

If civil society be the offspring of convention, that convention must be its law. That convention must limit and modify all the descriptions of constitution which are formed under it. Every sort of legislative, judicial, or executory power are its creatures. They can have no being in any other state of things; and how can any man claim under the conventions of civil society rights which do not so much as suppose its existence — rights which are absolutely repugnant to it? One of the first motives to civil society, and which becomes one of its fundamental rules, is *that no man should be judge in his own cause.* By this each person has at once divested himself of the first fundamental right of uncovenanted man, that is, to judge for himself and to assert his own cause. He abdicates all right to be his own governor. He inclusively, in a great measure, abandons the right of self-defence, the first law of nature. Men cannot enjoy the rights of an uncivil and of a civil state together. That he may obtain justice, he gives up his right of determining what it is in points the most essential to him. That he may secure some liberty, he makes a surrender in trust of the whole of it.

Government is not made in virtue of natural rights, which may and do exist in total independence of it, and exist in much greater clearness and in a much greater degree of abstract perfection; but their abstract perfection is their practical defect. By having a right to everything they want everything. Government is a contrivance of human wisdom to provide for human *wants.* Men have a right that these wants should be provided for by this wisdom. Among these wants is to be reckoned the want, out of civil society, of a sufficient restraint upon their passions. Society requires not only that the passions of individuals should be subjected, but that even in the mass and body, as well as in the individuals, the inclinations of men should frequently be thwarted, their will controlled, and their passions brought into subjection. This can only be done *by a power out of themselves,* and not, in the exercise of its function, subject to that will and to those passions which it is its office to bridle and subdue. In this sense the restraints on men, as well as their liberties, are to be reckoned among their rights. But as the liberties and the restrictions vary with times and circumstances and admit to infinite modifications, they cannot be settled upon any abstract rule; and nothing is so foolish as to discuss them upon that principle.

The moment you abate anything from the full rights of men, each to govern himself, and suffer any artificial, positive limitation upon those rights, from that moment the whole organization of government becomes a consideration of convenience. This it is which makes the constitution of a state and the due distribution of its powers a matter of the most delicate and complicated skill. It requires a deep knowledge of human nature and human necessities, and of the things which facilitate or obstruct the various ends which are to be pursued by the mechanism of civil institutions. The state is to have recruits to its strength, and remedies to its distempers. What is the use of discussing a man's abstract right to food or medicine? The question is upon the method of procuring and administering them. In that deliberation I shall always advise to call in the aid of the farmer and the physician rather than the professor of metaphysics.

The science of constructing a commonwealth, or renovating it, or reforming it, is, like every other experimental science, not to be taught *a priori*. Nor is it a short experience that can instruct us in that practical science, because the real effects of moral causes are not always immediate. [. . .] In states there are often some obscure and almost latent causes, things which appear at first view of little moment, on which a very great part of its prosperity or adversity may most essentially depend. The science of government being therefore so practical in itself and intended for such practical purposes — a matter which requires experience, and even more experience than any person can gain in his whole life, however sagacious and observing he may be — it is with infinite caution that any man ought to venture upon pulling down an edifice which has answered in any tolerable degree for ages the common purposes of society, or on building it up again without having models and patterns of approved utility before his eyes. [. . .]

The pretended rights of these theorists are all extremes; and in proportion as they are metaphysically true, they are morally and politically false. The rights of men are in a sort of *middle*, incapable of definition, but not impossible to be discerned. The rights of men in governments are their advantages; and these are often in balances between differences of good, in compromise sometimes between good and evil, and sometimes between evil and evil. Political reason is a computing principle: adding, subtracting, multiplying, and dividing, morally and not metaphysically, or mathematically, true moral denominations.

By these theorists the right of the people is almost always sophistically confounded with their power. The body of the community, whenever it can come to act, can meet with no effectual resistance; but till power and right are the same, the whole body of them has no right inconsistent with virtue, and the first of all virtues, prudence. Men have no right to what is not reasonable and to what is not for their benefit.

Notes

1. i.e. the British [Eds].
2. i.e. the exponents of natural rights, such as the Revolution Society and other supporters of the principles of the French Revolution of 1789 [Eds].

1.6

Paine: The Rights of Man

Natural rights

Natural rights are those which appertain to man in right of his existence. Of this kind are all the intellectual rights, or rights of the mind, and also all those rights of acting as an individual for his own comfort and happiness, which are not injurious to the natural rights of others. Civil rights are those which appertain to man in right of his being a member of society. Every civil right has for its foundation, some natural right pre-existing in the individual, but to the enjoyment of which his individual power is not, in all cases, sufficiently competent. Of this kind are all those which relate to security and protection.

Thomas Paine (1739—1809)
Source: From *The Rights of Man* (1969) Penguin, pp. 90—1, 165—6, 168, 185—7, 200, 240. First published in 1791—2 as a reply to Burke's *Reflections*.

From this short review, it will be easy to distinguish between that class of natural rights which man retains after entering into society, and those which he throws into the common stock as a member of society.

The natural rights which he retains, are all those in which the *power* to execute is as perfect in the individual as the right itself. Among this class, as is before mentioned, are all the intellectual rights, or rights of the mind: consequently, religion is one of those rights. The natural rights which are not retained, are all those in which, though the right is perfect in the individual, the power to execute them is defective. They answer not his purpose. A man, by natural right, has a right to judge in his own cause; and so far as the right of mind is concerned, he never surrenders it: But what availeth it him to judge, if he has not power to redress? He therefore deposits this right in the common stock of society, and takes the arm of society, of which he is a part, in preference and in addition to his own. Society *grants* him nothing. Every man is a proprietor in society, and draws on the capital as a matter of right.

From these premises, two or three certain conclusions will follow.

First, that every civil right grows out of a natural right; or, in other words, is a natural right exchanged.

Second, that civil power, properly considered as such, is made up of the aggregate of that class of the natural rights of man, which becomes defective in the individual in point of power, and answers not his purpose; but when collected to a focus, becomes competent to the purpose of every one.

Third, that the power produced from the aggregate of natural rights, imperfect in power in the individual, cannot be applied to invade the natural rights which are retained in the individual, and in which the power to execute is as perfect as the right itself. [. . .]

The nature of government

What is government more than the management of the affairs of a nation? It is not, and from its nature cannot be, the property of any particular man or family, but of the whole community, at whose expense it is supported; and though by force or contrivance it has been usurped into an inheritance, the usurpation cannot alter the right of things. Sovereignty, as a matter of right, appertains to the nation only, and not to any individual; and a nation has at all times an inherent indefeasible right to abolish any form of government it finds inconvenient, and establish such as accords with its interest, disposition, and happiness. [. . .] Every citizen is a member of the sovereignty, and, as such, can acknowledge no personal subjection; and his obedience can be only to the laws.

When men think of what government is, they must necessarily suppose it to possess a knowledge of all the objects and matters upon which its authority is to be exercised. In this view of government, the republican system, as established by America and France, operates to embrace the whole of a nation; and the knowledge necessary to the interest of all the parts, is to be found in the centre, which the parts by representation form: but the old governments are on a construction that excludes knowledge as well as happiness; government by monks, who know nothing of the world beyond the walls of a convent, is as consistent as government by kings. [. . .]

Whether the forms and maxims of governments which are still in practice, were adapted to the condition of the world at the period they were established, is not in this case the question. The older they are, the less correspondence can they have with the present state of things. Time, and change of circumstances and opinions, have the same progressive effect in rendering modes of government obsolete, as they have upon customs and manners. Agriculture, commerce, manufactures, and the tranquil arts, by which the prosperity of nations is best promoted, require a different system of government, and a different species of knowledge to direct its operations, than what might have been required in the former condition of the world. [. . .]

Of society and civilization

GREAT part of that order which reigns among mankind is not the effect of government. It has its origin in the principles of society and the natural constitution of man. It existed prior to government, and would exist if the formality of government was abolished. The mutual dependence and reciprocal interest which man has upon man, and all the parts of a civilized community upon each other, create that great chain of connexion which holds it together. The landholder, the farmer, the manufacturer, the merchant, the tradesman, and every occupation, prospers by the aid which each receives from the other, and from the whole. Common interest regulates their concerns, and forms their law; and the laws which common usage ordains, have a greater influence than the laws of government. In fine, society performs for itself almost everything which is ascribed to government.

To understand the nature and quantity of government proper for man, it is necessary to attend to his character. As nature created him for social life, she fitted him for the station she intended. In all cases she made his natural wants greater than his individual powers. No one man is capable, without the aid of society, of supplying his own wants; and those wants, acting upon every individual, impel the whole of them into society, as naturally as gravitation acts to a centre.

But she has gone further. She has not only forced man into society, by a diversity of wants, which the reciprocal aid of each other can supply, but she has implanted in him a system of social affections, which, though not necessary to his existence, are essential to his happiness. There is no period in life when this love for society ceases to act. It begins and ends with our being. [. . .]

Government is no farther necessary than to supply the few cases to which society and civilization are not conveniently competent; and instances are not wanting to show, that everything which government can usefully add thereto, has been performed by the common consent of society, without government.

For upwards of two years from the commencement of the American war, and to a longer period in several of the American states, there were no established forms of government. [. . .] So far is it from being true, as has been pretended, that the abolition of any formal government is the dissolution of society, that it acts by a contrary impulse, and brings the latter the closer together. All that part of its organization which it had committed to its government, devolves again upon itself, and acts through its medium. [. . .]

Formal government makes but a small part of civilized life; and when even the best that human wisdom can devise is established, it is a thing more in name and idea, than in fact. It is to the great and fundamental principles of society and civilization — to the common usage universally consented to, and mutually and reciprocally maintained — to the unceasing circulation of interest, which, passing through its million channels, invigorates the whole mass of civilized man — it is to these things, infinitely more than to anything which even the best instituted government can perform, that the safety and prosperity of the individual and of the whole depends. [. . .]

Man, with respect to all those matters, is more a creature of consistency than he is aware, or than governments would wish him to believe. All the great laws of society are laws of nature. Those of trade and commerce, whether with respect to the intercourse of individuals, or of nations, are laws of mutual and reciprocal interest.

They are followed and obeyed, because it is the interest of the parties so to do, and not on account of any formal laws their governments may impose or interpose.

Of the old and new systems of government

The only forms of government are the democratical, the aristocratical, the monarchical, and what is now called the representative.

What is called a *republic*, is not any *particular form* of government. It is wholly characteristical of the purport, matter, or object for which government ought to be instituted, and on which it is to be employed, RES-PUBLICA, the public affairs, or the public good; or, literally translated, the *public thing*. It is a word of a good original, referring to what ought to be the character and business of government; and in this sense it is naturally opposed to the word *monarchy*, which has a base original signification. It means arbitrary power in an individual person; in the exercise of which, *himself*, and not the *res-publica*, is the object.

Every government that does not act on the principle of a *republic*, or in other words, that does not make the *res-publica* its whole and sole object, is not a good government. Republican government is no other than government established and conducted for the interest of the public, as well individually as collectively. It is not necessarily connected with any particular form, but it most naturally associates with the representative form, as being best calculated to secure the end for which a nation is at the expense of supporting it.

Ways and means of improving the condition of Europe

Civil government does not consist in executions; but in making that provision for the instruction of youth, and the support of age, as to exclude, as much as possible, profligacy from the one, and despair from the other. Instead of this, the resources of a country are lavished upon kings, upon courts, upon hirelings, impostors, and prostitutes; and even the poor themselves, with all their wants upon them, are compelled to support the fraud that oppresses them.

Why is it, that scarcely any are executed but the poor? The fact is a proof, among other things, of a wretchedness in their condition. Bred up without morals, and cast upon the world without a prospect, they are the exposed sacrifice of vice and legal barbarity. The millions that are superfluously wasted upon governments, are more than sufficient to reform those evils, and to benefit the condition of every man in a nation, not included within the purlieus of a court. This I hope to make appear in the progress of this work.

1.7

Wollstonecraft: Vindication of the Rights of Women

The prevailing opinion of sexual character

I love man as my fellow; but his sceptre, real or usurped, extends not to me, unless the reason of an individual demands my homage; and even then the submission is to reason, and not to man. In fact, the conduct of an accountable being must be regulated by the operations of its own reason; or on what foundation rests the throne of God?

It appears to me necessary to dwell on these obvious truths, because females have been insulated, as it were; and while they have been stripped of the virtues that should clothe humanity, they have been decked with artificial graces that enable them to exercise a short-lived tyranny. Love, in their bosoms, taking place of every noble passion, their sole ambition is to be fair, to raise emotion instead of inspiring respect; and this ignoble desire, like the servility in absolute monarchies, destroys all strength of character. Liberty is the mother of virtue, and if women be, by their very constitution, slaves, and not allowed to breathe the sharp invigorating air of freedom, they must ever languish like exotics, and be reckoned beautiful flaws in nature. [...]

Brutal force has hitherto governed the world, and that the science of politics is in its infancy, is evident from philosophers

Mary Wollstonecraft (1759—97)
Source: From *Vindication of the Rights of Women* (1975) Penguin, pp. 121—2, 127, 139, 259—60. First published in 1792.

scrupling to give the knowledge most useful to man that determinate distinction.

I shall not pursue this argument any further than to establish an obvious inference, that as sound politics diffuse liberty, mankind, including woman, will become more wise and virtuous. [. . .]

The *divine right* of husbands, like the divine right of kings, may, it is to be hoped, in this enlightened age, be contested without danger; and though conviction may not silence many boisterous disputants, yet, when any prevailing prejudice is attacked, the wise will consider, and leave the narrow-minded to rail with thoughtless vehemence at innovation. [. . .]

I wish to sum up what I have said in a few words, for I here throw down my gauntlet, and deny the existence of sexual virtues, not excepting modesty. For man and woman, truth, if I understand the meaning of the word, must be the same; yet in the fanciful female character, so prettily drawn by poets and novelists, demanding the sacrifice of truth and sincerity, virtue becomes a relative idea, having no other foundation than utility, and of that utility men pretend arbitrarily to judge, shaping it to their own convenience.

Women, I allow, may have different duties to fulfil; but they are *human* duties, and the principles that should regulate the discharge of them, I sturdily maintain, must be the same. [. . .]

Of the pernicious effects which arise from the unnatural distinctions established in society

But to render her really virtuous and useful, [woman] must not, if she discharge her civil duties, want individually the protection of civil laws; she must not be dependent on her husband's bounty for her subsistence during his life, or support after his death; for how can a being be generous who has nothing of its own? or virtuous who is not free? [. . .]

Though I consider that women in the common walks of life are called to fulfil the duties of wives and mothers, by religion and reason, I cannot help lamenting that women of a superior cast have not a road open by which they can pursue more extensive plans of usefulness and independence. I may excite laughter, by dropping a hint, which I mean to pursue, some future time, for I really think that women ought to have representatives, instead of being arbitrarily governed without having any direct share allowed them in the deliberations of government.

1.8

Godwin: Enquiry Concerning Political Justice

Of promises

Few things can be more absurd than to talk of our having promised obedience to the laws. If the laws depend upon promises for their execution, why are they accompanied with sanctions? Why is it considered as the great arcanum of legislation to make laws that are easy of execution, and that need no assistance from the execrable intervention of oaths and informers? Again, why should I promise that I will do everything that a certain power, called the government, shall imagine it convenient, or decide that it is fitting, for me to do? Is there in this either morality, or justice, or common sense? Does brute force alone communicate to its possessor a sufficient claim upon my veneration? [...] There is but one power to which I can yield a heart-felt obedience, the decision of my own understanding, the dictate of my own conscience. The decrees of any other power, especially if I have a firm and independent mind, I shall obey with reluctance and aversion. [...]

Of obedience

Government can with no propriety be compared to the construction of a bridge or a canal, a matter of mere convenience and refinement. It is supposed to be of the most irresistible necessity; it is indisputably an affair of hardship and restraint. It constitutes other men the arbitrators of my actions, and the ultimate disposers of my destiny. Almost every member of every community that has

William Godwin (1756—1836)
Source: From *Enquiry Concerning Political Justice and its Influence on Modern Morals and Happiness* (1978) Penguin, pp. 228—9, 238—9, 247—8, 300—1, 304, 544—5, 550—1, 552—4. First published in 1793.

existed on the face of the earth might reasonably say, 'I know of no such contract as you describe; I never entered into any such engagement; I never promised to obey; it must therefore be an iniquitous imposition to call upon me to do something under pretence of a promise I never made.' [. . .] Government in reality, as has abundantly appeared, is a question of force, and not of consent. [. . .]

The true supporters of government are the weak and uninformed, and not the wise. In proportion as weakness and ignorance shall diminish, the basis of government will also decay. This however is an event which ought not to be contemplated with alarm. A catastrophe of this description would be the true euthanasia of government. If the annihilation of blind confidence and implicit opinion can at any time be effected, there will necessarily succeed in their place an unforced concurrence of all in promoting the general welfare. [. . .]

Of the cultivation of truth

It is also impossible that any situation can occur in which virtue cannot find room to expatiate. In society there is continual opportunity for its active employment. I cannot have intercourse with a human being who may not be the better for that intercourse. If he be already just and virtuous, these qualities are improved by communication. If he be imperfect and erroneous, there must always be some prejudice I may contribute to destroy, some motive to delineate, some error to remove. If I be prejudiced and imperfect myself, it cannot however happen that my prejudices and imperfections shall be exactly coincident with his. I may therefore inform him of the truths that I know, and, even by the collision of prejudices, truth is elicited. [. . .]

All these reasonings are calculated to persuade us that the most precious boon we can bestow upon others is virtue, and that the highest employment of virtue is to propagate itself. But, as virtue is inseparably connected with knowledge in my own mind, so by knowledge only can it be imparted to others. [. . .]

Hence it appears that the only species of sincerity which can in any degree prove satisfactory to the enlightened moralist and politician is that where the frankness is perfect, and every degree of reserve is discarded. [. . .]

Of the future of political societies

Government can have no more than two legitimate purposes, the suppression of injustice against individuals within the community, and the common defence against external invasion. The first of these purposes, which alone can have an uninterrupted claim upon us, is sufficiently answered by an association, of such an extent, as to afford room for the institution of a jury to decide upon the offences of individuals within the community, and upon the questions and controversies respecting property which may chance to arise. [. . .] It might be easy indeed for an offender to escape from the limits of so petty a jurisdiction; and it might seem necessary, at first, that the neighbouring parishes, or jurisdictions, should be governed in a similar manner, or at least should be willing, whatever was their form of government, to cooperate with us in the removal or reformation of an offender whose present habits were alike injurious to us and to them. But there will be no need of any express compact, and still less of any common centre of authority, for this purpose. General justice, and mutual interest, are found more capable of binding men than signatures and seals. In the meantime, all necessity for causing the punishment of the crime, to pursue the criminal would soon, at least, cease, if it ever existed. The motives to offence would become rare: its aggravations few: and rigour superfluous. The principal object of punishment is restraint upon a dangerous member of the community; and the end of this restraint would be answered by the general inspection that is exercised by the members of a limited circle over the conduct of each other, and by the gravity and good sense that would characterize the censures of men, from whom all mystery and empiricism were banished. [. . .]

Of national assemblies

The pretence of collective wisdom is among the most palpable of all impostures. The acts of the society can never rise above the suggestions of this or that individual, who is a member of it. [. . .] National assemblies, or, in other words, assemblies instituted for the joint purpose of adjusting the differences between district and district, and of consulting respecting the best mode of repelling foreign invasion, however necessary to be had recourse to upon certain occasions, ought to be employed as sparingly as the nature of the case will admit. [. . .]

Of the dissolution of government

IT remains for us to consider what is the degree of authority necessary to be vested in such a modified species of national assembly as we have admitted into our system. Are they to issue their commands to the different members of the confederacy? Or is it sufficient that they should invite them to cooperate for the common advantage, and, by arguments and addresses, convince them of the reasonableness of the measures they propose? The former of these might at first be necessary. The latter would afterwards become sufficient. [. . .]

Man is not originally vicious. He would not refuse to listen to, or to be convinced by, the expostulations that are addressed to him, had he not been accustomed to regard them as hypocritical, and to conceive that, while his neighbour, his parent, and his political governor pretended to be actuated by a pure regard to his interest or pleasure, they were, in reality, at the expense of his, promoting their own. Such are the fatal effects of mysteriousness and complexity. Simplify the social system in the manner which every motive but those of usurpation and ambition powerfully recommends; render the plain dictates of justice level to every capacity; remove the necessity of implicit faith; and we may expect the whole species to become reasonable and virtuous. It might then be sufficient for juries to recommend a certain mode of adjusting controversies, without assuming the prerogative of dictating that adjustment. [. . .]

The reader has probably anticipated the ultimate conclusion from these remarks. If juries might at length cease to decide, and be contented to invite, if force might gradually be withdrawn and reason trusted alone, shall we not one day find that juries themselves and every other species of public institution may be laid aside as unnecessary?

1.9

Hegel: Lectures on the Philosophy of World History

Only in the state does man have a rational existence. The aim of all education is to ensure that the individual does not remain purely subjective but attains an objective existence within the state. The individual can certainly make the state into a means of attaining this or that end. But the truth is realized only in so far as each individual wills the universal cause itself and has discarded all that is inessential. Man owes his entire existence to the state, and has his being within it alone. Whatever worth and spiritual reality he possesses are his solely by virtue of the state. For as a knowing being, he has spiritual reality only in so far as his being, i.e. the rational itself, is his object and possesses objective and immediate existence for him; only as such does he possess consciousness and exist in an ethical world, within the legal and ethical life of the state. For the truth is the unity of the universal and the subjective will, and the universal is present within the state, in its laws and in its universal and rational properties.

The subjective will — or passion — is the activating and realizing principle; the idea is the inner essence, and the state is the reality of ethical life in the present. For the state is the unity of the universal, essential will and the will of the subject, and it is this which constitutes ethical life. The individual who lives within this unity has an ethical existence, and his value consists solely in this substantiality. [. . .] The aim of the state is that the substance which underlies the real activity and dispositions of men should be recognized and made manifest, and that it should ensure its own continuity. The absolute interest of reason requires that this ethical whole should be present. [. . .] For the state is not an abstraction which stands in opposition to the citizens; on the contrary, they are distinct moments like those of organic life, in which no one

Georg Wilhelm Friedrich Hegel (1770—1831)
Source: From *Lectures on the Philosophy of World History* (1975) Cambridge University Press, pp. 94—7. First delivered in 1830.

member is either a means or an end. The divine principle in the state is the Idea made manifest on earth.

The essence of the state is ethical life. This consists in the unity of the universal and the subjective will. [. . .] The universal spirit is essentially present as human consciousness. Knowledge attains existence and being for itself in man. The spirit knows itself and exists for itself as a subject, and its nature is to posit itself as immediate existence: as such, it is equivalent to human consciousness.

It is customary to act in accordance with the universal will and to make one's aim a universal one which is recognized within the state. Even in primitive states the will is subordinated to another will, although this does not mean that the individual has no will of his own, but only that his particular will has no authority. [. . .] This is the first necessary moment in the existence of the universal — the element of knowledge and thought which emerges at this point within the state. Only in this environment, i.e. within the state, can art and religion exist. The nations we are concerned with here have acquired a rational internal organization, and world history takes account only of those nations which have formed themselves into states. But we must not imagine that this can occur on a desert island or in a completely isolated community. [. . .] The universal must be more than just the opinions of individuals. It must have an existence of its own, and as such, it is to be found in the state itself in the shape of all that is generally recognized. In the state, the internal becomes reality. Reality, of course, is outwardly varied, but in this case, we are considering its universal qualities.

The universal idea attains phenomenal reality in the state. [. . .] The phenomenal aspect of the spirit is its self-determination, which is the element of its concrete nature: the spirit which does not determine itself is merely an abstraction of the understanding. The self-determination of the spirit is its phenomenal aspect, which we have to consider here in the shape of states and individuals.

The spiritual individual, the nation — in so far as it is internally differentiated so as to form an organic whole — is what we call the state. This term is ambiguous, however, for the state and the laws of the state, as distinct from religion, science, and art, usually have purely political associations. But in this context, the word 'state' is used in a more comprehensive sense, just as we use the word 'realm' to describe spiritual phenomena. A nation should therefore be regarded as a spiritual individual, and it is not primarily its external side that will be emphasized here, but rather what we have previously called the spirit of the nation, i.e. its self-consciousness in relation to its own truth and being, and what it recognizes as truth in the absolute sense — in short, those spiritual powers which live within the nation and rule over it. The universal which emerges and becomes conscious within the state, the *form* to which everything in it is assimilated, is what we call in general the nation's *culture*. But the determinate *content* which this universal form acquires and which is contained in the concrete reality which constitutes the state is the *national spirit* itself. The real state is animated by this spirit in all its particular transactions, wars, institutions, etc. This spiritual content is a firm and solid nucleus which is completely removed from the world of arbitrariness, particularities, caprices, individuality, and contingency; whatever is subject to the latter is not part of the nation's character: it is like the dust which blows over a town or a field or hangs above it without changing it in any essential way. Besides, this spiritual content is the essential being of each individual, as well as constituting the spirit of the nation. It is the sacred bond which links men and spirits together. It remains one and the same life, one great object, one great end, and one great content, on which all private happiness and all private volition depend. [. . .]

When the state or fatherland constitutes a community of existence, and when the subjective will of men subordinates itself to laws, the opposition between freedom and necessity disappears. The rational, as the substance of things, is necessary, and we are free in so far as we recognize it as law and follow it as the substance of our own being; the objective and the subjective will are then reconciled, forming a single, undivided whole. For the ethical character of the state is not that of individual morality, which is a product of reflection and subject to personal conviction; reflective morality is more accessible to the modern world, whereas the true ethics of antiquity are rooted in the fact that everyone adhered to his prescribed duty. An Athenian citizen did virtually by instinct what was expected of him; if I reflect on the object of my activity, however, I must be conscious that my will has assented to it. But ethical life is duty, the substantial right, or second nature (as it has justly been called); for man's first nature is his immediate animal existence.

1.10

J. S. Mill: Representative Government

The criterion of a good form of government

And the one indispensable merit of a government, in favour of which it may be forgiven almost any amount of other demerit compatible with progress, is that its operation on the people is favourable, or not unfavourable, to the next step which it is necessary for them to take, in order to raise themselves to a higher level. [. . .]

The ideally best polity

There is no difficulty in showing that the ideally best form of government is that in which the sovereignty, or supreme controlling power in the last resort, is vested in the entire aggregate of the community; every citizen not only having a voice in the exercise of that ultimate sovereignty, but being, at least occasionally, called on to take an actual part in the government, by the personal discharge of some public function, local or general.

To test this proposition, it has to be examined in reference to the two branches into which . . . the inquiry into the goodness of a government conveniently divides itself, namely, how far it promotes the good management of the affairs of society by means of the existing faculties, moral, intellectual, and active, of its various members, and what is its effect in improving or deteriorating those faculties.

The ideally best form of government, it is scarcely necessary to say, does not mean one which is practicable or eligible in all states of civilization, but the one which, in the circumstances in which it is practicable and eligible, is attended with the greatest amount of

John Stuart Mill (1806—73)
Source: From *Utilitarianism, Liberty and Representative Government* (1910) Dent, Everyman's Library Series, pp. 197, 207—9, 218, 228—30, 239, 254—7. First published in 1861.

beneficial consequences, immediate and prospective. A completely popular government is the only polity which can make out any claim to this character. It is pre-eminent in both the departments between which the excellence of a political constitution is divided. It is both more favourable to present good government, and promotes a better and higher form of national character, than any other polity whatsoever. [. . .]

We need not suppose that when power resides in an exclusive class, that class will knowingly and deliberately sacrifice the other classes to themselves: it suffices that, in the absence of its natural defenders, the interest of the excluded is always in danger of being overlooked; and, when looked at, is seen with very different eyes from those of the persons whom it directly concerns. [. . .] When a subject arises in which the labourers as such have an interest, is it regarded from any point of view but that of the employers of ,labour? I do not say that the working men's view of these questions is in general nearer to the truth than the other: but it is sometimes quite as near; and in any case it ought to be respectfully listened to, instead of being, as it is, not merely turned away from, but ignored. [. . .]

Under what conditions representative government is inapplicable

WE have recognized in representative government the ideal type of the most perfect polity, for which, in consequence, any portion of mankind are better adapted in proportion to their degree of general improvement. As they range lower and lower in development, that form of government will be, generally speaking, less suitable to them; [. . .] Let us examine at what point in the descending series representative government ceases altogether to be admissible, either through its own unfitness, or the superior fitness of some other regimen. . .

Representative, like any other government, must be unsuitable in any case in which it cannot permanently subsist, i.e. in which it does not fulfil the three fundamental conditions . . . These [are] (1) that the people should be willing to receive it; (2) that they should be willing and able to do what is necessary for its preservation; (3) that they should be willing and able to fulfil the duties and discharge the functions which it imposes on them. [. . .]

Of the proper functions of representative bodies

The meaning of representative government is, that the whole people, or some numerous portion of them, exercise through deputies periodically elected by themselves the ultimate controlling power, which, in every constitution, must reside somewhere. This ultimate power they must possess in all its completeness. They must be masters, whenever they please, of all the operations of government. [. . .]

But while it is essential to representative government that the practical supremacy in the state should reside in the representatives of the people, it is an open question what actual functions, what precise part in the machinery of government, shall be directly and personally discharged by the representative body. [. . .]

There is a radical distinction between controlling the business of government and actually doing it. The same person or body may be able to control everything, but cannot possibly do everything; and in many cases its control over everything will be more perfect the less it personally attempts to do. [. . .]

Instead of the function of governing, for which it is radically unfit, the proper office of a representative assembly is to watch and control the government: to throw the light of publicity on its acts: to compel a full exposition and justification of all of them which any one considers questionable; to censure them if found condemnable, and, if the men who compose the government abuse their trust, or fulfil it in a manner which conflicts with the deliberate sense of the nation, to expel them from office, and either expressly or virtually appoint their successors. This is surely ample power, and security enough for the liberty of the nation. In addition to this, the Parliament has an office, not inferior even to this in importance; to be at once the nation's Committee of Grievances, and its Congress of Opinions; an arena in which not only the general opinion of the nation, but that of every section of it, and as far as possible of every eminent individual whom it contains, can produce itself in full light and challenge discussion. [. . .]

Of the infirmities and dangers to which representative government is liable

One of the greatest dangers . . . of democracy, as of all other forms of government, lies in the sinister interest of the holders of power: it is the danger of class legislation; of government intended for (whether really effecting it or not) the immediate benefit of the dominant class, to the lasting detriment of the whole. And one of the most important questions demanding consideration, in determining the best constitution of a representative government, is how to provide efficacious securities against this evil. [. . .]

If the representative system could be made ideally perfect, and if it were possible to maintain it in that state, its organization must be such that these two classes, manual labourers and their affinities on one side, employers of labour and their affinities on the other, should be, in the arrangement of the representative system, equally balanced, each influencing about an equal number of votes in Parliament. [. . .] The reason why, in any tolerably constituted society, justice and the general interest mostly in the end carry their point, is that the separate and selfish interests of mankind are almost always divided; some are interested in what is wrong, but some, also, have their private interest on the side of what is right: and those who are governed by higher considerations, though too few and weak to prevail against the whole of the others, usually after sufficient discussion and agitation become strong enough to turn the balance in favour of the body of private interests which is on the same side with them.

Of true and false democracy, representation of all, and representation of the majority only

In a really equal democracy, every or any section would be represented, not disproportionately, but proportionately. A majority of the electors would always have a majority of the representatives; but a minority of the electors would always have a minority of the representatives. Man for man they would be as fully represented as the majority. Unless they are, there is not equal government, but a government of inequality and privilege: one part of the people rule over the rest: there is a part whose fair and equal share of influence in the representation is withheld from them; contrary to all just government, but, above all, contrary to the principle of democracy, which professes equality as its very root and foundation.

1.11

Marx and Engels:
The Communist Manifesto

The history of all hitherto existing society is the history of class struggles. [. . .] Each step in the development of the bourgeoisie was accompanied by a corresponding political advance of that class. An oppressed class under the sway of the feudal nobility, an armed and self-governing association in the medieval commune; here independent urban republic (as in Italy and Germany), there taxable 'third estate' of the monarchy (as in France), afterwards, in the period of manufacture proper, serving either the semi-feudal or the absolute monarchy as a counterpoise against the nobility, and, in fact, cornerstone of the great monarchies in general, the bourgeoisie has at last, since the establishment of modern industry and of the world-market, conquered for itself, in the modern representative state, exclusive political sway. The executive of the modern state is but a committee for managing the common affairs of the whole bourgeoisie. [. . .]

The means of production and of exchange, on whose foundation the bourgeoisie built itself up, were generated in feudal society. At a certain stage in the development of these means of production and of exchange, the conditions under which feudal society produced and exchanged, the feudal organization of agriculture and manufacturing industry, in one word, the feudal relations of property became no longer compatible with the already developed productive forces; they became so many fetters. They had to be burst asunder; they were burst asunder. [. . .]

A similar movement is going on before our own eyes. Modern bourgeois society with its relations of production, of exchange and of property, a society that has conjured up such gigantic means of production and of exchange, is like the sorcerer, who is no longer able to control the powers of the nether world whom he has called up by his spells. For many a decade past the history of industry and

Karl Marx (1818—83) and Friedrich Engels (1820—95)
Source: From Marx and Engels *Selected Works in Two Volumes* (1958) Lawrence and Wishart, pp. 34—6, 39, 44, 54. First published in 1848.

commerce is but the history of the revolt of modern productive forces against modern conditions of production, against the property relations that are the conditions for the existence of the bourgeoisie and of its rule. [. . .]

All the preceding classes that got the upper hand, sought to fortify their already acquired status by subjecting society at large to their conditions of appropriation. The proletarians cannot become masters of the productive forces of society, except by abolishing their own previous mode of appropriation, and thereby also every other previous mode of appropriation. They have nothing of their own to secure and to fortify; their mission is to destroy all previous securities for, and insurances of, individual property.

All previous historical movements were movements of minorities, or in the interest of minorities. The proletarian movement is the self-conscious, independent movement of the immense majority, in the interests of the immense majority.

When, in the course of development, class distinctions have disappeared, and all production has been concentrated in the hands of a vast association of the whole nation, the public power will lose its political character. Political power, properly so called, is merely the organized power of one class for oppressing another. If the proletariat during its contest with the bourgeoisie is compelled, by the force of circumstances, to organize itself as a class, if, by means of a revolution, it makes itself the ruling class, and, as such, sweeps away by force the old conditions of production, then it will, along with these conditions, have swept away the conditions for the existence of class antagonisms and of classes generally, and will thereby have abolished its own supremacy as a class.

1.12

Engels: The Origin of the Family, Private Property and the State

The state is, therefore, by no means a power forced on society from without; just as little is it 'the reality of the ethical idea', 'the image and reality of reason,' as Hegel maintains. Rather, it is a product of society at a certain stage of development; it is the admission that this society has become entangled in an insoluble contradiction with itself, that it has split into irreconcilable antagonisms which it is powerless to dispel. But in order that these antagonisms and classes with conflicting economic interests might not consume themselves and society in fruitless struggle, it became necessary to have a power seemingly standing above society that would alleviate the conflict, and keep it within the bounds of 'order'; and this power, arisen out of society but placing itself above it, and alienating itself more and more from it, is the state.

As distinct from the old gentile order, the state, first, divides its subjects *according to territory*. As we have seen, the old gentile associations, built upon and held together by ties of blood, became inadequate, largely because they presupposed that the members were bound to a given territory, a bond which has long ceased to exist. The territory remained, but the people had become mobile. Hence, division according to territory was taken as the point of departure, and citizens were allowed to exercise their public rights and duties wherever they settled, irrespective of gens and tribe. This organization of citizens according to locality is a feature common to all states. That is why it seems natural to us; but we have seen what long and arduous struggles were needed before it could replace, in Athens and Rome, the old organization according to gentes.

The second distinguishing feature is the establishment of a *public power* which no longer directly coincides with the population organizing itself as an armed force. This special public power is necessary because a self-acting armed organization of the population has become impossible since the split into classes. The slaves also belonged to the population; the 90,000 citizens of Athens formed only a privileged class as against the 365,000 slaves. The people's army of the Athenian democracy was an aristocratic public power against the slaves, whom it kept in check; however, a gendarmerie also became necessary to keep the citizens in check, as we related above. This public power exists in every state; it consists not merely of armed men but also of material adjuncts, prisons and institutions of coercion of all kinds, of which gentile [clan] society knew nothing. It may be very insignificant, almost infinitesimal, in societies where class antagonisms are still undeveloped and in out-

Friedrich Engels (1820—95)
Source: From Marx and Engels *Selected Works in One Volume* (1968) Lawrence and Wishart, pp. 577—9. First published in 1884.

of-the-way places as was the case at certain times and in certain regions in the United States of America. It [the public power] grows stronger, however, in proportion as class antagonisms within the state become more acute, and as adjacent states become larger and more populous. We have only to look at our present-day Europe, where class struggle and rivalry in conquest have tuned up the public power to such a pitch that it threatens to swallow the whole of society and even the state.

In order to maintain this public power, contributions from the citizens become necessary — *taxes.* These were absolutely unknown in gentile society; but we know enough about them today. As civilization advances, these taxes become inadequate; the state makes drafts on the future, contracts loans, *public debts.* Old Europe can tell a tale about these, too.

Having public power and the right to levy taxes, the officials now stand, as organs of society, *above* society. The free, voluntary respect that was accorded to the organs of the gentile [clan] constitution does not satisfy them, even if they could gain it; being the vehicles of a power that is becoming alien to society, respect for them must be enforced by means of exceptional laws by virtue of which they enjoy special sanctity and inviolability. [. . .]

Because the state arose from the need to hold class antagonisms in check, but because it arose, at the same time, in the midst of the conflict of these classes, it is, as a rule, the state of the most powerful, economically dominant class, which, through the medium of the state, becomes also the politically dominant class, and thus acquires new means of holding down and exploiting the oppressed class. Thus, the state of antiquity was above all the state of the slave owners for the purpose of holding down the slaves, as the feudal state was the organ of the nobility for holding down the peasant serfs and bondsmen, and the modern representative state is an instrument of exploitation of wage labour by capital. By way of exception, however, periods occur in which the warring classes balance each other so nearly that the state power, as ostensible mediator, acquires, for the moment, a certain degree of independence of both. Such was the absolute monarchy of the seventeenth and eighteenth centuries, which held the balance between the nobility and the class of burghers; such was the Bonapartism of the First, and still more of the Second French Empire, which played off the proletariat against the bourgeoisie and the bourgeoisie against the proletariat. The latest performance of this kind, in which ruler and ruled appear equally ridiculous, is the new German Empire of the Bismarck nation: here capitalists and workers are balanced against each other and equally cheated for the benefit of the impoverished Prussian cabbage junkers.

In most of the historical states, the rights of citizens are, besides, apportioned according to their wealth, thus directly expressing the fact that the state is an organization of the possessing class for its protection against the non-possessing class. It was so already in the Athenian and Roman classification according to property. It was so in the medieval feudal state, in which the alignment of political power was in conformity with the amount of land owned. It is seen in the electoral qualifications of the modern representative states. Yet this political recognition of property distinctions is by no means essential. On the contrary, it marks a low stage of state development. The highest form of the state, the democratic republic, which under our modern conditions of society is more and more becoming an inevitable necessity, and is the form of state in which alone the last decisive struggle between proletariat and bourgeoisie can be fought out — the democratic republic officially knows nothing any more of property distinctions. In it wealth exercises its power indirectly, but all the more surely. On the one hand, in the form of the direct corruption of officials, of which America provides the classical example; on the other hand, in the form of an alliance between government and Stock Exchange, which become the easier to achieve the more the public debt increases and the more joint-stock companies concentrate in their hands not only transport but also production itself, using the Stock Exchange as their centre. The latest French republic as well as the United States is a striking example of this; and good old Switzerland has contributed its share in this field. But that a democratic republic is not essential for this fraternal alliance between government and Stock Exchange is proved by England and also by the new German Empire, where one cannot tell who was elevated more by universal suffrage, Bismarck or Bleichröder. And lastly, the possessing class rules directly through the medium of universal suffrage. As long as the oppressed class, in our case, therefore, the proletariat, is not yet ripe to emancipate itself, it will in its majority regard the existing order of society as the only one possible and, politically, will form the tail of the capitalist class, its extreme Left wing. To the extent, however, that this class matures for its self-emancipation, it constitutes itself as its own party and elects its own representatives, and not those of the capitalists. Thus, universal suffrage is the gauge of the maturity of the working class. It cannot and never will be anything more in the present-day state; but that is sufficient. On the day the thermometer of universal suffrage registers boiling point among the workers, both they and the capitalists will know what to do.

The state, then, has not existed from all eternity. There have been societies that did without it, that had no idea of the state and state power. At a certain stage of economic development, which was necessarily bound up with the split of society into classes, the state became a necessity owing to this split. We are now rapidly approaching a stage in the development of production at which the existence of these classes not only will have ceased to be a necessity, but will become a positive hindrance to production. They will fall as inevitably as they arose at an earlier stage. Along with them the state will inevitably fall. Society, which will reorganize production on the basis of a free and equal association of the producers, will put the whole machinery of state where it will then belong: into the museum of antiquities, by the side of the spinning-wheel and the bronze axe.

1.13

Marx: The Eighteenth Brumaire of Louis Bonaparte

The struggle between Bonaparte and the National Assembly

As soon as the revolutionary crisis had been weathered and universal suffrage abolished, the struggle between the National Assembly and Bonaparte broke out again. [. . .]

After 13 June [1850], Bonaparte had caused . . . requests [for increases in the allowance he received as elected, constitutional President of the Republic] to be voiced, this time without eliciting response. . . . Now, after 31 May, he at once availed himself of the favourable moment and caused his ministers to propose a Civil

Karl Marx (1818—83)
Source: From Marx and Engels *Selected Works in Two Volumes* (1958) Lawrence and Wishart, pp. 217, 293—5, 307—8, 312, 318—19, 332, 334—5. First published in 1852. The phrase 'Eighteenth Brumaire' refers to the date in the French Revolutionary calendar when Napoleon Bonaparte, Louis' uncle, seized power in 1799.

List of three millions in the National Assembly. [. . .] He practised regular *chantage*.[1] The National Assembly had violated the sovereignty of the people with his assistance and his cognizance. He threatened to denounce its crime to the tribunal of the people unless it loosened its purse-strings and purchased his silence with three million a year. [. . .] Could the National Assembly break with the President of the republic at a moment when in principle it had definitely broken with the mass of the nation? [. . .]

Bonaparte, . . . was . . . entitled to make tours of the French Departments, and according to the disposition of the town that he favoured with his presence, now more or less covertly, now more or less overtly, to divulge his own restoration plans and canvass votes for himself. On these processions, which the great official *Moniteur*[2] . . . naturally had to celebrate as triumphal processions, he was constantly accompanied by persons affiliated with the *Society of December 10*. This society dates from the year 1849. On the pretext of founding a benevolent society, the *lumpenproletariat* of Paris had been organized into secret sections, each section being led by Bonapartist agents, with a Bonapartist general at the head of the whole. [. . .] This Bonaparte, who constitutes himself *chief of the lumpenproletariat*, who here alone rediscovers in mass form the interests which he personally pursues, who recognizes in this scum, offal, refuse of all classes the only class upon which he can base himself unconditionally, is the real Bonaparte. [. . .]

Thus it proved that the party of Order[3] [in the National Assembly] had lost in conflicts with Bonaparte not only the ministry, not only the army, but also its independent parliamentary majority, that a squad of representatives had deserted from its camp, out of fanaticism for conciliation, out of fear of the struggle, out of lassitude, out of family regard for the state salaries so near and dear to them, out of speculation on ministerial posts becoming vacant . . . out of sheer egoism, which makes the ordinary bourgeois always inclined to sacrifice the general interest of his class for this or that private motive. From the first, the Bonapartist representatives adhered to the party of Order only in the struggle against revolution. [. . .]

[The party of order] were . . . reduced to moving within strictly parliamentary limits. And it took that peculiar malady which since 1848 has raged all over the Continent, *parliamentary cretinism,* which holds those infected by it fast in an imaginary world and robs them of all sense, all memory, all understanding of the rude external world — it took this parliamentary cretinism for those who had destroyed all the conditions of parliamentary power with their own hands, and were bound to destroy them in their struggle with the other classes, still to regard their parliamentary victories as victories and to believe they hit the President by striking at his ministers. They merely gave him the opportunity to humiliate the National Assembly afresh in the eyes of the nation. [. . .]

Only a partial revision [of the Constitution] which would prolong the authority of the President would pave the way for imperial usurpation. A general revision which would shorten the existence of the republic would bring the dynastic claims into unavoidable conflict, for the conditions of a Bourbon and the conditions of an Orleanist Restoration were not only different, they were mutually exclusive.

The parliamentary republic was more than the neutral territory on which the two factions of the French bourgeoisie, Legitimists and Orleanists, large landed property and industry, could dwell side by side with equality of rights. It was the unavoidable condition of their *common* rule, the sole form of state in which their general class interest subjected to itself at the same time both the claims of their particular factions and all the remaining classes of society. As royalists they fell back into their old antagonism, into the struggle for the supremacy of landed property or of money, and the highest expression of this antagonism, its personification, was their kings themselves, their dynasties. Hence the resistance of the party of Order to the *recall of the Bourbons.* [. . .]

The aristocracy of finance, therefore, condemned the parliamentary struggle of the party of Order with the executive power as a *disturbance of order*, and celebrated every victory of the President over its ostensible representatives as a *victory of order.* By the aristocracy of finance must here be understood not merely the great loan promoters and speculators in public funds, in regard to whom it is immediately obvious that their interests coincide with the interests of the state power. All modern finance, the whole of the banking business, is interwoven in the closest fashion with public credit. A part of their business capital is necessarily invested and put out at interest in quickly convertible public funds. [. . .]

The *industrial bourgeoisie,* too, in its fanaticism for order, was angered by the squabbles of the parliamentary party of Order with the executive power. After their vote of January 18 on the occasion of Changarnier's dismissal, Thiers, Anglas, Sainte-Beuve, etc, received from their constituents in precisely the industrial districts public reproof. [. . .]

When trade was good, as it still was at the beginning of 1851, the commercial bourgeoisie raged against any parliamentary struggle, lest trade be put out of humour. When trade was bad, as it continually was from the end of February 1851, the commercial bourgeoisie accused the parliamentary struggles of being the cause of stagnation and cried out for them to stop in order that trade might start again. The revision debates came on just in this bad period. [...]

The extension of the state

[The] executive power [in France] with its enormous bureaucratic and military organization, with its ingenious state machinery, embracing wide strata, with a host of officials numbering half a million, besides an army of another half million, this appalling parasitic body, which enmeshes the body of French society like a net and chokes all its pores, sprang up in the days of the absolute monarchy, with the decay of the feudal system, which it helped to hasten. The seignorial privileges of the landowners and towns became transformed into so many attributes of the state power. [...] The first French Revolution, with its task of breaking all separate local, territorial, urban and provincial powers in order to create the civil unity of the nation, was bound to develop what the absolute monarchy had begun: centralization, but at the same time the extent, the attributes and the agents of governmental power. Napoleon perfected this state machinery. [...]

Only under the second Bonaparte does the state seem to have made itself completely independent. As against civil society, the state machine has consolidated its position so thoroughly that the chief of the Society of December 10 suffices for its head, an adventurer blown in from abroad, raised on the shield by a drunken soldiery, which he has bought with liquor and sausages, and which he must continually ply with sausage anew. [...]

The role of the peasantry

The small-holding peasants form a vast mass, the members of which live in similar conditions but without entering into manifold relations with one another. Their mode of production isolates them from one another instead of bringing them into mutual intercourse. [...] Each individual peasant family is almost self-sufficient; it itself directly produces the major part of its consumption and thus acquires its means of life more through exchange with nature than in intercourse with society. A small holding, a peasant and his family; alongside them another small holding, another peasant and another family. A few score of these make up a village, and a few score of villages make up a Department. In this way, the great mass of the French nation is formed by simple addition of homologous magnitudes, much as potatoes in a sack form a sack of potatoes. In so far as millions of families live under economic conditions of existence that separate their mode of life, their interests and their culture from those of the other classes, and put them in hostile opposition to the latter, they form a class. In so far as there is merely a local interconnection among these small-holding peasants, and the identity of their interests begets no community, no national bond and no political organization among them, they do not form a class. [. . .]

Historical tradition gave rise to the belief of the French peasants in the miracle that a man named Napoleon would bring all the glory back to them. And an individual turned up who gives himself out as the man because he bears the name of Napoleon . . . After a vagabondage of twenty years and after a series of grotesque adventures, the legend finds fulfilment and the man becomes Emperor of the French. The fixed idea of the Nephew was realized, because it coincided with the fixed idea of the most numerous class of the French.

The Bonaparte dynasty represents not the revolutionary, but the conservative peasant; not the peasant that strikes out beyond the condition of his social existence, the small holding, but rather the peasant who wants to consolidate this holding, not the country folk who, linked up with the towns, want to overthrow the old order through their own energies, but on the contrary those who, in stupefied seclusion within this old order, want to see themselves and their small holdings saved and favoured by the ghost of the empire. It represents not the enlightenment, but the superstition of the peasant; not his judgment, but his prejudice; not his future, but his past.

Notes

1. Translation: blackmail [Eds].
2. Official journal of the Republic [Eds].
3. Marx earlier explained the party of Order and its parliamentary factions thus [Eds]: Legitimists and Orleanists . . . formed the two great factions of the party of Order. Was that which held these factions fast to their pretenders and kept them apart from one another nothing but lily and tricolour, House of Bourbon and House of Orleans, different shades of royalism, was it at all the confession of

faith of royalism? Under the Bourbons, *big landed property* had governed, with its priests and lackeys; under the Orleans, high finance, large-scale industry, large-scale trade, that is, *capital*, with its retinue of lawyers, professors and smooth-tongued orators.

1.14

Weber: I Politics as a Vocation

What is the state?

What is a 'state'? Sociologically, the state cannot be defined in terms of its ends. There is scarcely any task that some political association has not taken in hand, and there is no task that one could say has always been exclusive and peculiar to those associations which are designated as political ones: today the state, or historically, those associations which have been the predecessors of the modern state. Ultimately, one can define the modern state sociologically only in terms of the specific *means* peculiar to it, as to every political association, namely, the use of physical force.

'Every state is founded on force,' said Trotsky at Brest-Litovsk. That is indeed right. If no social institutions existed which knew the use of violence, then the concept of 'state' would be eliminated, and a condition would emerge that could be designated as 'anarchy,' in the specific sense of this word. Of course, force is certainly not the normal or the only means of the state — nobody says that — but force is a means specific to the state. Today the relation between the state and violence is an especially intimate one. In the past, the most varied institutions — beginning with the sib — have known the use of physical force as quite normal. Today, however, we have to say that a state is a human community that (successfully) claims the *monopoly of the legitimate use of physical force* within a given territory. Note that 'territory' is one of the characteristics of the state. Specifically, at the present time,

Max Weber (1864—1920)
Source I: From *Max Weber* (1970) H. H. Gerth and C. Wright Mills (eds), London, Routledge & Kegan Paul, and New York, Oxford University Press, pp. 77—9. First published in 1919.

the right to use physical force is ascribed to other institutions or to individuals only to the extent to which the state permits it. The state is considered the sole source of the 'right' to use violence. Hence, 'politics' for us means striving to share power or striving to influence the distribution of power, either among states or among groups within a state. [. . .]

Like the political institutions historically preceding it, the state is a relation of men dominating men, a relation supported by means of legitimate (i.e. considered to be legitimate) violence. If the state is to exist, the dominated must obey the authority claimed by the powers that be. When and why do men obey? Upon what inner justifications and upon what external means does this domination rest?

To begin with, in principle, there are three inner justifications, hence basic *legitimations* of domination.

First, the authority of the 'eternal yesterday,' i.e. of the mores sanctified through the unimaginably ancient recognition and habitual orientation to conform. This is 'traditional' domination exercised by the patriarch and the patrimonial prince of yore.

There is the authority of the extraordinary and personal *gift of grace* (charisma), the absolutely personal devotion and personal confidence in revelation, heroism, or other qualities of individual leadership. This is 'charismatic' domination, as exercised by the prophet or — in the field of politics — by the elected war lord, the plebiscitarian ruler, the great demagogue, or the political party leader.

Finally, there is domination by virtue of 'legality,' by virtue of the belief in the validity of legal statute and functional 'competence' based on rationally created *rules*. In this case, obedience is expected in discharging statutory obligations. This is domination as exercised by the modern 'servant of the state' and by all those bearers of power who in this respect resemble him.

It is understood that, in reality, obedience is determined by highly robust motives of fear and hope — fear of the vengeance of magical powers or of the power-holder, hope for reward in this world or in the beyond — and besides all this, by interests of the most varied sort . . . However, in asking for the 'legitimations' of this obedience, one meets with these three 'pure' types: 'traditional,' 'charismatic,' and 'legal.'

Weber: II Economy and Society

Bases of legitimacy

The actors may ascribe legitimacy to a social order by virtue of:

(a) *tradition*: valid is that which has always been;

(b) *affectual*, especially emotional, *faith*: valid is that which is newly revealed or exemplary;

(c) *value-rational* faith: valid is that which has been deduced as an absolute;

(d) positive enactment which is believed to be *legal*.

Such legality may be treated as legitimate because:

(α) it derives from a voluntary agreement of the interested parties;

(β) it is imposed by an authority which is held to be legitimate and therefore meets with compliance. [. . .]

1. The validity of a social order by virtue of the sacredness of tradition is the oldest and most universal type of legitimacy. The fear of magical evils reinforces the general psychological inhibitions against any sort of change in customary modes of action. At the same time the manifold vested interests which tend to favour conformity with an established order help to perpetuate it . . .

2. Conscious departures from tradition in the establishment of a new order were originally almost entirely due to prophetic oracles or at least to pronouncements which were sanctioned as prophetic and thus were considered sacred. This was true as late as the statutes of the Greek *aisymnetai*. Conformity thus depended on belief in the legitimacy of the prophet. In times of strict traditionalism a new order — one actually regarded as new — was not possible without revelation unless it was claimed that it had always been valid though not yet rightly known, or that it had been obscured for a time and was now being restored to its rightful place.

Source II: From *Economy and Society* (1978) University of California Press, Vol. 1, pp. 36—8; Vol. 2 pp. 921—2, 925—6. Written between 1910 and 1914.

3. The purest type of legitimacy based on value-rationality is *natural law.* The influence of its logically deduced propositions upon actual conduct has lagged far behind its ideal claims; that they have had some influence cannot be denied, however. Its propositions must be distinguished from those of revealed, enacted, and traditional law.

4. Today the most common form of legitimacy is the belief in legality, the compliance with enactments which are *formally* correct and which have been made in the accustomed manner. In this respect, the distinction between an order derived from voluntary agreement and one which has been imposed is only relative. For so far as the agreement underlying the order is not unanimous, as in the past has often been held necessary for complete legitimacy, the order is actually imposed upon the minority; in this frequent case the order in a given group depends upon the acquiescence of those who hold different opinions. On the other hand, it is very common for minorities, by force or by the use of more ruthless and far-sighted methods, to impose an order which in the course of time comes to be regarded as legitimate by those who originally resisted it. In so far as the ballot is used as a legal means of altering an order, it is very common for the will of a minority to attain a formal majority and for the majority to submit. In this case majority rule is a mere illusion. The belief in the legality of an order as established by voluntary agreement is relatively ancient and is occasionally found among so-called primitive people; but in these cases it is almost always supplemented by the authority of oracles.

5. So far as it is not derived merely from fear or from motives of expediency, a willingness to submit to an order imposed by one man or a small group, always implies a belief in the legitimate authority (*Herrschaftsgewalt*) of the source imposing it. [. . .]

6. Submission to an order is almost always determined by a variety of interests and by a mixture of adherence to tradition and belief in legality, unless it is a case of entirely new regulations. In a very large proportion of cases, the actors subject to the order are of course not even aware how far it is a matter of custom, of convention, or of law. In such cases the sociologist must attempt to formulate the typical basis of validity. [. . .]

The nation

The fervour of this emotional influence does not, in the main, have an economic origin. It is based upon sentiments of prestige, which often extend deep down to the petty-bourgeois masses of states rich in the historical attainment of power-positions. The attachment to all this political prestige may fuse with a specific belief in responsibility towards succeeding generations. The great power structures *per se* are then held to have a responsibility of their own for the way in which power and prestige are distributed between their own and foreign polities. It goes without saying that all those groups who hold the power to steer common conduct within a polity will most strongly instill themselves with this idealist fervour of power prestige. They remain the specific and most reliable bearers of the idea of the state as an imperialist power structure demanding unqualified devotion.

In addition to the direct and material imperialist interests there are the indirectly material as well as the ideological interests of strata that are in various ways privileged within a polity and, indeed, privileged by its very existence. They comprise especially all those who think of themselves as being the specific 'partners' of a specific 'culture' diffused among the members of the polity. Under the influence of these circles, the naked prestige of 'power' is unavoidably transformed into other special forms of prestige and especially into the idea of the 'nation.'

If the concept of 'nation' can in any way be defined unambiguously, it certainly cannot be stated in terms of empirical qualities common to those who count as members of the nation. In the sense of those using the term at a given time, the concept undoubtedly means, above all, that *it is proper* to expect from certain groups a specific sentiment of solidarity in the face of other groups. Thus, the concept belongs in the sphere of values. Yet, there is no agreement on how these groups should be delimited or about what concerted action should result from such solidarity.
[...]

Instead, we shall have to look a little closer into the fact that the idea of the nation for its advocates stands in very intimate relation to 'prestige' interests. The earliest and most energetic manifestations of the idea, in some form, even though it may have been veiled, have contained the legend of a providential 'mission.' Those to whom the representatives of the idea zealously turned were expected to shoulder this mission. Another element of the early idea was the notion that this mission was facilitated solely through the very cultivation of the peculiarity of the group set off as a nation. Therewith, in so far as its self-justification is sought in the value of its content, this mission can consistently be thought of only as a specific 'culture' mission. The significance of the 'nation' is usually anchored in the superiority, or at least the irreplaceability, of the culture values that are to be preserved and developed only through the cultivation of the peculiarity of the group. It therefore goes without saying that, just as those who wield power in the polity invoke the idea of the *state*, the intellectuals, as we shall tentatively call those who usurp leadership in a *Kulturgemeinschaft* (that is, within a group of people who by virtue of their peculiarity have access to certain products that are considered 'culture goods'), are specifically predestined to propagate the *'national'* idea.

1.15

Lenin: State and Revolution

State power

Engels elucidates the concept of the 'power' which is called the state, a power which arose from society but places itself above it and alienates itself more and more from it. What does this power mainly consist of? It consists of special bodies of armed men having prisons, etc, at their command.

We are justified in speaking of special bodies of armed men, because the public power which is an attribute of every state 'does not directly coincide' with the armed population, with its 'self-acting armed organization'.

Like all great revolutionary thinkers, Engels tries to draw the attention of the class-conscious workers to what prevailing philistinism regards as least worthy of attention, as the most habitual thing, hallowed by prejudices that are not only deep-rooted but, one might say, petrified. A standing army and police

Vladimir Illich Lenin (1870—1924)
Source: From *Selected Works* (1967) Vol. 2, Moscow, pp. 272—3, 335—6, 343—5. First published in 1917.

are the chief instruments of state power. But how can it be otherwise?

From the viewpoint of the vast majority of Europeans of the end of the nineteenth century whom Engels was addressing, and who had not gone through or closely observed a single great revolution, it could not have been otherwise. They could not understand at all what a 'self-acting armed organization of the population' was. When asked why it became necessary to have special bodies of armed men placed above society and alienating themselves from it (police and a standing army), the West-European and Russian philistines are inclined to utter a few phrases borrowed from Spencer or Mikhailovsky, to refer to the growing complexity of social life, the differentiation of functions, and so on.

Such a reference seems 'scientific', and effectively lulls the ordinary person to sleep by obscuring the important and basic fact, namely, the split of society into irreconcilably antagonistic classes.

Were it not for this split, the 'self-acting armed organization of the population' would differ from the primitive organization of a stick-wielding herd of monkeys, or of primitive men, or of men united in clans, by its complexity, its high technical level, and so on. But such an organization would still be possible.

It is impossible because civilized society is split into antagonistic, and, moreover, irreconcilably antagonistic, classes, whose 'self-acting' arming would lead to an armed struggle between them. A state arises, a special power is created, special bodies of armed men, and every revolution, by destroying the state apparatus, shows us the naked class struggle, clearly shows us how the ruling class strives to restore the special bodies of armed men which serve *it*, and how the oppressed class strives to create a new organization of this kind, capable of serving the exploited instead of the exploiters. [. . .]

Only in Communist society, when the resistance of the capitalists has been completely crushed, when the capitalists have disappeared, when there are no classes (i.e, when there is no distinction between the members of society as regards their relation to the social means of production), *only* then 'the state . . . ceases to exist', and '*it becomes possible to speak of freedom*'. Only then will a truly complete democracy become possible and be realized, a democracy without any exceptions whatever. And only then will democracy begin to *wither away*, owing to the simple fact that, freed from capitalist slavery, from the untold horrors, savagery, absurdities and infamies of capitalist exploitation, people will gradually *become accustomed* to observing the elementary rules of social intercourse that have been known for centuries and repeated for thousands of years in all copy-book maxims. They will become accustomed to observing them without force, without coercion, without subordination, *without the special apparatus* for coercion called the state. [. . .]

The withering away of the state

The expression 'the state *withers away*' is very well chosen, for it indicates both the gradual and the spontaneous nature of the process. Only habit can, and undoubtedly will, have such an effect; for we see around us on millions of occasions how readily people become accustomed to observing the necessary rules of social intercourse when there is no exploitation, when there is nothing that arouses indignation, evokes protest and revolts, and creates the need for *suppression.*

And so in capitalist society we have a democracy that is curtailed, wretched, false, a democracy only for the rich, for the minority. The dictatorship of the proletariat, the period of transition to Communism, will for the first time create democracy for the people, for the majority, along with the necessary suppression of the exploiters, of the minority. Communism alone is capable of providing really complete democracy, and the more complete it is, the sooner it will become unnecessary and wither away of its own accord.

In other words, under capitalism we have the state in the proper sense of the word, that is, a special machine for the suppression of one class by another, and, what is more, of the majority by the minority. Naturally, to be successful, such an undertaking as the systematic suppression of the exploited majority by the exploiting minority calls for the utmost ferocity and savagery in the matter of suppressing, it calls for seas of blood, through which mankind is actually wading its way in slavery, serfdom and wage labour.

Furthermore, during the *transition* from capitalism to Communism suppression is *still* necessary, but it is now the suppression of the exploiting minority by the exploited majority. A special apparatus, a special machine for suppression, the 'state', is *still* necessary, but this is now a transitional state. It is no longer a state in the proper sense of the word; for the suppression of the minority of exploiters by the majority of the wage slaves of *yesterday* is comparatively so easy, simple and natural a task that it will entail far less bloodshed than the suppression of the risings of slaves, serfs or wage-labourers, and it will cost mankind far less. And it is compatible with the extension of democracy to such an overwhelming majority of the population that the need for a *special machine* of suppression will begin to disappear. Naturally, the exploiters are unable to suppress the people without a highly complex machine for performing this task, but *the people* can suppress the exploiters even with a very simple 'machine', almost without a 'machine', without a special apparatus, by the simple *organization of the armed people* (such as the soviets of workers' and soldiers' deputies, we would remark, running ahead).

Lastly, only Communism makes the state absolutely unnecessary, for there is *nobody* to be suppressed — 'nobody' in the sense of a *class*, of a systematic struggle against a definite section of the population. We are not utopians, and do not in the least deny the possibility and inevitability of excesses on the part of *individual persons*, or the need to stop *such* excesses. In the first place, however, no special machine, no special apparatus of suppression, is needed for this; this will be done by the armed people themselves, as simply and as readily as any crowd of civilized people, even in modern society, interferes to put a stop to a scuffle or to prevent a woman from being assaulted. And, secondly, we know that the fundamental social causes of excesses, which consist in the violation of the rules of social intercourse, is the exploitation of the people, their want and their poverty. With the removal of this chief cause, excesses will inevitably begin to '*wither away*'. We do not know how quickly and in what succession, but we do know they will wither away. With their withering away the state will also *wither away.* [. . .]

Democracy

Democracy is a form of the state, one of its varieties. Consequently, it, like every state, represents, on the one hand, the organized, systematic use of force against persons; but, on the other hand, it signifies the formal recognition of equality of citizens, the equal right of all to determine the structure of, and to administer, the state. This, in turn, results in the fact that, at a certain stage in the development of democracy, it first welds together the class that wages a revolutionary struggle against capitalism — the proletariat, and enables it to crush, smash to atoms, wipe off the face of the earth the bourgeois, even the republican-bourgeois, state machine, the standing army, the police and the bureaucracy and to substitute for them a *more* democratic state machine, but a state machine nevertheless, in the shape of armed workers who proceed to form a militia involving the entire population.

Here 'quantity turns into quality': *such* a degree of democracy implies overstepping the boundaries of bourgeois society and beginning its socialist reorganization. If really *all* take part in the administration of the state, capitalism cannot retain its hold. The development of capitalism, in turn, creates the *pre-conditions* that *enable* really 'all' to take part in the administration of the state. Some of these preconditions are: universal literacy, which has already been achieved in a number of the most advanced capitalist countries, then the 'training and disciplining' of millions of workers by the huge, complex, socialized apparatus of the postal service, railways, big factories, large-scale commerce, banking, etc, etc.

Given these *economic* preconditions, it is quite possible, after the overthrow of the capitalists and the bureaucrats, to proceed immediately, overnight, to replace them in the *control* over production and distribution, in the work of *keeping account* of labour and products, by the armed workers, by the whole of the armed population. [. . .]

From the moment all members of society, or at least the vast majority, have learned to administer the state *themselves*, have taken this work into their own hands, have organized control over the insignificant capitalist minority, over the gentry who wish to preserve their capitalist habits and over the workers who have been thoroughly corrupted by capitalism — from this moment the need for government of any kind begins to disappear altogether. The more complete the democracy, the nearer the moment when it becomes unnecessary. The more democratic the 'state' which consists of the armed workers, and which is 'no longer a state in the proper sense of the word', the more rapidly *every form* of state begins to wither away.

1.16

Gramsci: Prison Notebooks

Relations of political forces

A subsequent moment is the relation of political forces; in other words, an evaluation of the degree of homogeneity, self-awareness, and organization attained by the various social classes. This moment can in its turn be analysed and differentiated into various levels, corresponding to the various moments of collective political consciousness, as they have manifested themselves in history up till now. The first and most elementary of these is the economic-corporate level: a tradesman feels *obliged* to stand by another tradesman, a manufacturer by another manufacturer, etc, but the tradesman does not yet feel solidarity with the manufacturer; in other words, the members of the professional group are conscious of its unity and homogeneity, and of the need to organize it, but in the case of the wider social group this is not yet so. A second moment is that in which consciousness is reached of the solidarity of interests among all the members of a social class — but still in the purely economic field. Already at this juncture the problem of the state is posed — but only in terms of winning politico-juridical equality with the ruling groups: the right is claimed to participate in legislation and administration, even to reform these — but within the existing fundamental structures. A third moment is that in which one becomes aware that one's own corporate interests, in their present and future development, transcend the corporate limits of the purely economic class, and can and must become the interests of other subordinate groups too. This is the most purely political phase, and marks the decisive passage from the structure to the sphere of the complex superstructures; it is the phase in which previously germinated ideologies become 'party', come into confrontation and conflict, until only one of them, or at least a single combination of them, tends to prevail, to gain the upper hand, to propagate itself throughout society — bringing about not only a unison of economic and political aims, but also intellectual and moral unity, posing all the questions around which the struggle rages not on a corporate but on a 'universal' plane, and thus creating the hegemony of a fundamental social group over a series of subordinate groups. It is true that the state is seen as the organ of one particular group, destined to create favourable conditions for the latter's maximum expansion. But the development and expansion of the particular group are conceived of, and presented, as being the motor force of a universal expansion, of a development of all the 'national' energies. In other words, the dominant group is coordinated concretely with the general interests of the subordinate

Antonio Gramsci (1891—1937)
Source: From *Selections from the Prison Notebooks* (1971) Lawrence and Wishart, pp. 181—2, 208—9, 210, 242—3, 246. Written between 1929 and 1937.

groups, and the life of the state is conceived of as a continuous process of formation and superseding of unstable equilibria (on the juridical plane) between the interests of the fundamental group and those of the subordinate groups — equilibria in which the interests of the dominant group prevail, but only up to a certain point i.e. stopping short of narrowly corporate economic interest. [. . .]

State and civil society

Every social form has its 'economic man', i.e. its own economic activity. [. . .] Between the economic structure and the state with its legislation and its coercion stands civil society, and the latter must be radically transformed, in a concrete sense and not simply on the statute-book or in scientific books. The state is the instrument for conforming civil society to the economic structure, but it is necessary for the state to 'be willing' to do this; i.e. for the representatives of the change that has taken place in the economic structure to be in control of the state. To expect that civil society will conform to the new structure as a result of propaganda and persuasion, or that the old economic man will disappear without being buried with all the honours it deserves, is a new form of economic rhetoric, a new form of empty and inconclusive economic moralism. [. . .]

Political parties

At a certain point in their historical lives, social classes become detached from their traditional parties. In other words, the traditional parties in that particular organizational form, with the particular men who constitute, represent, and lead them, are no longer recognized by their class (or fraction of a class) as its expression. When such crises occur, the immediate situation becomes delicate and dangerous, because the field is open for violent solutions, for the activities of unknown forces, represented by charismatic 'men of destiny'.

These situations of conflict between 'represented and representatives' reverberate out from the terrain of the parties (the party organizations properly speaking, the parliamentary-electoral field, newspaper organization) throughout the state organism, reinforcing the relative power of the bureaucracy (civil and military), of high finance, of the Church, and generally of all bodies relatively independent of the fluctuations of public opinion. How are they created in the first place? In every country the process is different, although the content is the same. And the content is the crisis of the ruling class's hegemony, which occurs either because the ruling class has failed in some major political undertaking for which it has requested, or forcibly extracted, the consent of the broad masses (war, for example), or because huge masses (especially of peasants and petit-bourgeois intellectuals) have passed suddenly from a state of political passivity to a certain activity, and put forward demands which taken together, albeit not organically formulated, add up to a revolution. A 'crisis of authority' is spoken of: this is precisely the crisis of hegemony, or general crisis of the state. [. . .]

Educative and formative role of the state

Its aim is always that of creating new and higher types of civilization; of adapting the 'civilization' and the morality of the broadest popular masses to the necessities of the continuous development of the economic apparatus of production; hence of evolving even physically new types of humanity. But how will each single individual succeed in incorporating himself into the collective man, and how will educative pressure be applied to single individuals so as to obtain their consent and their collaboration, turning necessity and coercion into 'freedom'? Question of the 'Law': this concept will have to be extended to include those activities which are at present classified as 'legally neutral', and which belong to the domain of civil society; the latter operates without 'sanctions' or compulsory 'obligations', but nevertheless exerts a collective pressure and obtains objective results in the form of an evolution of customs, ways of thinking and acting, morality, etc.

Political concept of the so-called 'Permanent Revolution', which emerged before 1848 as a scientifically evolved expression of the Jacobin experience from 1789 to Thermidor.[1] The formula belongs to an historical period in which the great mass political parties and the great economic trade unions did not yet exist, and society was still, so to speak, in a state of fluidity from many points of view: greater backwardness of the countryside, and almost complete monopoly of political and state power by a few cities or even by a single one (Paris in the case of France); a relatively rudimentary state apparatus, and greater autonomy of civil society from state activity; a specific system of military forces and of national armed services; greater autonomy of the national economies from the economic relations of the world market, etc. In the period after 1870, with the colonial expansion of Europe, all these elements change: the internal and international organizational relations of the state become more complex and massive, and the Forty-Eightist formula of the 'Permanent Revolution' is expanded and transcended in political science by the formula of 'civil hegemony'. The same thing happens in the art of politics as happens in military art: war of movement increasingly becomes war of position, and it can be said that a state will win a war in so far as it prepares for it minutely and technically in peacetime. The massive structures of the modern democracies, both as state organizations, and as complexes of associations in civil society, constitute for the art of politics as it were the 'trenches' and the permanent fortifications of the front in the war of position: they render merely 'partial' the element of movement which before used to be 'the whole' of war, etc. [. . .]

The state as educator

The conception of law will have to be freed from every residue of transcendentalism and from every absolute; in practice, from every moralistic fanaticism. However, it seems to me that one cannot start from the point of view that the state does not 'punish' (if this term is reduced to its human significance), but only struggles against social 'dangerousness'. In reality, the state must be conceived of as an 'educator', in as much as it tends precisely to create a new type or level of civilization. Because one is acting essentially on economic forces, reorganizing and developing the apparatus of economic production, creating a new structure, the conclusion must not be drawn that superstructural factors should be left to themselves, to develop spontaneously, to a haphazard and sporadic germination. The state, in this field, too, is an instrument of 'rationalization', of acceleration and of Taylorization.[2] It operates according to a plan, urges, incites, solicits, and 'punishes'; for, once the conditions are created in which a certain way of life is 'possible', then 'criminal action or omission' must have a punitive sanction, with moral implications, and not merely be judged generically as 'dangerous'. The Law is the repressive and negative aspect of the entire positive, civilizing activity undertaken by the state. The 'prize-giving' activities of individuals and groups, etc, must also be incorporated in the conception of the Law; praiseworthy and meritorious activity is rewarded, just as criminal actions are punished (and punished in original ways, bringing in 'public opinion' as a form of sanction).

Notes

1. Gramsci is referring to Marx's slogan from the period of revolutions in 1848 (when he anticipated immediate transition from bourgeois to proletarian revolution directed at the permanent overthrow of possessing classes), and to the period of the French Revolution (1789–94) when a nascent Parisian proletariat wrung temporary economic concessions out of the government [Eds].
2. Taylorization: a rigidly divided and supervized method of mass production.

1.17

Dahl: A Preface to Democratic Theory

In American politics, as in all other societies, control over decisions is unevenly distributed; neither individuals nor groups are political equals. When I say that a group is heard 'effectively' I mean more than the simple fact that it makes a noise; I mean that one or more officials are not only ready to listen to the noise, but expect to suffer in some significant way if they do not placate the group, its leaders, or its most vociferous members. To satisfy the group may require one or more of a great variety of actions by the responsive leader: pressure for substantive policies, appointments, graft, respect, expression of the appropriate emotions, or the right combination of reciprocal noises.

Thus the making of governmental decisions is not a majestic march of great majorities united upon certain matters of basic policy. It is the steady appeasement of relatively small groups. Even when these groups add up to a numerical majority at election time it is usually not useful to construe that majority as more than

Robert Alan Dahl (1915–   )
Source: From *A Preface to Democratic Theory* (1956) University of Chicago Press, pp. 145–50.

an arithmetic expression. For to an extent that would have pleased Madison enormously, the numerical majority is incapable of undertaking any coordinated action. It is the various components of the numerical majority that have the means for action.

As this is familiar ground, let me summarize briefly and dogmatically some well-known aspects of the constitutional rules: the groups they benefit, those they handicap, and the net result. When we examine Congress we find that certain groups are over-represented, in the sense that they have more representatives (or more representatives at key places) and therefore more control over the outcome of Congressional decisions than they would have if the rules were designed to maximize formal political equality. Equal representation in the Senate has led to over-representation of the less densely populated states. [. . .] Because of the operation of the single-member district system in the House [of Representatives], on the average, a net shift of 1 per cent of the electorate from one party to the other will result in a net gain of about 2.5 per cent of the House seats for the benefited party; and because of the operation of the two-member district in the Senate, a shift of 1 per cent will result in a net gain for the benefited party of about 3 per cent of the Senate seats. Hence when large heterogeneous groups, like the farmers, shift their party support the legislative effects are likely to be considerably exaggerated. [. . .]

The bureaucracies are much more complex. In varying degrees they must be responsive to both Presidential and Congressional politicians. But the Presidential and Congressional politicians to whom they must respond are themselves rather a narrow and specialized group. In Congress, typically, it is the chairmen of the House and Senate Appropriations Committees, of the relevant subcommittees, and of the relevant substantive committees. Among Presidential politicians, administrators must usually be responsive to the Budget Bureau, to the departmental secretary, and, of course, to the President himself. They must also be responsive to their own specialized clienteles. The most effective clientele obviously is one like the farmers, that is also well represented in Congress and even in the executive branch; sometimes bureaucracy and clientele become so intertwined that one cannot easily determine who is responsive to whom. [. . .]

This much may be said of the system. If it is not the very pinnacle of human achievement, a model for the rest of the world to copy or to modify at its peril, as our nationalistic and politically illiterate glorifiers so tiresomely insist, neither, I think, is it so obviously a defective system as some of its critics suggest.

To be sure, reformers with a tidy sense of order dislike it.

Foreign observers, even sympathetic ones, are often astonished and confounded by it. Many Americans are frequently dismayed by its paradoxes; indeed, few Americans who look upon our political process attentively can fail, at times, to feel deep frustration and angry resentment with a system that on the surface has so little order and so much chaos.

For it is a markedly decentralized system. Decisions are made by endless bargaining; perhaps in no other national political system in the world is bargaining so basic a component of the political process. In an age when the efficiencies of hierarchy have been re-emphasized on every continent, no doubt the normal American political system is something of an anomaly, if not, indeed, at times an anachronism. For as a means to highly integrated, consistent decisions in some important areas — foreign policy, for example — it often appears to operate in a creaking fashion verging on total collapse.

Yet we should not be too quick in our appraisal, for where its vices stand out, its virtues are concealed to the hasty eye. Luckily the normal system has the virtue of its vices. With all its defects, it does nonetheless provide a high probability that any active and legitimate group will make itself heard effectively at some stage in the process of decision. This is no mean thing in a political system.

It is not a static system. The normal American system has evolved, and by evolving it has survived.

1.18

Hayek: The Constitution of Liberty

Democracy

Like most terms in our field, the word 'democracy' is also used in a wider and vaguer sense. But if it is used strictly to describe a method of government — namely, majority rule — it clearly refers

Friedrich August von Hayek (1889—   )
Source: From *The Constitution of Liberty* (1960) Routledge & Kegan Paul and University of Chicago Press, pp. 103—4, 115—16, 130, 231—2.

to a problem different from that of liberalism. Liberalism is a doctrine about what the law ought to be, democracy a doctrine about the manner of determining what will be the law. Liberalism regards it as desirable that only what the majority accepts should in fact be law, but it does not believe that this is therefore necessarily good law. Its aim, indeed, is to persuade the majority to observe certain principles. It accepts majority rule as a method of deciding, but not as an authority for what the decision ought to be. To the doctrinaire democrat the fact that the majority wants something is sufficient ground for regarding it as good; for him the will of the majority determines not only what is law but what is good law. [. . .]

The liberal believes that the limits which he wants democracy to impose upon itself are also the limits within which it can work effectively and within which the majority can truly direct and control the actions of government. So long as democracy constrains the individual only by general rules of its own making, it controls the power of coercion. If it attempts to direct them more specifically, it will soon find itself merely indicating the ends to be achieved while leaving to its expert servants the decision as to the manner in which they are to be achieved. [. . .]

It is not the powers which democratic assemblies can effectively wield but the powers which they hand over to the administrators charged with the achievement of particular goals that constitute the danger to individual freedom today. Having agreed that the majority should prescribe rules which we will obey in pursuit of our individual aims, we find ourselves more and more subjected to the orders and the arbitrary will of its agents. [. . .]

It is one of the great tragedies of our time that the masses have come to believe that they have reached their highest standard of material welfare as a result of having pulled down the wealthy, and to fear that the preservation or emergence of such a class would deprive them of something they would otherwise get and which they regard as their due . . . In a progressive society there is little reason to believe that the wealth which the few enjoy would exist at all if they were not allowed to enjoy it. [. . .] A world in which the majority could prevent the appearance of all that they did not like would be a stagnant and probably a declining world. [. . .]

Law versus coercion

The range and variety of government action that is, at least in principle, reconcilable with a free system is thus considerable. The old formulae of *laissez-faire* or non-intervention do not provide us with an adequate criterion for distinguishing between what is and what is not admissible in a free system. [. . .]

A government which cannot use coercion except in the enforcement of general rules has no power to achieve particular aims that require means other than those explicitly entrusted to its care and, in particular, cannot determine the material position of particular people or enforce distributive or 'social' justice. In order to achieve such aims, it would have to pursue a policy which . . . determines for what specific purposes particular means are to be used.

This, however, is precisely what a government bound by the rule of law cannot do. If the government is to determine how particular people ought to be situated, it must be in a position to determine also the direction of individual efforts . . . If government treats different people equally, the results will be unequal . . . if it allows people to make what use they like of the capacities and means at their disposal, the consequences for the individuals will be unpredictable. The restrictions which the rule of law imposes upon government thus preclude all those measures which would be necessary to insure that individuals will be rewarded according to another's conception of merit or desert rather than according to the value that their services have for their fellows — or, what amounts to the same thing, it precludes the pursuit of distributive, as opposed to commutative, justice. Distributive justice requires an allocation of all resources by a central authority; it requires that people be told what to do and what ends to serve. Where distributive justice is the goal, the decisions as to what the different individuals must be made to do cannot be derived from general rules but must be made in the light of the particular aims and knowledge of the planning authority. As we have seen before, when the opinion of the community decides what different people shall receive, the same authority must also decide what they shall do.

Part 2

The Formation of Modern States

Introduction

JAMES ANDERSON

How have modern states been formed and how has the relationship between state and society changed in the process? Part 2 provides a variety of answers to these questions. It focuses on processes of state formation in different historical and geographical contexts, ranging from Western Europe in the sixteenth century to Africa in the 1960s.

The selections look at different, though often related, factors in state formation: at the internal conflicts and changing relationships between social classes and groups, including groups in the state apparatus itself; at the impact of wars and preparations for war; at the role of states in industrialization and the impact of industrialization on state forms and activities; at the significance of nationalism in establishing, maintaining and undermining states; and at the creation of new states through decolonization.

As well as covering different topics and social contexts the various authors adopt different approaches. However, while a variety of approaches are necessary in dealing with such a large and complex subject, a number of common features stand out. All the selections, for instance, bring out the importance of the international context, or 'external' factors, in state formation, rather than simply looking at 'internal' elements in isolation. Some interesting overlaps also occur, in that different authors bring somewhat different perspectives to bear on the same issues, such as the role of social classes, or of nationalism, or of mercantilist economic policy in the lead-up to the Industrial Revolution. In some cases these different perspectives are contradictory, but generally they are complementary — dealing with the same issue from a slightly different angle, or in a different historical or geographical context.

Moreover Part 2 as a whole addresses the question of what we mean by *modern* states. What constitutes their 'modernity'? Clearly it is not a simple question of historical time-periods, for each region of the world, indeed each individual country, has its own chronology. For example, the *absolutist* state, which we take as the precursor to the 'modern' state, had already been undermined in England — by the English Revolution of 1640 — virtually before it had even been established in Russia, and in Russia it continued in existence up to the socialist Revolution of 1917. This sort of variation over time and space certainly complicates the problem of understanding how modern states became 'modern', and it makes generalization a risky business. However, generalizing is not something which we can avoid. While each particular case of state formation is in some respects unique, each case also exhibits features which are general to a range of cases. Moreover, no modern state was formed in isolation from the world system of states.

One easy way of appreciating what modern states have in common is to contrast contemporary states with states in past historical eras. Looking at pre-modern states is also a good antidote to the tendency we all have to accept contemporary states and the world system of states as somehow 'natural' (because we have no direct personal experience of any alternatives). The best antidote to this is, of course, to study the *social* processes whereby states became 'modern'. To help in forming generalizations about these processes it is useful to think in broad terms about the transition from feudalism (and other pre-capitalist societies) to capitalism, and then to the period in which industrial capitalism came to dominate the world and socialism became a serious possibility (or was achieved as some claim).

Our starting point in examining the emergence of the modern state is Western Europe in the sixteenth century and the growth of the absolutist state. In many ways absolutism was the precursor of modern states. In Chapter 2.1, Perry Anderson shows that the absolutist state in Western Europe was a key element in the transition from feudalism to capitalism. Indeed it appears quite 'modern' in several respects: for example, it was characterized by the creation of regular armies, a centralized bureaucracy and taxation system, and state policies for trade and diplomacy — all things we tend to take for granted as 'natural', but which had not previously existed in the medieval states of Europe. However, Anderson shows that absolutism, while it was in part conditioned by the rise of a bourgeoisie, was in fact dominated by the continued rule of the traditional feudal aristocracy. Hence its modern appearance belies an essentially archaic structure; and bourgeois revolutions were necessary, Perry Anderson argues, to enable the development of modern states and the free expansion of capitalism.

Chapter 2.2 by Theda Skocpol compares the revolutions in France, Russia and China, which overthrew the state in what she calls agrarian bureaucratic societies. She sees weakness in the state structure as one of the basic causes of each of these revolutions, and a centralization and nationalization of the state as one of their main outcomes. Her approach, in contrast to Anderson's, suggests that there was nothing distinctively 'bourgeois' about the French Revolution.

Barry Supple, in Chapter 2.3, looks at the state in relation to the Industrial Revolution. He compares the part played by the state in the process of industrialization in nineteenth-century Britain and Germany, and he discusses the influence of industrialization in 'modernizing' the state. He also elaborates the connections between economic policy and nationalism.

Nationalism is the central subject of Chapters 2.4 and 2.5, by Edward Carr and Tom Nairn. Carr wrote his piece in 1945, and in it he traces how the social composition and status of the 'nation' changed in European history from its origins in absolutism to the Second World War. Nairn, in contrast, develops a theory to explain the rise of nationalism as a general phenomenon in the nineteenth century. He explains it as a populist response to the problems of the unevenness of development (e.g. of industrialization) across territories. He thus provides one way of explaining the division of territory between states where nationalism played a significant formative role (for example, in the unification of Germany, or in the creation of new states such as Czechoslovakia out of the ruins of the absolutist Austro-Hungarian Empire).

In recent times nationalism has often been associated with the creation of new states out of the former European colonies in Asia and Africa, most of which have gained independence since 1945. Nationalist struggles such as those against French rule in Algeria and Vietnam, and to a lesser extent the Kenyan struggle against the British, had a huge impact on world politics and they encouraged independence struggles in other colonies. However, many colonial territories were granted independence without such struggles, and in some cases nationalism only became important after independence. Ruth First (a long-standing opponent of South African apartheid who was killed by a letter bomb in 1982, sent 'presumably by the South African department of dirty tricks' to quote *The Guardian*, 18 August 1982) analyses in Chapter 2.6 the nature of post-colonial states in Africa. She focuses on how they achieved independence and why so many of them have experienced army coups d'état. The chapter on the formation of African states is extracted from her book *The Barrel of a Gun*, which was written in the 1960s (before, it should be noted, the success of nationalist struggles in Angola, Mozambique and Zimbabwe which run somewhat counter to her main argument).

The final chapter in Part 2 is by a member of the Course Team, Adam Westoby, and deals with the nature of Communist states (an issue already touched on by Skocpol). While official Marxist self-images of these states see them as socialist (a view shared by many of their opponents, as well as by supporters in the West) there are a number of critical Marxist theories which deny this claim. Westoby provides a succinct outline of these, together with a number of non-Marxist theories.

2.1
The Absolutist States of Western Europe

PERRY ANDERSON

In the course of the sixteenth century, the absolutist state emerged in the West. The centralized monarchies of France, England and Spain represented a decisive rupture with the pyramidal, parcellized sovereignty of the medieval social formations, with their estates and liege-systems. [. . .]

The absolute monarchies introduced standing armies, a permanent bureaucracy, national taxation, a codified law, and the beginnings of a unified market. All these characteristics appear to be pre-eminently capitalist . . . [and] they coincide with the disappearance of serfdom, a core institution of the original feudal mode of production in Europe[1] . . . [However] the end of serfdom did not thereby mean the disappearance of feudal relations from the countryside. Identification of the two is a common error. Yet it is evident that private extra-economic coercion, personal dependence, and combination of the immediate producer with the instruments of production, did not necessarily vanish when the rural surplus ceased to be extracted in the form of labour or deliveries in kind, and became rent in money: so long as aristocratic agrarian property blocked a free market in land and factual mobility of manpower — in other words, as long as labour was not separated from the social conditions of its existence to become 'labour-power' — rural relations of production remained feudal. [. . .]

Source: From 'The absolutist state in the West', in *Lineages of the Absolutist State* (1979) NLB 1974, Verso Edition, Ch. 1 pp. 15—42; and pp. 428—9. The footnotes and references have been excluded, and sub-headings added. The three Notes have been added by the editors.

Aristocracy and peasantry

The lords who remained the proprietors of the fundamental means of production in any pre-industrial society were, of course, the noble landowners. Throughout the early modern epoch, the dominant class — economically and politically — was thus the *same* as in the medieval epoch itself: the feudal aristocracy. This nobility underwent profound metamorphoses in the centuries after the close of the Middle Ages: but from the beginning to the end of the history of absolutism, it was never dislodged from its command of political power.

The changes in the *forms* of feudal exploitation which supervened at the end of the medieval epoch were, of course, far from insignificant. Indeed, it was precisely these changes which changed the forms of the state. Absolutism was essentially just this: *a redeployed and recharged apparatus of feudal domination*, designed to clamp the peasant masses back into their traditional social position — despite and against the gains they had won by the widespread commutation of dues. [. . .] But the dimensions of the historical transformation involved in the advent of absolutism must in no way be minimized. It is essential, on the contrary, to grasp the full logic and import of the momentous change in the structure of the aristocratic state, and of feudal property, that produced the new phenomenon of absolutism.

Feudalism as a mode of production was originally defined by an organic *unity* of economy and polity, paradoxically distributed in a chain of parcellized sovereignties throughout the social formation. The institution of serfdom as a mechanism of surplus extraction fused economic exploitation and politico-legal coercion at the molecular level of the village. The lord in his turn typically owed liege-loyalty and knight-service to a seigneurial overlord, who claimed the land as his ultimate domain. With the generalized commutation of dues into money rents, the cellular unity of political and economic oppression of the peasantry was gravely weakened, and threatened to become dissociated (the end of this road was 'free labour' and the 'wage contract'). The class power of the feudal lords was thus directly at stake with the gradual disappearance of serfdom. The result was a *displacement* of politico-legal coercion upwards towards a centralized, militarized summit — the absolutist state. Diluted at village level, it became concentrated at 'national' level. The result was a reinforced apparatus of royal power, whose permanent political function was the repression of the peasant and plebeian masses at the foot of the social hierarchy. This new state machine, however, was also by its nature vested with a coercive force capable of breaking or disciplining individuals and groups *within* the nobility itself. The arrival of absolutism was thus, as we shall see, never a smooth evolutionary process for the dominant class itself: it was marked by extremely sharp ruptures and conflicts within the feudal aristocracy to whose collective interests it ultimately ministered. At the same time, the objective complement of the political concentration of power at the height of the social order, in a centralized monarchy, was the economic consolidation of the units of feudal property beneath it . . . a compensatory strengthening of the titles of property . . . In other words . . . landownership tended to become progressively less 'conditional' as sovereignty became correspondingly more 'absolute'. The weakening of the medieval conceptions of vassalage worked in both directions: while it conferred new and extraordinary powers on the monarchy, at the same time it emancipated from traditional restraints the estates of the nobility . . . Individual members of the aristocratic class, who steadily lost political rights of representation in the new epoch, registered economic gains in ownership as the obverse of the same historical process . . . The royal states of the Renaissance were first and foremost modernized instruments for the maintenance of noble domination over the rural masses.

Aristocracy and bourgeoisie

Simultaneously, however, the aristocracy had to adjust to a second antagonist: the mercantile bourgeoisie which had developed in the medieval towns . . . It was precisely the intercalation of this third presence that prevented the Western nobility from settling its accounts with the peasantry in Eastern fashion,[1] by smashing its resistance and fettering it to the manor. The medieval town had been able to develop because the hierarchical dispersal of sovereignties in the feudal mode of production for the first time freed urban economies from direct domination by a rural ruling class. The towns in this sense were never exogenous to feudalism in the West . . . in fact, the very condition of their existence was the unique 'detotalization' of sovereignty within the politico-economic order of feudalism. [. . .]

[Towards the end of the fifteenth century] a sudden, concurrent revival of political authority and unity occurred in country after country. From the pit of extreme feudal chaos and turmoil of the Wars of the Roses, the Hundred Years War and the second

Castilian Civil War, the first 'new' monarchies straightened up virtually together, during the reigns of Louis XI in France, Ferdinand and Isabella in Spain, Henry VII in England[2] and Maximilian in Austria. Thus when the absolutist states were constituted in the West, their structure was fundamentally determined by the feudal regroupment against the peasantry, after the dissolution of serfdom; but it was secondarily *over-determined* by the rise of an urban bourgeoisie which, after a series of technical and commercial advances, was now developing into pre-industrial manufactures on a considerable scale. [. . .] The threat of peasant unrest, unspokenly constitutive of the absolutist state, was thus always conjoined with the pressure of mercantile or manufacturing capital within the Western economies as a whole, in moulding the contours of aristocratic class power in the new age. The peculiar form of the absolutist state in the West derives from this double determination.

Private property and public authority

The dual forces which produced the new monarchies of Renaissance Europe found a single juridical condensation. The revival of Roman law, one of the great cultural movements of the age, ambiguously corresponded to the needs of both social classes whose unequal power and rank shaped the structures of the absolutist state in the West. [. . .] [The revival started in twelfth-century Italy and had spread outwards to all the major countries of Western Europe by the end of the Middle Ages.] But the decisive 'reception' of Roman law . . . occurred in the age of the Renaissance, concurrently with that of absolutism. The historical reasons for its deep impact were two-fold [economic and political], and reflected the contradictory nature of the original Roman legacy itself.

Economically, the recovery and introduction of classical civil law was fundamentally propitious to the growth of free capital in town and country. For the great distinguishing mark of Roman civil law had been its conception of absolute and unconditional private property. [. . .] The full reappearance of the idea of absolute private property in land was a product of the early modern epoch. For it was not until commodity production and exchange had reached overall levels — in both agriculture and manufactures — equal to or above those of antiquity, that the juridical concepts created to codify them could come into their own once again. [. . .] The reception of Roman law in Renaissance

Europe was thus a sign of the spread of capitalist relations in towns and country: *economically*, it answered to vital interests of the commercial and manufacturing bourgeoisie. [. . .]

Politically the revival of Roman law corresponded to the constitutional exigencies of the reorganized feudal states of the epoch. In fact, there is no doubt that on a European scale, the primary determinant of the adoption of Roman jurisprudence lay in the drive of royal governments for increased central powers. For the Roman legal system . . . comprised two distinct — and apparently contrary — sectors: civil law regulating economic transactions between citizens, and public law governing political relations between the state and its subjects . . . The juridically unconditional character of private property consecrated by [civil law] found its contradictory counterpart in the formally absolute nature of the imperial sovereignty [enshrined in public law] . . . It was [the latter which particularly attracted] the new monarchies of the Renaissance. [. . .] The double social movement engraved in the structures of Western absolutism thus found its juridical concordance in the reintroduction of Roman law. [. . .]

In other words, the enhancement of private property from below was matched by the increase of public authority from above, embodied in the discretionary power of the royal ruler. The absolutist states in the West based their novel aims on classical precedents: Roman law was the most powerful intellectual weapon available, for their typical programme of territorial integration and administrative centralism. [. . .] [Roman public law] provided the juristic protocols for overriding medieval privileges, ignoring traditional rights, and subordinating private franchises. [. . .]

Archaic 'modernity'

The superior effect of juridical modernization was thus to reinforce the rule of the traditional feudal class. The apparent paradox of this phenomenon was reflected in the whole structure of the absolutist monarchies themselves — exotic, hybrid compositions whose surface 'modernity' again and again betrays a subterranean archaism. This can be seen very clearly from a survey of the institutional innovations which heralded and typified its arrival: *army, bureaucracy, taxation, trade, diplomacy* [Ed's emphasis]. These can be briefly considered in order.

Armies and warfare

It has often been remarked that the absolutist state pioneered the professional army, which with the military revolution introduced in the late sixteenth and seventeenth centuries by Maurice of Orange, Gustavus Adolphus and Wallenstein (infantry drill and line by the Dutchman; cavalry salvo and platoon system by the Swede; unitary vertical command by the Czech) grew immensely in size. Philip II's armies numbered some 60,000 or so, while a hundred years later Louis XIV's ran to 300,000. Yet both the form and the function of these troops diverged immensely from that which later became characteristic of the modern bourgeois state. They were not normally a national conscript force, but a mixed mass in which foreign mercenaries played a constant and central role. These mercenaries were typically recruited from areas outside the perimeter of the new centralized monarchies, often mountain regions which specialized in providing them: the Swiss were the Gurkhas of early modern Europe. French, Dutch, Spanish, Austrian or English armies included Swabians, Albanians, Swiss, Irish, Wallachians, Turks, Hungarians or Italians. The most obvious social reason for the mercenary phenomenon was, of course, the natural refusal of the noble class to arm its own peasants wholesale . . . [and] mercenary troops ignorant of the very language of the local population, could be relied on to stamp out social rebellion. German *Landsknechten* dealt with the East Anglian peasant risings of 1549 in England, while Italian arquebusiers ensured the liquidation of the rural revolt in the West country . . . The key importance of mercenaries, already increasingly visible in the later Middle Ages, from Wales to Poland, was not merely an interim expedient of absolutism at the dawn of its existence: it marked it down to its very demise in the West. In the late eighteenth century, even after the introduction of conscription into the main European countries, up to two-thirds of a given 'national' army could be composed of hired foreign soldateska. [. . .]

The function of these vast new agglomerations of soldiers was also visibly distinct from that of later capitalist armies. There has hitherto been no Marxist theory of the variant social functions of war in different modes of production. This is not the place to explore the subject. Yet it can be argued that war was possibly the most *rational* and *rapid* single mode of expansion of surplus extraction available for any given ruling class under feudalism. Agricultural productivity [and trade] . . . both grew very slowly for the lords, compared with the sudden and massive 'yields' afforded by territorial conquest, of which the Norman invasions of England or Sicily, the Angevin seizure of Naples or the Castilian conquest of Andalusia were only the most spectacular examples. It was thus logical that the social definition of the feudal ruling class was military. [. . .]

The nobility was a landowning class whose profession was war: its social vocation was not an external accretion but an intrinsic function of its economic position. The normal medium of inter-capitalist competition is economic, and its structure is typically additive: rival parties may both expand and prosper — although unequally — throughout a single confrontation, because the production of manufactured commodities is inherently unlimited. The typical medium of inter-feudal rivalry, by contrast, was military and its structure was always potentially the zero-sum conflict of the battlefield, by which fixed quantities of ground were won or lost. For land is a natural monopoly: it cannot be indefinitely extended, only redivided. The categorial object of noble rule was territory, regardless of the community inhabiting it. Land as such, not language, defined the natural perimeters of its power. The feudal ruling class was thus essentially motile, in a way that a capitalist ruling class later could never be. For capital itself is *par excellence* internationally mobile, thereby permitting its holders to be nationally fixed: land is nationally immobile, and nobles had to travel to take possession of it. A given barony or dynasty could thus typically transfer its residence from one end of the continent to the other without dislocation. Angevin lineages could rule indifferently in Hungary, England or Naples; Norman in Antioch, Sicily or England; Burgundian in Portugal or Zeeland; Luxemburger in the Rhineland or Bohemia; Flemish in Artois or Byzantium; Habsburg in Austria, the Netherlands or Spain. No common tongue had to be shared between lords and peasants in these varied lands. For public territories formed a continuum with private estates, and their classical means of acquisition was force, invariably decked out in claims of religious or genealogical legitimacy. Warfare was not the 'sport' of princes, it was their fate. [. . .]

The absolutist states reflect this archaic rationality in their inmost structure. They were machines built overwhelmingly for the battlefield. It is significant that the first regular national tax to be imposed in France, the *taille royale*, was levied to finance the first regular military units in Europe — the *compagnies d'ordonnance* of the mid-fifteenth century, of which the premier unit was composed of Scots soldiers of fortune. By the mid-sixteenth century, 80 per cent of Spanish state revenues went on military expenditure . . . By the mid-seventeenth century, the annual outlays

of continental principalities from Sweden to Piedmont were everywhere predominantly and monotonously devoted to the preparation or conduct of war, now immensely more costly than in the
Renaissance. Another century later, on the peaceful eve of 1789,
according to Necker two-thirds of French state expenditure were
still allocated to the military establishment. It is manifest that this
morphology of the state does not correspond to a capitalist
rationality: it represents a swollen memory of the medieval
functions of war. Nor were the grandiose military apparatuses of
the late feudal state left idle. The virtual permanence of international armed conflict is one of the hallmarks of the whole
climate of absolutism. [. . .]

Bureaucracy and taxation

The characteristic civilian bureaucracy and tax system of the
absolutist state was no less paradoxical. It appears to represent a
transition to Weber's rational legal administration, in contrast to
the jungle of particularist dependencies of the high Middle Ages.
Yet at the same time, the Renaissance bureaucracy was treated as
saleable property to private individuals: a central confusion of two
orders that the bourgeois state has everywhere kept distinct. Thus
the prevalent mode of integration of the feudal nobility into the
absolutist state in the West took the form of acquisition of 'offices'.
He who privately purchased a position in the public apparatus of
the state could then recoup himself by licensed privileges and
corruption (fee-system). [. . .]

Such office-holders, who proliferated in France, Italy, Spain,
Britain or Holland, could hope to make up to 300—400 per cent
profit, and perhaps very much more, on their purchase. The
system was born in the sixteenth century and became a central
financial support of the absolutist states during the seventeenth
century. Its grossly parasitic character is evident: in extreme
situations (France during the 1630s is an example), it could even
cost a royal budget something like as much in disbursements (via
tax-farms and exemptions) as it supplied in remunerations. The
growth of the sale of offices was, of course, one of the most
striking by-products of the increased monetarization of the early
modern economies and of the relative ascent of the mercantile and
manufacturing bourgeoisie within them. Yet by the same token,
the very integration of the latter into the state apparatus by the
private purchase and inheritance of public positions and honours,
marked its subordinate assimilation into a feudal polity in which
the nobility always necessarily constituted the summit of the social

hierarchy . . . Absolutist bureaucracy both registered the rise of mercantile capital, and arrested it.

If the sale of offices was an indirect means of raising revenue from the nobility and the mercantile bourgeoisie on terms profitable to them, the absolutist state also, and above all, of course, taxed the poor. The economic transition from labour dues to money rents in the West was accompanied by the emergence of royal taxes levied for war, which in the long feudal crisis at the end of the Middle Ages had already been one of the main provocations for the desperate peasant upheavals of the time. [. . .]

Economic policy

The economic functions of absolutism were not exhausted, however, by its tax and office system. Mercantilism was the ruling doctrine of the epoch, and it presents the same ambiguity as the bureaucracy which was intended to enforce it, with the same underlying reversion to an earlier prototype. For mercantilism undoubtedly demanded the suppression of particularistic barriers to trade within the national realm, and strove to create a unified domestic market for commodity production. Aiming to increase the power of the state relative to that of all other states, it encouraged exports of goods, while banning exports of bullion or coins, in the belief that there was a fixed quantity of commerce and wealth in the world . . . Its characteristic creations were the royal manufactures and state-regulated guilds in France, and the chartered companies in England. The medieval and corporatist lineage of the former scarcely needs comment; the telltale fusion of political and economic orders in the latter scandalized Adam Smith . . . [whose classical bourgeois doctrine of *laissez-faire* insisted on a] rigorous formal separation of the political and economic systems. [. . .]

For mercantilism exactly represented the conceptions of a feudal ruling class that had adapted to an integrated market, yet had preserved its essential outlook on the unity of what Francis Bacon called 'considerations of plenty' and 'considerations of power'. [. . .] Mercantilist theory . . . was heavily 'bellicist' emphasizing the necessity and profitability of warfare. [. . .] The mercantilist theories of wealth and of war were, indeed, conceptually inter-locked: the zero-sum model of world trade which inspired its economic protectionism was derived from the zero-sum model of international politics which was inherent in its bellicism.

Diplomacy

Trade and war were not the only external activities of the absolutist state in the West, of course. Its other great effort was invested in *diplomacy*. This was one of the great institutional inventions of the epoch — inaugurated in the miniature area of Italy in the fifteenth century, institutionalized there with the Peace of Lodi, and adopted in Spain, France, England, Germany and throughout Europe in the sixteenth century. Diplomacy was, in fact, the indelible birth-mark of the Renaissance state: with its emergence an international state system was born in Europe, in which there was a perpetual 'probing of the weak points in the environment of a state or the dangers to it emanating from other states'. Medieval Europe had never been composed of a clearly demarcated set of homogeneous political units — an international state system. Its political map was an inextricably superimposed and tangled one, in which different juridical instances were geographically interwoven and stratified, and plural allegiances, asymmetrical suzerainties and anomalous enclaves abounded. Within this intricate maze, there was no possibility of a formal diplomatic system emerging, because there was no uniformity or parity of partners. [. . .]

[But the] contraction of the feudal pyramid into the new centralized monarchies of Renaissance Europe produced for the first time a formalized system of inter-state pressure and exchange, with the establishment of the novel institutions of reciprocal fixed embassies abroad, permanent chancelleries for foreign relations, and secret diplomatic communications and reports, shielded by the new concept of 'extra-territoriality'. [. . .]

Yet these instruments of diplomacy, ambassadors or state secretaries, were not the weapons of a modern national state. The ideological conceptions of 'nationalism' as such were foreign to the inmost nature of absolutism. The royal states of the new epoch did not disdain to mobilize patriotic sentiments in their subjects, in the political and military conflicts which constantly opposed the various monarchies of Western Europe to one another. But the diffuse existence of a popular proto-nationalism in Tudor England, Bourbon France or Habsburg Spain was basically a token of bourgeois presence within the polity, and it was always manipulated by grandees or sovereigns more than it governed them. The national aureole of absolutism in the West, often apparently very pronounced (Elizabeth I, Louis XIV), was in reality contingent and borrowed. The ruling norms of the age lay elsewhere. For the ultimate instance of legitimacy was the *dynasty*, not the territory.

The state was conceived as the patrimony of the monarch, and therefore the title-deeds to it could be gained by a union of persons . . . The supreme device of diplomacy was therefore marriage — peaceful mirror of war, which so often provoked it. For, less costly as an avenue of territorial expansion than armed aggression, matrimonial manoeuvring afforded less immediate results (often only at one generation's remove) and was thereby subject to unpredictable hazards of mortality in the interval before the consummation of a nuptial pact and its political fruition. Hence the long detour of marriage so often led back directly to the short route of war. The history of absolutism is littered with such conflicts, whose names bear them witness: Wars of the Spanish, Austrian, or Bavarian Successions . . . In diplomacy, too, the index of feudal dominance in the absolutist state is evident.

Transition to capitalism

Immensely magnified and reorganized, the feudal state of absolutism was nevertheless constantly and profoundly over-determined by the growth of capitalism within the composite social formations of the early modern period. These formations were, of course, a combination of different modes of production under the — waning — dominance of one of them: feudalism. All the structures of the absolutist state thus reveal the action from a distance of the new economy at work within the framework of an older system. [. . .] The premonitions of a new political order contained within them was not a false promise. The bourgeoisie in the West was already strong enough to leave its blurred impress on the state, under absolutism. For the apparent paradox of absolutism in Western Europe was that it fundamentally represented an apparatus for the protection of aristocratic property and privileges, yet at the same time the means whereby this protection was promoted could *simultaneously* ensure the basic interests of the nascent mercantile and manufacturing classes. The absolutist state increasingly centralized political power and worked towards more uniform legal systems . . . It did away with a large number of internal barriers to trade, and sponsored external tariffs against foreign competitors . . . It provided lucrative if risky investments in public finance for usury capital . . . It mobilized rural property by seizure of ecclesiastical lands . . . It offered rentier sinecures in the bureaucracy . . . It sponsored colonial enterprises and trading companies . . .

In other words, it accomplished certain partial functions in the *primitive accumulation* necessary for the eventual triumph of the capitalist mode of production itself. The reasons why it could perform this 'dual' role lie in the specific nature of merchant or manufacturing capital: since neither rested on the mass production characteristic of machine industry proper, neither in themselves demanded a radical rupture with the feudal agrarian order which still enclosed the vast majority of the population (the future wage-labour and consumer market of industrial capitalism). In other words, they could develop within the limits set by the reorganized feudal framework. This is not to say that they everywhere did so: political, religious or economic conflicts could well fuse into revolutionary explosions against absolutism after a certain period of maturation, in specific conjunctures. There was, however, always a potential *field of compatibility* at this stage between the nature and programme of the absolutist state and the operations of mercantile and manufacturing capital. For in the international competition between noble classes that produced the endemic warfare of the age, the size of the commodity sector within each 'national' patrimony was always of critical importance to its relative military and political strength. Every monarchy thus had a stake in gathering treasure and promoting trade under its own banners, in the struggle against its rivals. Hence the 'progressive' character that subsequent historians have so often conferred on the official policies of absolutism. Economic centralization, protectionism and overseas expansion aggrandized the late feudal state while they profited the early bourgeoisie. They increased the taxable revenues of the one by providing business opportunities for the other. [...]

In nature and structure, the absolutist monarchies of Europe were still feudal states: the machinery of rule of the same aristocratic class that had dominated the Middle Ages. But in Western Europe where they were born, the *social formations* which they governed were a complex combination of *feudal and capitalist modes of production*, with a gradually rising urban bourgeoisie and a growing primitive accumulation of capital, on an international scale. It was the intertwining of these two antagonistic modes of production within single societies that gave rise to the transitional forms of absolutism. The royal states of the new epoch brought to an end the parcellization of sovereignty that was inscribed in the pure feudal mode of production as such, although without themselves ever achieving a fully unitary polity. [...]

The term 'absolutism' [was] in fact always technically a misnomer ... [for] one basic characteristic ... divided the absolute monarchies of Europe from all the myriad other types of despotic, arbitrary or tyrannical rule, incarnated or controlled by a personal sovereign, which prevailed elsewhere in the world. *The increase in the political sway of the royal state was accompanied, not by a decrease in the economic security of noble landownership, but by a corresponding increase in the general rights of private property.* The age in which 'absolutist' public authority was imposed was also simultaneously the age in which 'absolute' private property was progressively consolidated. It was this momentous social difference which separated the Bourbon, Habsburg, Tudor or Vasa monarchies from any Sultanate, Empire or Shogunate[3] outside Europe. [. . .]

The rule of the absolutist state was that of the feudal nobility in the epoch of transition to capitalism. Its end would signal the crisis of the power of its class: the advent of the bourgeois revolutions, and the emergence of the capitalist state.

Notes

1. The absolutist states in Eastern Europe — in Prussia, Austria and Russia — were 'device(s) for the consolidation of serfdom'; in the more backward social conditions of Eastern Europe, the aristocracy did not have to contend with a rising urban bourgeoisie, and Eastern absolutism was more militarized than in the West; for example, 'The Prussian bureaucracy . . . was born as an offshoot of the Army' (Anderson, pp. 195, 213, 430).
2. England 'the strongest medieval monarchy in the West . . . produced the weakest and shortest absolutism'. It did not develop a large standing army like Spain or France and 'therefore there was an exceptionally early demilitarization of the noble class . . .'. Henry VIII, in selling off most of the land seized from monastries, 'lost . . . the one great chance of English absolutism to build up a firm economic base independent of parliamentary taxation', and this also strengthened in size and wealth the landed gentry, who was converted to 'commercial activities long before any comparable rural class in Europe'. The English Revolution by 'a commercialized gentry, a capitalist city (London), a commoner artisanate and yeomanry' was able to defeat Charles I's attempt to strengthen absolutism precisely because he lacked a standing army and the resources independent of parliament to pay for one. 'Before it could reach the age of maturity, English absolutism was cut off by a bourgeois revolution' (Anderson, pp. 113, 125, 142).
3. Japan is probably the only case of indigenous feudalism outside Europe, and it is also the only area outside of Europe or European settlement which has achieved an advanced industrial capitalism. However, this was achieved only through contact with European and American capitalism. Anderson argues that the advanced nature of

Japanese feudalism enabled the rapid implantation of industrial capitalism after the 1868 Meiji Restoration, but that capitalism did not develop indigenously because Japanese feudalism did not evolve into an absolutist state. In the Tokugawa Shogunate (1603—1868) sovereignty remained fragmented between regional lords with their own armies, towns had less autonomy and merchants less status than in Europe, there was nothing like the concept of absolute private property derived from Roman law, and no centralized legal system, taxation or bureaucracy covering the whole country (Anderson, pp. 413—28).

2.2

States and Revolutions: France, Russia and China

THEDA SKOCPOL

Social revolutions in France, Russia and China occurred, during the earlier world-historical phases of modernization, in agrarian bureaucratic societies situated within, or newly incorporated into, international fields dominated by more economically modern nations abroad. In each case, social revolution was a conjuncture of three developments: (1) the collapse or incapacitation of central administrative and military machineries; (2) widespread peasant rebellions; and (3) marginal élite political movements. What each social revolution minimally 'accomplished' was the extreme rationalization and centralization of state institutions, the removal of a traditional landed upper class from intermediate (regional and local) quasi-political supervision of the peasantry, and the elimination or diminution of the economic power of a landed upper class . . . I shall attempt to explain the three great historical social revolutions, first, by discussing the institutional characteristics of agrarian states, and their special vulnerabilities and potentialities during the earlier world-historical phases of modernization, and second, by pointing to the peculiar characteristics of old regimes in France, Russia and China, which made them uniquely vulnerable among the earlier modernizing agrarian states to social-revolutionary transformations. Finally, I shall suggest reasons for similarities and differences in the outcomes of the great historical social revolutions.

An agrarian bureaucracy is an agricultural society in which social control rests on a division of labour and a coordination of

Source: From 'France, Russia, China: a structural analysis of social revolutions', in *Comparative Studies in Society and History: An International Quarterly* (1976), 18, 2, April, pp. 175–210. The footnotes and most references have been excluded.

effort between a semi-bureaucratic state and a landed upper class. The landed upper class typically retains, as an adjunct to its landed property, considerable (though varying in different cases) undifferentiated local and regional authority over the peasant majority of the population. The partially bureaucratic central state extracts taxes and labour from peasants either indirectly through landlord intermediaries or else directly, but with (at least minimal) reliance upon cooperation from individuals of the landed upper class. In turn, the landed upper class relies upon the backing of a coercive state to extract rents and/or dues from the peasantry. At the political centre, autocrat, bureaucracy, and army monopolize decisions, yet (in varying degrees and modes) accommodate the regional and local power of the landed upper class and (again, to varying degrees) recruit individual members of this class into leading positions in the state system.

Agrarian bureaucracies are inherently vulnerable to peasant rebellions. Subject to claims on their surpluses, and perhaps their labour, by landlords and state agents, peasants chronically resent both. To the extent that the agrarian economy is commercialized, merchants are also targets of peasant hostility. In all agrarian bureaucracies at all times, and in France, Russia and China in non-revolutionary times, peasants have had grievances enough to warrant, and recurrently spur, rebellions. Economic crises (which are endemic in semi-commercial agrarian economies anyway) and/or increased demands from above for rents or taxes might substantially enhance the likelihood of rebellions at particular times. But such events ought to be treated as short-term precipitants of peasant unrest, not fundamental underlying causes.

Modernization is best conceived not only as an *intra*-societal process of economic development accompanied by lagging or leading changes in non-economic institutional spheres, but also as a world-historic *inter*-societal phenomenon [. . .]

Of course, societies have always interacted. What was special about the modernizing intersocietal network that arose in early modern Europe was, first, that it was based upon trade in commodities and manufactures, as well as upon strategic politico-military competition between independent states, and, second, that it incubated the 'first (self-propelling) industrialization' of England after she had gained commercial hegemony within the Western European-centred world market.

In the wake of that first commercial-industrial breakthrough, modernizing pressures have reverberated throughout the world. In the first phase of world modernization, England's thoroughgoing commercialization, capture of world market hegemony, and expansion of manufactures (both before and after the technological Industrial Revolution which began in the 1780s), transformed means and stakes in the traditional rivalries of European states and put immediate pressure for reforms, if only to facilitate the financing of competitive armies and navies, upon the other European states and especially upon the ones with less efficient fiscal machineries. In the second phase, as Europe modernized and further expanded its influence around the globe, similar militarily compelling pressures were brought to bear on those non-European societies which escaped immediate colonization, usually the ones with pre-existing differentiated and centralized state institutions. [. . .]

But agrarian bureaucracies faced enormous difficulties in meeting the crises of modernization. Governmental leaders' realm of autonomous action tended to be severely limited, because few fiscal or economic reforms could be undertaken which did not encroach upon the advantages of the traditional landed upper classes which constituted the major social base of support for the authority and functions of the state in agrarian bureaucracies. Only so much revenue could be squeezed out of the peasantry, and yet landed upper classes could often raise formidable obstacles to rationalization of tax systems. Economic development might mean more tax revenues and enhanced military prowess, yet it channelled wealth and manpower away from the agrarian sector. Finally, the mobilization of mass popular support for war tended to undermine the traditional, local authority of landlords or landed bureaucrats upon which agrarian bureaucratic societies partly relied for the social control of the peasantry. [. . .]

All modernizing agrarian bureaucracies have peasants with grievances and face the unavoidable challenges posed by modernization abroad. So, in some sense, potential for social revolution has been built into all modernizing agrarian bureaucracies. Yet, only a handful have succumbed. Why? A major part of the answer, I believe, lies in the insight that 'not oppression, but weakness, breeds revolution'. It is the breakdown of a societal mode of social control which allows and prompts social revolution to unfold. In the historical cases of France, Russia and China, the unfolding of social revolution depended upon the emergence of revolutionary crises occasioned by the incapacitation of administrative and military organizations. That incapacitation, in turn, is best explained not as a function of mass discontent and mobilization, but as a function of a combination of pressures on state institutions from more modernized countries abroad, and (in two cases out of three) built-in structural incapacities to mobilize increased resources in response to those pressures. France, Russia and China were also special among all agrarian bureaucracies in that their agrarian institutions afforded peasants not only the usual grievances against landlords and state agents but also 'structural space' for autonomous collective insurrection. Finally, once administrative/ military breakdown occurred in agrarian bureaucracies with such especially insurrection-prone peasantries, then, and only then, could organized revolutionary leaderships have great impact upon their societies' development — though not necessarily in the ways they originally envisaged.

Breakdown of societal controls: foreign pressures and administrative/military collapse

If a fundamental cause and the crucial trigger for the historical social revolutions was the incapacitation of administrative and military machineries in modernizing agrarian bureaucracies, then how and why did this occur in France, Russia and China? What differentiated these agrarian bureaucracies which succumbed to social revolution from others which managed to respond to modernizing pressures with reforms from above? Many writers attribute differences in response to qualities of will or ability in governmental leaders. From a sociological point of view, a more satisfying approach might focus on the interaction between (a) the magnitude of foreign pressures brought to bear on a modernizing agrarian bureaucracy, and (b) the particular structural characteristics of such societies that underlay contrasting performances by leaders responding to foreign pressures and internal unrest.

Overwhelming foreign pressures on an agrarian bureaucracy could cut short even a generally successful government programme of reforms and industrialization 'from above'. Russia is the obvious case in point. From at least the 1890s onward, the Czarist regime was committed to rapid industrialization, initially government-financed out of resources squeezed from the peasantry, as the only means of rendering Russia militarily competitive with Western nations. Alexander Gerschenkron [1960] argues that initial government programmes to promote heavy industry had succeeded in the 1890s to such an extent that, when the government was forced to reduce its direct financial and administrative role after 1904, Russia's industrial sector was nevertheless capable of autonomously generating further growth (with the aid of foreign capital investments.) Decisive steps to modernize agriculture and free peasant labour for permanent urban migration were taken after the unsuccessful Revolution of 1905. Had she been able to sit out World War I, Russia might have recapitulated the German experience of industrialization facilitated by bureaucratic guidance.

But participation in World War I forced Russia to mobilize fully her population, including her restive peasantry. Army officers and men were subjected to years of costly fighting, and civilians to mounting economic privations — all for nought. For, given Russia's 'industrial backwardness . . . enhanced by the fact that Russia was very largely blockaded . . .', plus the 'inferiority of the Russian military machine to the German in everything but sheer numbers . . . , military defeat, with all of its inevitable consequences for the internal condition of the country, was very nearly a foregone conclusion' [Chamberlin, 1963, pp. 64—5]. The result was administrative demoralization and paralysis, and the disintegration of the army. Urban insurrections which brought first middle-strata moderates and then the Bolsheviks to power could not be suppressed, owing to the newly-recruited character and war weariness of the urban garrisons. Peasant grievances were enhanced, young peasant men were politicized through military experiences, and, in consequence, spreading peasant insurrections from the spring of 1917 on could not be controlled.

It is instructive to compare 1917 to the Revolution of 1905. Trotsky called 1905 a 'dress rehearsal' for 1917, and, indeed, many of the same social forces with the same grievances and similar political programmes took part in each revolutionary drama. *What accounts for the failure of the Revolution of 1905 was the Czarist regime's ultimate ability to rely upon the army to repress popular disturbances.* Skillful tactics were involved: the regime bought time to organize repression and assure military loyalty with well-timed liberal concessions embodied in the October Manifesto of 1905 (and later largely retracted). Yet, it was of crucial importance that the futile 1904—5 war with Japan was, in comparison with the World War I morass, circumscribed, geographically peripheral, less demanding of resources and manpower, and quickly concluded once defeat was apparent. The peace treaty was signed by late 1905, leaving the Czarist government free to bring military reinforcements back from the Far East into European Russia.

The Russian Revolution occurred in 1917 because Russia was too inextricably entangled with foreign powers, friend and foe, economically and militarily more powerful than she. Foreign entanglement must be considered not only to explain the administrative and military incapacitation of 1917, but also entry into World War I. That involvement cannot be considered 'accidental'. Nor was it 'voluntary' in the same sense as Russia's entry into the 1904 war with Japan. Whatever leadership 'blunders' were involved, the fact remains that in 1914 both the Russian state and the Russian economy depended heavily on Western loans and capital. Moreover, Russia was an established part of the European state system and could not remain neutral in a conflict that engulfed the whole of that system.

Foreign pressures and involvements so inescapable and overwhelming as those that faced Russia in 1917 constitute an extreme case for the earlier modernizing agrarian bureaucracies we are considering here. For France and China the pressures were surely no more compelling than those faced by agrarian bureaucracies such as Japan, Germany and Russia (1858—1914) which successfully adapted through reforms from above that facilitated the extraordinary mobilization of resources for economic and military development. Why were the Bourbon and Manchu regimes unable to adapt? Were there structural blocks to effective response? [. . .]

Inherent in all agrarian bureaucratic regimes were tensions between, on the one hand, state élites interested in preserving, using, and extending the powers of armies and administrative organizations and, on the other hand, landed upper classes interested in defending locally and regionally based social networks, influence over peasants, and powers and privileges associated with the control of land and agrarian surpluses. Such tensions were likely to be exacerbated once the agrarian bureaucracy was forced to adapt to modernization abroad because foreign military pressures gave cause, while foreign economic development offered incentives and models, for state élites to attempt reforms which went counter to the class interests of traditional, landed upper strata. Yet there were important variations in the ability of semi-bureaucratic agrarian states to respond to modernizing pressures with reforms which sharply and quickly increased resources at the disposal of central authorities. What can account for the differences in response?

Not the values or individual qualities of traditional bureaucrats: Japan's Meiji reformers acted in the name of traditional values and authority to enact sweeping structural reforms which cleared the way for rapid industrialization and military modernization. Russia's czarist officialdom was renowned for its inefficiency and corruption, and yet it implemented basic agrarian reforms in 1861 and 1905 and administered the first stages of heavy industrialization.

Leaving aside value-orientations and individual characteristics, we must look at the class interests and connections of state officials. *The adaptiveness of the earlier modernizing agrarian bureaucracies was significantly determined by the degree to which the upper and middle ranks of the state administrative bureaucracies were staffed by large land-holders.* Only state machineries significantly differentiated from traditional landed upper classes could undertake modernizing reforms which almost invariably had to encroach upon the property or privileges of the landed upper class. [. . .]

But where — as in Bourbon France and late Manchu China — regionally-based cliques of landed magnates were ensconced within nominally centralized administrative systems, the ability of the state élites to control the flow of tax resources and implement reform policies was decisively undermined. By their *resistance* to the mobilization of increased resources for military or economic purposes in modernization crises, such landed cliques of officials could engender situations of acute administrative/military disorganization — potentially revolutionary crises of governmental authority.

The French monarchy struggled on three fronts throughout the eighteenth century. Within the European state system, France's 'amphibious geography' forced her to compete simultaneously with the great continental land powers, Austria and (after mid-century) Prussia, and with the maritime powers, above all, Britain. Britain's accelerating commercial and industrial development put France at ever increasing disadvantage in trade and naval strength and the extraordinary efficiency of Prussia's bureaucratic regime, its special ability to extract resources from relatively poor people and territories and to convert them with minimal wastage to military purposes, tended to compensate for France's advantages of national wealth and territorial size. And the French monarchy had to fight on a 'third front' at home — against the resistance of its own privileged strata to rationalization of the tax system.

Perceptive as he was in pointing to rationalization and centralization of state power as the most fateful outcomes of the French Revolution, Alexis de Tocqueville surely exaggerated the extent to which monarchical authority already exhibited those qualities before the Revolution. [. . .] Such was the system in theory, an absolute monarch's dream. But in practice? Quite aside from general qualities which set the French administrative system in the eighteenth century in sharp contrast to the Prussian . . . the system afforded landlords (and wealth-holders generally) strategic points of institutional leverage for obstructing royal policies. [. . .]

The *parlements*, or sovereign courts, nominally a part of the administrative system, were the most avid and strategically located of the institutional defenders of property and privilege. 'The French monarchy never remedied its fatal error of having sold judicial offices just at the moment when it became master of the political machine. The monarch was almost completely powerless in the face of his judges, whom he could not dismiss, transfer, or promote' [Dorn, 1963, p. 26]. [. . .]

By their dogged defence of tax and property systems increasingly inadequate to the needs of the French state in a modernizing world, the *parlements* throughout the eighteenth century repeatedly blocked attempts at reform. Finally, in 1787—8, they '. . . opened the door to revolution' [Cobban, 1963, p. 155] by rallying support against now indispensable administrative fiscal reforms, and by issuing the call for the convening of the Estates General.

France fought at sea and on land in each of the general European wars of the eighteenth century: the War of the Austrian Succession; the Seven Years War; and the war over American Independence. In each conflict, her resources were strained to the utmost and her vital colonial trade disrupted, yet no gains, indeed losses in America and India, resulted. The War for American Independence proved to be the last straw. 'The price to be paid for American Independence was a French Revolution' [Cobban, 1963, p. 122]; royal treasurers finally exhausted their capacity to raise loans from financiers, and were forced (again) to propose reforms of the tax system. The usual resistance from the *parlements* ensued, and an expedient adopted by Calonne in an attempt to circumvent it — the summoning of an Assembly of Notables in 1787 — only provided privileged interests yet another platform for voicing resistance. A last-ditch effort to override the *parlements* (by Brienne in 1787—8) crumbled in the face of concerted upper-class defiance, popular demonstrations, and the unwillingness of army officers to direct forcible suppression of the popular resistance.

The army's hesitance was especially crucial in translating fiscal crises and political unrest into general administrative and military breakdown. Recruited from various privileged social backgrounds — rich noble, rich non-noble, and poor country noble — the officers had a variety of long-standing grievances, against other officers and, significantly, against the Crown, which could never satisfy them all. But it is likely that the decisive explanation for their behaviour lies in the fact that they were virtually all privileged, socially and/or economically, and hence identified during 1787—8 with the *parlements*. [. . .]

During its opening phases, until after the King had capitulated and agreed to convene the Estates General, the French Revolution pitted all strata, led by the privileged, against the Crown. The army officers' understandable reluctance to repress popular unrest during that period created a general crisis of governmental authority and effectiveness which in turn unleashed social divisions, between noble and non-noble, rich and poor, that made a subsequent resort to simple repression by the Old Regime impossible.

The officers' insubordination early in the Revolution was all the more easily translated into rank-and-file insubordination in 1789 and after, because of the fact that French soldiers were not normally insulated from the civilian population. Soldiers were billeted with civilians, and those from rural areas were released during the summers to help with the harvest at home. Thus, during 1789, the *Gardes Françaises* (many of whom were married to Parisian working-class women) were won over to the Paris revolution in July, and peasant soldiers spread urban news in the countryside during the summer and returned to their units in the autumn with vivid tales of peasant revolt.

Like the Bourbon Monarchy, the Manchu Dynasty proved unable to mobilize resources sufficient to meet credibly the challenges posed by involvement in the modernizing world. 'The problem was not merely the very real one of the inadequate resources of the Chinese economy as a whole. In large measure the financial straits in which the Peking government found itself were due to . . . [inability to] command such financial capacity as there was in its empire' [Feuerwerker, 1970, p. 41]. Part of the explanation for this inability lay in a characteristic which the Chinese state shared with other agrarian states: lower and middle level officials were recruited from the landed gentry, paid insufficient salaries, and allowed to engage in a certain amount of 'normal' corruption, withholding revenues collected as taxes from higher authorities. Yet, if the Manchu Dynasty had encountered the forces of modernization at the height of its powers (say in the early eighteenth century) rather than during its declining phase, it might have controlled or been able to mobilize sufficient resources to finance modern industries and equip a centrally controlled modern army. In that case, officials would never have been allowed to serve in their home provinces, and thus local and regional groups of gentry would have lacked institutional support for concerted opposition against central initiatives. But, as it happened, the Manchu Dynasty was forced to try to cope with wave after wave of imperialist intrusions, engineered by foreign industrial or industrializing nations anxious to tap Chinese markets and finances, immediately after a series of massive mid nineteenth-century peasant rebellions. The Dynasty had been unable to put down the

Taiping Rebellion on its own, and the task had fallen instead to local, gentry-led, self-defence associations and to regional armies led by complexly interrelated gentry who had access to village resources and recruits. In consequence of the gentry's role in putting down rebellion, governmental powers formerly accruing to central authorities or their bureaucratic agents, including, crucially, rights to collect and allocate various taxes, devolved upon local, gentry-dominated, sub-district governing associations and upon provincial armies and officials increasingly aligned with the provincial gentry against centre.

Unable to force resources from local and regional authorities, it was all Peking could do simply to meet foreign indebtedness, and after 1895 even that proved impossible. [. . .] The Boxer Rebellion of 1900, and subsequent foreign military intervention, only further exacerbated an already desperate situation.

Attempts by dynastic authorities to remedy matters through a series of 'reforms' implemented after 1900 — abolishing the Confucian educational system and encouraging modern schools; organizing the so-called 'New Armies' (which actually formed around the nuclei of the old provincial armies); transferring local governmental functions to provincial bureaux; and creating a series of local and provincial gentry-dominated representative assemblies — only exacerbated the sorry situation, right up to the 1911 breaking point. [. . .]

With each reform, dynastic élites thought to create powers to counterbalance entrenched obstructive forces, but new officials and functions were repeatedly absorbed into pre-existing local and (especially) regional cliques of gentry. The last series of reforms, those that created representative assemblies, ironically provided cliques of gentry with legitimate representative organs from which to launch the liberal, decentralizing 'Constitutionalist movement' against the Manchus.

What ultimately precipitated the 'revolution of 1911' was a final attempt at reform by the central government, one that directly threatened the financial interests of the gentry power groups for the purpose of strengthening central government finances and control over national economic developments. [. . .] Conspiratorial groups affiliated with Sun Yat Sen's T'eng Meng Hui, and mainly composed of Western-educated students and middle-rank New Army officers, joined the fray to produce a series of military uprisings. Finally:

> . . . the lead in declaring the independence of one province after another was taken by two principal elements: the

military governors who commanded the New Army forces and the gentry-official-merchant leaders of the provincial assemblies. These elements had more power and were more conservative than the youthful revolutionarists of the T'eng Meng Hui [Fairbank, 1971, p. 132].

The Chinese 'Revolution of 1911' irremediably destroyed the integument of civilian élite ties — traditionally maintained by the operation of Confucian educational institutions and the central bureaucracy's policies for recruiting and deploying educated officials so as to strengthen 'cosmopolitan' orientations at the expense of local loyalties — which had until that time provided at least the semblance of unified governance for China. 'Warlord' rivalries ensued as gentry interests attached themselves to regional military machines, and this condition of intra-élite disunity and rivalry (only imperfectly and temporarily overcome by Chiang Kai-Shek's regime between 1927 and 1937) condemned China to incessant turmoils and provided openings (as well as cause) for lower-class, especially peasant, rebellions and for Communist attempts to organize and channel popular unrest.

Peasant insurrections

If administrative and military breakdown in a modernizing agrarian bureaucracy were to inaugurate social revolutionary transformations, rather than merely an interregnum of intra-élite squabbling, then widespread popular revolts had to coincide with and take advantage of the hiatus of governmental supervision and sanctions. Urban insurrections provided indispensable support during revolutionary interregnums to radical political élites vying against other élites for state power: witness the Parisian *sans culottes*' support for the Jacobins; the Chinese workers' support for the Communists (between 1920 and 1927); and the Russian industrial workers' support for the Bolsheviks. But fundamentally more important in determining final outcomes were the peasant insurrections which in France, Russia and China constituted irreversible attacks on the powers and privileges of the traditional landed upper classes.

Agrarian bureaucracy has been the only historical variety of complex society with differentiated, centralized government that has, in certain instances, incubated a lower-class stratum that was *simultaneously strategic* in the society's economy and polity (as surplus producer, payer of rents and taxes, and as provider of corvée and military manpower), and yet *organizationally autono-mous* enough to allow the 'will' and 'tactical space' for collective insurrection against basic structural arrangements. [. . .]

If peasants are to be capable of self-initiated rebellion against landlords and state officials, they must have (a) some institutionally based collective solidarity, and (b) autonomy from direct, day-to-day supervision and control by landlords in their work and leisure activities. Agricultural regimes featuring large estates worked by serfs or labourers tend to be inimical to peasant rebellion — witness the East Elbian Junker regime — but the reason is not that serfs and landless labourers are economically poor, rather that they are subject to close and constant supervision and discipline by landlords or their agents. If large-estate agriculture is lacking, an agrarian bureaucracy may still be relatively immune to widespread peasant rebellion if landlords control sanctioning machineries, such as militias and poor relief agencies, at local levels. On the other hand, landlords as a class, and the 'system' as whole, will be relatively vulnerable to peasant rebellion if: (a) sanctioning machineries are centralized; (b) agricultural work and peasant social life are controlled by peasant families and com-munities themselves. These conditions prevailed in France and Russia and meant that, with the incapacitation of central admini-strative and military bureaucracies, these societies became suscep-tible to the spread and intensification of peasant revolts which in more normal circumstances could have been contained and repressed.

It is worth emphasizing that peasant actions in revolutions are not intrinsically different from peasant actions in 'mere' rebellions or riots. When peasants 'rose' during historical social revolutionary crises, they did so in highly traditional rebellious patterns: bread riots, 'defence' of communal lands or customary rights, riots against 'hoarding' merchants or landlords, 'social banditry'. Peasants initially drew upon traditional cultural themes to justify rebellion. Far from becoming revolutionaries through adoption of a radical vision of a desired new society, 'revolutionary' peasants have typically been 'backward-looking' rebels incorporated by circum-stances beyond their control into political processes occurring independently of them, at the societal 'centre'.

In the highly abnormal circumstances of social revolution, administrative breakdown, political rebellions of marginal élites, and peasant insurrections *interacted* to produce transformations that none alone could have occasioned or accomplished. Because peasants could rebel on their own in France and Russia, they did not have to be *directly mobilized* by urban radicals. In China, such mobilization was ultimately necessary, but it was for the most part a military mobilization which conformed with important modifications to an age-old pattern of élite/peasant coordination of effort to accomplish 'dynastic replacement'. [. . .]

Radical political movements and centralizing outcomes

Although peasant insurrections played a decisive role in each of the great historical social revolutions, nevertheless an exclusive focus on peasants — or on the peasant situation in agrarian bureaucracies — cannot provide a complete explanation for the occurrence of social revolutions. Russia and China were recurrently rocked by massive peasant rebellions, yet peasant uprisings did not fuel structural transformations until the late eighteenth century and after. Obviously agrarian bureaucracies were exposed to additional and unique strains and possibilities once English and then European commercialization-industrialization became a factor in world history and development. The stage was set for the entry of marginal élites animated by radical nationalist goals.

Who were these marginal élites? What sectors of society provided the social bases for nationalist radicalisms? *Not* the bourgeoisie proper: merchants, financiers and industrialists. These groups have had surprisingly little *direct* effect upon the politics of modernization in any developing nation, from England to the countries of the Third World today. [. . .]

Instead, nationalist radicals tended to 'precipitate out' of the ranks of those who possessed specialized skills and were oriented to state activities or employments, but either lacked traditionally prestigious attributes such as nobility, landed wealth, or general humanist education, or else found themselves in situations where such attributes were no longer personally or nationally functional. Their situations in political and social life were such as to make them, especially in times of political crises, willing to call for such radical reforms as equalization of mobility opportunities, political democracy, and (anyway, before the revolution) extension of civil liberties. [. . .]

In Bourbon France, radicals (of whom the Jacobins were the most extreme) came primarily from the ranks of non-noble, non-wealthy lawyers, professionals, or state functionaries, and disproportionately from the provinces.

In the market towns and small administrative centers a new

class of bourgeois (that is, non-noble) lawyers had grown up to defend the interests of the provincial members of the monarchial society. It was they who seem to have suffered most, or at least most consciously, from the delaying and obfuscating tactics of the aristocratic courts and therefore best understood the pall that privilege cast over all administrative efforts at reform. Through the famous corresponding societies, these provincial critics exchanged ideas and laid the intellectual foundation for much that happened in 1789 and after [Fox, 1971, pp. 89—90].

In Russia, by 1917, the revolutionary sects, such as the Bolsheviks and the Left Social Revolutionaries, constituted the surviving politically organized representatives of what had earlier been an outlook much more widespread among university-educated Russians: extreme alienation, disgust at Russia's backwardness, preoccupation with public events and yet refusal to become involved in the round of civil life. As Russia underwent rapid industrialization after 1890, opportunities for university education were extended beyond the nobility — a circumstance which helped to ensure that universities would be hotbeds of political radicalism — yet, before long, opportunities for professional and other highly skilled employments also expanded. Especially in the wake of the abortive 1905 Revolution, Russia's university-educated moved toward professional employments and liberal politics. Yet when events overtook Russia in 1917, organized radical leadership was still to be found among the alienated intelligentsia.

In China, as in Russia, radical nationalist modernizers came from the early student generations of university-educated Chinese. Especially at first, most were the children of traditionally wealthy and prestigious families, but urban and 'rich peasant' backgrounds, respectively, came to be overrepresented in the (pre-1927) Kuomintang and the Communist élites. With the abolition of the Confucian educational system in 1904, and the collapse of the imperial government in 1911, even traditionally prestigious attributes and connections lost their meaning and usefulness. At the same time, neither warlord regimes, nor the Nationalist government after 1927 offered much scope for modern skills or credentials; advancement in these regimes went only to those with independent wealth or personal ties to military commanders. Gradually, the bulk of China's modern-educated, and especially the young, came to support the Communist movement, some through active commitment in Yenan, others through passive political support in the cities.

Two considerations help to account for the fact that radical leadership in social revolutions came specifically from the ranks of skilled and/or university-educated marginal élites oriented to state employments and activities. First, agrarian bureaucracies are 'statist' societies. Even before the era of modernization official employments in these societies constituted both an important route for social mobility and a means for validating traditional status and supplementing landed fortunes. Second, with the advent of economic modernization in the world, state activities acquired greater-than-ever objective import in the agrarian bureaucratic societies which were forced to adapt to modernization abroad. For the concrete effects of modernization abroad first impinged upon the state's sphere, in the form of sharply and suddenly stepped up military competition or threats from more developed nations abroad. And the cultural effects of modernization abroad first impinged upon the relatively highly educated in agrarian bureaucracies, that is upon those who were mostly either employed by the state or else connected or oriented to its activities. [. . .]

The earlier modernizing agrarian bureaucracies that (to varying degrees) successfully adapted to challenges from abroad did so either through revolution, or basic reforms 'from above' or social revolution 'from below'. Either traditional bureaucrats successfully promoted requisite reforms or else their attempts precipitated splits within the upper class which could, if the peasantry were structurally insurrection-prone, open the door to social revolution. In the context of administrative/military disorganization and spreading peasant rebellions, tiny, organized radical élites that never could have created revolutionary crises on their own gained their moments in history. As peasant insurrections undermined the traditional landed upper classes, and the old regime officials and structures tied to them, radical élites occupied centre stage, competing among themselves to see who could seize and build upon the foundations of central state power. [. . .]

No political élite not able or willing to accept the peasants' revolutionary economic gains could hope to emerge victorious from the intra-élite or inter-party conflicts that marked revolutionary interregnums. Elites with close social or politico-military ties to traditional forms of landed upper-class institutional power (i.e. the privileged rentier bourgeoisie of France, the Kerensky regime in Russia, the [post-1927] Kuomintang in China) invariably lost out.

The historical social revolutions did not culminate in more liberal political arrangements. At opening stages of the French, Russian (1905) and Chinese revolutions, landed upper-class/middle-strata political coalitions espoused 'parliamentary liberal' programmes. But events pushed these groups and programmes aside, for the organized élites who provided the ultimately successful leadership in all social revolutions ended up responding to popular turmoil — counterrevolutionary threats at home and abroad, peasant anarchist tendencies, and the international crises faced by their societies — by creating *more* highly centralized, bureaucratized and rationalized state institutions than those that existed prior to the revolutions. This response, moreover, was entirely in character for élites adhering to world views which gave consistent primacy to organized political action in human affairs.

The strengthening and rationalizing of central state powers was the result of the French Revolution as surely as of the Russian and Chinese. [. . .]

France:

> came out of the revolutionary-Napoleonic crisis with its administrative organization profoundly and . . . irreversibly altered. . . . After 1815, France retained a set of budgetary procedures, a network of departmental prefects, and a system of centrally appointed judges in the place of the deficit financing ex post facto, the quaint chaos of provincial powers, and the court system based on ownership of office with which the old monarchy had lived for centuries [Ford, 1963, pp. 22—3]. [. . .]

Thus, what changed most thoroughly in *all* of the historical social revolutions was the mode of societal control of the lower strata. Landed upper classes lost (at least) their special socio-political authority and their roles in controlling the peasantry (however feebly) through local and regional quasi-political institutional arrangements — the *parlements* and seigneurial courts in France; *zemstvos* and landed estates in Russia; clans, associations, sub-district, district and provincial governments in China. The peasantry and the urban lower strata were directly incorporated into now truly *national* polities and economies, institutionally and symbolically.

But wasn't the French Revolution a 'bourgeois' revolution, in contrast to the 'Communist' Chinese and Russian Revolutions? Throughout, this essay has emphasized patterns common to all three of the great historical revolutions, thus violating much of the common wisdom about the special 'bourgeois' nature of the French Revolution. The traditional argument about the French Revolution holds that it was in some sense made by a 'strong' bourgeois economic class, and 'cleared the way' politically, judicially and socially for capitalist industrialization in France.

Proponents of the view that the French Revolution was a 'bourgeois revolution' can point to evidence which seems to support their position. The French Revolution did *not* result in the complete elimination of property-owning upper classes. Neither did political élites take direct control of the economy to spur national industrialization. Regional, estate and guild barriers to the formation of a national market were eliminated. And, in time, France did undergo capitalist industrialization.

Yet there are equally important facts which contradict the thesis of the 'bourgeois revolution'. Before the Revolution, French 'industry' was overwhelmingly small-scale and non-mechanized, and commercial and financial capital coexisted non-antagonistically, indeed symbiotically, with the more settled and prestigious 'proprietary' forms of wealth (land, venal office, annuities). During the Revolution, political leadership for the Third Estate was overwhelmingly recruited from the ranks of professionals (especially lawyers), office-holders, and intellectuals, not commercial or industrial bourgeois. The men who ruled France after the Revolution were bureaucrats, landowners, soldiers, commercial and financial capitalists, much as before. [...]

From the point of view of what might have optimized conditions for French national industrialization, the French Revolution seems best interpreted as either overwrought or premature. A few ministerial reforms under the Old Regime might well have optimized chances for France quickly to emulate British industrial developments (especially since Old Regime officials were leaning toward a system of international free trade, as exemplified by the Commercial Treaty of 1786). Social revolution in France, as in Russia and China, strengthened national political institutions, equipped them to mobilize people and resources to meet the crises of modernization, to guarantee order at home, and to counter foreign threats. Yet in Russia and China, emerging from revolutionary crises in the twentieth century, strengthened national political institutions could be used *directly* to promote enterprises already implanted by foreign capital and employing models and advanced technologies from abroad. But in post-Revolutionary France, resources mobilized by strengthened national institutions were dissipated in the adventuristic Napoleonic Wars, while France lost ground against her chief economic competitor, Great Britain. The outcome could hardly have been different. A French economy consisting entirely of small-scale agricultural and (mostly non-mechanized) industrial units could hardly be directed from above (as the Jacobin interlude proved), especially when foreign models of large-scale industry were as yet in world history entirely lacking.

The French Revolution was remarkably similar to the Russian and the Chinese in its basic *causes* — failure of old regime officials to mobilize sufficient national resources to promote national economic development and/or counter military competition or threats from more developed nations abroad — and in its *structural dynamics* — peasants and marginal political élites against a traditional landed upper class. That *outcomes* differed — that in France no Communist Party emerged to displace fully landed wealth, collectivize agriculture, and direct industrialization — is not only attributable to factors stressed by traditional theories of revolution, such as the shape of the pre-revolutionary class structure and the established ideological aims of avowed revolutionary élites, but also to the *opportunities* and *requirements* for state initiatives in industrialization presented by the *world* political economy *at the time* each agrarian bureaucratic society was incorporated into a modernizing world and experienced social revolutionary transformation 'in response'.

Let me sum up what this essay has attempted to do. To explain the great historical social revolutions, I have, first, conceptualized a certain type of society, the agrarian bureaucracy, in which social control of the lower strata (mainly peasants) rests with institutions locally and regionally controlled by landed upper classes, together with administrative and military machineries centrally controlled; and second, I have discussed differences between agrarian bureaucracies which did and those which did not experience social revolutions in terms of (a) institutional structures which mediate landed upper-class relations to state apparatuses and peasant relations to landed upper classes and (b) types and amounts of international political and economic pressures (especially originating with more developed nations) impinging upon agrarian bureaucracies newly incorporated into the modernizing world. According to my analysis, social revolutions occurred in those modernizing agrarian bureaucracies — France, Russia and China — which *both* incubated peasantries structurally prone to autonomous insurrection *and* experienced severe administrative and military disorganization due to the direct or indirect effects of military competition or threats from more modern nations abroad. [. . .]

This comparative historical analysis has been meant to render plausible a theoretical approach to explaining revolutions which breaks with certain long-established sociological proclivities. While existing theories of revolution focus on discontent, and its articulation by oppositional programmes or ideologies, as the fundamental cause of revolutions, I have emphasized mechanisms and dynamics of societal social control through political and class domination. Moreover, while other theories view the impact of modernization (as a cause of revolution) in terms of the effects of processes of economic development on class structures, 'system equilibrium', or societal members' levels of satisfaction, my approach focuses on the effects of modernization — viewed also as an inter-societal politico-strategic process — upon adaptive capacities of the agrarian bureaucratic states and upon the opportunities open to political élites who triumph in revolutions.

References

Chamberlin, William Henry (1963) *The Russian Revolution,* Vol. 1, New York, Grosset and Dunlap, originally published in 1935.

Cobban, Alfred (1963) *A History of Modern France, Volume 1: 1715—1799,* Baltimore, Maryland, Penguin, originally published in 1957.

Dorn, W. L. (1963) *Competition for Empire, 1740—1763,* New York, Harper and Row, originally published in 1940.

Fairbank, John King (1971) *The United States and China,* 3rd edn, Cambridge, Massachusetts, Harvard University Press.

Feuerwerker, Albert (1970) *China's Early Industrialization,* New York, Atheneum, originally published in 1958.

Ford, Franklin L (1963) 'The revolutionary-Napoleonic era: how much of a watershed?', *American Historical Review* 69(1), October.

Fox, Edward Whiting (1971) *History in Geographic Perspective: The Other France,* New York, W. W. Norton.

Gerschenkron, Alexander (1960) 'Problems and patterns of Russian economic development', pp. 42—72 in Cyril E. Black (ed.) *The Transformation of Russian Society,* Cambridge, Massachusetts, Harvard University Press.

Hampson, Norman (1963) *A Social History of the French Revolution,* Toronto, University of Toronto Press.

Hampson, Norman (1968) *The Enlightenment,* Baltimore, Maryland, Penguin.

Robinson, G. T. (1969) *Rural Russia under the Old Regime,* Berkeley and Los Angeles, University of California Press, originally published in 1932.

2.3

States and Industrialization: Britain and Germany in the Nineteenth Century

BARRY SUPPLE

In the long perspective of history the Industrial Revolution is an *international* phenomenon — extending, in its processes and consequences, over the whole world . . . However, it is customary for economists and historians to examine its origins and impact in terms of individual nations . . . The flow of goods and men and ideas, the patterns of culture and ambitions, the elements of social structure, are all best understood, in the first instance at least, in terms of the distinctive frameworks created by national boundaries [. . .]

It is therefore through the history of nations that we must begin any empirical study of the role of the state in the international phenomenon which we call the Industrial Revolution.

Modern industrial society originated in Britain when *laissez-faire* was an important part of the emerging economic ideology. This is not to say that the British classical economists ignored the case in favour of direct participation by the state in the workings of the economy. But the balance of their argument . . . came down heavily on the side of non-interference. Even more important than this was the associated fact that the initial phase of modern economic growth in Britain was a market-based phenomenon — owing little directly to the activity of the state.[1] On the other hand,

Source: From 'The state and the industrial revolution 1700—1914' in Carlo M. Cipolla (ed.) *The Industrial Revolution 1700—1914* (1976), The Fontana History of Europe, Hassocks Harvester Press/Barnes and Noble. Most of the footnotes have been excluded and sub-headings added.

however, although other nations imported Britain's Industrial Revolution with vigour and enthusiasm, they did not on the whole adopt the official policy — or, rather, the lack of policy — which was associated with the pioneer episode of industrialization. Indeed, in the context of modern world history, a *laissez-faire* economic policy seems less like an orthodoxy than a brief aberration from a norm of detailed government intervention in economic affairs. [...]

[However], the nation-state was 'modernized' by the advent of industrialization, with its enormous impact on social structures and ambitions and its revolutionary implications for worldwide networks of power. Some relationship between the state and industrialization is, in fact, necessarily involved in the idea of modernity. Britain's relatively brief but spectacular period of unchallenged economic supremacy, French history after the Revolution, the creation of a powerful, imperial Germany and its industrial rivalry with late Victorian Britain, the unification of Italy — all exemplify the role of the national concept in modern history. The state — in the sense of the sovereign institutions of society — was an obvious expression of that concept in the international arena. At the same time, however, it was a potential instrument of nationhood and of industrial power, since its sovereignty (where it could be successfully asserted) implied an ability both to transform national institutions and to dispose of economic resources by legislative or administrative means.

The extent of state political and economic activity obviously varied from country to country. Yet, even where it was at its most extreme, it cannot be treated as an entirely independent element in socio-economic processes — i.e. as an institution which, with or without consent, imposes its will on all other institutions. Although its power *was* virtually absolute, the state must also be seen as *part* of society, reflecting particular social forces and representing (however confusedly or narrowly) specific group or class interests. Such an institution can conceivably act arbitrarily in the political sense. But it cannot act entirely independently of causes located in the society with which it is associated. Hence, although in some respects 'the state' shapes 'society', it is more useful to envisage 'the state' as the institutional arrangements which a group or interest (or shifting alliances of groups or interests) within society uses in order to exercise its dominance in the political arena. This is not to say that the state always, or ever, reflects the exact distribution of effective power within a society. (For example, in Britain the political authority and influence of the industrial middle classes lagged behind their effective economic power for much of the nineteenth century.) But it *is* to say that a government draws its aims as well as its legitimacy from existing elements in a particular society. [. . .]

Therefore, the important question becomes: in what circumstances will groups or classes in the society use the state to encourage industrial development? And the important point to remember is that the state enters the arena of industrial development not as an arbitrary and unpredictable force, but as the agent of 'old' or 'new' forces or classes within society, acting either in their own self-interest or in pursuit of an ostensibly national purpose, within which their own role can be rationalized . . .

Historically, the most important way in which the state stimulated industrial growth in a capitalist setting was through its ability to restructure the institutions of society — i.e. through its ability to *create* a capitalist setting in the first instance . . . [by] the eradication of the power of feudal institutions (land tenures, guilds, etc.) in revolutionary France, the abolition of internal tariffs in France and Germany, the maintenance of an orderly system of law in Britain, the political unification of Germany and Italy . . . state aid to formal technical education (which occurred much earlier on the Continent than in Britain) . . . official information services such as some German states used to diffuse technological ideas . . .

The state could manipulate taxes, subsidies or markets in order to stimulate the development of private enterprise. It could, for example, protect favoured industries by customs duties, provide specific firms or industries with subsidies or monopolistic privileges, guarantee sales or the payment of interest on private investment in order to attract capital to particular ventures, or itself lend money on favourable conditions. Finally, although it rarely did so outside the field of railways, the state could directly assume the tasks of investment and enterprise.

Britain 1815—70

The main countries of Western Europe emerged from the Napoleonic Wars with a framework of socio-economic institutions which were far better suited to the needs of economic growth than those of the mid-eighteenth century [e.g. feudal practices and internal barriers to trade were removed] . . . Yet the removal of potential obstacles to industrialization was not, alone, sufficient to promote it — although it *was* sufficient to encourage the beginnings of the emergence of a newly important class of entrepreneurs in industry, finance and commerce. What actually stimulated industrial growth in Western Europe in the early nineteenth century was a combination of Britain's continuing example, economic pressure and national ambition.

For most of this period, the British economy, which had initiated the Industrial Revolution without the direct intervention of the state, prolonged and heightened its supremacy on the basis of market forces. Indeed, the main trend of British legislation after the Wars (which, if anything, increased the industrial gap between the British and Continental economies) was precisely in the direction of a continued dismantling of the structural, fiscal and economic barriers to the mobility of men and resources. Flexible use of land had, of course, already been achieved (it was confirmed by the General Enclosure Act of 1801 which aimed at a simplification of agricultural reorganization). And in the post-war years a formidable series of reforms took place. Tariffs were reduced from the 1820s and the campaign for free trade led to the repeal of the Corn Laws (1846) and later to the virtual abolition of significant duties on almost all imports. The Navigation Laws were liberalized in the 1820s and abolished within a generation. In the mid-1820s the remaining laws ostensibly regulating the manufacture and quality of various goods were repealed. A new Poor Law in 1834 was in part designed to 'free' labour from the enervating pull of local wage-subsidies and relief payments, by substituting the disincentive of harsh workhouse conditions. The capital market was made much more efficient by easier facilities for forming joint-stock companies, which culminated in limited liability legislation in 1856. And the confidence of British manufacturers was reflected not merely in the advent of free trade, but in the abolition of the Combination Acts (1824), which had hindered trade union development, in the further liberalization of trade union laws, and in the repeal of the legislation (which was in any case by then somewhat ineffective) forbidding the emigration of skilled artisans (1825) and the unlicensed export of machinery (1843). [. . .]

[As] far as the allocation and flow of productive resources were concerned, there was no doubt that Britain was closer to the ideal of liberal capitalism in 1851 than it had been in 1815 — and that the task of shaping the institutional prerequisites of the move had been willingly adopted by a state which proved admirably accommodating to new economic forces and social trends.

Sustained by an environment which was outstandingly favourable to their private enterprise, British businessmen forged ahead in the industrial race. In fact, it seems likely that growth rates, capital accumulation and accompanying social change were at their most rapid in the 1830s, 1840s and 1850s. Yet the dramatic qualities of Britain's industrialization were not — indeed, could not be — ignored on the Continent, while the new pressures of demand and supply (of men and capital and techniques as well as goods) which flowed from Britain's Industrial Revolution were also powerful stimulants of change. Emulation and competitive forces therefore served to diffuse industrialization in Western Europe in the first half of the nineteenth century. By the 1850s it had begun decisively to transform the economies of France, Belgium and parts of Holland, while its influence was already felt in various of the German states.

This transformation was based in large part on domestic resources and skills. And even when resources or skills were lacking, Continental entrepreneurs were active and ambitious enough to secure them from Britain. As a result, British capital, sometimes accompanied by entrepreneurs, flowed into Continental industries and, from the 1840s, railways. [. . .]

Germany

Yet the considerable potential of private enterprise and market forces on the Continent in the years after 1815 did not mean that the role of the state was as neutral as in Britain. [. . .] Writing in 1841, Friedrich List, the German political economist, argued that:

> At a time when technical and mechanical science exercise such immense influence on the methods of warfare, when all warlike operations depend so much on the condition of the national revenue, when successful defence greatly depends on the questions, whether the mass of the nation is rich or poor, intelligent or stupid, energetic or sunk in apathy; whether its sympathies are given exclusively to the fatherland or partly to foreign countries; whether it can muster many or but few defenders of the country — at such a time, more than ever before, must the value of manufactures be estimated from a political point of view.[2]

Industrialization thus became an adjunct of political policy. Second, there were still some areas even in North-Western Europe where institutional reform was needed [and in Germany] the basic political prerequisite of unified nationhood still had to be achieved. Underlying both these ambitions — for national power and for national coherence and independence — was a newly important force in European ideology: nationalism. The concept of the unity, character and uniqueness of individual nations had roots which went far back in European history. But with the opening of the post-Revolutionary age, with the sense of opportunity and threat derived from the twin forces of modernization and economic growth, the drive for national strength became a pervasive force in Continental Europe. To some, the idea of the nation was largely a metaphysical concept; but many also recognized its economic implications. As List argued:

> . . . between the individual and entire humanity . . . stands THE NATION, with its special language and literature, with its peculiar origin and history, with its special manners and customs, laws and institutions, with the claims of all these for existence, independence — reflection and continuance for the future . . . Meanwhile, however, an infinite difference exists in the condition and circumstances of the various nations . . . but in all of them . . . exists the impulse of self-preservation, the striving for improvement which is implanted by nature. It is the task of politics to civilise the barbarous nationalities . . . to secure to them existence and continuance. It is the task of national economy to accomplish *the economical development of the nation,* and to prepare it for admission into the universal society of the future.[3]

Consequently, while a desire to defend and extend the nation-state provided a reason for governments' concern with the Industrial Revolution, the relative backwardness of those seeking to imitate Britain, combined with the importance of achieving a fairly rapid growth rate, provided a strong incentive for its positive encouragement. Finally, and again in contrast to Britain, the early nineteenth-century governments of Continental Europe shared a tradition of direct participation in industrial and technological development. Their institutions and their official outlook both meant that it was logical for them to play an active role at a time of genuinely modern industrialization.

[In] the German states . . . the state itself invested money in industrial enterprises . . . In Prussia, the state ironworks and coal-mines in Silesia retained their importance [in the eighteenth century, absolutist states such as Prussia had directly promoted selected industries] . . . and new government funds were ploughed into transport . . . and manufacturing industry — including Prussia's first mill to weave worsted with power looms, in 1842. Yet even here there was a reaction: by the 1840s the use of official subsidies to industry was under attack as a threat to 'pure' private enterprise and as a losing proposition. By the mid-1850s the Overseas Trading Corporation (*Seehandlung*) which had handled most of these funds had disposed of the bulk of its investments. As far as direct investment in manufacturing industry was concerned, state action in the leading economies of Western Europe — France, the Low Countries, Prussia — was becoming less necessary, and therefore less desired by industrial entrepreneurs who were increasingly capable of raising needed capital privately.

There was, however, another type of state action which was eminently acceptable to private enterprise and which was of *increasing* relevance to the needs of industrializing societies. This was the pattern of aid to technical education and to the diffusion of technological and business ideas which had been established in the eighteenth century. The authorities in France and the German states, for example, sent officials to Britain and the United States to bring back technical information, and shaped their trading, taxation and patent policies to encourage and subsidize inventors, immigrant businessmen and imported machinery and ideas. [. . .]

This participation in the technological and educational externalities of manufacturing industries . . . suggests that the reluctance of the . . . Prussian government to invest money directly in manufacturing was a pragmatic rather than an ideological response to economic circumstances. And this is confirmed by the attitude of Continental governments towards the railway.

Railways

European governments had, of course, long been concerned with the social overhead capital embodied in national transport systems. Now, from the 1830s onwards, the relationship between the state and the creation of nineteenth-century railway networks provides a striking example of government 'intervention' in a capitalist system. In this respect it is significant that Britain — less overtly nationalistic, more explicitly individualist — was once again an exception. There, private market forces determined the shape and extent of the railway network and provided the necessary resources for its construction. But in Britain the railways *followed* the Industrial Revolution: they came to a powerful and wealthy society which did not need the help of the government to mobilize financial resources. On the Continent, by contrast, the timing of the technological 'availability' of the railway, and its potential importance for rapid economic growth, meant a new role for the state. Thus, on the one hand, it was clear that the pattern, as well as the extent and speed of construction, of railways systems would help determine the pattern and coherence of national development itself. Railways could unite a nation as could no other technological development, and their potential role in military hostilities was soon apparent. National consciousness and national strategy therefore combined to give the state a crucial basis for action — especially where large land masses emphasized the superiority of rail over water transport. On the other hand, the economic incentive to railway construction encountered financial difficulties precisely because of its timing: although they were potential stimulants of general economic growth, railways were themselves large and expensive investments, the return on which might take years to appear. Private costs were unprecedently high; private benefits conceivably remote, certainly risky. In these circumstances there was a straightforward economic motive for government participation to reduce private costs or guarantee private benefits. As a consequence of these twin incentives — the political-strategic and the economic — the state played an important part in the development of railways in the newly industrializing nations. [. . .]

[But in Germany] the early years of the railway were also years of political fragmentation. And the lack of national unity was reflected in the fact that the various states made no attempt to plan a national system when the first railways were constructed in the 1830s and 1840s. On the other hand, public and private needs were clearly recognized: by 1850 there were almost 6000 kilometres of line in the various German states (compared to only 3000 in France) . . . [However the] German railways were 'mixed' systems, with private and public companies running separate lines. In Prussia, there was, in fact, no state enterprise until the early 1840s, when the financial difficulties of the early lines led to government investment in, and guarantees to, private companies. The first Prussian state railway was initiated in 1847. Thenceforth the government rapidly extended its control over large parts of an expanding network. The drive for Prussian dominance in Germany, the military implications of German nationhood, and the concept of economic unification and growth all played a part. Altogether, by 1875 there were some 28,000 kilometres of railways in Germany (by now a federal entity); the federal states controlled almost half (12,000 kilometres), private owners about as much (12,600 kilometres), and the balance was privately owned but managed by the various federal railway administrations. [. . .]

The cost, external economies and strategic implications of railways gave them a special importance in nineteenth-century economic development, and readily explains the involvement of public authorities in their construction and management. Yet, distinctive as they were, they really only provide a particular example of a general situation: the state's necessary concern with nation-building and market unification. [. . .]

Market unification

In the case of Germany the basis of ultimate unification was laid (even before the individual states had begun to play a crucial role in the creation of their various railway networks) by the establishment of the *Zollverein*, or Customs Union (1834). Here, as in so much of subsequent German history, the lead was taken by Prussia — where the government had already unified and energized the domestic market in 1818 by abolishing a complex mixture of duties levied at provincial and town boundaries and replacing them with a single (albeit very low) tariff at the state frontier. In fact, the abolition of tariff barriers within Germany was widely acknowledged to be a prerequisite of extensive development — although interstate rivalries held up the attainment of this end for many years. Ultimately, after smaller customs unions had been founded, the *Zollverein* came into operation on 1 January, 1834, with its duties based upon the Prussian tariff and Prussia undertaking its negotiations with foreign countries. The free trade area created by these moves covered about four-fifths of Germany and contained about 33 million people. By facilitating interregional mobility, competition and specialization, and by strengthening Prussia's hand in international commercial negotiations, the *Zollverein* — a classic example of market creation by the state — greatly encouraged private industrialization.

In the long run the Prussian-dominated *Zollverein,* which grew in size as it was extended to more states, was a powerful agent of political as well as economic change: the unification of political institutions in Germany was based upon the unification of market institutions. [. . .]

The 1860s saw the birth of modern Germany under Prussian hegemony, and while France was being defeated by Prussia in the war of 1870–1, the German Empire was formally established in January 1871. The creation of the new state was underpinned by the forces of economic growth. Prussia, the most powerful of German states, naturally took the lead externally as well as internally; the economic prospects of unification anticipated the political reality; and the *Zollverein* and the railway — two structural prerequisites of the extension of the market — shaped the framework of the new state. Moreover, the ideology of nationalism took close account of its economic implications: not merely in envisaging that national power had to be based upon national wealth, but in asserting that economic achievement (e.g. tariff policy and industrial growth) could be both cause and effect of nationhood . . .

One should guard against an exaggeration of the role of the state in Germany's industrialization. Certainly, the actual processes and proximate causes of industrial growth were firmly embedded in market forces — not merely in the sense that (with the main exception of the railways) the principal units of production were privately managed and financed, but also in that some of the most important agents of change for the industrial sector — the joint-stock banks — were successful innovations of private enterprise to overcome the problems of capital mobilization. Nevertheless . . . the state institutions of Germany did exercise a considerable influence on the course of economic development. In terms of direct actions this was achieved through help to industry in its early stages, the sponsoring of technical education and information, and participation in the construction and, even more, the management of railways. Less directly, but in the last resort more significantly, the state was responsible for creating the very fabric of nationhood — a fabric within which market forces could be unleashed to produce industrialization. [. . .]

Laissez-faire and economic nationalism

By the 1850s and 1860s the twin forces of nationalism and industrialism had changed the political appearance and economic prospects of Europe. The Industrial Revolution, initiated in Britain with little direct help from the state, had spread almost everywhere as an idea, and in a few countries as a reality — but compared with Britain, it had done so with more, and sometimes far more, explicit encouragement from the state. To some extent collective action can be seen as the consequence of relative economic backwardness. Yet substantial direct government activity had taken place only in one area where capital and technological needs were considerable: the railways . . . It would, in fact, be wrong to contrast a *laissez-faire* Britain and other European countries committed on doctrinaire grounds to the use of state resources for growth purposes. First, because the extent of government intervention can be best explained, not in terms of basic [doctrines] of political economy, but as the outcome of economic needs and national ambitions. Second, because what might be called 'negative intervention' — the use of the state to make *institutional* adjustments designed to encourage market activity — was a common feature of British and Continental economic history. We have already seen that in the early nineteenth century, successive British governments, without abandoning their theoretical commitments to *laissez-faire*, greatly improved the framework and liberalized the pattern of commercial policy within which goods, capital, enterprise and labour could flow freely. And it is a strong feature of Continental economic development in the middle years, and particularly the third quarter, of the nineteenth century that they exemplified a comparable liberalization of trading relationships and of the legal institutions of a nascent industrial capitalism. [. . .]

Economic liberalism was [however] only a brief episode in the history of industrial capitalism. In the last quarter of the nineteenth century the tide turned in the leading industrial economies. Thenceforth a larger and much more 'positive' economic and social role was found for the state. To differing degrees in such countries as Germany, Britain, France and Belgium, economic nationalism took a far more restrictive turn as tariff barriers were raised and the intensified rivalry of the international economy led to the nationalistic control of markets and the extension of exclusive empires. Meanwhile, the state moved to tackle the economic and social problems of growth, to salvage railways systems, to bolster weak sections of the economy, and to ameliorate the increasingly apparent social tensions and problems of urban and industrial maturity, which demanded more welfare legislation and social reform. Obviously, all these developments — and notably the rise of protection and the increasing knowledge of the structural imperfections of liberal capitalism — greatly extended the scope of the state's economic role, as governments wrestled with the problem of instability, poverty and urbanism. *Laissez-faire*, which in any case only ever existed in a very specific form, was dead; killed not by the prerequisites but by the consequences of industrialization.

Notes

1. However, the state played a crucial, albeit *indirect*, role in creating and defending the British Empire and making Britain by the 1760s the centre of the world's biggest free trade area, developments critical to her pioneer role in the Industrial Revolution (Supple, pp. 315—16).
2. List, Friedrich (1904 edn) *The National System of Political Economy*, pp. 168—9.
3. *Ibid*, pp. 141—2.

2.4

States and Nationalism: The Nation in European History

EDWARD CARR

The modern history of international relations [up to 1945] divides into three partly overlapping periods, marked by widely differing views of the nation as a political entity. The first was terminated by the French Revolution and the Napoleonic wars, having the Congress of Vienna as its tailpiece and swan song; the second was essentially the product of the French Revolution and, though its foundations were heavily undermined from 1870 onwards, it lasted on till the catastrophe of 1914, with the Versailles settlement as its belated epilogue; the third period, whose main features first began to take shape after 1870, reached its culmination between 1914 and 1939. [. . .]

The first period

The first period begins with the gradual dissolution of the medieval unity of empire and church and the establishment of the national state and the national church. In the new national unit it was normally the secular arm which . . . emerged predominant; but there was nothing anomalous in a bishop or prince of the church exercising territorial sovereignty. *The essential characteristic of the period was the identification of the nation with the person of the sovereign* [Eds' emphasis]. Luther regarded the bishops and princes as constituting the German nation. Louis XIV thought that

Source: From 'The climax of nationalism' in E. H. Carr, *Nationalism and After* (1945) London, Macmillan, (reprinted 1968) pp. 1—34. Footnotes have been excluded and sub-headings added.

the French nation 'resided wholly in the person of the King'. [. . .]
In much of Eastern Europe the restriction of the nation to the
upper classes still held good in the nineteenth century. It was said
of a Croat landowner of the nineteenth century that he would
'sooner have regarded his horse than his peasant as a member of
the Croat nation' . . . In the middle of the nineteenth century, and
even later, the distance which separated the Polish gentry from the
Polish-speaking peasantry was still so great that the latter did not
as a rule look on themselves as part of the Polish nation. [. . .]

International relations were relations between kings and princes;
and matrimonial alliances were a regular instrument of diplomacy.
The behaviour of the seventeenth- and eighteenth-century
sovereigns conformed perfectly to this prescription. The absolute
power of the monarch at home might be contested. Even Frederick
the Great described himself as the 'first servant' of his state. But
nobody questioned that in international relations with other
monarchs he spoke as one having authority over his 'subjects' and
'possessions'; and these could be freely disposed of for personal or
dynastic reasons. The doctrine of sovereignty made sense so long
as this authority remained real and 'our sovereign lord the king'
had not yet become a ceremonial phrase. These were the auspices
under which international law was born. It was primarily a set of
rules governing the mutual relations of individuals in their capacity
as rulers. [. . .]

The 'international of monarchs', all speaking a common
language, owning a common tradition, and conscious of a common
interest in maintaining the submissiveness of their subjects, was
not wholly a fiction, and secured at any rate formal recognition of
a common standard of values . . . Claiming the sanctity of law as
the basis of their own authority, they could not afford openly and
flagrantly to flout it in their relations with one another. It was not a
seventeenth- or eighteenth-century autocrat, but a nineteenth-
century American democrat, who coined the slogan 'My country,
right or wrong'. [. . .]

A sovereign waging war no more desired to inflict injury or loss
on the subjects of his enemy than a citizen going to law desires to
inflict them on the servants of his adversary. They might indeed,
and commonly did, suffer from the rapacity and savagery of his
pressed or hired soldiers; but his own subjects were also not
immune from these hazards. A large part of the early history of
international law consists of the building up of rules to protect the
property and commerce of non-combatants. Civilians were in
effect not parties to the quarrel. The eighteenth century witnessed
many wars; but in respect of the freedom and friendliness of

intercourse between the educated classes in the principal European countries, with French as a recognized common language, it was the most 'international' period of modern history, and civilians could pass to and fro and transact their business freely with one another while their respective sovereigns were at war. [. . .]

Mercantilism

Equally characteristic were the national economic policies of the period, to which the name 'mercantilism' was afterwards given. The aim of mercantilism, both in its domestic and in its external policies, was not to promote the welfare of the community and its members, but to augment the power of the state, of which the sovereign was the embodiment. Trade was stimulated because it brought wealth to the coffers of the state; and wealth was the source of power, or more specifically of fitness for war. As Colbert, the most famous and consistent exponent of the system, put it, 'trade is the source of finance, and finance is the vital nerve of war'. *Internally, mercantilism sought to break down the economic particularism, the local markets and restrictive regulations, which underlay the uniformity of the medieval order, to make the state the economic unit and to assert its undivided authority in matters of trade and manufacture throughout its territory* [Eds' emphasis]. Externally, it sought to promote the wealth and therefore the power of the state in relation to other states. Wealth, conceived in its simplest form as bullion, was brought in by exports; and since, in the static conception of society prevailing in this period, export markets were a fixed quantity not susceptible of increase as a whole, the only way for a nation to expand its markets and therefore its wealth was to capture them from some other nation, if necessary by waging a 'trade war'. War thus became an instrument of mercantilist policy as well as its ultimate end. It is a mistake to contrast mercantilism with *laissez-faire* as if the one were directed to national, the other to individual, ends. Both were directed to national ends; the difference between them related to a difference in the conception of the nation. Mercantilism was the economic policy of a period which identified the interest of the nation with the interest of its rulers. Its aim . . . was 'wealth for the nation, but wealth from which the majority of the people must be excluded'.

The second period

The second period, which issued from the turmoil of the

Napoleonic Wars and ended in 1914, is generally accounted the most orderly and enviable of modern international relations. [...]

Looked at in one way, it succeeded in delicately balancing the forces of 'nationalism' and 'internationalism'; for it established an international order or framework strong enough to permit of a striking extension and intensification of national feeling without disruption on any wide scale of regular and peaceful international relations. Put in another way, it might be said that, while in the previous period political and economic power had marched hand in hand to build up the national political unit and to substitute a single national economy for a conglomeration of local economies, in the nineteenth century a compromise was struck between political and economic power so that each could develop on its own lines. Politically, therefore, national forces were more and more successful throughout the nineteenth century in asserting the claim of the nation to statehood, whether through a coalescence or through a break-up of existing units. Economically, on the other hand, international forces carried a stage further the process inaugurated in the previous period by transforming a multiplicity of national economies into a single world economy. From yet a third angle the system might be seen as a compromise between the popular and democratic appeal of political nationalism and the esoteric and autocratic management of the international economic mechanism. The collapse of these compromises, and the revelation of the weaknesses and unrealities that lay behind them, marked the concluding stages of the second period. The failure since 1914 to establish any new compromise capable of reconciling the forces of nationalism and internationalism is the essence of [the crisis that has culminated in world war].

The 'democratization' of nationalism

The founder of modern nationalism as it began to take shape in the nineteenth century was Rousseau, who, *rejecting the embodiment of the nation in the personal sovereign or the ruling class, boldly identified 'nation' and 'people'* [Eds' emphasis]; and this identification became a fundamental principle both of the French and of the American revolutions. It is true that the 'people' in this terminology did not mean those who came to be known to a later epoch as the 'workers' or the 'common people'. The Jacobin constitution, which would have substituted manhood suffrage for the substantial property qualification of the National Convention, was never operative. [French political writers of the eighteenth century, including Rousseau, had been opposed to a democracy of *universal* suffrage; and the North American Revolution had established only a property-owners' suffrage. In France] the solid and respectable middle class, which made up the 'Third Estate', retained through a large part of the nineteenth century a rooted fear and mistrust of the masses.

Nevertheless this middle-class nationalism had in it from the first a democratic and potentially popular flavour which was wholly foreign to the eighteenth century. The distance in this respect between Frederick the Great and Napoleon, two ambitious and unscrupulous military conquerors separated in time by less than half a century, is enormous. Frederick the Great still belonged to the age of legitimate monarchy, treated his subjects as instruments of his ambition, despised his native language and culture and regarded Prussia not as a national entity but as his family domain. Napoleon, by posing as the champion and mandatory of the emancipated French nation, made himself the chief missionary of modern nationalism. He was in many senses the first 'popular' dictator. Intellectually the transition from Frederick to Napoleon was paralleled by the transition from Gibbon to Burke, or from Goethe and Lessing to Herder and Schiller; the cosmopolitanism of the Enlightenment was replaced by the nationalism of the Romantic movement. The implications of the change were far-reaching. The nation in its new and popular connotation had come to stay. International relations were henceforth to be governed not by the personal interests, ambitions and emotions of the monarch, but by the collective interests, ambitions and emotions of the nation.

The 'democratization' of nationalism imparted to it a new and disturbing emotional fervour. With the disappearance of the absolute monarch, the personification of the nation became a necessary convenience in international relations and international law. But it was far more than a convenient abstraction. The idea of the personality and character of the nation acquired a profound psychological significance. Writers like Mazzini thought and argued about nations exactly as if they were sublimated individuals. [. . .]

Nationalism contained

[Yet] the dynamite of nationalism did not produce its catastrophic explosion for a full century after the downfall of Napoleon, so that this second period of modern international relations looks today like an idyllic interlude between the turbulent first period of warring monarchies and the [third], and apparently still more turbulent, period of warring nations . . . [How is this relative tranquility to be explained?]

The ruling middle classes who were the bearers of the nineteenth-century nationalism entertained almost everywhere throughout the middle years of the century a lively fear of revolution from below. The rights of property were scarcely less sacrosanct than the rights of man and the functions of the bourgeois democratic state — the 'night-watchman state' in Lassalle's sarcastic phrase — were largely concerned with its protection. Property, sometimes described as 'a stake in the country', was a condition of political rights and — it might be said without much exaggeration — of full membership of the nation: the worker had, in this sense, no fatherland. When Marx appealed to the workers of the world to unite, he was fully conscious of the strength which unity gave to his adversaries. The nineteenth-century bourgeoisie of the propertied classes in Western Europe formed a coherent entity, trained to the management both of public and of business affairs (the modern English public school, like the French *lycée*, dates from this period), and united by ties of common ideals and common interests. In their competent hands the democratized nation was still proof for many years to come against the disruptive turbulence of popular nationalism.

The second explanation of the pacific character of nineteenth-century nationalism goes deeper and is fundamental to the whole nineteenth century. What happened after 1815, though through no particular merit of the peace-makers of Vienna, was nothing less than the gradual development of a new kind of economic order which, by making possible a phenomenal increase of production and population, offered to the newly enfranchised nations of Europe the opportunity to expand and spread their material civilization all over the world, and, by concentrating the direction of this world economic order in one great capital city, created an international — or, more accurately, supra-national — framework strong enough to contain with safety and without serious embarrassment the heady wine of the new nationalism . . . Not only were the middle-class governments of the Western nations united by a common respect for the rights of property and for the principle of non-interference in the management of a world economy which was so triumphantly advancing the wealth and authority of the middle classes, but even Habsburg and Romanov relicts of eighteenth-century autocracy did not disdain the financial crumbs that fell from prosperous bourgeois tables and became humble hangers-on of the bourgeois economic order.

This new international economic society was built on the fact of progressive expansion and on the theory of *laissez-faire*. The expansion of Europe, consisting both in a startling increase in the population and production of Europe itself and in an unprecedentedly rapid dissemination of the population, products and material civilization of Europe throughout other continents, created the fundamental change from the static order and outlook of the eighteenth century to the dynamic order and outlook of the nineteenth. The initial divergence which explains the whole opposition of principle between mercantilism and *laissez-faire* is that, while the mercantilists believed that the size of the cake was fixed, the philosophers of *laissez-faire* believed in a cake whose size could and should be indefinitely extended through the enterprise and inventiveness of individual effort. Restriction and discrimination are the natural reaction of producers to a limitation of demand. In the nineteenth century most people were convinced, on the plausible evidence around them, that a continuously increasing production would be absorbed by a progressively and infinitely expanding demand.

In a world of this kind, goods could pass freely from place to place — and not only goods, but men. Freedom of migration was an even more vital factor in the nineteenth-century economic and political system, and more necessary to its survival, than freedom of trade. Newcomers were made welcome by their prospect of their contribution to an expanding production; unlimited opportunity for all who were willing to work was an accepted item in the nineteenth-century creed. The same kind of welcome awaited new nations, whether formed, as in Germany, by a belated application of the mercantilist policy of breaking down internal barriers to unity, or, as in Eastern Europe, by splitting off from former multinational units. [. . .]

The success of this nineteenth-century compromise between a closely-knit world economic system and unqualified recognition of the political diversity and independence of nations was rendered possible by two subtle and valuable pieces of make-believe which were largely unconscious and contained sufficient elements of reality to make them plausible. These two salutary illusions were, first, that the world economic system was truly international, and second, that the economic and political systems were entirely separate and operated independently of each other.

'Pax Britannica'

The international system, simple in its conception but infinitely complex in its technique, called into being a delicate and powerful financial machine whose seat was in the City of London. [. . .] All gold-standard countries had to keep pace with one another in expanding and contracting the flow of money and trade; and it was the London market which inevitably set the pace. Just as mercantilism in the seventeenth and eighteenth centuries had transformed local economies into a single national economy, so in the nineteenth century the merchants, brokers and bankers of London, acting under the sovereign responsibility of the 'old lady of Threadneedle Street', transformed the national economies into a single world economy . . . Here was the seat of government of the world economy of the so-called age of *laissez-faire* . . . And because it was not consciously directed to anything but the day-to-day task of ensuring the maintenance of sound currency and balanced exchanges — the control which made the whole system work — it was autocratic, without appeal and completely effective. Nor was it, properly speaking, international, much less representative. It was at once supra-national and British.

The second illusion which secured acceptance of the nineteenth-century world order sprang from the formal divorce between political and economic power . . . Yet it was precisely because economic authority was silently wielded by a single highly centralized autocracy that political authority could safely be parcelled out in national units, large and small, increasingly subject to democratic control. This economic authority was a political fact of the first importance; and the British economic power of which it was a function was inseparably bound up with the political power conferred by the uncontested supremacy of the British Navy. But these interconnexions of political and economic power were overlooked [. . . and on the] supposed separation of political and economic power, and this real blend of freedom and authority, the nineteenth-century order rested.

In the 1870s the first subterranean rumblings began to shake this splendid edifice. Germany emerged beyond challenge as the leading Continental power; and it was in Germany that Friedrich List had sown many years before the first seeds of rebellion against Britain's world economic system. The last imperfect triumphs of free trade were left behind in the 1860s. The German tariff of 1879 was long remembered as the first modern 'scientific' tariff — a piece of economic manipulation in the interests of national policy. After 1870 the constructive work of nationbuilding seemed complete. Nationalism came to be associated with 'the Balkans' and with all that that ominous term implied. When the British commercial and British naval supremacy were first seriously challenged in the 1890s, ominous cracks soon began to appear in the structure. When this supremacy in both its forms was broken by the First World War, the nineteenth-century economic system collapsed in utter and irretrievable ruin . . .

The third period

The third period brings yet another change in the character of the nation. The catastrophic growth of nationalism and bankruptcy of internationalism which were the symptoms of the period can be traced back to their origins in the years after 1870, but reach their full overt development only after 1914. This does not mean that individuals became in this period more outrageously nationalist in sentiment or more unwilling to cooperate with their fellow-men of other nations. *It means that nationalism began to operate in a new political and economic environment. The phenomenon cannot be understood without examination of the three main underlying causes which provoked it: the bringing of new social strata within the effective membership of the nation; the visible reunion of economic with political power; and the increase in the number of nations* [Eds' emphasis].

The 'socialization' of nationalism

The rise of new social strata to full membership of the nation marked the last three decades of the nineteenth century throughout Western and Central Europe. Its landmarks were the development of industry and industrial skills; the rapid expansion in numbers and importance of urban populations; the growth of workers' organizations and of the political consciousness of the workers; the introduction of universal compulsory education; and the extension of the franchise. These changes, while they seemed logical steps in a process inaugurated long before, quickly began to affect the content of national policy in a revolutionary way. [. . .]

Henceforth the political power of the masses was directed to improving their own social and economic lot. The primary aim of national policy was no longer merely to maintain order and conduct what was narrowly defined as public business, but to minister to the welfare of members of the nation and to enable them to earn their living. The democratization of the nation in the second period had meant the assertion of the political claims of the dominant middle class. The socialization of the nation for the first time brings the economic claims of the masses into the forefront of the picture. The defence of wages and employment becomes a concern of national policy and must be asserted, if necessary, against the national policies of other countries; and this in turn gives the worker an intimate practical interest in the policy and power of his nation . . .

The twentieth-century alliance between nationalism and socialism may be traced back to its first seed in the revolutionary nationalism of the Jacobins; and in France, where the Jacobin tradition remained potent, the Left has asserted itself in successive national crises — in 1871, in 1917 and again in 1940 — as the custodian of the national interest against the compromisers and defeatists of the Right. In its modern form, however, the alliance dates from Bismarck, who, schooled by Lassalle, showed the German workers how much they had to gain from a vigorous and ruthless nationalism . . . In the same period the word 'jingoism' was coined in Great Britain to describe something that had not hitherto existed — the nationalism of the masses . . . The successes of Tory democracy, the career of Joseph Chamberlain and the adoption by the Liberal Party after 1906 of far-reaching measures of social reform were all straws in the wind. National policy was henceforth founded on the support of the masses; and the counterpart was the loyalty of the masses to a nation which had become the instrument of their collective interests and ambitions. [. . .]

In the nineteenth century, when the nation belonged to the middle class and the worker had no fatherland, socialism had been international. The crisis of 1914 showed in a flash that, except in backward Russia, this attitude was everywhere obsolete. The mass of workers knew instinctively on which side their bread was buttered; and Lenin was [one of the few socialists] proclaiming the defeat of his own country as a socialist aim and crying treason against the 'social-chauvinists'. International socialism ignominiously collapsed. Lenin's desperate rearguard action to revive it made sense only in Russia, and there only so long as revolutionary conditions persisted. Once the 'workers' state' was effectively established, 'socialism in one country' was the logical corollary. The subsequent history of Russia and the tragi-comedy of the Communist International are an eloquent tribute to the solidarity of the alliance between nationalism and socialism. [. . .]

The link between 'economic nationalism' and the socialization of the nation emerged clearly in the decisive and fateful step taken by all the great industrial countries after 1919 — the closing of national frontiers to large-scale immigration. The middle-class governments of the nineteenth century, concerned with the importance of cheap and abundant labour to swell the tide of production and profits, had been under no political compulsion to give prior consideration to the wage-levels and standards of living of their own workers . . . Now the prohibition was imposed, contrary to the patent interests of employer and capitalist, almost without opposition; and one of the most effective and necessary safety-valves of the nineteenth-century international order, the avenue of escape opened to the enterprising and the discontented, was closed with a snap. No single measure did more to render a renewal of the clash between nations inevitable. No single measure more clearly exhibited the inherent drive of the new and powerful labour interests towards policies of exclusive nationalism. When in the 1930s humanitarian pressure demanded the admission of alien refugees to Great Britain, consent was given on the condition that they did not 'seek employment'. [. . .] The attitude of the workers was precisely imitated by the professional middle class in similar conditions. Medical opposition in Great Britain to the immigration of refugee doctors in the 1930s was a conspicuous and not particularly creditable example. [. . .]

Workers became interested equally with employers in measures of protection and subsidies for industry. Advocacy of such measures proved a fruitful meeting-ground for the hitherto conflicting forces of capital and labour; and national and social policies were welded more firmly than ever together . . . 'Planned economy' is a Janus with a nationalist as well as a socialist face; if its doctrine seems socialist, its pedigree is unimpeachably nationalist. [. . .]

Nations multiply

The third cause of the inflation of nationalism — the startling increase in the number of nations during our third period — is one of which sufficient account is rarely taken. Here too the year 1870 marks a significant turning-point. Down to that time the influence of nationalism had been to diminish the number of sovereign and independent political units in Europe. In 1871 after the unification of Germany and Italy had been completed there were 14; in 1914 there were 20; in 1924 the number had risen to 26. It would be an understatement to say that the virtual doubling in 50 years of the number of independent European states aggravated in degree the problem of European order. It altered that problem in kind — the more so since the convention ruling in 1871 that only five or at most six Great Powers were concerned in major European issues no longer commanded general acceptance. Nor could the settlement after the First World War be regarded as in any way final or conclusive. National self-determination became a standing invitation to secession. The movement which dismembered Austria-Hungary and created Yugoslavia and Czechoslovakia was bound to be succeeded by movements for the dismemberment of Yugoslavia and Czechoslovakia. Given the premises of nationalism the process was natural and legitimate, and no end could be set to it. After 1914 it spread rapidly to the Arab world, to India, to the Far East; though elsewhere the British Dominions offered the more impressive spectacle of separate nations growing to maturity within the unsevered bonds of the Commonwealth. Moreover, this dispersal of authority occurred at a time when both military and economic developments were forcing on the world a rapid concentration of power: it not only ignored, but defied, a trend deeply rooted in the industrial conditions of the period. The bare fact that there are in Europe [in 1945] more than 20, and in the world more than 60, political units claiming the status of independent sovereign states, goes far by itself to explain the aggravation of the evils of nationalism in our third period.

Although, however, this multiplication of national frontiers in Europe and the extension throughout the world of a conception hitherto limited to Western Europe and its direct dependencies have given an immense impetus to 'economic nationalism', it may well seem unfair to apply this term in an invidious sense to the natural and legitimate determination of 'backward' nations to share in advantages hitherto monopolized by those who had had so long a start in industrial development. The nineteenth-century concentration of industry in a few great countries in Western Europe, which furnished their industrial products to the rest of the world and consumed in return its food and raw materials, may have been a highly practical example of the division of labour. But this privileged status of the industrial nations was self-destructive in so far as it was bound sooner or later to create a desire and capacity for industrial production and a development of national consciousness in the less privileged countries. List had argued as long ago as 1840 that, while free trade might be the interest of industrially mature nations, protective tariffs were a necessary and legitimate instrument for developing backward industries and countries to a state of maturity. In the nineteenth century, Germany and the United States had both learned and profited by this lesson. It was now taken up by new and smaller nations all over the world, and the whole machinery of economic nationalism was set in motion to develop their industries and bring them some fraction of the power and prestige which went with industrial development. Such procedures inevitably curtailed international trade and multiplied competition for narrowing markets. [...]

These three factors — the socialization of the nation, the nationalization of economic policy and the geographical extension of nationalism — have combined to produce the characteristic totalitarian symptoms of our third period. The combination of these factors has found expression in two world wars, or two instalments of the same world war, in a single generation ...

'Total war'

The World War of 1914 was the first war between socialized nations and took on for the first time the character of what has since been called 'total war'. The view of war as the exclusive affair of governments and armies was tacitly abandoned. Before hostilities ended, the obliteration of the traditional line between soldier and civilian had gone very far; attack on civilian morale by propaganda, by mass terrorism, by blockade and by bombing from the air had become a recognized technique of war. Popular national hatreds were for the first time deliberately inflamed as an instrument of policy, and it came to be regarded in many quarters as a legitimate war aim, not merely to defeat the enemy armed forces, but to inflict punishment on members of the enemy nation. In the Second World War any valid or useful distinction between armed forces and civilian populations disappeared almost from the outset; both were merely different forms of man-power and woman-power mobilized for different tasks and on different 'fronts' in the same struggle. [...]

The re-establishment of national political authority over the economic system, which was a necessary corollary of the socialization of the nation, was no doubt one of the factors contributing to the situation which produced the two world wars. But it received from them so powerful an impetus that its relation to them is as much one of effect as of cause. The immediate and revolutionary consequence of the outbreak of war in 1914 was the assumption by every belligerent government of the right to create and control its own national money and the deposition of sterling from its role as the universal currency ... After 1914 both personal relations and commercial transactions, direct or indirect, with enemy citizens became a criminal offence; and for the first time in the history of modern war enemy private property was confiscated — a devastating blow at the foundations of *laissez-faire* society and bourgeois civilization. [...]

As custodians of the living standards, employment and amenities of their whole populations, modern nations are, in virtue of their nature and function, probably less capable than any other groups in modern times of reaching agreement with one another. [. . .] In peace, as in war, the international law of the age of sovereigns is incompatible with the socialized nation. The failure to create an international community of nations on the basis of international treaties and international law marks the final bankruptcy of nationalism in the West.

2.5

Nationalism and the Uneven Geography of Development

TOM NAIRN

Nationalism is *as a whole* quite incomprehensible outside the context of that process's *uneven* development . . . it is mobilization *against* the unpalatable, humanly unacceptable truth of grossly uneven development. [. . .]

Nationalism in general is 'a phenomenon connected not so much with industrialization or modernization as such, but with its uneven diffusion' (Gellner, 1964, p. 166). It first arose as a *general* fact (a determining general condition of the European body politic) after this 'uneven diffusion' had made its first huge and irreversible impact upon the historical process, that is, after the combined shocks engendered by the French Revolution, the Napoleonic conquests, the English Industrial Revolution, and the war between the two super-states of the day, England and France. This English— French 'dual revolution' impinged upon the rest of Europe like a tidal wave. What Gellner calls the 'tidal wave of modernization'. Through it the advancing capitalism of the more bourgeois societies bore down upon the societies surrounding them — societies which predominantly appear until the 1790s as buried in feudal and absolutist slumber.

Nationalism was one result of this rude awakening. For what did these societies — which now discovered themselves to be in-tolerably 'backward' — awaken into? A situation where polite universalist visions of progress had turned into means of domination . . . The spread of free commerce from which so much had been hoped was turning (as Friedrich List pointed out) into the

Source: From *The Break-Up of Britain: Crisis and Neo-Nationalism* (1977) New Left Books; pp. 96—105, 'Scotland and Europe' (written in 1974); pp. 184—92 and pp. 176—9 (in that order), 'Old and new Scottish nationalism' (written in 1975). Some of the sub-headings have been added.

195

domination of English manufactures — the tyranny of the English 'City' over the European 'Country'. In short, there was a sort of imperialism built into 'development'. And it had become a prime necessity to resist *this* aspect of development.

Enlightenment thinkers had mostly failed to foresee this fatal antagonism . . . They imagined continuous diffusion from centre to periphery . . . The metropolis would gradually elevate the rustic hinterland up to its level, as it were . . .

In fact, progress invariably puts powerful, even deadly weapons in the hands of this or that particular 'advanced' area. Since this is a particular place and people, not a disinterested centre of pure and numinous culture, the result is a gulf (far larger than hitherto, and likely to increase) between the leaders and the hinterland. In the latter, progress comes to seem a hammer-blow as well as (sometimes instead of) a prospectus for general uplift and improvement. It appears as double-edged, at least. So areas of the hinterland, even in order to 'catch up' (to advance from 'barbarism' to the condition of 'civil society', as the Enlightenment put it), are *also* compelled to mobilize against progress. That is, they have to demand progress not as it is thrust upon them initially by the metropolitan centre, but 'on their own terms'. These 'terms' are, of course, ones which reject the imperialist trappings: exploitation or control from abroad, discrimination, military or political domination, and so on.

'Nationalism' is in one sense only the label for the general unfolding of this vast struggle, since the end of the eighteenth century. Obviously no one would deny that nationalities, ethnic disputes and hatreds, or some nation-states, existed long before this. But this is not the point. The point is how such relatively timeless features of the human scene were transformed into the general condition of national*ism* after the bourgeois revolutions exploded fully into the world. Naturally, the new state of affairs made use of the 'raw materials' provided by Europe's particularly rich variety of ethnic, cultural and linguistic contrasts. But — precisely — it also altered their meaning, and gave them a qualitatively distinct function, an altogether new dynamism for both good and evil.

In terms of broad political geography, the contours of the process are familiar. The 'tidal wave' invaded one zone after another, in concentric circles. First Germany and Italy, the areas of relatively advanced and unified culture adjacent to the Anglo-French centre; it was in them that the main body of typically nationalist politics and culture was formulated. Almost at the same time, or shortly after, Central and Eastern Europe, and the more peripheral regions of Iberia, Ireland, and Scandinavia. Then Japan and, with the full development of imperialism, much of the rest of the globe. [. . .] [Some of the reactions] may, or may not, have involved socialist revolutions and projected a non-national and Marxist image; there is no doubt that every one of them involved a *national* revolution quite comprehensible in the general historical terms of national*ism* (even without reference to other factors).

Europe's bourgeoisies

We have glanced at the political geography of uneven development. What about its class basis and social content? Sociologically, the basis of the vital change we are concerned with obviously lay in the ascendancy of the bourgeoisie in both England and France: more exactly, in their joint rise and their fratricidal conflicts up to 1815. Their Janus-headed 'modernity' was that of bourgeois society, and an emergent industrial capitalism.

And it was upon the same class that this advancing 'civil society' everywhere had the principal impact. In the hinterland too there were 'rising middle classes' impatient with absolutism and the motley assortment of *anciens régimes* which reigned over most of Europe. Naturally, these were far weaker and poorer than the world-bourgeoisies of the West. The gross advantages of the latter had been denied them by history's unequal development. Now they found themselves in a new dilemma. Previously they had hoped that the spread of civilized progress would get rid of feudalism and raise them to the grace of liberal, constitutional society. Now (e.g.) the German and Italian middle classes realized that only a determined effort of their own would prevent utopia from being marred by *Manchestertum* and French bayonets. Beyond them, in the still larger Europe east of Bohemia and Slovenia, the even weaker Slav middle classes realized that 'progress' would in itself only fasten German and Italian fetters upon their land and people more firmly. And so on.

This 'dilemma' is indeed the characteristic product of capitalism's uneven development. One might call it the 'nationalism-producing' dilemma. Given the premise of uneven growth, and the resultant impact of the more upon the less advanced, the dilemma is automatically transmitted outwards and onwards in this way. The result, nationalism, is basically no less necessary. [. . .]

The role of intellectuals

Equally naturally, nationalism was from the outset a 'bourgeois' phenomenon in the sense indicated. But two further qualifications are needed here, to understand the mechanism at work. The first concerns the intelligentsia, and the second concerns the masses whose emergence into history was — behind and beneath the more visible 'rise of the bourgeoisie' — the truly decisive factor in the transformation we are dealing with . . . [As Hobsbawm points out (1962, pp. 133—5)] the motor role is provided by 'the lesser landowners or gentry and the emergence of a national middle and even lower-middle class in numerous countries, the spokesmen for both being largely professional intellectuals . . . (above all) . . . the *educated* classes . . . the educational progress of large numbers of "new men" into areas hitherto occupied by a small élite. The progress of schools and universities measures that of nationalism, just as schools and especially universities become its most conspicuous champions.'

Nationalism and the masses

But if the intellectuals are all-important in one sense (spreading nationalism from the top downwards as it were), it is the masses — the ultimate recipients of the new message — that are all-important in another. As a matter of fact, they determine a lot of what the 'message' is. [. . .] [The intellectuals have to mobilize the masses.[People is all they have got: this is the essence of the under-development dilemma itself.

Consequently, the national or would-be national middle class is always compelled to 'turn to the people'. It is this compulsion that really determines the new political complex ('nationalism') which comes forth. For what are the implications of turning to the people, in this sense? First of all, speaking their language (or, over most of Europe, what had hitherto been viewed as their 'brutish dialects'). Secondly, taking a kindlier view of their general 'culture', that *ensemble* of customs and notions, pagan and religious, which the Enlightenment had relegated to the museum (if not to the dustbin). Thirdly — and most decisively, when one looks at the process generally — coming to terms with the enormous and still irreconcilable *diversity* of popular and peasant life.

It is, of course, this primordial political compulsion which points the way to an understanding of the dominant contradiction of the era. Why did the spread of capitalism, as a rational and universal ordering of society, lead so remorselessly to extreme fragmentation, to the exaggeration of ethnic-cultural differences, and so to the *dementia* of 'chauvinism' and war? Because that diffusion contained within itself (as it still does) the hopeless antagonism of its own unevenness, and a consequent imperialism; the latter forces mobilization against it, even on the part of those most anxious to catch up and imitate; such mobilization can only proceed, in practice, via a popular mass still located culturally upon a far anterior level of development, upon the level of feudal or pre-feudal peasant or 'folk' life — that is, upon a level of (almost literally) 'pre-historic' diversity in language, ethnic characteristics, social habits, and so on. [. . .] Political nationalism of the classic sort was not necessarily democratic by nature, or revolutionary in a social sense (notoriously it could be inspired by fear of Jacobinism, as well as by Jacobinism). But it *was* necessarily 'populist' by nature.

Thus, we can add to the 'external' (or geo-political) co-ordinates of nationalism mentioned above, a set of 'internal' or social-class co-ordinates. The former showed us the 'tidal wave' of modernization (or bourgeois society) transforming one area after another, and soliciting the rise of nationalist awareness and movements. The latter shows us something of the mechanism behind the 'rise': the bourgeois and intellectual populism which, in existing conditions of backwardness where the masses are beginning to enter history and political existence for the first time, is ineluctably driven towards ethnic particularism. Nationalism's forced 'mobilization' is fundamentally conditioned, at least in the first instance, by its own mass basis. [. . .]

Let me now point out some important implications of this model of nationalism . . . Its main virtue is a simple one. It enables us to decide upon a materialist, rather than an 'idealist' explanation of the phenomenon. In the question of nationalism, this philosophical point is critical. This is so, because of the very character of the phenomenon. Quite obviously, nationalism is invariably characterized by a high degree of political and ideological voluntarism. Simply because it *is* forced mass-mobilization in a position of relative helplessness (or 'under-development'), certain subjective factors play a prominent part in it. It is, in its immediate nature, idealistic. It always imagines an ideal 'people' (propped up by folklore studies, antiquarianism, or some surrogate for these) and it always searches urgently for vital inner, untapped springs of energy both in the individual and the mass. Such idealism is inseparable both from its creative historical function and its typical delusions. Consequently a generally idealist mode of explanation has always been tempting for it. It lends itself rather to a Hegelian and romantic style of theorizing, than to a rationalist or Marxist one. This is one reason why Marxism has so often made heavy weather of it in the past. [. . .]

The nation and romanticism

[Nevertheless it] is a fact that, while idealist explanations of the phenomenon in terms of consciousness or *Zeitgeist* (however acute their observation may be, notably in German writers like Meinecke) never account for the material dynamic incorporated in the situation, a materialist explanation can perfectly well account for all the most 'ideal' and cultural or ideological symptoms of nationalism (even at their most berserk). Start from the premise of capitalism's uneven development and its real class articulation, and one can come to grasp the point even of chauvinist lunacy, the 'irrational' elements which have played a significant role in nationalism's unfolding from the outset to the end. Start from the lunacy itself and one will end there, after a number of gyrations — still believing, for instance, that (in Hegelian fashion) material development exists to serve the idea of 'spiritual development'. [. . .]

The politico-cultural necessities of nationalism, as I outlined them briefly above, entail an intimate link between nationalist politics and *romanticism*. Romanticism was the cultural mode of the nationalist dynamic, the cultural 'language' which alone made possible the formation of the new inter-class communities required by it. In that context, all romanticism's well-known features — the search for inwardness, the trust in feeling or instinct, the attitude to 'nature', the cult of the particular and mistrust of the 'abstract', etc. — make sense. But if one continues to adopt that language, then it becomes impossible to get back to the structural necessities which determined it historically. And of course, we *do* largely speak the language, for the same reason that we are still living in a world of nationalism.

Lastly let me point out an important limitation of the analysis. So far I have been concerned with the earlier or formative stages of nationalism. That is, with the nationalism which was originally (however much it has duplicated itself in later developments) that of Europe between 1800 and 1870. But it is certainly true that after 1870, with the Franco-Prussian war and the birth of Imperialism (with a large 'I'), there occurred further sea-changes in nationalist development. These were related, in their external coordinates, to a new kind of great-power struggle for backward lands; and as regards their internal coordinates, to the quite different class struggle provoked by the existence of large proletariats within the metropolitan centres themselves. [. . .]

I have stated that we still live in a climate of nationalism [but] it would, of course, be more accurate to say we still inhabit the universe of late nationalism: that is, nationalism as modified by the successive, and decisive, mass experiences of imperialism and total war. [. . .]

The imperial countries had their own version of nationalism, as a creed of conquest. Both sides in the great contest came to make use of the same ideas, and this created the notorious ambiguity that still haunts them: nationality had become the basis for both 'national liberation' and 'narrow nationalism', both the sacred principle of self-determination and Fascism.

'Relative over-development'

But the semantic confusion does not end there. From quite early on in the process there was a third cross-category. This neglected but significant group turned nationalist in order to liberate themselves from alien domination — yet did so, typically, not from a situation of colonial under-development but from one of relative progress. They were nationalities who struggled to free their own strong development from what they had come to perceive as the backwardness around them — from some larger, politically dominant power whose stagnation or archaism had become an obstacle to their further progress.

Certain other characteristics usually attach to this nationalism of 'relative over-development'. The peoples and territories concerned are small. They tend to be in 'sensitive' zones of a larger political economy, alongside or inbetween powerful neighbours. They usually develop so rapidly through the discovery and exploitation of subsoil resources — coal and iron in the nineteenth century, petroleum today. And sometimes they occupy a particularly favourable 'crossroads' position in terms of trade patterns.

Capitalizing on these resources, such areas drive forward developmentally. They feel held back and exploited by the backward state power controlling them. Yet they are most often too small and powerless, too isolated or eccentrically located, to shake free and evolve into members of the world élite. Thanks to their bourgeois development, they are too strong to submerge or liquidate; but not strong enough to fight free. Hence they tend to remain stranded, like unassimilable problem—children of the international order.

Belgium was the first important case of this sort, in the post-Industrial Revolution era. The Belgian revolution of 1830—2 and the new state it created represented much more than a Catholic protest against the overlordship of the Calvinist Netherlands. At that period Belgium had developed rapidly into the most advanced centre of the new industrialism on the Continent. The exploitation of coal and iron, and the country's strategic position across the great rivers, had bred an active entrepreneurial middle class — a restless, forward-looking bourgeoisie impatient with Dutch bureaucracy and backwardness.

The Holland of the early nineteenth century . . . was a decaying mercantile empire given to indulgent contemplation of past glories, and very little inclined to put up with the disruptive strains of industrialization. The liberal Belgian middle class wanted to escape from this palsied grip. They asked originally for limited home rule, and, when this was resisted by King William I, soon escalated their demands to complete independence . . . [successfully] . . .

Later small-country middle-class movements had a harder time, in the fiercer and more imperialist climate which prevailed from the later nineteenth century to the present.

From mid-century onwards, the relatively developed region of Bohemia reacted against the dead hand of Hapsburg absolutism in a similar fashion. The Czech-speaking middle class formulated a nationalism of its own, and fought for a modern bourgeois state capable of liberating them from the incorrigible parasitism of Austria-Hungary. Although superficially like the other Slav nationalisms in the backward lands of the empire — Slovenia, Slovakia, Serbia — Bohemian-based separatism actually stood on different, more developed ground. This is why the Czech state that eventually appeared in the post-1918 settlement was to be the success story of Central Europe between the wars.

But this success was short-lived, and difficult . . . Their relative over-development remained an intolerable threat to the dominant political powers. They emerged from German occupation in 1945 only to become a new challenge within the Soviet bloc. [. . .]

In two other cases, achievement was even more fleeting. In the Iberian peninsula the Basque and Catalan regions had been the natural focus of industrial revolution. Both nationalities enjoyed a relatively privileged situation, either in resources or in trade location; and both straddled the existing political frontiers of the

French and Spanish states. Again, varieties of nationalism arose to exploit this advantage and build middle-class states capable of effective modernization. This implied of course breaking from the backward, ex-imperial land-mass mainly dominating them, the old Spanish state.

These countries have never obtained independence. They knew only brief periods of limited 'home rule' in the early 1930s, under the liberal republic. Then the ferocious reaction from the centre subjected them to a still-continuing colonial régime of forced integration. [. . .]

[Another category is] the relative over-development linked to settler implantation. [Because of] a combination of social and geographical factors . . . colonization [occasionally resulted in] self-sustaining, middle-class societies . . . more or less complete social formations, capable of independence and self-reference, and with their own variety of nationalism. Like the other small nations mentioned . . . they have become so many islands of relative over-development in relation to backward areas around them . . . [and some of them, e.g. White South Africa, Israel] pose what may be the most anguishing and intractable problems of contemporary history . . . 'It is through them that the forces of historical development break into actual conflict and trouble. Nor is there the slightest chance of this category of awkward nationalisms diminishing — on the contrary,' as world development accelerates 'it is certain to grow'.

The British Isles already have one such centre of turbulence, in Northern Ireland. There, the British Empire fostered the development of a relatively advanced industrial mini-society on the basis of an old settler community, the Ulster Protestants . . . [but] has the further decline of the old empire state now created another conflict of broadly the same sort? Will Scotland in turn become a centre of disruptive development, outpacing the somnolent failure to the south of it — and compelled, therefore, along a path of political separation?

Few would now deny that relative over-development in the United Kingdom context has something to do with the startling rise of the Scottish National Party. This is not wholly due to the discovery of North Sea oil . . . [though] few would deny that the dramatic new prospects disclosed by petroleum development made a big difference. They encouraged a revolution of rising expectations and a new self-confidence (affecting the middle classes most tangibly).

At the same time, the London state and the southern economy have lurched several leagues further on the downward track they have been following for decades. It would be exaggerated, admittedly, to claim that the UK state is yet quite like the Hapsburg Empire or the old Castilian state. But the similarities are notable enough: there is a recognizable composite of archaism, incorrigible economic failure, backward-looking complacency, indurate social conservatism and blind will to survive in the same historic form. Culture has become largely the celebration of these values. The main 'opposition' party, British Labour, is as addicted to them as the overt conservatives. [. . .]

The Scots know quite well that the North Sea will be sucked dry mainly to keep [the British] Model-T Leviathan going. The chances of the new resources being employed effectively for the long-awaited modernization of Britain's industrial economy are absolutely zero . . . A large part of the Scottish people are now looking towards a future of separate development. But so far they have only voted for it; we do not know how many of them would be prepared to fight for it, if the going became harder . . . [nor do we] know at what point the British state will resist such claims with more decision. [. . .]

'Neo-nationalism'

'Neo-nationalism' . . . is a phenomenon which now affects a definite area of Western Europe, most notably the Spanish, French and British states, and the Low Countries. The position in Italy and Germany is significantly different, for reasons associated with the more recent (and prototypically nationalist) development of these countries, with their defeat in the Second World War, and with the relatively advanced forms of regional government both have adopted since 1945. The other, older states were all constituted in certain key respects *before the age of nationalism proper*. They are, as a matter of fact, the 'original' nation-states which fostered modern capitalism, and whose impact upon the rest of the world precipitated the process of general 'development' (imperialism and counter-imperialism) with which nationalism became inextricably linked. For this very reason, as many scholars have indicated, they belong in a rather special category. They themselves evolved prior to the general conditions of uneven development which they foisted on the world. They are not really so much 'nation-states' as 'state-nations', in which the factors of nationality had played a role quite distinct from that they would assume in nationalism proper.

Put at its most simple: they were in fact multi-ethnic assemblages in which, through lengthy processes of conquest and absorption, one or another nationality had established ascendancy (normally in late-feudal times, through the machinery of absolute monarchy). Then, when these entities were exposed to the new circumstances of the nationalist age (nineteenth—early twentieth century) they normally reacted by the maximization of this ascendancy, by reinforcement of French (Langue d'Oïl), Spanish (Castilian), British (English), or Belgian (Wallon) patriotism, most often in a new imperialist framework.

This new situation enabled the historically 'composite' nature of such states to be buried politically for a time (though of course the interment was never as total as it seemed from the vantage-points of London, Paris, etc.). Now, however, with the further prolonged era of capitalist expansion since 1950 and the formation of the European Common Market, the external conditions which did so much to consolidate the old state-nations have largely gone. Their empires have disappeared, with a few insignificant exceptions. They have dwindled in status to mediocre, second-rate powers whose pretentions far outrange their capabilities. [. . .] These areas are not large enough, in relation to the operations of modern multinational capitalism and the dominant states of our time, and their powers are feeble and antiquated by the same token. Their 'metropolitan' culture draws every day closer to that ageless joke: the village idiot convinced, against all the evidence, that he still has a thing or two to teach the world. [. . .]

Thus, the bourgeois modes of domination which held such polities together have wilted. There is a most important corollary to this, which must not be overlooked. The decline of bourgeois hegemony has not been accompanied by the rise of an alternative — that is, by the emergence of an effective socialist power at the level of the old states. Had the class struggle accelerated politically at the same time, it is doubtful if Scottish and other neo-nationalist movements would have made much headway. [. . .] Two factors in combination . . . created the conditions for nationalist resurgence: the multinational petroleum business, and the degeneration of United Kingdom politics. But the failure of socialism is surely another way of regarding the second of these. It is the failure of the Left to advance far enough, fast enough, on the older state-nation platforms which history had provided, it is the inability of great-nation socialism to tackle advanced contradictions properly, that has made this 'second round' of bourgeois nationalisms inevitable.

References

Gellner, E. (1964) 'Nationalism', in *Thought and Change,* London, Weidenfeld & Nicolson.
Hobsbawm, E. J. (1962) *The Age of Revolution: Europe 1789—1848,* London, Weidenfeld & Nicolson.

2.6

Colonialism and the Formation of African States

RUTH FIRST

The crisis of Africa's independence governments, which one after the other have fallen victim to army coups d'état, cannot be discussed without a close look at . . . the state structures built up during the colonial period . . . In the phase of decolonization power was transferred, through virtually unchanged institutions of government, to largely hand-picked heirs. These heirs are the new ruling groups of Africa.

The colonial sediment

Independence is seen as a watershed in the development of the contemporary African condition. And so it was. In 1960 there occurred changes scarcely credible ten years before. But despite the great wave from colonial to independent government, there remained a continuity between the old dependence and the new. Many of the means and ends that made up colonial administration were inherited virtually intact by the independence governments. For the sediment of colonialism lies deep in African society. The armies are colonial products; the political system is largely a transplant, and a bad one at that; while the political rulers were trained or constrained by the colonial system. Africa was a continent of bureaucratic rule, with armies behind the administrators ready to prove whenever necessary that government existed by conquest.

Source: From *The Barrel of a Gun* (1970) Harmondsworth, Penguin, pp. 27−73, but mainly from 'Ways and means of decolonization', pp. 41−58, half of which is reproduced. Footnotes have been excluded and sub-headings added.

Conquest, diplomatically and officially speaking, became a sustained venture of the European powers after the Berlin conference of 1884—5, although the slaver, the trader, the fortune-hunter and the missionary had all come before the imperial army, each in his turn or all together softening up the continent for conquest. The division of Africa was an extension of the struggle among the European powers of the nineteenth century, and Africa under colonialism was ruled as a promontory of European interests. Colonialism was trade, investment and enterprise for the benefit of an alien society. Power lay outside the country. African trade, African free enterprise, far from being encouraged, were ousted, or permitted to operate only as very junior partners . . .

The patents for the administrative grids fashioned in London or Paris, in Brussels or in Lisbon, varied in style and design, [but] colonialism in its different variations was more like than unlike in the form of rule it imposed. This was, whether conscious or not, military in conception and organization. More than anything else, colonial administrations resembled armies. *The chain of authority from the top downwards was untouched by any principle of representation or consultation* [Eds' emphasis]. For long periods in some territories, indeed, the colonial administrations not only resembled armies, in their para-military formation and ethos; they were, as in the Sudan, the instruments of military men . . . Military conquest was followed by military administration . . .

The colonial system functioned in the conviction that the administrator was sovereign; that his subjects neither understood nor wanted self-government or independence; that the only article of faith on which administrators could confidently depend was that all problems of 'good government' were administrative, and that disaster would follow from attempts to conceive of them as political . . .

If there was any training and adaptation before independence, it was a schooling in the bureaucratic toils of colonial government, a preparation not for independence, but against it. It could not be otherwise. Colonialism was based on authoritarian command; as such, it was incompatible with any preparation for self-government. Africa was the continent of bureaucratic rule. In that sense, every success of administration was a failure of government. Government was run not only without, but despite the people.

Ways and means of decolonization

The Second World War broke shatteringly into the staid pace of colonial rule. The Dutch tried holding on to Indonesia, by massive force, as the French tried in Indo-China, and subsequently in Algeria, at disastrous cost. The sporadic troubles of the British Empire, previously put down by punitive expeditions, were tending to grow into prolonged guerrilla war . . . The longer the Empire lasted, the higher the expenditure on retaining it seemed to grow . . .

In the 1950s and the 1960s, constitutional formulae, constitutional conferences and bargaining dominated African politics. It began with cautious changes, like allowing Africans to enjoy unofficial majorities in legislative councils, and it ended with the cascade of independence constitutions in the 1960s . . .

A former colonial governor and head of the African division of the Colonial Office, Sir Andrew Cohen, [had argued that] Britain . . . should recognize that 'successful co-operation with nationalism' was the 'greatest bulwark against Communism'. The transfer of power to colonial people need not be a defeat, but a strengthening of the Commonwealth and the Free World.

Decolonization came to Africa in two phases. The first, in the first decade after the end of the war, occurred in those regions which European armies had used as actual theatres of war: Ethiopia, Libya, Egypt, the Sudan, Morocco and Tunisia. The defeat of the Italian army restored to Ethiopia an independence dating from the eleventh century and interrupted only by the Italian invasion of 1935. Libya, another former Italian colony, found herself independent in 1951 by vote of the United Nations, because the big powers could not decide what to do with her. (During the final negotiations, a UN delegate is supposed to have remarked to a colleague, 'At three o'clock this afternoon we free Libya.' His colleague replied, 'Impossible. We freed Libya yesterday.')

Uniquely in Africa, and for reasons closer to Middle East than African developments, Egypt in 1952 achieved more than formal independence in a seizure of power by an army coup d'état that set afoot a social revolution . . . Egypt's social order, like China's, had been ripe for toppling; but whereas in China, a political movement with a finely articulated policy for social revolution adopted mass armed struggle to seize power, in Egypt army officers seized the state in one sharp blow at the apex, and then looked about for a political force and a policy to express the change. From his first conventional disavowal of the political interest and role of soldiers, Nasser graduated by 1962 to the thesis that the role of the army was to clear the path of the revolution.

The ensuing years were to show — not only in Egypt, but also in the Sudan and Algeria — how far an army could 'clear the path of the revolution'; or for reasons intrinsic to the control and style of armies, and such interests as were represented in Egypt's officer corps, it might proceed instead to undermine it . . .

In the French African Empire, it was the independence struggle in the Maghreb that was principally responsible for France's accommodation to new policies. In both Morocco and Tunisia — though not in Algeria — France astutely timed independence offers to forestall guerrilla actions and install moderate leaderships.

Ghana and Guinea attained independence in the tail years of this first decade. Then came the avalanche of West and Central African independence in 1960, when 17 colonies of the British and French Empires in Africa became independent, and even Belgium, seemingly the most intransigent of the colonial powers, suddenly shortened her timetable for the independence of the Congo from 30 years to seven months. Another five countries became independent during the next two years; then Kenya in 1963, a full 10 years after the armed rebellion that disturbed the pace of negotiated independence; then in East and Central Africa, the states of Tanganyika, Malawi, Zambia and Zanzibar, the latter one month before an armed uprising in 1964. The ensuing years saw the conclusion of the process, as small states like Gambia, Botswana, Lesotho, Swaziland and Mauritius joined the independence round.

It looked deceptively easy, this evacuation of empire. True, members of the West African élites . . . had been meeting spasmodically in Pan-Africanist conferences: in 1900, after the First World War, and, more intensively, after the Second World War. They had launched students' federations in London and Paris; nationalist newspapers; and finally, fully fledged political independence movements which, for long patient, mild and pliant, received a stiffening of ex-servicemen, trade union and radical agitation after the war . . . In Ghana Nkrumah catapulted a positive action campaign into the orderly pace of constitution-making; there were demonstrations by ex-soldiers, with riots and boycotts, in the late 1940s, at a cost of 29 killed and 237 injured . . .

But inside Africa, apart from Algeria and the other countries of the Maghreb, Kenya, the Cameroun and Madagascar, *it was hard to find turbulence enough to explain why, having earlier seemed so resolved to keep the continent, the colonial powers* — with the exception of Portugal and the settler-dominated communities — *now, after the war, seemed so preoccupied with how to get out of it* [Eds' emphasis] . . .

Kenya and Algeria

In East Africa, the tempo was accelerated by the 'Mau Mau' rising; in French Africa, by Algeria's war for independence. It was the struggles in these two countries, though different in scale and duration, that provided the exceptions to Africa's licensed advance to constitutional independence. Both countries, significantly, were dominated by White settler power that had ruthlessly dispossessed the colonial peasantry, and enjoyed a voluble say in metropolitan decisions.

In Kenya, a dominant local White community and the colonial regime between them met African grievances with repression and precipitated the very revolt that these measures had been designed to deny . . . The state of emergency unleashed in 1952 against the underground movement that was preparing for armed resistance was intended to savage the leadership and terrorize discontent into submission. It did the opposite. A plan for revolt, only partly prepared, was triggered into action by lower levels of the leadership, who escaped the police net by moving into the forests and turning them into bases of operation for a guerrilla war. But . . . the fighting groups that remained in the forest after 1956 were small isolated bands, constantly pursued by government troops and offering little co-ordinated resistance . . . [and] by the time that independence constitution-making for Kenya was begun, less than a decade later, the peasant revolt was defeated, and its aims were all but obliterated. In the space of a few devious years, Kenyatta, once execrated as a Black nationalist leader to darkness and death, had become the grand old man of the settlers . . .

Despite the armed rebellion, therefore, independence for Kenya came only after the colonial power had prepared the timing and the manner of the take-over. It came not with victory, at the climax of the military rising, but only five years later, when settler intransigence had turned to 'realism', and the policy of confrontation with African demands had become one of bargaining and negotiation. The generation of militant fighters was dead, imprisoned or blacklisted. In its place was a generation that, for the most part, was ready to accept independence as a gentleman's agreement, with the political process as the prerogative of a privileged élite. The 'Mau Mau' had fought a war, but lost it, and the landless poor which that struggle had represented were given no place in the independence settlement.

Algeria's war, by contrast, lasted twice as long and ended in the victory of independence. Far from her conflict being blockaded in the forests, it spread to France, brought down the Fourth Republic and threatened the survival of the Fifth, in a decisive display of the dangers in the settler slogan *'L'Algérie, c'est la France'* (or *Algérie Française*) . . . Alone in Africa, Algeria fought a national liberation war for independence which struck at the very basis of French settler-colonialism. But the seizure of power through armed struggle was not followed by a period of concentrated mass mobilization, without which a revolutionary transition to independence cannot be secured. In part this was because Algeria emerged from the war economically exhausted . . . but, above all, Algeria's revolution was stunted because her leadership was locked in conflict . . . [and] could not agree on the post-liberation restructuring of Algerian society.

Crisis of empire, American pressure

Despite her own setback, it was Algeria's war for independence that achieved more for the other French colonies than anything that they dreamt of doing for themselves. And yet, in the main, the tempo for change in Africa was accelerated more *outside* the continent than within it, in Asia rather than in Africa; France's colonies gained their independence as a direct consequence of crisis in other parts of the French empire . . . The French had been defeated at Dien Bien Phu, and this altered the French course not only in Indo-China, in Asia, but also in Africa. Faced with a Dien Bien Phu, Frantz Fanon has written, a veritable panic overtakes colonial government:

> Their purpose is to capture the vanguard, to turn the movement of liberation towards the right, and to disarm the people: quick, quick, let's decolonise. Decolonise the Congo before it turns into another Algeria . . .

Independence was breaking out all over the French Empire, and the British; and over the Dutch and the Belgian, as well. There were international reasons why. Already by 1945 the war had fundamentally altered the pre-war structure of power. United States policy was to supplant European imperialisms with paternalist and profitable economic ties; in place of old-style colonies, would be put the new containment, in United States free enterprise. There was, thus, a perceptible shift in the priorities of Western powers, which had to take their cue from the most powerful among them. The United States was interested, for its own reasons, in confining traditional European power and its financial freedom to pursue an independent course . . . Decolonization was a move to shore up 'stabilizing' forces in restless regions, rather than a recognition of the right of peoples to the independence and the freedom that the phrases of the United Nations so eloquently embodied . . .

African élites, European models

Africa's rapid transition to independence, if it made the early 1960s heady with optimism, left behind a damaging legacy of myth and illusion. Independence came by too many to be seen as a single, sharp act, like running the national flag up the flag-pole. The constitutional agreement once signed, an African state was independent. Indeed, independence was seen by the political careerists not as the beginning, but as the end in a process of change. To them independence was reduced to a constitutional formula in which contesting élites, serviced by lawyers and public relations men, bargained on terms and fixed indemnities for the departing power, which for their part were intent on handing over political power as long as this did not affect their economic stakes . . . [This] is not, to be sure, invariably the whole story in each individual country. But, on the whole, the experience of decolonization in Africa is not one of grass-root struggle, except for brief, unsustained periods.

In much of Africa, the leaders of the independence movement accepted without undue perturbation the form of independence ordained by the departing colonial authority. 'Gabon is independent,' President M'ba is reputed to have said, 'but between Gabon and France nothing has changed; everything goes on as before . . .' British or French or Belgian constitutional traditions seemed the only permissible, even possible, form. Regular electoral competition within a European-type constitution became the 'pubertal rite' on the independence scene; though, so shortly before independence, the colonial system had been busy locking up its opponents and had never dreamt of paying them salaries to oppose.

Transferring the so-called Westminster model was an exercise of dubious value. The British constitution, unwritten just because it is rooted in age-old precedent and tradition uniquely British, serves a society which could scarcely be less like those for which its export model was prepared. The Parliament at Westminster owes its present character to a civil war and several centuries of bitter struggle. The legislature is anything but the sole seat of power; beyond it function the great institutions of the economy from the banks to the stock exchange; the civil service; the education system; the great families; the newspaper chains; the Institute of Directors and the Trade Union Congress; all forms of power diffused through the society. In new African states, patterns of power — or lack of them — are quite different; and, most often, unsettled and unresolved . . . The fact that few of the models lasted more than a few years in Africa reflected on the value of the original exercise. From the end of 1960 to the beginning of 1962, 13 states revised their constitutions or produced altogether new ones.

The assumptions of the imported systems proved untenable in the new states. With the onset of independence, African parliaments seemed notoriously to debate the least important issues of the day. This was because the parliamentary convention of government and opposition politely exchanging the seats of office assumes that the crucial ideological questions have been settled; but, neither settled nor even debated in Africa, they tended to drop into oblivion. Land and economic policy were not scrutinized; social policies and administration were inherited from colonial days, and, for the most part, kept intact. Caught in the parliamentary round, the politicians devoted themselves to electioneering and party manoeuvring, rather than to national mobilization for national needs . . .

One country after another sank into political crisis. The political parties seemed to be dying on their feet, till army juntas swept them away altogether. The causes lay deeper, by far, than a failure of the parliamentary model. Yet, so firm was the faith in the transfer of 'superior' and tested Western systems of government, that many continued to seek explanations in the inability of Africans to govern themselves.

Post-colonial fantasy and real continuity

The apologia of colonialism, that it was a preparation for independence, is, in fact, largely fantasy. Studies of particular colonial records, wrote Schaffer, 'show that it is very difficult to trace any continual preparatory process at work, or any signs of a prepared policy until after the war'. Even then the post-war years were too late for preparation, save as a purely political, almost desperate effort to provide an ideology of delay (in the granting of independence). The notion of preparation was to justify the colonial record, as a tactic of delay in the sense that 'you would not seem to be delaying, only training and educating'. The theory of preparation 'emerged after the event', Lord Hailey [a British colonial administrator] agreed. A decade after the end of the war, he wrote that there was no trained machinery of administration ready to hand.

In any event, if independence was to provide Africa with Western European-styled political systems, the 'preparation' period should have encouraged direct elections, free political campaigning, full opportunities for all political parties to solicit the support of the electorate with their programmes . . . [In fact] colonial administrators fought delaying actions against direct elections, precisely because they wanted checks on the so-called 'professional politician' . . . [they] manipulated local, regional and ethnic differences to emphasize divisive rather than unifying national interests. And such divisions were deposited in independence constitutions, to assail the cohesion and survival of the new states from their inception.

Independence arrived already crippled by the colonial past. And most serious, that heritage was assumed virtually intact by many of the new rulers. Judging by the structures which they took over and left almost unchanged, the new governments of Africa were planning not to break with the pre-independence past, but to maintain close continuity with it, unaware — or, if they were aware, unable to do much about it — that the 'experience' gained under the colonial administration was not only irrelevant, but dangerous, to the new needs of African states . . .

It was ultimately this curious identity of interest between the new élite and the colonial oligarchy that facilitated the peaceful transfer of power to African régimes in most of colonial Africa. Once it had become apparent that the trade and economic policies of the colonial power could be conducted without the apparatus of direct political control, decolonization as a bargaining process with cooperative African élites did not end with the onset of independence, but continued beyond. The former colonial government guarded its options and interests; the careerist heirs to independence preoccupied themselves with an 'Africanization' of the administration which, more than even the transfer of political power, gave them openings previously filled by White men. Africanization, like the transfer of power, occurred within the largely unaltered framework of the colonial system . . .

In some newly independent African states, African leaders and parties harboured a more radical purpose. They saw decolonization as only the first step. Mass parties were built in Ghana, Guinea, Mali and Tanzania as explicitly anti-colonial instruments. They aimed not to inherit but to transform the system . . . [and] Africa has had her political martyrs as well as her political careerists.

But taking the continent as a whole, the independence

'revolution' in Africa was brief, makeshift and leaky. *It came precipitated as much if not more by thrusts from beyond the continent as by sustained and articulated social revolution from within* [Eds' emphasis]. This does not mean that independence was unwanted in Africa, or that her peoples were any less ready for it than any other peoples in the Third World. It means that, in the circumstances of its coming, it could accomplish and change only so much, and no more.

White power, Black parody

When government was transferred to Africans in the era of independence, there existed, in each independent state, a select circle of heirs. Except in circumstances like those in Northern Nigeria, where the new men of politics were linked with traditional sources of power, political control passed to a Western-educated élite which headed independence movements of relatively recent, effectively post-Second World War origin . . .

For the greater period of colonial rule, the chiefs and traditional heads were the most malleable instruments of the alien government. Running the administration through the chiefs was 'colonialism-on-the-cheap' . . . [But] by the time that power came to be transferred, however, the colonial governments had abandoned the chiefs as the main medium of political authority and had decided to use instead a new élite, more directly sprung from the needs of the colonial system . . .

Mostly they had acquisitive aspirations, if not resources, and envious eyes fixed on the White man and his estate, together with a marked inability to conceptualize the promise of independence other than in terms of their own immediate interest . . . Here and there a section of the élite had a firmer commitment to national rather than to narrow goals, but over time it encountered obstacles either under-estimated or blithely ignored . . .

European education

It was Western education that disengaged an élite and drove the cleavage in colonial society between the chosen minority and the ranks of the commoners . . .

Education was the ladder to a post in the administration or the rank above labourer in the money economy; and because education was free, the sons of humble parents could climb the rungs.

The early élites maintained their footholds; but new entrants fast outnumbered them, and the members of the present élites in the African states are drawn predominantly from humble homes. Most rapid expansion occurred in the late 1940s, when the colonial administrators began responding to pressures within the colonies, and in the late 1950s, as independence approached . . . As members of the imported oligarchy left, Africans stepped in to fill their jobs, play their roles, inherit their rates of pay and their privileges, and assume their attitudes, in particular the conviction that the educated in power have a divine right to rule and to prosper.

The educational system was geared not to Africa but to Europe. School textbooks were written and published in metropolitan capitals; students wrote the examinations of metropolitan universities. In British colonies, African children recited the tables of English kings and the dates of English wars . . . In pre-independence days, the cries of the intellectuals were vibrant and their needs passionate after what the continent had suffered . . . African students, especially those who studied abroad, talked, and even planned revolution in Paris and London, as Europe's 1848 generation had done in the same cosmopolitan meeting-grounds . . . Then came independence. Students who had been volubly dissident went home to be absorbed in the élite. Some of the most politically skilful renounced their opposition to the regimes in power and were rewarded with appropriate posts. Some found it too difficult to leave at all and remained in the metropolis. Sometimes victimization awaited them at home if they persisted in their radicalism . . .

The language of the élite was the language of the colonial power. Education and a white collar were the gateway to the White world; and what that world practised, the pupils imitated. Before independence, these standards were regulated by the colonial order. After independence, they were retained virtually intact by an élite that needed to entrench itself behind them . . .

The conditioning was not only to set an élite apart from and above the common people, but against them. Yet, like an emergent bourgeoisie everywhere, the African élite identified the general interest with its own . . . Personal initiative was the key to individual success; and individual achievement, a credit to the society as a whole. Within the élite, the preoccupation with personal initiative was a short step to policies that talked of African socialism but really meant private ownership — by Africans. The members of the African élite were spiritually company directors or property-owners long before they became them in reality . . . [With independence] they had become heirs to a successor state that they had, with few exceptions, little inclination to change. They had criticized not so much the system as its incumbents. With independence, they were the incumbents . . .

White eminence, army coup d'état

Always brooding over African society is the presence of the Whites. After independence, when they vacated political and administrative seats, metropolitan economic interests stayed behind, and so, too, did a deeply enduring subservience to colonial standards and attitudes . . . Administrators model themselves on systems devised for European conditions; and military men think of what Alexander, or Napoleon, a Sandhurst or St Cyr instructor might do in their place. Direct or snide criticism from London, Paris or Brussels, wounds deeply. Approval from Europe compensates for estrangement from the poor and illiterate at home . . .

Whites also make their influence felt more permanently and directly . . . In many African states, if permanent secretaryships were fairly rapidly Africanized, the command of army, police and security remained the last in White hands. Major decisions hinged frequently not on the purposiveness of the independence government but on the equivocations of White officials. Above all, especially in the French territories, the ultimate arbiters in political crisis were the French military forces. This was so before independence, and afterwards . . .

[One after the other independence governments fell victim to army coups d'état and] more than any institution left behind by colonialism, the armies of Africa were set in the colonial pattern. More than this, the armies of the new states were the identical armies that the colonial powers had built to keep their empires quiescent. After independence they retained, with few exceptions, their colonial pattern of army organization; their dependence on the West for officer training, specialist advice and equipment; and their affinity with the foreign and defence policies of the metropolitan countries. Even when Africanized and run by commanders-in-chief who were nationals of their own countries, Africa's armies were an extension of the West. Where they had gone into battle in the pre-independence period, it had been for, not against the colonial power. And, except for Algeria and to some extent Morocco, they played no part in the independence struggle.

2.7

Conceptions of Communist States

ADAM WESTOBY

This note attempts an overview of *general* conceptions of Communist states — ideas and theories which seek to elucidate their character, their overall relations to society, their essential principles of internal structure, and to place them within larger historical trajectories. Far from being comprehensive, the intention is rather to suggest, by comparison and contrast, some of the core problems which different thinkers commonly encounter.

An obvious feature of Communist states is the extent to which state and society interpenetrate. The party-state monopoly of tolerated political activity, and state control over almost all economic activity, provide the premises, but not the limits, of this intimacy. One result is that almost all theories of Communist states cannot avoid also being, in important measure, theories of Communist society. And both political and social theories differ, notoriously, not only in the answers they provide but in the ways they pose their questions. Many arise within a relatively well defined tradition, which conditions their choice and framing of questions. Moreover theories of Communist states evolve both in mutual contention, and in parallel with, and in imperfect reflection of, the objects they conceptualize. The attempt to make analytical comparisons lucid, therefore, also requires — and cross-cuts with — some linkages of intellectual history. It also, inevitably, involves a measure of critical assessment on the part of the author. Thus, like all *tours d'horizon*, this one has a point of view; however it is content to emerge, rather than claim precedence as an axiom.

Specially commissioned for this volume
© Adam Westoby, January 1983

The scope[1] and order may (approximately) be summarized as follows.

(1) Marxism, seeing modern society as in travail between capitalism and socialism, generally conceives of Communist states through one or other of these categories: 'state capitalism', or a form (if 'degenerated') of 'workers' state'.

(2) The latter has affinities with criticisms from reform Communists, raising problems of distribution, economic inequality and, perhaps, class; Western proponents of a *new* dominant class extend the implications to questions of exploitation and property.

(3) The concept of 'totalitarianism', set in a different framework, sees the concentration of political power, and not economics, as essential; 'bureaucratic collectivism' and its relatives attempt syntheses of economics and politics (or of property and the state).

(4) Ideas of 'convergence' raise questions of what, if any, general historical sequences Communist states may be placed within; 'oriental despotism' exemplifies concepts of a fundamentally different itinerary for East and West.

(5) Shifting from structure to genesis, various ideas argue the roots of the political volition that goes into the making of Communist states.

(6) Last, I review implications for Communist states' international action; and suggest some general conclusions.

In Communist states it is the state which owns and controls most major components of the economy. State planning, rather than private investment, is the motor of industrialization and economic development. This substitution is central to most Marxist theories of Communist states (as, indeed, it is to many socialist political programmes). The most important ideas are those of 'state capitalism', and of various types of 'workers' states'. Two linked preoccupations recur in them: the sense that state types are apposite or functional to particular forms and/or levels of economic development; and that the state acts as guardian of the property of the dominant class.

'State capitalism'

The notion of state capitalism goes back many years. From the first months of the Soviet state, opponents of the Bolsheviks protested that the revolution had resulted in a new state capitalism, with the new regime bringing back into authority the managers, and even the proprietors, of capitalist enterprises.[2] The term 'state capitalism' was also used, in this period, by Lenin, but not derogatively; it expressed his view that the New Economic Policy (1921 on) could advantageously emulate the enlargement of the German state's economic role during the war, assuming control over private enterprises in the interests of the nation as a whole.[3] Lenin varied the usage mainly in that he regarded the German state as representative of the German bourgeoisie, while the Soviet government exercised a 'dictatorship of the proletariat and peasants'. Later development as a theory, though, has almost always had a critical edge. The Menshevik current within Russian social democracy had always argued that it would be impossible, or at least disastrously mistaken, to short-cut the next necessary phase of Russian economic development: capitalist industrialization within a bourgeois—democratic political system. The smallness of the Russian working class, and the generally low level of economic development and culture, would make a mirage of any direct push for socialism. Mensheviks interpreted the state the Bolsheviks built in this light, though the man who spelt out this view most fully in the early 1920s was their mentor Karl Kautsky. Bolshevik terror during the civil war (1918—20) impressed him not only morally, but sociologically. It reflected the state's attempt to substitute for social classes, and it facilitated a fusion of the new state and party officialdom with former capitalist managers and proprietors.[4]

The idea of 'state capitalism' recurred repeatedly during the inter-war years.[5] For example in the 1930s the then social democrat Lucien Laurat amended Marx's schema of distribution in *Capital* to account for the privileged salaries of the Soviet élite.[6] But its most systematic development, applied not only to the Soviet Union but to the satellite states formed in Eastern Europe after the war, and to Communist China, came from dissident Communists (mainly Trotskyists) after the Second World War. The best known is that which Tony Cliff put forward from 1948, in which he tied the notion more directly to the impetus for industrialization.[7] According to Cliff capitalism was *restored* in the Soviet Union about 1928, only not in the form of private capital but as its agglomeration into state property. This was the significance of Stalin's turn to forced collectivization and industrialization during the first five-year plans. The growth of the state's bureaucracy was, together with Stalin's personal ascendancy, the necessary mechanism in substituting state coercion for market forces and extracting the surplus for industrialization from the peasantry. Cliff also depicted the Russian state (in particular) as an *imperialist* 'state capitalist' state, colonizing Eastern Europe and imposing on it similar structures and similar programmes for industrialization.[8]

As a *Marxist* theory, 'state capitalism' faces the problem of how to account for economic accumulation in the absence of the main mechanisms Marx examined in *Capital* — profits, market competition among independent capitals; more generally the operation of the 'law of value'. Thus Cliff and his co-thinkers, such as Michael Kidron, developed the idea of the 'permanent arms economy': *economic* competition between private capitals is being superseded (to differing extents) by military—political competition between capitalist states.[9] In Communist societies internal competition is entirely suppressed and the arms race is the main spur pushing, for example, Soviet planners to raise the productivity of their 'one big factory'.[10]

Variants of the Marxist theory of imperialism have also been applied to Soviet industrialization. Alvin Gouldner's concept of 'internal colonialism' posited a relationship of industrializing Soviet cities and their dominant political bureaucracy to the exploited countryside, analogous to that between metropolitan countries and their exploited colonies. The surplus for industrial accumulation was realized by political control which allowed the imposition of low agricultural sale prices, and high prices for factory-produced consumer goods, upon the peasants. Gouldner's account is close, in its essentials, to the idea of the 'scissors' invoked by Soviet planners in the 1920s: a free grain market inflates agricultural prices and causes industry to founder, as happened during the civil war and war communism (1918—21).[11] Soviet planners, however, employed the notion with a distinct political thrust: to one degree or another they favoured extraction of a surplus from the countryside.[12]

Ideas of 'state capitalism' have also been applied to Chinese industrialization after the Second World War. But the main point of departure remained the Soviet Union.

'Degenerated workers' states'

If Communist states are not capitalist, perhaps they must be socialist? The other main group of Marxist views forms a spectrum, shading from these states' own official fictions to more realistically critical conceptions of them as quasi- or proto-socialist. To take perhaps the most influential example among the latter: the notion of the 'degenerated workers' state' developed by Trotsky after his exclusion from power in the 1920s.[13] Trotsky, an eloquent defender of the regime up to the early 1920s, identified the essential 'degeneration' of the Soviet state in the growth of a privileged bureaucracy which found its political representative in Stalin. Economic backwardness, shortage, and the isolation of the Russian revolution had produced, not a new type of capitalist ruling *class*, but a bureaucratic *caste*. This rested both on the existence of socialist economic foundations (state control of the economy, which Trotsky saw as dependent on the Party's monopoly of political power), but also on the insecurity of these foundations, and the hostile pressure of a surrounding capitalist world.[14] The essential antagonism (or 'deformation') is between socialist production and unequal distribution. With very long queues, it is necessary to appoint a 'policeman' to keep order; the state bureaucracy becomes 'a bourgeois organ in a workers' state' and 'draws off the cream for its own use'.[15]

Ideas of a 'degenerated workers' state' resemble those of 'state capitalism' in that both link the privileges and the dictatorial methods of the state bureaucracy to economic backwardness: the state, directly or as a surrogate for the market, must coerce the surpluses for industrialization. But the further question thus arises of why the political regime endures once industrialization is achieved and extreme shortages recede.

There is also the problem of how the working class can be (as one of Trotsky's modern followers puts it) 'institutionally excluded from the administration of its own state'[16] by a stable regime in the very long term. Analogies have been proffered (for example by Ernest Mandel) with the great variety of state forms (liberal republic, monarchy, military dictatorship, Fascism) which have proved consistent with the social domination of the capitalist class.[17]. If the German bourgeoisie suffered under 'their' Hitler, might not Russian or Chinese workers suffer under 'their' Stalin or Mao?

In Trotsky's earlier version, however, the stress was on impermanence. Inequality and the political regime alienated the working class from the state even though it remained, in an historical sense, a 'workers' state'. This increased the dangers to both the political regime and the economic base by defeat in external war, a military coup, recrudescence of private property rights, or some combination of these. (Similar dangers have often been invoked by the rulers of Communist states.)

Reform Communists' ideas

Trotsky offered a vivid portrait rather than a clear-cut theory. Where he depicted Stalin's regime as specific to the earlier stages of industrialization he anticipated a number of post-war reform Communists who have argued the need for political and intellectual liberalization as a precondition of economic reform, especially with the expansion of creative mental work central to 'post-industrialism'. The concept of a state formed by its need to control the economy as the essential lever of industrialization leads, naturally, into ideas which distinguish different phases of industrialization and see some of the crucial strains within Communist states as arising from transitions from earlier into later ones. The difficulties of centralized 'command' economies multiply as the number and variety of products increase, and the relationships between them do so much faster. Thus, in the 1960s, stagnating rates of industrial growth brought home to economic planners in the Soviet Union and Eastern Europe problems both of decentralized control, and of effective accounting, which led them to reinstate ideas in which freer markets were seen as complementing state direction.[18]

Something of a renaissance, albeit brief, resulted in several related fields: economic and planning theory; public administration; aspects of law. These provided the intellectual underpinnings of the moves towards market decentralization widely prepared in the Soviet bloc during the 1960s, but thoroughly enacted only in some countries, such as Hungary. In Czechoslovakia, where the economic reform was aborted when it began to unwind into political liberalization unacceptable to the Soviet leadership, ideas were pushed even further. Paralleling notions of 'post industrialism' put forward by sociologists in the West, a group of reform-minded Czech social scientists argued that in industrially advanced societies (such as theirs) industrial production would be progressively overshadowed in importance by science and technology as independent factors in the productive process, and more generally by creative mental employment. Increasing numbers of highly skilled intellectual workers would require, ever more insistently, a more liberal regime and freer interchange of ideas if their input to production were to be realised effectively.[19] This was an argument somewhat distinct from the (slightly earlier) economists' arguments for decentralization, which did not necessarily involve political relaxation, but rather devolution of practical measures of control. Such arguments, from those with official and/or academic status within Communist states, did not, of course, directly challenge official characterizations of the state. Nonetheless, on slightly different and more concrete planes, they questioned both the capacity of the socialist state to substitute itself for markets, and the 'leading role' of the industrial working class throughout the transition from capitalism to full Communism.

Inequality, exploitation, class, property

Czech (and other) economic reformers were viewed with reserve by industrial workers. One reason was their advocacy of pay differentials. Like owners and their managers in capitalist societies, the efforts of the administrators and 'intellectual workers' of socialism were to be spurred by economic rewards. The linked questions of differences in pay and other benefits and of the mechanism (if any) of exploitation in socialist society have been central to many theories of Communist states, including several quasi-Marxist ones. Marx originally provided a theoretical justification (most fully in the *Critique of the Gotha Programme*, 1875) in which he linked economic inequality to the persistence of the state for some time after the capture of political power by the working class. The impossibility of eliminating scarcity immediately meant that labour would have to be rewarded not 'according to need' but in accordance with 'bourgeois right' (by which he meant paying more skilled or energetic workers more, rather than profits on capital).[20] It would be necessary for a state to regulate rights of distribution and their inequalities. The idea is continued by Lenin, even in his most 'anarchist' essay on the state, *State and Revolution* (1917).

There is in these ideas, however, no suggestion that economic inequality will assume the form of *exploitation*, or that social differentiation linked with it will give rise to an antagonistic social structure, or new *classes*. However, from rather early in the life of the Soviet regime it began to seem to some that its institutionalized and linked inequalities of income and power denoted precisely this. Yet the economic mechanism involved, linked as it evidently was to the state's overwhelming role in employment, did not easily lend itself to a general theoretical account.

Modification of the Marxist theory of capitalist exploitation seemed to offer one solution. But there is a crucial difference between, for example, early theories of 'state capitalism', which see a fusion between the bureaucracies of state trusts and persistent and growing private capital, and later ones (such as Cliff's) which recognize the elimination of large-scale private property as permanent.[21] But in the latter case the essential mechanisms Marx postulated, of commodities exchanging at or near their labour values, and the competition of capitals in quest of profit, is lacking. State direction overrides many prices; during Soviet industrialization in the 1930s, for example, labour and other resources were channelled into heavy industry despite exceedingly low 'prices' for its outputs.

The notion of the 'degenerated workers' state', on the other hand, denies that exploitation is — as it would be under capitalism — rooted in the system of production. It results only from 'deformation' of the system of *distribution*, in antagonism with the (potentially socialist) organization of production. The state bureaucracy enjoy their privileges as, so to speak, a form of organized pilferage. And this is what makes them a *caste* rather than a class. In Marxism's view of previous social formations, the systematic extraction of a surplus by a minority has involved not only a specific mechanism of exploitation, but also an exploitative class reproducing itself from generation to generation, usually through property inheritance. Thus discussion of whether it is possible to identify a 'ruling class' in Soviet-type societies has often turned on its self-reproduction, its property forms, and their relations with the state. Trotsky's account of the 'degenerated workers' state', for example, saw systematic inheritance as dependent on the re-emergence of private property and, thus, on the eventual restoration of capitalism over socialist economy.

Clearly, however significant inheritance of privilege has developed without private property. One family of conceptions (broadly speaking that of 'bureaucratic collectivism', see below) account for this through notions of 'class' property, collectively controlled (and therefore 'owned') by a ruling stratum through the state. The question of *individual* family inheritance does not arise. Most versions of 'state capitalism' argue similarly. And a somewhat distinct line of thinking — with roots which pre-date the Russian revolution — stresses the joint capacity of educational differences and the social division of labour to form the basis of a generalized differentiation of the social structure, reproducing itself across generations.[22] Among recent writers, for example, Alvin Gouldner argues the global rise of a 'new class' distinguished by its 'culture of critical discourse', embodied in a form of 'human capital'.[23] This is the basis both of its higher productivity and its higher salaries. Gouldner's 'new class' in Communist societies resembles the growing scientific élite described by Czech theorists of 'post industrialism', but seen under a more critical aspect.

Where Gouldner identifies discrete divisions, the East German dissident Rudolf Bahro analyses the social division of labour as a continuum through a hierarchical pyramid.[24] There is a ranking of social locations, but no divisions into a small number of classes. Education acts as a multiplex factor of inheritance: not only have more upper-class children the cultural 'head start' enjoyed by the middle classes in the West, but education's associations with state or party office bring opportunities for direct manipulation of one's offspring's education and life chances.

Marx, seconded by Lenin, licensed higher economic rewards in so far as these reflected greater productivity. But, especially in the absence of the market, privileged positions of office can arise in the state or party bureaucracy which have no sensible connection with the productivity of the individual and since, in many cases, higher education leads to bureaucratic office, the two effects — even if they were conceptually distinct[25] — are almost impossible to disentangle empirically. The elaborate state-party hierarchies of appointment and promotion are thus seen by 'new class' theorists both as an essential *part* of economic differentiation, and as *representative* of those who benefit from it.

'Totalitarianism'

The concept of 'totalitarianism', by contrast, emphasizes the capacity of state bureaucracy to dominate society directly, independently of roots in property forms or ruling classes. The general sociology of bureaucracy, in particular of its internal mechanisms, has a large, but unfortunately largely oblique, bearing on theories of Communist states. Much of it is (for obvious reasons of accessibility) derived from studies of corporate and state bureaucracies in the West. Moreover much of 'organization theory' is pragmatic, aimed at improving administration and work organization, and therefore focuses more on the alterable than the quintessential features of bureaucracy. Weber commented on the effects of the simultaneous growth of state and private bureaucracies, and the 'unchecked' development of state bureaucracy that was to be expected if private property was eliminated.[26] The scope he saw for liberal politics to control bureaucratic structures lay largely in their mutual counter-balancing. His view may be taken as preamble to theories of 'totalitarianism' as the characteristic form of Communist states. The concept comes with many variants and nuances, but all shift their primary emphasis from the economy and property relations to political and administrative structures and the disposition of power. Power, when too far concentrated, ceases to be limitable by other powers, and destroys institutional and social pluralism throughout society.

The word 'totalitarianism', although it came to be one applied mainly to Communist states by their liberal critics, was actually launched as a term of approbation. Mussolini, from the mid-1920s, made *'lo stato totalitario'* (the totalitarian state) part of the language of Italian fascism, denoting by it his intention of principle to eliminate political rivals and form a one-party state. German Nazis similarly referred to their regime as *'totalitar'* in the 1930s (though Hitler preferred the word *'authoritar'*).[27] 'Totalitarianism' was then adopted by social scientific literature before the Second World War as descriptive of Stalin's one-party state as well (though Soviet writers did not, of course, accept this).

The post-war development of the term in application to Communist states consists of a mixture of description and theory, embracing a family of linked characteristics, though not necessarily taken as defining conditions of 'totalitarianism' in the state.[28] Because the nature of *political* regimes has varied more than property relations both over time and as between different Communist states (and because politics is a less exact discipline than economics) the attempt to define a single category primarily via the polity rather than the economy necessarily produces even less clear-cut and general results.

Concentration of political power is essential to the idea of totalitarianism. In the sense of many of its exponents, it implies a concentration not only in one party but in the hands of the individual leader who, subordinating the party to his own purposes, rules through a network of more personal connections. Fascist states are particularly clear examples of this, but the 'Führerprinzip' is present also in the cults of Stalin's, or Mao's, personality. This recrudescence within a contemporary state of earlier forms involves — what is rather general in Communist parties — the recurrence of conflict between individual leaders or aspirants and the administrative apparatuses. It has affinities with the ascendancy of a single political leader in, for example, nineteenth-century France — Bonapartism — though the domination of totalitarian leaders in and through the party is distinct from Bonapartism's rule 'above party'. Linked with the concentration of power in the state is the attempt to destroy it at other and alternative levels. Totalitarianism, in this sense, aims also at the elimination, containment, neutering or assimilation of intermediate social institutions which could act as rival sources of power. The elimination of private capital and employment is, thus, one specific — if centrally important — case of something more general, which includes the assimilation of religious institutions, or trade unions, for example. At a more microscopic level, totalitarianism seeks also to weaken direct connections and solidarity between individuals, atomizing society so that the state's monopoly of control over the major, and formal, institutions renders the individual more directly dependent upon it, without personal connections in civil society to fall back on.

There are two other important shifts in the relations between state and society. First, the subordination of law, understood as an impersonal and independent system of adjudication, so that even though legal forms are preserved, the legal system is, in effect, under the control of the party leadership. And, secondly, the enforcement of an official 'ideology', provided by the state with a monopoly of authority in many areas of intellectual life, and claiming validity as a universal system of doctrine: Marxism—Leninism. The doctrine must be the more energetically defended by the state in that its democratic formulae are in tension with the actual political regime; it sets limits to private, as well as public, intellectual life.

If these features characterize totalitarianism as an ideal type, it is clear that many Communist states, in many periods, do not conform to it. The concentration of political power in one single leader is often circumscribed by a ruling oligarchy's wish to avoid the dangers of a 'cult of personality'. In respect of the state's pressure on the individual, there is clearly an enormous gulf between, say, high Stalinism and the relatively low-profile rule of Janos Kadar in Hungary. Similarly, the elimination of other powers is not a necessary condition of Communist rule: Polish Communism has co-existed ever since the war (as Mussolini earlier did) with a deeply entrenched Catholic church with which it has had to discover and continually renegotiate a *modus vivendi*. Whether, however, Communist rule could for long tolerate, for example, independent trade unions, which tend more directly to rival its economic and social powers, is more doubtful — as the case of Poland again testifies. The independence of the judiciary appears to be only a temporary and unstable phenomenon — as, again, in brief periods in Poland, or in Czechoslovakia before the Soviet invasion of 1968. But there are several instances when the political authorities have relaxed too stringent a control of intellectual life, and have allowed assent to Marxism—Leninism to decline to the point where it is merely polite, or less. Nonetheless, rival intellectual currents do, it is clear, always act as irritants of Communist states; as with independent social institutions the authorities have, if not an absolute intolerance of them, at least an 'allergy' towards them.

Suppressing rivalry creates its own problems for state authorities, partly analogous to those of eliminating free markets:[29] they lack the sort of 'sounding boards' which give democratic states warning of social pressures and shifting interests, and allow them to respond. Defence of the political monopoly imposes, as one of its costs, a species of 'numbness' in the perception of social processes; the tension between these is a perennial problem of Communist states.

Most senses of 'totalitarianism' see social atomization as a means for direct control of the central state power over individuals. Recently Alexander Zinoviev (an exiled Soviet logician and student of his former society) has urged a corrective emphasis on the individual's more immediate social environment: what social atomization produces is, in fact, an *active* (though rather cynical) participation.[30] The individual lives his life not in the state alone but within much smaller 'communes', the 'cells' of social life; within these his life chances depend on competition with others for leverage within a structure of power. Unlike economic competition in the West, where the performance of one individual does not necessarily worsen the situation of others, competition for power is a 'zero sum game'; consequently, in Communism's war of each against all, mendacity and mistrust are endemic. These are fought out within, and reinforce, the larger official frameworks of control. There is a curious and pessimistic asymmetry: where, in much political theory, the state is morally enlarged by its affinity with the people, in Zinoviev's account the totalitarian state, in imposing an affinity with its own ethos on the people, morally diminishes them.

'Bureaucratic collectivism'

Zinoviev's view (like Bahro's) reminds us that the social structures and interdependencies within Communist states (and the differences among them) elude neat categorization into a small number of classes. The problems of pinpointing a (politically) ruling class and an (economically) exploiting one have often been linked, and sometimes identified. The striking but very rough correlation of privilege and power, and the absence of any simple criterion (such as private property) have led to much involved discussion. The problems involved have produced a strand (with roots in Marxism, but growing well beyond it) which depicts — sometimes metaphorically and sometimes almost literally — the state power itself as a form of property capable of appropriation, if not by individuals then by a class collectively. The alignment of political with economic primacy is thus, so to speak, semantically assured. Christian Rakovsky developed a comment of Marx on the Prussian bureaucracy ('owns the state as private property') along these lines in characterizing the Soviet system in 1930.[31] The Italian Brumo Rizzi, in 1939, described the 'class property' of a new 'bureaucratic collectivist' ruling class as the hallmark of a distinct social form, to which modern societies, led by the Fascist and Communist states, were tending.[32] A similar, but more famous, view was echoed a little later by James Burnham in *The Managerial Revolution* (1941).[33] In his construction two (perhaps over-determining) elements are combined: the managers owe their ascent to their necessity in production, but secure their position by the monolithic possession of the state power. The internal metabolism of the ruling group, and their relations to the rest of society, are little discussed.

Historical sequences and 'convergence'

Rizzi and Burnham offer early examples of the idea of a general 'convergence' of different state types towards a common condition[34] — which they both took Stalin's Russia in the 1930s to have approximated most closely. Evidently questions of Communist states' placing within sequences of historical development relate, but in a complex way, to those of their location within the world system of states. We take the former first.

For Marxist theories, historical sequences pose problems. Most variants take as fundamental a definite succession for modern societies, each defined by its characteristic mode of production: feudalism yields to capitalism, which in turn is transformed into socialism. More or less complex interrelations and combinations between these forms are recognized; for example, in Russia after the 1905 revolution, Parvus' and Trotsky's theory of 'permanent revolution' recognized the late and feeble development of economic capitalism within a political order inherited from the past, and envisaged that the bourgeois-democratic 'stage' might, in this national instance, be largely by-passed; many Russian Marxists before 1917 also anticipated (or feared) that economic backwardness would require dictatorial methods for any attempt to leap a stage direct to socialism. But as far as contemporary Communist states are concerned, Marxism's fundamental scenario tends to impose on its adherents a view of them as either a form (the last?) of capitalism — 'state capitalism' — or else as a variant (even if early, atypical, or deformed) of socialism. To view them as a social form distinct from either capitalism or socialism, or even an intervening stage between the two, disrupts the logic of Marx's analyses of capitalism, which see the premises of socialism being created organically within it. Certain Marxists — Rizzi, for example — do bluntly interpose 'bureaucratic collectivism' as an extra stage, but most opt either in the direction of 'state capitalism', or for a sort of proto-socialism.

Most ideas involving a notion of 'totalitarianism' have, however, a less closely defined historical sequence as background. The period of apparently greater liberalism under Kruschev in the Soviet Union, especially, gave rise to a distinct post-war sense of 'convergence' of which Talcott Parsons' functionalist sociology may be taken as an instance.[35] For Parsons, world history has evolved through three stages: primitive, intermediate and modern, and both Communist and Western states are now obliged to adapt to the exigencies of the modern period, with increasingly sophisticated industrial production and patterns of life. The increasing weight of the state and the bureaucratization of social functions in the West is reflected in a mirror-opposite evolution of Communist societies, towards greater differentiation, liberalization of the political regime, the emergence of competing interest groups, and so on.

Convergence in this sense, however, need neither lead to close similarities, nor affect all portions of society: in particular, industrial society may rely very heavily, or far less, on state direction of economic activity. This sense of 'convergence' — to a degree away from 'totalitarianism' — is distinct from that advanced, for example, by Marcuse: here high levels of technological development both require and secure integration of the mass of the population, not only into work but mentally, into functionally useful patterns of feeling and thought.[36] Deviance need less and less be repressed since it is increasingly isolated: one-dimensional thought rules. Like Parsons, Marcuse projected a reduction in state coercion in Communist societies, but in an account with a far more pessimistic coloration. Rather than the recurrent emergence of competing groups, he anticipated increasing passive homogeneity, East and West.

Oriental despotism

Ideas of any strict sequence of modes of production with their corresponding states, each functional in traversing a given level of economic development, run aground on the evident parallelisms of, for example, industrialization. America and Russia, during the last hundred years, have both covered a great deal of common ground in basic industrialization, but the former with a capitalist mode of production and state, and the latter with 'socialist' ones. Perhaps this has to do with national histories going back much further, and specifically with the non-feudal character of Russia before capitalism developed within it? This is the suggestion of the (aberrant) Marxist Karl Wittfogel, in *Oriental Despotism*.[37] Russian social relations, both prior to and after Peter the Great's reforms, were only superficially feudal and 'Western'; fundamentally they were shaped by relations of the state to society characteristic of the 'asiatic mode of production', in which strong intermediate proprietors are lacking, and the centralized state has a powerful role both in the extraction of the economic surplus (through taxes, etc.) and in the organization, or at least regulation, of production.[38] The connected notions of oriental despotism and the asiatic mode of production have a twin force: they emphasize the existence of forms of society (recognized but never examined in depth by Marx) in which both political dominance and economic exploitation occur through the state, without any substantial role for private property. And secondly, they stress that state forms can endure over the very long term, producing parallelisms across widely separated economic levels. Wittfogel's outlook is that of an (anti-Bolshevik) Marxist; however, the conception of profound and long-lasting differences of state, culture and temperament dividing authoritarian East from liberal West is widespread.[39]

Such views have a particular 'edge' for Eastern Europe: its states represent the imposition of an alien political order on societies and cultures which, having developed as part of Europe, are intrinsically unfitted for them; the broader extent of social and national rebellion in Eastern Europe compared with the Soviet Union since the war is taken as confirmation of this difference.

Wittfogel's view bridges two schools in that, while schematically loyal to Marx, he also makes fundamental use of the term 'totalitarian'. As a concept, 'totalitarianism' is more commonly associated with liberal political outlooks and is, hence, grounded in different views of the long-term historical background from Marxism: different both in terms of the stages perceived, and in the extent to which they are perceived as necessary, particularly in the modern period.

The will to power

Much of the discussion so far has run in terms of Communist states as related to objective social structures. One can also tease out a strand of thinking which stresses the subjective characteristics, in particular the political volition, of a 'new class' — very variously defined — in both the genesis and internal development of Communist states. Usually the sources of the 'new class' are found in processes already under way in non- or pre-Communist societies: the growth of an educated but unpropertied middle class grounded in specialist professional and bureaucratic occupations, particularly in the state. The pioneer of this view deserves mention: the Russian-Polish radical Jan Makhaisky, exiled to Siberia in the 1890s, there discerned from reading *Capital*, not the benefits of socialism, but the dangers represented by the new class of 'white hands' with their 'intellectual capital', exploiting manual labour through their higher salaries, who aimed to ride the working class to power through socialism and, once there, establish both their dictatorship and their privileges through state offices.[40] The idea has often been renewed, often with greater sociological sophistication. Djilas' *The New Class*,[41] written from the privileged position of a former close lieutenant of Marshall Tito, emphasizes its conscious unity of will, so effective in gaining power. Gouldner's portrait of the 'new class' distinguishes the 'critical' educated strata, in scientific, cultural and social employment, from old-style managers. Its 'problem-solving' outlook and abilities explain its varied impulses and achievements from, for example, the Chinese Communist revolution to the American 'new left' of the 1960s. Ivan Szelenyi discovers represented in the Eastern European Communist states the interests of an historically much older stratum: an intelligentsia separated from both large-scale property and the mass of the population, but with a propensity for politics as 'rational re-distribution'.[42] Recent neo-conservative writers, particularly in the United States, have seen in the growth of state-financed middle-class occupations the roots of 'interventionism' and leftism aiming at their protection and expansion.[43] Similar interests are, it is argued, crucial to Communism as a political movement, and are embodied triumphant in its states. Students of intellectuals more narrowly defined have found in them both the wellspring of Communist state totalism and of the ideologies aiming at the rational-utopian reconstruction of society which enable them to mobilize much larger social forces.[44]

In the international arena

What implications do different theories of Communist states — most of which start from their internal structure — have for their international action? The range is considerable: from the picture of the 'degenerated workers' state' as essentially vulnerable and defensive, seeking an illusory isolation; through views that Soviet international conduct (for example) is a new form of imperialism; to Cornelius Castoriadis' characterization of the Soviet state as a 'stratocracy' — i.e. one in which the commanding military caste dominates society as a whole, dividing the economy into civilian and military sectors, siphoning off the best of the former to supply the latter, and in which geographical expansion and conquest (partly to appropriate the more efficient economies of capitalist rivals) is a fundamental objective of the system.[45]

Views of the international action of Communist states turn not only on their internal characteristics but also on wider questions of their relationships with other societies, in particular the developed market democracies of the West. Difference need not necessarily imply fundamental rivalry: it may equally entail a degree of complementary symbiosis, as in the 'Vodka-Cola' thesis popularized by Charles Levinson.[46] Equally similarity (as implied, for example, by many versions of 'state capitalism') need not entail mutually pacific relations. Ideas of the intrinsic defensiveness of *all* Communist states suffer problems in explaining hostilities between them: for example, the proxy Sino—Soviet war fought out between China and Vietnam, or the Vietnamese—Cambodian conflict. Equally, ideas which deduce foreign expansionism as fundamental, for economic or political reasons or a mixture of the two, cannot be applied in any common way to the very large Communist states, acting as world powers, and the smaller ones, generally dependent on one of the former. The analogy of a Soviet colonial system in Eastern Europe is limited in one crucial respect: there are no formal colonial relations, each Eastern European state remains, constitutionally, sovereign. (Several, however, include a clause prescribing 'friendship' with the Soviet Union in their constitutions.) Soviet control is a continuous system of guidance-suggestion-intervention through the upper reaches of the party apparatuses. It depends, thus, on the party and state's internal cohesion, and the authority of the state; it is when this is threatened that the Soviet leadership intervenes most directly. China has never acquired an analogous constellation of dependent powers, with the possible and temporary exception of Albania. It is doubtful whether one can provide a single framework of explanation of even Communist *super*states' international action; motives and pressures on many levels interact, and combine very differently for the first, and later, comers. One general point is, however, stressed by many writers (reversing economic accounts of capitalist imperialism): a basic impulse towards foreign expansionism lies in Communist states' economic *in*efficiency relative to market economies. While the state's monopoly of power is — through inefficiencies in the planning system — a disadvantage on the economic plane, it is a pronounced advantage on the military and political ones. Nor do Communist governments have to fear the same internal opposition to external war as many Western ones.

Conclusions

What might we distil from the variety of ideas above? My conclusions would, I think, be fourfold.

(1) Conceptions of Communist states reflect, profoundly, the 'realist' sea-change in political thought which preceded them; all aim, at some level, at empirical explanation. They are seldom free of normative appetites, but unlike classical theories their justifications (or indictments) attach to the shape or methods, and not the very existence, of the state's sovereign power.

(2) In them recurs the urge, repeatedly frustrated, to single out one or a few aspects — economic or political — as the decisive ones; when other theorists criticize or react against this they often over-emphasize *other*, equally partial, features.

(3) From their interplay a certain consensus-across-differences emerges: the interpenetration of state and society compels a 'seamless robe' approach; conceptions of the one very commonly extend into a general view of the other.

(4) But, paradoxically and in parallel, there also emerges a sense that the typical Communist state has become — from a rational, functional or moral point of view, or some combination of these — superfluous to or parasitic upon the life of society; and, perhaps, that this is one of the things that the determination and comprehensiveness of its political grip reflects.

But such points, in so far as they do emerge, are by no means unique to thinking about Communist states.

Notes

1. Even among general conceptions I have selected harshly and, in compression, been unfair to all — I hope equally so. More empirical and so-called 'middle-range' theories are entirely omitted. The expression, '*Communist* states' simply denotes the coverage.
2. For examples of anarchist criticisms of this sort, see Paul Avrich (ed.) (1973) *The Anarchists in the Russian Revolution,* London, Thames and Hudson, and (1967) *The Russian Anarchists*, Princeton, Princeton University Press. Similar criticisms came later from certain left-wing Bolsheviks; see Robert V. Daniels (1960) *The Conscience of the Revolution,* Cambridge, Massachusetts, Harvard University Press. At this time the idea of 'state capitalism' was not clearly distinguished from that of a new, but non-capitalist, ruling class.
3. See, for example (1921) 'The tax in kind' in *Collected Works* (1963—70) Moscow, Progress Publishers, Vol. XXXII. But Nikolai Bukharin (who in turn drew on the ideas of the German social democrat Rudolph Hilferding) was the Bolshevik who earlier developed the idea of the bourgeois state as 'a direct exploiter, organizing and directing production as a collective capitalist'; related views clearly underlay his later fear that Stalin's Russia was becoming a 'Leviathan state'; see Stephen F. Cohen (1975) *Bukharin and the Bolshevik Revolution,* New York, Vintage Books.
4. See his (1920) *Terrorism and Communism,* London, Allen & Unwin; his views on the Soviet state are discussed in Massimo Salvadori (1979) *Karl Kautsky and the Socialist Revolution, 1880—1938,* London, New Left Books.
5. Early views are described in Adam Buick and William Jerome (1967) 'Soviet state capitalism? The history of an idea', *Survey* No. 62, January.
6. His views are summarized in English in Lucien Laurat (pseudonym, i.e. Otto Machl) (1940) *Marxism and Democracy,* London, Left Book Club.
7. Republished (1974) as *State Capitalism in Russia,* London, Pluto Press. Cliff's views on China are in Ygael Gluckstein (i.e. Tony Cliff) (1957) *Mao's China,* London, Allen & Unwin, whose arguments are refreshed in Nigel Harris (1978) *The Mandate of Heaven,* London, Quartet Books. A more orthodox Marxist criticism is David Purdy (1976) *The Soviet Union — State Capitalist or Socialist?,* London, Communist Party of Great Britain.
8. Ygael Gluckstein (1952) *Stalin's Satellites in Europe,* London, Allen & Unwin; see also Chris Harman (1974) *Bureaucracy and Revolution in Eastern Europe,* London, Pluto Press.
9. Cliff (1957) 'Perspectives of the permanent war economy', *Socialist Review,* Vol. VI, No. 8, and Michael Kidron (1970) *Western Capitalism Since the War,* Harmondsworth, Penguin, Ch. III.
10. Cliff, *State Capitalism in Russia,* p. 209.

11. Alvin Gouldner (1977—8) 'Stalinism: a study of internal colonialism', *Telos*, No. 34, Winter. The idea preceded the events; Bukharin warned in 1925 against the working class 'degenerating into a real exploiting class', treating the peasant economy 'as a "proletarian" colony' (quoted in Cohen, *Bukharin and the Bolshevik Revolution*, p. 172).

12. See Alexander Erlich (1960) *The Soviet Industrialisation Debate*, Cambridge, Massachusetts, Harvard University Press; also Moshe Lewin (1968) *Russian Peasants and Soviet Power, 1924—8*, London, Allen & Unwin.

13. It was developed mainly in opposition to the theory of 'socialism in one country', whose first chief advocate was Bukharin, and sponsor Stalin. Ideas akin to Trotsky's have recently been embraced by 'eurocommunist' theorists of Western Communist parties.

14. The main statement is (1972) *The Revolution Betrayed*, New York, Pathfinder Press, written in 1936. Trotsky's thinking is well surveyed in Baruch Knei-Paz (1978) *The Social and Political Thought of Leon Trotsky*, Oxford, Oxford University Press.

15. *The Revolution Betrayed*, pp. 112—13.

16. Paul Bellis (1979) *Marxism and the USSR*, London, Macmillan, p. 234 — a useful critical exploration. Post-war disagreements (more involved than fruitful) among Trotsky's followers on the nature of Communist states are overviewed by Bruno Bongiovanni (1982) 'The dissolution of Trotskyism', *Telos*, No. 52, Summer.

17. See, for example, E. Mandel (1979) *On Bureaucracy: A Marxist Analysis*, London, The Other Press.

18. An interesting account, relating back to earlier arguments, is in Moshe Lewin (1974) *Political Undercurrents in Soviet Economic Debates*, Princeton, Princeton University Press. See also Michael Ellman (1969) *Economic Reform in the Soviet Union*, London, PEP.

19. Radovan Richta, *et al* (1969) *Civilisation at the Crossroads*, White Plains, New York, IASP.

20. Marx-Engels (1968) *Selected Works*, London, Lawrence and Wishart, Vol. I.

21. Recent variants, also recognizing the elimination of *private* capital as permanent, have seen Lenin as the architect of 'a particular type of capitalist revolution', the only type of which a backward country such as Russia was capable; see, for example, Charles Bettelheim (1982) *Luttes de Classes en URSS*, Paris, Maspero, Vol. 3 and (1982) *Le Monde Dimanche*, 3 Octobre.

22. Bakunin was an early example; for others see Adam Westoby (1981) 'Education, inequality and the question of a Communist "new class"', in Roger Dale *et al.* (eds) *Education and the State*, Vol. I, Brighton, Falmer Press.

23. (1979) *The Future of Intellectuals and the Rise of the New Class*, London, Macmillan.

24. (1978) *The Alternative in Eastern Europe*, London, New Left Books.

25. A recent essay of theoretical economics, John Roemer's (1982) *A*

Theory of Exploitation and Class, Cambridge, Massachusetts, Harvard University Press, distinguishes two forms of exploitation in socialism, due to greater skill and privileged office respectively.

26. 'Parliament and government in a reconstructed Germany', in Weber (1968) *Economy and Society,* New York, Bedminster, Vol. III.

27. Leonard Schapiro (1969) 'The concept of totalitarianism', *Survey,* No. 73, Autumn.

28. More a term than a theory, 'totalitarianism' has long had a momentum of its own in ordinary parlance, outside the voluminous academic literature. Classic post-war statements are Hannah Arendt (1951) *The Origins of Totalitarianism,* New York, Harcourt Brace, and Carl Freidrich and Zbigniew Brzezinski (1957) *Totalitarian Dictatorship and Autocracy,* Cambridge, Massachusetts, Harvard University Press.

29. An early and influential criticism of state economic monopoly is Ludwig von Mises' (1920) 'Economic calculation in a socialist commonwealth' (originally published in German) in F. A. Hayek (ed.) (1935) *Collectivist Economic Planning,* London, George Routledge.

30. Zinoviev's views are set out (1981) in *Communisme comme realité,* Paris, Julliard, and in his satirical novel (1979) *Yawning Heights,* Harmondsworth, Penguin. An interpretative summary is Philip Hanson (1982) 'Alexander Zinoviev: totalitarianism from below', *Survey,* Vol. 26 No. 1, Winter.

31. Statement translated (1930) in *Luttes de Classes,* Paris, September— December.

32. (1939) *La Bureaucratisation du Monde,* Paris, Hachette.

33. Max Shachtman, co-dissident with Burnham among Trotskyist intellectuals in the 1930s, further developed the Marxist 'bureaucratic collectivist' criticism of the Soviet Union; see his essays in (1962) *The Bureaucratic Revolution,* New York, Donald Press. Among later variants Antonio Carlo (1974) in 'The socio-economic nature of the USSR', *Telos,* No. 21, Fall, sees it as a phase in the regression of the Soviet Union to capitalism, while Moshe Machover and John Fantham (1979) *The Century of the Unexpected*, Liverpool, Big Flame, view 'state collectivism' as specific to underdeveloped societies.

34. Writings on 'convergence' are reviewed in Alfred G. Meyer (1970) 'Theories of convergence', in Chalmers Johnson (ed.) *Change in Communist Systems,* Stanford, Stanford University Press.

35. See, for example (1960) *Structure and Process in Modern Societies,* Glencoe, Illinois, Free Press.

36. (1968) *One Dimensional Man,* London, Sphere Books.

37. (1957) New Haven, Yale University Press; revised edition (1981) New York, Vintage Books; his was an important influence on Bahro's view, mentioned above.

38. The adventures of Marx's 'asiatic mode of production' within Marxism are recounted in Marian Sawer (1977) *Marxism and the Question of the Asiatic Mode of Production,* The Hague, Martinus Nijhoff.

39.   A recent example is Robert Conquest's (1980) *We and They,* London, Temple Smith. The conception of the Soviet regime as a specific outcome of the Russian state's 'patrimonial' relation to society is set out in Richard Pipes' (1977) *Russia under the Old Regime,* Harmondsworth, Penguin.

40.   See Marshall S. Shatz (1968) 'J. W. Machajski and "Makhaevshchina", 1866—1926', PhD thesis, Columbia University; extracts from Machajski's main work, *The Intellectual Worker* (1898—1905) are in Alexander Skirda (ed.) (1979) *Le socialisme des intellectuels,* Paris, Le Seuil.

41.   Milovan Djilas (1968) *The New Class,* (2nd edn) London, Allen & Unwin.

42.   Ivan Szeleny, and George Konrad (1979) *The Intellectuals on the Road to Class Power,* Brighton, Harvester.

43.   A selection is in B. Bruce-Biggs (ed.) (1979) *The New Class?,* New Brunswick, New Jersey, Transaction Books.

44.   See, for example, Raymond Aron (1957) *The Opium of the Intellectuals,* London, Secker and Warburg, and Lewis Feuer (1975) *Ideology and the Ideologists,* Oxford, Basil Blackwell.

45.   (1981) *Devant la Guerre,* Paris, Fayard. Castoriadis' earlier views are in (1973) *La Société bureaucratique,* Paris, Union Générale d'Editions.

46.   Charles Levinson (1980) *Vodka-Cola,* Horsham, Biblios. The central idea is that Western capital, through loans and co-ownership of plants, shares in the exploitation of Communist states' more disciplined labour force, realizing profits through exports to the West.

Part 3
Citizenship, Society and the State

Introduction

STUART HALL

The main theme of Part 3 is the relation between 'state' and 'civil society'. The first three chapters deal with 'representative' aspects of the state. They address the thorny question of the relationship between *representative democracy* and *capitalism*. The paradox is posed most sharply by Göran Therborn in Chapter 3.2, as indicated by his title: 'The rule of capital and the rise of democracy'. What Therborn points out is that capitalism as an economic system implies a society in which the imperatives of capital accumulation are dominant. Wealth accumulates to a tiny capitalist class which naturally plays a leading role in society. This is what he means by 'The rule of capital'. The 'Rise of democracy', on the other hand, implies a form of state in which electoral power has been equally distributed on the democratic principle of 'one person, one vote' and where the basis of representation is not wealth and influence, but universal suffrage and the 'sovereign will of the people'. Can these two principles coexist? Are they compatible or will they always conflict? And if they conflict, which will win?

Chapter 3.1 offers an optimistic answer to those questions. T. H. Marshall's 'Citizenship and social class' is *the* classic treatment of the relation between capitalism and democracy from a *reformist* perspective. Basically, Marshall argues, reform can modify the worst aspects of economic inequality and make the system more equal and just, without overthrowing it altogether. His principal evidence for this is the history of the modern welfare state. Marshall sees a long, uneven, but persistent trend towards the expansion of the rights of 'citizenship'. He traces this in terms of the expansion of civil, political and social rights to the popular masses, culminating in the great redistributive achievements of the post-war welfare state. The latter, he acknowledges, does not weaken the basic drive of market capitalism towards the creation of inequality. But, he argues, politics and economics *are* to some degree separate in the liberal democratic state. This enables movements of reform to use the state to create greater equality for the vast majority who do not do so well out of the free market; and to provide some support — and thus some stake in the system — for those who would otherwise rapidly fall into the trap of poverty and insecurity. In this way, he suggests, the dynamic of class inequalities stemming from the capitalist market organization of society can be 'moderated' to some degree. The worst excesses of class inequality can be successfully 'abated' through the expansion of democratic social rights.

Therborn, in Chapter 3.2, explores the apparent contradiction between the dynamic of capitalism and the drive towards democratization from a different orientation. This contradiction, and how to resolve it, poses a problem for both Marxist and non-Marxist types of explanation. Non-Marxists have to explain how it comes about that power can be said to be 'democratized', when the capitalist economy tends to concentrate wealth and power in a few hands and when society must therefore be dominated by the strategic interests of a minority capitalist class. They also need to explain why, in the nineteenth century, when the popular struggles for the extension of the franchise first began, it was argued by many capitalists that capitalism and universal democracy were mutually antagonistic (a position advanced at that time even by liberals committed to some widening of the franchise, like John Stuart Mill); whereas today defenders and apologists for capitalism, like Hayek or Friedman, are likely to insist that it is *only* under the conditions of the free play of market forces that political freedom and democracy can be ensured.

Marxists, on the other hand, are also confronted by a paradox. How does a small, minority capitalist class maintain its dominant position in society if power has been genuinely 'democratized'? If, as is claimed, it is 'the people' who exercise popular sovereignty in the state, why do the masses still appear to consent to be 'ruled' by capital and its 'representatives' — the bourgeoisie? These fundamental questions penetrate deep into the heart of modern liberal democracy.

Therborn's approach is really to explore the great diversity of actual historical circumstances through which the liberal democratic state and universal suffrage have come into existence within capitalist societies. In its early phases, bourgeois society established market freedoms — but it strongly resisted the freedom for every citizen to vote, or full-scale democracy. So the two do not logically or historically entail one another. Universal suffrage was never achieved except through various forms of popular struggle.

However, these rarely took the form of open confrontations with the bourgeoisie. More often they occurred when the nation-state was in the process of formation; or when the nation was being mobilized to deal with war or an external threat; or as a consequence of the construction of alliances between the working class and other class strata, like the peasantry; or where advantage could be taken of fissures within the ruling bloc itself. However, though democracy had to be forced — or as the leading political scientist, C. M. Macpherson has put it, 'grafted' — on to liberal capitalism, Therborn insists that 'bourgeois representative democracy' is *not* a sham. There are real tendencies within capitalist development which favour the emergence of liberal—democratic representative institutions, even if at the time of their appearance, they were bitterly resisted by the bourgeoisie and only conceded (as in the successive reforms of male and female suffrage in Britain) after prolonged struggle, and at the eleventh hour.

The main thrust of Therborn's argument is therefore against any schematic approach to the question of the relation of capitalism and democracy. Bob Jessop's chapter, 'Capitalism and democracy: the best possible political shell?' takes this approach several steps further. Jessop's starting point is Lenin's surprising observation, in *Imperialism*, that bourgeois democracy is not a brake or a limitation on capitalism, but rather provides it with its 'best shell' (i.e. the most favourable political institution for capitalism's further development). Jessop criticizes the 'functionalism' which he believes to be implicit in Lenin's observation. Capitalism does not, in his view, logically and inevitably get the form of the state which best 'fits' it and most effectively meets its functional needs. Indeed, Jessop is dubious as to whether there is ever *any* such necessary correspondence between the political forms of the state and the 'needs of capital'. The form of the state, he suggests, cannot be logically derived from an analysis of the 'laws and tendencies' of the economy alone. Rather, it must be seen as the result of the whole economic, political and ideological configuration of society. The state is related to the social formation as a whole, not simply to the mode of production. In general, Jessop is rejecting here both a type of 'functionalism' common to many Marxists and non-Marxists alike, and a 'logic of capital' approach which has gained great currency among some Marxists in recent years.

Jessop is sympathetic to the proposition that there is a tendency for some types of state to be more commonly associated with some stages of capitalist economic development: for example, the *laissez-faire* state with liberal market capitalism; the interventionist state with advanced corporate capitalism. But he insists, with Therborn, that the actual historical variations and combinations have been remarkably wide. For Jessop, then, representative democracy is not *necessarily* 'the best political shell' as Lenin argued. It does, however, allow the subordinate classes to be represented within the state, and thus gives them a voice and a stake in society — a fact which helps to incorporate popular democratic forces and strengthens the popular legitimacy of the state without changing the fundamental structures of society. On the other hand, Jessop points out that even democratic representation cannot always guarantee capitalism stability or growth, and that in fact it has often been combined with instabilities and 'crises' of the system.

Jessop's overall conclusion is that Lenin's dictum is tenable *only* in those circumstances where bourgeois domination has already been secured and can be effectively maintained. This makes the capitalism/democracy relationship much more *conditional* — though some may feel that the argument still concludes with a tautology: democracy works well for the bourgeoisie provided the bourgeoisie can maintain its hegemony over it!

The final two chapters in Part 3 deal more with 'interventionist' themes. (The principal readings on state intervention in the economy are to be found in Part 4.) Eli Zaretsky's chapter on 'The place of the family in the origins of the welfare state' offers a review of the changing relations between the state and the family in American history. The family is, of course, one of the principal sites where the shifting boundaries between the 'public' and the 'private' can be traced, and where the expansion of the state or its penetration into institutions often regarded as quintessentially 'domestic' can be most vividly observed. Zaretsky outlines the shifts and changes in the context of the origins and development of what he calls the American 'welfare state'. He shows how, in the 'liberal' era, family forms and functions were assimilated to the prevailing doctrines of self-sufficiency and economic individualism. In the progressive era, the formative period for American conceptions of welfare, social and 'corporate' approaches to welfare support were added to the core 'economic individualist' conceptions of family support and care, without fundamentally displacing them. The feminism of the period, he argues, played a paradoxical role, in reconciling the demands for greater individual opportunities for women with a protection and defence of the family. Zaretsky's major general thesis is that the overwhelming thrust of American welfare state policy has been, not to invade the space and functions of the family and displace them, but rather to preserve it as an economically independent private unit.

Finally we include two extracts from a recent collection of

essays and papers by the French philosopher and historian, Michel Foucault. Foucault advances a set of novel and contentious propositions about the nature of power and the modalities of the state. He challenges the traditional language of political philosophy, which has always put the question of the sovereignty of the state above that of its role as the agent of domination. But, more controversially, he questions many of the traditional conceptions of power. Power, he argues, is not a thing which some groups (e.g. the bourgeoisie) can exclusively possess and impress on others. Power circulates throughout society. Everyone is caught somewhere or other in its circuits. It is sustained as much in the small but significant interplay of power as in the grand strategies of the state. We should therefore study it at this 'micro' level: what he calls 'the micro mechanisms of power'. It follows also that in Foucault's view, power is dispersed throughout the body politic, and is not simply to be found centralized and monopolized in the state, and radiating outwards from that centre. Finally, he attempts to shift the methodology of studying power away from the aim, intention or purposes for which the state might exercise power, to the study of *how it works*: its techniques and procedures, the mechanisms and apparatuses of 'regulation' involved. These are key terms for Foucault, and they challenge the normal conceptions of the function of state intervention. In his view, the function of the exercise of power by the state is neither to 'represent' nor to 'secure an interest' nor to 'repress and coerce', but rather to *regulate* and *discipline* civil society.

Foucault's terminology — difficult as it is, at times — not only opens to question traditional modes of analysis of the state: it also provides a radical challenge to conventional notions of the distinctions between 'state' and 'society', and therefore questions what the value is of framing our analysis of the state in terms of how it 'intervenes in' society.

3.1

Citizenship and Social Class

T. H. MARSHALL

The sociological hypothesis latent in Alfred Marshall's essay[1] postulates that there is a kind of basic human equality associated with the concept of full membership of a community — or, as I should say, of citizenship — which is not inconsistent with the inequalities which distinguish the various economic levels in the society. In other words, the inequality of the social class system may be acceptable provided the equality of citizenship is recognized. [. . .]

He recognizes only one definite right, the right of children to be educated, and in this case alone does he approve the use of compulsory powers by the state to achieve his object. He could hardly go further without imperilling his own criterion for distinguishing his system from socialism in any form — the preservation of the freedom of the competitive market. [. . .] His sociological hypothesis lies as near to the heart of our problem today as it did three-quarters of a century ago — in fact nearer. The basic human equality of membership [. . .] has been enriched with new substance and invested with a formidable array of rights. It has developed far beyond what he foresaw, or would have wished. It has been clearly identified with the status of citizenship. [. . .]

Is it still true that basic equality, when enriched in substance and embodied in the formal rights of citizenship, is consistent with the inequalities of social class? I shall suggest that our society today assumes that the two are still compatible; so much so that citizenship has itself become, in certain respects, the architect of

Source: From *Citizenship and social class and other essays* (1950) Cambridge, Cambridge University Press. Originally delivered in Cambridge as the Marshall Lecture for 1949.

legitimate social inequality. Is it still true that the basic equality can be created and preserved without invading the freedom of the competitive market? Obviously it is not true. Our modern system is frankly a socialist system[2] not one whose authors are, as Marshall was, eager to distinguish it from socialism. But it is equally obvious that the market still functions — within limits. Here is another possible conflict of principles which demands examination. And thirdly, what is the effect of the marked shift of emphasis from duties to rights? Is this an inevitable feature of modern citizenship — inevitable and irreversible? [. . .]

I shall ask whether there appear to be limits beyond which the modern drive towards social equality cannot, or is unlikely to pass, and I shall be thinking, not of the economic cost (I leave that vital question to the economists), but of the limits inherent in the principles that inspire the drive. But the modern drive towards social equality is, I believe, the latest phase of an evolution of citizenship which has been in continuous progress for some 250 years. [. . .]

The development of citizenship to the end of the nineteenth century

[. . .] I shall be running true to type as a sociologist if I begin by saying that I propose to divide citizenship into three parts. But the analysis is, in this case, dictated by history even more clearly than by logic. I shall call these three parts, or elements, civil, political and social. The civil element is composed of the rights necessary for individual freedom — liberty of the person, freedom of speech, thought and faith, the right to own property and to conclude valid contracts, and the right to justice. The last is of a different order from the others, because it is the right to defend and assert all one's rights on terms of equality with others and by due process of law. This shows us that the institutions most directly associated with civil rights are the courts of justice. By the political element I mean the right to participate in the exercise of political power, as a member of a body invested with political authority or as an elector of the members of such a body. The corresponding institutions are Parliament and councils of local government. By the social element I mean the whole range from the right to a modicum of economic welfare and security to the right to share to the full in the social heritage and to live the life of a civilized being according to the standards prevailing in the society. The institutions most closely

connected with it are the educational system and the social services.
[...]

By 1832 when political rights made their first infantile attempt to walk, civil rights had come to man's estate and bore, in most essentials, the appearance that they have today.[3] 'The specific work of the earlier Hanoverian epoch', writes Trevelyan, 'was the establishment of the rule of law; and that law, with all its grave faults, was at least a law of freedom. On that solid foundation all our subsequent reforms were built'. This eighteenth-century achievement, interrupted by the French Revolution and completed after it, was in large measure the work of the courts, both in their daily practice and also in a series of famous cases in some of which they were fighting against Parliament in defence of individual liberty. The most celebrated actor in this drama was, I suppose, John Wilkes, and, although we may deplore the absence in him of those noble and saintly qualities which we should like to find in our national heroes, we cannot complain if the cause of liberty is sometimes championed by a libertine.

In the economic field the basic civil right is the right to work, that is to say the right to follow the occupation of one's choice in the place of one's choice, subject only to legitimate demands for preliminary technical training. This right had been denied by both statute and custom; on the one hand by the Elizabethan Statute of Artificers, which confined certain occupations to certain social classes, and on the other by local regulations reserving employment in a town to its own members and by the use of apprenticeship as an instrument of exclusion rather than of recruitment. The recognition of the right involved the formal acceptance of a fundamental change of attitude. The old assumption that local and group monopolies were in the public interest, because 'trade and traffic cannot be maintained or increased without order and government', was replaced by the new assumption that such restrictions were an offence against the liberty of the subject and a menace to the prosperity of the nation. [...]

By the beginning of the nineteenth century this principle of individual economic freedom was accepted as axiomatic. You are probably familiar with the passage quoted by the Webbs from the report of the Select Committee of 1811, which states that:

> no interference of the legislature with the freedom of trade, or with the perfect liberty of every individual to dispose of his time and of his labour in the way and on the terms which he may judge most conducive to his own interest, can take place

without violating general principles of the first importance to the prosperity and happiness of the community.[4] [. . .]

The story of civil rights in their formative period is one of the gradual addition of new rights to a status that already existed and was held to appertain to all adult members of the community — or perhaps one should say to all male members, since the status of women, or at least of married women, was in some important respects peculiar. This democratic, or universal, character of the status arose naturally from the fact that it was essentially the status of freedom, and in seventeenth-century England all men were free. Servile status, or villeinage by blood, had lingered on as a patent anachronism in the days of Elizabeth, but vanished soon afterwards. This change from servile to free labour has been described by Professor Tawney as 'a high landmark in the development both of economic and political society', and as 'the final triumph of the common law' in regions from which it had been excluded for four centuries. Henceforth the English peasant 'is a member of a society in which there is, nominally at least, one law for all men'.[5] The liberty which his predecessors had won by fleeing into the free towns had become his by right. In the towns the terms 'freedom' and 'citizenship' were interchangeable. When freedom became universal, citizenship grew from a local into a national institution.

The story of political rights is different both in time and in character. The formative period began, as I have said, in the early nineteenth century, when the civil rights attached to the status of freedom had already acquired sufficient substance to justify us in speaking of a general status of citizenship. And, when it began, it consisted, not in the creation of new rights to enrich a status already enjoyed by all, but in the granting of old rights to new sections of the population. [. . .]

It is clear that, if we maintain that in the nineteenth century citizenship in the form of civil rights was universal, the political franchise was not one of the rights of citizenship. It was the privilege of a limited economic class, whose limits were extended by each successive Reform Act. [. . .]

It was, as we shall see, appropriate that nineteenth-century capitalist society should treat political rights as a secondary product of civil rights. It was equally appropriate that the twentieth century should abandon this position and attach political rights directly and independently to citizenship as such. This vital change of principle was put into effect when the Act of 1918, by adopting manhood suffrage, shifted the basis of political rights from economic substance to personal status. I say 'manhood' deliberately in order to emphasize the great significance of this reform quite apart from the second, and no less important, reform introduced at the same time — namely the enfranchisement of women. [. . .]

The original source of social rights was membership of local communities and functional associations. This source was supplemented and progressively replaced by a Poor Law and a system of wage regulation which were nationally conceived and locally administered. [. . .]

As the pattern of the old order dissolved under the blows of a competitive economy, and the plan disintegrated, the Poor Law was left high and dry as an isolated survival from which the idea of social rights was gradually drained away. But at the very end of the eighteenth century there occurred a final struggle between the old and the new, between the planned (or patterned) society and the competitive economy. And in this battle citizenship was divided against itself; social rights sided with the old and civil with the new. [. . .]

In this brief episode of our history we see the Poor Law as the aggressive champion of the social rights of citizenship. In the succeeding phase we find the attacker driven back far behind his original position. By the Act of 1834 the Poor Law renounced all claim to trespass on the territory of the wages system, or to interfere with the forces of the free market. It offered relief only to those who, through age or sickness, were incapable of continuing the battle, and to those other weaklings who gave up the struggle, admitted defeat, and cried for mercy. The tentative move towards the concept of social security was reversed. But more than that, the minimal social rights that remained were detached from the status of citizenship. The Poor Law treated the claims of the poor, not as an integral part of the rights of the citizen, but as an alternative to them — as claims which could be met only if the claimants ceased to be citizens in any true sense of the word. For paupers forfeited in practice the civil right of personal liberty, by internment in the workhouse, and they forfeited by law any political rights they might possess. This disability of defranchisement remained in being until 1918, and the significance of its final removal has, perhaps, not been fully appreciated. The stigma which clung to poor relief expressed the deep feelings of a people who understood that those who accepted relief must cross the road that separated the community of citizens from the outcast company of the destitute.

The Poor Law is not an isolated example of this divorce of social rights from the status of citizenship. The early Factory Acts show the same tendency. Although in fact they led to an improvement of working conditions and a reduction of working hours to the benefit of all employed in the industries to which they applied, they meticulously refrained from giving this protection directly to the adult male — the citizen *par excellence*. And they did so out of respect for his status as a citizen, on the grounds that enforced protective measures curtailed the civil right to conclude a free contract of employment. Protection was confined to women and children, and champions of women's rights were quick to detect the implied insult. Women were protected because they were not citizens. If they wished to enjoy full and responsible citizenship, they must forgo protection. By the end of the nineteenth century such arguments had become obsolete, and the factory code had become one of the pillars in the edifice of social rights. [. . .]

By the end of the nineteenth century, elementary education was not only free, it was compulsory. This signal departure from *laissez faire* could, of course, be justified on the grounds that free choice is a right only for mature minds, that children are naturally subject to discipline, and that parents cannot be trusted to do what is in the best interests of their children. But the principle goes deeper than that. We have here a personal right combined with a public duty to exercise the right. Is the public duty imposed merely for the benefit of the individual — because children cannot fully appreciate their own interests and parents may be unfit to enlighten them? I hardly think that this can be an adequate explanation. It was increasingly recognized, as the nineteenth century wore on, that political democracy needed an educated electorate, and that scientific manufacture needed educated workers and technicians. The duty to improve and civilize oneself is therefore a social duty, and not merely a personal one, because the social health of a society depends upon the civilization of its members. And a community that enforces this duty has begun to realize that its culture is an organic unity and its civilization a national heritage. It follows that the growth of public elementary education during the nineteenth century was the first decisive step on the road to the re-establishment of the social rights of citizenship in the twentieth. [. . .]

The impact of citizenship on social class

Citizenship is a status bestowed on those who are full members of a community. All who possess the status are equal with respect to the rights and duties with which the status is endowed. There is no universal principle that determines what those rights and duties shall be, but societies in which citizenship is a developing institution create an image of an ideal citizenship against which achievement can be measured and towards which aspiration can be directed. The urge forward along the path thus plotted is an urge towards a fuller measure of equality, an enrichment of the stuff of which the status is made and an increase in the number of those on whom the status is bestowed. Social class, on the other hand, is a system of inequality. And it too, like citizenship, can be based on a set of ideals, beliefs and values. It is therefore reasonable to expect that the impact of citizenship on social class should take the form of a conflict between opposing principles. If I am right in my contention that citizenship has been a developing institution in England at least since the latter part of the seventeenth century, then it is clear that its growth coincides with the rise of capitalism, which is a system, not of equality, but of inequality. Here is something that needs explaining. How is it that these two opposing principles could grow and flourish side by side in the same soil? What made it possible for them to be reconciled with one another and to become, for a time at least, allies instead of antagonists? The question is a pertinent one, for it is clear that, in the twentieth century, citizenship and the capitalist class system have been at war. [. . .]

It is true that class still functions. Social inequality is regarded as necessary and purposeful. It provides the incentive to effort and designs the distribution of power. But there is no overall pattern of inequality, in which an appropriate value is attached, *a priori*, to each social level. Inequality therefore, though necessary, may become excessive. As Patrick Colquhoun said, in a much-quoted passage: 'Without a large proportion of poverty there could be no riches, since riches are the offspring of labour, while labour can result only from a state of poverty . . . Poverty therefore is a most necessary and indispensable ingredient in society, without which nations and communities could not exist in a state of civilization.[6] [. . .]

The more you look on wealth as conclusive proof of merit, the more you incline to regard poverty as evidence of failure — but the penalty for failure may seem to be greater than the offence warrants. In such circumstances it is natural that the more unpleasant features of inequality should be treated, rather irres- ponsibly, as a nuisance, like the black smoke that used to pour unchecked from our factory chimneys. And so in time, as the social conscience stirs to life, class-abatement, like smoke-abate- ment, becomes a desirable aim to be pursued as far as is compatible with the continued efficiency of the social machine.

But class-abatement in this form was not an attack on the class system. On the contrary it aimed, often quite consciously, at making the class system less vulnerable to attack by alleviating its less defensible consequences. It raised the floor-level in the basement of the social edifice, and perhaps made it rather more hygienic than it was before. But it remained a basement, and the upper stories of the building were unaffected. [. . .]

There developed, in the latter part of the nineteenth century, a growing interest in equality as a principle of social justice and an appreciation of the fact that the formal recognition of an equal capacity for rights was not enough. In theory even the complete removal of all the barriers that separated civil rights from their remedies would not have interfered with the principles or the class structure of the capitalist system. It would, in fact, have created a situation which many supporters of the competitive market economy falsely assumed to be already in existence. But in practice the attitude of mind which inspired the efforts to remove these barriers grew out of a conception of equality which overstepped these narrow limits, the conception of equal social worth, not merely of equal natural rights. Thus although citizenship, even by the end of the nineteenth century, had done little to reduce social inequality, it had helped to guide progress into the path which led directly to the egalitarian policies of the twentieth century. [. . .]

This growing national consciousness, this awakening public opinion, and these first stirrings of a sense of community membership and common heritage did not have any material effect on class structure and social inequality for the simple and obvious reason that, even at the end of the nineteenth century, the mass of the working people did not wield effective political power. By that time the franchise was fairly wide, but those who had recently received the vote had not yet learned how to use it. The political rights of citizenship, unlike the civil rights, were full of potential danger to the capitalist system, although those who were cautiously extending them down the social scale probably did not realize quite how great the danger was. They could hardly be expected to foresee what vast changes could be brought about by the peaceful use of political power, without a violent and bloody revolution. The 'planned society' and the welfare state had not yet risen over the horizon or come within the view of the practical politician. The foundations of the market economy and the contractual system seemed strong enough to stand against any probable assault. In fact, there were some grounds for expecting that the working classes, as they became educated, would accept the basic principles of the system and be content to rely for their protection and progress on the civil rights of citizenship, which contained no obvious menace to competitive capitalism. Such a view was encouraged by the fact that one of the main achievements of political power in the later nineteenth century was the recognition of the right of collective bargaining. This meant that social progress was being sought by strengthening civil rights, not by creating social rights; through the use of contract in the open market, not through a minimum wage and social security.

But this interpretation underrates the significance of this extension of civil rights in the economic sphere. For civil rights were in origin intensely individual, and that is why they harmonized with the individualistic phase of capitalism. By the device of incorporation groups were enabled to act legally as individuals. This important development did not go unchallenged, and limited liability was widely denounced as an infringement of individual responsibility. But the position of trade unions was even more anomalous, because they did not seek or obtain incorporation. They can, therefore, exercise vital civil rights collectively on behalf of their members without formal collective responsibility, while the individual responsibility of the workers in relation to contract is largely unenforceable. These civil rights became, for the workers, an instrument for raising their social and economic status, that is to say, for establishing the claim that they, as citizens, were entitled to certain social rights. But the normal method of establishing social rights is by the exercise of political power, for social rights imply an absolute right to a certain standard of civilization which is conditional only on the discharge of the general duties of citizenship. Their content does not depend on the economic value of the individual claimant. There is therefore a significant difference between a genuine collective bargain through which economic forces in a free market seek to achieve equilibrium and the use of collective civil rights to assert basic claims to the elements of social justice. Thus the acceptance of collective bargaining was not simply a natural extension of civil rights; it represented the transfer of an important process from the political to the civil sphere of citizenship. But 'transfer' is, perhaps, a misleading term, for at the time when this happened the workers either did not possess, or had not yet learned to use, the political right of the franchise. Since then they have obtained and made full use of that right. Trade unionism has, therefore, created a secondary system of industrial citizenship parallel with and supplementary to the system of political citizenship. [. . .]

A new period opened at the end of the nineteenth century,

conveniently marked by Booth's survey of Life and Labour of the People in London and the Royal Commission on the Aged Poor. It saw the first big advance in social rights, and this involved significant changes in the egalitarian principle as expressed in citizenship. But there were other forces at work as well. A rise of money incomes unevenly distributed over the social classes altered the economic distance which separated these classes from one another, diminishing the gap between skilled and unskilled labour and between skilled labour and non-manual workers, while the steady increase in small savings blurred the class distinction between the capitalist and the propertyless proletarian. Secondly, a system of direct taxation, ever more steeply graduated, compressed the whole scale of disposable incomes. Thirdly, mass production for the home market and a growing interest on the part of industry in the needs and tastes of the common people enabled the less well-to-do to enjoy a material civilization which differed less markedly in quality from that of the rich than it had ever done before. All this profoundly altered the setting in which the progress of citizenship took place. Social integration spread from the sphere of sentiment and patriotism into that of material enjoyment. The components of a civilized and cultured life, formerly the monopoly of the few, were brought progressively within reach of the many, who were encouraged thereby to stretch out their hands towards those that still eluded their grasp. The diminution of inequality strengthened the demand for its abolition, at least with regard to the essentials of social welfare.

These aspirations have in part been met by incorporating social rights in the status of citizenship and thus creating a universal right to real income which is not proportionate to the market value of the claimant. Class-abatement is still the aim of social rights, but it has acquired a new meaning. It is no longer merely an attempt to abate the obvious nuisance of destitution in the lowest ranks of society. It has assumed the guise of action modifying the whole pattern of social inequality. It is no longer content to raise the floor-level in the basement of the social edifice, leaving the superstructure as it was. It has begun to remodel the whole building, and it might even end by converting a skyscraper into a bungalow. It is therefore important to consider whether any such ultimate aim is implicit in the nature of this development, or whether, as I put it at the outset, there are natural limits to the contemporary drive towards greater social and economic equality. [. . .]

The degree of equalization achieved [by the modern system of welfare benefits] depends on four things: whether the benefit is offered to all or to a limited class; whether it takes the form of money payment or service rendered; whether the minimum is high or low; and how the money to pay for the benefit is raised. Cash benefits subject to income limit and means test had a simple and obvious equalizing effect. They achieved class-abatement in the early and limited sense of the term. The aim was to ensure that all citizens should attain at least to the prescribed minimum, either by their own resources or with assistance if they could not do it without. The benefit was given only to those who needed it, and thus inequalities at the bottom of the scale were ironed out. The system operated in its simplest and most unadulterated form in the case of the Poor Law and old age pensions. But economic equalization might be accompanied by psychological class discrimination. The stigma which attached to the Poor Law made 'pauper' a derogatory term defining a class. 'Old age pensioner' may have had a little of the same flavour, but without the taint of shame. [. . .]

The extension of the social services is not primarily a means of equalizing incomes. In some cases it may, in others it may not. The question is relatively unimportant; it belongs to a different department of social policy. What matters is that there is a general enrichment of the concrete substance of civilized life, a general reduction of risk and insecurity, an equalization between the more and the less fortunate at all levels — between the healthy and the sick, the employed and the unemployed, the old and the active, the bachelor and the father of a large family. Equalization is not so much between classes as between individuals within a population which is now treated for this purpose as though it were one class. Equality of status is more important than equality of income. [. . .]

I said earlier that in the twentieth century citizenship and the capitalist class system have been at war. Perhaps the phrase is rather too strong, but it is quite clear that the former has imposed modifications on the latter. But we should not be justified in assuming that, although status is a principle that conflicts with contract, the stratified status system which is creeping into citizenship is an alien element in the economic world outside. Social rights in their modern form imply an invasion of contract by status, the subordination of market price to social justice, the replacement of the free bargain by the declaration of rights. But are these principles quite foreign to the practice of the market today, or are they there already, entrenched within the contract system itself? I think it is clear that they are. [. . .]

Conclusions

I have tried to show how citizenship, and other forces outside it, have been altering the pattern of social inequality. [. . .] We have to look, here, for the combined effects of three factors. First, the compression, at both ends, of the scale of income distribution. Second, the great extension of the area of common culture and common experience. And third, the enrichment of the universal status of citizenship, combined with the recognition and stabilization of certain status differences chiefly through the linked systems of education and occupation. [. . .]

I asked, at the beginning, whether there was any limit to the present drive towards social equality inherent in the principles governing the movement. My answer is that the preservation of economic inequalities has been made more difficult by the enrichment of the status of citizenship. There is less room for them, and there is more and more likelihood of their being challenged. But we are certainly proceeding at present on the assumption that the hypothesis is valid. And this assumption provides the answer to the second question. We are not aiming at absolute equality. There are limits inherent in the egalitarian movement. But the movement is a double one. It operates partly through citizenship and partly through the economic system. In both cases the aim is to remove inequalities which cannot be regarded as legitimate, but the standard of legitimacy is different. In the former it is the standard of social justice, in the latter it is social justice combined with economic necessity. It is possible, therefore, that the inequalities permitted by the two halves of the movement will not coincide. Class distinctions may survive which have no appropriate economic function, and economic differences which do not correspond with accepted class distinctions. [. . .]

Notes

1. Alfred Marshall, a distinguished Professor of Economics at Cambridge, whose lecture on 'The future of the working classes' (1873) provided T. H. Marshall with his point of departure.
2. Marshall, writing in 1949, in the heyday of the welfare state, means by this 'social democratic'.
3. G. M. Trevelyan, *English Social History,* p. 351.

4. Sidney and Beatrice Webb (1920) *History of Trade Unionism,* p. 60.
5. R. H. Tawney (1916) *The Agrarian Problem in the Sixteenth Century,* pp. 43—4.
6. P. Colquhoun (1806) *A Treatise in Indigence,* pp. 7—8.

3.2
The Rule of Capital and the
Rise of Democracy

GÖRAN THERBORN

The relationship between advanced capitalism and democracy contains two paradoxes — one Marxist and one bourgeois. Any serious Marxist analysis has to confront the following question: How has it come about that, in the major and most advanced capitalist countries, a tiny class — the bourgeoisie — rules by means of democratic forms? The bitter experiences of Fascism and Stalinism, and the enduring legacy of the latter, have taught the firmest revolutionary opponents of capitalism that bourgeois democracy cannot be dismissed as a mere sham. Does contemporary reality then not vitiate Marxist class analysis? Present-day capitalist democracy is no less paradoxical from a bourgeois point of view. In the nineteenth and early twentieth centuries, as both political practice and constitutional debate clearly demonstrate, prevailing bourgeois opinion held that democracy and capitalism (or private property) were incompatible. Even such a broad-minded liberal as John Stuart Mill remained a considered opponent of democracy for this very reason. He advocated the introduction of plural votes for entrepreneurs, merchants and bankers, as well as their foremen-lieutenants and professional hangers-on, in order to forestall proletarian 'class legislation'. In modern times, however, since at least the outbreak of the Cold War, bourgeois ideologists have maintained that *only* capitalism is compatible with democracy. What has happened? Is this perhaps just a *post hoc* rationalization of a historical accident?

Source: From *New Left Review* (1977) No. 103, May/June.

Basic problems

Before going any further, we should make absolutely clear what we understand by 'democracy'. The term is here used to denote a form of state with all the following characteristics. It has (1) a representative government elected by (2) an electorate consisting of the entire adult population, (3) whose votes carry equal weight, and (4) who are allowed to vote for any opinion without intimidation by the state apparatus. Such a state is a bourgeois democracy in so far as the state apparatus has a bourgeois class composition and the state power operates in such a way as to maintain and promote capitalist relations of production and the class character of the state apparatus.

It is notoriously difficult to delimit precisely the democratic form of government, but the above definition seems adequate to locate the crucial variables: popular representation and free, universal and equal suffrage. It further includes, as necessary prerequisites, the important legal freedoms of speech, assembly, organization and the press. The definition is intentionally formal, since the problem here is not to expose the 'seamy side' of bourgeois democracy but to elucidate how a democratic form of government has arisen in a society where a tiny minority determine whether, where, how and for how much the majority of the population work, as well as how and where they live.

Democracy is one of the key words of contemporary ideological discourse, despite — or perhaps precisely because of — the fact that so little serious research has been devoted to it. It is hardly surprising that the classical Marxist writers produced almost nothing of substance on the question, for none of them had personal experience of a fully-fledged bourgeois democracy. Subsequently, the preponderant role of the Soviet Union and the acute threat of Fascism were not conducive to deeper study of the problem within the international labour movement. What is more remarkable is the lack of fundamental analysis following the Western Communist Parties' reappraisal of bourgeois democracy and the rise of a new Marxist intelligentsia in the capitalist countries since the mid-1960s. Discussion has instead centred mainly on the capitalist state in general, usually treated at a very high level of abstraction. [. . .]

However, these questions cannot be avoided by the labour movement in its current strategic discussion of the relationship between democracy and socialist revolution. In the developed capitalist countries, all major sections of the revolutionary labour movement have now openly acknowledged that bourgeois democracy cannot be dismissed as a mere sham. It is now seen as an important popular conquest, which lays the basis for further advance. This in turn poses a challenge for historical study and analytical research.

It is even more striking that the problematic relationship between democracy and the rule of capital has attracted so little attention from bourgeois social scientists, historians and constitutional theorists. Here one may speak of a real regression in analytical courage and perceptiveness. As is shown by the struggles for constitutional reform that broke out in all countries, the issue was very seriously and heatedly debated by bourgeois thinkers and politicians in the nineteenth and early twentieth centuries. It is tempting to regard the present lack of interest in the way in which the contradiction between democracy and minority privilege was eventually resolved as, at least in part, determined by repressed and inconsolable memories — memories of an unexpected escape, which is best forgotten lest it reawaken the old spectre: the working masses. [. . .]

The democratic principle of popular representation implies the existence of either a republic or a parliamentary monarchy. The predominant régime of nineteenth-century Europe — a constitutional monarchy in which the Cabinet had no clear-cut responsibility to Parliament — cannot then be held to fulfil the conditions of democracy . . . For representative government clearly implies popular sovereignty. In our sample of 17 countries, the process of attainment of representative government stretched over a period of two centuries: from the mid-eighteenth century, when a parliamentary cabinet was consolidated in Britain, to 1952, when US occupation of Japan was terminated and the 1947 democratic constitution took effect as the basis of a sovereign state.

The introduction of universal suffrage required the dismantling of a number of restrictions . . . Of a certain importance were limitations based on standards of literacy (as in Italy until the new electoral law of 1911, and in the southern states of the USA well into the twentieth century) or on membership of a particular sex (invariably the female), race (Blacks in the USA, Chinese in the USA and Canada), or (parts of) a given class (wage-labourers with a household of their own in Denmark and Britain) . . . The achievement of equal suffrage also involved the abolition of plural voting — which survived in Britain until 1948, although it was of little import after 1918 — and the elimination or emasculation of a privileged upper House. [. . .]

The establishment of democracy

Now that we have defined the criteria of bourgeois democracy, we should attempt to locate the period of establishment in the 17 countries. (Tables 3.2.1 and 3.2.2). [. . .]

TABLE 3.1.1 Year of Establishment of Democracy

Country	First attainment of democracy	Male democracy (if prior)	Reversal (excl. foreign occupation)	Beginning of present-day democracy
Australia	(1903)			
Austria	1918		1934	1955
Belgium	1948	1919		
Canada	(1920)		(1931)	(1945)
Denmark	1915			
Finland	(1919)		1930	1944
France	1946	1884		
Germany	1919		1935 (1956)	1949 (1968
Italy	1946	(1919)	[1922]	1946
Japan	1952			
Netherlands	1919	1917		
New Zealand	1907			
Norway	1915	1898		
Sweden	1918			
Switzerland	1971	c.1880	([1940])	([1944])
UK	1928	1918		
USA	c.1970			

Note: Brackets denote qualifications, square brackets a process of reversal or re-establishment of male democracy.

In the history of democratization, two features are striking by their absence. First, the fact that none of the great bourgeois revolutions actually established bourgeois democracy. It is not only of the early Dutch and English Revolutions that this is true: the democratic constitution produced by the French Revolution remained a dead letter from beginning to end of its brief existence. The July Revolution did not even manage to draft one, although it did stimulate the development of a male democratic movement in

TABLE 3.2.2 Timing of Female Enfranchisement

Before First World War	During or after First World War	In aftermath of Second World War	Later
Australia	Austria	Belgium	Switzerland
Finland	Canada	France	
New Zealand	Denmark	Italy	
Norway	Germany	Japan	
	Netherlands		
	Sweden		
	UK		
	USA		

Switzerland. The international popular upsurge of 1848 was rapidly stifled by feudal-dynastic reaction — and also by the bourgeoisie itself. For example, in 1850 the Second French Republic deprived 2.5 million adult males of the vote by the introduction of lengthy residence qualifications. Similarly, the Danish bourgeois National Liberals eagerly assisted in clipping the wings of the popular chamber in the 1860s. The American Republic was established by White propertied gentlemen, and the only Blacks enfranchised by the Civil War were male northerners. Unified Italy took over the extremely narrow franchise of the kingdom of Sardinia. And when, despite the misgivings of the bourgeois liberals, Bismarck introduced universal male suffrage in Reich elections, a regime of parliamentary democracy was neither the object nor the outcome of the measure.

The second striking absence in the history of bourgeois democracy is that of a steady, peaceful process accompanying the development of wealth, literacy and urbanization. On the eve of the First World War, only three peripheral capitalist states could have been characterized as democracies: Australia and New Zealand (where rampant racism was able to turn outwards rather than inwards) and Norway . . . The long-standing British parliamentary régime had still not enfranchised the whole male working class, and was only slowly beginning to relax after its repression of the first democratic mass movement in history. In the United States, the process of democratization had suffered two reverses: one in the North, directed against new illiterate immigrants, the other turned against the Blacks and poor White opposition of the South.
[. . .]

Contributory factors to democratization

National mobilization

National mobilization of the people for the purposes of war has been related to the development of democracy in two basic ways. On the one hand, measures of democratization have been introduced as a *means* towards the end of national mobilization; on the other, they have been produced as *effects* of the process of integration (military, economic and ideological) expressed in popular mobilization for the national effort. The two clearest examples of the former are Giolitti's franchise reform in Italy and the Canadian War Times Elections Act of 1917 — both part of political preparations for war. The second relationship is illustrated by the establishment of male democracy in Belgium, the Dutch reforms of 1917—19, the Danish Right's acceptance of democracy in 1915, the British Reform Act of 1918, and the introduction of female suffrage in the United States in 1919 (perhaps also in France and Belgium after the Second World War). In all these cases, a process of democratization already under way was speeded up and facilitated by a wartime *union sacrée*. [. . .]

In other cases as well, national mobilization has played an important role in extension of the suffrage. Bismarck, for example, wrote in his memoirs: 'The acceptance of general suffrage was a weapon in the struggle against Austria and the rest of the foreign powers, a weapon in the struggle for national unity'. But his intention was that only candidates for the propertied classes should be allowed to compete for the votes of the masses. [. . .]

The agrarian classes

Two internal factors seem to have been of the most immediate strategic importance: the independent strength of the agrarian petty and small bourgeois landowners, and divisions within the ruling-class (or power) bloc. This statement should at once be qualified by mentioning the enormous role of the labour movement. The Second International went down in ignominious disarray in 1914, but its contribution to the development of bourgeois democracy was certainly not insubstantial. Indeed, this may be said to have been its principal historical accomplishment. However, although the labour movement was the only consistent democratic force on the arena, it was nowhere strong enough to achieve bourgeois democracy on its own, without the aid of victorious foreign armies, domestic allies more powerful than itself, or splits in the ranks of the enemy.

It is hardly surprising that the tiny privileged minority constituted by the mercantile and industrial bourgeoisie and the feudal and capitalist landowners should have been almost invariably hostile to democracy — hence the exclusivist outcome of the bourgeois revolutions. By contrast, the urban *artisanat* and petty bourgeoisie generally tended in a democratic direction and provided the striking force of both the Jacobins and the 1848 revolutions. But, as these examples also show, they were too weak to hold out against feudal and bourgeois reaction. The peasantry, however, constituted an absolutely decisive force in the still largely agrarian capitalist countries of the nineteenth and early twentieth centuries. [. . .]

However, as the case of Britain shows most clearly, the existence of a vigorous agrarian small and petty bourgeoisie is by no means a necessary condition of democratization. In fact, Britain, like France, although in a rather different way, provides an excellent example of the second critical internal factor mentioned above — a divided ruling class. There have been at least two ways in which, under certain circumstances, splits have come to play an important determining role. As long as there is no serious threat from below, divisions can lead to intense vying for popular support; and provided that there exists a degree of underlying unity (if only because of previous disastrous experiences of violent conflict), they may help to promote institutional procedures securing peaceful coexistence and opposition.

Divisions within the ruling classes

The waves reaching Britain from revolutionary France and the first steps of the labour movement were all effectively crushed by a unified ruling class. However, the early and immature bourgeois revolution resulted in the establishment, by the nineteenth century, of a deeply rooted parliamentary pattern based on competition within the ruling class between landed and urban capital. When the counter-revolutionary panic subsided, and especially when popular agitation re-emerged in more cautious forms, this rivalry developed into a struggle for broader mass support. The important extension of the franchise by the Conservative Disraeli government in 1867 offers a brilliant illustration of this feature. Parliament and the Tory Party itself were caught in an unstable balance of power, while outside popular pressure for electoral reform was mounting. After a series of complicated manoeuvres, in which Disraeli's main objective was to out-trump his Liberal rivals and to secure the leading position within his own party, the government-sponsored bill was finally carried by a parliamentary majority. In mid nineteenth-century Britain, a Conservative politician could possess such enormous class self-confidence that a handful of parliamentary radicals, playing the competitive game of the ruling class, managed shrewdly and inostensibly to extend the suffrage further than the government had intended. The key thing for Disraeli was to beat the Liberals, who opposed the bill from the right. [. . .]

Finally, it should be stressed that underlying all these patterns was a common, consistent force: the working class. In a certain sense, different patterns may be said to express the different allies necessary for the success of the working-class struggle for democracy. [. . .]

Capitalism and democracy: inherent tendencies

Bourgeois democracy has been attained by such diverse and tortuous routes that any straightforward derivation from the basic characteristics of capitalism would be impossible, or at best seriously misleading. Nevertheless, the facts that democracy in the sense defined above did not appear anywhere prior to capitalism; that some capitalist countries have experienced a purely internal development of democracy; and that all major advanced bourgeois states are today democracies — these naturally call for some elucidation of the tendencies inherent within capitalism. [. . .]

1. Bourgeois democracy has always succeeded mass struggles of varying degrees of violence and protractedness. The first inherent tendency, then, will be found in *the conditions favouring popular struggle*. Legal emancipation of labour and the creation of a free labour market, industrialization, concentration of capital are all intrinsic tendencies which simultaneously lay the basis for a working-class movement of a strength and stability inachievable by the exploited classes of pre-capitalist modes of production. In accordance with Marx's analysis of the growing contradictions of capitalism, the working class is, *ceteris paribus,* strengthened by the advance and development of capitalism. This explains the traditional sociological correlations of democracy with wealth,

literacy and urbanization — factors which bear upon the relationship of forces in the class struggle. And, as we have already seen, the labour movement has itself played a vital role in the struggle for democracy.

2. However, we also remarked that in general the working class has not won a share in the political process in the heat of battle. On the contrary, it has been more common for the bourgeoisie to make concessions after a period of successful resistance to reform. [. . .]

3. National unification and liberation have everywhere been seen by the bourgeoisie as a strategic necessity for the development and protection of trade and industry and the breaking of feudal dynastic power. And for these aims it has often found it invaluable to enlist popular support. [. . .]

4. Feverish development of the productive forces is another feature peculiar to the capitalist mode of exploitation. One of the main reasons why nineteenth- and early twentieth-century liberals could deny the compatibility of democracy with private property was their dread that popular legislatures and municipal bodies would greatly increase taxation. However, they were disregarding the elasticity and expansive capacity of capitalism . . . Rises in productivity make possible a simultaneous increase of both rates of exploitation and real incomes of the exploited masses. This is, of course, not in itself conducive to democracy. But it is relevant in so far as it provides the bourgeoisie with an unprecedentedly wide room for manoeuvre in dealing with the exploited majority.

5. So far we have deliberately talked in very general terms of popular mobilization and incorporation of the working class into the political process. But such mobilization need not be democratic. In their very different ways, wartime Wilhelmine Germany, Fascism, and Third World 'populism' all testify to that. What makes capitalist democracy at all possible is a characteristic unique among known modes of production. [. . .]

The rule of capital requires a state — for both internal and external support and protection — but, as long as it upholds the separate realm of capitalist 'civil society', this state does not have to be managed personally by bourgeois. And in the long history of democratization, bourgeois politicians have learnt the many mechanisms at their disposal to keep the state in harmony with the needs of capital.

6. This last-mentioned feature of capitalism may explain why the impersonal rule of a tiny minority is conceivable in democratic forms — why, for example, the rule of capital is compatible with a Labour Party government, whereas a feudal aristocracy cannot be governed by a peasant party . . . Capitalist relations of production tend to create an *internally competing, peacefully disunited ruling class*. In its development, capital is divided into several fractions: mercantile, banking, industrial, agrarian, small and big. Except in a situation of grave crisis or acute threat from an enemy (whether feudal, proletarian or a rival national state) bourgeois class relations contain no unifying element comparable to the dynastic kingship legitimacy and fixed hierarchy of feudalism. [. . .]

In the absence of a single centre, some kind of elective, deliberative and representative political machinery became necessary. Therefore, propertied republics or parliamentary monarchies developed at an early stage in the formation of capitalist states — for example, the Italian, German and Swiss city republics, the United Provinces of the Low Countries, Britain, the United States, France and Belgium (the latter after 1830). [. . .]

Nevertheless, bourgeois democracy is no mere accident of history, and capitalism does contain a number of tendencies which are conducive to processes of democratization. Thus, it has frequently, and correctly, been observed that bourgeois democracy entails a competitive division within a basic framework of unity . . . But the concrete economic and political dynamic of the rise of capitalism does involve the struggle for and development of a new divided unity. This appears as the *nation-state*, freed of the barriers and boundaries of dynastic legitimacy, feudal enfiefment and provincial tradition. The establishment of national sovereignty and unity resulted from struggles against royal absolutism, foreign dynasties and provincial separatism. These were the stakes of the Dutch wars against Spain in the sixteenth and seventeenth centuries; the seventeenth-century English Revolution and Civil War; the US Declaration of Independence; the French Revolution of 1789; the 1830 August Revolution in Belgium; the unification of Switzerland, Italy, Germany, and of the Canadian, Australian and New Zealand colonies; the Meiji Restoration in Japan; the establishment of the constitutional Eider state in Denmark; the emancipation of Norway and Finland; and even the constitutional struggles within the Habsburg Empire. [. . .]

Freedom of trade and industry created a network of divisive competitive relationships which ran through the new ruling class of the unified and sovereign states. The market replaced the hierarchical pyramid of medieval and absolutist feudalism. And it was in this unity-division of national state and market that the process of democratization originated. [. . .]

However, the working-class movement was nowhere capable of achieving democracy by its own unaided resources . . . Only in conjunction with external allies were the non-propertied masses able to gain democratic rights; and it was above all the propertied minorities who in the end answered the critical questions of timing and form — of when and how democracy was to be introduced. Thus, the process of democratization unfolded within the framework of the capitalist state, congealing in the form of bourgeois democracy rather than opening the road to popular revolution and socialist transformation. [. . .]

The two paradoxes explained

We are now in a position to confront the two paradoxes with which we started. For Marxists, it will be remembered, the problem appeared as one of explaining how a tiny social minority has come to rule predominantly in democratic forms; while for bourgeois liberal thought, it seemed an insoluble mystery that classical liberals were convinced of the incompatibility of capitalism and democracy, whereas contemporary bourgeois opinion maintains that *only* capitalism is compatible with democracy.

The solution to the Marxist problem is by now fairly clear. Bourgeois democracy has always and everywhere been established in struggle against (hegemonic fractions of) the bourgeoisie, but through political means and channels provided for by the capitalist state. Moreover, when it has been threatened or destroyed, the labour movement has taken up the struggle anew against the leading fraction of the ruling class (as in Austria, Finland, France, Germany and Italy). Thus, although bourgeois democracy is democratic government plus the rule of capital, its democratic component has been achieved and defended against the bourgeoisie.

The bourgeois paradox is resolved when we grasp a feature of the process to which classical liberalism quite naturally paid scant attention. Democracy developed neither out of the positive tendencies of capitalism, nor as a historical accident, but out of the *contradictions* of capitalism. Bourgeois democracy has been viable at all only because of the elasticity and expansive capacity of capitalism, which were grossly underestimated by classical liberals and Marxists alike.

3.3

Capitalism and Democracy: the Best Possible Political Shell?

BOB JESSOP

[...] The state is the principal locus of political power in *capitalist societies* and cannot be derived from an abstract consideration of the *pure capitalist mode of production* (CMP). Indeed, it is one of the principal difficulties in the capital logic school of analysis of the capitalist state, that it neglects the more concrete problem of *state power in a given social formation* in favour of the *ideal collective capitalist in the CMP*. This makes it impossible for the school to grasp the nature of the capitalist state.

It is important to recognize the nature of the state in this respect. Three points merit special emphasis. These are (a) the state is a structural ensemble rather than a subject, (b) the state is a system of political domination rather than a neutral instrument, and (c) state power is a complex social relation that reflects the changing balance of social forces in a determinate conjuncture. Let us consider these points in turn.

First, the state is a set of institutions and apparatuses of political representation and intervention that cannot, as a set of structures, exercise power. In this context it is acceptable to define the institutional boundaries of the state in terms of the legal distinction between 'public' and 'private' provided one neither sees it as an originating subject endowed with an essential unity nor neglects the role of private institutions and bodies in securing political domination. This is especially important in the analysis of capitalist democracies. For to treat the state as a real (as opposed to legal) subject is to exclude from consideration political struggles within

Source: From G. Littlejohn *et al.* (eds) (1978) *Power and the State*, London, Croom Helm.

and between state apparatuses, as well as the effects of its institutional structure on political struggles in general. Likewise, to endow the state with an essential unity or inevitable bourgeois character is to engage in crude reductionism and to suggest that the only valid form of political struggle is one concerned to smash the existing state apparatuses. Moreover, if one adopts such an essentialist position or simply argues that all institutions of class domination or social cohesion should be included in one's definition of the state, then it becomes impossible to differentiate between democratic and non-democratic forms of domination and to discuss the effects of changes in the institutional boundaries of the state.

Second, even though the state has been defined in institutional terms rather than as a subject capable of exercising power, this should not be interpreted as an argument that the state is a *neutral instrument* that can be used with *equal facility and equal effectiveness* by all classes and social forces regardless of their location in the social formation or their political goals. For the institutional structure of the state has unequal and asymmetrical effects on the ability of different social forces to realize their interests through political struggle. This argument against a crude instrumentalist view of the state is reinforced through consideration of the various ways in which political forces themselves are constituted in part through the constraints associated with different forms of state. This means that classes should not be seen as already constituted political forces which exist outside and independently of the state and which are capable of manipulating it as an instrument. For, although classes are defined at the level of relations of production, their political weight depends on the forms of organization and means of intervention through which economic interests are expressed. These considerations also apply to other political forces besides wage-labour and capital. Thus the state should be viewed as a system of political domination whose structure has a definite influence on class struggle through its impact on the balance of social forces and the forms of political practice.

Third, although the state is not a real subject that exercises power, state power certainly exists and, indeed, constitutes the principal focus of political class struggle. State power is a complex social relation that reflects the changing balance of social forces in a determinate conjuncture in so far as they are concerned to control, reorganize, and restrict state apparatuses and state intervention. It is always contingent upon the circumstances in which the political struggle between such forces occurs as well as the correlation of forces — circumstances which are influenced in part by the institutional structure of the state itself. This view involves a firm rejection of any attempt to differentiate between 'state power' and 'class power' either as descriptive concepts or principles of explanation. This distinction can be sustained only by treating the state itself as a subject and/or ignoring the continuing class struggle within the state as well as that outside it. One should treat state power as a complex social relation whose changing nature depends on various interrelated factors.

It is within this context that we must locate the second term in the relation between capitalism and democracy. This can be seen as a determination of the state and/or state power. Thus democracy can be treated as an aspect of the institutional structure of representation and intervention and/or as a system of effective self-administration by the people. Indeed, if radical democratic theories focus on self-administration or popular control of government, liberal democratic theories emphasize the role of institutional mechanisms that enable the people at best to choose passively between political élites and government policies. Likewise, if Marx advocated genuine democracy based on government from below, he also criticized the formalism of bourgeois democracy and stressed its contribution to the continued rule of capital. The implications of formal democratic institutions in a capitalist society will therefore differ from those of substantive self-government in a classless society and it is correspondingly necessary to maintain the distinction between institutional forms and effective state power or political control.

What does democracy entail? In the institutional context of the capitalist state it refers to the legal entitlement of 'citizens' to participate in the determination of the policies to be executed by the state in its capacity as sovereign legal subject; and, in addition, to the legal conditions of existence of such participation. Citizenship involves the institution of an individual juridical subject endowed with specific political rights as well as obligations and the extension of this legal status to all adult members of the society without reference to their class position or other attributes. In this sense the institutionalization of citizenship can vary across social formations in terms of the scope and specification of the political rights of participation and in terms of the inclusiveness of the citizenry in relation to the total adult population. Democracy also has other legal preconditions. These focus on the institutionalization of certain political freedoms (e.g. freedom of association, freedom of speech, free elections) and of parliamentary (or equivalent) control over the executive and administration. They are the necessary juridical supports to the formal exercise of the citizen's rights of political participation. The popular-democratic struggle in capitalist societies takes the form of struggles to extend the scope of citizens' rights of participation, to include more of the 'people' within the category of citizens, and to institute the legal conditions appropriate to democracy. Moreover, because formal democratic institutions do not guarantee real control by the 'people', popular-democratic struggle also encompasses struggle to establish and maintain the social conditions in which such control can be realized. In this connection the 'people' is not a formal juridical subject (as in *People* v. *Dunleavy*) but a real political force constituted during the struggle to democratize the relations of political and ideological domination in a given social formation. To the extent that its struggle is successful, state power itself becomes more democratic. [. . .]

The correlation between capitalism and democracy

Several attempts have been made to correlate capitalism and democracy and to deduce the one from the other. Such efforts can be found among radical and Marxist writers as well as among conservative and liberal theorists. Indeed, given the contrasting political and ideological positions of such authors, it is surprising to discover a series of parallels in their analyses. This can be illustrated with reference to the work of social market economists and of various left-wing theorists.

Milton Friedman has argued on both historical and logical grounds that economic freedom is correlated with political freedom. He argues that the typical state of mankind is tyranny, servitude, and misery and that the nineteenth and early twentieth century in the Western world are remarkable exceptions to this general trend. This suggests that the free market and the development of capitalist institutions are a necessary condition of political freedom. Moreover, even though the dominance of private enterprise has been associated with authoritarian regimes such as Italian Fascism, Bismarckism and Tsarist autocracy, the degree of freedom available to citizens in such cases was much greater than is true of totalitarian states like communist Russia or Nazi Germany. And, with the introduction of collective economic planning since the end of World War II, there has been a corresponding reduction in political freedom for the individual. But, since historical evidence by itself can never be convincing, Friedman also tries to establish certain logical links between capitalism and political freedom. He argues that:

> the kind of economic organization that provides economic freedom directly, namely, competitive capitalism, also promotes political freedom because it separates economic power from political power and in this way enables the one to offset the other (1962, p. 9).

This is possible because the market removes the organization of economic activity from the control of political authority and so reduces, rather than reinforces, the concentration of power. [...]

The arguments of the 'capital logic' school are similar in certain respects to those of the 'social market economy' theorists. The former derives the nature of the capitalist state from the nature of the capital relation. It argues that, although competition between capitals secures some of the conditions necessary to capital accumulation (especially in terms of realizing the law of value[1]), it is also essential that there be an institutional complex that is not directly subordinate to the law of value to accomplish the conditions that competition does not secure. These include the provision of an appropriate legal framework for generalized commodity production, the creation of the general material conditions of production (infrastructure), the regulation of the conflict between wage-labour and capital, and the protection and expansion of the total national capital on the world market (cf. Altvater, 1973). Thus, despite the appearance of institutional separation and political autonomy, the state is actually an ideal collective capitalist and a necessary political moment in the social accomplishment of capital. This view is not dissimilar from that of Friedman. But, whereas he is committed to the view that capitalist production is non-exploitative and essentially crisis-free, Marxist writers argue that capitalism is exploitative and that the most fundamental barrier to continued accumulation is not misguided state intervention but capital itself. This implies, contrary to the view of the social market theorists, that the liberal democratic state is not the co-guarantor (together with competitive capitalism) of individual freedom. Indeed, as Macpherson has argued:

> the more nearly the society approximates Friedman's ideal of a competitive capitalist market society, where the state establishes and enforces the individual right of appropriation

and the rules of the market but does not interfere in the operation of the market, the more completely is political power being used to reinforce economic power (1973, pp. 148—9).

Thus, far from the separation of political from economic power underwriting individual freedom, it is a ruse of capital whose effect is to secure the conditions in which the working class can be subjected to the exploitation of capital. This is the basis for Moore's generalisation that, '[where] exploitation takes the form of exchange, dictatorship tends to take the form of democracy' (1957, p. 85). [. . .]

Now, if there is no one-to-one correlation between capitalism and democracy in specific societies, it is clear that the relation between them must be contingent, rather than a relationship of logical entailment. Moreover, if the latter were indeed the case, history would be reduced to an effect of the self-realization of a concept (capitalism) in true Hegelian fashion. This means that the question must be posed as follows: given that democracy is a possible form of state in societies dominated by the capitalist mode of production, what determines the extent to which this possibility is realized or not, as the case may be? It is to this problem that we now turn. [. . .]

Capital accumulation and forms of capitalist state

Democracy has been found in the most dissimilar social formations: in primitive communist groups, in the slave states of antiquity, and in mediaeval communes. And similarly absolutism and constitutional monarchy are to be found under the most varied economic orders. When capitalism began, as the first production of commodities, it resorted to a democratic constitution in the municipal communes of the Middle Ages. Later, when it developed to manufacturing, capitalism found its corresponding political form in the absolute monarchy. Finally, as a developed industrial economy, it brought into being in France the democratic republic of 1793, the absolute monarchy of Napoleon I, the nobles' monarchy of the Restoration Period (1815—1830), the bourgeois constitutional monarchy of Louis Phillippe, then again the democratic republic, and again the monarchy of Napoleon III, and finally, for the third time, the republic . . . No absolute and general relation can be constructed between capitalist development and democracy. The political form of a given country is always the result of the composite of all the existing political factors, domestic as well as foreign. It admits within its limits all variations of the scale from absolute monarchy to the democratic republic (R. Luxemburg, 1970, pp. 72—4).

In this passage from 'Reform or revolution', Rosa Luxemburg notes that democratic institutions are found in pre-capitalist societies and need not be found in capitalist societies. But she also notes that the relation is not random but contingent on the general political conjuncture. This is certainly correct but, before we consider the specifically political factors, it is worthwhile considering whether specific forms of capitalism are more or less conducive to democratic forms of government. This is implied in Luxemburg's own analysis — where simple commodity production and industrial production are associated with the democratic form and manufacturing is associated with absolutism. In short, given that capitalism does not exist in its pure form, is there nonetheless an association between specific variant forms or stages of capitalism and the forms of state with which they are associated?

One of the most interesting answers to this question has been suggested by Holloway and Picciotto in a series of papers. They attempt to establish the nature of the capitalist state in terms of the development of capital accumulation. For example, since capitalism is a historically specific form of production, there is necessarily a transition period during which its preconditions are established. This requires state intervention and compulsion — for it is only once these conditions are secured that capital accumulation can proceed on the basis of exchange between 'equals'. In transitional conjunctures, therefore, an absolutist state pursuing mercantilist policies is the appropriate form of capitalist state. However, once the conditions of existence of capital accumulation have been assured, the appropriate form of state is a liberal state which gives the fullest possible freedom to individual capitals compatible with securing the general conditions for capital accumulation. This implies a combination of general *laissez-faire* with specific interventions to redress the effects of unfettered competition (e.g. factory legislation). The liberal state, it should be noted, need not be a liberal *democratic* state. But it is common for the liberal state to be associated with parliamentarism. However, the further development of capital accumulation is associated with the increasing importance of the tendency of the rate of profit to fall[2] and the need for state intervention to restructure capital in a way that facilitates the renewal of capitalist exploitation. The liberal state is, under those conditions, replaced by the interventionist state (Holloway and Picciotto, 1977). [. . .]

The effects of democratic representation

[. . .] If one accepts the view that the state is neither an originating subject nor a neutral instrument, but a system of apparatuses and institutions that have determinate effects on the political struggle, it is essential to consider the effects of democratic representation on the class struggle between wage-labour and capital in capitalist societies. In this respect it should be noted immediately that 'representation' is not an expressive relationship in which representer and represented are related in a manner that guarantees the accurate representation of the views or interests of the represented. For the means of representation have their own effects on the process of representation in exactly the same way that the means of scientific enquiry affect the representation of the real world in the production of scientific knowledge. Nor can one side-step this problem through a resort to reductionist or essentialist arguments that determine the interests of a given class without reference to the means of representation in a determinate political situation and then assess the extent to which a given form of representation distorts these interests. For the means of representation are themselves part of the conjuncture that determines class interests (cf. Hirst, 1976 and Hindess, 1978). Indeed, it is precisely this problem that is at the heart of the long-standing debate in the socialist movement concerning the correct strategies and tactics of revolutionary struggle in bourgeois democratic republics. Let us now consider the effectivity of the means of representation.

Lenin stated his belief in *The State and Revolution* that:

[a] democratic republic is the best possible political shell for capitalism, and therefore capital, once in possession . . . of this very best shell, establishes its power so securely, so firmly, that *no* change of persons, of institutions, or of parties in the bourgeois democratic republic can shake it (1963, p. 296).

This view was anticipated by Engels, who referred to the bourgeois democratic republic as 'the logical form of bourgeois rule' (Engels to Bernstein in Zurich, 24 March 1884); and it is shared by many other Marxists past and present. Thus, in a recent issue of *New Left Review*, Perry Anderson argued that 'the general form of the representative state — bourgeois democracy — is itself the principal ideological lynch-pin of Western capitalism' (1977, p. 28). [. . .]

Likewise, Poulantzas claims that 'juridico-political ideology holds a dominant place in the dominant ideology of this [i.e. capitalist] mode of production, taking a place analogous to religious ideology in the dominant ideology of the feudal mode of production' (1972, p. 128). And, in the words of Perry Anderson, 'the existence of the parliamentary state thus constitutes the formal framework of all other ideological mechanisms of the ruling class. It provides the general code in which every specific message elswhere is transmitted' (1977, p. 28). In short, these theorists argue that the effect of bourgeois law in general and parliamentarism in particular is to misrepresent and mystify the nature of bourgeois political domination as well as of bourgeois economic exploitation. [. . .]

However, far from seeing political fetishism as an automatic effect of the parliamentary republic, with its constitution of formally equal citizens and a sovereign state representing the national interest, it is vital to examine the ideological social relations and ideological class struggles that are involved in the reproduction (and transformation) of this phenomenon. This requires the analysis of political parties, trade unions, and pressure groups as well as the more obviously ideological apparatuses.

But even to talk about political parties, trade unions, and pressure groups is to presuppose an important material basis of political fetishism, namely, the institutional separation in capitalist societies between the economic and political instances of the social formation. This is a generic feature of such societies but nonetheless has specific effects in liberal democratic regimes. For the latter involve a clear demarcation between private and public spheres, and thereby separate economic and political class struggle to the advantage of capital and the detriment of labour. The growth of economic intervention by the state weakens this separation and threatens to unify the two forms of struggle. From the viewpoint of capital, the ideal position is one in which economic class struggle is confined within the limits of the market relation and political class struggle is confined within the limits of bourgeois parliamentarism. There would be a clear division between trade union struggles concerned with wages and conditions and political struggles to promote social reforms through parliamentary majorities and the mobilization of public opinion. To the extent that these struggles are unified, it would be through a social democratic movement. But even this would involve a division of labour between the industrial and political wings of the movement: industrial power would be confined to industrial disputes rather than be employed to reinforce parliamentary action; state power would be confined to the 'public' sphere and not employed to interfere in private disputes. For, given such an institutional separation and its corresponding forms of class struggle, the prospects for the economic and political domination of capital would be much enhanced. It was the recognition of this that motivated the ruling-class strategy aimed at 'constitutionalizing' the labour movement in Britain and vindicated in the outcome of the General Strike (cf. J. Foster, 1976, *passim*). [. . .]

The discussion so far has focused on the effects on the system of representation in the democratic republic. But there is another side to the state. This is state intervention. For, although a system of self-government would entail a fusion between representation and intervention, it is an essential characteristic of the liberal democratic state (and, indeed, other forms of capitalist state) that representation is separate from administration. This is not to deny that the class struggle is reproduced within the administrative apparatuses of the state itself, but simply to assert that capitalist democracy is characterized by a formal separation of representative and administrative institutions and the presupposition of official neutrality, in contrast to the partisanship of the elected representatives in charge of the state. This has been noted forcibly by Max Weber in his analyses of bureaucracy. For, if we ignore his twin tendencies to treat bureaucracy as a technically efficient, neutral instrument and bureaucrats as an originating collective subject interested in the usurpation of political power, Weber provides an incisive account of the nature and effects of bureaucracy. He argues that the most significant feature of the modern state is bureaucratic domination and that the most significant check to the domination of bureaucrats is the consolidation of a strong parliament based on universal suffrage. [. . .]

The fundamental importance of bureaucracy in this respect is the separation of the masses from the means of administration — the separation of bureaucrats themselves from possession of such means being secondary. This applies as much to the means of economic intervention and welfare administration as it does to the means of coercion and repression. The growth of bureaucracy in general and the growing concentration and centralization of state power in particular therefore reinforce the political subordination of the people as a whole. For it separates them from the exercise of state power and leads to their individuation and isolation as clients or consumers of the administration and its services. [. . .]

The contradictions of capitalist democracy

The preceding discussion suggests that the mechanism of democratic representation through parliaments combined with bureaucratic administration is optimal for capital accumulation. But several qualifications are necessary. For, contrary to the implications of the theory of political fetishism, bourgeois democratic republics are not automatic guarantors of consent and stability. This should be apparent from the formal character of democratic institutions. These do not exist in a political vacuum but receive substance from the conjuncture of which they form part. This implies that the adequacy of the bourgeois democratic republic is contingent on the overall political, economic and ideological situation. It is therefore imperative to determine the conditions under which democracy is (or is not) adequate to securing the rule of capital. [. . .]

In the context of parliamentary democracy two aspects of bourgeois domination are especially important. These are the attachment of the working class and other subordinate classes to parliamentary forms of representation and the articulation of working class and popular-democratic demands into political programmes and ideologies conducive to the ideological domination of a power bloc organized under the hegemony of the bourgeoisie or one of its fractions. In the absence of these conditions we find a 'representational crisis' and a crisis of hegemony.

A *representational crisis* has been defined by Poulantzas as a 'split between the political parties and the classes and class fractions they represented' (1976, p. 102). It is characterized by the development of extra-parliamentary forms of organization and political action and the transformation of parties into parliamentary coteries. In the rise of Fascism and Nazism, for example, we find the proliferation of 'corporate-economic' organizations that directly confront the executive as well as paramilitary organizations that engage in open violence and political intimidation. The origins of such crises clearly vary from case to case. But their content is typically *a crisis of hegemony* (cf. Gramsci, 1971, p. 210), [Eds' emphasis]. This is reflected in the questioning of the dominant ideology and the detachment of popular-democratic movements from subordination to the dominant forms of ideological discourse and practice. For, as Laclau has argued in a paper on 'Fascism and Ideology', a fundamental condition of ideological hegemony is the ability to integrate popular-democratic values and demands into an ideology and programme that secures the representation of bourgeois interests (1977).

Much the same point is made by Gamble in relation to the articulation of the 'politics of support' and the 'politics of power'. Thus, in the rise of both Fascism and Nazism, we find that the petite bourgeoisie detaches itself from the dominant ideology in a general ideological crisis and regroups around the Fascist and Nazi parties which articulate an ideology and programme that *appeals* more directly to petit bourgeois sentiments (although it does not necessarily realize their interests in its policies once in power). Likewise, in the case of military dictatorships in Latin America, a major factor leading to *coups d'état* has proved to be an organic crisis of the ruling class and the failure of the bourgeoisie to consolidate its own hegemony in parliamentary regimes (cf. Nun, 1967, pp. 77–109, and Murphy, 1976, *passim*). In the case of both Fascist and military regimes, the crisis of representation is ended through the simple expedient of dissolving political parties and resorting to repression. But this does not solve the problem of representation as such and it is necessary to develop new forms of representation that do not threaten the rule of capital. This problem is particularly clear in military regimes in relation to the return to 'civilian' rule (cf. Huntington, 1968, pp. 241–63). It appears in different guise in Fascist regimes — particularly in relation to the role of economic-corporate groups such as the Italian corporations and the German Labour Front and middle-class guilds. In the case of Fascist parties, it is important to reject the mythology of totalitarian rule and examine the forms assumed by class and popular-democratic struggles within the party itself. For, regardless of the form of regime in capitalist states, some mechanism of representation is necessary to ensure the flexibility and cohesion of the social formation in the face of crises.

We are now in a position to define the conditions under which democracy is the best possible political shell for capital. These are dependent on the political conjuncture within which democratic institutions are situated and not on the innate qualities or effects of such institutions. They are tied to the class practices of the various classes in the social formation and their articulation to popular-democratic and other political and ideological practices. In short, the bourgeois democratic republic is the best possible political shell for capital to the extent that the bourgeoisie is politically and ideologically dominant. This view is not, of course, original. It has also been expressed quite explicitly by José Nun in an essay on the middle-class military coup. He writes that:

> the validity of the classical Marxist proposition according to which representative democracy is the form of government which most closely corresponds to the interests of the bourgeoisie depends on the previous consolidation by the latter of its hegemonic supremacy, its development of a metaphysical justification of its leading role, and its demonstration of its efficacy as a ruling class (Nun, 1967, p. 99).

However, where the bourgeoisie is not politically dominant in political struggle (i.e. at the level of political forces rather than political institutions) and ideologically dominant in ideological struggle (i.e. in terms of the articulation of ideologies rather than the system of ideological apparatuses), the democratic republic poses serious threats to the rule of capital in relation to the appropriation and exercise of state power. Whether or not capital can consolidate its rule through the institution of an exceptional form of state, or the working class can institute a socialist republic, is then contingent on the balance of forces in the particular conjuncture then obtaining. [. . .]

Conclusions

1. Democracy refers to the legal entitlement of 'citizens' to participate in the determination of policies to be executed by the state in its capacity as sovereign legal subject; and, in addition, to the legal conditions of existence of such participation.

2. Parliamentary democracy refers to a democratic system in which 'citizens' participate through the exercise of voting rights in relation to a parliament from which the political executive is then recruited from representatives who command a majority in parliament; for the purposes of this chapter the term has been extended to include presidential systems of the American kind

where citizens elect the political executive separately from the legislature. The key factor in both cases is the participation of citizens as individual electors.

3. Corporate democracy refers to a democratic system in which 'citizens' participate through the exercise of voting rights in relation to a corporation which represents their interests in the formulation of state policy; the unit of representation is the corporation rather than the constituency organized on a territorial basis and citizens participate in their capacity as economic agents.

4. Contemporary capitalist democracies are characterized in varying degrees by the contradictory unity of parliamentary and corporatist forms of democratic representation; there has been a gradual displacement of representation from parliamentary to corporatist forms in parallel with the growing centralization and concentration of state power.

5. The fundamental precondition of continued bourgeois domination in democracy is the political and ideological domination of the bourgeoisie: in the case of parliamentarism, this takes the form of the attachment of the electorate to political parties that are committed to the rules of parliamentary politics and whose programmes are articulated with the dominant ideology; in the case of corporatism, this takes the form of an 'economic-corporate' orientation, i.e. representation of the interests of the corporation or those of a class (represented by several corporations) on a purely economic level — this involves the problem of state power 'but only in terms of winning politico-juridical equality with the ruling groups: the right is claimed to participate in legislation and administration, even to reform these — but within the existing fundamental structures' (Gramsci, 1971, p. 181). In both cases the domination of the bourgeoisie is secured through acceptance of the existing fundamental structures and the articulation of popular-democratic claims with pursuit of the interests of the bourgeoisie in capital accumulation on an expanded scale.

6. In the absence of bourgeois political and ideological domination, democratic forms of representation cannot secure the conditions required for expanded reproduction. This is indicated by representational and ideological crises: the detachment of the masses from bourgeois political parties (social democratic parties included) and from trade unions or 'corporations' and/or the collapse of

ideological hegemony on the part of bourgois intellectuals, ideological apparatuses, and so on. Crises do not engender their own solutions. How they are resolved, if at all, depends on the balance of forces in each case. The manner of their resolution determines the forms of appearance of subsequent crises.

7. Liberal democratic representation based on parliamentarism is appropriate only to certain stages of capital accumulation at certain points in the total world economy; thereafter corporate democratic representation may prove more adequate to securing the conditions necessary for capital accumulation. And, in other social formations outside the metropolitan centres, 'exceptional' forms of state may be typical. The transition from parliamentarism to corporatism is not automatic but has specific origins in the continuing play of political forces in each society. The current situation in Britain is characterized by the contradictory unity of parliamentarism and corporatism under the dominance of the former mediated through the Cabinet.

8. Since democracy is a form of representation that acquires substance only in specific conjunctures, it is necessary for socialist and popular-democratic forces to struggle for the realization of those legal and social conditions necessary to popular control of government. But this is a struggle that must be articulated with the struggle against inequality in the sphere of production if the end-result is not to be a more perfect bourgeois democratic shell for capital accumulation. In this context corporatism represents a critical area of political struggle. For the exact nature and significance of corporatism and the extent of its democratization are still open issues.

Notes

1. The law of value is the most important principle regulating the process of commodity production and is itself an effect of commodity production. It determines the pattern of investment, i.e. the circuit of capital between different branches of production, according to the deviation of their specific rate of profit from the average rate of profit. The average rate of profit is the effect of competition between capitals which ensures that each capital appropriates a part of the total surplus-value proportionate to the fraction of total social capital which it represents. The need for each capital to make at least the average rate of profit to ensure its long-term reproduction ensures the

subordination of the labour-process to the valorization (or surplus-value production) process within each enterprise.
2. The tendency of the rate of profit to fall is a fundamental tendency of capital accumulation analysed in terms of value theory. It refers to the effect of an increasing organic composition of capital on the value rate of profit considered in isolation from changes in the rate of exploitation, the value of wage-labour and the technical composition of capital. For, given these restricted conditions and the assumption that labour-power is the sole source of added value, it necessarily follows that the average rate of profit expressed in value terms must fall as the value of constant capital (means of production, raw materials, etc.) increases in relation to the value of variable capital (labour-power). It is important to realize, however, that this effect is tendential. It is possible to avoid or offset this tendency in so far as the rate of exploitation can be increased, the value of labour-power decreased, etc. It is the mobilization of these counter-tendencies that constitutes the crux of state intervention in late capitalism.

References

Aims of Industry (1967), *The Case for Capitalism,* London.
Altvater, E. (1973) 'Notes on some problems of state interventionism', *Kapitalistate,* 1 and 2.
Anderson, P. (1977) 'The antinomies of Antonio Gramsci', *New Left Review,* 100.
Balibar, E. (1973) 'Sur la dialectique historique', *La Pensée.*
Brittan, S. (1975) 'A "manifesto" for 1975', in *Crisis '75?,* London, Institute of Economic Affairs.
Bunyan, T. (1976) *The Political Police in Britain,* London, Freemann.
Centre for Policy Studies (1975) *Why Britain Needs a Social Market Economy,* London, Centre for Policy Studies.
Engels, F. (1968) *The Role of Force in History,* New York, International Publishers.
Fernbach, D. (1973) 'Introduction', in K. Marx, *Surveys from Exile,* Harmondsworth, Penguin.
Finer, S. E. (1976) *Electoral Reform and Adversary Politics,* London, Antony Wigram.
Foster, J. (1976) 'The state and ruling class during the general strike', *Marxism Today,* May.
Friedman, M. (1962) *Capitalism and Freedom,* London, University of Chicago Press.
Gamble, A. (1974) *The Conservative Nation,* London, Routledge & Kegan Paul.
Gramsci, A. (1971) *Prison Notebooks,* London, Lawrence and Wishart.
Hailsham, Lord (1976) 'Elective dictatorship', Richard Dimbleby Lecture, 14 October.

Hansard Society (1976) *The Report of the Hansard Society Commission on Electoral Reform,* London, Hansard Society.

Hindess, B. (1978) 'Classes, politics, and the state in contemporary Marxist theory', in G. Littlejohn *et al.* (eds) (1978) *Power and the State,* London, Croom Helm.

Hirst, P. Q. (1976) *Social Evolution and Sociological Categories,* London, Allen & Unwin.

Hirst, P. Q. (1976) 'Althusser and the theory of ideology', *Economy and Society,* 5.

Holloway, J. and Picciotto, S. (1976) 'Capital, the state, and European integration', mimeo.

Holloway, J. and Picciotto, S. (1977) 'Capital, crisis and the state', *Capital and Class* 2.

Huntington, S. P. (1968) *Political Order in Changing Societies,* London, Yale University Press.

Kline, R. (1973) *Can Socialism Come Through Parliament?,* London, I. S. Pamphlet.

Laclau, E. (1977) *Ideology and Politics in Marxist Theory,* London, New Left Books.

Lenin, V. I. (1963) *The Agrarian Programme of Social Democracy* (1907) and *The State and Revolution* (1917) in *Selected Works,* Vol. 1, Moscow.

Luxemburg, R. (1970) *Rosa Luxemburg Speaks,* New York, Pathfinder Press.

Mcpherson, C. B. (1973) *Democratic Theory,* London, Oxford University Press.

Mandel, E. (1975) *Late Capitalism,* London, New Left Books.

Marx, K. (1962) 'A review of Guizot's book, why has the English Revolution been successful?' in K. Marx and F. Engels, *On Britain,* Moscow.

Marx, K. (1852) *The Eighteenth Brumaire of Louis Bonaparte.*

Marx, K. and Engels, F. (1975) *Selected Correspondence,* London, Lawrence & Wishart.

Moore, B. Jr. (1968) *The Social Origins of Dictatorship and Democracy,* London, Allen Lane.

Moore, S. W. (1957) *The Critique of Capitalist Democracy,* New York, Paine-Whitman.

Murphy, S. D. (1976) 'Argentina: the impact of monopoly capitalism on the political structure', MA Dissertation, University of Essex.

Nun, J. (1967) 'The middle class military coup', in C. Veliz (ed.) *The Politics of Conformity in Latin America,* London, Oxford University Press.

Offe, C. and Ronge, V. (1975) 'Theses on the theory of the state', *New German Critique,* 6.

Ollman, B. (1971) *Alienation,* London, Cambridge University Press.

Pahl, R. and Winkler, J. (1974) 'The coming corporatism', *New Society,* 10 October.

Pashukanis, E. B. (1968) 'The Marxist theory of law and the state', in

H. Babb (ed.) *Soviet Legal Philosophy,* Cambridge, Massachusetts, Harvard University Press.

Poulantzas, N. (1972) *Political Power and Social Classes,* London, New Left Books.

Poulantzas, N. (1976) *The Crisis of the Dictatorships,* London, New Left Books.

Weber, M. (1968) *Economy and Society,* New York, Bedminster Press.

Wengraf, T. (1970) 'Notes on Marx and Engels theories of the development of the capitalist state', mimeo.

Wright, E. O. (1974—5) 'To control or to smash bureaucracy: Weber and Lenin on politics, the state, and bureaucracy', *Berkeley Journal of Sociology,* xix.

3.4

The Place of the Family in the Origins of the Welfare State

ELI ZARETSKY

The history of the welfare state viewed in the context of the history of the family

I begin by distinguishing those aspects of the family that are historically specific — especially its emergence as a private economic unit and the domestic ideology that accompanies its economic role — from the more deeply rooted biological, psychological, and social necessities that the historically modern family now accommodates. The historic tendency in America — the result of the market (i.e. the frontier) and of industrialization — has been to weaken or destroy primary bonds of kinship and community and to make the economically independent individual or family responsible for his or her welfare and for the care of those (especially children) who cannot care for themselves. Changes in state policy and in the law have reflected this tendency. Such scholars as Nancy Cott and Carl Degler have traced the 'birth' of the modern American ideal of the family as a private institution to the late eighteenth and early nineteenth centuries, and it is widely agreed that the nineteenth-century liberal state fostered and presupposed ideals of individual or familial autonomy.[1] I argue that this is also true of the welfare state; it fostered individualism and familial autonomy, but in a historically specific form that weakened the primary human ties of interdependence on which individualism and autonomy ultimately depend. [. . .]

Ties of sexuality, kinship, and biological and psychological dependence are inevitable; self-supporting nuclear families are

Source: Abridgement of 'The Place of the Family in the Origins of the Welfare State' by Eli Zaretsky. From *Rethinking the Family: Some Feminist Questions* edited by Barrie Thorne with Marilyn Yalom. Copyright © 1982 by Longman Inc. Reprinted by permission of Longman Inc., New York.

not. The relevance of this distinction recurs throughout the history of the American family. Herbert Gutman's *The Black Family in Slavery and Freedom* demonstrates how the slave community built and maintained elaborate systems of kinship after the African systems were destroyed by the passage. Primary bonds between mothers and children, as well as between men and their families, were sustained through being imbedded in a larger kin-based community. The psychological effectiveness of these ties survived the physical disruption of the couple or the family unit. Of course, slaves could not maintain independent, self-supporting economic units; kinship, not the family, supplied the 'normal idiom of social relations'.[2] Even at present among the welfare mothers studied by Carol Stack, one of the groups least integrated into the labour force, family life is organized around kinship, reciprocity, and female networks, rather than around an employed head of household.[3]

Similar themes pervade the history of the working-class family. Social historians of immigration such as Rudolph Vecoli, Tamara Haraven, and Virginia Yans-McLaughlin have pointed to the importance of kinship ties and of the ethnic community among the immigrants, and in contrast to previous scholars, have argued that these survived the entry into an industrial society. But there is a vast difference between a society *organized* around ties of kin and community and the *survival* of kin and community in a society organized around wage-labour. The classic works in the history of immigration — William I. Thomas and Florian Znaniecki's *The Polish Peasant in Europe and America* and Oscar Handlin's *The Uprooted* — rightly argue that the kinship ties and communal obligations of traditional peasant society were giving way, even before immigration, to the individualizing pressures of a wage-labour based economy. [...]

The American political system, overall, has sought to foster independent, self-supporting units (individuals or families) rather than a particular family form. Social reformers and philanthropists throughout the nineteenth century took private property to be the basis of a 'normal' (i.e. self-supporting) family, properly divided in role and function according to sex. When the rise of industry in the late nineteenth century threw the possibility of familial autonomy and self-sufficiency into question, many traditions and interests converged on a new solution during the progressive years. Just as private property was assumed as the basis of the independent political or social individual, according to eighteenth- and nineteenth-century reformers, so a wage or salary was assumed to play that role by twentieth-century reformers; this assumption has been incorporated into the reforms of the welfare state. The fact that wage-labour has made family life possible at all supplied the crucial mediation that made the middle-class preaching concerning the family and domesticity even plausible to working-class immigrants, and led both the middle class and the working class to support a more active role for the state. Rather than the state undermining the family, it is difficult to imagine how any form of the family could have survived the enormously destructive uprooting that accompanied industrialization without some intervention from the state. The issue is not whether the welfare state eroded the family, but rather in what form it preserved it. My argument is that the family has been preserved as an economically private unit and that most of the normative aspects of state policy are based on that. [. . .]

Liberalism and the family

The modern English and American liberal tradition broke with the patriarchal assumption of continuity between families and the state. Already in 1685 Locke mocked Filmer's belief that authority was vested in a kind of transhistorical fatherhood: 'a strange kind of domineering phantom,' Locke called it, 'a gigantic form'.[4] In Locke's view it was property that gave the 'political quality to personality'. In the development of the modern state the ownership of property was taken to establish a sphere of autonomy around the individual or family, into which the state could not intrude. 'Property', over time, acquired many meanings, including labour and ultimately one's personhood.

Only with the attempt to establish the market as an autonomous sphere of society did the ideal of the family as a private (i.e. non-governmental) unit take hold. De Tocqueville in 1835 contrasted the father in an aristocratic family with his 'political right to command' to the father in a democracy, 'the legal part of parental authority vanish[ed]'.[5] It was only after a boundary was drawn between civil or private society (individuals and their families) and the state, that one can begin to speak of state intervention into the family, much less of the state replacing the family.

The various ways in which the state began to take over responsibilities from families in the early nineteenth century, or to intervene into the family, should not be understood solely in terms of the expansion of state authority. These new forms of intervention simultaneously involved a drastic limitation on the state when compared to the powers of seventeenth- and even eighteenth-century governments to intervene. The terms on which the *laissez-faire* state could intervene into the family were similar to those by which it could intervene into the economy. The liberal or *laissez-faire* state had the responsibility for establishing the arena and the formal rules within which private (i.e. economic or otherwise civil) activity proceeded (e.g. it was responsible for international relations or currency). The *laissez-faire* state was permitted to intervene into the economy where private means were inadequate, for example, in the building of canals or public education. Finally, the *laissez-faire* state was obliged to intervene where misbehaviour had taken place, as in an obstruction of trade.

In order to understand the individualistic character of the welfare state, I would cite three currents of nineteenth-century reform that, while based on *laissez-faire* or liberal principles, nonetheless called for governmental intervention into the family. The first, which was the most purely *laissez-faire*, was the feminist effort to establish a non-patriarchal family by unblocking obstacles to equality and freedom of contract in the realms of marriage, divorce, custody law, and economic rights. The second, a more direct precursor to the welfare state, was the transfer of responsibility for the poor and the dependent from families and the community to what became state institutions. David Rothman has termed this process 'the discovery of the asylum', and Michael Katz has called it 'the rise of the institutional state'. These phrases are misleading because these reforms were not meant to build institutions, but rather to rehabilitate and perfect individuals, largely by encouraging a certain kind of private family, and in that way ultimately to eliminate the need for institutions. The third is the development of the principle of 'scientific charity' in the late nineteenth century that, in my view, supplies a bridge between the early nineteenth-century emphasis on rehabilitation and the reforms of the progressive era. By the end of the nineteenth century the idea that a living wage for individuals or families was a 'right' rather than 'charity' began to be accepted and is generally taken to mark the beginnings of the interventionist welfare state. [. . .]

Feminism and marital reform

The pre-Civil War feminist redefinition of individualism to include women was perhaps the most important, though also the most removed, contribution that *laissez-faire* thinking made to the welfare state. Morton Horowitz has described the general shift in the antebellum period from a 'protective, regulative, paternalistic' conception of law to one 'thought of as facilitative of individual desires'.[6] Beginning in the 1840s, feminists sought to extend this conception of contract into the sphere of the family. They challenged the patriarchal common-law presumption of marital unity by which husband and wife were taken to be one person — and that one the husband, as Blackstone had put it. They sought to revoke the husband's legal right to sexual services from his wife, and the presumption that child custody should be inevitably awarded to the father in case of divorce. They achieved some success in the passage of the Married Women's Property Acts of the 1840s in New York, California, and other states, which gave women the right to trade and contract on the marketplace, to earn wages and to spend them. The same period saw the beginnings of divorce reform. The general idea underlying these movements was expressed by Stanton: to make democracy 'the law of the family as well as the state'.[7]

After the Civil War and Reconstruction, the idea that government should intervene to protect individual rights gained much wider currency. During the late nineteenth century, there was an upsurge in legislative and judicial action concerning the family, reflecting an ever-rising number of women (and children) who called on the state to protect their rights against patriarchal authority, as well as a rising number of fathers who called on the state to aid them in maintaining their authority. These laws and cases touched not only on property rights but on the nature and limits of parental authority and obligations. The most important issue was divorce, as the rate rose by more than 600 per cent between 1860 and 1920.

The relevance of these currents to the twentieth-century welfare state became clear during the progressive era when judges, social workers, and government officials, who were at least influenced to think of the family in terms of individual rights for women and children, encountered the traditional, often pre-liberal families of the immigrants. [. . .]

Economic liberalism and 'moral treatment'

The dramatic construction of non-familial institutions for the dependent poor, the orphaned, the sick, and the insane in the early nineteenth century is a more direct precursor of the twentieth-century welfare state. But the historical significance of these institutions is poorly described in terms of a transfer of functions from families to the state. The basic outlook of the asylums was as much rooted in early nineteenth-century political economy, with its attack on patriarchal and community charity, and its aim of a society of self-supporting individual family units, as in religious forms of humanitarianism. As the spread of the market broke down older paternalistic and community traditions, such as apprenticeship, it created a new form of dependency largely unique to market societies: individuals outside families. At the same time, the market supplied a new model of social health: the self-supporting individual or family, which the nineteenth-century agencies of rehabilitation took as their goal. [. . .]

The concept of individual rehabilitation that these asylums were built to effect is much more important for understanding the nature of the welfare state than the fact that they ultimately expanded the domain of the state. The philanthropists and reformers who built these asylums rejected the idea that mental illness or poverty were inevitable in any community, and instead tried to think through the causes of deviance and dependency and their cure. According to their conception, both the person's heredity and environmental history (particularly the family history) established the context within which his or her free will or moral faculty expressed itself. The asylums were a way of changing people's environment so that they became responsible for themselves once again. This principle of individual responsibility, not the growth of tutelary institutions, marks the early nineteenth century as the seedbed of what Lasch has called 'the therapeutic state'.[8] The doctors, penologists, reformers, neurologists, and philanthropists who built the early asylums shared an optimistic, perfectionist — and ultimately *laissez-faire* — outlook similar to the emphasis on self-reliance and self-help that characterized other reformers and radicals during the antebellum period. [. . .]

Orphan asylums and reform schools did abrogate the rights of parents and others from the 'abnormal' (i.e., broken or non-self-supporting) families they sought to help. Many nineteenth-century Americans believed that the children of the poor were better off in institutions. In 1838, in an important case, a Pennsylvania court upheld the right of magistrates to commit children to a house of refuge over parental opposition. These tendencies are important. But there is a difference between the state's weakening or restriction of parental authority and the state's weakening of the family . . .

The same institutions that threatened the parental authority of the poor, also valorized family life in general, as in the case of the director who sought to model his asylum after the 'well-regulated family' or the orphan asylum that sought to cultivate a 'home feeling'. The emphasis of these institutions on individual treatment through the reform of character both encouraged and embodied the same ethical principles and scientific theories that reformers were then urging upon the family, suggesting that the causal element does not rest with the asylums. [. . .]

The schematic model of the state replacing the family obscures the sense in which government intervention, as it developed, was accompanied by an increasingly sharp delineation of the 'normal' family as a private and autonomous (i.e., self-supporting) institution. The transfer of responsibility for the poor and other dependent groups from the family and community to asylums and state institutions was accompanied by an intensified emphasis on the role of the family in educating both men and women for their different places in a market-based society, a role for which women were held responsible. While economic independence was highly prized in society as a whole, within family units the theme was self-sacrifice for women, and a new level of attention was paid to the nurturant role of mothers and the special needs of children.

The late nineteenth-century critique of charity

If the building of asylums in the early nineteenth century expressed the outlook of political-economic individualism more than of paternalism, this was no less true of the spread of principles of rationalization and scientific management among charity workers in the late nineteenth century, principles that clearly anticipate the outlook of progressive era reform.

Beginning with the Civil War, 'business principles' — strict administration, careful control of funds, and, closely related, a faith in social science — became the leading principles governing work with the poor. [. . .]

Concurrently, principles of scientific management came to dominate private philanthropy. In 1877, the Reverend Humphrey S. Gurteen, drawing, as usual, on British precedent, founded the Charity Organization Societies (COS) in Buffalo, New York. The COS sought to replace the old philanthropy that fostered dependence by 'intelligence', which would foster independence. Responding to the depression of the 1870s, they recognized that poverty was systematic and social, but held to a faith in the personal rehabilitation of the poor. The COS sought to turn themselves into a 'machine' of rehabilitation, 'to do in charity what is done in commerce and industry — so to arrange its different agencies, and so to coordinate its different forces as to attain a certain end with the least possible waste of energy'. Encouraging city-wide organizations, dividing the city into districts, and keeping careful records on those seeking relief, the COS sent forth thousands of volunteers into the poorer districts of the city with the hope that individual contact would encourage the rehabilitation of the poor.

The purpose of the movement was to turn the poor into self-supporting citizens. 'Not alms but a friend' was its well-known slogan. H. L. Wayland, one of its leaders, wrote in 1887 that 'next to alcohol . . . the most pernicious fluid is indiscriminate soup'. [. . .]

Human nature, wrote Josephine Shaw Lowell, 'is so constituted that no man can receive as a gift what he should earn by his own labour without a moral deterioration'. Only a society organized around independent, self-supporting individuals and families could effect the 'reunion between the classes' that Lowell saw as the point of the new philanthropy.[9]

The 'scientific charity' movement of Gilded Age America was the direct descendant of the antebellum humanitarianism it attacked, as well as the progenitor of the settlement house and social work movements of the progressive era that attacked it. All three movements were organized around an attack on charity on the grounds that charity fosters dependence. The proponents of 'scientific charity' accepted governmental action or social reform so long as it was not 'charity' (i.e. handouts). Early progressive thinking, as expressed by the settlement house workers, continued to look toward regeneration through personal relationships, although this became less and less important with the development of professional social work. At the same time, the reformers of the progressive era developed the idea that independence was a social right — not a charitable gift — and that government was responsible for guaranteeing that right.

In 1891 John Dewey, in his *Outlines of a Critical Theory of Ethics,* attacked charity as an effort to control the character of the recipient and urged instead a change of conditions to make possible self-support. Dewey, in common with many other thinkers of his epoch, used Darwinian premises to redefine character as 'the organized capacity for social functioning'.[10] George Herbert Mead supplied the deepest progressive era critique of charity in his 1918

'Psychology of punitive justice' and later in his contribution to
Ellsworth Faris's *Intelligent Philanthropy.* [. . .]

The impulse to give, Mead argued, must be socialized. Charity
should be replaced by social service and social work. This was a
task of social organization, of reform, of politics; it was the
achievement of civilization, of 'social order', to replace the
voluntary character of charity with an obligation. 'Social service',
Mead wrote, was 'still in some communities hardly more than an
artificial island, scientifically fabricated, as it were, in an ocean of
primitive impulsiveness'. By the early years of the twentieth century
even the word charity had come into disfavour to be replaced by a
series of euphemisms: first, social work, and later, aid, pensions,
welfare, and human resources. [. . .]

Progressivism and the modern family

The vast transformation of American life wrought by late
nineteenth-century industrialization led to the great expansion of
the state that we identify with progressivism. The principle that
government should intervene into social and economic conditions
on behalf of 'the public' existed in the nineteenth century, but the
progressive era marked a shift, above all in the extended regulation
of business, protection for consumers and, beginning during World
War I, protection of the collective bargaining process. Within this
context, urban and state governments enacted a series of measures
aimed at protecting the health, housing and neighbourhood
conditions, and educational opportunities of working-class and
immigrant families. The most important new forms of 'intervention'
into the family were the abolition of child labour and the enactment
of protective legislation for women. In contrast to the reform
tradition of the nineteenth century, progressive reforms were not
directed at the 'poor' but sought to shore up the 'normal', self-
supporting family as well. In this sense, progressive reforms
anticipated and laid the basis for the comprehensive governmental
intervention of the twentieth century as expressed during the New
Deal and post-New Deal eras in such areas as social security,
housing, and education reform.

Beneath the diversity of thought of that era lay a common grid
of assumptions shared by most thinkers and made explicit among
those at Hull House and the University of Chicago, such as Jane
Addams, William I. Thomas, and John Dewey. These progressives
relied on a Darwinian model of social interdependence to repudiate

the individualistic political economy that underlay so much nineteenth-century thought. In their view, the rise of industry had destroyed the self-sufficiency of the old, petit bourgeois family, making it necessary to develop other institutions, particularly schools and neighbourhoods, to perform many tasks once performed by the family. They hoped that any such new institutions would reflect the general evolutionary tendency toward a more specialized and interdependent division of labour.

While fostering governmental intervention, their key concept was that of the 'social', and they drew upon the contemporaneous development of sociology for such notions as custom, mores, and folkways. According to George Herbert Mead, 'we must recognize that the most concrete and most fully realized society is not that which is presented in institutions but that which is found in the interplay of social habits and customs, in the readjustments of personal interests that have come into conflict, and which takes place outside of court, in the change of social attitude that is not dependent upon an act of legislature'. [. . .]

Using the concept of the social, progressive thinkers sought to redefine individualism in order to free it from its political-economic and masculinist integument. As we have seen, their view of people as intrinsically social was based on a denial of the aggressive and sexual bases of the individual. Their critiques of political-economic individualism and war tended to ignore the aggressiveness taken for granted by most previous thinkers. Progressive reform looked to pragmatic regulation, compromise, 'balancing acts', and 'rules of reason'. The spirit of adjustment and compromise can be seen in the vast extension of discretionary powers granted to the juvenile courts and in the creation of regulatory agencies; ironically, both reforms tended to intensify the process of corruption, manipulation, and special pleading they were in part designed to eliminate.

Similarly, the attempt to redefine individualism to include women minimized the importance of biological differences between the sexes, when compared to the central place that these differences held for nineteenth-century thinkers. The reform of society, they expected, would lead to the reform of the family as well. Through a recognition of its place in a democratic, interdependent, and functionally divided society, it would become more sociable, more democratic and cooperative, more personal and informal, and less private and self-contained. 'Industrialization', wrote the evolutionary socialist and family historian Arthur Calhoun in 1919, has led to the 'general democratization of society' and the 'waning of domestic monarchy'. As women gained 'economic opportunity outside of marriage', they would become more independent within the home. The modern family would be based on a recognition of the individual rights of its members, especially women and children.[11]

At this point we can see the extent to which the general attack on dependence converged with the history of feminism. Jane Addams was one of the thinkers of the period most sensitive to the contradictions involved in the critique of paternalism; nevertheless, that critique was the central theme of her early work. In 1902 she put *Democracy and Social Ethics* together out of a series of magazine articles she had written during the 1890s that contains six critical discussions of paternalistic relationships: father/daughter, mistress/maid, ward boss/immigrant, teacher/student, charity worker/recipient, and company town boss/worker. She offered a parable of the welfare state in contrasting a good-natured but poor landlord and a hard-hearted but rich landlord. The rich landlord 'collects with sternness . . . accepts no excuse, and will have his own', while the good-natured landlord 'pities and spares his poverty pressed tenants'. Though the rich landlord is unloved, he commands admiration; the good-natured landlord is treated with a 'certain lack of respect. In one sense he is a failure.' Intermingled with the love his tenants bear him, there is contempt. Quite properly, they suspect that his behaviour is weak at its root, that it is not based upon reality, and that it hides unacknowledged motives, perhaps a fear of standing one's ground or an excessive need to be loved. For Addams, the development of relations of individual integrity among people depended on their recognition of their real economic position. A society organized around wage-labour, she believed, made possible a kind of equality and independence that paternalism foreclosed.[12] [. . .]

The shift the progressives helped accomplish from a *laissez-faire* outlook to one appropriate to a highly integrated corporate capitalist welfare state masked the continuity of market relations both in society and as incorporated into governmental reforms. The idea that government should guarantee a job was different from the *laissez-faire* state's responsibility for guaranteeing the market but, like it, was based on the accommodation of collectivist arrangements to the capitalist property system. As with government intervention into business, government intervention into social life presupposed wage-labour and private property. The paradox is that the progressive attempt to reshape the family and individualism in line with increasing social cooperation and interdependence not only preserved the economic individualism of the nineteenth-century marketplace but intensified it . . .

Feminism and progressivism

A key source for Addams's attack on paternalism was her immersion in the politics of the late nineteenth- and early twentieth-century women's movement. When that movement is remembered in all its diversity, to include not only suffrage but temperance, the social purity movement, women's labour organizations, and women's clubs, it can be ranked with labour, populism, and urban reform (with all of which it overlapped) as among the largest and most influential social movements of the period. The central problem that all tendencies of the women's movement faced was that of reconciling the spread of the marketplace, with its emphasis on individualism and competition, with the traditional values of 'women's sphere' — benevolence and selfless nurturance. The spread of market relations promised to free women from the backwardness of the patriarchal family but at the same time threatened to corrode and undermine family life and the values it embodied. For the first generation of college-educated women, entering the labour force in the 1890s, the contradictions between the family and the market or, put psychologically, between dependence and autonomy, were particularly acute. One expression of this was the search for a politics that could combine wage-labour and economic independence, especially for middle-class women, with state protection of the family, especially among the poor.

Jane Addams, one of the most important feminists of the period, as well as a leader of progressivism, spoke to this issue. Government, she wrote, was simply 'enlarged housekeeping'. [. . .]

In a single metaphor, Addams combined the progressive view that society was moving toward increasing interdependence and a more socially oriented ethics, with the feminist view that women, who once took private responsibility for nurturance, would carry this value into the world of work and government. In this way, she brought the 'separate sphere' ideology of feminism into the corporate era. She was able to defend both the entry of women as individuals into the world of work and the obligation of the new government services to protect the family (particularly its most dependent members, women and children) and particularly the families of the poor. [. . .]

The family wage

In the progressive period, as earlier, government policies continued to respond to pressures to protect both the individual man or woman and the family. However, the great expansion of government intervention in this period coincided with the vast and unremitting growth in women working, and the beginning of the elimination of children and young people from the labour force. This posed in graphic terms the contradiction between women as individuals (i.e. wage earners) and women as the radiating core of the family. The most important recognition of this contradiction in government policy was protective labour legislation for working women, upheld after a series of efforts by the US Supreme Court in the case of *Muller* v. *Oregon* in 1908. [. . .]

Heidi Hartmann's 'Capitalism, patriarchy and job segregation by sex' puts the issue of protective legislation at the centre of a critique of the welfare state. According to Hartmann, men, acting as a gender (specifically, working-class men coopted by employers) excluded women from the trade union movement during the late nineteenth century and supported protective legislation to enforce occupational segregation by sex.[13] [. . .]

But these conflicts must be understood alongside the simultaneous struggle shared by working-class women and men for a decent family life. At a time when it required everyone within the household to support a family, the idea of a single wage for a single breadwinner was viewed as extremely desirable. At a time when most of a woman's adult life span corresponded to the years of pregnancy and child rearing, many if not most women shared the idea that this breadwinner should be the man. The growth in women working during the early twentieth century, in so far as it was a necessity imposed on working-class women, was viewed as a social evil by every feminist organization of the period, as well as by a great many working-class women themselves, as Leslie Tentler's work has shown.[14] The slogan of the Women's Trade Union League, the primary organization of working women, was 'the eight-hour day; a living wage; to guard the home'. [. . .]

More important than the history of the family wage issue is the history of working people's aspirations for a family. The goal of the family wage combined the feminist emphasis on the importance of motherhood and the family with the trade union emphasis on the dignity and self-reliance of the male breadwinner. Its ethical and social origins certainly included traditions of community more characteristic of working-class than middle-class life, and probably also drew upon expectations of cooperation and sharing between the sexes. In the 1880s, when the first modern investigations of working-class family life were undertaken by the Massachusetts Bureau of Labor Statistics, one of the findings that most shocked and dismayed the middle-class male investigators was that working-class men would cook, clean, and care for the children while their wives were at work and they were not. [...]

Explaining the modern family as the result of 'capitalism' is no longer adequate. Many scholars have observed that the organization of modern family life around wage-labour conformed to the needs of an ascendant capitalist class and a new imperialist state that proclaimed children as its most important national resource and that considered education and population policy as essential props of national strength. But state policy toward the family was not dictated by any capitalist conspiracy. Rather, it was the outcome of a series of single-issue reform movements, each one of which was 'realistic' enough and 'pragmatic' enough to take the rise of corporate capitalism and the accompanying individualistic structure of family life for granted and to seek to attain a specific goal — even goals that had major impact, such as the abolition of child labour — within its confines. A common historical process shaped the acquiescence of feminists in the domination of capital at the workplace and the acquiescence of labour in the domination of men within the home, but neither of these was an inevitable outcome.

Far from the state 'invading' or 'replacing' the family, a certain kind of alienated public life and a certain kind of alienated private life have expanded together. The form in which the welfare state expanded was public, the content private. The vast expansion of government spending that marked the New Deal and post-New Deal eras has scarcely eliminated the strength of market forces in our society, and in many ways has strengthened them. [...]

The spread of a society organized around self-reliance, the market, and wage-labour marked a great advance, perhaps especially for women, but we should also mark its costs and limits. By the time our nation reached the early twentieth century, the attempt to shore up independence through economic means had become largely defensive, and in our own time economic individualism largely betrays the promise it once held out. Neither the attempt to extend the traditionally male ideal of individual independence to women nor the attempt to extend the traditionally female ideal of nurturance to men can be based on an economic system that fosters a one-sided ideal of economic independence and a correspondingly hollow collectivity. True independence, for both sexes, is based on an acceptance of our dependence on others and is realized through our ability to nurture and give to others without conflict within ourselves.

Notes

1. Nancy F. Cott (1977) *The Bonds of Womanhood: 'Woman's Sphere' in New England, 1780—1835,* New Haven, Yale University Press; and Carl N. Degler (1980) *At Odds: Women and the Family in America from the Revolution to the Present,* New York, Oxford University Press.
2. Herbert Gutman (1978) *The Black Family in Slavery and Freedom, 1750—1925,* New York, Pantheon. The quote is on Gutman's p. 217 from Sidney W. Mintz and Richard Price (1974) 'An anthropological approach to the study of Afro-American history', unpublished paper, February.
3. Carol Stack (1974) *All Our Kin,* New York, Harper and Row.
4. John Locke (1966) *Two Treatises of Government,* Thomas I. Cook (ed.), New York, Hafner, p. 11.
5. Alexis De Tocqueville (1954) *Democracy in America,* New York, Vintage, Ch. 2, p. 203.
6. Morton J. Horowitz (1977) *The Transformation of American Law 1780—1860,* Cambridge, Massachusetts, Harvard University Press, p. 253.
7. Quoted in Ellen DuBois (1975) 'The radicalism of the woman suffrage movement: notes toward the reconstruction of nineteenth-century feminism', *Feminist Studies 3,* No. 1/2, Fall, pp. 66—8.
8. Christopher Lasch (1980) 'Life in the therapeutic state', *New York Review of Books,* June.
9. Josephine Shaw Lowell (1884) *Public Relief and Private Charity,* New York, p. 66; and Marion E. Gettleman (1963) 'Charity and social classes in the United States, 1874—99,' *American Journal of Economics and Sociology,* 22, April, pp. 313—30; July, pp. 417—26.
10. John Dewey (1969) *Outlines of a Critical Theory of Ethics,* New York, Greenwood, and Merle Curti (1935) *Social Ideas of American Educators,* New York, Scribner's, p. 523.
11. W. Arthur Calhoun (1919) *A Social History of the American Family,* Cleveland, Ch. 3, p. 157; cf. Eli Zaretsky (1979) 'Progressive Thought on the Impact of Industrialization on the Family and Its Relation to the Emergence of the Welfare State, 1890—1920', PhD. dissertation, University of Maryland.
12. Jane Addams (1901) *Democracy and Social Ethics*, New York, Macmillan, pp. 24—5.

13. Heidi Hartmann, 'Capitalism' in Anthony Giddens and David Held (eds) (1982) *Classes, Power and Conflict,* London, Macmillan.
14. Leslie Woodcock Tentler (1979) *Wage-Earning Women: Industrial Work and Family Life in the United States, 1900—1930,* New York, Oxford University Press. Hartmann, agreeing with William O'Neill, dismisses the 'social feminists' as 'not primarily interested in advancing the cause of women's rights'.

3.5

Power, Sovereignty and Discipline

MICHEL FOUCAULT

I Two features

The essential role of the theory of law,[1] from medieval times onwards, was to fix the legitimacy of power; that is the major problem around which the whole theory of law and sovereignty is organized . . . The essential function of the discourse and techniques of law has been to efface the domination intrinsic to power in order to present the latter . . . on the one hand, as the legitimate rights of sovereignty, and on the other, as the legal obligation to obey it . . .

My general project over the past few years has been . . . to show not only how law is, in a general way, the instrument of this domination — which scarcely needs saying — but also to show the extent to which, and the forms in which, the law (not simply the laws but the whole complex of apparatuses, institutions and regulations responsible for their application) transmits and puts in motion relations that are not relations of sovereignty, but of domination. Moreover, in speaking of domination I do not have in mind that solid and global kind of domination that one person exercises over others, or one group over another, but the manifold forms of domination that can be exercised within society. Not the domination of the King in his central position, therefore, but that of his subjects in their mutual relations: not the uniform edifice of sovereignty, but the multiple forms of subjugation that have a place and function within the social organism.

The system of law, the domain of law, are permanent agents of these relations of domination, these polymorphous techniques of

Source I: From 'Two features', in Colin Gordon (ed.) *Power/Knowledge*, (1980) New York, Pantheon Books, and Brighton, Harvester Press.

subjugation. Law should be viewed, I believe, not in terms of a legitimacy to be established, but in terms of the methods of subjugation that it instigates . . .

The analysis in question should not concern itself with the regulated and legitimate forms of power in their central locations, with the general mechanisms through which they operate, and the continual effects of these. On the contrary, it should be concerned with power at its extremities, in its ultimate destinations, with those points where it becomes capillary, that is, in its more regional and local forms and institutions. Its paramount concern, in fact, should be with the point where power surmounts the rules of law, which organize and delimit it and extends itself beyond them, invests itself in institutions, becomes embodied in techniques, and equips itself with instruments and eventually even violent means of material intervention . . .

Secondly, the analysis should not concern itself with power at the level of conscious intention or decision; it should not attempt to consider power from its internal point of view and should refrain from posing the labyrinthine and unanswerable question: 'Who then has power and what has he in mind? What is the aim of someone who possesses power?' Instead, it is a case of studying power at the point where its intention, if it has one, is completely invested in its real and effective practices. What is needed is a study of power in its external visage, at the point where it is in direct and immediate relationship with that which we can provisionally call its object, its target, its field of application, there — that is to say — where it installs itself and produces its real effects.

Let us not, therefore, ask why certain people want to dominate, what they seek, what is their overall strategy. Let us ask, instead, how things work at the level of on-going subjugation, at the level of those continuous and uninterrupted processes which subject our bodies, govern our gestures, dictate our behaviours etc. In other words, rather than ask ourselves how the sovereign appears to us in his lofty isolation, we should try to discover how it is that subjects are gradually, progressively, really and materially constituted through a multiplicity of organisms, forces, energies, materials, desires, thoughts etc. We should try to grasp subjection in its material instance as a constitution of subjects. This would be the exact opposite of Hobbes' project in *Leviathan*, and of that, I believe, of all jurists for whom the problem is the distillation of a single will — or rather, the constitution of a unitary, singular body animated by the spirit of sovereignty — from the particular wills of a multiplicity of individuals . . .

A third precaution relates to the fact that power is not to be taken to be a phenomenon of one individual's consolidated and homogeneous domination over others, or that of one group or class over others . . . Power must be analysed as something which circulates, or rather as something which only functions in the form of a chain. It is never localized here or there, never in anybody's hands, never appropriated as a commodity or piece of wealth. Power is employed and exercised through a net-like organization. And not only do individuals circulate between its threads; they are always in the position of simultaneously undergoing and exercising this power. They are not only its inert or consenting target; they are always also the elements of its articulation. In other words, individuals are the vehicles of power, not its points of application.

The individual is not to be conceived as a sort of elementary nucleus, a primitive atom, a multiple and inert material on which power comes to fasten or against which it happens to strike, and in so doing subdues or crushes individuals. In fact, it is already one of the prime effects of power that certain bodies, certain gestures, certain discourses, certain desires, come to be identified and constituted as individuals. The individual, that is, is not the *vis-à-vis* of power; it is, I believe, one of its prime effects . . .

When I say that power establishes a network through which it freely circulates, this is true only up to a certain point . . . We are not dealing with a sort of democratic or anarchic distribution of power through bodies . . . The important thing is not to attempt some kind of deduction of power starting from its centre and aimed at the discovery of the extent to which it permeates into the base, of the degree to which it reproduces itself down to and including the most molecular elements of society. One must rather conduct an *ascending* analysis of power, starting, that is, from its infinitesimal mechanisms, which each have their own history, their own trajectory, their own techniques and tactics; and then see how these mechanisms of power have been — and continue to be — invested, colonized, utilized, involuted, transformed, displaced, extended etc, by ever more general mechanisms and by forms of global domination. It is not that this global domination extends itself right to the base in a plurality of repercussions: I believe that the manner in which the phenomena, the techniques and the procedures of power enter into play at the most basic levels must be analysed, that the way in which these procedures are displaced, extended and altered must certainly be demonstrated; but above all what must be shown is the manner in which they are invested and annexed by more global phenomena and the subtle fashion in which more general powers or economic interests are able to engage with these technologies that are at once both relatively autonomous of power and act as its infinitesimal elements.

In order to make this clearer, one might cite the example of madness. The descending type of analysis, the one of which I believe one ought to be wary, will say that the bourgeoisie has, since the sixteenth or seventeenth century, been the dominant class; from this premise, it will then set out to deduce the internment of the insane. One can always make this deduction, it is always easily done and that is precisely what I would hold against it. It is in fact a simple matter to show that since lunatics are precisely those persons who are useless to industrial production, one is obliged to dispense with them . . . These kinds of deduction are always possible. They are simultaneously correct and false. Above all they are too glib . . .

I believe that anything can be deduced from the general phenomenon of the domination of the bourgeois class. What needs to be done is something quite different. One needs to investigate historically, and beginning from the lowest level, how mechanisms of power have been able to function. In regard to the confinement of the insane, for example, . . . we need to see the manner in which, at the effective level of the family, of the immediate environment, of the cells and most basic units of society, these phenomena of repression or exclusion possessed their instruments and their logic, in response to a certain number of needs. We need to identify the agents responsible for them, their real agents (those which constituted the immediate social *entourage*, the family, parents, doctors etc.) and not be content to lump them under the formula of a generalized bourgeoisie. We need to see how these mechanisms of power, at a given moment, in a precise conjuncture and by means of a certain number of transformations, have begun to become economically advantageous and politically useful. I think that in this way one could easily manage to demonstrate that what the bourgeoisie needed, or that in which its system discovered its real interests, was not the exclusion of the mad . . . but rather, the techniques and procedures themselves of such an exclusion. It is the mechanisms of that exclusion that are necessary, the apparatuses of surveillance, the medicalization of sexuality, of madness, of delinquency, all the micro-mechanisms of power, that came, from a certain moment in time, to represent the interests of the bourgeoisie . . .

What in fact happened . . . was that the mechanisms of the exclusion of madness . . . began from a particular point in time, and for reasons which need to be studied, to reveal their political usefulness and to lend themselves to economic profit, and that as a natural consequence, all of a sudden, they came to be colonized and maintained by global mechanisms and the entire state system . . .

To put this somewhat differently: the bourgeoisie has never had any use for the insane; but the procedures it has employed to exclude them have revealed and realized — from the nineteenth century onwards, and again on the basis of certain transformations — a political advantage, on occasion even a certain economic utility, which have consolidated the system and contributed to its overall functioning. The bourgeoisie is interested in power, not in madness, in the system of control of infantile sexuality, not in that phenomenon itself. The bourgeoisie could not care less about delinquents, about their punishment and rehabilitation, which economically have little importance, but it is concerned about the complex of mechanisms with which delinquency is controlled, pursued, punished and reformed etc. . . .

By way of summarizing . . . I would say that we should direct our researches on the nature of power not towards the juridical edifice of sovereignty, the state apparatuses and the ideologies which accompany them, but towards domination and the material operators of power, towards forms of subjection and the inflections and utilizations of their localized systems, and towards strategic apparatuses. We must eschew the model of Leviathan in the study of power. We must escape from the limited field of juridical sovereignty and state institutions, and instead base our analysis of power on the study of the techniques and tactics of domination . . .

As long as a feudal type of society survived, the problems to which the theory of sovereignty was addressed were in effect confined to the general mechanisms of power, to the way in which its forms of existence at the higher level of society influenced its exercise at the lowest levels . . . In effect, the mode in which power was exercised could be defined in its essentials in terms of the relationship sovereign—subject. But in the seventeenth and eighteenth centuries, we have the production of an important phenomenon, the emergence, or rather the invention, of a new mechanism of power possessed of highly specific procedural techniques, completely novel instruments, quite different apparatuses, and which is also, I believe, absolutely incompatible with the relations of sovereignty . . .

This type of power is in every aspect the antithesis of that mechanism of power which the theory of sovereignty described or sought to transcribe. The latter is linked to a form of power that is exercised over the earth and its products, much more than over human bodies and their operations. The theory of sovereignty is something which refers to the displacement and appropriation on the part of power, not of time and labour, but of goods and wealth. It allows discontinuous obligations distributed over time to be given legal expression, but it does not allow for the codification of a continuous surveillance. It enables power to be founded in the physical existence of the sovereign, but not in continuous and permanent systems of surveillance. The theory of sovereignty permits the foundation of an absolute power in the absolute expenditure of power. It does not allow for a calculation of power in terms of the minimum expenditure for the maximum return.

This new type of power, which can no longer be formulated in terms of sovereignty, is, I believe, one of the great inventions of bourgeois society. It has been a fundamental instrument in the constitution of industrial capitalism and of the type of society that is its accompaniment. This non-sovereign power, which lies outside the form of sovereignty, is disciplinary power. Impossible to describe in the terminology of the theory of sovereignty from which it differs so radically, this disciplinary power ought by rights to have led to the disappearance of the grand juridical edifice created by that theory. But in reality, the theory of sovereignty has continued not only to exist as an ideology of law, but also to provide the organizing principle of the legal codes which Europe acquired in the nineteenth century, beginning with the Napoleonic Code . . .

Modern society, then, from the nineteenth century up to our own day, has been characterized on the one hand, by a legislation, a discourse, an organization based on public law, whose principle of articulation is the social body and the delegative status of each citizen; and, on the other hand, by a closely linked grid of disciplinary coercions whose purpose is in fact to assure the cohesion of this same social body. Though a theory of law is a necessary companion to this grid, it cannot in any event provide the terms of its endorsement. Hence these two limits, a right of sovereignty and a mechanism of discipline, which define, I believe, the arena in which power is exercised. But these two limits are so heterogeneous that they cannot possibly be reduced to each other . . .

The discourse of discipline has nothing in common with that of law, rule, or sovereign will. The disciplines may well be the carriers of a discourse that speaks of a rule, but this is not the juridical rule deriving from sovereignty, but a natural rule, a norm. The code they come to define is not that of law but that of normalization . . .

I believe that in our own times power is exercised simultaneously through the law of sovereignty and these disciplinary techniques, and that these techniques and these discourses, to which the disciplines give rise, invade the area of law so that the procedures of normalization come to be ever more constantly engaged in the colonization of those of law. I believe that all this can explain the global functioning of what I would call a *society of normalization* . . .

II Truth and power

Thus to pose the problem of power in terms of the state means to continue posing it in terms of sovereign and sovereignty, that is to say in terms of law. If one describes all these phenomena of power as dependent on the state apparatus, this means grasping them as essentially repressive: the army as a power of death, police and justice as punitive instances, etc. I don't want to say that the state isn't important; what I want to say is that relations of power, and hence the analysis that must be made of them, necessarily extend beyond the limits of the state. In two senses: first of all because the state, for all the omnipotence of its apparatuses, is far from being able to occupy the whole field of actual power relations, and further because the state can only operate on the basis of other, already existing power relations. The state is superstructural in relation to a whole series of power networks that invest the body, sexuality, the family, kinship, knowledge, technology and so forth. True, these networks stand in a conditioning—conditioned relationship to a kind of 'meta-power' which is structured essentially round a certain number of great prohibition functions; but this meta-power, with its prohibitions, can only take hold and secure its footing where it is rooted in a whole series of multiple and indefinite power relations that supply the necessary basis for the great negative forms of power . . .

I would say that the state consists in the codification of a whole number of power relations which render its functioning possible, and that revolution is a different type of codification of the same relations. This implies that there are many different kinds of

Source II: From 'Truth and power' in Colin Gordon (ed.) *Power/Knowledge* (1980) New York, Pantheon Books, and Brighton, Harvester Press.

revolution, roughly speaking as many kinds as there are possible subversive recodifications of power relations, and further that one can perfectly well conceive of revolutions which leave essentially untouched the power relations which form the basis for the functioning of the state.

Editor's note

Where Foucault's translator has consistently translated the French term 'droit' into the English 'right', I have rendered it into the more general and colloquial form 'law'. 'Right' is technically the more accurate translation, since Foucault, writing within the tradition of Roman law, is using the distinction, common in that discourse, between *civil* law, regulating the relations between citizens (*jus*), and *public* law, governing the relations between the state and its subjects (*lex*). This distinction is much less clear in English legal tradition. Hence, a phrase like 'the theory of right' may sound strange to any reader other than one trained in legal discourse. However, the rendering, 'law', in my edited version should be taken to refer to those public aspects of law which define and regulate sovereignty, political and legal obligation, powers of the state and the rights of citizens and legal subjects.

Part 4
The State and the Economy

Introduction

LAURENCE HARRIS

A distinctive characteristic of modern theories of the state is the prominence of economic factors. The manner in which relations between the state and 'civil society' are considered, invariably has the economic processes of the latter at the forefront, or else as a pervasive shadow over the explicitly political, cultural or more general social connections. This is no less true of non-Marxist than of Marxist approaches. The chapters which follow are concerned quite explicitly with that economic dimension of the connections between the state and civil society.

The classical Marxist view is that the manner in which the state is constituted and state power organized corresponds in some way to the conditions of the economic base; and in the broadest terms the idea of a correspondence is shared by other schools of thought. The persuasiveness of the general idea, however, meets its stiffest test when it is confronted with the specific variations in the state that arise in the course of economic change and that appear in the differences between one state and another.

The very changed conditions of capitalist societies in the decades after the Second World War posed the greatest challenge to the general formulations of the correspondence view; the development of more specific concepts was one response. While the theories of Offe and Altvater and new concepts of state monopoly capitalism marked a Marxist response, concepts of 'the corporatist state' have been a major development in non-Marxist writings (with Marxist contributions from authors such as Panitch).

The 'corporatist' label was first applied to the political and economic structure of Hitler's Germany, Mussolini's Italy and Franco's Spain, but in the 1970s writers such as Pahl and Winkler in Britain identified the development of corporatism as a significantly new form of state power. The corporatism they identified was different from that of the Fascist states and Chapter 4.1 by

317

Colin Crouch which opens Part 4 sets out the differences and discusses the modern corporatist thesis.

The idea that the state in capitalist societies had become corporatist related institutional changes to the economic exigencies, principally to the question of harnessing and regulating the conflict between capital and labour. Keith Middlemas's book, *Politics in Industrial Society*, is a rich historical study of the development of corporatist type arrangements for the integration of capital and labour in relation to the British state, arrangements which did seem to many to be a fundamental part of the modern landscape until the 1979 Conservative government downgraded the tripartite institutions that brought state, capital and labour together. He examines the growth and vicissitudes of these arrangements since 1911 but rejects the schematic corporatism thesis of a new type of state in favour of a closely related, but more flexible idea that the British state has been marked by 'corporate bias'. Chapter 4.2 is an extract from his book which gives the broad outlines of his concept and its application.

The changes in the form of the state which some identified as corporatist were matched by the rise of state policies towards the economy articulated around Keynesian views of the state's role. The exact nature of Keynesianism is problematic and Tomlinson has even questioned whether it did mark a distinctive phase in the state's relation to the economy. Kerry Schott's chapter attempts to counter Tomlinson's negative answer. Her reference point is the development of economic policy in Britain between 1940 and 1964, and in her examination of the record she links the demand management and budgetary policy that characterizes narrow Keynesianism with the development of corporatist-type arrangements and with the construction of a 'concordat' between the interests of capital and labour. An additional characteristic of the long post-war boom that earned Keynesianism a place in history was state intervention at the international level, providing stable monetary and commercial conditions for the development of world trade, and Schott's account of developments in Britain is strengthened if placed in that context.

The interests of capital and labour are a major concept in Schott's analysis and one outcome of their interplay is new forms of organization. Peter Hall's chapter, however, stands that common conception on its head, for he argues that the forms of organization of labour and capital (and of the state) have an autonomous influence of their own: in fact, that the interests of different classes and fractions of classes in some respects do not even exist independently of the form of organization through which they are articulated. He argues that his theory, outside the mainstreams but drawing upon them, has the virtue of accounting for differences in the formulation of economic policy in different countries and a comparative study of Britain and the Federal Republic of Germany is offered in support. An additional feature of this essay is that, like Marxist studies which derive from Hilferding, undifferentiated capital and labour are not the only economic actors in civil society, for financial and industrial capital are distinguished and their relation with each other as well as with labour affects the formulation of economic policy (and, in a broader perspective, could be said to affect the structure of the state). Hall's thesis opens up several possible lines of enquiry, but as it stands it has some weaknesses. The comparative study can be no more than illustrative, rather than a test since, first, the differences between the cases cannot be attributed to a single crucial variable such as the organizational structure and, second, the evidence does not permit us to discriminate between the idea that the organizational form's influence is autonomous and the idea that the form is derived and symptomatic. Moreover, the concept of organization itself needs close scrutiny if it is to mean more than an institutional set-up with a voice.

Whereas Hall compares the state and the formulation of economic policies in different capitalist societies, Rakovski draws a comparison with a broader brush. If it is the case that the economic system underlies the nature of the state, we would expect the sharp differences in the ways Soviet-type and capitalist societies are ruled to be linked to marked differences in their economies and the social divisions that relate to them. The thesis that there was some convergence between East and West after the former adopted some measure of decentralized planning, and the latter adopted Keynesian and welfare policies, is critically examined by Rakovski who applies a Marxist perspective to socialist and capitalist societies alike. His rejection of the convergence thesis is based upon the argument that the economic systems and corresponding class structure are very different; in consequence (although this has to be explicitly drawn out from the text) the position of the state and the character of state power are quite different and far from having converged. It is a strong statement of the thesis that there is a correspondence between the form of the state and the economic system. Although it does not share with some of the other chapters in this part the deployment of historical and institutional material in support of the argument, the rigorous application of his theoretical concepts gives Rakovski's contribution a distinctive strength.

4.1

The State, Capital, and Liberal Democracy

COLIN CROUCH

It is remarkable to what extent the recent spread of interest in the state has led to the elaboration of social theory solely within the Marxist tradition. There have been *writings* on the subject from a range of other positions, some of which are discussed below, but little attempt at systematic theory. It is particularly strange that so little has emerged from the American pluralist tradition of political science, which has for so long dominated the subject and prided itself on the superiority over Marxism of its ability to conceptualize the political. True, much of its empirical work has been in the area of 'community power' rather than of the nation-state . . . but then the Marxist literature has also contributed at the former level through the studies of urban political economy of the French school . . . The reason may be that only Marxism has a theoretical apparatus capable of tackling the relationship between the political and the economic, which is particularly important in any study of the state in contemporary Western society.

The Marxist tradition therefore provides the best starting point for work in this field. There remain, however, several highly unsatisfactory aspects in most of this literature as it has so far developed. In particular, and rather surprisingly, there is no acceptable answer to the fundamental question: why must the state in a capitalist society serve the interests of capitalism? Further, the reluctance of most Marxist theory to admit any element of genuine pluralism within the polities of the liberal democracies leads to a convoluted process of redefinition and circumlocution.

Source: From Colin Crouch (ed.) *State and Economy in Contemporary Capitalism,* (1979) London, Croom Helm, pp. 13—53.

Much of the present chapter will be taken up with an elaboration of these and other criticisms and an attempt to reformulate parts of state theory to meet them.

But it is in the interests of neither Marxist sociology nor the subject as a whole for Marxist literature to be regarded as isolated and self-contained; it is part of a more general corpus. Where current writing on the state is concerned this involves two main strands: the thesis of 'overloaded government' and (a field that includes several Marxist writers) theories of the corporate state. [The latter will] be discussed in order to trace ideas overlapping with the Marxist literature and points to which [it] might pay more attention. [. . .]

The revival of interest in the corporate state reinforces the impression that with the apparent passing of the Keynesian period of post-war economic development the capitalist world is returning to some of the political preoccupations of earlier decades — broadly those from 1870 to 1940. It was from the 1870s onwards that the industrializing countries of Western Europe began to come to terms with two developments which had not been part of the canon of early capitalism: the inevitability of the organization of labour; and the need to be able to ensure the viability and progress of a particular national economy within the potentially destabilizing context of international trade, particularly during periods of recession. The capacity and willingness of industrial polities to respond to these issues varied with the extent of the commitment of their institutions to classical *laissez-faire* capitalism. The question cannot be argued in full detail here, but a good contrast is provided by the cases of Britain and Germany. In the former country a lengthy development of industrialization in a context of individualism and restricted state involvement imparted a deep liberalism to political, legal and economic institutions to which neither corporatist industrial relations nor state-regulated capitalism could be easily wedded. In Germany industrialism was from the outset led from above by a strong state which was building at the same time a modern economy and a new nation on the basis of institutions and legal codes which had changed little since medieval times. As a result the liberal phase of German capitalism was brief, possibly non-existent, and the country was well equipped for a corporatist integration of labour and state-aided, state-protected industry . . .

In the period before World War I the main result of these new orientations was the policy of imperialism. Although this was associated with policies of trying to produce a nationalistically integrated and hierarchically ordered society at home, corporatist labour relations remained largely an ideological aspiration, primarily of Roman Catholic social thought trying to find a way between the conflictual individualism of capitalism and the disruptive, anti-hierarchical (not to mention atheistic) aspirations of the growing socialist movement of organized labour.

If the Great War ended the age of imperialism (though not the fact of empires) it also provided the basis for a new integration of state, capital and labour. In modern wars of total mobilization, all capitalist societies are corporatist: the need to win the war creates an overwhelming moral unity and defines an external enemy so clearly that internal conflicts pale into insignificance; the state engages in a degree of propaganda and popular activation not normally seen in capitalist societies — politics ceases to be a mere 'sideshow in the circus of life' . . . and becomes literally a matter of life and death; the degree of economic regulation in which the state engages increases massively since it has to ensure the needs of the single overriding extra-economic priority of fighting the war; and the working class is taken into a highly corporatist relationship, with civil liberties restricted because of war needs, but concern for its physical and moral welfare considerably increased.

During the extreme crises of the 1920s and 1930s these models of state action to incorporate organized labour and to protect industry remained relevant to economic and social policy, though with very different emphasis in different countries. For example, in Italy it was under the Fascist regime, with its self-conscious adoption of corporatist rhetoric, that a system of organized industrial interests responsive to state direction was established, after the crushing by force of the oppositional labour movement. In Germany corporatist organizations involving the autonomous labour movement, together with protective measures for private industry, were developed by the centre-left governments of the Weimar republic, and it was largely the petit bourgeois forces left *outside* that system who gave support to the Nazi movement. This was thus in certain important respects hostile to corporatism in the name of a more inclusive state unimpeded by interest groups — an important and often overlooked difference between the Italian and German Fascist movements . . . In contrast again, in Britain a policy of industrial protection, cartelization and restriction was adopted only with extreme reluctance by governments and industrialists still preferring a liberal economic system, while a corporatist strategy towards labour was pursued only fitfully — for much of the period the high level of unemployment and the demoralization of labour after the General Strike of 1926 seemed to make political recognition of organized labour unnecessary.

During World War II the Fascist countries were already under a form of corporatism; in Britain the war effort had the implications for domestic organization discussed above; while in the occupied countries the labour movement and those sections of capital which did not collaborate forged a unity in the Resistance that facilitated corporatist developments in the early post-war years. However, as I have discussed elsewhere . . . the wartime build-up of corporatist potentialities petered out during the 1950s as the years of unprecedented economic growth and mass prosperity provided an original and apparently secure basis of social integration for advanced capitalist societies. Apart from a motley collection of countries including Spain and Portugal, the Netherlands, Peronist Argentina and possibly Sweden and Norway . . . the concept of corporatism became of declining relevance as an element in the analysis of contemporary politics.

During the past decade all that has changed. The decline in economic fortunes and associated rise of detailed state economic activity, together with the resurgence of industrial conflict and government attempts to regulate it, have revived the concept of the corporate state. Although the various authors who have contributed to the theme differ among themselves, and everyone has contributed his own classification of types of corporatism, there is a reasonably wide and fruitful area of agreement, which may be summarized in the following terms.

1. Corporatism is best regarded as a strategy pursued by capitalism when it cannot adequately subordinate labour by preventing its combination and allowing market processes to work. If liberal capitalism operates through individualism and the rigorous separation of the economic, political and ideological (or normative) spheres, corporatism entails the opposite. Subordinates and other economic actors are organized, and order is secured by the hierarchical control of organization. Regulation through organization almost necessarily involves the state as the only institution capable of securing centralized order (the merging of the political and the economic); while a high degree of normative integration is also necessary to ensure consensus over hierarchy. It is this *reversal* of some of the achievements of the liberal phase of capitalism that imparts the element of medievalism so important to corporatist ideology.

2. It follows from the above that corporatism is a *class* concept and belongs to the analysis of capitalist society. It has to do with ensuring the subordination of labour and represents an alternative strategy for capital when the classic pattern of control through markets is unavailable (or is for other reasons not pursued). Most analyses of corporatism have adopted this approach, but an important exception is J. T. Winkler. His primary focus is on industrial rather than industrial relations policy. This is in itself not objectionable, but he detaches the concept entirely from class relations, regarding it as essentially a relationship of tension between the state and private industry; industry remains in private *ownership* but subject to *control* by the state — a new formulation of the division between ownership and control. There are two problems with such an analysis. First, it ignores the fact that the regulation of labour in the interests of capital has been an important aspect of most corporatist policies. Second, it leaves implicit and poorly theoretized the relationship between capital and the state. Whose interests does the state serve and why? If . . . there are good reasons for believing that most actions of the state are taken in the interests of at least certain sections of capital, then the idea of corporatism being a matter of the state, as a separate entity, imposing constraints on industry becomes highly suspect. On the other hand, to anticipate subsequent arguments, Winkler's arguments are not to be as easily disposed of as current versions of Marxist theory assume, and it is the problematic status of corporatist strategies within liberal democratic capitalist societies which leads us to raise certain queries of the Marxist account.

3. While corporatism certainly has to do with industrial relations, it would be wrong to regard it as a concept which can be analysed within the variables of industrial relations in isolation. Some of the conditions of corporatism may reflect developments in other areas of the economy, such as: defensive rationalization and cartelization; an increasing degree of concentration in industry to take advantage of modern technology and the economies of scale; state participation in economic planning; and other processes which at least partially suspend the full force of market competition. The reason for this is as follows. One does not need to accept the Marxist labour theory of value to recognize that ultimately every price reflects the cost of the labour input of the good in question. Any policy which partially suspends market forces needs to find alternative means of restraining prices — ultimately the price of

labour. Where imported goods are concerned, this is achieved through tariffs and other protectionist measures. Within the domestic market in an economy with an organized labour movement, similar control can be secured only by incorporating labour's organizations within the structure of economic regulation. Where labour is weak and non-disruptive, the general economic policies associated with corporatism may be able to dispense with a labour relations policy — as was perhaps the case in Britain for much of the 1920s — but this is likely to be temporary; if the corporatist policies are at all successful in stabilizing the economy in conditions of suspended competition, labour will become powerful.

It will be noted that not all the developments associated with corporatism immediately involve the state — indeed some of the more idealistic versions of corporatist theory virtually ignored the state and envisaged a corporatist system emerging out of a chain of autonomous agreements between employers and workers. This is as naive as syndicalist theory, to which it is not unrelated, but it is important to regard the state's activity as *part* of a wider pattern of developments which reduce the fragmentation, atomization and competition among economic units which characterized classical capitalism. Particularly useful here is a concept closely related to that of the corporate state which is also enjoying a revival of interest — that of 'organized capitalism' developed in Weimar Germany by Hilferding, Naphtali and others. Hilferding discerned a series of related processes taking place within modern capitalism, some involving the state, others not. Included were concentration in industry, trade and banking; the bureaucratization of and introduction of planning into the firm consequent on the emergence of professional management; the increasing organization and extension to a national basis of industrial conflicts; growing state intervention to restore the economic equilibrium constantly disrupted by the chaos of capitalist markets; state intervention in social policy to reduce insecurity; imperialism; the growing importance of political parties and an expansion of the role of the state to embrace general guidance (*Leistung*) of the whole society rather than simply the maintenance of order (*Ordnung*); the development of ideologies of scientific efficiency.

Hilferding considered that these processes would mean increasing economic stability and a societization of processes formerly left to the autonomous regulation of the market. As a reformist Marxist he believed that this marked the start of the transformation of capitalism into a planned, rational socialist economy, especially as increasing participation by the labour movement was necessary in the institutions established to secure stability. Concomitantly he saw a need for workers to share control in running industry at the level of the firm — a contribution of his thought which has survived in the German labour movement's advocacy of *Mitbestimmung*.

Clearly, Hilferding is discussing the same processes as those usually labelled as corporatism: the establishment of a capitalist order secured through organized co-ordination rather than through markets, with labour's organizations integrated into the process of control. However, where most concepts of corporatism see this process as one in which labour is subordinated, Hilferding considered that through such mechanisms labour *might* succeed in transforming capitalism and gaining dominance. His optimism and, as a result, his overall theory are generally considered to have been discredited by the eventual fate of Weimar — though certainly no more discredited than the official international Communist policy at that time of, first, conniving at any crisis in the fragile structure of German liberal democracy and then temporarily co-operating with the Nazi regime. It has also been observed that the defensive measures of European capitalism in the 1920s did not have the stabilizing and progressive, let alone transformative, potentialities that Hilferding believed; however, the same critics point out that the Keynesian economic policies which became dominant by the 1940s did provide the kind of politicized stabilization of capitalist economies for which he had been looking.

4. Hilferding's arguments that an organized capitalism presents opportunities to organized labour has interesting implications for corporatist theory — implications which are echoed in much recent literature. Because of its origins in nineteenth-century anti-liberal Conservatism, and even more because of its use by Fascist regimes in Italy, Spain and Portugal, the corporatist state is often regarded as highly hierarchical with few elements of pluralism. This assumes that a corporatist strategy employed by dominant élites is actually successful. There is one major condition for this success: the organizations which simultaneously represent and discipline the working class have to operate primarily downwards, ordering and controlling their members. If in fact they instead (or even also) work upwards, conveying demands to the state and to organized capital, not only do they impart a strong element of pluralism, but it is a pluralism which is less constrained by the market and by the institutional segregation of polity and economy characteristic of liberal capitalism.

In classic corporatist ideology this problem was overcome by envisaging that all classes of society would be united morally and normatively, usually through the agency of the Catholic Church, in a manner that was considered to have been characteristic of medieval, feudal society before the disruptive impact of liberal, individualistic capitalism. The ambition was always improbable; the construction of a positive ideological unity in a capitalist society has proved to be a difficult task. Some success was achieved with the creation of a Catholic labour movement in opposition to the existing socialist one throughout Continental Western Europe, though even this never saw its role in entirely collaborationist terms.

The Fascist countries had greater scope for creating ideological unity than those with essentially liberal political systems, through their intensive use of state propaganda and popular mobilization under nationalist slogans. However, this was heavily buttressed by the use of massive coercion which in principle has no place in corporatism. To a certain extent the widespread repression of dissidence was a condition for the success of ideological mobilization. In a society where autonomous groups are allowed to organize themselves, attempts at mobilization by the right will be countered by similar attempts by the left, leading to a raising of political tension and a threat to social stability: hence the tendency for mass mobilization to be inversely related to the degree of liberal freedoms present in a society.

These considerations lead us to predict two different destinies for corporatist strategies, depending on whether the social context in which they are launched is liberal or authoritarian. By liberal I here mean a society in which organizations (of capital, labour and other groups) develop autonomously within civil society, deriving their self-definitions and their power from their constituent parts — ultimately from individuals. By authoritarian is meant a system in which organizations are defined, allocated power and probably even created by the state, their base in civil society being weak. Clearly a scale of that kind is a continuum rather than a two-fold classification: for example while the Federal Republic of Germany and the United Kingdom would both be classified as liberal, the latter would rest more unambiguously near the liberal pole. Further, of course, the positions of individual countries change over time. However, for the purpose of the present discussions we shall speak in terms of the two extreme cases: liberalism and authoritarianism.

If the ruling classes of an authoritarian society make use of corporatist strategies they will do so through the creation of more or less artificial organizations — at least on the side of labour — whose scope and power will be subject to the whim of the state for as long as the state can remain effectively authoritarian. Repression can be easily mobilized to deal with dissidents. The corporatism will be hierarchical and relatively untroubled, though it will not really correspond to the ambitions of classical corporatist ideology which saw the necessary unity of such a system emerging spontaneously from the organism of civil society.

Against this, corporatism in a liberal society means coming to terms with autonomous organizations which will never be entirely successfully subjected to ideological hegemony and which must always do something to represent their members. Relations between the state and these organized interests are therefore always likely to be characterized by bargaining: something has to be exchanged for the social peace which the organizations are expected to deliver. This has at least two important implications. First, this kind of shifting, bargained relationship is very different from both the moral order of pure corporatism and the rigid control of Fascism. Second, the fact that the bargaining takes place between organized labour and the state, and between peak organizations of capital and labour, opens up a range of issues to working-class demands which go way beyond the limited, institutionally segregated economistic demands of collective bargaining under liberal capitalism — Hilferding's argument. It is for this reason that capitalist interests within liberal societies enter corporatist arrangements with great reluctance — they are corporatists *malgré eux*. They may be driven to corporatist strategies because these offer the only hope of coming to terms with a militant labour movement, or (as outlined under 3, above) economic problems not immediately connected with labour relations may lead them into that pattern of state intervention, organization as interest groups and suspension of competition which entails corporatism.

This ambiguity in corporatism within liberal societies, and the different patterns produced by corporatist strategies within liberal and authoritarian contexts has been captured by several recent commentators, most notably by Schmitter . . . The theory of the corporate state is thus able to contribute much to an understanding of contemporary developments, placing them in historical context and relating changes in the role of the state to wider economic changes. However, by themselves, accounts of corporatism do not explain why the state responds to capital's needs — especially since these needs are so reluctantly expressed. At this point one needs to turn to Marxist theory — bearing in mind that the distinction between liberal democracy and authoritarianism identified in the corporatist literature will create problems.

4.2

Corporate Bias

KEITH MIDDLEMAS

[. . .] During the crisis of political values and the state itself which afflicted all industrial nations in Europe in the 1900s and 1910s, and culminated in the manpower and production crises of the First World War, British governments stimulated institutional growth among bodies representing business and labour interests, in order to maintain public consent. Afterwards, these institutions continued to grow, acquiring new representative functions on behalf of their members, among employers and trade unions, and as intermediaries of central government. In spite of the failure of the National Industrial Conference in 1919, and of subsequent attempts to create a formal 'parliament of industry' or to impose a corporative system, the political relationship between increasingly powerful and legitimate interests developed into a complicated ritual, where earlier, simplistic ideas about collective bargaining and class representation were modified under the influence of the search for public consent by party governments, and the 'higher interests' of the nation-state.

Under the double stimulus of government's needs and the changing economic and social conditions of their membership, what had once been interest groups outside the formal constitution — what Hobbes called 'lesser Common-wealths in the bowels of a greater, like worms in the entrayles of a naturale man' — became governing institutions, existing thereafter as estates of the realm, committed to cooperation with the state, even if they retained the customary habit of opposition to specific party governments. As a necessary condition of their transformation, other institutions which had once shared these functions, voluntary societies,

Source: From K. Middlemas, *Politics in Industrial Society* (1979) London, André Deutsch, pp. 371—82.

churches, the press and to some extent parties themselves, declined in political significance.

Yet the governing institutions failed to become wholly representative of their various constituencies, remaining exposed to popular discontent and members' rights of recall. For the purpose of central government they could not be relied on as if they had been estates in the classic corporatist model of the state, largely because they did not supersede the political parties or, indeed, come to resemble them. They did not, for example, develop ideologies, claiming only to represent the sum of members' individual wills. Hence the slow, tentative, often secretive patterns chronicled above, informal, flexible and highly sensitive to changes in the balance of power.

Before attempting to generalize, therefore, it is necessary to emphasize again the tentative, even fragile character of the system. Physical growth of an institution does not by any means result in an increase in its political power. Progress towards institutional collaboration, and the avoidance of economic competition and class conflict is a tendency, not an irreversible trend. Schematically, the process may be described as a series of interactions of declining importance: first, the triangular cooperation between government and governing institutions (in this case employers and trade unions); secondly, between these institutions and their constituents (TUC and unions, BEC or FBI and federations of particular industries); thirdly, between individual members (federations and firms, unions and branch officials or shop stewards).

In a different, but intersecting plane lie the relationships between government and party, government and state bureaucracy (of which local government is an extension); and in yet another those between all three and the public or, in parliamentary terms, the mass electorate. In direct contrast to the rigid linkages laid down — though not necessarily implemented — in the Fascist constitutions of Italy or Portugal, or the totalitarian systems of Hitler's Germany and Stalin's Russia, the British system in the half-century after 1916 depended on a multiple bargaining process at all levels — the first being the most important — even though its aims of social harmony, economic wellbeing and the avoidance of crisis were not dissimilar.

The phrase 'governing institution' is to be understood as a description of a body which assumes functions devolved on it by government, shares some or all of the assumptions about national interests held by government, and accepts aims similar to those laid down by government; with the fundamental qualification that this form of association is not compulsory, but voluntary to the extent that it takes place within general limits derived, negatively, from the evidence of what the institution's constituent members will or will not accept. Prevailing economic and social circumstances, like the conditions which led to the shop-stewards' movement in the First World War, or to the employers' *volte-face* on state intervention in the late 1920s, rather than theoretical considerations of where collaboration conflicted with their natural or primordial interests, governed the speed with which institutions succumbed to government's desires.

To put it simply, what had been merely interest groups crossed the political threshold and became part of the extended state: a position from which other groups, even if they too held political power, were still excluded. Because recognition by government meant so much, and since classical theory did not allow for it, it follows naturally, that attempts were made, often in a partisan way, to define at law the legitimacy of such an association. Certain governments sought to define the constitutional status of trade unions (1906, 1927), or employers' organizations (cartels and monopoly legislation, or Ministry of Labour's delegated powers, after 1940). These often disruptive attempts to circumscribe governing institutions were, of course, distinct from, and supplementary to, the permanent process of brokerage between them and government which continued virtually unchecked, since both *normally* preferred to legal definition something much closer to the concept of free collective bargaining, as understood between employers and union leaders, albeit on a more complex, national scale.

In order to sustain their new role, the governing institutions acquired administrative trappings; and BEC/FBI and TUC began to resemble each other and also the governments with which they associated. Yet, as their variable performance over 50 years suggests, their role was not governed by the size and density of their bureaucracies; the TUC remained until the 1960s (and perhaps still remains) poor and ill-staffed compared, say, with the TGWU or AUEW, the CBI by comparison with the Engineering Employers' Federation. A theory of bureaucratization cannot explain more than the *appearance* of certain administrative habits, and the outlook these engendered towards their own constituencies; the institutions' place in relation to the state was dictated almost entirely by the needs of governments and by their own representative function. The weaknesses which came from their lack of power to enforce discipline on their own members was not necessarily to governments' advantage; but their strengths, where they existed, remedied the weaknesses of the state, complementing in time of crisis its ability to persuade or coerce the mass of the population or impose its requirements on the industrial, business or financial communities.

This system is not corporatism, but one where *corporate bias* predominates. The association of governing institutions, committed ultimately to a consensual view of the national interest, reduced sharply and permanently the power of interests and organizations still outside the threshold: and the harmony which was achieved, as a result, enabled governments of the 1930s and 40s to maintain order and consent and to survive the Second World War as no other European state did. Corporate bias can be detected at all levels of political activity, as pervasive a phenomenon as the oligarchic tendencies which led Michels to elaborate his iron law of oligarchy. It is, of course, inseparable from the decline of party and parliamentary politics and is, necessarily, sustained by continuous opinion management. By 1945 it had replaced, for all *practical* purposes, classical democratic theory as that had been understood in 1911.

But that was not the only change. Corporate bias tended to negate more obvious manifestations of class conflict, blurring what had been seen in the 1900s as sharp lines of social and economic cleavage. The relatively simple class structure of Edwardian England was replaced by a denser, overlapping and sometimes contradictory set of alignments, often apparently dissociated from economic causes and lacking articulation. [. . .] Contradictions in the political order were transposed to a broader sphere; and when political equilibrium between power groups had been achieved, 'the state was primarily responsive to group interests, leaving no one group to press for the national interest or general good'.

In such conditions, the state bureaucracy operates in a vacuum, defining the general good by default; and control over public opinion reaches a point at which, 'from the perspective of scientific research, which is making great strides in this area, there are neither factual nor normative limits to manipulation'. Consequently, legitimate rule tends to be maintained, not through traditional free-market economies, nor economic management (the 'neutral' state asserting a sort of collective capitalist will) but through the political system, in which avoidance of crisis is made the highest priority. The class struggle is diffused and transposed, as 'concrete constellations' (rather than parliamentary-democratic parties, which have become merely filtering devices for popular opinion or agencies for government propaganda) bargain over the distribution of social and economic rewards. The state itself becomes enmeshed with the institutions out of which the system is now constituted, its tasks becoming primarily managerial . . .

At the same time, however, the state cannot allow those excluded from political bargaining to become too large or hostile a group, and it develops methods to compensate for politically intolerable consequences, either by paying perpetual Danegeld, or incorporating them as new power groups. The problem occurs if and when marginal groups like the unemployed or immigrants cannot be accommodated; for a return to the politics of class, whether from Right or Left, would be inherently destructive of the compromises already achieved — as it proved to be across Europe in the 1900s. In Britain, at least until the late 1960s, it was solved with remarkable cunning: governing institutions and parties combined to take issue with the excluded, not on the question of the threat to their own role in the composition of the state, but of the threat to the already obsolescent parliamentary system — forcing them, almost by definition, to attack from outside the confines of what the great mass of the electorate still accepted as the legitimate centre of political activity.

Pursuing the argument empirically through half a century of history makes it clear that corporate bias in the British state ensured a uniquely low level of class conflict, compared with the countries of comparable social and economic development in Western Europe. Britain was the one society to survive the collapse of political values in the 1900s, the First World War, and the depression of the 1930s, without lapsing into authoritarian rule like Italy and Germany, or political decay like France. It is reasonable to assume a relationship between internal political harmony and national survival, if only to explain the absence in the 1930s of effective revolutionary discontent, and in the 1940s of opposition to the rigours of war: Dunkirk, after all, was the symbol of national reconciliation, not its cause.

In the circumstances after the great European 'civil war' of 1914–18, corporate bias offered the only practical alternative to Fascism or totalitarianism and, given the possibly ephemeral nature of the war settlement of 1945, may perhaps still do so. But if the argument is prolonged, it leads to the conclusion that while a balance sheet taken in 1945 would have shown on the credit side the accomplishment of a 'British Revolution' in economic and social life (for which the parliamentary democratic system received the credit), the debit should have been the admission that there still existed an innate conservatism, almost unchanged since the greater crisis of 1915—22. Backward-looking in its aims, gradual in method, revisionistic in theory, the new system accommodated itself to change by moving at the least speed commensurate with the interests of each governing institution, while each vied with the rest to ostracize dissent and manage, or accommodate, mass opinion. Only in this sense did it cope with the stresses imposed on it, as if in response to Marx's own dictum that 'men do not pose questions which they cannot answer.' The price, as C. Wright Mills observed more than a decade ago, was that the countervailing power of the public to control government diminished grievously — a development which had gone a long way in Britain before 1939.

But if the system failed the individual, or the minority group, lacking the means 'to articulate the inarticulate cry', it is also true to say that it put the state in perpetual pawn: on occasions when institutional compromise broke down, government broke down also. After 50 years in which the state's organization and functions had been extended on the basis of corporate harmony, withdrawal of consent by any one of the participants necessarily impaired the most vital functions of government, a situation which could not be remedied by the law and all the paraphernalia of coercion, either in imposing conscription on Ireland in 1917, or enforcing the UAB scales in February 1935 — or for that matter industrial relations legislation in 1968 or 1971. Government and institutions had grown up, like Siamese twins, displaying two separate bodies and heads to the world outside but sharing the heart of power. [. . .]

The evidence I have given does permit a certain degree of historical theorizing. First, it is necessary to distinguish corporate bias from theories of the corporate state, as expounded on the Fascist model, in practice most clearly in Italy in the 1920s, and Portugal under Salazar, or by neo-Fascists and quasi-corporatists in Britain and elsewhere . . .

Second, corporate bias should be seen as having political substance in its own right, rather than being simply a matter of economic practice, or 'redistributive corporatism' as it is sometimes called. Several recent commentators have related modern corporatism primarily to government control of economic planning, and to centripetal tendencies in the economic thinking of both major parties in Britain . . . This is a presentation which, when applied historically, tends to ignore both the political element in economic decision making and the power of governing institutions strongly evident at least 40 years ago. [. . .]

Between 1911 and the present day, central government has undeniably moved from a position of facilitating to one of supporting economic change, and finally to direction — but only with the agreement of the governing institutions, whose formal, representative structures have consistently relieved government of the impossible task of dealing with, and harmonizing the clash of wills of large numbers of heterogeneous interest groups at all levels of political life. Indeed, from the late 1920s until about 1965, the trend was for governments to try to ensure public compliance in the process rather than to seek to drum up — as they could easily have done — popular protest against 'blackmail' by the institutions. Because the system of government was created as the sum of separate forces, each motivated by its component parts, operating in growing equilibrium within the matrix of the state itself, the question whether change occurred as a result of state neutrality or dynamism should be rephrased. It occurred in the form described here because the existing pluralist system no longer worked, and because the divergent interests could no longer be harmonized without bringing the more powerfully based ones into the orbit of government.

Third, corporate bias, as it is presented here, is not an ideology, even when it encompasses the nature of the state. Too great a variety of behaviour patterns existed, and the system of the 1940s was still too unstable, to allow the title 'corporatism'. Corporate bias which, like the bias of a wood at bowls, is in itself no more than a tendency always to run to one side, must suffice, rather than the typology of aims, unity, order, nationalism, and success, suggested by Winkler when analysing British government in the late 1970s. Admittedly, a great deal of research needs to be done to develop a convincing historical analysis of the underlying patterns of behaviour of trade unions or employers' organizations, and their leadership or cadres; but the result is unlikely to reveal a coherent ideology for either. The usual example chosen to suggest the existence of ideology is the industrial parliament concept. But merely to string together a list of its advocates from Lloyd George onwards, including the 'Tory corporatists' and trade unionists like Arthur Henderson, proves nothing. The 'alternative to parliament' even when put forward collectively by the TUC Research Department or the NCEO Council was a purely mechanical device for embodying practices which the authors knew already existed, or which they believed could be introduced to promote harmony and crisis avoidance. It was not an assertion of the role of institutions within a coherent intellectual system.

In spite of these qualifications, analysis of corporate bias does reveal much about the nature of the British political system and of the state that developed after the first major twentieth-century crisis. The central tenet of classical democratic theory, that choices were made through the electoral system utilizing the mechanisms of party and parliament was, of course, modified by Joseph Schumpeter more than 30 years ago, when he pointed out that electors were actually restricted to infrequent acts of choice between opposing and stylized party presentations; policy was made continuously by party governments, in between elections, virtually independent of any general will. But the concept of democracy needs to be modified much further to account for participation by institutions in the governing process, and for the phenomenon of opinion management by the state in its bureaucratic aspect. As institutions crossed the threshold separating pressure groups from a share of the state's powers and authority, they enhanced the tendency already present among governments to categorize political choices in terms of the national interest, over and above class or sectional interests, and to accept as necessary an interdependence almost as binding as the medieval doctrine of organic society. Even by the 1930s it had become impossible to argue, as Baldwin did at the time of the General Strike, that the role of government was simply to hold the ring, protecting alike the interest of the state and the public at large against the evil consequences of sectional rivalry. [. . .]

It may be too much to assert that the governing institutions became *part* of the state in the sense that government departments are a part, or the armed services. Yet political parties whose function is to mediate between state and society are part of the state only in so far as their leaders form the personnel of cabinets. Without in any way asserting that the governing institutions resembled parties, their leaders, at given times, took up similar positions in the expanded state. For, in response to the crisis of the 1900s and the First World War (which was in essence a crisis of the state), and in contrast to the narrowing of the area of the state which authoritarian rule in Germany and in Italy implied, British governments gave way to, or actually encouraged, corporate bias in order to overcome problems which the classical democratic system could not solve.

4.3

The Rise of Keynesian Economics: Britain 1940—64

KERRY SCHOTT

Why, how, and when Keynesian policy was introduced and consolidated in Britain has recently received less attention than its subsequent demise.[1] Within economics, the Keynesian decline is usually linked quite directly to the theoretical takeover by the monetarists and the subsequent rise of Thatcher economics. In scenarios of this type, practical economic policy simply follows theoretical developments with a time lag.[2] The underlying premise of this interpretation of recent economic history is the rather naive notion that the state is little more than an active respondent to the advice of its economists. The government, in formulating and carrying out economic policy, is also assumed to be virtually omnipotent. It not only does do as it is told, but it *can* do as it is advised by economists.[3]

The necessity for developing a wider political economy analysis of what has occurred has now been stressed by many writers, but the difficulties in doing so are not trivial.[4] First, an understanding of the demise of Keynesianism would probably be facilitated by an understanding of its introduction and consolidation into British policy. Second, there is some confusion over whether or not there even was a Keynesian revolution. Tomlinson (1981), despite widespread agreement to the contrary, has suggested there never was a Keynesian policy in Britain, and indeed probably never could be. Thus, whatever policy alterations there have been need some scrutiny.

Third, whatever the policy changes in the post-war period they did not simply occur in the limited atmosphere of economic theory

Source: From *Economy and Society,* (1982) Vol. 11, No. 3, August.

debates. These were, and are, important: but the way in which theory and practice are related, and how these relations influence and are influenced by the state, and other groups, is not obvious. Perry Anderson, partly following Gramsci, has argued that in Britain the industrial bourgeoisie and the old aristocracy form an amalgam which is the ruling class.[5] This class then exerts a powerful hegemony over all society and this dominance is partly expressed in a cultural supremacy. This cultural hegemony, Anderson argues, contrary to Raymond Williams and E. P. Thompson, results in an ideological development of the working class which is inevitably stunted.[6] It is shaped and formed and limited by the ruling class — not just directly, but by the definitions of the limits within which life is conducted under capitalism. Thus 'the real historical content of the working-class movement has not in the main been articulated ideologically at all, but institutionally.'[7] The ruling class imposes its own goals and values on society. What follows is addressed to these three issues. [. . .]

Was there a Keynesian revolution?

Whether or not the Keynesian era ever existed is clearly dependent on what we mean by Keynesian. Jim Tomlinson (1981) defines it as an economic policy that is principally concerned with getting full employment by the manipulation of budgetary aggregates. This is all right as far as it goes, though to be pedantic perhaps other types of theories might strictly qualify as Keynesian on this definition.[8] In any case what this rather narrow view of Keynesian policy does is to avoid the different economic and political nuances that exist amongst Keynesians. These differences seem to me to be of some interest because they raise the question of why one type of Keynesianism, namely the neoclassical synthesis, came to dominate economic thinking.

Looking at Keynesianism in this rather broader way also brings out the point that some Keynesian economists have considered the political and economic constraints that their policies would face and not all of them have been optimistic. Kalecki, for one, was pretty gloomy about the longer term prospects for Keynesian policy in a capitalist economy.[9] His work is quite topical, not because of his gloom which seems a currently popular sentiment, but because he tried to analyse the way in which prevailing economic conditions affected the manner in which economic theory and policy was used by the state.

There is obviously a wide range of ways in which Keynesianism can be defined but the most currently acceptable seems to be that spelled out by Franco Modigliani (1977, p. 1): 'The fundamental practical message of the *General Theory* [is] that a private enterprise economy using an intangible money *needs* to be stabilized, *can* be stabilized, and therefore *should* be stabilized by appropriate monetary and fiscal policies.'

The first basic proposition is that, left to its own devices, capitalism is an unstable economic system in the sense that it alternates between periods of protracted stagnation and unemployment, and bursts of booming economic activity and inflation. Capitalism cannot be counted on to provide full employment or even socially adequate capital utilization without state intervention. It is this proposition that is at the heart of all Keynesian analysis. Capitalist investment decisions have an inherent tendency to produce fluctuations in economic activity and with it recurring and possibly lengthy bouts of unemployment.

Within the broad church of Keynesianism, differences are then apparent over *the form* that state intervention should take to achieve economic stability and full employment, and *how viable* these policies are likely to be. The differences in the form of policy range from quite limited state intervention, where the state simply influences private investment indirectly by managing aggregate demand, to a wider state role, where state expenditure itself supplants private investment as the principal driving force behind economic activity. The more limited variant of Keynesianism is the neoclassical synthesis, and is associated with writers like Tobin, Samuelson and Modigliani.[10] It is also the variant spelled out in numerous macroeconomic textbooks.

The state plays what has become its conventional role in economic theory: when aggregate demand is too low to call forth sufficient private investment for full employment, effective demand is expanded. This is done mainly via tax and public expenditure decisions which may lead to a public sector deficit. In any case the increase in demand aimed for is that which is sufficient to stimulate private investment and employment. In an analogous way when demand is excessive, in an economic boom, the state steps in to decrease demand. Taxes may be raised and state expenditure cut: the public budget deficit is cut or a surplus is aimed for. When effective demand falls the overheated economy is restrained.

The simultaneous appearance in the mid-1950s of unemployment and rising wages and prices (though not on the same scale as more recent experience) led to some modification in the neoclassical synthesis. In particular the Phillips curve was added to the policy tool-box.[11] This relationship purported to show that there was a trade-off between unemployment and inflation and this trade-off meant that the full employment target was necessarily accompanied by some inflation. Less than full employment positions meant also less inflation but zero inflation and full employment were incompatible. Both policy goals could not be reached together. At the same time the long-run trade-off appeared to be less favourable than the short-run trade-off between these two objectives; though this particular dilemma was not investigated in any detail until the late 1960s and 1970s.[12]

What this implied for the dominant Keynesian analysis was that achieving full employment was not such a straightforward matter. Attaining full employment meant accepting a level of inflation which also would probably increase over time. If inflation was to be controlled in this scenario then the full employment target had to be abandoned, at least up to a point. In practice in Britain this problem did not really plague Keynesian policy until the 1970s. The Callaghan—Healey Labour administration, when faced with a 25 per cent inflation rate which was rising, sacrificed the full employment target.

For Keynesians of this dominant ilk the way to get both full employment and stable prices is via an incomes policy or wage and price policies. These policies, in addition to the demand management already mentioned, would theoretically permit both economic objectives to be reached at the same time. Full employment is then conceptually possible, with stable prices, but only if wage-price policies are effective. But on this score most Keynesians are not particularly optimistic. They do not regard an incomes policy as automatically politically viable and many conventional assessments of these policies in practice rate them as 'disappointing'.[13] As far as Keynesians are concerned, incomes policies have not worked and this is largely because of what are perceived to be political difficulties in their implementation. This impasse leads Modigliani to comment in this context that 'the design of better alternatives is probably the greatest challenge presently confronting those interested in stabilization.'[14] In Britain work on these alternatives is being pursued, notably by Professors James Meade and Richard Layard, and their suggestions are being noted by the SDP and the Liberal parties.[15] Thus this dominant variant of Keynesianism has been concerned with full employment as a policy goal, but the viability of the target has also been discussed at length, and not particularly optimistically for both economic and political reasons.

The wider variant of Keynesianism is more socialist, at least in a narrow economistic sense, and is associated with writers like Kalecki and Joan Robinson.[16] To achieve economic stability and full employment, and especially to maintain it in the longer run, the limited state role of simply stimulating private investment is not thought likely to be sufficient. In this case, as even Keynes noted, 'a comprehensive socialization of investment will prove the only means of securing an approximation of full employment' (Keynes, 1936, p. 378). In this theoretical Keynesian variant the state takes over from the capitalist investors as the principal economic force. Large public investments occur which would ultimately replace much capitalist investment over time. Institutional changes on a large scale would need to be accommodated for full employment to be maintained.

Now Kalecki was rather sanguine about the political viability of this wider Keynesian vision. He certainly believed that his policies were economically viable and that they could achieve and maintain full employment. What appears to have bothered him is first the likely necessity for 'wider Keynesianism' if full employment were to be achieved — the narrow variant of Keynesian policy was not going to be sufficient.[17] Second, he thought the political and social constraints under capitalism were immense. They might be overcome, he thought, writing in 1943, but he appears to have been very doubtful. What he expected was a political business cycle where large bouts of unemployment would be engineered by policy and used by capitalists to discipline their work force.[18] Such heavy handedness occurred because sustained full employment, over a decade or more, would breed a powerful working class who would not only resist wage cuts but continually demand and get wage increases. This behaviour he suspected would be controlled under capitalism if unemployment bouts were permitted. Once the work force was more docile, economic activity would be stimulated. The ensuing political business cycle, he expected, would be less severe than the pre-Keynesian cycle but it would exist, and he for one did not welcome it. He wished to see more planning, the socialization of investment and an economy that was managed for the welfare of *all* its members. But he did not necessarily assume that this was going to occur.

> If capitalism can adjust itself to full employment a fundamental reform will have been incorporated in it. If not, it will show itself an outmoded system which must be scrapped.[19]

This wider variant of Keynesianism, calling for more planning, would necessarily have been less aggregative in its approach than narrow Keynesianism. The overall budgetary aggregates were still vitally important, of course, but once any far-reaching socialization of investment began, it would require decisions about what sectors of the economy to prioritize. Planning decisions, at least at sub-aggregate levels, would have been necessary.

This variant of Keynesianism really never got off the ground in practice. But its very existence, even as a theoretical concept, raises the more intriguing issues of why Britain got the economic policy it did. Why did the neoclassical synthesis dominate and why did it decline? This will be discussed shortly, but first it is necessary to refute the Tomlinson (1981) position.

Jim Tomlinson (1981) has argued that economic policy in Britain, especially over the 1950s and 1960s, was not Keynesian even in the narrow sense I have defined. He rests his argument on two main propositions. First, the full employment of these decades was caused by an autonomous investment boom; second, when the government attempted Keynesian policy, it was so constrained in its behaviour that it could not follow these policies even if it wanted to.

It is correct that the 20 years after the Second World War were accompanied by very high investment activity and, as Matthews (1968) has suggested, this contributed largely to full employment. The economy was, in this period, marked by a high level of aggregate demand. Private investment and consumption were high. There was more or less continuous full employment and gradually rising prices.[20] The 1950s and 1960s were a long and sustained boom period.

In this economic climate a Keynesian economic policy would principally have been concerned with dampening demand pressures and it would be a surprise to see public budgets that were in large or growing deficit. There were, throughout this period, odd years of mild recession but overall the economy was booming. Government policy would have been lunatic on Keynesian grounds, if it had run large deficits in these circumstances. It therefore is not particularly telling to note, as Jim Tomlinson does, that the public sector deficit was small or even non-existent. If the private sector is generating sufficient demand for full employment, then the public sector is clearly not, on narrow Keynesian grounds, required to add to this demand.

What Matthews (1968) does mention is that the boom in the private sector was encouraged by the state. Its policies were broadly expansionary and Dow (1964) has argued that they were frequently too expansionary. Also balance of payments difficulties were not always dealt with by a deflationary fiscal stance but by other measures of direct controls which allowed the boom to continue.[21] It is also an open question as to how much government subsidy, aid, and tax relief to industry aided the boom; and even how much the very commitment to Keynesianism encouraged investment to meet what would have been expected to be high demand.[22]

Whatever the answer to this, the fact that full employment was largely sustained by private economic activity does not refute the proposition that Keynesian policy was operative. And as Matthews (1968) remarks in his conclusion, the full employment years up to 1968 are 'something for which economists and the Keynesian revolution can take some credit.'

The other point that Jim Tomlinson (1981) makes is that constraints on policy, and in particular public borrowing constraints, were so severe that Keynesian budget deficits were not run. He argues that 1975—6 was a time of rising unemployment and a time when a government of Keynesian hue should have been increasing its deficit to finance and encourage employment. The attempts by the Labour government to do this were thwarted. The domestic money markets would not lend in sufficient quantity; the balance of payments constrained external borrowing; and the IMF, as the going source of funds, then imposed conditions forcing a fiscal contraction. Instead of being expansionary as desired, the fiscal stance forced on the government was deflationary and unemployment duly rose.

Now what this interpretation of events leaves out is the 1975—6 inflation rate which was at peak levels.[23] In this economic position, of both high unemployment and inflation, a conventional Keynesian advising the state would be urging reflation only if an incomes policy restraining prices in some way could be simultaneously made to work. It was at this juncture that the 'Social Contract', the then prevailing form of incomes policy, was coming unstuck. Wages and prices were rising. Faced with this situation, the only alternative for a Keynesian would be to advise fiscal restraint. The lack of a workable incomes policy meant that an expansionary budget was out of the question; had aggregate demand been stimulated at this time, without inflationary controls, the inflation rate would have accelerated and, it was thought, then beyond all control.

But for narrow Keynesians the perceived constraint was the

political one related to the ineffectual nature of the incomes policy. If an incomes policy cannot be made to work, then aggregate demand management is severely limited in an inflationary context. But this is all part of conventional Keynesian theory as we have already noted. In inflationary periods demand management policy is necessarily different from when prices are stable.

This is more obvious if you compare the 1975—6 experience with that in 1952. In 1952—3 price rises were moderate and the economy appeared to be in an underemployed position, with 2 per cent (!) of the workforce out of work. The 1953 budget was expansionary in tone. Income tax was cut, tax allowances for private investment were increased, government expenditure, especially on housing, went up. Subsequently unemployment fell to 1.3 per cent in 1954. In a period where inflation is not of great concern the better chances of managing demand to increase employment are apparent.

Thus, it is correct that Keynesian policy faces constraints — and in an inflationary period these can inhibit planned increases in demand which would otherwise be pursued to increase employment. But these particular constraints, and indeed others, are part of Keynesian analysis.[24] It is not part of Keynesian policy to increase demand when prices are rising and are at high levels. This is only advised to increase employment when there is a complementary and effective incomes policy restraining prices. Hence it is not particularly convincing to argue that Keynesian policy was not being pursued throughout the 1950s and 1960s, and even in the early 1970s. It was being pursued in its neoclassical synthesis form.

British Keynesianism

The Keynesian variant first introduced into British economic policy was far from being this neoclassical synthesis type. The first Keynesian budget was introduced in 1941 in the midst of the Second World War and was part of a reform package principally aimed at establishing some workable manpower policy. In the context of a war economy it involved industrial planning in a major way. The state was not only tinkering with the private economy at this juncture, but virtually directing every aspect of it. This needed a major planning apparatus, which was duly established.

The second phase of Keynesianism followed the war when the industrial planning associated with war and direct economic controls were dismantled. Aggregative budget formulation on neoclassical synthesis lines became the order of the day and the state virtually withdrew from industrial planning to the manipulation of broader economic aggregates.

This type of policy embodied inherent contradictions which were both political and economic. By the mid-1960s these were becoming serious, and attempts to confront them finally delivered us to monetarism in its 1979 Thatcher form. All along the line conflicts between the working class and its rulers were apparent, and this did particularly show up in the form of institutions that arose to make and implement policy. However, there were also conflicts within the working class and the ruling class, as well as unrest amongst groups of people who were unrepresented in the structures of power.

All these matters did influence what occurred both within the state and outside it. Ultimately Keynesian policy was replaced because, in its accepted form, it could not deal with changes in the economy at the same time as overcoming or defusing the conflicts within society. There was nothing automatic about the replacement of Keynesianism by monetarism and other scenarios could have conceptually occurred. What did happen was the result of conflicts between different groups wielding different powers at that particular juncture. And in this struggle economic theory, not surprisingly, was used by several groups as an ancillary ideological weapon. In this more minor sideshow the cultural supremacy of the ruling class was certainly obvious.

The introduction of Keynesianism: 1940–5

The early part of this period was marked by a working class which was in a fairly powerful position, and a Conservative government, under Chamberlain, which was in a crisis. There was a distinct possibility that the war might be lost and Chamberlain's conduct of it was under fire, both from within his own party and from without. One of the more important features of this period was the inability of the government to achieve a manpower policy and by early 1940 this was emerging as critical.[25]

Domestically, the basic problem was not unfamiliar, and had in fact been faced during the First World War. The cost of living was rising, there were excessive profits on war contracts and wage demands were increasing. Industry was fearful of inflation and its subsequent effects on wage demands. The Trades Union Congress for its part, had neither the will nor the power to instruct its members to restrict wage demands in the presence of rising costs of living. And Treasury policy to suppress inflation by curbing wage demands was simply unenforceable without the TUC and its members' assistance. On top of all this some workable and non-inflationary method had to be found to move workers into those parts of industry essential for the war effort.[26]

Economically, not all was an unmitigated disaster and indeed, in contrast to the earlier French position, productive potential was good. Rearmament was well underway and reasonably balanced with other productive needs; financial resources, and particularly credit abroad, was substantial; fighter defence and the use of radar was proving successful after a major effort. The one missing and vital component was a workable manpower policy.[27]

Chamberlain's refusal to face up to this issue, along with his patronizing attitude and contempt of the unions, contributed to his own demise, and early in 1940 he was replaced by Churchill at the head of a coalition government.[28] Churchill's political activities in the 1920s and 1930s certainly made him no great friend of the unions, but he was nevertheless aware of their current power and of the necessity of bargaining with them.[29] Wage restraint could only be gained in return for price controls and subsidies to offset any rapid price increases.

It is generally thought that the resulting political concordat was a trade by the people for sacrifice now in return for social reforms after the war; and the contract is usually linked with patriotic sacrifice and a hatred of Fascism, fuelled by the spirit of Dunkirk and Churchill's oratory. But the fact is that, at least in 1940−1, when manpower policy was set, this interpretation does not appear to be correct. In its assessment of public opinion in 1941, the Ministry of Information concluded that material matters counted more to people than ideals. The standard of living and security of the home was more important than belief in victory, equality of sacrifice, a just cause, or the integrity of national leadership. '[The public] is unable, and has apparently no great wish, to picture the details of the post-war world. It speculates relatively little about the end of the war.'[30]

By 1943 this public attitude had been replaced by a widespread and radical demand for social reforms after the war but this development, comparable to similar pressures in the mid−1920s, came after the initial manpower policy.[31] The shift in public attitude was an important factor in the election of the 1945 Labour government but it had little impact on the economic policy of 1940−1.[32]

The industrial concordat that was established gave workers

material gains, both in the form of wages and better working conditions, in exchange for strict and almost draconian controls of industrial production. The already existing ban on strikes and lock-outs continued, and transfers of labour from one industry to another were controlled by the Ministry of Labour. In return the low wages of agricultural workers and railwaymen were raised; the excess profits tax was put up from 60 per cent to 100 per cent; factory inspections were used to force employers to improve conditions and to contact workers' opinions. Employers were forbidden to hire labour except via trade unions or official labour exchanges. Wages and conditions, against Treasury advice, were to be set by free collective bargaining at the factory level and in the event of disagreement by compulsory government arbitration with the result binding on both sides. The Treasury was to control prices through policy, focusing on dividends and profits and by direct price controls and these in turn would limit wage demands.[33]

What seems especially pertinent about this period is that the reforms that were enacted, for instance, specifically controlling inflation via price controls rather than wage controls, were brought about by considerable union strength. Major concessions by the working class were made, but the resulting concordat certainly reflected working-class strength at this time. Labour's consent was vital to win the war and this, along with union strength, enabled certain reforms which otherwise would not have been enacted.

The state machinery that was set up at this stage also reflected this position. The powerful overseer of the concordat was the Ministry of Labour, headed by Ernest Bevin, a staunchly anti-communist union leader, who soon became a Labour MP. His influence and vision of the future, with all its limitations, runs through the whole proceedings. He sought, and was largely successful in establishing, a machinery that would control industry and give organized labour a base through which it would work when the war ended.[34] The policy was not without conflicts, particularly with miners and dockers and certain skilled workers who were in short supply, but overall the policy did meet both the requirements of the war effort as defined by the state, and the expressed material demands of the labour force as a whole.[35] During the war years wage rates rose faster than prices and actual earnings because of long overtime, increased rapidly. On the other hand salaries declined by 21 per cent in the 1938—47 period, and income from property fell by 15 per cent.[36]

Two pieces of the Bevin machinery are worth noting. The Joint Consultative Committee was set up and met twice a month, with

Bevin in the chair, presiding over seven representatives from the employers' associations and seven from the union leadership. This was a smaller and more powerful group than the National Joint Council which was made up of people from the Trades Union Congress and the British Employers' Confederation. This larger National Joint Council had existed prior to 1941 but had functioned in an essentially powerless way and had rarely influenced policy.[37] The Joint Consultative Committee, on the other hand, brought the union leadership into government on a consultancy basis with roughly equal power to that of employers for the first time. Consultancy with unions was nothing new, but even in the First World War (partly due to splits between union leadership and the rank and file), they had never achieved power parity with employers and had had much less influence on government policy.[38]

Bevin also established Joint Production Committees on an area basis which forced joint consultation between employers and unions at regional levels and which undoubtedly contributed to the material gains and conditions of workers in particular industries such as retail distribution and textiles. The Ministry of Labour became immensely powerful, with access to all information on the war effort. It not only had the ability to enforce consultation between employers and workers but also the ability to insist on the implementation of agreements.[39] The need for labour, as a resource to win the war, had won the union leadership more power than ever before; and the Bevin machinery as a post-war legacy was to influence later changes in this power.

The other major development of the war years was concurrent with this industrial policy and this was the acceptance of Keynesian economic principles in budget formation and economic policy. The national budget of 1941 was, for the first time, based on Keynesian theory, albeit within the context of war and a heavily planned economy. The 1941 fiscal deal involved the 100 per cent excess profits tax, a 10 shilling income tax, price controls and clothes rationing in return for wage moderation under the tripartite wage bargaining system. Income distribution, as already noted, was shifting in favour of the workforce.

From a long-term perspective, the Keynesian input into reconstruction plans for the post-war period was more important. The Nuffield College Reconstruction Survey, headed by G. D. H. Cole, received financial support from the Treasury in 1941. The liberal impact of Beveridge and Keynes on reconstruction policy is well known, but they were supported by a strong collegiate cast of technocrats including Roy Harrod, Dudley Stamp, Nicholas Kaldor and Joan Robinson.[40] The Trades Union Congress, the Federation of British Industry and the British Employers' Confederation all supported the general drift of this policy and contributed to it.[41] Most employers recognized that after the war enormous amounts of investment would be required for capital reconstruction and without government guarantees for credit, reconstruction would be difficult if not impossible.[42] At the same time, labour cooperation would be required if inflation and excessive consumer demands were to be avoided and social reforms were the obvious exchange.

Indeed, by 1943 public opinion also demanded such a strategy. Army education programmes and the publicity given to Beveridge raised and sustained the expectation that the country would be a better place for everyone after the war.[43] Virtually no-one wanted a return to the 1930s and a survey of business in 1942 found that while few employers thought that the proposed welfare system would offer them much benefit, 75 per cent of them thought it should be adopted.[44]

The majority of the nation seemed agreed but there was dissent. In particular, Aims of Industry, a conservative business grouping which is still active, and the Society of Industrialists, led by Lord Perry of Ford Motors, Lord Leverhulme and the publisher Ernest Benn, were opposed.[45] They saw the emerging policy as an unnecessary control of trade and private life. As they saw it, unemployment after the war would only be avoided by unhampered trade and the resulting economic growth. The left of the Labour Party was also unhappy. Led by Aneurin Bevan they attacked the Keynesian policy as a simple transformation of capitalism which would only serve to prolong the *status quo*.[46] They sought its burial, not its rebirth.

But the dissenters from both sides were not strong enough to prevail and in 1945 when the Labour Party swept to power, with its first ever outright majority over all other party combinations, the blueprint for the future was obvious. Keynesian policy would prevail along with the acceptance by government of the objectives of full employment, price stability and growth. This policy also obviously suited the electorate as shown by the election results and by intelligence reports in 1945.[47] These reports indicated that the public had lost some of its 1943 radical fervour, but certainly expected legislative reforms and economic gains from the government. But these demands were reformist and a rejection of the 1930s. They were not a call for the immediate establishment of socialism.[48]

Thus, in this period what was achieved by the working class

appeared to be a commitment to full employment, via Keynesian policy, and a relatively powerful consultative machinery for the unions to use in dialogues with the state about economic policy. These were both reforms and Aneurin Bevan was correct to point out that there was nothing inherently socialist about them. But they were at least gains that had not existed in prior periods. Unemployment was now no longer perceived as a social problem — it was an economic problem which the state was obliged to eradicate. Furthermore the legacy of Ernest Bevin's institutions was to provide unions with a direct forum through which they could attempt to influence government policy. These organizations worked in an institutional sense until Thatcherism, though in a changed form.

Moving from Keynesian planning to Keynesian budget management: 1946—64

The dismantling of the planned wartime economy and its transition to the more familiar Keynesian form is a fascinating historical period. There seem to have been several major influences at work. First, the United States threw a major financial spanner in the works with amazing repercussions. Second, the union movement, though not always united, concentrated on getting short-term material gains for its members and on protecting and maintaining the consultative machinery that, under Ernest Bevin in the Ministry of Labour, had been established. Third, the importance of maintaining full employment was recognized and accepted by governments of both Conservative and Labour hue. Finally, the more right-wing and less reformist sections of industrialists had very little influence, along with the more socialist elements of the Labour party and the trades unions. A middle-of-the-road reformist consensus appeared to have arrived.

At the end of the war, the newly elected Labour government, under Attlee, was preoccupied with the required restructuring of the British economy. The efficient war production machine, largely financed by lend lease loans from the United States, had to be transformed to a peacetime economy geared to the production of goods and services for trade. It was generally thought that the massive investment that was required would be financed by the continuation of United States lend lease loans and these would enable both exports and internally consumed production to increase.[49] At the conclusion of the European hostilities the balance of payments was in deficit on the current account to the tune of

£2500 million and the industrial base for civil production was very weak.[50] This had to be strengthened for future industrial viability and to pay off previous national debts.

The task was immense and it was expected to be accompanied by a relatively ordered demobilization of the armed forces. The war in the Pacific continued and this implied that some troops would continue to be deployed while industrial regeneration began.[51] But as it turned out, these British ideas were not shared by their United States allies. President Truman both suspended lend-lease arrangements and promptly finished the war in the Pacific by dropping atomic bombs on Nagasaki and Hiroshima.

The prospect for Britain of the immediate mass demobilization of the armed forces was of less concern than the suspension of US finance, and the new Labour government had a crisis on its hands. A new loan arrangement was quickly established, but the British government was in no position to bargain and the conditions attached to the new loan pleased neither the Conservatives nor the Labour Party.[52] The House of Commons was dismayed and Mr Stanley, speaking for the opposition, put it bluntly:

> We are sitting here today as the representatives of a victorious people, discussing the economic consequences of victory. If a visitor were to come . . . from Mars . . . he might well be pardoned for thinking that he was listening to the representatives of a vanquished people discussing the economic penalties of defeat.[53]

In some senses this was not a bad assessment of the position. The economic penalties referred to are interesting. In commercial terms the new loan arrangement looked attractive. It was for £3700 million, which may have been too little, but the interest was a mere 2 per cent. Repayment was to be over 50 years and neither repayment nor interest was to begin until 1951. The rest of the negotiated arrangement was in contrast more unpalatable and restrictive. Two conditions in particular are worth mentioning. First, the loan was dependent on acceptance of the Bretton Woods proposals for the establishment of the International Monetary Fund and the International Bank. The British were not in principle opposed to these institutions, but the United States in effect gave Parliament just five days to think about them. This meant that the establishment of these institutions got little debate, and in any case Britain was not in a position to alter their proposed *modus vivendi* which greatly favoured the United States.[54]

The second condition was insistence that sterling convertibility with the dollar be established within 12 months. Since Britain was the only European belligerent to be forced into convertibility so early, and since dollars were in heavy world demand, the upshot of this condition was an easily foreseeable and massive run on British foreign reserves. In fact by the day convertibility was met, $3.6 billion had already drained from British reserves and the original loan, meant to last three years, barely lasted 18 months. Its contribution in this period to industrial investment was small, and in retrospect its major effect was a balance of payments crisis on the capital account.[55]

As this particular disaster unfolded, it appeared that the United States wanted to ensure that Britain would never become an industrially competitive threat. The US was in a powerful position to enforce its hegemony over Europe and it quite blatantly shaped the Bretton Woods Agreement and the IMF so that this power would be exerted. In addition, the policies of the Attlee government were perceived, across the Atlantic, to be extremely socialist. They were not to be encouraged and certainly not financially underwritten by decisions taken in the US Congress.[56]

This US financial policy had long-term consequences for Britain, and indeed the rest of the world, but in the short term it certainly put a damper on the British economy.[57] The government was committed to sweeping social reforms and the establishment of a welfare state with a considerable nationalization programme. Many of these policies in fact proceeded, but their pace of introduction and their breadth were severely constrained.

This direct financial constraint was also supported by the British financial sector who were particularly opposed to price controls and wanted these replaced by either free market outcomes or wage restraints. After the war these price controls gradually disappeared, along with the physical planning and central co-ordination of production that had marked the war economy. This disappearance was associated with an increase in the power of the Treasury within the civil service at the expense of the old Ministry of Labour.[58] Capital requirements now dominated the need for labour and the Ministry of Labour was no longer a crucial actor. The gradual abandonment of price controls accompanied Treasury backed moves towards wages policy as the instrument to control inflation.[59] There was in no sense a conspiracy between domestic financial capital, the US government, and the British Treasury, but in practice their aims concerning controls and planning were not dissimilar and their combined influence was powerful.

It is also obvious that the existence of a widespread planning apparatus after the war was a threat to what British industrialists saw as their right to manage.[60] They were fearful that this right would be challenged, but in the event there was little pressure for the maintenance of central planning or controls. The trade unions were remarkably submissive on these issues in this period, and with the exception of the radical miners' union and the electrical workers, they principally concentrated their efforts on wage demands.[61] In theory the TUC was committed, after the war, to further economic planning, a National Investment Board and some form of wages policy.[62] But it was only the radical unions who were willing to accept a National Investment Board if it meant, as it necessarily must have done, wage restraint in return for a planned investment policy. All other unions went on to press wage demands which employers generally conceded to keep production going: as long as full employment was maintained it is hard to escape the impression that the TUC cared little about or recognized any wider economic implications.

The Labour Party was also dominated by a Morrisonian view of industry which accepted the right of managers to manage and the assumption that they would do so efficiently.[63] Various industries were nationalized, but they were to operate on hierarchical lines like private firms with recognized business talent in charge. The actual importance of business cooperation was highlighted by the steel industry's nationalization where a complete mess resulted after a lack of business cooperation. Consultation between management and workers at various levels within these nationalized industries was envisaged, but the structures for it were not particularly influential.[64] In the event, the managers' right to manage was not challenged in public industry, let alone in the private sector.

The general flow of events was solidly towards some form of a mixed economy which was not to be characterized by central planning or the establishment of a more socialist form of Keynesianism. This general drift was also noticeable in changes in the economics literature of the period. Socialism in the 1930s and 1940s had been associated with planning and one of the main arguments revolved about the immorality of capitalism. This type of outlook was replaced by a stress on economic efficiency as the overriding concern and socialism, in so far as it was advocated, was argued for in terms of its economic superiority.[65] Socialism was a better system because it was more efficient, not simply because capitalism was wrong. But if the stress was simply efficiency, any system that provided reasonable material rewards was a contender on these grounds.

The commitment to full employment was certainly upheld and it was really only challenged once in this period. This occurred in 1957. The Conservatives won the 1951 and 1955 elections and in 1957 the Macmillan government, with Thorneycroft as Chancellor of the Exchequer, attempted to institute a relatively mild squeeze, along with curbs on government expenditure aimed at stabilizing prices.[66] The resulting fall in demand and higher unemployment was accompanied by a run on reserves because of an expected devaluation. This latter development was in part a reaction to the Suez crisis and its handling, but also seems simply to have occurred because the expectations of devaluation subsequently built up pressures that led to its necessity.[67]

In this air of crisis, Thorneycroft was faced by a hostile party as well as by union protests. The TUC refused to cooperate and would not urge wage restraint, and the number of days lost from strikes increased.[68] Many small businesses also went bankrupt during 1956—8 and the failure of the Conservatives to help this portion of their party faithful caused problems.[69] The general tone was not helped by loud protests from the British Employers Federation, many of whom were large industrialists, saying that wage and price restraint was vital.[70]

Thorneycroft, along with Enoch Powell and Nigel Birch, resigned over the issue. Price stability was not to be the number one priority and economic policy based on this aim was rejected.[71] In addition, the efficacy of monetary policy was being questioned and the influential Radcliffe Report in 1959 added to the downgrading of monetary policy as an anti-inflation device.[72] Indeed, the use of monetary policy in this way was not really to occur again until the mid-1970s.

The commitment to full employment was kept up by democratic pressures through the ballot box as well as by union pressure, and this on-going commitment, along with the dismantling of the planning apparatuses of the war, and the movement away from price controls, necessarily ushered in budget management on narrow Keynesian lines. As a political sort of policy the Keynesianism that manipulates broad aggregates is far more acceptable to private industry than the planning variety.[73] The latter involves meddling in industry in quite specific ways and the visible favouring of some industrial groups over others. It is thus fiercely opposed by some industrial groups who perceive they will not benefit by it. And of course there is the more general form of opposition because it directly questions the perceived right of managers to manage.

Manipulating broad aggregates, on the other hand, does not challenge managerial prerogatives and its impact is seen to be roughly the same for all industries. Thus as long as full employment was to be maintained, and this did represent a working-class victory of some note, the Keynesian management of budgetary aggregates was a far more acceptable policy from the collective point of view of British capital.

It would be wrong to suggest that there was no dissent to this policy but the protests, both from right and left, had little influence. On the right, groups like Aims of Industry, and sometimes the British Employers Federation were vocal in opposition.[74] They wanted free enterprise on pre-Keynesian lines. However, their power was never overwhelming. The Federation of British Industry favoured the Keynesian reforms and correctly perceived that nationalization was no real threat to private industry.[75] There was also strong support for Keynesian objectives from the electorate at large and the trades unions.

On the left the debates about socialism coming from the Tribune Group and some unions were effectively stifled by both the event and the promise of economic growth. Living standards rose and the vision of technical progress, industrial regeneration and continued Keynesian economic intervention to maintain full employment dulled class issues. Consensus had apparently been found and so long as living standards rose and full employment was upheld, the consensus was not under threat.

The consultative machinery between unions, business and government which had been firmly established in the war continued. Initially the TUC attempted to tie the 1945 Labour government to an industrial contract which would formally create an institution for advice and participation in state policy.[76] But Attlee's resistance to this, in his Prime Ministerial role, was accepted. The unions may have found formalized acceptance by the Labour Party difficult because it could have identified them too closely with the parliamentary Labour Party and implied their exclusion from government when the Conservatives were in power. The issue was not pressed, although finally in 1961 a Conservative government established the National Economic Development Council.[77] The formation of this tripartite body seems to have been initiated by the Federation of British Industry though the TUC and the government readily accepted it as a forum and it still continues to function though its influence now seems much diminished.

Despite the lack of formalized union influence before 1961, there was considerable *ad hoc* consultation and this continued even after the 1951 Conservative election victory. Indeed, by 1958 the unions had parity with employers on 850 government committees including a National Production Advisory Council and all Economic Planning boards.[78] This parity, however, did not necessarily signify equal power, though the continued existence of the Bevin-type machinery was, along with full employment, one of the main outcomes of this period. What had been achieved by the working class was a full employment commitment and a consultative machinery of some influence. There was, however, virtually no direct working-class input into investment or pricing decisions.

Comments

The Keynesian policy era thus seems to have been related to a dominant political consensus that was built on several foundations: a commitment to full employment, economic growth and increasing living standards, and consultation for unions and business in the process of economic policy formulation. Since the mid-1960s there has been an increasing strain on these foundations and they have subsequently crumbled. The situation now is one of minimal economic growth, vast unemployment and little consultation over policy. The consensus is gone along with the Keynesianism that contributed to it. Conflict in society is more open and it frequently involves groups outside the structures we have been discussing.

What is of particular interest from this past Keynesian experience is the shifts in policy that occurred and the varying influences in these changes that different groups exerted at different times. A particular form of Keynesianism was implemented and there seems to be some evidence to support the notion, derived from Perry Anderson, that working-class gains in this period were mostly reflected in the institutions for making economic policy.[79] A consultative machinery was established and, at least partly through its influence, the material gains of full employment and rising living standards were won for some time. However, the working class seemed to pay little attention to the economic and social theory behind the policy and perhaps partly because of this, few demands were articulated about investment and pricing decisions. The cultural hegemony of the ruling class seems to have encompassed economic theory and this hegemony was rarely questioned.

These ideas are only really superficially touched upon in this chapter and it would be wild to make too much of them, but they do seem to be worth further investigation.

Notes

1. See Crouch (ed.) (1979), Modigliani (1977), Tobin (1981), Johnson (1971) for discussions of the demise of Keynesianism.
2. This point is also made in Tomlinson (1981).
3. See Peacock (1979, pp. 5—8) for a longer discussion of this viewpoint.
4. See Gold (1977), Martin (1979), Skidelsky (1979) and Crouch (1979).
5. Anderson (1964). This argument is critically discussed in Goldthorpe (1979).
6. See Anderson (1964), Williams (1961) and E. P. Thompson (1965).
7. Anderson (1964, pp. 44—5).
8. The monetarism of David Laidler (1981) for example comes close to satisfying it. It is not fair to assert that all non-Keynesians care little about full employment.
9. See Kalecki (1943).
10. See Tobin (1981), Modigliani (1977) and Samuelson (1964) for examples of the genre.
11. The original paper was Phillips (1958) but this was elaborated and developed in Lipsey (1960) and Tobin (1972).
12. This work was largely influenced by Friedman (1977) though Keynesians were critical of it. See Solow (1976).
13. See Modigliani (1977, p. 15).
14. Modigliani (1977, p. 15).
15. Layard (1981).
16. Kalecki (1943); Kalecki (1971); Robinson (1979) for examples of their approach.
17. Though not stated explicitly in Kalecki (1943) this view is implicit in his argument. The technical problems of maintaining full employment in a simple Keynesian model have also been investigated by Harrod (1939), though this work is not at all concerned with political consequences.
18. See Kalecki (1943).
19. Kalecki (1943, p. 331).
20. The performance of the British economy is discussed in detail in Dow (1964); Caves and Krause (1980); Caves *et al.* (1968).
21. These controls related to capital flows as well as to current account items.
22. An empirical study by Feldstein and Flemming (1971) suggests, not surprisingly, that the concessions and industrial subsidies of various sorts were beneficial to industry.
23. The inflation rate accelerated from 9.2 per cent in 1973 to 24.2 per cent in 1975. See Caves and Krause (1980, p. 5).

24. For a recent rendering of Keynesianism see Tobin (1981) or Modigliani (1977). The difference between monetarists and Keynesians are explored in Morgan (1978).
25. See Middlemas (1979, pp. 267—70).
26. See Milward (1977).
27. Parker (1954).
28. Milward (1977).
29. Churchill was considered a die-hard Conservative after the 1926 strike and he was not the Labour Party's preferred candidate either. Like George VI they would have preferred to work with Lord Halifax but Halifax conceded that a Prime Minister could not hold office from the Lords and he did not stand. P. Addison (1976).
30. Stephen Taylor, head of the Ministry of Information's Home Intelligence, INF I/292. Appendix to weekly report 22—9 September 1941; quoted in Addison (1976, p. 185).
31. Middlemas (1979, p. 273).
32. This is in conflict with the usual interpretation which can be found for example in W. K. Hancock and M. M. Gowing (1949, p. 541). The position taken here is in agreement with Middlemas (1979, Ch. 10).
33. See Pollard (1962, pp. 344—5).
34. See Bullock (1960, Vol. 1, p. 653).
35. Bevin's clashes with various groups are discussed in Bullock (1960). See pp. 30, 60—2 for a discussion of the dockers' disputes. Engineering apprentices also were in dispute. See Macdonald (1976, p. 125).
36. Pollard (1962, pp. 344—5). Quoted in Middlemas (1979, p. 279).
37. Middlemas (1979, p. 267).
38. *Ibid*, Chs 3 and 4.
39. Bullock (1960, Vol. 2, p. 118); Middlemas (1979, pp. 266—7).
40. Nuffield College Reconstruction Survey, 1943, *Employment Policy and the Organization of Industry After the War,* Eighth Conference. TJ C22.
41. Different groupings offered up different variants of reconstruction policy including industry's *A National Policy for Industry,* the Nuffield College study as on p. 303, and the TUC's *Postwar Reconstruction,* 1944 report.
42. Middlemas (1979, p. 297) quotes Roy Harrod as pointing out that post-war reconstruction could alone cost £1000 million per year.
43. Middlemas (1979, p. 271).
44. Addison (1976, p. 218).
45. Middlemas (1979, p. 299).
46. *Parliamentary Debates,* Commons, Vol. 401, col. 527.
47. Addison (1976, pp. 247—8).
48. Addison (1976, pp. 120—3); Middlemas (1979, p. 301).
49. Dow (1964, pp. 9—14).
50. *Ibid*, p. 19.
51. *Ibid*, pp. 13—29.

52. *Ibid,* p. 18.
53. House of Commons Debate, 13 December 1945, 652—3.
54. Dow (1964; p. 18 and footnote 1).
55. *Ibid,* Ch. 2.
56. These issues are dealt with at length in Gardner (1956).
59. Dow (1964, pp. 13—29).
60. Middlemas (1979, pp. 398—9).
61. *Ibid,* p. 403.
62. TUC, *Reconstruction Report,* 1945.
63. *Parliamentary Debates,* Commons, Vol. 458, col. 60.
64. See Jenkins (1959).
65. Examples of the earlier socialist literature are Cripps (1934), G. D. H. Cole (1935), Dalton (1935) and Wootton (1934). The shift in socialist attitudes is typified by Cole (1935) about whom Wootton remarks 'he writes — not so much of wrongs as of muddles' (Wootton, 1934, p. 104).
66. The Thorneycroft Budget is discussed at some length in Dow (1964, pp. 90—111).
67. Dow (1964, pp. 95—7).
68. A. H. Halsey, *Trends in British Society,* Tables 4.10, 4.11, 4.14.
69. *Economic Surveys,* 1956—8.
70. Middlemas (1979, p. 409).
71. See, for example, Eden (1960, pp. 262—3) and Macmillan's behaviour in the late 1950s described in Middlemas (1979, pp. 408—10).
72. 1959 Cmnd. 827, Treasury, *Committee on the Working of the Monetary System, Radcliffe Report,* HMSO, London.
73. This is also pointed out in the US case by Gold (1977).
74. Middlemas (1979, pp. 399—401).
75. *Ibid.*
76. TUC, *Report on Reconstruction,* 1944.
77. Middlemas (1979, p. 343).
78. Beer (1965, p. 337).
79. Anderson (1964).

References

Addison, P. (1976) *The Road to 1945: British Politics and the Second World War,* London, Quartet.
Anderson, Perry (1964) 'Origins of the Present Crisis', *New Left Review,* No. 23.
Beer, S. H. (1965) *Modern British Politics,* (1st edn) London, Faber.
Blackaby, F. (ed.) (1979) *British Economic Policy, 1960—74,* London, Cambridge University Press.
Bullock, A. C. C. (1960) *The Life and Times of Ernest Bevin,* Vols 1 and 2, London, Hodder & Stoughton.

Caves, R. E. *et al.* (1968) *Britain's Economic Prospects,* Washington, Brookings Institution.

Caves, R. E. and Krause, L. B. (eds) (1980) *Britain's Economic Performance,* Washington, Brookings Institution.

Cole, G. D. H. (1935) *Principles of Economic Planning,* London, Macmillan.

Cripps, Sir Stafford (1934) *Why This Socialism?* London, Gollancz.

Crouch, Colin (ed.) (1979) *State and Economy in Contemporary Capitalism,* London, Croom Helm.

Crouch, Colin (1979) 'The State, Capital and Liberal Democracy', in Colin Crouch (ed.) (1979) *State and Economy in Contemporary Capitalism.*

Dalton, H. (1935) *Practical Socialism for Britain,* London, Routledge.

Dow, J. C. R. (1964) *The Management of the British Economy 1945–60,* Cambridge, Cambridge University Press.

Eden, Anthony (1960) *Memoirs,* Part 2, *1951–7; Full Circle,* London, Cassell.

Feldstein, M. and Flemming, J. S. (1971) 'Tax policy, corporate saving and investment behaviour in Britain', *Review of Economic Studies,* October.

Friedman, M. (1977) 'Nobel Prize Lecture: inflation and unemployment', *Journal of Political Economy.*

Gardner, R. N. (1956) *Sterling Dollar Diplomacy,* Oxford, Clarendon Press.

Gold, D. A. (1977) 'The Rise and Decline of the Keynesian Coalition', *Kapitalistate,* No. 6.

Goldthorpe, John (1979) 'Intellectuals and the working class in modern Britain', *The Fuller Bequest Lecture,* University of Essex.

Hancock, W. K. and Gowing, M. M. (1949) *British War Economy,* London, HMSO.

Harrod, Sir Roy F. (1939) 'An essay in dynamic theory', *Economic Journal.*

Jenkins, C. (1959) *Power at the Top: A Critical Survey of the Nationalised Industries,* London, MacGibbon & Kee.

Johnson, Harry G. (1971) 'The Keynesian revolution and the monetarist counter revolution', *American Economic Review.*

Kalecki, M. (1943) 'Political aspects of full employment', *Political Quarterly.*

Kalecki, M. (1971) *Selected Essays on the Dynamics of the Capitalist Economy,* Cambridge, Cambridge University Press.

Keynes, J. M. (1936) *The General Theory of Employment, Interest and Money,* London, Macmillan.

Laidler, David (1981) 'Monetarism: an interpretation and an assessment', *Economic Journal.*

Lancaster, K. (1973) 'The dynamic inefficiency of capitalism', *Journal of Political Economy.*

Layard, Richard (1981) 'Is incomes policy the answer to unemployment?', *LSE Inaugural Lecture,* 1981.

Lipsey, R. G. (1960) 'The relationship between unemployment and the rate of change of money wage rates in the UK, 1862—1957', *Economica*, Vol. 27.

Macdonald, D. F. (1976) *The Trade Unions and the State*, (2nd edn) London, Macmillan.

Martin, Andrew (1979) 'The dynamics of change in a Keynesian political economy: the Swedish case and its implications', in Colin Crouch (ed.) *State and Economy in Contemporary Capitalism*.

Matthews, R. C. O. (1968) 'Why has Britain had full employment since the war?', *Economic Journal*, September.

Middlemas, Keith (1979) *Politics in Industrial Society*, London, Deutsch.

Milward, A. S. (1977) *War Economy and Society 1939—45*, London, Allen Lane.

Modigliani, Franco (1977) 'The monetarist controversy or, should we forsake stabilization policies?', *American Economic Review*, March.

Morgan, B. (1978) *Monetarists and Keynesians*, London, Macmillan.

Niskanen, W. A. (1979) 'Review of "corruption: a study in political economy" by Susan Rose-Ackerman', *Journal of Economic Literature*, June.

Parker, H. M. D. (1954) *Manpower: A Study of Wartime Policy and Administration*, London, HMSO and Longmans.

Peacock, Alan (1979) *The Economic Analysis of Government*, Oxford, Martin Robertson.

Phillips, A. W. (1958) 'The relation between unemployment and the rate of change of money wages in the UK', *Economica*.

Pollard, A. (1962) *The Development of the British Economy 1914—50*, London, Edward Arnold.

Robinson, Joan (1979) *Collected Economic Papers*, Oxford, Blackwell, (esp. Part 3).

Samuelson, P. A. (1964) 'A brief look at post Keynesian developments', in R. Lekachman (ed.) *Keynes' General Theory Reports of Three Decades*, New York, Macmillan.

Sargent, Thomas J. (1979) *Macroeconomic Theory*, New York, Academic Press.

Skidelsky, Robert (1979) 'The decline of Keynesian politics', in Colin Crouch (ed.) (1979) *State and Economy in Contemporary Capitalism*.

Solow, R. M. (1976) 'Down in the Phillips curve with gun and camera', in R. L. Teigen (ed.) (1978) *Readings in Money, National Income and Stabilization Policy*, Homewood, Illinois, Irwin, (4th edn).

Thompson, E. P. (1965) 'The peculiarities of the English', *Socialist Register*.

Tobin, James (1972) 'Inflation and unemployment', *American Economic Review*, March.

Tobin, James (1981) 'The monetarist counter-revolution today — an appraisal', *Economic Journal*, March.

Tomlinson, Jim (1981) 'Was economic policy ever Keynesian?', *Economy and Society*, Vol. 10, No. 1.

Williams, Raymond (1961) *The Long Revolution*, London, Chatto & Windus.

Wootton, Barbara (1934) *Plan or No Plan*, London, Gollancz.

4.4
Patterns of Economic Policy: an Organizational Approach

PETER HALL

The interruption in economic growth of the 1970s brought to the advanced industrial nations of Western Europe a renewed concern for the relationship between the economy and the polity. This relationship had been obscured in the preceding two decades of almost unparalleled prosperity by two sorts of factors. In the first instance, impressive rates of economic growth acted as a solvent for the political tensions associated with underlying conflicts of interest over the distribution of the national product (cf. Lipset, 1964). [. . .] Thus it was often difficult to see the relationship between such conflicts and the economic policies of the period. Secondly, economic growth was presented in many influential formulations as the result of a demographic or technological dynamic virtually independent of political machination (Carré *et al*, 1972). [. . .] Accordingly, the role of the state seemed to be negligible in the face of a self-equilibrating economic system.

The economic crisis of the recent period, however, has called both of these notions into question and raised again a twin set of issues which for many years have been obscured, namely: What are the political determinants of economic policy; What is the role of the state in the capitalist economy? These are the questions which this chapter addresses. They are large issues which deserve much longer treatment than is possible here, and indeed there has been a resurgence of work on this subject. One of the objects of this chapter is to provide a preliminary review of this work, to place its disparate elements in some relation to one another and to

Source: From S. Bornstein *et al.* (eds) *The State in Capitalist Europe* (1983) London, Allen & Unwin, Ch. 2.

indicate the contribution each has made to the resolution of these issues. But its purpose is also to go slightly beyond the existing literature to develop the outlines of a new approach which argues that the distribution of power among social groups implicit in the specific organization of capital, labour and the state, has a determining influence on the economic policies adopted in the advanced industrial nations. Since this approach builds on existing theories, it may be useful to begin with a review of the current literature, before proceeding to brief case studies of Germany, France, and Britain which are presented as a stimulus to further research. We find that the literature falls into two broad groups each of which encompasses several different approaches to a common set of problems.

Theories of the state

The first group consists of theories of the state often, although not exclusively, associated with neo-Marxist analyses. This body of literature represents the most ambitious attempt to describe the role of the state in the capitalist economy and has undergone an extensive development in recent years. In general, these theories are united by their concentration on a common aim, namely the 'attempt to establish theoretical guarantees that the state in a capitalist society necessarily functions on behalf of capital' (Jessop, 1977, p. 352). This is an important issue, not least because it has been contested by those on the right who argue that the activities of the state in recent years constitute not an advantage, but a threat to the interests of capital (Bacon and Eltis, 1976).

Since these theories have been reviewed in detail elsewhere (Gold, Lo and Wright, 1975; Jessop, 1977; Jessop, 1982) . . . only their main lines of argument will be noted here. Three such lines of argument have emerged, each of which represents a step forward in the attempt to move beyond the classic observations that the state is 'a committee for managing the common affairs of the bourgeoisie' (Marx and Engels), the 'ideal collective capitalist' (Engels), or a 'machine for the oppression of one class by another' (Lenin). The first line of argumentation, often labelled 'instrumentalist theories' and associated with Domhoff . . . and Miliband (1969) maintains that the state can be relied upon to pursue policies which further the interests of capital, because the organization of politics in pluralist systems places capitalists in privileged positions both inside and outside the state from which they can exercise a decisive influence over policy making. These theories emphasize such factors as the social interaction of political and business élites, the role of financial advantages in the electoral arena and the commercial bias of the media.

A second line of argument, which might be labelled 'functionalist', suggests that the influence which capitalists are able to exercise over policy via their role in the political arena is, in the words of Poulantzas 'not the important side of the matter'. Rather, the functions which the state is compelled to perform by virtue of the exigencies of the capitalist system itself, dictate that the policies of the state will conform to the interests of capital. Whereas instrumentalist theories emphasize the constraints imposed by the operation of a pluralist political system, functionalist theories emphasize the constraints entailed by the operation of a capitalist economic system, and in particular those associated with the requisites of accumulation or the reproduction of capital. Poulantzas (1972, 1975, 1978) is the most distinguished defender of this position, but it has been adopted with varying emphasis by Altvater (1973) and Yaffe (1973), and in versions which stress the political requirements of capitalism by O'Connor (1973), Offe (1972, 1974) and Hirsch (1978).

Finally, a group of theorists who might be termed '*synthetics*' explains the behaviour of the managers of the state in terms of a direct link between pluralist politics and capitalist economics. They argue that, under a capitalist mode of production, the prosperity of all classes depends ultimately upon the profitability of the private sector and hence on the wellbeing and cooperation of individual capitalists. In order to remain in power under a liberal democratic electoral system, the state managers must secure such prosperity and cater to the interests of the private owners of the means of production. Transformation to a socialist system of production is ruled out by the politically intolerable period of economic hardship which the resistance of capital to any such attempt would impose. In other words, political survival within a capitalist democracy dictates the pursuit of prosperity via profit. Block (1977), Lindblom (1977) and Przeworski and Wallerstein (1980) are the most prominent exponents of this position.

There are some unresolved difficulties in these theories. In particular, neither instrumentalists nor functionalists have been able to present a convincing account of how the highly individualized interests of the actors who populate the state apparatus are aggregated in order to ensure that they act in the interests of a particular class. Instrumentalists tend to imply, rather implausibly, that social background confers a highly integrated class consciousness or to assume that even left-wing politicians will be responsive to the personalized inducements of the representatives of capital. Functionalists, on the other hand, tend to neglect the question of how individual interests are integrated into class interests and to imply that occupancy of positions in the state apparatus itself confers an understanding of, and concern for, the requisites of the capitalist economic system. Although the reproduction of a social or economic system is undoubtedly contingent on the performance of certain functions by the individuals within it, even functionalist theories must contain a plausible explanation for why individuals act in such a way as to perform those functions. And any such explanation must ultimately be couched in terms of the consciousness of individual subjects, even if in totality their actions constitute an objective function. It is on these grounds that synthetic theories may be seen as an advance on their predecessors. These theories are able to explain the performance of functions central to the reproduction of a class-based economic system in terms of the concrete interests of the managers of the state in retaining power. Accordingly this line of analysis is very persuasive.

But the very persuasiveness of these theories poses a problem. They suggest that the state in the capitalist societies of Western Europe can be expected to act so as to reproduce the economic system and to serve the interests of capital. But when we compare the experience of several European nations, such as Britain, France and Germany in the post-war period, we find there has been wide variation in the range of policies adopted by these states and in the efficacy of these policies for capitalist reproduction. The basic theories of the state are unable to explain this variation. Indeed, to the extent that some of the policies adopted in this period were counter-productive, the fundamental thesis of these authors is called somewhat into question. In general, theories of the state have provided a powerful set of explanations for why the state tends to function on behalf of capital; but when confronted with the need to account for systematic variation among the policies of different nations, these theories explain too much.

Studies of economic policy

The second body of literature to which we might turn for an explanation of this variation in policy is the more detailed comparative studies of macroeconomic and industrial policy which have appeared in recent years. Here, too, there are three kinds of study, each of which takes a slightly different approach to the explanation of variation in the economic policies of the European nations. All have made a substantial contribution to our understanding of the European economies.

The first group consists of comparative studies by *economists* of the economic policies pursued by several European governments. Representative works in this group range from the pioneering studies of Kirschen (1964, 1975) and Hansen (1969) to the more recent investigations of Krause and Salant (1977), Lieberman (1977) and the OECD (1977). These works provide valuable accounts of the economic policies implemented in post-war Europe and, in some cases, useful insights into the differences between the policy-making procedures of various nations. But the capacity of these accounts to provide a systematic comparison of the political factors underlying the differences in economic policy across nations is limited by their tendency to treat policy primarily as a response to prevailing economic circumstances, and policy making as a process that is determined by the resolution of a set of technical issues. There is very little room for the influence of political variables in such analyses (cf. Kirschen, 1964; Keohane, 1978), yet unless economic policy making is peculiarly immune to the sort of influences found in other policy areas (Heidenheimer *et al,* 1977) political variables can be expected to exert a decisive impact on national patterns of policy.

As a result, the work of a second group of analysts represents a significant advance in this sphere. These are the *political economists,* such as Cowart (1978), Hibbs (1980), and Tufte (1979) . . . who have developed formal models to measure the impact of different political parties on macroeconomic policies and outcomes and to assess the impact of electoral competition on such policies. In most cases, their results suggest that we can expect the economic policies of a state to be affected by the approach of an election, by cross-national differences in the preferences of the electorate, and by the entry into office of a different political party. These are important findings. But, leaving aside problems associated with model specification and parameter measurement here, the ability of these studies to explain economic policy making is limited by their concentration on the electoral arena and by the assumption into which they are forced by this kind of modelling that the state is a unitary and relatively rational actor. Such models inevitably neglect the non-electoral modes of interest intermediation which can be of substantial importance to policy making (Schmitter and

Lehmbruch, 1979), and are susceptible to the sorts of criticisms which Allison (1971) levelled at rational actor models in the foreign policy sphere.

Some of the problems of both these lines of analysis have been resolved by a third body of literature which might be described as *institutionalist*. An influential series of cross-national analyses organized by Shonfield (1969), MacLennan *et al.* (1968), Vernon (1974), Hayward and Watson (1975), and Warnecke and Suleiman (1975) have drawn attention to the institutional differences in economic policy making among the European states in such a way as to reveal broadly different national patterns of decision making. By moving beyond the description of discrete policies to identify distinctive national patterns of policy, these analysts have made an important contribution to our understanding of the variations in European economic policy. But, ultimately, their work has been limited by the difficulty they have had in locating the *sources* of these national differences. In several instances (cf. especially Hayward and Watson, 1975, Ch. 1; Shonfield, 1969), these authors have resorted to a form of explanation which attributes differences in policy and policy making to the culturally specific attitudes or aptitudes of national élites. But the national specificity of these attitudes remains nebulous and unproven and, to the extent that they exist, their origins remain unexplained (Hall, 1981b).

In general, if theories of the state seem to explain too much, these studies of economic policy ultimately seem to explain too little. We are confronted, on the one hand, with a set of theories which effectively link the operation of the state to broad structural determinants within the polity and the economy but at a level of generality which is unable to explain particular national patterns of policy. And, on the other hand, we face explanations for particular policies which do not fully capture the structural factors which may lie behind cultural accounts of the national patterns of policy. Is there any way of bridging this gap?

An alternative approach

What is needed is an alternative view of the political determinants of economic policy that links those policies to the structural constraints implicit in the socio-economic organization of each nation. Equipped with such a view, we could explain the broad differences in the patterns of economic policy among the European nations by reference to the distribution of power among the key social groups affected by such policy, since the socio-economic organization of a nation both conditions and reflects this distribution of power. This section develops the broad lines along which such a view could be constructed, and subsequent sections assess its effectiveness for explaining the patterns of policy in Britain . . . and Germany.

The construction of such a view begins with the observation that national economic policy is influenced most significantly, first, by what a government is *pressed*, to do, and second, by what it *can* do in the economic sphere. To a large extent, in a liberal democracy the former defines what is desirable and the latter defines what is possible. This dualism reflects the fact that implementation is the obverse of the formulation of policy. Governments are frequently prevented from adopting a particular policy by the absence of any means to implement it.

To this observation should be added the hypothesis that both the pressures for a particular policy and the possibility of implementing it are most fundamentally affected by the organization of three basic facets of the socio-economic structure of a nation, namely, the organization of labour, the organization of capital, and the organization of the state itself. The first refers primarily to the organization of the working class in the labour market. The second refers principally to the organizational relationship between financial and industrial capital. And the third refers to the internal organization of the state apparatus as well as to the organization of the electoral arena.

Why is organization so important? Four reasons can be adduced. First, policy is generally formed in response to pressures from various groups according to the interests those groups have in the outcomes of policy making. But the facility with which particular interests can be articulated and the force with which they can be pressed on policy makers is dependent upon the organization of the structures within which they are expressed. Secondly, and of equal importance, the very interests of the actors themselves are critically affected by the organization of the economic and political structures within which they operate. Interests of the sort relevant to economic policy do not exist independently of the organization of particular markets. Thirdly, economic policy making is invariably a collective endeavour. That is to say, economic policy is the output, not of individuals, but of organizations which aggregate the endeavour of many individuals in particular ways. Accordingly, the structure of these organizations has an immense impact on the nature of the policies produced. It is an 'organizational intelligence' rather than the intelligence of individuals which ultimately determines such factors as the capacity of the state for strategic thinking or the quality of policy. Finally, in order to implement economic policy, the state relies on access to organizational resources in both the public and private sectors. Variations in organization among these sectors put significant constraints on the ability of the state to secure acquiescence for its policies from both the electorate and producers' groups.

It should be apparent that this approach draws some inspiration from a recent line of analysis in the literature which explains differing economic policies in terms of the broad coalitions of economic interests that converge around specific policy alternatives. Maier has examined the coalitions which lie behind inflation policy in these terms. Gourevitch uses a similar approach to explain tariff policy in the late nineteenth century (1977) and economic responses to the Great Depression (1980). And Esping-Anderson and Friedland (1981) suggest that changing economic coalitions under-lie the contemporary economic crisis in Western Europe. The antecedents for this work are analyses which have stressed the impact of the evolving power of the working class on public policy (cf. Martin, 1975; Gough, 1975).

The approach adopted here accepts the contention of this body of literature that economic policies are often a response to the demands of groups with particular economic interests. In contrast to some of these analyses, however, it regards the process whereby those interests are defined, articulated, and aggregated as especially problematic. Such an approach posits that the organization of both economic and political arenas plays a critical role in determining which interests will be most effectively articulated and what sort of response they will elicit from the state. Organization does more than transmit the preferences of particular groups; it combines and ultimately alters them. Accordingly, economic policy may not faithfully reflect a struggle among competing economic interests precisely because organization refracts that struggle. Thus, for instance, the notion that the state embodies the 'institutionalization of class conflict' or a 'condensation of class forces' (Poulantzas, 1978) must be modified to take into account the fact that the state acts as a distorting mirror to reproduce a highly imperfect reflection of these conflicts and one which imprints its own image on their resolution. In the long run, of course, organization itself is shaped by the conflicts which underlie it. But this is rarely a rapid process, and in the meantime the institutions which organize intergroup relations act as a kind of social memory, imprinting the conflicts of the present with the institutional legacy of the past.

Let us turn from the general elaboration of this approach to the concrete experiences of Germany . . . and Britain in the post-war period. The object is to see if an account of the organization of capital, labour, and the state in each nation can contribute to the explanation of some of the most significant differences in the economic policies they have adopted over this period.

The Federal Republic of Germany

The most distinctive features of the German states with relevance for economic policy are the strict division of control over fiscal and monetary policy between the Ministry of Economics and the *Deutsche Bundesbank*, the central bank, and the entrenched power of the latter within the German system. The independence of the *Bundesbank* is guaranteed by the German constitution which has given it a mandate to protect the value of the currency and established it as a special part of the executive, entrusted as an autonomous body with responsibility for monetary and credit policy (Wadbrook, 1972, p. 89). Since the majority of its Board of Directors is chosen by the central banks of the German *Länder*, and those chosen by the Federal Government are given minimum terms of eight years, the Bank is relatively insulated from pressure from the Ministry of Economics. Most authorities agree that the officers of the Bank are on a par with the highest federal authorities and not subject to instructions from the federal government (Wadbrook, 1972 p. 89). As a consequence, while the operation of fiscal policy remains in the hands of the government, the instruments of monetary policy, which are also potent weapons for influencing the level of economic activity, are in hands that are subject to an entirely different set of influences than those normally associated with the parliamentary arena.

The organization of capital in Germany is also distinctive in important respects. Among our cases, the most salient feature of that organization is the relationship between the institutions of financial and industrial capital. In Germany this relationship is characterized by the concentration of financial capital itself and by arrangements which permit financial capital, represented primarily by the major banks, to exercise a high degree of detailed control over the operations of industrial capital at the economic level. Although there are over 3000 quasi-banking institutions in

Germany, the financial world is dominated by three large 'commercial' banks — *Deutsche Bank, Dresdner Bank,* and *Commerzbank* — which work closely together to exert vast leverage over the rest of the banking sector and much of industry (Medley, 1981; Shonfield, 1969, Ch. 11). A series of legal provisions and customary business practices combines to make this possible. German banks, unlike their American counterparts, are allowed to hold equity in other firms. Moreover, almost 85 per cent of all shareholders in Germany generally deposit their shares with a bank which, in the absence of specific instructions to the contrary, enjoys the privilege of voting those shares as it likes. In addition, these banks are entitled to lend their voting rights to other banks and are accustomed to doing so. Since, under German law, the votes of 25 per cent of the shares in a company are sufficient to block any measure coming before the shareholders, the banks are generally in a position to influence the major decisions of a firm. At most recent count, the banks voted 70 per cent of the shares of the 425 largest firms in Germany, accounting for three quarters of the value of all the shares on the stock exchange. And 318 of the top 400 companies had on average two bankers on their supervisory boards (Medley, 1981, p. 48, and see Document 1).

Two consequences of particular importance follow from this. First, by virtue of these arrangements, the German banks have a direct and extensive interest in the long-term performance of the major firms within German industry. Secondly, the banks, and in particular the big three, are in a position to exercise immense influence over the activities of these firms. In keeping with this, the banks have developed considerable technical expertise in industrial matters and the capacity to provide detailed direction to the firms whose shares they hold. Similarly, the banks have become accustomed to collaborating with each other on their plans for particular industries (Shonfield, 1969, Ch. 11). This stands in stark contrast to the situation in Britain or America where commercial banks are prohibited from taking shares in companies, where competition is more common than collusion in the banking sector, and where the debtor—creditor relationship is a more distant one, based less on the assessment of a firm's strategy and more on a mechanical consideration of the creditworthiness of its balance sheet.

The organization of labour in Germany is distinguished by the concentration of the labour-market organizations and the highly regularized nature of their collective bargaining arrangements. Following the Second World War, the German working class was reorganized into 16 large unions, each covering entire industries with up to several million members in them. Almost all became affiliated to a central federation, the *Deutschegewerkschaftsbund* (DGB). In the view of most authorities, these two organizational innovations — unions organized along industrial lines and a unitary union movement — set the basic framework for the coordination present in the industrial relations of post-war Germany. [...] On this framework has also been built a system for collective bargaining which is highly regulated by statute and quasi-judicial procedures. Its principal features include the use of legally-sanctioned contracts running as long as two or three years during which strikes are prohibited, regulations which render wildcat strikes illegal and the employment of a Federal Labour Court as well as arbitration procedures to adjudicate many disputes (cf. Müller-Jentsch and Sperling, 1978). In most of these respects, the organization of the German labour market differs substantially from that in Britain or France.

Is there any relationship between these features of the organization of political and economic activity in Germany and the distinctive patterns of German economic policy? To answer this, we must first identify the patterns in German policy which most broadly distinguish it from the policies of Britain . . . and then locate the roots of the differences. For this purpose, it will be useful to break economic policy down into its three major components, macroeconomic policy, industrial policy, and incomes policy, and examine each in turn.

To begin with the macroeconomic sphere, German policy for most of the post-war period has been distinguished by two unusual characteristics. The first has been the persistent maintenance of the Deutschmark at an undervalued level on the foreign exchange markets. The second has been the presence of bias in favour of deflationary macroeconomic policies consistent enough to constitute a repudiation of Keynesian anti-cyclical policy and severe enough to culminate in the artificial creation of the peculiarly German recession of 1966–7 (Kreile, 1978; Wadbrook, 1972).

The long-standing undervaluation of the Mark was not dictated by economic circumstances. On the contrary, it was a controversial policy with distinctive costs and benefits for different segments of society and real risks for the German economy as a whole. In distributive terms, the effect of the policy was to provide an immense subsidy to export sectors and a measure of protection to domestic capital financed by imposing higher costs on German workers and consumers in the form of higher priced imports. Over a period of time, the policy dramatically strengthened the export sector of the economy. As a percentage of GDP, exports rose from 8 per cent in 1955 to 25 per cent in 1980. By 1975, exports accounted for 47 per cent of sales in investment goods, 36 per cent in chemicals, 56 per cent in machine tools, and 52 per cent in automobiles (Kreile, 1978, p. 201). This brought clear employment benefits, but it caused a series of balance of payments problems and rendered the economy especially vulnerable to imported inflation (Wadbrook, 1972, p. 251). Since the German populace is generally supposed to be hypersensitive to the risk of inflation (Kraus and Salant, 1977, p. 591), the adoption of such a policy especially requires explanation.

As early as 1955, it became apparent to many observers that the Mark was undervalued, and several prominent economic institutes, mindful of the inflationary consequences, began to urge that the Mark be repegged (Kaufman, 1969). In 1966, even Ludwig Erhardt, the Minister of Economics known as the 'father of the social market economy' and a man of considerable influence, began to urge revaluation. Throughout the late 1950s, most of the senior economic officials in the unions and both major parties, the CDU and the SPD, also began to advocate *de facto* or *de jure* revaluation (Kaufman, 1969, pp. 199–200). But nothing was done until 1961, and then a half-hearted revaluation of 5 per cent continued to keep the Mark below its natural parity. Two forces converged to ensure that this would be the case. The first was the power of the *Bundesbank* which, while unable to initiate a revaluation, could effectively veto one. The second was the singular relationship between financial and industrial capital in Germany which meant that they could combine to oppose the move.

Since undervaluation shields the profit levels of both export and domestic sectors, industry tends to support it in most countries. But whereas financial capital in Britain supported an overvalued exchange rate, the German banking community joined with industry against revaluation. In part this may be attributed to the natural aversion of central banks to exchange-rate movements, but it is also apparent that the German banking community had an equity interest in the industrial sector and thus an immediate concern for its performance, which was more intense than that of the British banks. In Germany, the two segments of capital interpreted their interests as congruent, and together they were a potent political force. Accordingly, the President of the German Federation of Industry (the BDI) announced that an open or concealed revaluation of the Mark could result in a catastrophe for the entire economy (Kaufman, 1969, p. 205), and the President of the *Bundesbank,* acting on behalf of the banking community, opposed revaluation, declaring that exchange rate parity is sacrosanct (Kaufman, 1969, p. 191). The President of the BDI and the influential leader of the *Deutsche Bank* both put pressure on the Chancellor, Konrad Adenauer, who vetoed the plans of his Minister of the Economy for revaluation (Kreile, 1978, p. 214).

Throughout the 1950s and 1960s, this combination of *Bundesbank* influence and pressure from a coalition of industrial and financial capital effectively maintained the Mark at an undervalued level. The revaluation to which Adenauer consented in 1961 in the face of overwhelming inflationary pressures was barely half that which had been expected, and revaluation was secured again in December 1961, only after it had been made a central issue between the two major political parties in the preceding election. Only by means of an election were the interests of consumers and workers able to prevail over those of capital and the central bank. This situation prevailed for 25 years during which the pattern for post-war German economic policy was largely set. And it changed in 1973, with the floating of the Mark, primarily because the *Bundesbank* itself switched sides in the face of new economic circumstances which meant that without a floating exchange rate it lost virtually all its power to control monetary policy (cf. Kreile, 1978, p. 216).

The second noteworthy feature of German macroeconomic policy was that until 1967 it remained relatively contractionary. On the fiscal side, the federal government tended to run a budgetary surplus, and a comparative study of the 1955—65 period chides the German authorities for failing to use fiscal policy as a counter-cyclical device (Hansen, 1969, pp. 233, 254). To a certain extent, this can be explained by the anti-Keynesian doctrines of Germany's economic leaders, who believed that a 'social market economy' would stabilize itself (Zinn, 1978). But the *Bundesbank* played an important role here as well. For most of this period, it countered any laxity on the fiscal side with tight monetary policies. Its officials tended to regard recession as 'a necessary purge which restored labour discipline as well as confidence in the currency' (Kreile, 1978, p. 209), and their ability to counteract constraint on the central government's behaviour.

This *pas de deux* became explicit in 1965—6, when the *Bundesbank* played a central role in creating the first real recession Germany had experienced since the war. Angered by increases in public expenditure which preceded the 1965 election, and concerned that the accompanying expansion would lead to inflationary wage increases, Bank officials introduced a restrictive monetary policy in August 1964, and strengthened it during the following 18 months. In the words of the President of the *Bundesbank*: 'As late as May 1966 the *Bundesbank* felt obliged to raise the discount rate from 4 to 5 per cent although private capital spending was already stagnating. It did so because government expenditure was still too high at that time . . . The bodies responsible for the public budgets did not see reason until the capital market, and later also the money market, failed them' (Klöten *et al*, 1978, p. 31). As a result, GDP fell by 15 per cent and unemployment rose from 140,000 to 600,000 in the space of a year (Lieberman, 1977, p. 207). Alone among the European nations, Germany experienced a recession at this time. Although German fiscal policy took on an anti-cyclical aspect with the enactment of the Stability and Growth Act of 1967, the *Bundesbank* continued to act as a restraint on expansionary policy in the following years, most notably in 1973—4 when it adopted a restrictive monetary stance in the wake of the oil price increases of that year.

In the sphere of industrial policy, the German experience has been distinguished by relatively limited forms of state intervention leaving the details of industrial reorganization up to the financial sector, and in particular to the three large banks. Thus, for instance, regional development aid in Germany is distributed via a system in which the banks play an active part in helping to choose the recipient (Shonfield, 1969, p. 263). Applications for aid must first be approved by one of the banks. If granted by the Ministry of Economics, aid is then administered in the form of a subsidized loan by the bank, which pockets a portion of the subsidy as a fee for service. Similarly, a number of schemes for sectoral rationalization, such as those for the steel industry in 1962—3 and again in 1971—4, were orchestrated almost entirely by the three big banks. In each case, the government facilitated the reorganization when requested, but left the banks to play the directing role (Shonfield, 1969, p. 255; Medley, 1981, p. 53). Similar procedures were followed for the shipbuilding industry in the early 1970s when the government provided a set of basic subsidies to German yards, but left the nature of the reorganization itself up to the shipyards and their bankers (Medley, 1981, p. 58ff.). This contrasts strongly with the techniques used by both French and British governments for rationalization of the same sectors.

It should be clear that this overall approach has been possible only by virtue of the unusual relationship between finance and industrial capital in Germany. As a result of the organization of capital, the banks have had the interest, expertise, and influence to make such an approach work. In Shonfield's words (1969, p. 261): 'The big banks have always seen it as their business to take an overall view of the long-term trend in any industry in which they were concerned, and then to press individual firms to conform to certain broad lines of development.' The banks were especially effective at this since they had the ability to plan for an entire sector and to impose cuts where necessary, a capacity which individual firms or even trade associations lacked, and since they were free from many of the political pressures to safeguard regional interests and employment that the government would have faced if it were seen as the instigator.

Finally, in the sphere of incomes policy, German policy making is characterized by a pattern that might be described as one of 'tacit tripartism'. The distinguishing characteristics of this pattern are that, on the one hand, the unions generally exercise a substantial degree of restraint in wage negotiations, and on the other hand, usually do so without the need for any explicitly or centrally negotiated bargain with the state to tie acquiescence to the delivery of other goods to them in return. Once again this pattern stands in contrast to both the French and British cases. Two sorts of explanations are often adduced for this. One stresses the unusual fear of inflation which was Weimar's legacy to the *Bundesrepublik,* and the other emphasizes the establishment of a procedure for 'concerted action' (*Konzertierte Aktion*) in the years following 1967. But neither of these are entirely convincing: the former because workers in many countries have reason to fear inflation, and the latter because the pattern of 'tacit tripartism' characterized German wage agreements long before the procedures for concerted action were established. Indeed, many knowledge-able observers, including the present Chancellor, have suggested that concerted action is a facade for something with deeper roots (Vogel, 1973, p. 186).

We should look for those roots in the organization of German labour, whose structure makes it rational on an individual level for German workers to accept wage restraint, while the equivalent organizational forms in Britain and France do not. To establish this, a brief analysis of the factors involved in consensual wage regulation is necessary. In general, wage restraint can be seen as a public good — just as inflation is a public bad. It is a 'good' to the extent that, if achieved, it reduces subsequent price inflation and so raises real income, but it is 'public' in the sense that the benefits of restraint do not accrue only to those who exercise it but to everybody . . . However, wage restraint is an especially vicious public good because it must be exercised by almost everybody for *any* benefits to accrue; and if it is not, then those who exercise it not only fail to receive any benefit, but also suffer disproportionately greater losses of real income in the subsequent inflation.

In the face of this, the most effective way to secure wage restraint is to turn it from a . . . public good into at least a semi-private good — that is, a good of the sort that those who pay for it can be assured of receiving its benefits. This is effectively what incomes policies do. By enforcing a measure of restraint on everyone, they provide assurance that a corresponding reduction of inflation will follow from an act of restraint. Depending on its form, the policy may also guarantee that others will not make disproportionate gains at the expense of those who exercise restraint. And it may offer certain key actors, such as union leaders, an additional set of goods in exchange for their acquiescence in restraint. These may range from organizational goods, which enhance the power of union organizations, to other sorts of public goods, such as fiscal or social policies of the sort that union leaders value. These supplementary elements may be a significant component of particular bargains; but survey data indicate that the assurance that restraint will be universal is one of the most important factors in mobilizing support for restraint among rank-and-file workers.

In the terms of this analysis, the organization of German labour is particularly conducive to the achievement of wage restraint in several respects. The centralized character of the German unions and the legal procedures available to enforce a particular wage bargain increase the likelihood that, once restraint is agreed upon, it will be widespread and thus have a pay-off for rank-and-file actors. From their point of view, the risks associated with restraint are consequently lower, and the returns likely to be higher, than they would be under a system where the reduction of inflation was conditional on the acquiescence of many more unions competing within a less regularized set of bargaining procedures. Accordingly, restraint is proportionately more attractive to the rank-and-file. In addition, since the leadership of the German unions is relatively concentrated, to arrive at a norm, agreement must be secured from a relatively small number of people and their subsequent compliance is relatively easily monitored. Similarly, the availability of alternative leaders is restricted, and any challenge to an agreement must go through the difficult process of finding alternative leadership before it can be expressed in an organized way. As the events of the 1969—71 period illustrate, this does not eliminate challenges, but it inhibits them (Müller-Jentsch and Sperling, 1978).

In such a context, once a reasonable wage norm has been identified, a series of organizational factors facilitates translation into policy with little need for an elaborate and intensely negotiated bargain at the centre. Attention focuses on the identification of the norm rather than on political manipulation to secure consent for it. This has, in fact, been the German pattern. Here it is termed 'tacit tripartism', but it has also appropriately been called an 'incomes policy from below' (Kindleberger, 1965, p. 248). In the early 1960s, when inflation first became a problem, the *Bundesbank* took the lead in suggesting a norm; but when its conservative biases became suspect, a Council of Economic Experts was established in part to perform this function (cf. Roberts, 1979). It continues to do so. The operation of policy in this sphere has not been entirely unproblematic for the Germans, and from time to time other instruments, including the occasional induced recession and the unions' relationship with the SPD, have been used to bolster support for wage restraint. But overall, the distinctiveness of the German pattern of incomes policy, especially in contrast to the experiences of the British and the French, seems most attributable to factors associated with the organization of labour. [. . .]

Great Britain

Turning to Britain, we can see the impact of organizational factors on policy once again. In the organization of the British state, two factors are especially significant. First, as in Germany, there is a strict separation between the organ responsible for fiscal policy, the Treasury, and that responsible for monetary policy, the Bank of England. And although its independence is not as constitutionally entrenched as that of the *Deutsche Bundesbank*, the Bank of England enjoys considerable autonomy and substantial influence over policy. This derives from its role as the principal manager of monetary policy, and as the spokesman within Whitehall for the financial markets. The Bank was nationalized after the war and its decisions formally subjected to Treasury approval. But, according to most inside observers, this in no way legislated for a revolution in relations between the Bank and the Treasury . . . (Select

Committee, 1970). The Bank retained a virtual monopoly of expertise on both domestic and international monetary matters, which made it difficult for any other political body to question its judgment on such issues, especially in the midst of a crisis. Moreover, the Governor of the Bank enjoys the unique rights of immediate access to the Prime Minister, which he exercises on a weekly basis, and/or making his institution's views known to the public. Accordingly, when issues of confidence in sterling or the public debt arise, the Bank can both contribute to the definition of the conditions on which 'financial confidence' is deemed to rest, and interpret these conditions directly to the government of the day. In the face of this, as successive Prime Ministers have testified, formal limits on the Bank's authority dwindle into insignificance (Keegan and Pennant-Rae, 1979, p. 99).

Secondly, in contrast to both the German and French cases, where the central economic ministry has been charged with responsibility for industrial performance, the main responsibility of the British Treasury for the most of the post-war period has been the control of public expenditure. Until 1962, the internal organization of the Treasury was geared almost exclusively to the performance of this function; and the National Economy Group, which was established at that time to oversee the impact of government operations on the real resources of the nation, was still oriented to the management of aggregate consumption and investment rather than to the sectoral organization or performance of British industry (cf. Shonfield, 1969, p. 104). Until 1975, the Treasury had virtually no capacity for assessing the detailed impact of its measures on industry. Indeed, for much of the post-war period, the British government lacked a Cabinet-level Minister of Industry as well. The first steps to remedy this were taken in 1962 when the Board of Trade was given increased responsibilities for regional development. Not until the late 1960s, when the Ministry of Technology began to assemble a staff of industrial experts, did the British government develop a capacity for the coordination of industrial policy. Moreover, the Treasury continued to exercise a kind of bureaucratic hegemony over economic policy making within Whitehall throughout this period, despite the short-lived experiment with a Department of Economic Affairs (Shanks, 1978; Budd, 1977).

With respect to the organization of capital, the British situation is notable for the relatively strict division of interest and operations that persists between the managers of financial and of industrial capitals. It is often suggested that financial capital is more powerful than industrial capital in Britain and exercises control over the latter's operations (cf. Thompson, 1977, p. 196). But, in fact, the relative strength of financial capital is at the political level, that is, in . . . relations with Whitehall where its representatives enjoy superior access and wield more tangible sanctions in negotiations with the government than do industrialists. At an economic level, however, the large clearing banks that account for most of British lending exercise none of the detailed control over the affairs of industry that is evident in Germany or France.

This situation is attributable to two sorts of factors. On the one hand, UK firms generally rely on internally-generated funds for capital investment. Between 1950 and 1972, 76 per cent of gross capital formation in Britain was funded from earnings compared to 62 per cent in Germany and 49 per cent in France. Furthermore, when forced to seek external sources of funds, UK firms have traditionally turned to equity rather than to debt. The average ratio of fixed interest capital to variable dividend capital of British firms in 1972 was only 0.55 compared with 0.74 in Germany and 0.92 in France (Thompson, 1977, p. 196; Lever and Edwards, 1980). As a result, industrial capital in Britain has been much less dependent on the banks for finance than its Continental counterparts. Secondly, what capital *is* provided by the banks to British industry has been funnelled primarily through short-term loans; in fact, a substantial portion of the funds available to even the largest corporations is still provided via regularized overdraft facilities. In 1972, for instance, 73 per cent of borrowing by non-financial enterprises in the UK was short term, compared with 49 per cent of the borrowing in France and 30 per cent in Germany (Thompson, 1977, p. 263) . . . This is significant because when a bank grants short-term credit, it does not usually look closely at the details of a firm's performance or market strategy, as it might in connection with a long-term loan. Instead, it extends funds on more mechanical principles of creditworthiness associated with balance-sheet figures such as the ratio of liquid assets to liabilities (cf. Thompson, 1977, p. 196). As a consequence, in comparison with the banks of Germany and France, the British banks appear to have more limited knowledge about the operations of British industry and less of a stake in the profitability of particular industrial sectors. British finance capital is thus more likely to define its interests in a way that is separate from those of industry.

The organization of labour in Britain is also somewhat different to either France or Germany. In contrast to the French case, there is a central Trades Union Congress (TUC) in Britain, to which most organized workers are affiliated, and which has considerable moral authority among them, but it is a loose confederation with very limited bureaucratic resources and few sanctions to apply against its members. And in contrast to the German case, 112 separate unions are affiliated to the TUC, many of them still organized along craft lines. Within many of these affiliates a contest for control over union policy also continues between frequently autocratic leaders and an influential network of shop stewards (Taylor, 1978). In broad social terms, however, this is a powerful union movement. At the economic level, over 50 per cent of the labour force is unionized, and in such key sectors as coal, railways, and road transport over 95 per cent of the work force belongs to a trade union. In the face of severe inflation, most of these unions have been able to bargain for and secure real wage gains for their members. Similarly, at the political level, the union movement has substantial influence within the Labour Party which has been in office for at least 18 of the last 36 years, and its ability to stymie the policies even of Conservative governments has been demonstrated on several occasions in recent years (Crouch and Pizzorno, 1978).

How are these factors related to the patterns of British economic policy? In the eyes of most commentators, the principal feature of British post-war macroeconomic policy has been the recurrence of a 'stop—go' cycle of reflation followed by sharp deflation (Hansen, 1969; Caves *et al*, 1968; Brittan, 1971). Expansion in 1950 and early 1951 based on rearmament for the Korean War was followed, in 1952, by sharp increases in the Bank Rate, control on instalment buying ('hire purchase') and cuts in capital investment. The income tax cuts and investment allowances of 1953—4 led to renewed hire purchase controls, decreases in public investment, and sales tax increases in 1955—6. The budgets of 1958 and 1959 employed direct and indirect tax cuts to initiate another expansion, but in 1960 brought successive increases in the Bank Rate, a more restrictive budget and hire purchase controls, plus tax increases and reductions in public expenditure in 1961. In 1962—3 the Chancellor embarked on another expansion but this, too, came to a halt as the new Labour government imposed increasingly deflationary measures in the years between 1964 and 1970. In the 1970s a similar pattern was pursued as the deflationary policies of 1970—1 were followed by rapid expansion of public spending in 1972—4, deflation in 1975—7, expansion in 1978—80, and deflation in 1981. If these measures had been timed so as to moderate the effects of the business cycle on the British economy we might attribute this 'stop—go' pattern to the application of Keynesian principles of economic management. But detailed analyses of the period suggest that these policies were timed in such a way as to reinforce, rather than reduce, the effect of cyclical fluctuations on investment and output (Caves *et al*, 1968; Hansen, 1969, p. 443).

Accordingly, we have to turn elsewhere for an explanation — to factors which ultimately lead us back to the organization of the British polity. The expansionary policies pursued during the 'go' side of these cycles can be traced to the policy-makers' interest in stimulating economic growth. But this sort of stimulus invariably sucked imports into the economy which threw the balance of payments into deficit and precipitated an outflow of the foreign exchange reserves of the nation. Confronted with this situation, British policy makers faced a choice between letting the exchange rate decline, or deflating the economy so as to reduce expenditure on imports relative to exports. In similar situations, the French devalued. But for almost 30 years after the war, British policy makers refused to devalue, except in 1948 and 1967 when they no longer had a choice. They consistently defended an exchange rate which by the end of the 1950s was seriously overvalued (Brittan, 1971, p. 299). And in tandem with this, they maintained a policy of borrowing short-term funds to finance long-term capital outflows and a £3.5 billion overhang of overseas sterling balances which exacerbated the effects of speculative pressure on the reserves (cf. Pollard, 1969, Ch. 8). This meant that whenever the exchange rate came under pressure, British authorities moved to deflate the economy. It seems that in every one of these cases deflation was undertaken in response to an outflow of foreign reserves rather than as a result of domestic developments (Caves *et al*, 1968, p. 78). The appearance of a 'stop—go' cycle in British policy was directly related to the defence of a high exchange rate and the maintenance of extensive international financial obligations (Blank, 1978).

The consequences for British industry were adverse in two respects. First, the increasingly frequent and severe deflations entailed by this policy discouraged capital investment which might have improved productivity and thus may have limited the nation's general economic growth. Secondly, the policy saddled industrialists with particularly high export prices while subsidizing the price of competing imports. British export prices rose by 14.5 per cent more than the average price of world exports in the decade after 1953. Pollard (1969, p. 44) and others argue that this differential, rather than the sectoral distribution of British manufacturing, was the decisive element handicapping Britain's export industries. Moreover, deflation consistently depressed domestic investment in Britain, and the suggestion that it may have helped restrain prices is belied by the fact that prices rose as quickly in deflationary periods as at other times (Pollard, 1969, p. 483).

In short, for most of the post-war period, the British pursued a policy which appeared to be in the interests of finance capital and was detrimental to those of industry. Until the 1970s, the representatives of the British financial community believed that the maintenance of a high exchange rate, of the overseas balances and of unfettered capital flows was essential to the profitability of British finance capital and to the survival of London as an international financial centre. At each turning point, spokesmen for the City and for the Bank of England pressed the government to deflate rather than devalue (Brittan, 1971), and in each instance their views prevailed. To a large extent, the position they took, and their success in defending it, must be attributed to the organization of British capital and of the state. The arms-length relationship between financial and industrial capital in Britain was certainly conducive to the different definitions of interests which emerged on the two sides when such issues arose. In this context, the comments of a senior industrialist interviewed by Grant and Marsh (1978, p. 69) are revealing. He declared: 'There is a false assumption that all businessmen have common interests. Yet to me it is patently obvious that the interests of manufacturing business and the City are sometimes not coincident'. The contrast is with Germany where the banks' direct stake in the profitability of industrial enterprise and their familiarity with its needs have led the two sides to join in support of a low exchange rate.

At the same time, the organization of the British state was such that the views of financial capital were more likely to be influential on macroeconomic policy questions than were the views of industrial capital. As we have seen, the Bank of England, which considers itself to be the guardian of the interests of the financial community, was vested with primary responsibility for exchange rate questions. In contrast with the French *Trésor*, the Treasury had little expertise in this area and was accustomed to relying on the Bank (Keegan and Pennant-Rae, 1979). In times of crisis the authority of experts is especially enhanced. The Bank used the crisis situations engendered by pressure on the reserves to impress its demands for deflation on the government (Blackaby, 1979, p. 312). Similarly, even within the Treasury, there were few officials with specific responsibility for, or detailed knowledge of, the interests of manufacturing industry who might have successfully opposed deflation. On the contrary, the preoccupation of most Treasury officials with the control of public expenditure predisposed them to deflationary episodes during which public expenditure might be cut back. The organization of Whitehall was conducive to the formation of a consensus on the desirability of deflation over devaluation of the sort that Blank (1978) has found. The closed nature of the British bureaucracy, moreover, minimized the impact of outside advice from industry . . . Although politicians were ultimately responsible for these decisions, the power they wielded was, in many respects, illusory. It was difficult for even the most radical of them to contravene the received wisdom of many years and the advice of the most senior authorities in the field when it seemed that the country was in crisis and its financial viability was at stake (Brittan, 1971, p. 197).

In the sphere of industrial policy, the British experience has displayed three distinctive characteristics. First, a coordinated policy aimed at the rationalization of key industrial sectors was not developed until late in the post-war period. Following the Labour government's failure to use the Industrial Organization and Development Act of 1947 to enforce a measure of planning on industry (Shonfield, 1969, pp. 98ff), the British government made only sporadic attempts to encourage rationalization in the private sector through the 1950s. The measures which were taken in shipbuilding, or in the textile industry via the Cotton Industry Act of 1959 were mainly extensions of programmes begun in the 1930s (Grove, 1967; Blackaby, 1979, p. 403). Not until a growing concern about Britain's relatively slow rate of economic growth prompted the establishment of the National Economic Development Council (NEDC) in 1962 and the creation of a Secretary of State for Industry, Trade and Regional Development in 1963, did the British state attempt to mount an industrial policy aimed at the large-scale regeneration of British industry (Brittan, 1971, Ch. 6).

Secondly, even after 1962, most of the government's activities in this area were oriented to the maintenance of employment in economically depressed areas rather than to the reorganization of industry (McCrone, 1969, p. 119). Regional considerations have continued to be the guiding principle behind British industrial policy. Even in the most recent period, the vast majority of funds have gone to firms in declining sectors of the economy . . . This contrasts with the activities of the French and the Germans who have focused most of their attention and a large portion of their funds on high growth sectors of industry.

Finally, the extent to which British policy has been seriously 'interventionist' is very limited. There was no attempt by the state to force industrial reorganization on critical sectors as in France. Even Britain's principal attempt at planning, associated with the National Economic Development Council in the 1960s, was a tripartite exercise based on mutual persuasion. As Hagen and White (1966, cited in Black, 1978, p. 113) note, the British government approached producer groups 'not as a representative of the public interest seeking the recommendations of groups with special interests before it exercised its authority, but as one association approaching two other associations to ask them what they would be willing to do'. The Economic Development Committees and Sectoral Working Parties spawned by the NEDC operated on the same basis, and it is not surprising that they seem to have enhanced the influence of industry over government rather than *vice versa*.

This pattern of policy can be linked to several facets of the organization of British capital and the state. Most importantly, the British state lacked the instruments with which to enforce an active policy of sectoral reorganization even if it could have formulated one. Financial capital in Britain has been relatively independent of the state. The Bank of England attempts to influence the total quantities of credit extended in the economy and has occasionally suggested that the banks give priority to export industries in their lending, but the state lacks the detailed control over the flows of funds in the economy which the French state enjoys. Moreover, industry itself has been less dependent on debt, and thus on the banking sector, for finance in Britain than in France, although this may be changing (*Bank of England Quarterly Bulletin*, June, 1979, p. 185). Thus, even if the state had nationalized the banks, its leverage over industry would still have been limited. The tax allowances on which the British have relied for most of the post-war period to stimulate investment cannot be focused on individual firms in such a way as to enforce a rationalization programme. And the subsidies which several governments have made available to industry are not a substitute for more extensive control over an industry's sources of external finance.

At the same time, the division of responsibility and allocation of expertise within the British state has not been conducive to the development of a strategy for industrial rejuvenation capable of being sustained in the face of conflicting economic demands. Power over the direction of economic policy and the allocation of public funds remained with the Treasury which, until 1975, had little responsibility for, or knowledge of, the needs of British industry. While the Department of Economic Affairs and NEDC were mandated to develop such a strategy, control over the priorities of economic policy never left the Treasury (cf. Budd, 1977; Brittan, 1971), and many of its decisions ultimately frustrated the planners (Leruez, 1975). Without an apparatus committed to sectoral planning and entrenched within Whitehall, the British state proved attentive to sectoral problems only in crisis situations. Initiative in this area remained at the political level where concerns naturally focused on the short-term alleviation of unemployment rather than on the long-term reallocation of investment toward growth sectors of industry.

In the field of incomes policy, the British pattern has displayed three distinctive characteristics. First, the government has made extensive efforts to secure an incomes policy at a number of junctures in the post-war period, and has implemented either voluntary or statutory wage norms in 1948, 1961—2, 1965—6, 1966—7, 1972—3 and 1975—8. Secondly, in each case, the imposition of a norm has been preceded by a serious attempt on the part of the government to reach agreement with the TUC and the Confederation of British Industry (CBI) on the need for a norm and on the outlines of a broader economic strategy. And finally, after one to two years under a wage norm, rank-and-file resistance to the policy has forced the union leadership to withdraw its support for such a policy, and impelled the government to return to free collective bargaining. Thus the British pattern has been one of alternation between incomes policy negotiated from above and free collective bargaining.

Once again, the roots of this pattern can be traced to the organization of the British labour market. On the one hand, the British government found it necessary to attempt to reach agreement on an incomes policy because of the power of the union movement. This power is reflected in the high proportion of the labour force which is organized, especially in the key industrial sectors, and in the influence of the unions over the Conference of the Labour Party. At a political level this has meant that the unions have had the ability to turn the electorate, and in some cases a party's own supporters, against the government through widespread industrial disruption. A Labour government learned this lesson during the defeat of its industrial relations legislation in 1968; and a Conservative government had it confirmed when a confrontation with striking mineworkers contributed to its electoral defeat in February 1974 (Jenkins, 1970; Hurd, 1979). Of equal significance is the fact that at an economic level, British workers have had an ability to maintain their real wages through periods of both inflation and state-induced recession (Turner and Wilkinson, 1972). Both of these factors have limited the usefulness of imposing deflation on the economy to deter the unions from seeking higher wages and have forced the government to look to negotiations over an incomes policy as an alternative.

If these negotiations have been made necessary in Britain by the power of the unions, however, they have also been made possible by the existence of a single union confederation. In both respects, Britain stands in contrast to France where the weakness of the union movement limits the need for negotiations, and the multiplicity of unions discourages any one of them from reaching an agreement with the state.

In part, these factors explain the attachment of British officials to 'tripartism,' which Grant and Marsh (1978, p. 389) define as 'a belief that the peak organizations representing management and the trade unions are of special importance among all producers' groups, that negotiations should take place with these peak organizations on the major issues of economic policy, and that agreement with these groups will provide a basis for the successful implementation of the government's economic policy'. It is also intrinsically difficult to secure adherence to a voluntary incomes policy in Britain without a substantial amount of bargaining. In contrast to Germany, where the acquiescence of a few major union leaders is sufficient to assure all concerned that restraint will be widespread and returns in the form of reduced inflation at least will be forthcoming, the TUC must persuade a large number of its affiliates to support a policy, before any can be assured that it will stick. This requires a substantial effort at the mobilization of consent. Similarly, even if the CBI is involved primarily in order to lend weight to the government's demands for wage restraint, an institutional framework within which bargaining can take place on a regularized basis is essential if the British state is to realize a strategy of semi-voluntary restraint. In the absence of bargaining, the generalized distribution of positive incentives to the unions has proved ineffective at securing restraint. An institutional framework, of the sort the NEDC or TUC—Labour Party Liaison Committee provides, has made it possible for the state to demand a *quid pro quo* for each of the goods it distributes, to exact the maximum returns in exchange for those goods and to monitor any ensuing agreement. Once one turns from brandishing 'sticks' to offering 'carrots,' bargaining produces more of a return than simple bribery.

While the TUC can strike a wage bargain with the government, however, there is an intrinsic limit to how long the bargain can be kept. Because the TUC is a loose confederation of affiliated unions with few sanctions, short of expulsion, to use against them, an enormous expenditure of organizational resources and institutional authority is required if it is to persuade its member unions — and they their members — to limit wage demands. After a period, those resources are exhausted, and a rank-and-file backlash begins to find alternative leadership with which to challenge prevailing personnel and policy. The existence of a large number of decentralized unions means that alternative leadership is more readily available in Britain than in Germany. Thus, any tripartite arrangement is bound to break down, and a period of free collective bargaining, often under more militant leadership, ensues before another tripartite bargain is attempted. Hence the alternation between incomes policy and free-for-all which has characterized the British experience in the post-war period.

Conclusion

In conclusion, although only a preliminary analysis has been possible here, the economic policies of Germany . . . and Britain seem to have followed distinctive patterns throughout most of the post-war period; and these, in turn, can be related to peculiar features of the organization of capital, labour and the state in each nation. A comprehensive analysis would have to deal with several facets of these nations' policies which are not covered here. In particular, within the context of these broad patterns, the individual policies of each nation have changed direction at several points since the war, and this internal dynamic should be accounted for as well. What seems striking, however, is not the occasional variation in a country's policies, but the persistence of broad patterns which differentiate the policies of one country from those of another. In a world of flux, it is underlying continuities which most merit explanation; and the parallel persistence of both these patterns and specific organizational forms strongly suggests that the two are related.

To some extent, the effect of these organizational factors on political outcomes is independent of the power of individual groups but in three respects they are clearly related to the distribution of power among social groups. First, the relative power of capital and labour at critical historical junctures, when the organization of key institutions is in flux, can have an important impact on the organizational relations . . . which emerge during the period and are institutionalized. The political power of British capital in the critical years following the war, for example, played an important role in blocking the establishment of planning mechanisms there (Shonfield, 1969). Secondly, once a given pattern of socio-economic organization is established, it instantiates a particular balance of power among key social groups and exercises a continuing influence over their ability to mobilize, to form coalitions and to wield power in the political arena. Finally, as in the case of German revaluation, the dimensions of socio-economic organization which specify the relations one group has to another, can define the interests those groups will perceive themselves to have in a policy and thus structure their demands even before the groups mobilize to bring pressure to bear in a political forum. In this respect, these facets [of such] organizations can be thought of as intermediate factors in the determination of economic policy, lying somewhere between more transitory interest group pressures and the structural limits to policy making in a capitalist state that structuralist or synthetic theories identify . . .

References

Allison, G. (1971) *The Essence of Decision,* Boston, Little Brown.
Altvater, E. (1973) 'Some problems of state interventionism', *Kapitalistate,* Vol. 2.
Bacon, R. and Eltis, W. (1976) *Britain's Economic Problem: Too Few Producers?,* London, Macmillan.
Blackaby, F. T. (ed.) (1979) *British Economic Policy 1960—74,* London, Cambridge University Press.
Blank, S. (1978) 'Britain and the politics of foreign economic policy: the domestic economy, and the problem of pluralistic stagnation', in P. J. Katzenstein, (ed.) *Between Power and Plenty,* Maddison, University of Wisconsin Press, pp. 89—138.
Block, F. (1977) 'The ruling class does not rule: notes on the Marxist theory of the state',*Socialist Review,* No. 33, May—June, pp. 6—28.
Brittan, S. (1971) *Steering the Economy,* Harmondsworth, Penguin.
Budd, A. (1977) *The Politics of Economic Planning,* Manchester, Manchester University Press.
Carré, J. J., Dubois, A. and Malinvand, E. (1972) *La croissance française,* Paris, Editions du Seuil.
Caves, R. E. *et al.* (1968) *Britain's Economic Prospects,* Washington, DC and London, Brookings Institution and Allen & Unwin.

Caves, R. E. *et al.* (1979) *The Changing System of Industrial Relations in Great Britain,* Oxford, Basil Blackwell.

Cowart, A. (1978) 'The economic policies of European governments', *British Journal of Political Science,* Vol. 8, Part 3, 4, pp. 285–311, 425–39.

Cowart, A. (1978) 'The intensification of industrial conflict in the United Kingdom', in C. Crouch and A. Pizzorno (eds), Vol. 1, pp. 191–256.

Crouch, C. and Pizzorno, A. (eds) (1978) *The Resurgence of Class Conflict in Western Europe Since 1968,* 2 Vols, New York, Holmes & Meir.

Esping-Andersen, G., Friedland, R. and Wright, E. O. (1976) 'Modes of class struggle and the capitalist state', *Kapitalistate,* Vol. 4, 5.

Gold, D. A., Lo, C. Y. H. and Wright, E. O. (1975) 'Recent developments in Marxist theories of the capitalist state', *Monthly Review,* October–November, pp. 29–43, 36–51.

Gough, I. (1975) 'State expenditure in advanced capitalism', *New Left Review,* Vol. 92, July–August, pp. 53–92.

Gough, I. (1979) *The Political Economy of the Welfare State,* London, Macmillan.

Gourevitch, P. A. (1977) 'International trade, domestic coalitions, and liberty: comparative responses to the Great Depression of 1873–1896', *Journal of Interdisciplinary History,* Vol. 8, No. 1, August.

Gourevitch, P. A. (1980) 'The politics of economic policy in the Great Depression of 1929: some comparative observations'. Paper presented to the American Political Science Association, Washington, DC, August.

Gowland, D. (1978) *Monetary Policy and Credit Control,* London, Croom Helm.

Grant, W. and Marsh, D. (1978) *The Confederation of British Industry,* London, Hodder & Stoughton.

Grove, J. W. (1967) *Government and Industry in Britain,* London, Longmans.

Hagen, E. E. and White, S. F. T. (1966) *Great Britain: Quiet Revolution in Planning,* Syracuse, Syracuse University Press.

Hall, P. A. (1981a) 'Economic planning and the state: the evolution of economic challenge and political response in France', in G. Esping-Andersen and R. Friedland (eds) *Political Power and Social Theory,* Vol. III, Greenwich, Connecticut, Jai Press.

Hall, P. A. (1981b) *'Miti culturali e realtà economiche: la programmazione francese nel confronto con l'esperienza Brittannica',* Stato e Mercato, Vol. I, No. 1 April.

Hansen, B. (1969) *Fiscal Policy in Seven Countries 1955–1965,* Paris, OECD.

Hayward, J. and Watson, M. (eds) (1975) *Planning, Politics and Public Policy: The British, French and Italian Experience,* London, Cambridge University Press.

Heidenheimer, A. J. Heclo, H. and Adams, C. T. (1977) *Comparative Public Policy: The Politics of Social Choice in Europe and America,* New York, St. Martin's Press.

Hibbs, D. A. (1980) 'On the demand for economic outcomes: macro-economic performance and mass political support in the United States, Great Britain and Germany'. Paper presented to the American Political Science Association, Washington, DC, August.

Hirsch, H. (1978) 'The state apparatus and social reproduction: elements of a theory of the bourgeois state' in J. Holloway and S. Picciotto (eds) *State and Capital,* London, Edward Arnold, pp. 57—107.

Hurd, D. (1979) *An End to Promises,* London, Collins.

Jenkins, P. (1970) *The Battle of Downing Street,* London, Charles Knight.

Jessop, B. (1977) 'Recent theories of the capitalist state', *Cambridge Journal of Economics,* Vol. I, pp. 343—73.

Jessop, B. (1982) *The Capitalist State,* Oxford, Martin Robertson.

Kaufmann, H. (1969) 'A debate over Germany's revaluation, 1961: a chapter in political economy', *Weltwirtschaftliches Archiv,* Vol. 103, pp. 181—212.

Keegan, W. and Pennant-Rae, R. (1979) *Who runs the economy?: Control and influence in British economic policy,* London, Maurice Temple Smith.

Keohane, R. O. (1978) 'Economics, inflation, and the role of the state', *World Politics,* Vol. 3, No. 1, October, pp. 108—28.

Kindleberger, C. D. (1965) 'Germany's persistent balance-of-payments disequilibrium', in R. E. Baldwin (ed.) *Trade, Growth and the Balance of Payments,* Chicago, Amsterdam, pp. 230—48.

Kirschen, E. S. (ed.) (1964) *Economic Policy in Our Time,* 2 Vols, Amsterdam, North Holland.

Kirschen, E. S. (ed.) (1975) *Economic Policies Compared,* 2 Vols, Amsterdam, Elsevier.

Klöten, N., Kellerer, H-H. and Vollmer, R. (1978) 'The political and social factors of Germany's stabilization performance'. Paper presented to a Brookings Conference on the Politics and Sociology of Global Inflation, Washington, DC, December.

Krause, L.B. and Salant, W.S. (eds) (1977) *Worldwide Inflation,* Washington, DC, Brookings Institution.

Kreile, M. (1978) 'West Germany: the dynamics of expansion', in P. J. Katzenstein (ed.) *Between Power and Plenty,* Maddison, University of Wisconsin Press, pp. 191—224.

Leruez, J. (1975) *Economic Planning and Politics in Britain,* London, Martin Robertson.

Lever, H. and Edwards, G. (1980) 'Why Germany beats Britain', *Sunday Times* 2 November, pp. 16—17.

Lieberman, S. (1977) *The Growth of European Mixed Economies 1945—1970,* New York, John Wiley.

Lindblom, C. E. (1977) *Politics and Markets,* New York, Basic Books.

Lipset, S. M. (1964) 'The changing class structure and contemporary European politics', *Daedalus,* Vol. 93, No. 1, Winter, pp. 271—303.

McCrone, G. (1969) *Regional Policy in Britain,* London, Allen & Unwin.

MacLennan, M., Forsyth, M. and Denton, G. (1968) *Economic Planning and Policies in Britain, France and Germany,* New York, Praeger.

Martin, A. (1975) 'Is democratic control of capitalist economies possible?', in Leon Lindberg *et al.* (ed.) *Stress and Contradiction in Modern Capitalism,* Lexington, Massachusetts, Lexington Books.

Medley, R. (1981) 'Monetary stability and industrial adaptation in Germany'. Prepared for the US Congress, Joint Economic Committee, June.

Miliband, R. (1969) *The State in Capitalist Society,* London, Weidenfeld & Nicolson.

Müller-Jentsch, W. and Sperling, H-J. (1978) 'Economic development, labour conflicts and the industrial relations system in West Germany', in C. Crouch and A. Pizzorno (eds) *The Resurgence of Class Conflict in Western Europe Since 1968,* Vol. 1, London, Macmillan, pp. 257—306.

O'Connor, J. (1973) *The Fiscal Crisis of the State,* New York, St. Martin's Press.

OECD (1977) *Towards Full Employment and Price Stability,* Paris, OECD.

Offe, Claus (1972) 'Political authority and class structure', *International Journal of Sociology,* Vol. 2, No. 1.

Offe, Claus (1974) 'Structural problems of the Capitalist State', *German Political Studies,* Vol. 1.

Pollard, S. (1969) *The Development of the British Economy, 1914—1967* (2nd edn) New York, St. Martin's Press.

Poulantzas, Nicos (1972) 'The problem of the capitalist state', in R. Blackburn (ed.) *Ideology in Social Science,* London, Fontana.

Poulantzas, Nico (1973) *Political Power and Social Classes,* London, New Left Books.

Poulantzas, Nicos (1975) *Classes in Contemporary Capitalism,* London, New Left Books.

Poulantzas, Nicos (1978) *State, Power, Socialism,* London, New Left Books.

Przeworski, A. and Wallerstein, M. (1980) 'The structure of class conflict in advanced capitalist societies'. Paper presented to the American Political Science Association, Washington, DC, August.

Roberts, C. C. (1979) 'Economic theory and policy-making in West Germany', *Cambridge Journal of Economics,* Vol. 3, pp. 83—9.

Schmitter, P. and Lehmbruch, G. (eds) (1979) *Trends Toward Corporatist Intermediation,* New York, Sage.

Select Committee on Nationalized Industries (1969—70) *First Report,* Vol. IV, House of Commons.

Shanks, M. (1978) *Planning and Politics,* London, Allen & Unwin.

Shonfield, A. (1969) *Modern Capitalism,* London, Cambridge University Press.

Taylor, R. (1978) *Labour and the Social Contract,* Fabian Tract 458, London, Fabian Society.

Thompson, G. (1977) 'The relationship between the financial and industrial

394   *The State and the Economy*

sectors in the United Kingdom economy', *Economy and Society,* Vol. 6, No. 3, August.

Tufte, E. (1979) *Political Control of the Economy,* Princeton, Princeton University Press.

Turner, H. A. and Wilkinson, F. (1972) *Do Trade Unions Cause Inflation?,* Cambridge, Cambridge University Press.

Vernon, R. (ed.) (1974) *Big Business and the State,* Cambridge, Massachusetts, Harvard University Press.

Vogel, F. (1973) *German Business after the Economic Miracle,* London, Macmillan.

Wadbrook, W. P. (1972) *West German Balance of Payments Policy,* New York, Praeger.

Warnecke, S. J. and Suleiman, E. N. (eds) (1975) *Industrial Policies in Western Europe,* New York, Praeger.

Yaffe, D. (1973) 'The Marxian theory of crisis, capital and the state', *Economy and Society,* Vol. III.

Zinn, K. G. (1978) 'The social market in crisis', in S. Holland (ed.) *Beyond Capitalist Planning,* Oxford, Basil Blackwell, pp. 85–105.

4.5

Capitalist and Socialist States: a Critique of the Convergence Thesis

MARC RAKOVSKI

The idea of the convergence of the two world systems is almost as old as their coexistence. Of the numerous versions of this theory, that of 'industrial society' is the most widespread. In the heroic age of large-scale machine industry (so the theory runs), primitive technology did not yet unambiguously determine the social organization of production. At the beginnings of the development of contemporary 'industrial society', therefore, differences which were historical in origin could play a significant role in the organization of society. Where the industrial revolution took place within the context of private enterprise, capitalism evolved; where it took place on the basis of state ownership of the means of production, socialism evolved. But when technical development reaches the stage at which it is based on science, the differences between the respective points of departure lose their significance. Modern technology leaves no freedom of choice for the social patterns of the division of labour and cooperation. It directly defines the appropriate labour process and, through this, defines the wider social relations as well. In every mature industrial society there is the same technical division of labour, the same pattern of consumption, stratification and social mobility; the relation between the economy and politics is the same; and most important, specialized technical and scientific knowledge play the same role in the administration of social processes.

These prophets of industrial society were not motivated by the similarity of observable characteristics in the two systems. They

Source: Abbreviated and edited extract from M. Rakovski *Towards an East European Marxism* (1978) Allison and Busby and St Martin's Press.

were, in reality, interested in an ideological justification of Western capitalism. They wanted to prove that modern capitalism was no longer capitalism but, from the class point of view, a neutral industrial society, that it was not the interests of the bourgeoisie which governed social processes but the requirements of techno-logical and economic rationality.

But as far as empirical facts are concerned, even the Marxists now accept the predictions of the theory of industrial society: the trends of technological development in the two societies are becoming more and more parallel, and consequently the similarity is ever greater in the field of the division of labour and the pattern of consumption, and it is becoming increasingly clear that real social power in both societies is being transferred into the hands of some sort of technocracy. The only difference is that, in keeping with the different structure of the explanation, the theories of the left do not conclude that neither system is capitalist any longer, but rather that both are.

The left-wing convergence theory does not state that there are no differences in the social, institutional and class structure of the two societies. The theory's adherents argue that these differences are inconsequential, since they do not have significant results in the observable behaviour of the two systems. Thus the procedure for a critique of the theory should be as follows. As a first step, a socio-economic model of the two societies should be worked out. Then the behavioural regularities, both different and similar (though developed under the influence of different causes), should be deduced from the two models. If we succeed in deducing the similarities mentioned by the left-wing convergence theory from this particular model, then this gives us an explanation for something the convergence theory only describes. If we also succeed in deducing systematic differences from this particular model and the deductions from this model can also be verified empirically, then we can also use the model for other phenomena which contradict the convergence theory.

The aim of this chapter is more modest than this. It does not attempt a systematic elaboration of these models, but merely tries to establish some very important differences in the fields of economic organization and class structure. We cannot therefore provide strict deductions about the behavioural regularities of the two systems. We must content ourselves with a short discussion of behavioural regularities in the light of the distinctions indicated. At most this will make these theoretical distinctions plausible. But, as a beginning, this is perhaps something, especially if we consider that with the help of models sketched in this way we can succeed in showing significant differences among the very phenomena which the Marxist convergence thesis is fond of quoting.

Our approach will be to bring into the model only those differences which are not the subject of debate among Marxists. Furthermore, we shall only consider general differences in the models. That is, we shall set aside differences which are associated with initial historical conditions, the socio-economic backwardness of Soviet-type societies, the world economic and political background of the original process of accumulation in the Soviet Union, etc. Thus we shall handle our model as if there were no difference in the point of departure. This abstraction narrows still further the group of social processes that we can explain, but as a first step it seems expedient to do it. In this way, we can get round the danger of trying to explain by means of our model those differences which in reality result from differences of historical circumstance and not from the peculiarities of the systems.

The structural differences that we are going to consider are all related to the following very orthodox assertion: under capitalism it is the private ownership of the means of production that is dominant, whereas in Soviet-type societies the means of production are under state ownership. By 'the domination of private property' we mean that rights to a share in the surplus product are bought and sold on the capital market; that shareholders can influence the use to which their capital is put, at least in so far as they can withdraw their capital from one enterprise and invest it in another; that the shares of a section of the enterprises are either entirely or for most part in the hands of private individuals or other private enterprises so that the state cannot directly influence them; and finally, that this private sphere of economic activity can be seen to influence the macroeconomic behaviour of the whole system, the trend of changes in the level of employment, income, prices and wages and the cyclical fluctuations round this trend. By state ownership of the means of production we mean that, apart from certain exceptions which are insignificant from the standpoint of the economy as a whole, every economic organization is subordinate to a unified state administrative hierarchy, and the allocation of productive resources is arranged among the different levels and branches of this hierarchy. Neither income, nor decision-making rights stem from any sort of capital market. (It goes without saying that state property as defined here is not the only possible form of non-capitalist property relation.)

Economic organization

The models of a capitalist economy can be ranged on a scale between two extremes. In the one ideal type a perfectly competitive market links the enterprises with the consumers, while in the other the enterprises are powerful corporations which can cut themselves off completely from market conditions. In the former model, as far as the enterprise is concerned, the market parameters are an objective datum which has to be adapted to. In the latter model the enterprises do not adapt themselves to the economic environment, but rather mould the economic environment to suit their own investment, development and production programmes.

It is clear that the latter ideal type is closer to the model of the Soviet economy than the 'pure competition' ideal type. It is also a commonplace to say that historical development by now is in the process of passing from the situation of the first ideal type to that of the second. At most, what is disputed is the degree of concentration and centralization that has been reached. Both standpoints incline us to assume for the purposes of the present study that independence from market forces has proceeded as far as is possible under capitalism. Thus we ought only to set out those limitations to development which can in no way be transgressed while private ownership of the means of production is dominant.

Under capitalism the joint effect of two things hinders the elimination of the mechanisms of supply and demand. One of these is the uncertainty of the conditions of economic activity. No growth and integration of corporations is entirely indifferent to unforeseeable changes in the economic environment. There are always incalculable changes in the sphere of the supply of raw materials, in technological development and in the structure of the labour supply. That is, even the biggest corporations cannot completely control the input of production factors. Neither can consumer demand be perfectly manipulated. Manipulation is merely one of the factors that affect consumer preferences, and no one can say for certain how manipulation influences the structure of demand and its overall size. As a result, the possibilities for both investment and profits fluctuate, and do so, moreover, in a way which cannot be completely foreseen and is not always the same. It is not possible, therefore, to be entirely free from the uncertainties of the supply of and demand for capital.

The second thing which limits the changeover to programmed

production is the institutional system of the capitalist economy. Complicated relationships of dependence are created between capitalist enterprises by the overlapping of shareholdings and board membership. One corporation buys a significant portion of the shares of another; a significant portion of the shares of two corporations are in the property of one person or family group; two enterprises have common members on their boards or in their executive management, etc. Similar links can exist between a private enterprise and the state as well. The state can buy shares in a private enterprise and, *vice versa*, private enterprises and private individuals can buy shares in state enterprises. But these relations of mutual dependence do not conquer the whole of the economy. Many big groups exist in the capitalist economy which really are independent of each other and of the state. It follows from this that capitalist enterprises are typically self-financing, that is, they must cover their expenditure by their income. Thus they cannot shift the risk costs on to other economic organizations, but must accommodate themselves to the unforseeable changes of environment, that is to market conditions.

The only economic organization for which this condition does not hold true in the strict sense is the state. The majority of the state's income does not come from productive, service or commercial activities, and usually the use of income is not determined by the aim of creating new income from it. State budgeting can therefore play the role of a shock-absorber when, for example, a mammoth enterprise is on the verge of bankruptcy. In the interests of ensuring employment and averting negative market reaction (or simply as a result of lobby pressure) the state can give the enterprise temporary tax concessions or can even aid it with exceptional credits and advantageous orders. What is more, the state can act relatively freely when it decides on this kind of intervention, for not only is it able to use the financial and physical resources at its disposal to cover its costs, but it can, for example, also impose an exceptional tax or increase the money supply at a rate faster than that of economic growth, etc. On top of this, it can aid the economy by such methods as a statutory wages policy or by the use of statutory price regulation. But the freedom of the capitalist state is severely limited. It cannot raise taxes as it likes, since this decreases what is usually called the desire to invest. It cannot permanently keep the money supply above the level of growth, because this would lead to uncontrollable inflation and the destruction of the economic mechanism. Statutory wage and price regulations always lead to dubious results, unless control is extended to every sort of economic transaction, and the capitalist state is only capable of doing this in a war economy. In short, the capitalist state can only intervene in economic processes to the extent that it is allowed to by the behavioural patterns of the private economy. The private economy reacts to state intervention according to its own rules. If the state does not bring its actions into line with these patterns, then these actions become counterproductive; for example, anti-cyclical measures which are overdone or badly timed can have a destabilizing effect.

The possibilities of independence from the economic environment are not unlimited in the Soviet-type system either, but they are nevertheless substantially greater. Here too it is impossible to foresee exactly the changes going on among production factors and consumer preferences. The principle of self-financing is valid too, at least in the context of the economy as a whole, for, to be sure, it is a tautology that in any closed system total expenditure cannot be bigger than total income plus total accumulated savings. But at the level of the individual enterprise it is not necessary to put this into effect. With the exception of significant small-scale industrial and commercial services, the whole economy is organized under a single, unitary administrative hierarchy. As with the capitalist economy, this also has two ideal types, and here too development is from one towards the other. The first is the centralized ideal type. Here the central powers prescribe in detail what to produce, in what quantities, to what standard, using what quality of tools and what materials, and in accordance with these orders, with a separate planning order on each occasion, they put the necessary resources at the enterprises' disposal. In this case the enterprises are, by definition, not self-financing, for they do not operate with resources which are permanently at their disposal. They are not financially responsible for their losses. The accumulation of unsold goods is not for them an indication of the need to change the structure of production. The second is the decentralized ideal type. Here the central powers set only very general targets for the enterprises (for example, they must achieve a given profit) and the enterprises dispose of their own resources, with which they fulfil their targets. In this case the enterprises can be self-financing, but the economy can also function normally if, *de facto*, no single enterprise is self-financing (which naturally is not the same as saying that total growth is negative, for the surpluses taken by the state can be greater than the losses incurred by the enterprises).

The decentralization of the command system does not mean

that the enterprises gain institutional autonomy from the state. Dependence remains, even if it is not accompanied by the right of command over every detail of enterprise activity. Enterprise directors are appointed and dismissed, rewarded and punished, by the central powers: that is, by just those same units of the hierarchical organization which, by the manipulation of the state budget and bank credits, control the investment possibilities of the enterprises, while on the other hand also controlling, via the party and the trade unions, the consensus between the interest groups within the enterprise.

Let us consider the example of investments. Suppose that the investment system is ideally decentralized: that is to say, discounting all infrastructural and non-economic investments, that every investment decision originates at enterprise level. From this it does not yet follow that every investment will be covered from its own savings. Just like the capitalist corporation, the Soviet-type enterprise is dependent on external investment sources. But while the search for external investment sources renders the capitalist enterprise dependent on the capital and money markets where the state and private capital compete with one another, the Soviet-type enterprise becomes dependent on the state administrative hierarchy. A Soviet-type enterprise can, in principle, draw on three sources: another enterprise's capital, bank credits and support from the state budget. The first possibility in reality is insignificant, even in the extreme case of there being no legal barriers to it. It is not in the interests of the individual departments directing the economy to agree to allow outside enterprises, which they cannot directly control, to gain influence over enterprises under their supervision by investing capital in them. Nor is it in the interests of the enterprises to invest their capital in an area where the power of a distant branch of the administrative hierarchy holds sway. As far as the other two sources are concerned, the central powers exercise exclusive control over them. The enterprises can compete with one another for budget support or bank credits, but the central apparatus does not compete with anyone for investment demand. Real investment decisions, in consequence, generally originate with the participation of the central authorities, even if the investment system is ideally decentralized.

There is no legal autonomy of enterprises to limit the Soviet-type state's direct influence on enterprise behaviour. This influence is not even restricted by the fact that obedient enterprises are recompensed for relative or absolute losses incurred by state intervention. In the first place, it has at its disposal a larger arsenal of instruments with which to balance enterprise finances. On top of the measures that the capitalist state can use (tax concessions, credit supports) the Soviet-type state can take further specific measures because it controls the interest to be paid on productive capital, determines the wage fund to be used by the enterprise and its mode of distribution, and also regulates the price system. Secondly, the Soviet-type state can use these tools more freely than the capitalist one can use its tools. The only things which limit its actions are those such as the *de facto* macroeconomic ratios of the budget (for example, it cannot curtail for a long period the portion allocated to ensure a socially acceptable level of consumption), but it is not restricted by the anticipations and unpredictable reactions of enterprises. To stay with the example of investments, the state does not have to be afraid of the desire to invest falling because of frequent disturbances in the price system or the redistribution of the whole of the surplus to loss-making enterprises. First of all, the overwhelming majority of investments are conceived with the participation of the state, so the state can thus influence them directly. Secondly, the enterprises are not deterred by unsatisfactory demand, as they can count on state support in the case of making a loss.

Both economies, capitalist and Soviet, are mixed economies. In both, some mixture of market and non-market relations coordinates the processes of production, service and consumption. However, the private property barrier in capitalism does not allow non-market relations to come to gain precedence. However much the freedom of the state and the large corporations is increased, the market always remains the primary frame of reference to which non-market actions must adapt themselves. State property (as defined above) is not a barrier to non-market actions. Rather, the hierarchical relations of dependence between the central command and the enterprises put restrictions on the market becoming the dominant frame of reference. And if this difference holds even in this imaginary marginal case, where the two systems are closest to each other, then *a fortiori* it must stand in all other cases, that is, the comparison between really existing capitalist and really existing Soviet societies.

The class structure

At first glance the difference seems to be that each class, including the working class, has its own economic and political organizations under capitalism, while in Soviet-type societies no class, not even the ruling class, is capable of organizing itself independently. But there would be no point in incorporating this difference in the explanatory model. The part of this statement referring to capitalist societies, though valid for most developed Western nations, is true only with important exceptions: Fascism and military dictatorships. Rather, we should go back to very general differences to find the reason why it is so common, under capitalism, for independent class organizations to be incorporated into the reproduction process of society, and why, in Soviet-type societies, it never occurs.

If we set aside the problems of the organizations of classes, a single essential structural difference remains, namely the differences in the ruling class's relation to property. In brief, under capitalism the ruling class has a property-owning stratum, in Soviet-type societies, on the other hand, it does not.

Those Marxists who say that the two systems work in an essentially similar way do not attribute any significance to this difference. They either argue that in modern capitalism real economic power does not lie in the hands of the property-owning group, or they argue that the ruling class of Soviet-type societies is a property-owning class as well, that it is in command of the forces of production of the whole society in the same way as the shareholders of a large corporation are in command of the corporation's capital. Let us consider the former contention first. It is based on the well-known thesis of academic sociology and economics on the separation of ownership and control. The bigger the corporations, the more fragmented the ownership of capital and the smaller the proportion of shares that remain in private hands. As a result, the growth of corporations inevitably reaches a point where the shareholders cannot already influence the economic strategy of the enterprise with their votes. From that point onwards it is not the corps of owners that makes real economic decisions, but the summit of the enterprises' organizational hierarchy, the upper management. Private property becomes a mere epiphenomenon; it has its effects on the field of the distribution of income and differences of consumption, but it has no influence on economic and political power. Real power, just as in Soviet-type societies, is linked to key positions in the large organizations, the corporations and the state.

In accordance with our method of reasoning, we shall accept that this thesis of the separation of ownership and control is in fact valid, even though we realize that the empirical evidence to back up the thesis is extremely controversial and that precisely among sociologists the opposite thesis has much support. But if, even in this marginal case, we find significant differences in the structure of the capitalist and socialist ruling class, then we do not have to prove separately that the difference holds when we look at other individual cases.

Now let us suppose that shareholders cannot in fact influence positively the behaviour of management with their votes. They can still, however, influence it in a negative way. If they are dissatisfied with their dividend, they can withdraw their capital from the company. Therefore, as long as capital is freely alienable, that is to say, as long as the capital market exists, the managers of large corporations will be forced to behave, by and large, exactly as the owner-directors of the traditional profit-maximizing enterprises. The economic power of management is indeed linked to organizational roles and not to legal property rights, but behind the organizations stand separate property interests. In the case of the complete separation of ownership and control, these interests control decision making by means of an anonymous power only: the power of the capital market. But this power is enough to keep the corporations in their sphere of influence. Therefore, management cannot simply merge with the state technocracy; it cannot become the representative, at company level, of interests linked to the state apparatus. Under capitalism, a not insignificant portion of the ruling class is made up of private individuals, who as a social group, supported by independent economic power, manoeuvre against the other classes and groups within the ruling class.

The other proposition remains, according to which the ruling class of Soviet-type societies is nothing more than a kind of 'collective property' class. And indeed, all the power that under capitalism is attached to private enterprises, in these societies is divided between the various levels and branches of the administrative hierarchy. However, we should not forget that in Soviet-type economic systems there are no functional equivalents to such institutions as general meetings of shareholders or the capital market. There are no specialized organizations which might call the efficiency of the utilization of invested capital to account, and which can freely transfer their capital from one enterprise to the other if they are dissatisfied with the results. Ownership functions are distributed between the various parts of the administrative apparatus and are, at the same time, impossibly intertwined with their non-ownership functions: for example, the tasks of ensuring political stability and macroeconomic balances. In Soviet-type societies a person belongs to the ruling class inasmuch as, and only inasmuch as, he plays a role in making and/or preparing decisions within the state administrative hierarchy. All his power is tied to his office or to informal relationships which have been established during his official activities. His power has no private backing separate from the state administrative hierarchy. Therefore it is misleading to call the ruling class a 'collective property' class.

In Soviet-type societies, all sections of the ruling class are clearly subordinate to the top political élite, which monopolizes the summits of the state administrative hierarchy. Decentralization of the command system does, of course, increase the freedom of decision of the lower branches, but it does not create independent economic powers which would cut across the relations of sub- and superordination of the administrative apparatus. Even the enterprise managements in an ideally decentralized system do not stand at the head of autonomous economic organizations. They are not controlled by the capital market, and not even by some sort of functional equivalent of it, but by the uniform administrative hierarchy, and in the last analysis by the political élite of the ruling class. And if we find that the chances of class organization and the possible forms of class struggle are substantially different even in this marginal case, in which the two class structures are closest to each other, then the difference must stand *a fortiori* in all other cases as well.

Class struggle

[What are the full consequences of the different class structures for the question that is at the centre of every Marxist enquiry: what are the possibilities in both systems for organized class struggle?]

We have already touched on the basic difference in the political institutional system of the two societies, in our outline of the models. In the majority of capitalist societies, every social group has the means of representing its own interests in relation to decisions of state power via its own political organizations, while in Soviet-type societies not even the ruling class has such organizations. Now, in conclusion, we must relate these characteristics in the behaviour of the two systems to the explanatory model.

The economic activity of the bourgeoisie takes place in the private sector of society. This economic activity naturally always influences the decisions of the state authority, and this influence, as we suggested when we sketched out our model, is becoming stronger. But we also suggested that the private nature of the workings of capitalist economic organizations does not change, which also means that within the bourgeoisie there are groups which stand in a competitive relation to one another. Each one would like to secure for itself the advantages of cooperation with the state, would like the infrastructural investments of the state to be decided in its favour, would like itself to be the one to receive advantageous state orders, etc. But they are not all equally strong in their competitive struggle to influence the state's economic policy. And the weaker groups would be forced to look on helplessly as the links of the stronger lobby with the state became closed and more exclusive, if they could not resort to other mechanisms for influencing the decisions of the state authority which might make it possible for them to balance their economic disadvantages with certain non-economic advantages. These mechanisms are guaranteed to the opposing groups of the bourgeoisie by the system of so-called representative democracy. The ratios of representation are defined by the exercise of political rights attached to the individual; the competing groups of the bourgeoisie thus have the opportunity not merely to measure their own strength against that of the others, but also to try and gather behind themselves the forces of the other classes in society. And because of the very inequality of the positions of economic power, there are always, within the bourgeoisie, not insignificant groups who have an interest in maintaining the representative system as a mechanism for balancing the power relations within the ruling class.

Naturally, individuals invested with equal political rights in a system based on the exercise of political rights attached to the individual do not all influence the decisions of the state authority with equal weight. The strength of the political organizations and tools for influencing public opinion are determined to a great extent by the weight of the economic power behind them. To this extent, the ratios of the economic power of the various capitalist interest groups are realized even in the public sphere of political competition. But to some extent, economic strength in this field can be balanced by appeals to the interests of the electors.

What is more, the contest does not necessarily remain the internal affair of the competing groups of the bourgeoisie. Once institutions of political democracy exist, the other classes, including the working class, cannot be prevented from creating their own political organizations and tools for influencing public opinion.

The political behaviour of the working class thus becomes less spontaneous and more predictable, and is enacted increasingly within a legal framework. The political content of the struggle within this framework decides what this means for the stability of the whole of the system. It can just as easily mean the growing integration of the aspirations of the working class as the intensification of the class struggle. But even in the latter case, the bourgeoisie cannot easily dismantle the institutional system of representative democracy, even if it is slowly becoming dangerous. The transformation of political institutions towards dictatorship affects the interests of the various groups among the bourgeoisie in different ways. Even within the capitalist class, therefore, factions evolve which adhere to the political institutional system that is advantageous for them, though by this they put the rule of the whole class at risk.

The political rights of the individual are by and large the same in Soviet-type societies as they are in liberal democracies. But no special group, not even the ruling class, has either the right or the means to influence the exercise of these rights through organizations and means of information which are centred solely on the interests of that group. So the exercise of political rights becomes an empty ritual. The formally existing representative institutions perform a symbolic function only. The ruling class does not need to enforce its influence on state power by way of any kind of political representation. Its rule is not based on its position in the private sector of the economy, but on its position in the state administrative hierarchy which abolishes the private nature of the economy. Naturally, the ruling class in Soviet-type societies is not unified either. Interest groups around the various levels and branches of the administrative hierarchy are continually struggling with each other for control over an increasingly large proportion of social resources. In normal circumstances, however, as far as we can see on the basis of our model at least, the structure of the system makes it disadvantageous for any group to break the unity of the administrative hierarchy.

If any group wanted to free itself from the administrative apparatus and tried to stand up as an independent economic power, it would not only find itself in opposition to the pressure of the other parts of the ruling class, but would also become defenceless against the oppressed class as well. The patronage of the political leaders does not only mean restrictions for the managers of productive and service enterprises, for example, but also defence against the workers. The upper economic administration guarantees that the 'normal' demands of the workers can always be satisfied, and is able to mobilize sufficient force to break 'excessive' demands. In normal circumstances the lower level managers desire, at most, the decentralization of decision-making rights within the administrative hierarchy, and not the dismantling of the unity of the hierarchy.

As long as the unity of the administrative hierarchy remains, the oppressed class cannot create for itself an independent organizational base, for it always finds itself faced with the united pressure of the whole institutional system. The most important political consequence of our model, therefore, is that although the polarization of the ruling class is a necessary precondition for any social force to organize itself, no developmental tendencies can be deduced from the general structure of the system which might point to the growth, with time, of the probability of such a polarization.

For all that, the structure of the system does not exclude the appearance of crisis situations in which the unity of the ruling class is shaken. It was after such a crisis as this that the contemporary version of Soviet-type societies, the subject of our model, evolved. In the transition period immediately following the death of Stalin, that section of the ruling class which wanted to destroy the system of mass terror which threatened it too, tried, on occasions at least, to mobilize groups outside the ruling class against the old élite, which was directly involved in the exercise of terror. This was made possible by the fact that the ending of Stalinist mass terror was in the primary interest of all the large social groups. The experiment, however, set off potentially revolutionary processes which threatened the very basis of ruling-class power and which in some countries could only be stopped by military means.

The political unity of the ruling class was re-established as a result of these shocks. No single interest group dared undertake so audacious an experiment. In the post-Stalinist system that has taken root since the overcoming of the crisis, there is no ruling-class group at all whose interests might coincide with the aspirations of broader social strata. The contradictions are no longer so simple or clear-cut as they were at the time of the struggle for the ending of mass terror, when the whole 'people' stood in opposition to a narrow political élite. Every social group is set on its own course now, determined by its partial interests. The target of the lower-level economic managers and political leaders, the chief forces in the destalinization process, is to increase their economic power and their say in the preparation of upper-level decisions.

For the masses the consequence is no longer manifest only in the ending of the mobilization of everyday life, in the fact that basic consumer needs are relatively continuously satisfied, but in ever-increasing social differentiation, in ever-increasing contrasts of income, lifestyle and consumer habits. It is probable, therefore, that the behaviour of lower-level managers will gradually fit into the pattern that follows from our model; they will consciously orientate themselves towards decentralization in the hierarchy, and cut themselves off from any attempt to break up the unity of the hierarchy.

It is not to be expected, therefore, that new crises in Soviet-type societies, that is, crises of the established post-Stalinist system itself, will stem from shifts within the ruling class. Any new disruption of the ruling class can only conceivably take place, if at all, as the result of a crisis which has already exploded in reality. The crisis will thus either be the result of development tendencies which lead to the economic collapse of the system or to an increase in the capacity of the oppressed class to resist, or it will be the result of a change in external conditions which the system is no longer capable of adapting to. As far as the latter is concerned, the forecasting of such changes is not the task of abstract model building, but of concrete historical and sociological analysis. As far as the former two possibilities are concerned we have no reason, on the basis of our model, to predict that the collapse of the economic growth of Soviet-type societies must follow. We can make certain cautious predictions concerning the growth of the relative autonomy of the oppressed class (on the basis of the spread of intellectual non-conformism and the strengthened position of the workers' household), but we cannot deduce from our model alone that this tendency will transcend the limits of the system's tolerance. However, it does follow clearly from our model that once (for whatever reason) a political crisis evolves again, similar to the crisis of the transition period, it will be enacted at a higher level, among more differentiated forms. The ruling class has become more articulated as a result of decentralization. Some of its groups have got used to greater independence. Ready oppositional ideologies have been developed in the subculture of the sub-intellectuals which, at the right moment, could have a mass effect. Illegal movements born in such an environment can have a certain importance in this sort of situation. The greater reserves of the workers' household give greater room for the emergence and consolidation of non-conformist ideas among groups of the younger generation now growing up in the working class.

Not sufficient? To be sure, it is not much. For post-Stalinist development has only just begun, and there are scarcely any usable antecedents for a Marxist theory of Soviet-type societies as *sui generis* class societies. Can people for whom the two systems are essentially the same say as much? Can they formulate in any way the problem of why there is no organized workers' movement, either revolutionary or reformist, in Eastern Europe? Can they explain why the members of the ruling class only realize their private interests by way of the role that they play in the administrative apparatus and not by way of independent political organizations? Can they account for the social basis of intellectual non-conformism? Do they recognize the possibilities latent in the rise of mass consumption? Can they explain the peculiar dynamic of economic cycles and their particular political effects? If not, the left-wing version of the convergence thesis must be discarded, and further progress must be made towards the elaboration of a theory of Soviet-type societies as *sui generis* class societies.

Part 5
Power, Legitimacy and the State

Introduction

PAUL G. LEWIS

Power and legitimacy are aspects of the state which are closely linked with its activity and position in society. According to Weber's definition (p. 111) the state is that human community which '(successfully) claims the *monopoly of the legitimate use of physical force* within a given territory' (original italics). Thus power (which may be seen as the capacity to exert force effectively) and the legitimacy of the claim to exercise it are the very base on which the state's existence rests. It is fairly clear why power and the monopolistic claim to physical force should be so basic to the existence of the state. States which are unable to enforce their monopolistic claim are on the verge of disintegration and face the threat of civil war and dissolution. Examples may be drawn from the fall of the Roman Empire (and even earlier) to the rebellion of East Pakistan and its secession to form the new state of Bangladesh. A state without power is, therefore, merely a political fiction and not the dominant unit whose activity we are exploring in this Reader.

The position of the state with regard to legitimacy is somewhat more complex. Weber does not really spell out the logical grounds on which the state's monopoly of physical force requires legitimation. Having stated that 'if the state is to exist, the dominated must obey the authority claimed by the powers that be' he then merely goes on to ask: 'When and why do men obey? Upon what inner justifications and upon what external means does this domination rest?' (p. 112). The requirement of legitimacy and the need to transform 'physical force' into 'authority' seem to be assumed. One reason for this is that authority, the capacity to inspire, suggest or compel a course of action without resort to the use of physical force, is often held to be as important an element of statehood and political rule as the command of physical powers empasized by Weber. Thus Machiavelli: 'There are two ways of fighting: by law

413

or by force. The first way is natural to men, and the second to beasts' (p. 66). A more complex view of the matter, which reflects the apparent paradox of the state — requiring not only a monopoly of the use of physical force but also that this monopoly be viewed as legitimate — is taken by Rousseau who notes: 'Man is born free, and he is everywhere in chains. Those who think themselves the masters of others are indeed greater slaves than they. How did this transformation come about? I do not know. How can it be made legitimate? That question I believe I can answer' (p. 71).

There is not space here to go into Rousseau's own answer (Rousseau was discussed in the Introduction) but we can examine some of the perspectives on this question offered by the chapters in Part 5 and see how they illuminate the relationship that holds between the state and power and legitimacy.

The first two chapters address the issue of legitimacy in the Communist party-states of Eastern Europe and the Soviet Union. As Bialer suggests in Chapter 5.1 ('The question of legitimacy') and his allusion to Napoleon's awareness of the transience of his rule, the issue of legitimacy is very much to the fore in political systems established by revolutionary conquest. Equally, in the Soviet Union, 'the regime arose from a revolution guided by a small minority. It developed into a full-fledged dictatorship that for more than a decade waged against society a social, economic, cultural, and political revolution from above. It utilized mass terror as an everyday instrument of societal management until just 25 years ago'. Yet despite, or perhaps because of this, the Soviet system has shown considerable success in legitimating itself. Factors assisting in this process were the national authenticity of the Bolshevik Revolution, the normative power exerted by the unbroken period of Communist party leadership, and the weathering of several major political crises, including the Nazi invasion of 1941 and several periods of leadership succession (the dramatic *absence* of crisis during the recent Andropov succession further adds to the argument for the legitimation of the Soviet regime). Bialer goes on to discuss the question of whose consent to the relevant principles of legitimation is most important, and of what the modes of integration are that sustain the legitimization of the claims of power-holders in the élite and within the diverse institutions of Soviet society. To this extent his analysis contributes a good deal in answering the question posed by Rousseau.

Chapter 5.2 ('Legitimacy and the Polish Communist state') analyses a case where the legitimation process has been far less successful, due at least in part to the lack of national authenticity in the process that encompassed the establishment of the Polish Communist party regime and to the problematic way in which successive political and leadership crises were managed. The contrast between the modern Soviet Union and Poland thus reflects the fundamental antithesis between legitimacy and usurpation stressed in the 'Legitimacy' entry in the *International Encyclopaedia of the Social Sciences,* an antithesis which is traced back to the early medieval period and which is claimed to lie at the root of the concept of legitimacy: 'Revolutions, unlike usurpation or *coups d'état,* are not necessarily illegitimate. If they succeed they introduce a new principle of legitimacy that supercedes the legitimacy of the former regime' (Sternberger, 1968, p. 244). Such can be seen as an achievement of the Bolshevik Revolution. The contrast between the Soviet and Polish cases, however, bears not only on the legitimation of their respective regimes, but also on their capacity to retain, enhance and exercise state power. It is true that particular geopolitical considerations enter into the problems surrounding the Polish state (though certain contingencies will influence the position of *any* specific state); nevertheless Lewis's discussion does suggest that the persistence of a legitimation problem is likely to bear negatively on the retention and exercise of state power. This particularly concerns the inability of a regime to achieve a degree of national authenticity on a relatively stable basis and to solve successive crises in such a way as to enhance political leaders' authority and to extend their freedom of action.

Moving to a quite different social and geographical context (albeit to one which shares some political similarities with the earlier examples), Chapter 5.3 examines the position of the state in post-colonial societies. In 'The state in post-colonial societies: Tanzania', Saul suggests that such systems stand in need both of territorial unity and legitimacy and that it is the post-colonial state's particular task, as it was in the early years of the Communist party regimes, to create those conditions. Saul then proceeds to examine conflicting arguments as to whether state economic power is devoted to some general process of economic development or rather to furthering the interests of particular social classes. E. P. Thompson, in 'The secret state', Chapter 5.4, again directs attention to a different kind of state and to the conditions under which its power is exercised. This fourth chapter argues for the existence of a 'state within a state' in modern Britain, one, moreover, which is able to wield its power undisturbed by changes of government or electoral defeats and victories. Thompson's argument for the existence of a secret state within an advanced capitalist society shows a perhaps surprising correspondence to the Soviet case in terms of its legitimation or, as Thompson puts it, its 'settled habit of power, a composure of power, inherited from generations of rule'. For, as Bialer emphasizes 'the centrality of the *élite dimension* of legitimization of power for the stability of political regimes', so Thompson suggests that the power of those who operate the secret British state is sustained not by the British public (they have no access to it) but by a 'deeply engrained reflex of deference towards the "real" guardians of British interests' held by many members of both Labour and Conservative Parties.

Chapter 5.5, 'Accumulation, legitimation and the state', introduces the ideas of two recent theorists of the advanced capitalist state. The approaches of Offe and Habermas (which have many features in common) highlight the importance of the legitimation process in advanced capitalist society and locate the issue of legitimacy at the centre of the conflicts and contradictions within advanced capitalism. While other readings, for example Bialer and Saul, tend to treat the acquisition and retention of state power as the central factor, Offe and Habermas see the problematic nature of the legitimation process as a crucial factor in the capacity of the capitalist system to survive its contemporary contradictions. Why should this be so? In Offe's view, the state is increasingly forced to intervene in the economy to manage economic crisis and to sustain the interests of those involved in exercising state power within the context of late capitalism. This, however, conflicts with the capitalists' concern for economic freedom and challenges the ethic of private enterprise and capitalism which provides the legitimation for the whole social order. By virtue of these contradictory tasks Offe views the survival of the capitalist state as highly problematic. The approach of Habermas, also discussed by Held in Chapter 5.5, is similar and the notion of legitimation crisis is also central to his view of the conflicts which challenge the contemporary capitalist state. More than Offe, however, Habermas indicates the importance of the political dimension of the capitalist state in its need to maintain a certain level of mass loyalty. The contradiction here is clearly a class one: the advanced capitalist state acts in the interest of capital whilst claiming, with reference to the ballot box, legitimation from the populace. The contradiction becomes critical not just because of the legitimation deficit but also because of a motivation deficit ('the requisite quantity of action-motivating meaning not being created'). Whilst it is not easy to distinguish the motivation crisis from the legitimation crisis introduced above, the conclusion is clear: the capitalist state is faced with insoluble contradictions and is unable to legitimate itself or gain sufficient support to sustain its activity. This controversial view of the state in capitalist society thus draws a further link between the capacity of the state to legitimate itself and its ability to retain a monopoly of power within a given territory.

Reference

Sternberger, D. (1968) 'Legitimacy' in *International Encyclopaedia of the Social Sciences,* New York, Macmillan.

5.1
The Question of Legitimacy

S. BIALER

If the question of legitimation, its formation, persistence, or possible disintegration is central to the long-run fate of any political regime, it is especially so with regard to the Soviet regime. After all, the regime arose from a revolution guided by a small minority. It developed into a full-fledged dictatorship that for more than a decade waged against society a social, economic, cultural, and political revolution from above. It utilized mass terror as an everyday instrument of societal management until just 25 years ago. Napoleon's famous words addressed to Metternich in 1813 sound very relevant in the Soviet context: 'Your sovereigns, born to the throne, may suffer twenty defeats and still keep returning to their capitals. I cannot. I am an upstart soldier. My rule will not survive the day on which I have ceased being strong and feared.'

But how can one test whether a 'revolutionary' regime which virtually abandons the policies of 'revolution from above' in favour of 'system management', which advances as its major goal the reproduction of existing societal relations, and which renounces mass terror as an instrument of rule has attained the degree of legitimacy denied it previously? Is the internal test of legitimacy discernible only when major challenges to the legitimizing principles surface in violence and explicit systemic opposition? More importantly, can the practical test of modern legitimacy be acquired only in competitive free elections? One author has remarked: 'An analysis of society's legitimating principles is similar to a surgical probing for that which is unseen, but nevertheless crucial for survival.'[1]

To begin with, a number of general factors work to favour the

Source: From Seweryn Bialer, *Stalin's Successors: Leadership, Stability and Change in the Soviet Union* (1980) Cambridge University Press, pp. 183–201.

418

development of the Soviet political regime's legitimacy or make it possible to evaluate the major tendencies in this respect. First, although conducted by a minority, the Soviet revolution contained the minimal prerequisite for developing a legitimate regime (at least for the Russian majority), that is, *national authenticity*. It was at least possible, therefore, to tap the traditional sources of support and compliance which could have been initially very far removed from the professed goals of the revolutionary élite.

Second, the existence of a political system over a long period of time can, and usually does, contribute to the system's acceptance by the population. Moreover, this acceptance may not be simple habituation; political institutions can come to exert *normative* power merely by their prolonged existence. In this regard the Soviet political regime has obviously passed the point where generational changes of the population have created the aura of the 'naturalness' of political institutions.

Third, an important factor in evaluating the development of legitimacy is the regime's survival of major systemic tests, points of crisis which place the question of the regime's legitimacy under enormous stress. Such a critical test for the Soviet Union was World War II. Whatever one thinks about how and why the Soviet Union survived World War II, its survival and victory provide a powerful (probably the most powerful) stimulus for the development of that legitimacy which in many respects came to fruition only after Stalin's death. Another such critical, although incomparably less costly, test was the most dangerous point of transition in any developed dictatorship, the death of the dictator and the succession. One has only to recall that fear of Soviet leaders about possible reactions to Stalin's death which underlay the notorious public appeal 'not to panic'. The Soviet political regime also weathered this test; by any standards it survived at a rather low cost. The last decade has marked the emergence of another such test, the first open appearance of dissent in the post-war Soviet Union; and one has to judge that the Soviet political regime has so far shown the ability to repress or neutralize it without major *internal* negative consequences for the stability of the system.

Without any doubt, the factors mentioned above bear witness to the stability of the Soviet political regime with regard to its survival. Yet in what sense do they attest to the manner and degree of legitimation? In what sense, especially, do they affirm the legitimation of the regime not only with regard to key crisis situations but in terms of everyday functioning and 'normal', long-range policies. Legitimacy entails a relatively stable margin of operation as well as error, even if particular policies are recognized as contrary to the interests of major groups of citizens.

At this point the concept of legitimacy has to be examined more closely. Most important theories of legitimacy can be differentiated by what they regard as the key legitimizing principles of consent; but, with very few exceptions, they do not ask the question 'whose consent', which is crucial for the establishment and especially for the sustenance of the legitimizing principles of a political regime, or they answer it in a non-differentiated, generalized way, referring to the 'population', 'subjects', 'citizens', and so forth.

Such a generalized understanding of legitimacy seems unsatisfactory, in my view, especially for the most promising level of social studies, the middle-range approaches. Instead, one should distinguish among: (1) *the substance of the legitimizing principles* of a particular political regime or type of regime; (2) *the identity and location* in the social structure of the strata or groups whose acceptance of these principles is crucial to the regime's legitimacy; (3) the *'mechanism'* by which the legitimization among these strata or groups is maintained; (4) *the level and type* of legitimacy attained and sustained by the political regime.

When discussing legitimacy, Huntington, Moore and Lowenthal concentrate their analysis of the 'mature' Soviet system on the first question, that is, on the substance of the legitimizing principles. I should like to start with the second question — 'whose consent'. The absolutely essential distinction that has to be made with regard to this question concerns the process of formation and sustenance and the extent of legitimization of the political regime among societal élites on the one hand and among large social strata, the 'publics', on the other hand. We have already made the argument and will extend it here that the Soviet regime has evolved in the course of its development a base of mass, popular support. This base consists in a combination of the existence of a relatively large stratum which actively identifies with the system together with a public which recognizes as legitimate and 'natural' the freedom of the regime to act on its behalf. Both of these elements are evident in the phenomenon of mass political participation in the Soviet Union which is central to an evaluation of the regime's popular legitimacy.

Depending on one's point of view, an analyst could maintain with equal justification that political participation in the Soviet Union is very high indeed or that it is almost non-existent. The choice would depend first of all on the difference which we previously noted between 'high politics' and 'low politics' — where something close to popular apathy is the rule in the former and highly developed activity the rule in the latter. The choice would depend even more on how one defines participation itself. If one were to define 'real', 'authentic' participation as consisting of spontaneous actions alone, fully voluntary and largely uncoordinated from a centre, one would describe the Soviet phenomenon as 'penetration' of the society by the authorities, 'mobilization' of the society by the party, 'transmission belts', and other such terms; but one would not use the term participation.

If, on the other hand, one looked simply at the activities of Soviet citizens which are socially oriented, that is, are neither private nor occur within the family, and define them as participation, one would be struck by their relatively high level. Under Soviet conditions, moreover, where most social activities have political undertones because of the form in which they originate or because of the way in which the authorities view their effects, one would describe this phenomenon as 'political participation'.

The first way of looking at Soviet popular participation seems too restrictive in the age of mass movements, popular dictatorships, and inclusionary authoritarian regimes. It is also a very ethnocentric point of view which simply defines an idealized Tocquevillian participation which takes place in advanced liberal democracies as the only 'real' and 'authentic' one.

This is not to say that terms like 'penetration', 'mobilization', 'controlled', and 'coordinated' to describe Soviet participation are incorrect. Far from it, by and large they are very true. However, the question is whether, after granting all this, one may not argue that political participation in Soviet society performs for the system functions similar to those performed by the 'authentic' participation in democratic societies. The point is that an absolute distinction between 'authentic' and 'controlled' participation shifts the focus of attention away from the functions and effects it has on the participants and the system to the manner in which it originates. Without being diverted by definitional and terminological distinctions, it is exactly the functions of participation which concern us here. [. . .]

I have postulated that broad strata of the population exhibit a basic identification with the Soviet system as it is. This identification is to a dominant extent unconscious, amorphous, and unfocused. I am not suggesting, therefore, that it represents a commitment to the system, a readiness to invest in it one's effort. It is for the majority at most an acceptance which goes hand in hand with such actual behaviour as mass absenteeism, lack of labour discipline, turnover at the workplace — all of which testify to dissatisfaction with many policies and, most importantly, to the overwhelmingly private concern of the working man with his own wellbeing. Such self-centred orientation may not be appropriate to collectivistic behaviour and to the image which the directors of the system seek for their society. To the extent that it signifies political apathy, however, that it is concerned with the question 'what do I get?' rather than with abstract questions of justice and equality, and that it goes hand in hand with basic acceptance of the regime's political formula, it signifies an acceptable legitimizing base with which the directors of the system have no reason to be dissatisfied.

The existing evidence about all types of regimes demonstrates the direct relationship between the level of legitimization of political regimes among groups and individuals and the degree of their participation in political activities and the management of societal affairs. Most problems of legitimization in modern societies, moreover, concern the legitimacy of some decision-making apparatus (rather than of individuals), that is, the *claims* of collective power centres to have the right to utilize physical resources for specific purposes and to have the right to demand a certain kind of consent behaviour from particular individuals, collectivities, groups, and so on. The main question here is what is decisive in making these claims hold. I fully agree here with Arthur L. Stinchcombe's proposition that what is crucial is the legitimacy of these claims in the other centres of power and not their legitimacy among the people who must take the consequences.

A legitimate right or authority is backed by a *nesting of reserve sources of power* set up in such a fashion that the power can always overcome opposition. The crucial function of *doctrines of legitimacy* and norms derived from them is to create a readiness in other centers of power to back up the actions of a person with a certain right. Doctrines of legitimacy serve the crucial function of setting up that nesting of powers which usually makes appeals to physical force unnecessary ... *A power is legitimate to the degree that, by virtue of the doctrines and norms by which it is justified, the power-holder can call upon sufficient other centers of power, as reserves in case of need, to make his power effective.* Some of these reserves may, or may not, be the popularity of a man's powers in public opinion or the acceptance of a doctrine of legitimacy of his powers among subordinates. The doctrine of legitimacy limits a power in so far as the exercise of the power is dependent on its being backed up, for this backing will be available only on terms accepted in other centers of power.[2]

Experience of Communist and authoritarian as well as democratic societies confirms in my opinion the centrality of the *élite dimension* of legitimization of power for the stability of political regimes with regard both to their survival and effectiveness. This is not to say that the 'popular' dimension of legitimization is unimportant. What is proposed is merely that it is secondary to the élite dimension in many respects of which two are most important. First, as long as the claims of a particular power centre or a particular élite are considered legitimate by other power centres, other élites, the low level of popular legitimacy or its decline do not endanger the stability of the political regime. Second, the decline in popular legitimacy, let alone a vocal or violent expression of such decline, is in itself more often than not preceded by and associated with the decline of élite legitimacy and very seldom with its increase.

Max Weber, who is the source of much of the current theorizing about the legitimacy of power, seems to be ambivalent on this point. On the one hand, in his general definitions and theory, the legitimacy of power is considered in terms of the acceptance by subordinates of the rights of superiors to control them. But 'in his concrete analyses of power phenomena, Weber was very little concerned with any estimations of the state of public opinion or of the ideological enthusiasm of subordinates and subjects. Rather, he analysed the reactions of other centres of power.'[3]

It is the élite dimension of legitimacy that seems to be more crucial from the point of view of the stability of the system and especially its potential for transformation. Most importantly, it is the decline or disintegration of élite legitimacy that either leads to the decline of mass legitimacy or transforms the lack of popular support into an effective popular opposition. The revolutions, revolts, and bloodless 'Springs' and 'Octobers' in Eastern Europe were first and foremost basic crises of legitimacy within the Communist élites. By contrast, the changes in outlook of the Soviet élite that occurred in the post-Stalin era and their internal conflicts did not take the form of a basic crisis of legitimacy among a majority or a crucial segment of the élite.

The Soviet political élite is, of course, not a homogeneous body; it joins varied interests, diverse outlooks and sympathies. During times of internal crisis and severe stress it tends to divide. Yet one may suggest that a core set of attitudes and beliefs which are strong and persistent permeate the élite stratum as a whole. When speaking about groups and interests in Soviet society, there is an understandable tendency to concentrate on the parameters of conflict relationships among different groups. This, after all, is the ingredient of experience which gives groups their uniqueness and variety. But when considering the context of élite group activity in the Soviet Union, it seems important to suggest that it refers to a relationship among groups who fundamentally accept the system but who compete for advantages within it. These groups exist within consensus relationships of a more general and durable kind than their conflict relationships. The difference here between the Soviet political élite and Communist élites of Eastern Europe is as striking as the difference between the Soviet and East European societies.

The most important legitimizing principles and preferences of the Soviet political regime which, it is suggested, are shared by diverse élites include:

(1) opposition to a liberal-democratic political organization of society;

(2) the commitment to a one-party state and to the leading role of the party within the state;

(3) A deep-seated fear and mistrust of spontaneity in political and social behaviour, which induce an interventionist psychology and stress the need of strong central government, of organization, of hierarchy, and of order;

(4) the cult of national unity and the condemnation of individuals and groups who threaten to impair that unity;

(5) deep-seated nationalism and a great-power orientation which provides the major effective durable bond among the élites and between the élite and the masses;

(6) the commitment to a Soviet East European empire;

(7) the radical decline of the impulse to reshape society and a commitment to the basic structure which Soviet society has attained;

(8) the withering away of utopianism and a commitment to the rationalization of the system;

(9) the belief in and commitment to progress understood particularly in a highly material and technical way and combined with a technological and scientific ethos . . .

As was stressed before, the responsiveness of other centres of power is crucial for the legitimacy of the claims of power-holders.

We now turn to the question: What is the 'mechanism' by which the legitimizing process is maintained? To express it differently, what are the *modes of integration* of norms and values which sustain the legitimization of claims among diverse functional and organizational segments of the élite, among its diverse institutions? [. . .]

Much useful insight into the modes of integration is provided by Hans Gerth and C. Wright Mills in their *Character and Social Structure,* a work which has not been sufficiently appreciated. The relations of the units are constructed by them in terms of means-ends schemata which involve the dimension of power.[4] They identify four principal modes of integration:

(1) *Correspondence:* when the integration of legitimizing values is achieved by the working out in several institutional orders of a common structural principle, which thus operates in a parallel way in each;

(2) *Coincidence:* when different values, different structural principles or developments in various orders result in their combined effects in the same, often unforeseen, outcome of unity for the whole society;

(3) *Convergence:* when two or more segments or values of diverse institutional orders coincide to the point of fusion, they become one institutional set-up;

(4) *Coordination:* when the integration is achieved by means of one or more institutional orders which become ascendant over other orders and direct them; thus other orders are regulated and managed by the ascendant order or orders.

The authors then add:

It should, of course, be understood that in any concrete social structure, we may well find mixtures of these four types of structural integration or structural change. The task is to search within and between institutional orders for points of correspondence and coincidence, for points of convergence and coordination, and to examine them in detail. The presence of one type does not exclude the possibility of others. We do not believe that there is any single or general rule governing the composition and unity of orders and spheres which holds for all societies. Reality is not often neat and orderly; it is the task of analysis to single out what is relevant to neat and orderly understanding.[5]

We propose to apply these four modes of integration to the Soviet Union. The most explicit case of *correspondence* among the diverse institutional orders of Soviet society with regard to legitimizing values is represented by the idea of hierarchy and organization. The basic legitimization of instituted conduct in each of these orders is very much the same — the subordination of the autonomous individual's free initiative for rational and moral self-determination to collective demands expressed by hierarchical structures between and within formal organizations. Thus the symbolic spheres of the various orders run in parallel or corresponding fashion.

The correspondence of the diverse orders, even assuming that they are relatively autonomous (and, as some students of Soviet society argue, they are becoming relatively more autonomous than in the past), is the outcome of processes in which all the significant orders develop in the direction of an integrated principle of planning, hierarchical subordination, and organization. (Another basic legitimation of instituted conduct in each of these orders which leads to a correspondent integrating principle is represented by the idea of 'mobilization', that is, the disposition of the resources calculated to bring forth the maximum expenditure of efforts and energy.)

In a provocative article, Zbigniew Brzezinski proposes that:

> The Bolshevik revolution not only was not a break from the predominant political tradition, but was, in historical perspective, an act of revitalized Restoration. The late Romanov period was a period of decay, of the gradual weakening of the hold of the state over society . . . and of internal loss of vitality within the top élite, not to speak of the autocrat's own personal weaknesses. The overthrow of that ruling élite brought to power a new group, much more vital, much more assertive, and imbued with a new sense of historical mission. The political result of the Bolshevik revolution was thus revitalized restoration of long dominant patterns.[6]

Brzezinski lists eight central elements of the pre-revolutionary tradition which, he argues, are continued in the post-revolutionary Russian experience. It is notable that one element that is not mentioned, and in our opinion rightly so, has to do with the question of Great Russian nationalism.

It is exactly in the interaction between the legitimizing idea of nationalism on the one hand and the modernizing values propagated by the Soviet party-state on the other hand that the integration of legitimizing values through *coincidence* occurs. Such a legitimization (as Hans Rogger argues convincingly) was absent in tsarist Russia, where the formation of a modern political centre was already caught up in the contradiction between the existing traditional state and modern nationalism.

Speaking about nationalism as a *political phenomenon,* that is, about convictions, attitudes, or movements, Rogger proposes that in sharp contrast to the West, where in the nineteenth century nationalism became a major factor of political loyalty and social integration, the dilemma of pre-revolutionary Russian nationalism consisted in that:

> . . . it could only with difficulty, if at all, view the tsarist state as the embodiment of the national purpose, as the necessary instrument and expression of national goals and values, while the state, for its part, looked upon every autonomous expression of nationalism with fear and suspicion . . . This was the case not only when the state was confronted by versions of nationalism formulated by radicals or liberals but even, and here the dilemma is most strikingly expressed, when it was defined by those who were most vocal in their support of the established order.[7] [. . .]

In the Soviet Union the dynamic, mobilizational, collectivistic, and future-goal-oriented nature of the legitimizing values of the political and economic orders coincided and became integrated with the inherited values of national identity latent in the cultural order and were reinforced by and fused with the new sense of historical mission propagated by the party's doctrine. The stage of Soviet system-building coincided with modern nation-building; the 'mature' stage of Soviet system management coincides with Soviet global-power aspirations.

The integration of legitimizing values through *convergence* occurs, often in unplanned ways, when values of different institutional orders, of diverse organizational or functional segments of élites, coincide to the point of fusion. In my opinion a possible example of such convergence in the Soviet case may be represented by the 'defence—heavy industry complex'. This complex constitutes above anything else a value, belief, and policy orientation that cuts across the organizational and functional lines of the élite establishment.

Tradition and the present status and ambitions of the Soviet

Union in the international arena combine to make the weight of the interests of the defence complex very great. The lingering insecurities of the past and the new insecurities of the present, the commitment to hold at any price a potentially explosive empire in Eastern Europe, and the pride of accomplishment in the defence— heavy industry area (by far the single most important area of real attainment by the Soviet regime) guarantees the prominence of the defence sector. The fact that the defence sector is the most modern societal sector, that it concentrates more scientific, technical, and managerial talent and more labour skill than all other sectors combined, adds to its weight. Defence-oriented education is incredibly highly weighted within the general educational establishment. The theme of patriotic nationalism is relatively more effective than the traditional ideological theme in mobilizing support. It exploits the past and present glories of the defence complex. Many former associates or 'graduates' of the defence complex, who today retain their association, are present within all segments of the élite and leadership. That is, they are to be found among the generalist politicians and the planners, among the ideologues and leaders of the scientific establishment, among the leading regime writers and famous plant directors. All these factors combine to make the weight of the interests of the defence complex much greater than the weight of the representation of the military—heavy industry élite segments in the leadership institutions and policy-making bodies. Even more important, they also serve to instill the values and beliefs of this 'complex' among diverse institutional orders, institutions, and élite segments. The effect is to create a policy orientation, one apparently embedded now in the political culture, which responds almost automatically to the defence—heavy industrial needs on a first-priority basis.

Integration through *coordination* is achieved 'by the subordination of several orders to the regulation of direction management of other orders'. Integration through coordination by the Soviet political order finds many expressions of which I shall mention two. First, one of its major and most visible expressions is the high level of what Etzioni calls 'political intensity',[8] that is, the ratio of societal activities which are fully or partially controlled politically as compared to those which are not. What probably is the most important dimension of political intensity has to do with the relations between the political and economic spheres, political and economic goals.

A chief goal of the Soviet political regime throughout its history has been economic, especially industrial, growth at the most rapid attainable rate and regardless of the social cost. Lenin's dictum 'politics cannot but have primacy over economics' meant initially that economic growth must be correlated with and subordinated to social change, to socialist transformation of society. In Stalinist Russia it came basically to mean that economic growth was too important a goal of the system to be left to managers, technocrats, and economists. Another Soviet slogan which viewed 'politics as condensed economics' expressed rather better the dominance of economic growth among the systemic goals of the regime. The issues of economic growth still permeate the entire Soviet political decision-making process. Economic growth (and the military power that is to proceed from it) constitutes the chief indicator of the political leadership's success and failure. The economic development desired and later achieved has constituted the historical justification of both the social transformation decreed by the leadership and the political order established by it.

Yet while *economic growth* is a decisive systemic goal, *economic criteria* for deciding what, how fast, and at what cost it should develop is not a primary consideration. The key characteristic of the Soviet economic sphere and economic growth is its lack of *economic* self-generating, self-regulating, and adjusting features. To run at all, let alone to perform well, it has required and still requires an enormous political edifice of regulation, supervision, and coordination. In fact, the Soviet political system as we know it was developed largely to run the economy and was shaped by running the economy in line with the chosen growth strategy.

The second and most important expression of the directly coordinative role of the political sphere is the proposition already mentioned: The symbolic sphere of all orders is centrally managed and controlled from the political sphere, and no rival claims to legitimate symbolic communications are recognized. Building on Shils's definition of a societal centre, Eisenstadt makes a contrast in this sense, it seems, between the weak and strong societal centre: 'A "strong" centre is one which enjoys access to other centres and can derive its legitimation from them — either by monopolizing and controlling them or by some more autonomous interdependence with them — and can accordingly command some commitment both within, but also beyond, its own specific sphere.'[9]

Notes

1. Claus Mueller (1975) *The Politics of Communications: A Study in the Political Sociology of Language, Socialization, and Legitimation,* London, Oxford University Press, p. 128.
2. Arthur L. Stinchcombe (1968) *Constructing Social Theories,* New York, Harcourt, Brace and World, pp. 160—2.
3. *Ibid,* p. 161, n.6.
4. Hans Gerth and C. Wright Mills (1953) *Character and Social Structure: The Psychology of Social Institutions,* New York, Harcourt, Brace, pp. 354—66.
5. *Ibid,* p. 366.
6. Zbigniew Brzezinski (1976) 'Soviet politics: from the future to the past?' in Paul Cocks, Robert V. Daniels, Nancy Whittier Heer (eds) *The Dynamics of Soviet Politics,* Cambridge, Massachusetts, Harvard University Press, p. 340.
7. Hans Rogger (1962) 'Nationalism and the state: a Russian dilemma', *Comparative Studies in Society and History,* 4, No. 3, April, pp. 253, 256.
8. Amitai Etzioni (1968) *The Active Society: A Theory of Societal and Political Processes,* New York, Free Press, p. 670.
9. S. N. Eisenstadt (ed.) (1971) *Political Sociology: A Reader,* New York, Basic Books, p. 18.

5.2
Legitimacy and the
Polish Communist State

PAUL G. LEWIS

The pressure of the state machine is nothing compared with
the pressure of a convincing argument.
C. Milosz, *The Captive Mind*

Legitimacy in Poland and Eastern Europe

Legitimacy may be defined as that political condition in which
power-holders are able to justify their holding of power in terms
other than those of the mere fact of power-holding. According to
one view such justifications are increasingly tenuous due to the
conditions under which the modern state has arisen and the means
it employs in order to persist. Theories of legitimacy typically view
power from two aspects — from that of its origins and from that of
its ends. More concretely, this invariably involves, on the one
hand, some discussion of the degree to which a regime of a
government can be said to rest on democratic consent and, on the
other, of the extent to which the regime or government guides its
actions by some notion of the common good or public interest.
Neither of these focuses, in Schaar's view, are likely to provide
adequate justifications for power under modern conditions:
'criticism and hard events have done their work: both concepts
have been reduced to rubble'.[1]

The argument on which this conclusion is based refers equally

Source: From Paul G. Lewis 'Obstacles to the establishment of political legitimacy
in Communist Poland', *British Journal of Political Science* (1982) XII, pp. 125—47,
amended and updated.

to developments in pluralist and Communist states; however, it is clear that it is modern Western, and particularly American, society with which it is most concerned. Yet Communist, and particularly East European, states provide an equally valid focus for studying the contemporary crisis of legitimacy. Whilst West European and American societies can be described as experiencing a legitimacy crisis in that the consensual basis of political rule is increasingly open to doubt and the ability of power-holders to satisfy the expectations of the electorate is viewed with growing scepticism, the grounds of legitimacy in Communist states, slim and unstable at the best of times, have of late been further attenuated. The attempt to legitimate the Communist regimes of Eastern Europe in terms of their origins has been a barren exercise and it is with reference to their capacity to further the common national interest that most East European regimes have tried to base their claim to legitimacy. The growing problems of the world economy during the 1970s, however, have affected Eastern as well as Western economies and have dealt a sharp blow to their rulers' aspiration to legitimate their powers by demonstrating their ability to produce a society of satisfied consumers. If the claims of pluralist power-holders to legitimacy are seen as weak, those of Communist rulers are frequently far weaker. I propose to examine in this discussion a case where rulers have consistently been unable to legitimize their position but where, due to the meagre power resources at their disposal, few alternative sources of political authority have been available. Obstacles to the establishment of legitimacy in Communist Poland and the progressive erosion of the authority of Gierek's administration provide an extreme example of political crisis — one which starkly demonstrates the need to establish grounds for legitimacy if power itself is not to be dispersed.

The position of Communist systems with regard to the establishment of political legitimacy is curiously ambiguous. The mere longevity of their regimes (well over 60 years in the Soviet Union and more than 30 years in Eastern Europe) itself helps the process, while particular events and processes that have taken place during the period have also served to enhance legitimacy. These may include, in the case of the Soviet Union, the experience of the 'Great Patriotic War' (1941–5) which helped to strengthen the links between Party and people, and the rise of the USSR to the position of second world power. The East European regimes draw less legitimacy from this source because their existence dates only from the 1940s and in most cases were imposed by the USSR rather than springing from national sources. However, even in their case, the Romanian regime has gained a certain popularity with its adoption of a nationalist stance while the Kadar regime in Hungary has gained some degree of legitimacy with its economic success and the skill of its leaders. At the same time some of these processes, notably the development of an established Communist system and the course of socio-economic growth, stimulate demands which the system finds difficult to cope with and which threaten to reduce its legitimacy. Several such aspects have been identified by R. Lowenthal.[2] They include the recognition of the irrelevance of the Party's identification with 'the dictatorship of the proletariat' and its dedication to class warfare, the unattractiveness to modern intellectual and technical élites of the ideological stress on the 'enemy' (frequently ill-defined), the lack of a real function for the Party rank and file except in times of crisis and the consequent predominance in the parties of self-seeking careerists. The difficulty the regimes face due to their inability to amend the ideology and to adapt the system of rule to contemporary conditions serves to intensify their problems of legitimacy. As suggested above, the legitimacy problems faced by the East European regimes are generally greater than those of the Soviet Union due both to their shorter history and to the fact that the regimes were, in general, imposed by force of Soviet arms.

The relevance of the latter fact is, of course, nowhere clearer than in Poland itself and this knowledge explains a great part of its legitimacy problem. However, despite several violent outbreaks of opposition and the menacing character of the conditions under which most leadership changes have taken place, it is notable that it was in the GDR (1953), Hungary (1956) and Czechoslovakia (1968) that Soviet forces intervened militarily to maintain Communist rule. Increasingly lethargic in these matters — it took the Soviet leadership some six months to make up its mind what to do about Czechslovakia — an equally threatening situation existed for at least double that time in Poland, without Soviet intervention. This is generally regarded as a major bonus for Poland. The impression held is that intensely patriotic and fervently Catholic Poles press their interests to the utmost and, with the aid of adroit Party leadership (such as that of Gomułka in 1956), stave off Soviet intervention. To an extent this impression is accurate, but it is far from complete. If it were the full picture, for example, one would expect a closer relationship between Party and people and not the widening gap that was evident in the late 1970s in relations between the leadership and the Party rank and file as well as with the nation as a whole. For the major point at issue here is less the nature of Polish—Soviet relations, important as these are, but more relations between Poland's Communist leaders and Polish society as a whole. These largely derive from a sequence of historical developments which makes it highly unlikely that a Communist regime would be able to gain legitimacy in the eyes of its subjects. Such factors include the dismemberment of Poland as a state in the late eighteenth century and Poles' subsequent suspicion of the state as an alien entity, the long history of Polish-Russian political antagonism which was resumed between 1919 and 1941 with the Soviet invasion of Poland in 1920, the re-annexation of Eastern Poland in 1939, and the sacrifice of Polish interests and demands by the Allies during the war to those of its more powerful Soviet neighbour. Moreover, fully conscious of this background, early Communist leaders failed to press for full totalitarianization between 1949 and 1953 and left many elements of the former social structure relatively intact. Yet this did not create a trusting or more positive relationship between Party leaders and the society or create stronger grounds for legitimacy. Further developments only served to weaken any grounds that did exist.

Lacking adequate domestic sources of legitimacy, the threat of Soviet military intervention has served as a partial support for the political rule of the Polish regime ('better us than the Russians'). It is true, however, that Moscow is genuinely unwilling to intervene militarily. Poland is by far the largest country in Eastern Europe and has great strategic and military importance. It has a long western border and controls communications with Germany (East and West). Any resort to military combat within Poland would leave the Warsaw Pact countries dangerously vulnerable, particularly if, as would be likely, Polish resistance were fierce and prolonged and the restoration of orthodox Communist leadership hard-fought. Such a prospect is considerably more menacing than the displeasing sight of a reformist Party. Thus, in the knowledge of the political recalcitrance of the Poles, the threat of Soviet intervention has been chosen by Kremlin leaders in preference to its application. This was apparently the case in 1956 and was also true of 1980—1. As noted above the existence of a constant Soviet threat has served as a partial source of legitimacy for the Polish Communist regime. (The 'geopolitical' argument for political compliance has been regularly aired during times of political crisis in order to stifle discussion of genuine change. It was notable that Solidarity officials and members refused all discussion of the possibility of Soviet intervention and persisted with exchanges on specific domestic issues.) On the other hand the perpetual use of a diffuse threat (what would the Soviets *not* tolerate?) has probably proved sufficiently comfortable for the leadership not to strain excessively to draw up and implement measures which might have bolstered domestic sources of legitimacy. The number of aborted economic reforms since 1956 has been conspicuous and has undoubtedly contributed to Poland's persistent economic failure. Where the limits of the permissible are vague, Polish leaders have veered towards conservatism. This may be contrasted with the necessity for Kadar to work out a *modus vivendi* with the Hungarians after 1956, which culminated in the introduction of the New Economic Mechanism in 1968 and rapidly climbing living standards. Moreover, the threat of Soviet intervention must by its nature decline in effectiveness and have only a temporary value in compensating for the regime's lack of legitimacy. In this sense the successor rulers following the invasions of Hungary and Czechoslovakia had an easier task in having a defeated population to control and knowing, themselves, the limit they could reach before provoking further Soviet intervention in their attempts to re-establish their regime's legitimacy. Enjoying neither genuine popular support nor the compliance of a people to whom Soviet force has directly shown the need for obedience, a high degree of political skill has been called for on the part of the Polish leadership.

There can now be little doubt that the political skills of Polish leaders have not been adequate to solve the problems facing them. Over several years Gomułka struggled to maintain Party unity until he found it slipping away from him after 1968. Gierek launched a programme of massive growth which soon ran into considerable difficulties, a situation which Gierek apparently found himself unable to master. Indeed, both periods suggest the fundamental importance of economic mismanagement and ineffective political leadership in bringing about the crises of 1970 and 1980. Economic mismanagement, political misjudgments and the decline in the effectiveness of leadership certainly played a part in both leadership cycles and suggest that political skills were not adequate for what was demanded. But in themselves such explanations of the outcome in 1980 do not seem to me convincing. The cycle of failure in Poland since 1956 suggests that a deeper process was at work, perhaps throwing up problems which no leadership was capable of solving satisfactorily. I have suggested earlier that the legitimacy problems of Communist Poland made strong demands on its political leaders, probably stronger than those placed on other leaders. The roots of the legitimacy problem may be traced back several centuries. Their relevance to Communist Poland became evident at an early stage when, uniquely in Eastern Europe, the totalitarian drive was weakened in order to mitigate the problems of Communist rule. As I shall attempt to demonstrate, this provided no solution and the inadequate grounds of the Communist regime's legitimacy continued to lie at the roots of its problems until the final backdown of its leadership in 1980.

The historical roots of regime weakness

Part of the explanation for the Polish United Workers' Party's inability to legitimize its rule relates to what many have seen as the general weakness of political authority in Poland. Due to a variety of factors, some lying far back in history, Poles have viewed those wielding political power with some suspicion and have been unwilling to follow their prescriptions. Due to the lengthy partition of Poland between Prussia, Russia and Austria-Hungary — dating (in its final form) from 1795 — the Polish nation developed as a stateless entity throughout the nineteenth century. Until 1918, although to a varying extent, patriotism was equated with resistance to government and state power. In terms of political techniques and the skills of government, Poles had no chance at all for 60 (in the case of Austro-Hungarian territories) or a 100 years (in that of the Russian) to participate in central parliamentary bodies. Correspondingly, the penetrative capacity of the political systems covering the territory occupied by the Poles was limited and the political authority they represented relatively weak. In the terminology of the theorists of political development associated with the Social Science Research Council's Committee on Comparative Politics, the processes of participation and penetration thus met with considerable obstacles and were not only separate from, but also antagonistic to, the other key development process of identity formation. This separation 'produced a crisis of legitimacy that could not be properly resolved until after the state was restored',[3] a process which therefore had to be postponed until the twentieth century before any resolution could even be contemplated. [. . .]

But if the partitions acted to weaken the authority of the modern Polish state they strengthened immeasurably that of another national institution — the Church. The fact that the religions of the two most repressive and culturally aggressive partition powers

— Prussia and Russia — were, respectively, Protestantism and Orthodoxy made it remarkably easy for the indigenous population to identify Roman Catholicism with Polish nationality. In this way the Church tapped a strong source of quasi-political support. In doing so it followed deep-rooted traditions established in the twelfth century, when national integration had been threatened by internal divisions and early German tribal expansionism. In the absence of a nationally accepted monarch it was the Church primate who acted as head of state and maintained national unity. Not only has the development of modern political authority been a process of unusual difficulty, but its central institution and incarnation, the state, is faced with a rival religious authority whose national role stretches back to the middle ages and whose roots in society are also unusually deep.

The attempt to legitimize the Communist regime therefore encountered two obstacles whose foundations were deeply buried in Polish history. These were, firstly, the fact that Communism came from the East and was brought by Russians, a people whose state had been in competition with that of Poland since the sixteenth century. The early years both of the modern Polish state and the revolutionary Soviet Republic were marked by armed conflict in 1920, which recapitulated earlier competition and foreshadowed later struggles. The second factor was that Soviet actions were, as least formally, guided by Marxism—Leninism, an outlook whose principles were fundamentally at odds with those of Catholicism. But later developments served to intensify this existing antagonism and to provide further obstacles to the accumulation of authority by the Communist regime. Crucial to this was the position of Poland during the Second World War. Unlike Hungary, Rumania and Bulgaria, Poland did not choose any form of alliance with Nazi Germany and was the first nation to fight German troops in 1939. Its resistant forces were large and well organized although almost wholly non-Communist, which was not surprising in view of Stalin's dissolution of the Polish Communist Party in 1938 and the occupation of Eastern Poland by Soviet Russia for virtually the first two years of the war. Thus the experience of the war left the Poles with no feelings of complicity in the Nazi domination of the Continent and with a record of anti-Nazi resistance far stronger than that, for example, of Czechoslovakia. Yet the nature of that resistance had been quite different from that in Yugoslavia, where a strong Communist movement had virtually liberated the country and forged strong links with the people. When the Soviet army entered Poland and preparations began for the establishment of a

Communist regime, it could not do so on the pretext that it was concerned to replace one compromised by ties with Nazi Germany. The legitimacy of Communism was little enhanced by Soviet actions with respect to Poland during the war, which included the murder of a large part of its officer corps at Katyń and acquiescence in the Nazi quelling of the Warsaw uprising.

The problems facing the newly-installed Polish Communist regime in legitimizing its position were therefore immense and there can be little doubt that Polish Party leaders have themselves been acutely aware of this. Croan notes that even the *attempt* to bring about some degree of congruence between regime and society has not been made, unlike in the GDR, where congruence has been achieved 'from the top down' with the construction of a socialist nation, and Czechoslovakia, where an attempt was at least made to build congruence 'from the bottom up'.[4] The weight of Stalinist totalitarianism was considerably lighter than in the other countries of Eastern Europe: there were no showtrials or executions of disgraced Communist leaders despite apparent pressure in that direction from Moscow. Poland's peasantry remained largely uncollectivized and a 'peasant party' was retained which had somewhat greater autonomy than equivalent organizations in Bulgaria, the GDR and Czechoslovakia. Neither, of course, had Kremlin agents the opportunity to purge and reshape Polish society in quite the same way as they did when dealing with defeated enemies. Compared with the other nations of Eastern Europe, Poland has retained a greater degree of separation between 'state' and 'society', permitting the preservation of a relatively coherent social tradition and enabling the reassertion of social authority in the political sphere under the conditions of weakened central power which characterized the latter years of Gierek's regime. A Polish writer has pointed to the four main factors which have sustained this social autonomy: the survival of private agriculture which has, if indirectly, helped to restrict the influence of bureaucracy on the life of the country; the existence of a powerful Church which has acted to counteract tendencies of social disintegration; the persistence of deep respect for Western institutions; and, a strong instinct for self-preservation nourished by the experiences of the nineteenth century.[5]

A number of factors emerging from the pre-Communist history of Poland have thus contributed to the weakness of Party authority during the Communist period and to the problems it has encountered in attempting to legitimize its position. This weakness has, in turn, given rise to further political problems. 'The failure of the Communist polity fully to penetrate Polish society' was itself a major contributory factor to the crisis of 1956, the first of several crises which have punctuated the history of Communist Poland. This has stemmed from a number of factors which included the general weakness of political authority and the strength of the Church, the historic Polish—Russian antagonism which was only intensified with the renewal of Polish statehood and the adoption by Russia of Marxist—Leninist ideology, and the particular injustice (as felt by Poles) of the nation's post-war status following its consistent record of opposition to Nazi Germany. As a result, successive groups of Communist leaders have correctly perceived the obstacles to enhancing Party authority in Poland. Equally aware of the dangers, Soviet leaders have so far shown some reluctance to exert the power they command with the full vigour of which they are capable. Thus Khrushchev eventually acquiesced in the return to power of Gomułka in 1956 despite initial opposition, while Brezhnev refused Gomułka's request 14 years later for Soviet assistance in putting down the workers' revolt of 1970. Despite hard-line statements and considerable sabre-rattling, Soviet leaders in fact adopted a relatively *laissez-faire* attitude to the Polish position. But Polish and Soviet Party leaders have been aware of the problems they faced in consolidating Communist power over Polish society and tended to explore the alternative path of legitimizing Party rule. As the events of 1980 showed, their efforts met with little success.

In the absence of any decisive application of power by the Soviet Union (as occurred in 1956 and 1968 in Hungary and Czechoslovakia) or any convincing grounds for the legitimacy of Communist rule the authority of the Party has grown increasingly weak. It was in recognition of this tendency, following the ominous events which preceded his succession to power and the hard political struggle of the following months, that Gierek undertook the massive investment programme of the early seventies in order that the regime could at least be seen as an efficient manager of the economy and gain legitimacy as successful provider for the population. The December revolt of 1970 showed how dangerous previous failures to confront the political tensions in Polish society were. It had long been clear that the abandonment only of the repressive features of Stalinism was by no means sufficient to overcome the gulf between people and 'partocracy' in Poland. These early reforms largely comprised the reduction of the security police's powers, the virtual abandonment of the attempt to collectivize agriculture by force and the permission of greater freedom for the Church. This relaxation, however, took place between December 1954 and December 1956. By the 1960s it was apparent that a depressing slide towards economic stagnation and greater political repression was under way, the economic failure leading to the workers' revolt of 1970. In this sense Party rule under Gomułka's second period of leadership (October 1956— December 1970) was in the nature of a confidence trick, and popular recognition of this fact helps explain why the contemporary opposition has adopted such an unyielding attitude. The 'peaceful revolution' of 1956 ('Spring in October') had at the time appeared a great popular victory — involving the return to power of Gomułka against Soviet inclinations and to the accompaniment of diverse democratic slogans. But, as suggested above, the liberalization went into reverse almost as soon as the 'victory' had been won — the gains had been made before Gomułka's return to power. By giving in to popular pressure for his return, the leadership was attempting to recover its authority without acceding to what was really being demanded.

1956 — A crisis suppressed

The crisis in Party authority of 1956 — reflected in the Poznań revolt of angry workers, the growing dissatisfaction and outspokenness of both Party and non-Party intelligentsia and the spontaneous dissolution of collective farms by their peasant members — could have been resolved only be endowing the Party with some new, hitherto untapped form of legitimacy or by enhancing the power resources available to the Party leadership. The latter option, however, was demonstrably not available in 1956. The general crisis within the Communist bloc following Stalin's death in 1953 was to a large extent itself a product of the post-Stalin leadership's decision to abolish terror, reduce security police powers, and unfreeze at least to some extent the cultural climate. The point at issue in 1956 was how far this thaw would be allowed to go — there was no possibility at this point of reinforcing the power apparatus and by these means enforcing obedience to Party directives. What presented itself as the obvious solution to the crisis was a move towards acquiring legitimacy for Party rule by acceding to popular demands for greater Polish independence from the Soviet Union, for the dilution of Marxist—Leninist orthodoxy in cultural and public life, for general liberalization in the mass media and for greater opportunities for grass-roots democracy. This, however, placed the leadership in a considerable dilemma for they knew that by giving in to these pressures and gaining legitimacy as the executor of the public will, they would ultimately be endangering both the limited autonomy that Poland enjoyed and their own position, as the Party would not long survive under conditions of political freedom and the unfettered expression of public opinion. The June riots in Poznań, however, indicated that some fairly drastic measures (or what at least could be publicly presented as such) had to be taken if the regime was not to collapse. In this situation there was one factor unique to Poland in the process of East European de-Stalinization. This was the continuing presence of Gomułka, disgraced and jailed for treason but not executed like many of the other early East European leaders. Gomułka's reputation as a victim of Stalinism had been spread in the revelations of Swiatlo, a senior secret policeman who defected in 1953 and had actually arrested Gomułka in 1951. Gomułka's importance in the contemporary context had been recognized from April 1956 by Communists and non-Communists alike, although suggestions that he return to political life were not made until June (shortly before the events in Poznań). His presence constituted what his British biographer describes as a 'trump card' in the political pack — one moreover that could be played by various protagonists.[6] [. . .]

It was this capacity of Gomułka — due to his unusual history which itself was associated with Communism's dubious claim to the Polish state — to act as the expression of diverse and conflicting claims which enabled the leadership to survive the legitimacy crisis, if at the cost of avoiding any real attempt actually to reconcile those claims and thus produce a more viable resolution to the crisis. [. . .] The relations between different factions within the leadership and Gomułka are therefore by no means clear, but none of the actors could be described as unambiguous representatives of the social forces which had played such a large part in bringing the situation to crisis point. No further articulation or representation of social group aspirations was achieved by the Party and in this respect no further development of its legitimacy was achieved. The regime appeared to have been strengthened but the crisis was hardly resolved. A quantitative study of the rate of turnover in Central Committee membership (the extent to which those elected onto the Committee retained their position up to and during the next Congress) shows a 'most interesting, and somewhat unexpected' stability between 1954 and 1959, a finding at variance with the more marked changes in personnel at the level of the top leadership.[7] Poland, in fact, showed the lowest rate of turnover in Central Committee membership in Eastern Europe until 1968. If, then, the Polish October was a revolution it was one of the palace variety which brought little change further down the major institution of rule.

The return of Gomułka, however, did preserve the rule of the Worker's Party in Poland whilst bringing some satisfaction to the non-Party population and avoiding the intervention of Soviet forces. It was an example of what J. Staniszkis has termed the system's 'learning by crisis', which 'does not imply a change in structure or functioning, but only a momentary lowering of the level of tensions'.[8] What it did not do was to base the Party's power on any firm grounds of legitimacy: the regime grew increasingly illiberal, disinclined to introduce institutional innovation or to encourage genuine participation and fostered increasingly closer ties with the Soviet Union. As a result the authority of the Party derived no lasting gains from the October experience and proved less, rather than more, competent to manage and direct Polish society. This was reflected by, amongst other things, the economic stagnation of the 1960s and the fact that Polish workers gained the lowest rise in earnings of all the East European countries throughout the decade, including the Soviet Union. In political terms the weakness of the Party leadership and frustration of the apparat gave rise to factional struggles which led to the anti-intellectual and anti-semitic purge of 1968, followed two and a half years later by the massacre of shipyard workers in the northern cities. Lacking authority and any real justification for the exercise of its power, the Party leadership — more precisely Gomułka and a handful of cronies — thus had no option but to apply brute force as a means of expressing its will. The developments of 1970 served to demonstrate the fragility of such power.

Gierek's strategy and the deepening legitimacy crisis

Gierek's inheritance when Gomułka was removed from power was a mixed one. The political situation to which Gomułka's tenure had given rise was, of course, deeply depressing. But in some ways the outlook for Gierek was bright and was frequently perceived as such by a number of Western observers. In 1974, for example, the political climate was described by A. Bromke as being 'exceptionally favourable'.[9] As late as 1978 it was possible to read a 'cautious prediction' that Poland would take a path of development 'similar to that of Hungary'.[10] For the Polish population Gierek had one great virtue — he was not Gomułka. Moreover his mammoth session with the Szczeciń strikers in early 1971 when a Party/state team argued with and harangued the workers in an attempt to get them to return to work did earn him a measure of respect. However, the institution with which he had to work — the Party — was a weak instrument of rule, lacking authority and even further depleted in legitimacy — having just shot down, as representative of working-class interests, dozens if not hundreds of workers (the official death toll was 28 workers). The economy was relatively stagnant, with low wages and poor productivity, although (unlike the current situation) with a balanced foreign trade account. The apparent slack in the economy presented Gierek with what many saw as his, the Party's and Poland's great chance — a massive economic renewal (rather similar in this respect to Edward Heath's contemporary 'dash for growth') which would help to stabilize the political situation and give the Party a stronger claim to legitimacy as efficient manager of the Polish economy. This, indeed, was why Gierek's bid for the leadership had been successful. As First Secretary of the Party organization of Katowice, one of seventeen Polish provinces, he had presided over the most industrialized area of the country (dubbed the 'Polish Katanga') and had gained a reputation for efficient management and for securing high wages for its workforce. Gierek's approach was from the outset one of determined though cautious reform — of the economy, of the Party, of representative organs and state administration. Despite this marked difference from Gomułka's outlook, the result was little better.

As suggested earlier, the first years of Gierek's policy achieved considerable success in terms of growing output and rising wage levels. Nevertheless, it was evident from a fairly early date that Gierek's ambitious programme involved considerable risks. As R. Dean aptly wrote, 'the Gierek leadership has mortgaged its own political legitimacy, and . . . the country's economic future as well'.[11] It was certainly an unfortunate coincidence that while foreign indebtedness was reaching high levels but before investment paid off in terms of productivity and greater exports, the Polish economy was affected by the international inflation and recession that followed the first energy crisis. It was estimated that the acceptable ceiling for foreign indebtedness (with repayment between 25—30 per cent of earnings from exports) was reached in 1975. No significant corrective measures were taken that year and, in the light of the events of 1970, it remains a mystery why the first major steps to restore economic balance were taken in the sensitive area of food prices with virtually no preparation of public opinion. Soundings were taken but, according to Babiuch, an ex-Politburo member, there was simply insufficient time to effect a 'reliable consultation'. The rises of December 1970 had been eventually withdrawn by Gierek the following February in the face of recurring strikes and a commission was set up to look into the whole area of prices and wages. Few concrete suggestions emerged and only a few general statements about the need to restore market equilibrium were made before the announcement of new price rises in June 1976. Strikes and demonstrations immediately followed, most notably in Ursus and Radom, and with equal alacrity these price rises were also withdrawn. More concerted steps to tackle production and supply problems were taken in December within the framework of the 'economic manoeuvre'. Its basis was to be a general cutting back of investment funds which would facilitate the reduction of foreign indebtedness, rein back the rise in domestic demand and help secure stability on the market. It would enable investment resources to be transferred to favour production directly for the market, to increase the supply of foodstuffs and provide more housing — all areas crucially important for the satisfaction of popular demands. If, indeed, these goals had been achieved, Gierek's reputation as an economic manager would have been vindicated and the authority of the Party enhanced. As it was, the problems diagnosed at the time of the introduction of the manoeuvre by the present vice-premier, Rakowski, persisted. It appeared that plant directors were simply not following central directives and were submitting artificially low costings to central planners, boosting investment and inflating their employees' earnings. Many in the government apparatus and economic administration were accused of not taking the current problems seriously and indeed did not believe that they could be successfully tackled under present conditions.

Thus the economic problem was also a political one: central decisions quite simply proved impossible to implement. As regards Party authority and the attempt to base legitimacy on consumerism, Gierek's problem was that of the chicken and the egg — the legitimacy of the regime and the authority of the Party would probably be enhanced if living standards could continue to rise and the Communist economy were to function smoothly. But to achieve this, the grand development plan had to be followed by those who were responsible for its implementation, and the authority of the Party leadership and its economic representatives had to be effective.

Gierek had not ignored the problem of the functioning of Party and state institutions and reforms had been introduced in three stages between 1972 and 1975. [. . .]

Why, however, was this institutional reform unsuccessful in enhancing the effectiveness of Party work and facilitating the implementation of decisions taken by the central leadership? Part of the answer was that the centralizing process and drive for Party control instituted by Gierek was not accompanied by any appeal to principles other than those of the Party's authority and its ability to master the socio-economic system. Having no viable basis of legitimacy on which to base his appeal for renewal, Gierek simply had to pin his hopes on the belief that economic success would bring its own political dividends. This priority had been noted at an early stage of Gierek's administration. The growing difficulties for the economy by the mid-1970s meant that the result of the reforms for the population was not material progress but merely further control and bureaucratization. The fact that the failure of the economic strategy was becoming increasingly clear from 1975 onwards meant that Gierek's claim to exercise authority was as threadbare as his predecessor's had been, whilst the sequence of elevated claims followed by failure to deliver was turning the public mood into one of intolerant anger. The roots of this are described by a writer in one of the unofficial journals which have been proliferating since the establishment of the Workers' Defence Committee (KOR) in 1976: 'The events of 1976 showed that Gierek's technocratism was worth as much as the patriotism of Gomułka . . . that, in short, the leaders of the PUWP have only one authentic ideology: power. The years 1971—6 have further brought a return to the conceptions of the Stalinist period'.[12] Kuron, one of the founding members of KOR, writing in November 1976, pinpointed the importance of the events of 1976 in revealing the regime's lack of legitimacy: 'deception cannot be repeated. The political crisis we are living through manifests itself as the paralysis of authority but rests on the exhaustion of the effectiveness of the methods by which authority has been exercised in Poland beginning in 1957 or 1959'.[13]

The débâcle

The measures which sparked off the strike movement and paved the way for the formation of the free trade union were not in themselves unreasonable. Their effect was to raise the price of meat from 1 July 1980, by which time meat subsidies were swallowing up 3 per cent of the entire national budget while the commodity itself could only be obtained in the shops with the utmost difficulty. The economic imbalance and political sensitivity of the consumer market was such that 40 per cent of the state budget went on subsidies for retail goods in early 1980. But economic experiences during the preceding 10 years of Gierek's rule made these price rises particularly painful for the Polish population. In the early years of Gierek's administration (which began with the removal of Gomułka in the wake of opposition to an earlier batch of rises) living standards had risen considerably. Official statistics show a 42 per cent rise in the average real wage paid to employees in the socialized economy between 1970 and 1975.[14] The same series shows a declining rate of growth after 1975 turning into a 2.7 per cent fall in the real wage during 1978. There was also a fall of 2 per cent in national income in 1979, the first such decline in the history of People's Poland and an event parallelled in post-war Eastern Europe only by the performance of the Czechoslovak economy in 1963, an experience which was to lead to the development of its ill-fated reform movement. In 1980 Polish national income fell a further 4 per cent. Exports were also stagnating — indeed, export growth between 1976 and 1979 was lower not only than during 1971—5 but also than the 1961—70 period, that of the much criticized Gomułka leadership. Gierek's attempt to justify his administration by successfully reinvigorating the economy and fostering material progress — one of the major slogans of the early seventies had been 'Let us build a second Poland' — ran out of steam in the middle of the decade. Thus, it began heading for disaster some time before the introduction of the 1980 price rises, which only served to throw a spark in a highly combustible atmosphere. Indeed, despite the undoubted material advances made during the seventies as a whole, a survey of the occupationally active population showed that 34 per cent thought that their family's condition had remained unchanged or had actually worsened between 1970 and 1978 (51 per cent of pensioners polled also falling into this category), whilst 52 per cent of those working and 37 per cent of pensioners felt that their situation had slightly improved.[15] Clearly, Gierek's attempt to provide a firmer basis for Party rule by achieving a dramatic rise in living standards and thus assuring popular satisfaction had fallen far short of target.

It is ironical that a leader who had placed such reliance on economic growth and consumption as a means of legitimizing his position (indeed, he had little choice) should fall like his predecessor as a result of strikes called after food price rises. It was his second attempt to raise food prices (the first having been in 1976) and it was a sign of the shambles that had developed in the economy that no-one since Gomułka's attempt in 1970 had denied that price adjustment was essential for balanced economic development. The obstacles to this happening, of course, were primarily political. It was unfortunate, to say the least, that the time eventually chosen to do so was one when living standards were stagnant if not declining and the benefits of higher income were less evident, if not already forgotten. Factors in contemporary Polish society also gave rise to feelings of relative deprivation. One was the irritating 'propaganda of success' — the claims in the media and particularly on television that life was continually improving and had become so much better, while proof to the contrary was all around. A second was the widespread knowledge that corruption pervaded the Party élite and administration and that state funds were swelling private purses as the economy plunged further into chaos and the incomes of others were being cut back.

These factors help to explain why the strike movement of 1980 showed such tenacity and a determination not to bow to further threats. Somewhat more puzzling is the apparent unwillingness (rather than incapacity) of the higher Party-state officials to take effective remedial action in a situation which threatened national and political, as well as economic, disaster. Thus in 1979 an authoritative report pinpointed the Party's conscious attempt to rule without permitting any popular participation in the exercise of power or assuming any genuine leading role legitimated by popular support[16] . . .

Whatever the cause, the official Party account of the events surrounding the strikes admits that at the peak of the crisis, in August, the government 'practically ceased to function'. But indications of such irresponsibility had emerged much earlier. The economic calculations on which the massive foreign loan and investment programme was based were open to considerable doubt from the very beginning. One indicative example, a reflection on the decisions taken by the very highest leadership, concerned the purchase of a licence to produce Berliet buses from the French firm. It had earlier been acknowledged that Hungarian vehicles were both more suitable to Polish conditions and much cheaper in terms of foreign exchange. But in 1972 the first high-level official visit to France was being arranged and, in a ludicrous distortion of traditional Polish politeness, it was felt that the leaders 'could not arrive empty-handed'. The net result was a planned production of the buses in 1980 (which was itself unlikely to have been achieved) at only one fifth of the level envisaged in 1972 when the licence was purchased, enormous foreign debt, crippling transport problems and remedial purchase of Hungarian buses.

Such irresponsibility permeated the whole politico-economic system. The meaning of the ill-fated economic manoeuvre itself, wrote one journalist, was that the more powerful interest groups agreed to lower total investment in order to give priority to their own investment plans which were then effectively unrestricted by central planning organs. Such 'particularism' ran rife and was a constant cause for complaint in official publications towards the end of the 1970s. But its eradication was inconceivable under existing conditions. It is notable that in 1980 24 per cent of continuing production investment was concentrated in Katowice, one of 49 Polish provinces (although admittedly the largest and endowed with a developed industrial infrastructure). It was unlikely to be a coincidence that Katowice was also the Silesian power-base of the First Secretary, Edward Gierek. Frequently, particularly in the *sauve qui peut* atmosphere of the late 1970s, particularism fell into open criminality. The scandal surrounding Maciej Szczepański, a Party official formerly responsible for broadcasting and the owner of several private cars, a helicopter and yacht, etc, is well known in the West; that concerning Tyrański, former director of a major export department and an actual dollar millionaire, less so. Such cases were the most extreme, of course, but similar behaviour was exhibited by officials and administrators at all levels, the scope of the misdemeanour being commensurate with the extent of the power exercised. The administrative reform probably gave a boost to these practices by increasing the number of second-level Party functionaries and state officials. This pattern explains why over half the local Party chiefs have been replaced since August 1980, frequently under pressure of public opinion, as have many equivalent state officials. In a country with one of the worst housing records in Europe (30 per cent fewer housing units per 1,000 inhabitants were built in 1972 in Poland than in the Soviet Union) the construction of private villas by managers and administrators out of public funds (one of the most popular élite perks) aroused strong emotions.

This blatant abuse of office is alluded to here not to bring in local colour but to illustrate the degree of cynicism with which many power-holders regarded their posts under Gierek. The slim base of legitimacy on which Party rule rested in Poland will have been evident from the earlier historical account and it was clear that power-holders in Poland were aware of their tenuous position. In the 1970, however, a qualitative change seemed to take place, as many of those in authority appeared to think it not even worthwhile to maintain the pretence that they legitimately occupied positions of power or that they wielded their authority in a rightful manner. An awareness seemed to have spread that their claims were empty and that the façade was not even worth erecting. The continuing legitimacy crisis of Communist rule in Poland thus resulted in the virtual elimination of the Party's authority. The erosion of the Gierek regime and its eventual collapse were attributable both in a distant and a more proximate sense to the maintenance of a coherent social tradition, and the name of the independent trade union, Solidarity, aptly referred to that fact. The miscalculations and irresponsibility of the Gierek leadership only served to forge links between the workers and the intelligentsia, groups whose opposition had previously been isolated and on previous occasions largely defeated. As W. Connor correctly noted shortly before the strikes: 'No other East European state currently faces the "mobilization", albeit quite partial, of such a diversity of social strata and groups, as does Poland under Gierek'.[17] Another factor in this mobilization was the rapid growth of the dissident movement and its literature after 1976. Particularly important in this was the work of coordination of KOR, and its role in maintaining contacts with the dissident workers who were activated by the experiences of 1970 and 1976. The price rises and lackadaisical handling of the subsequent strikes served to transform partial mobilization into a more complete social movement. In this the diagnosis of the pseudonymous Polish sociologist, Marek Tarniewski,[18] proved particularly relevant. Controlled political evolution in Poland, he suggested, was only possible if a constant 'social pressure' on the authorities was maintained. Any evolution not controlled by society could be transformed into stagnation or regression, as a system with severe limitations on the circulation of information hampers the perception and analysis of current situations and prevents accurate prediction. The outcome of earlier crises did not alter the political structure: 'the basic structural features of Party and state, the role of the Party, the role of the propaganda mirage and of the ideological dogmatists — all remained, although giving rise to inefficiency, even from the point of view of the authorities' achievement of their objectives'. The recurrent legitimacy crises of Communist Poland have served to foster an awareness of this also amongst the Polish population at large and the events of 1980 show that a new stage of Poland's political development has begun.

'Solidarity' and martial law

The strike movement which was responsible for the emergence of the free trade union and the latter's legal registration on 11 November 1980 ushered in a new stage in Poland's political development. For the first time in a Communist state, there now existed a national political institution which had grown out of mass popular movement and which had deep roots of legitimacy in Polish society. Despite its unconventional birth, the legitimacy of its origins in the eyes of Poles was shown by a survey, carried out by two professional sociologists, whose results were published soon after the Gdańsk agreement. The two most common assessments of the August events were that they were 'an inevitable consequence of the former policy' and a justified protest of the working people carried out in permissible form'.[19] These judgments were endorsed by 66 per cent of those with elementary education but by 86 per cent of those with basic occupational training or incomplete secondary education and by 83 per cent and 82 per cent of those with secondary and higher education respectively. As might have been expected from the readiness with which workers followed Solidarity's directives on industrial action, the trade union continued to attract a high level of support. The following March a survey indicated that 70 per cent of qualified workers were Solidarity supporters, while 75 per cent of Solidarity members (now totalling over ten million) supported the union leadership without reservation. Subsequent polls continued to demonstrate a high degree of support, testifying to its close relationship with the Polish people. Following the Church, Solidarity was the institution in which Poles 'placed most trust'. Way behind the army, parliament, the Council of State and government came the Party, lowest on the list.

With such indicators it was difficult to see how the Party could establish any greater legitimacy after August 1980. Two other factors entered into this. The first concerns the Party leadership's grudging acceptance of Solidarity and the vacillation shown by it in diverse dealings and actions with the union. Having decided the legal character and rights of Solidarity, during hard-fought negotiations at Gdańsk and protracted discussions at the registration offices, a positive attitude to cooperation with the union following the VI Plenum of the Party's Central Committee (October 1980) gave way to one that was more combative. At that meeting the Party's urgent need to re-establish its credibility was stressed and an apparent commitment to social and political renewal was made. Yet, having attempted to compel Solidarity to acknowledge the leading role of the Party in its statute, at the following Plenum in December Kania attempted once more to convince his audience of the reality of his Party's leadership by the unlikely statement that 'the Central Committee, in accordance with the expectations and aspirations of the great majority of the *aktiv* and members of the Party, chose the line of mutual understanding and renewal during the July—August crisis'. Nevertheless, the strikes had continued for over two months whilst the Central Committee followed the directions of Gierek as he attempted first to ignore and then to neutralize the strike movement. Such attempts to show that the Party leadership had viewed the strike committees and the establishment of the free union favourably from the beginning convinced no-one and only served to perpetuate suspicion of the Party and doubts concerning the nature of its pronouncements. When Solidarity's programme was published, it came under criticism for appearing to usurp the role of the Party. It was also pointed out, however, that the Party had only acted positively when under pressure from Solidarity. The second major factor which continued to undermine the Party's apparent desire to re-establish its credibility was the slow speed with which 'renewal' was occurring and the persistent suspicions that many Party and state officials had little if any commitment to that process, and felt greater sympathy for the system that prevailed under Gierek. Indeed Kania himself had talked at the December Plenum of the 'considerable obstacles' that stood in the way of socialist renewal. These he identified with 'conservative resistance', whose nature, however, was not spelt out in any further detail. In early 1981 Rakowski, future vice-premier under General Jaruzelski, was more specific. He suggested that the government (under Pińkowski) had failed to consult sufficiently with Solidarity over the issue of free Saturdays and over the multiplying complaints about governmental sluggishness and ineffectiveness. It was, he wrote, the national political leadership which needed to show the greatest patience in dealings with Solidarity. Two months later, in the midst of the crisis precipitated by Solidarity's threat of a general strike over the Bydgoszcz affair, he placed the greater part of the blame for the worsening situation in Poland directly on the clumsiness of the national authorities and their inability to cast off the old methods of government which they had developed under Gierek. Current developments were, he said, simply forging stronger and stronger links between local Party organizations and Solidarity.

This was not surprising, as the doubts concerning the genuineness of the leadership's desire for renewal were shared equally, if not more, by the Party rank and file. In their case this particularly concerned the holding of the special Party Congress, which had been agreed soon after the downfall of Gierek but had been postponed on several occasions. There were clear signs that higher Party officials were prepared for it to take place only if control over the agenda, participants and the election of Party leaders could be maintained. Directives concerning the organization of the Congress had been received by local Party organizations from the Central Committee early in the year and these were judged highly unsatisfactory by many Party groups. They provided for only limited rights on the part of local organizations to propose delegates, and the restricted use of secret voting procedures, and they contained no mention of limited terms of office-holding — a device called for to prevent the re-emergence of yet another self-perpetuating élite. Yet, in a situation where trust in the Party leadership was continuing to decline, it was only the promise of the Extraordinary Congress that was keeping many members in the Party. [. . .]

When the Party Congress finally met in July 1981 its achievements and consequences were curiously ambiguous and the role of the Party in the months following the Congress was open to considerable speculation. In terms of its procedures the IX (Extraordinary) Congress of the Polish United Workers' Party offered some reassurance to the democratically minded rank and file, while the representation accorded Solidarity in their results gave rise to hopes of a *rapprochement* of the Party with this new 'leading social force'. The conference delegates, 80 per cent of whom were freely elected by regional conferences and 20 per cent of whom were Solidarity members, elected an almost wholly new Central Committee. Only 18 members of the former Central Committee (on which 146 persons had sat) were re-elected and a large number of élite Party officials (who were normally very well represented) were absent from the new Committee, which was dominated by a combined majority of workers and peasants. The new Politburo, elected by the whole Congress, also included one Solidarity member. Meanwhile, in the midst of such unprecedented change in the Party's top bodies, continuity with the official line of gradual though determined reform was indicated by the level of support given to Kania and Jaruzelski (Party and government chiefs respectively). With the Congress based on procedures of free election and inner-Party democracy, many demands of the rank and file appeared to be satisfied, whilst in the representation given to Solidarity it seemed to promise some accommodation with the new social movement and the restoration of a certain degree of Party legitimacy.

However, as the summer of 1981 wore on and Solidarity held its first National Congress in September and October, relations between Solidarity and the Party worsened. The mood of the public was also becoming more bitter and aggressive as food became more difficult to obtain, prices of many commodities continued to rise and everyday life in general became even more of a struggle. The Party's authority over Polish society in the post-Congress period seemed no greater — as one writer pointed out 'if the party managed to relegitimate itself anywhere, it was in the Western press'.[20] Disagreements were not absent from the new Party leadership and in October Kania's offer of resignation was accepted by the Central Committee who installed General Jaruzelski, already Prime Minister and Minister of Defence, in his place. Indeed, in the midst of the changes that had taken place both in the Party leadership and amongst the ranks of Party officials throughout the country, the military *within* the Party (the 'comrades in uniform' whom Kania had singled out for praise in June 1981) were becoming an increasingly important element of continuity and organizational strength.[21] Whilst the changes that had taken place within the Party during 1981 had facilitated the emergence of a more coherent and aggressive leadership strategy it was clear, given the continuing public support shown for Solidarity and the latter's refusal to accept the Party's evidently spurious claim to the leadership of Polish society, that even the post-Congress Party had little chance of re-establishing its authority over society. Thus the weight of the Party leaders' strategy shifted to the goal of delegitimizing Solidarity as part of a more general plan for the preservation of state power.

To a certain extent the attempt was not unsuccessful. There were signs that the Polish public was becoming generally dis-illusioned with the failure of all political forces to offer some solution to the society's problems and their inability to reach some kind of agreement. In particular there was a growing unwillingness to use strike action, which was Solidarity's primary weapon in any conflict situation. Nevertheless, when martial law (a 'State of War') was declared by Jarulzelski on 13 December 1981 in a situation of growing tension and in the face of supposed threats by Solidarity leaders to resort to violence, it was clear that Solidarity still enjoyed massive support and that resistance to martial law was widespread. The critical nature of the legitimation crisis faced by the Polish regime was shown by the virtual abandonment of all Marxist—Leninist rhetoric by the martial rulers and the justification for the unprecedented shift in the basis of state power in terms rather of *raison d'état.* Thus, in his address during the first hours of military rule, Jaruzelski claimed that the continued existence of the Polish state itself was at risk: 'The achievements of many generations, the house erected from Polish ashes, are being destroyed. The structures of state are ceasing to function'. The legitimating principle, such as it was, of the military rulers was a confused one. Jaruzelski, head of both Polish government and Party, based his claim to power rather on his position as a soldier and his responsibility for the state itself. The novelty of this lies in the fact that the element of claimed legitimacy is different from and 'external to the ideology of the regime and to the communist world'.[22] This, however, gave rise to further problems in the Communist state.

For one thing, as was pointed out relatively soon after the declaration of the state of war, the exceptional powers taken had meant 'a disproportionate growth in the powers of the PUWP executive organs'. It was all too easy for power-holders to become accustomed to their exceptionally wide sphere of authority. But this was very similar to the situation that had given rise to the strike movement of August 1980 and it was significant that 13 December was already at this stage described as having created 'a real psychopolitical barrier between the Party, the broadly constituted authorities, and significant segments of particular social groups'. The real dangers inherent in this situation were subsequently indicated in the continuing decline of the Polish economy and the regularly occurring demonstrations of opposition. The legitimacy of such 'exceptional powers' tended to decline the longer they were exercised. A second problem concerned the diversity of the grounds on which Jaruzelski held power and the degree of confusion that existed about them. The considerable uncertainty that surrounded the Jaruzelski leadership in terms of its nationalist and reformist credentials undoubtedly acted to its advantage in terms of political authority and popular compliance. In large part the authority it claimed derived from the Extraordinary Congress of the Party and the reformist programme adopted there. It was still possible for Central Committee Secretary Barcikowski to state, nine months into military rule, that 'the actuality of the Congress documents is not contradicted by the fact that precisely under exceptional conditions it was temporarily necessary to reach for an exceptional solution'. Nevertheless the prolongation of such exceptional powers had itself a delegitimizing effect and attenuated the claim of the Jaruzelski leadership to exercise authority on the basis of the Party's reform programme.

Notes

1. J. Schaar (1970) 'Legitimacy in the modern state', in P. Green and S. Levinson (eds) *Power and Community,* New York, Vintage Books, p. 288.
2. R. Lowenthal (1974) 'On "established" Communist Party regimes', *Studies in Comparative Communism,* VII, 335–58, pp. 351–3.
3. R. Szporluk (1978) 'Poland' in R. Grew (ed.) *Crises of Political Development in Europe and the United States,* Princeton, New Jersey, Princeton University Press, p. 415.
4. M. Croan (1976) 'The leading role of the Party' in A. Janos (ed.) *Authoritarian Politics in Communist Europe,* Berkeley, Institute of International Studies, p. 170.
5. A. Szczypiorski (1979) 'The limits of political realism', *Survey,* XXIV, 21–32, p. 26.
6. N. Bethell (1972) *Gomułka,* Harmondsworth, Penguin, p. 202.
7. D. Pienkos (1975) 'Party elites and society', *Polish Review,* XX, 27–42, p. 37.
8. J. Staniszkis (1979) 'On some contradictions of socialist society', *Soviet Studies,* XXXI, 167–87, p. 177.
9. A. Bromke (1974) *'La nouvelle élite politique en Pologne',* Revue de l'est, July, 7–18, p. 17.
10. S. Tellenback (1978) 'The logic of development in socialist Poland', *Social Forces,* LVII, 436–56, p. 449.
11. R. Dean (1974) 'Gierek's Three Years', *Survey,* XX, 59–75, p. 67.
12. A. Macierewicz (1980) *'Walka o prawa obywatelskie',* Glos, Paris, Kultura, p. 131.
13. J. Kuron (1978) *Zasady ideowe,* Paris, Kultura, p. 29.
14. *Rocznik Statystyczny* (1979) p. 77.
15. *Nowe Drogi* (1980) June, p. 142.
16. *Raport o stanie narodu i PRL,* (1980) Paris, Kultura, p. 52.

17. W. Connor (1980) 'Dissent in Eastern Europe', *Problems of Communism,* XXIX, 1—17, p. 14.
18. M. Tarniewski (1975) *Ewolucja czy rewolucja,* Paris, Kultura, pp. 274—5.
19. *Polityka* (1980) 13 September. The survey findings are also discussed in *European Political Data Newsletter,* No. 37.
20. A. Arato (1982) 'Empire vs. civil society: Poland 1981—82', *Telos* XL, 19—48, p. 34.
21. See Section 6 of P. G. Lewis (1983) 'Institutionalisation and Political Change in Poland', in N. Harding (ed.) *The State in Socialist Society,* London, Macmillan.
22. C. Castoriadis interviewed by P. Thibaud (1982) *'Le plus dur et le plus fragile des régimes', L'Esprit,* LXIII, 140—6, p. 141.

5.3

The State in Post-colonial Societies: Tanzania

J. SAUL

There are three points which define the crucial significance of the state in post-colonial societies — two of which can be drawn directly from Alavi. For the first, we quote at length:

> The bourgeois revolution in the colony, in so far as that consists of the establishment of a bourgois state and the attendant legal and institutional framework, is an event which takes place with the imposition of colonial rule by the metropolitan bourgeoisie. In carrying out the tasks of the bourgeois revolution in the colony, however, the metropolitan bourgeoisie has to accomplish an additional task which was specific to the colonial situation. Its task in the colony is not merely to replicate the superstructure of the state which it had established in the metropolitan country itself. Additionally, it had to create a state apparatus through which it can exercise dominion over *all* the indigenous social classes in the colony. It might be said that the 'superstructure' in the colony is, therefore, 'over-developed' in relation to the 'structure' in the colony, for its basis lies in the metropolitan structure itself, from which it is later separated at the time of independence. The colonial state is therefore equipped with a powerful bureaucratic-military apparatus and mechanisms of government which enable them through its routine operations to subordinate the native social classes. The post-colonial society inherits that over-developed apparatus of

Source: From John S. Saul *The State and Revolution in Eastern Africa,* (1979) Heinemann and Monthly Review Press.

state and its institutionalized practices through which the operations of indigenous social classes are regulated and controlled.[1]

Much about this formulation is exemplary — and immediately illuminates the historical basis of the situation in East Africa.

A second, complementary, point also can be drawn from Alavi, for the state's prominent place in post-colonial society is rooted not only in the colonial legacy, but also in the contemporary production process. 'The apparatus of the state, furthermore assumes[s] also a new and relatively autonomous *economic* role, which is not parallelled in the classical bourgeois state. The state in the post-colonial society directly appropriates a very large part of the economic surplus and deploys it in bureaucratically directed economic activity in the name of promoting economic development.' Since these two features characterize the East African situation, they also serve there, in Alavi's words, to 'differentiate the post-colonial state fundamentally from the state as analysed in classical marxist theory'.[2]

There is a third feature, about which Alavi says little. In advanced capitalist countries the state is the 'dominant classes' political power centre' and in this respect comes to have an important ideological function. For in fact it symbolizes the unity of the social formation, seeming to transcend any narrow class or sectional interest and thus helping to legitimize the *status quo*. It is for this reason that Poulantzas has conceived the state as being 'not a class construct but rather the state of a society divided into classes', a fact which does not negate the further reality that such a capitalist state 'aims precisely at the political disorganization of the dominated classes'.[3] But the state's function of providing an ideological cement for the capitalist system is one which has evolved slowly and surely in the imperial centres, in step with the latter's economic transformation. In post-colonial societies, on the other hand, and particularly in Africa, this hegemonic position *must be created*, and created within territorial boundaries which often appear as quite artificial entities once the powerful force of direct colonial fiat has been removed. Peripheral capitalism, like advanced capitalism, requires territorial unity and legitimacy, and the post-colonial state's centrality to the process of *creating* these conditions (like its centrality in 'promoting economic development') further reinforces Alavi's point about that state's importance. Indeed, when viewed from a Marxist perspective, this is what all the fashionable discussion of 'nation-building' in development literature is all about![4]

These three points, taken together, help define the centrality of the state in the post-colonial social formation. And this centrality, in turn, is sufficient to suggest the importance of *those who staff the state apparatus* within such a formation. In Alavi's terms, the latter are members of 'the military-bureaucratic oligarchy', who thus come to play a semi-autonomous role in the situation created by the lifting of direct metropolitan control. The nature and extent of this autonomy — of the state and of those who staff it — from the determinations of other classes more directly rooted in the production process (Alavi identifies these as 'the indigenous bourgeoisie, the metropolitan neo-colonialist bourgeoisie, and the landed classes') is more controversial. [. . .]

[There follows a discussion of the relationship of the state to these three classes, with Saul noting that some theorists hold that in East Africa 'the real "socio-economic base" of those elements who directly control the state lies "in the international bourgeoisie"'. Saul states that:]

There is, of course, much truth in such an emphasis, but it remains an overstatement. True, Alavi's attempt to premise an explanation of the relative 'autonomy' of those elements which cluster around the state upon the nature of the interplay of other classes in post-colonial society is not entirely convincing, particularly with reference to East Africa. But some measure of autonomy does remain to those elements nonetheless — an autonomy rooted in the centrality of the state in these societies which Alavi's other arguments, cited earlier, do in fact help to illuminate. Indeed, some analysts would strengthen the point by extending the argument concerning the nature of the state's stake in the production process beyond Alavi's rather bland statement that it deploys surpluses 'in the name of promoting economic development'. Rather, they suggest that the strategic position which the state occupies *vis-à-vis* the economy, including the privileged access to the surplus which is thus available to the oligarchy, defines the latter's interest as being that of a *class*. Perhaps this is what Poulantzas has in mind when he cites 'the case of the *state bourgeoisie* in certain developing countries: the bureaucracy may, through the state, establish a specific place for itself in the existing relations of production. But in that case it does not constitute a class by virtue of being the bureaucracy, but by virtue of being an effective class'.[5]

Indeed, in East Africa, where other indigenous classes are so relatively weak, the position articulated by Debray in his discussion of the Latin American 'petty bourgeoisie' may seem to such analysts to be quite apropos: 'It does not possess an infrastructure of economic power before it wins political power. Hence it transforms the state not only into an instrument of political domination, but also into a source of economic power. The state, culmination of social relations of exploitation in capitalist Europe, becomes in a certain sense the instrument of their installation in these countries'.[6] Thus the use of the state — through special financing arrangements, training programmes, manipulation of licenses and the like — by newly powerful elements in post-colonial Kenya to parachute themselves into the private sector at the expense of the Asians is instructive in this respect. Moreover, Shivji suggests that *a very similar logic* leads to a somewhat different result in Tanzania, merely because of certain features distinctive to the political economy of the latter country. But on the essential similarity of the process he is quite outspoken. At the same time it must be emphasized that there are others, equally convinced of the relative autonomy of the state in many post-colonial African settings, who would draw rather different conclusions. In doing so, such observers have extended the notion of autonomy far beyond anything conceived by Alavi, arguing that it can actually provide the initial lever for mounting *socialist development strategies* in parts of Africa — including Tanzania! We must now turn directly to these various formulations.

Models for Africa

Implicitly, some crude notion of the autonomy of the state lies at the root of modernization theory, for example. Much the least interesting of the three broad formulations we shall mention in this section, it is a model which conceives of those who inherit the post-colonial state as 'benign élites' — the 'new middle class' or the 'modernizers'. Their role, within the trickle-down process of enlightenment from advanced countries to backward countries, is naturally to facilitate the 'development', the 'modernization', of their new nation. In addition, there is a left variant of this essentially benign interpretation — an interpretation which, quite uncritically, sees this new stratum as a force for socialism! Of course, this has been the stuff of much political rhetoric in many centres of

'African socialism', but [Reg] Green has recently given this argument an academic formulation (albeit with primary reference to Tanzania). Quite aware that 'the élite' in many parts of Africa may, in the service of its own self-interest, abuse both its opportunity for service and the trust of the mass of the people, Green nonetheless concludes that, for some unexplained reason, this does not occur in a country like Tanzania. [. . .]

At the opposite end of the spectrum from the 'benign' school are those who perceive in parts of Africa the crystallization of a fully formed class around the apparatus of the state — a class with an interest quite distinct from and antagonistic to the interests of the mass of the population.[7] Fanon hints at some such formulation, but it has been given its most vigorous scientific statement by Claude Meillassoux in his important 'class analysis of the bureaucratic process in Mali'.[8] He focuses on 'the bureaucrats', defining them as 'a body generated by the colonizers to carry out the tasks which could not (or would not) be undertaken by the Europeans themselves'. In this capacity they were entrusted with some of the instruments of power, notably with expertise. In other words, education and government (and business) *employment* are the crucial features. He then argues that in Mali,

> having been the instrument of the colonial power, and having turned against it to become the mouthpiece of the exploited Malian peasantry, the bureaucracy was gaining (with its access to power) some of the characteristics of a social class: control of the economic infrastructure and use of it as a means of exploitation, control of the means of repression involving a resort to various devices to maintain dominance. Some of its features are original: its opposite class is not yet socially well defined; it does not own the means of production on a private judicial basis, but controls them on a constitutional basis. There is no room here for a parliamentary system, regulating conflicts between a great number of private owners or corporations. The situation is better controlled through the single-party machine, within which open conflicts can be reduced to inner struggles between hidden factions. Appropriation of the economic bases of power cannot come from individual endeavour or entrepreneurship, nor from inheritance. It can come through co-operation by the people in position, or as the bargain lot of a *coup d'état.*

Meillassoux's findings parallel those of Alavi in several respects.

There is, for example, the subordination to imperialism of this 'class':

> Given the economic dependence of the country, the bureau-cracy is itself a dependent group, and its origin as an instrument of Western interests continues to influence its development. Instead of striving towards a real independence after winning the right to assert itself as political inter-mediaries with the outside world, the bureaucrats are content to return (with a higher international rank) under the rule of the old master.

Furthermore, their position is consolidated in contestation with (weak) indigenous classes: in the Mali class, an aristocracy (formerly slaveholders — a class for which there is no equivalent in East Africa) and a fairly well-developed trading class. However, having gone so far, Meillassoux remains reluctant in the end to call this group a class outright: 'It is also crucial that a distinction be made between the class proper and the dependent social elements which are the out-growth of classes, but which may, in specific historical circumstances, assume important historical functions'. Others, as we shall see, are prepared to go further in this direction, but for the moment another of Maillassoux's points may be cited. In noting the bureaucracy's attempt 'to gain certain positions of control in the modern economy and to eliminate opposition spreading from the Malian historical classes', he comments on their moves 'to infiltrate the national economy through the creation of a nationalized economic sector' as follows:

> This was done under the label of 'socialism' which provided them with a convenient ideology to bring the economy under their control, supposedly of course on behalf of the entire population. 'Socialism' permitted them to put the bureaucracy into the position of a managerial board of a kind of state corporation.

This is striking; it is almost identically the analysis that Shivji seeks to document with respect to 'Tanzanian socialism'!

It also bears a remarkable resemblance to the analysis by Fitch and Oppenheimer of Ghanaian developments under Nkrumah.[9] It is therefore interesting to note that a third model of the role of the oligarchy — he does not, of course, use that term — was articulated by Roger Murray precisely in the context of a brilliant critique of

Fitch and Oppenheimer's position.[10] Murray's is a model which falls somewhere between the polar opposites of the 'benign' and the 'class' models sketched above, and, like Meillassoux's argument, is of particular interest because it too foreshadows an approach to Tanzanian developments, in this case an approach very different from Shivji's. Murray is well aware of 'the sedimenting of new and gross class and power dispositions centering upon the state' in Ghana. Yet he is uneasy with Fitch and Oppenheimer's reduction of the socialist impulse there to the status of *'mere* manipulation', suggesting that in so arguing the authors lapse into 'pseudo-Marxist determinism'. A richer, more complex picture of those who inherit the over-developed state in the post-colonial period is needed.

What he sees instead is 'the accession to *state power* of unformed classes'. Concentrating on the CPP leadership and cadres, he notes that:

> they were drawn from the *petty bourgeois salariat* (clerks, primary schoolteachers, PWD storekeepers, messengers, etc.) — a mixed stratum which concentrated many of the political and cultural tensions of colonial society. It is precisely the socially ambiguous and unstable character of this stratum which helps us to understand its *relative autonomy and volatility* in the political arena. The CPP 'political' class did not express or reflect a determinate economic class. [. . .]

[Saul comments that given the indeterminate character of this class it is therefore possible that there be a struggle *within* this 'class-formation' between those who favour a neo-colonial set-up and those who oppose it.]

Socialism and the state in Tanzania

Turning to Tanzania, we may note at the outset that each of the models sketched in the second section has found its echo in the wide-ranging debate about the nature of Tanzania's 'socialism.' Thus, the right-benign interpretation is seen at its most sophisticated in the writings of Cranford Pratt, who eventually gives most bureaucrats and politicians in Tanzania high marks as 'developers', despite what to him appear as the unnerving hi-jinks of some few 'political ministers' and the occasional dangers of a 'doctrinaire determination of policies'. We have already taken note of Green's left-benign variant. Both wings of this approach present much too oversimplified an account to warrant their further discussion here. Rather, the really significant differences of scientific opinion lie between what are, in effect and broadly speaking, the protagonists of the Meillassoux and of the Murray/Cabral models.

On the one hand, and closer to Meillassoux, are the *Maji Maji* socialists, most notably Issa Shivji, author of two of the most important papers to have emerged from the Tanzanian debate.[11] It is in point to recapitulate his argument concerning the nature of class struggle in post-colonial Tanzania, for it is also a significant statement concerning the nature of the state there. As noted earlier, Shivji's scepticism about the socialist vocation of wielders of state power in Tanzania first found theoretical expression in his attempt to view these elements as quite straightforward agents of the international bourgeoisie. His second paper continues to stress the extent to which such elements service the interests of international capitalism, but he has gone on to develop a much more sophisticated analysis of their own stake in the system.

The class which takes power is, once again, the petty bourgeoisie, particularly its upper level (the intelligentsia) identified, rather eclectically, as comprised of intellectuals, teachers, higher civil servants, prosperous traders, farmers, professionals, higher military and police officers. The inclusion of the (African) traders and farmers in this class and in the nationalist coalition is not crucial, however. 'One of the outstanding features of the petty bourgeoisie was that they overwhelmingly came from the urban-based occupations, with some education and some knowledge of the outside world'. This class spearheads the struggle against the colonial state. In doing so, their interests merely 'coincide with those of the broad masses'. The same is true, Shivji states, for the next stage of development — the struggle with the Indian 'commercial bourgeoisie'. The role of the latter class-cum-ethnic group — which has controlled the intermediate sectors of the economy — is analysed by Shivji with great subtlety; in fact, he has provided the first really convincing class analysis of the Asian community in East Africa to date. On the African side he extends his analysis in a manner which is much more controversial.

For the confrontation which Shivji sees to be taking place between petty bourgeoisie and commercial bourgeoisie for economic power is complicated by a further development, one which emerges precisely with the accession to state power (at independence) of this petty bourgeoisie:

In an underdeveloped African country with a *weak petty bourgeoisie,* its ruling section, which comes to possess the instrument of the state on the morrow of independence, relatively commands enormous power and is therefore very strong. This was precisely the case in Tanzania . . . The Tanzanian scene . . . comes closer to the 'Bonapartist' type of situation where the contending classes have weakened themselves, thus allowing the 'ruling clique' to cut itself off from its class base and *appear* to raise the state above the class struggle. Of course, it is not that the contending classes had weakened themselves in the independence struggle. But a somewhat similar situation resulted from the fact that the petty bourgeoisie was weak and had not developed deep economic roots. This allowed the 'ruling group' a much freer hand. In other words the control of the state became the single decisive factor. For these and other reasons . . . it is proposed to identify the 'ruling group' and the 'bureaucratic bourgeoisie'. Before the Arusha Declaration, this would comprise mainly those at the top levels of the state apparatus — ministers, high civil servants, high military and police officers and such like. One may also include the high level bureaucrats of the Party and the cooperative movement, because of the important role the latter played in the pre-Arusha class struggles.

Shivji does note that the weakness of the petty bourgeoisie referred to here 'is due to the fact that it is still "embryonic"; the whole class structure is in *the process of* formation'. The same *caveat* is introduced with reference to the bureaucratic bourgeoisie. Is it 'a class *as distinct* from the petty bourgeoisie'? Not quite. 'Suffice to say that the post-independence class struggles (including the Arusha Declaration) were themselves a process leading to the emergence of the "bureaucratic bourgeoisie". The process may not be complete.' But having noted this, Shivji, unlike Murray, does not draw back from his terms. He is unconcerned with the weight of teleology which they bear. As he proceeds with his analysis, classes-in-formation behave, unambiguously, like fully formed classes. And this is the chief weakness of his argument.

For Shivji, in sum, the 'historical moment' is by no means 'uncertain'. On the contrary, he now uses this conception of Tanzania's class structure — straightforwardly and however much the 'structure' may be 'in the process of formation' — to explain the history of post-colonial Tanzania: it is the case of 'a *non-*

proletarian class after coming to political power ... now trying to wrest an economic base' from the commercial bourgeoisie. Half-measures, like the encouragement of the cooperatives, having failed, 'the only alternative, both for further struggle against the commercial bourgeoisie and for further penetration of the economy, was state intervention': 'it was thus that the Arusha Declaration was born in 1967'. With it, and with the attendant nationalizations, a new stage in the class struggle, à la Shivji, is reached:

> Up until the Arusha Declaration the 'bureaucratic bour-geoisie' was essentially of the politico-administrative type. Although the state played an important role in the economy it was mostly a regulatory one. With the Arusha Declaration the state and state institutions (including parastatals) became the dominant actors in the economy. Thus a new and more important wing of the bureaucratic bourgeoisie was created. Political power and control over property had now come to rest in the same class.

Socialism as '*mere* manipulation' — Shivji comes very close to such a position. Nevertheless, he does recognize that there is some difficulty in reconciling this with the Arusha Declaration Leadership Code, a code designed to prevent leaders from involving themselves — profitably — in the private sector. Here Shivji's explanation, in order to save his hypothesis, is that 'the ideology had gained the upper hand, for even a rhetoric has its own momentum and can have important effects on concrete measures'. This would also appear to be his 'explanation' for the very real constraints (certainly as compared with other parts of Africa) on élite income and consumption which have been a part of Tanzania's 'socialism'. In addition, Shivji states, as if to reinforce his general argument, that the code has often been flouted since its inception. This, in turn, suggests (quite accurately) that there was a 'spontaneous' tendency for 'leaders' to overlap into the private sector — as in neighbouring Kenya. Yet such a reality seems to contradict Shivji's emphasis. Why didn't the petty bourgeoisie use the state to facilitate their own movement in upon the Asians on a private basis — again, as in Kenya — rather than publicly and collectively?

Shivji is aware of this problem, of course, and his explanation is of considerable interest:

> In Kenya, there were important sections of the petty

bourgeoisie — yeoman farmers and traders, for example — besides the urban-based intelligentsia, who had already developed significant 'independent' roots in the colonial economy. Thus the petty bourgeoisie itself as a class was strong and different sections within it were more or less at par. This considerably reduced the power of the 'ruling clique' irrespective of its immediate possession of the state apparatus and kept it 'tied' to its class base — the petty bourgeoisie.

But this does not convince. Even if the entrepreneurial elements were stronger in transitional Kenya, the difference from Tanzania was not so striking as Shivji suggests, and in any case these Kenyan Africans' commercial opponents (European and Asian) were themselves much stronger than any counterparts in Tanzania; thus the *relative* economic weight of the African entrepreneurs cannot have been that much different. Moreover, it is quite unnecessary to make such subtle distinctions. As noted, it seems obvious that large sections of Shivji's bureaucratic bourgeoisie continues to cast envious glances at their civil servant and political counterparts in Kenya and at the gross (and rewarding) 'conflicts of interest' which serve to characterize Kenyan economic and political life. And, being disproportionately drawn from commercialized, cash-cropping and rural areas like Kilimanjaro and Bukoba, they do in fact have intimate (familial) connections with a 'yeomanry'. Unless contested, such a group would have had Tanzania gravitate in the Kenyan direction, a point made by Nyerere himself on more than one occasion. It is difficult, in fact, to avoid the conclusion that the Arusha Declaration package of policies — the opting for collective solutions to the Tanzanian development problem — represented, first and foremost, an *initial victory* for a *progressive wing* of the petty bourgeoisie (and the announcement of its continuing commitment to the interests of the workers and peasants), rather than some cold-blooded fulfilment of the class interests of that stratum's bureaucratic core.

This difference of opinion requires detailed exploration of a kind that is beyond the scope of the present chapter. Suffice to say that for Shivji this kind of 'manipulation' also tends to characterize each of the specific arenas of post-Arusha policy making, while for each such arena it can be shown that this is an oversimplification. Take, for example, the *'ujamaa* village' programme (designed to promote a Tanzanian brand of agricultural collective), in Shivji's eyes merely a calculated and perfunctory gesture — an expression of 'intermittent ideological hostility' to 'kulaks' — designed to maintain for the petty bourgeoisie its 'popular peasant base'. But this was not an immediately popular policy even among much of the peasantry; support for it would have to be *created*, sometimes in a manner (as in Ismani) which challenged the local dignitaries of the party itself. Nor is it entirely true that this policy was 'not basically against the interests of the petty bourgeoisie'. The fact that in practice bureaucrats often worked hard to defuse the policy by directing it away from the 'advanced' areas (Kilimanjaro and Bukoba mentioned above) and towards more defenceless, backward regions (with many fewer kulaks) testifies to their uneasiness. Nor were the extensive nationalizations of 1967 merely a charade. International capitalism was stung and the conventional wisdom of most civil servants visibly affronted. In other words, these and other intiatives represented real achievements in a transition toward socialism. That the full potential of these policies' possible contribution to such a transition has not been realized is, of course, also true, a point to which we shall return.

However, there is one crucial area of inquiry which cannot be passed over here, and which also sheds considerable light on the issue under discussion. Thus, Shivji argues that the main contradiction in Tanzania is now between the working class and the bureaucratic bourgeoisie, and cites the dramatic assertions of Tanzania's working class in recent years. Indeed, the further investigation of this subject by Shivji's colleague, Henry Mapolu, reveals a level of proletarian action in Tanzania which is virtually unparallelled elsewhere in Africa. [. . .]

But where did such a high level of consciousness come from? This too must be explained, especially when one compares this development with experience elsewhere in Africa. Moreover, the Tanzanian working class is small, even by continental standards, and, in the past, not marked by notably radical leanings. Once again, the conclusion suggests itself that initiatives taken by a certain sector of the leadership — notably by Nyerere and his supporters — played an important role in bringing about this development and in facilitating the emergence of what Shivji calls 'the proletarian line'. Unlike their Ghanaian counterparts, such a leadership did sense, albeit haltingly, that 'the oppressed' could 'alone have provided the conscious support for a socialist path of development' and they therefore sought to create such a base. Initiatives designed to facilitate 'workers' participation' (workers' councils) and peasant participation (*ujamaa* and decentralization) reflected this concern, despite the distortion in practice of these programmes by the dead hand of the bureaucracy. However, most significant in this respect has been *Mwongozo,* the TANU Guidelines of 1971 — a crucial document in crystallizing worker consciousness and in legitimizing, *even demanding*, the unleashing of popular pressures against oligarchical tendencies on the part of wielders of state power ('leaders'). Yet the drive for these measures did not come from below. Even Shivji must come part way to meet that reality.

> In the international situation where capitalism has become a global system and socialism has been established in a large area of the world: where both internally and externally physical and intellectual wars are raging between the capitalist and socialist lines, the world-wide circulation of progressive ideas has become commonplace. It is not surprising therefore that even capitalism and neo-colonialism have to be wrapped up in socialist rhetoric and vocabulary. But more important is the fact that though material *class* forces may not immediately warrant it, a few progressive and revolutionary leaders manage to push through (officially) radical ideas and policies. The adoption of the Mwongozo by TANU, with its progressive features, was such an event.

But who are these 'few progressive and revolutionary leaders'? As Shivji suggests, they do shape and crystallize, rather than merely reflect, popular consciousness; moreover, they seem to be cutting sharply against the interests of the bureaucratic bourgeoisie. It is precisely because Shivji's approach cannot fully illuminate such matters that other analysts have felt some other formulation than his to be necessary in order to explain, in class terms, the 'socialist' dimensions of Tanzania's experiment.

Indeed, it is only because it is much too evocative and dismissive a phrase that one avoids applying to Shivji's analysis Murray's epithet, 'pseudo-Marxist determinism'. Nonetheless, Murray's critique of Fitch and Oppenheimer is in many respects the best approach to Shivji. And Murray's positive formulations can also serve to promise much the most effective alternative approach to Tanzanian reality. In this respect it is worth noting that even the definitional problem (which Murray himself approached somewhat too obliquely) has been faced, quite straightforwardly, by Micheala von Freyhold — working from what is in effect a closely related viewpoint to that of Murray. Her solution, in a recent paper, is to use the term 'nizers'.

As she explains it:

> 'Nizers' or 'nizations' (from Africanization) is a term applied by Tanzanians to refer to that stratum or class which social scientists have called 'educated élite', 'labour aristocracy', or 'petty bourgeoisie' — those who took over important administrative and economic positions when colonialism was defeated.[13] [. . .]

[She then suggests that there are conflicts among the 'nizers' over alternative policies and class allegiances.] It is precisely to this 'still on-going struggle among the nizers' that von Freyhold traces the socialist impulse in Tanzania: 'In 1967 an enlightened political leadership had decided that Tanzania should not turn into a neo-colonial society. The Leadership Code was to cut the links between public office-holders and petty capitalism and nationalizations were to bring foreign capital under control . . . Both measures were . . . a vital first step.' And the direction of further steps also remains, in her eyes, a contested matter:

> While the transformation of the nizers is an obvious prerequisite for the promised creation of a socialist society it is obvious that it will not proceed without a protracted struggle within that educated stratum itself. What the progressive parts of Tanzania's nizers envisage as their future is not yet reality. As long as the future is undecided there are still two ways in which one can look at the present educated stratum: as a nascent petty bourgeoisie which will not only be a faithful agent of international capital but which will eventually solidify into a class with petty capitalist connections and orientations or as the precursors of a socialist avantgarde.

Of course, the general definitional problem has probably not been laid to rest by von Freyhold's coinage, suggestive though it is; nor does she directly address herself to Shivji's prognosis of bureaucratic consolidation *without* 'petty capitalist connections'. But the emphasis seems to me to be basically correct.

To argue so is not to ignore the contradictions which mitigate, and even undermine, the achievements of Tanzania's progressive nizers. Quite the reverse. I have stressed the extent to which various pressures — international and domestic — do play upon the system in such a way as to strengthen the least progressive elements in the 'present educated stratum' and to 'solidify' that stratum into a privileged class. It is quite true, as Shivji has demonstrated in another of his papers, that international capitalism can make adjustments and begin to shape to its own purposes the fact of nationalization. Corporations join with aid agencies and international economic institutions in reactivating 'conventional wisdom' and coopting those 'oligarchs' who are inclined to be so tempted. In addition, the expansion of the state sector has had the *result* (but, to repeat, not the primary purpose) of expanding the number who are prepared merely to feed off it, in the absence of countervailing tendencies. If, unlike Ghana, some more real effort has been made to create a new base for the state among the workers and peasants, the pace of bureaucratic consolidation seems to be outstripping that attempt. In consequence, demobilization of the peasantry becomes the more likely result, while workers find themselves set, not merely against the most conservative of managers, but against the state itself and the increasingly homogeneous class which defends it.

The negative weight of 'objective conditions' has been reinforced by subjective conditions. As Murray's analysis would suggest, ideological contestation in Tanzania has been a creative factor of great importance, with Nyerere's formulations in particular being crucial to facilitating a move to the left. But this ideology of the progressive nizers has also been marked by inadequacies which some might like to term petty bourgeois in nature: a hostility to Marxism, for example, and the consequent lack of a fully scientific analysis of imperialism and class struggle. And this problem has been compounded by a much too sanguine reliance on existing institutions of the inherited state (ministries and cabinets, an untransformed party) which cannot easily be turned to purposes of socialist construction. These factors too have made it difficult for Nyerere and others to consolidate their original initiatives. The results are paradoxical (and not preordained, à la Shivji). The conservative wing of the nizers now threatens to inherit a socialist initiative (and an even more 'overdeveloped' state than existed at the moment of independence) in the creation of which it had little hand, but which it has sought to warp to its own purposes from the moment of the policy's first being announced. All of which is to approach Shivji's conclusion, though not by Shivji's route:

> This marks the beginning of the political struggle and the rise of the proletarian line. There is bound to be increasing opposition to bureaucratic methods of work and 'management's' dominance, themselves a reflection of the neo-colonial

structure of the economy and the corresponding class structure. The struggles of the workers and peasants against internal and external vested class interests will characterize the subsequent class struggles in Tanzania.[14]

For it is necessary to reaffirm that much about this continuing class struggle has been shaped by the reality of struggle within the stratum of the nizers — within the 'oligarchy-in-the-making', if you like — during the first post-colonial decade.

The critique of Shivji is also a qualification of Alavi's approach. Apart from points made earlier concerning the important differences in context which East Africa presents, and some of the implications of these differences, it can now be argued that Alavi's approach is too rigid to comprehend fully the uncertainties which define the historical process in the immediate post-colonial period. In Tanzania, his 'oligarchies' become such only more slowly and with much more ambiguous results than his model would lead one to expect. At the same time it can be firmly stated that the pressures which move the situation toward such an unsavoury result as he seeks to theorize are indeed powerful. And, as noted, there is no doubt that these pressures have been, and are continually, making themselves felt upon Tanzania. As a result, 'oligarchical' tendencies — the consolidation of Shivji's 'bureaucratic bourgeoisie' (self-interested and ever more subservient to imperialism) — seem to have been the increasingly obvious result.

Has the further development of this trend altered perspectives on practice in Tanzania? Writing two years ago, I felt confident to conclude a survey of Tanzania's efforts at socialist construction in the following terms: 'Indigenous radicals will decide their own fates. Yet the fact that almost all have chosen to work within the established structures and upon the regime is no accident.'[15] And there is still some significant contestation within the 'petty bourgeoisie' and within the established institutions. But where, for example, one could then argue with some confidence that the control of working-class organization by party and state had played, despite the costs, a positive role in curbing consumptionism and raising worker consciousness, there is now reason to be more sceptical about the logic of continuing control. Faced with nizers more bent than ever upon consolidating their power, independent organization of the working class may seem an increasingly important goal. Similarly, the time may be approaching when the independent political organization of progressive elements, already a (difficult) priority in most other one-party and military/administrative regimes in Africa, becomes a priority for Tanzania as well. Smash the post-colonial state, or use it? But this is really a question which can only be asked, and answered, by those engaged in significant *praxis* within Tanzania itself.

Notes

1. Hamza Alavi (1972) 'The state in post-colonial societies — Pakistan and Bangladesh', in *New Left Review,* No. 74, July/August, pp. 59—81.
2. This quotation and others in this section are from Alavi, 'The state in post-colonial societies', unless otherwise indicated.
3. Nicos Poulantzas (1973) *Political Power and Social Classes,* London, New Left Books and Sheed and Ward, p. 191.
4. Richard Sklar (1967) 'Political science and national integration', *Journal of Modern African Studies 5,* No. 2 and John S. Saul, 'The dialectic of class and tribe' in John S. Saul (1979) *The State and Revolution in Eastern Africa,* London, Heinemann, p. 391.
5. Poulantzas, *Political Power and Social Classes,* p. 334.
6. Regis Debray (1967) 'Problems of revolutionary strategy in Latin America', *New Left Review,* No. 45, September/October, p. 35.
7. The most prominent of these is Issa Shivji (1970) author of 'Tanzania: The silent class struggle' in *Cheche,* Special Issue, Dar-es-Salaam, September; reprinted in L. Cliffe and J. S. Saul (eds) (1973) *Socialism in Tanzania*, Vol. 2, Nairobi, Tanzanian Publishing House, pp. 304—30; and (1973) 'Tanzania: The class struggle continues' (mimeo) Department of Development Studies, University of Dar-es-Salaam. See also his (1976) *Class Struggles in Tanzania*, New York, Monthly Review Press, and London, Heinemann. The interesting work of Henry Mapolu and Karim Hirji among others can also be cited in this connection.
8. C. Meillassoux (1970) 'A class analysis of the bureaucratic process in Mali', *Journal of Development Studies,* January.
9. R. Fitch and M. Oppenheimer (1966) *Ghana: End of an Illusion,* New York, Monthly Review Press.
10. Roger Murray (1967) 'Second thoughts on Ghana', *New Left Review,* No. 42, March/April.
11. J. K. Nyerere (1968) 'Introduction' to *Freedom and Socialism,* Nairobi, London, New York, Oxford University Press.
12. Henry Mapolu (1973) 'The workers' movement in Tanzania', *Maji Maji,* No. 12, September. See also Mapolu's (1972) 'Labour unrest: irresponsibility or worker revolution', *Jenga,* Dar-es-Salaam, No. 12, and Nick Asili (1971) 'Strikes in Tanzania', *Maji Maji,* No. 4, September.

13. M. von Freyhold (1973) 'The workers and the nizers' (mimeo) University of Dar-es-Salaam.
14. Shivji, 'Tanzania: The class struggle continues', p. 107.
15. Giovanni Arrighi and John S. Saul (1973) 'African socialism in one country' in *Essays on the Political Economy of Africa,* New York, Monthly Review Press, p. 312.

5.4
The Secret State

E. P. THOMPSON

It is difficult to disclose the operations of the 'servants' (in practice often *masters*) of modern states because these are generally defined by the operators themselves as 'official secrets'; what the operators themselves wish to secrete from public view they are empowered to classify as forbidden materials, and to defend from publicity by a number of sanctions — not only, as a final resort, the implementation of the Official Secrets Act, but also the recourse to 'D Notices', pressure (or favours) towards journalists and editors, the deportation of insubordinate aliens (such as Agee and Hosenball), the disciplining of civil servants (who have already passed through the screens of 'positive vetting'), and so on. And if, by the careful accumulation of evidence from public sources, independent investigators are able to reconstruct these operations with some accuracy, then they instantly become possessed of an 'official secret' which they publish at their own hazard.

This is the double-bind within which the British public has been held, for many years, by its own security services, and increasingly in recent years by the police and other agencies of government. It has worked so well that, whereas the CIA is now a household word, many people have only the haziest notion as to the character and functions of MI5, MI6 or the Special Branch of the police. Indeed, for a large part of the public, these organizations might not exist; or, if they do, they are thought of as either counter-espionage agencies, playing a John Le Carré game of spooks with the Russians, or as emergency flying squads brought into being, on an *ad hoc* basis, to counter evident threats from hi-jackers, bombers, or alien terrorists. It would amaze many British citizens

Source: From 'Introduction' to the *Review of Security and the State 1976* (1978) the corrected edition of *State Research* Bulletins 1977—8, Julian Friedmann Books.

475

to learn that these and other organizations are only at the end of a long historical line of ruling-class institutions, with agents or informants in trade unions, educational institutes, and political organizations (especially of the left), and with direct access to the postal and telephone systems of the country; that they are larger and more powerful, and less subject to ministerial or parliamentary control than they have ever been; and that a large part of their function has always been to invigilate the British people themselves.

The most satisfactory conditions for the effective operation of these organs of the state — and also for the operation of private information-gathering organs such as the Economic League — are ones in which they can lie low, beneath the threshold of public consciousness and concern. [. . .]

I have already said that operators of the British security services are 'some of the most secretive and arrogant' to be found in modern bureaucratic states. My words were chosen with care, and are intended to be neither complacent nor alarmist. I am insisting upon a peculiar combination of invisibility, lack of accountability, and the consequent composure of an antique ruling group which has been bred to govern from behind a wall of silence. The situation could, very certainly, be worse, and, if we are not alert, it will become worse. The German security organs are blatant and massively visible, in an old Prussian statist tradition; and they have seized gratefully upon the opportunity provided by Baader-Meinhof to enlarge their brutal presence in civil life. In Russia and in several parts of Eastern Europe it is never possible to disentangle the motives of administration from those of 'security' and control, and in significant areas it is not possible to speak of civil rights or of a rule of law at all. In the United States we have witnessed three decades of the frightening enlargement of agencies of 'security' (including massive espionage, provocation, 'dirty tricks', and possibly even assassinations, committed against their own citizens); but this has at length been met, by the American liberal tradition, in a very vigorous counter-attack, in which some journalists and lawyers have played an honourable part. Without this counter-attack, which included the massive 'leakage' and then the legally enforced disclosure of 'secret' documents and tapes, the mountain of official excreta known as 'Watergate' would never have been exposed to public view. And it is now possible, under the US Freedom of Information Act, for victims of these organs (such as Alger Hiss or the sons of the Rosenbergs) to gain access to some part of the documentation necessary for their vindication.

Thus the United States security organs are more powerful and more intrusive, but they have suffered a public check, are disgraced in the eyes of many American citizens, and are at last subject to some legal accountability. In this area at least, the American liberal tradition has turned out to be much tougher than the British. It is now a platitude — but one which bears repeating — that in Britain a 'Watergate' could not have occurred exactly in that way; but if it had occurred, in a more 'British' way, the British press would neither have been able nor have dared to disclose the facts about it, and the British public would have been told only so much as certain 'wise men' of the establishment thought it safe to allow them to know.

Thus British security operations are distinguished by their invisibility and their lack of accountability. (This is so much the case that even sections of the British left customarily denounce — as they should — the conspiracies of 'the CIA', overlooking the fact that for decades the invisible British counterparts have collaborated unreservedly with United States agents, fed them with information on British subjects, and shielded them from exposure behind the same screen that protects themselves.) They are also distinguished by a peculiar quality of ruling-class composure and arrogance.

A historian is bound to reflect upon the particular route which led us into this situation. Not much more than 100 years ago, the British people were distinguished throughout the world for their resistance — at least on their own home ground — to the pretentions of the state. This resistance stemmed not only from 'Radical' but also from 'Tory' sources. The settlement of 1688 had been marked, above all, by jealousy of the Crown, and, hence, of the central powers of the state. The gentry emerged as the rulers of England, and (more selectively) of Scotland and Wales also. In the eighteenth century, as the limited resources of parliamentary democracy became obstructed and corrupted, and as the aristocracy and great gentry enlarged their lands and wealth and their purchase upon interest and patronage, so both Whig and Tory magnates enlarged their hostility to a bureaucratized and rationalized state: they wished to be left free to govern in their own way within their own spheres of influence. This was very far from being a democratic impulse; but it did, in the Whig tradition, afford shelter for libertarian modes of thought, in continued jealousy of central power and in vigorous resistance to the examples of absolutism provided by Continental monarchies.

By the end of the eighteenth century, this was an all-pervasive

Whiggish rhetoric, shared by Tories, Whigs and Radicals alike. Moreover, it was a rhetoric taken over and applied to greatly more democratic ends, by the rising popular reform movement. The parliamentary oligarchs wished to contain their debates within the privacy of the walls of Parliament; they did not wish the British people to overhear how their governors talked, in private, about them. Wilkes and the printers defied 'the law' and breached this privacy; we owe *Hansard* to this defiance. In area after area, the 'common people' insisted that the civil rights of the 'freeborn Englishman' were not the privileges of an élite but were the common inheritance of all: freedom of press, speech and conscience, rights of assembly, inhibitions upon the actions of military or police against crowds, freedom from arbitrary imprisonment or unwarranted arrest and entry upon private premises. The insurgent British working-class movement took over for its own the old Whiggish bloody-mindedness of the citizen in the face of the pretentions of power. Even when labouring under the manifest class discrimination of the Combination Acts, the secretary of an illegal trade-union branch of framework knitters in Mansfield in 1812 was able to protest against a clause in a Bill proposed by the workers' representatives themselves, which authorized the search for shoddy goods in the houses of manufacturers: 'if iver that bullwark is broke down of every english mans hous being his Castil then that strong barrer is for iver broke that so many of our ancesters have bled for an in vain'. The workers had appropriated the democratic precedents and practices of past generations for their own; the ancestors were not 'theirs' but 'ours'.

And this was how matters continued for at least 100 years. The Chartist, Radical Liberal, Irish Nationalist, and formative Labour movements were distinguished by their sensitivity to libertarian issues, and their suspicion of the polity of statism. When the police forces were enlarged and rationalized (or as some would have it today, 'modernized') in the mid-nineteenth century, this was a victory for bourgeois utilitarian bureaucratic policy in the face of intense resistance extending from old Tory localism through Radical Liberalism to outright Chartist opposition — for Chartists and trade unionists very well understood what kind of imperatives dictated government policies. As a consequence of this opposition, the presence of the police in British public life remained unusually subdued. They must be seen as 'servants' of . . . either the gentry or 'the public', and they must in no circumstances exhibit a brash public presence. And, as a more concrete evidence of the old libertarian tradition, which endures to this day, the British police (at least in Britain) must usually go about the streets unarmed.

There were some anticipations of the statism of the twentieth century in the increasingly intrusive and punitive presence of the police in Britain in the 1880s. This was a natural reaction of the propertied classes, who reacted to the rumour that there were now socialist agitators in the streets (making speeches against *their property*!) with seemly terror. In general the police were impartial, attempting to sweep off the streets with an equable hand street-traders, beggars, prostitutes, buskers, pickets, children playing football, and free-thinking and socialist speakers alike. The pretext, very often, was that a complaint of interruption of trade had been received from a shopkeeper. William Morris remarked on the impatience of 'the more luxurious part of society' to 'clear the streets of costermongers, organs, processions, and lecturers of all kinds, and make them a sort of decent prison corridors, with people just trudging to and from their work'.

Less evidently impartial were the statements and actions of Sir Charles Warren, who, in the face of mounting demonstrations by unemployed, Radicals, Socialists and Irish Nationalists, was appointed Chief Commissioner of the London Metropolitan Police in 1886. Here he engaged in exercises of 'public relations' quite as vigorous as any subsequently set in motion by Sir Robert Mark or Sir David McNee. He presided over the processionals which culminated in his banning all meetings in Trafalgar Square (on the grounds that it was Crown property) and the subsequent episode of 'Bloody Sunday' when demonstrators were scattered by massive police and military forces, and with a violence which, in any accounting, was unnecessary and inexpedient. But Warren had overplayed his hand, the Liberal Party was shocked and riven down the middle. The general dislike of his methods was fuelled by the public's dislike of the police treatment of women, and by the conspicuous failure of Warren's forces to solve the 'Jack the Ripper' murders. When Warren refused outright to accept the instructions of the Home Secretary, he was forced, with the *douceur* of a KCB, to exchange the command of London for the command of Singapore (1889).

I do not mind about the KCB. I am perfectly willing for all over-mighty security officers and police to be given KCBs, so long as they are dismissed. I have introduced the case of Sir Charles Warren for two other reasons. First, it is a reminder — and an important reminder, in the face of a certain pessimistic determinism which is in fashion on the left — that it is not absolutely foreclosed and prescribed that ordinary people will lose every contest with power. The history of the past 90 years is not an unrelieved record of the enlargement of the powers of the state, and of the impudence of its officers. Because people made enough row, Warren was sacked; Trafalgar Square was re-opened and in the main has stayed open (apart from demonstrations about Ireland); the battle for free speech in the streets was, largely, won, for the Radicals and Socialists at least.

The second reason, however, is less comforting. Sir Charles Warren signals the feedback of imperialism — its experience and its consequences — to the streets of the imperial capital itself. Glancing at the DNB I see that, before serving as Metropolitan Police Commissioner, he had gained military experience in Gibraltar and Griqualand West; had commanded the Diamond Fields Horse in the Kaffir War (1877—8); and had been military and civil administrator of the Bechuanaland protectorate. He came from Suakin to London, and departed thence to Singapore; he served with distinction in the Boer War ('he cleared the country between the Orange River and the Vaal'), and was a founder-member of the Boy Scouts. He was, in short, a representative figure of the imperialist climax; and he reminds us of the inter-recruitment, cross-posting, and exchange of both ideology and experience between those who learned to handle crowds, invigilate subversives, and engage in measures of 'pacification' in the external Empire, and those who struggled with the labour problem, the unemployed question, the women problem, and sometimes just the people problem, at home.

We are entering the world of a John Buchan novel — British imperial interests are endangered by alien agents and by subversive rotters at home (perhaps even by milksops in the Cabinet?), but our hero knows that he can rely upon a few absolutely trustworthy people — men who went to the same privileged school, served together on the North-West Frontier or between the Orange River and the Vaal, and who bump up against each other in select London clubs or deer-stalking on the Scottish moors. These people know better than 'the politicians', and very much better than the public, what British interests are. They accept, with a grimace of resignation, the duty to save Britain from herself.

That is the novelettish way of seeing it. But in fact it remains true that the growth of an unrepresentative and unaccountable state within the state has been a product of the twentieth century. Its growth was, paradoxically, actually aided by the unpopularity of security and policing agencies; forced by this into the lowest possible visibility, they learned to develop techniques of invisible influence and control. It was also aided by the British tradition of civil service neutrality; this sheltered senior civil servants from replacement or investigation when administrations changed, and afforded to their policies the legitimation of 'impartial, non-political' intent. Ministers, and Prime Ministers, increasingly became putty, on questions of 'security', in their senior advisers' hands. They were handed their briefs, and — often, in the press of business, with the haziest understanding of these — they knew that it was their first business in the House to defend their own advisers or departments. And it must be admitted that Labour Ministers have shown the greatest eagerness to learn the same lessons of loyalty to their 'servants', and no one has been more eager than Mr Merlyn Rees.

A complex of forces has impelled the increasing statism of the past decades, and I will mention only two or three. Very obviously, two world wars have not only habituated people to uniform and to the arguments of national interest, but have also facilitated such lesser (but significant) perquisites as the busy exchanges between Oxford and Cambridge colleges and Whitehall, as scholars have done their bit in Intelligence. The rapid erosion of Empire had perforce retracted the imperial ideology, has brought it back home, into the security services, the army, and the police, where experience gained in Ireland, India, or Rhodesia, looks restively for new fields of application — these services are the last refuges of imperialism, within which a ghostly imperial ideology survives its former host.

There is also the very substantial, and very seldom mentioned, legacy of the British phase of 'McCarthyism' in the high Cold War. This resulted in extensive 'positive vetting' procedures in the public services, which were subjected to an opaque and pusillanimous inquiry, under the chairmanship of the late Lord Radcliffe, in 1961—2. The brief of this committee was to inquire into the measures of safeguarding information in the civil service against the intelligence services of foreign powers — although not, it seems, of the CIA — and against 'subversive organizations in this country, of which in current conditions the most formidable is the Communist Party of Great Britain, with its fringe of associated bodies and sympathizers'. This was a flexible definition, for 'current conditions' may change, and in the past 15 years, as the Communist Party has become increasingly less 'formidable', one wonders what other organizations, fringes and sympathizers have been added to the subversive list. In any case, the Radcliffe committee proceeded on the assumption that any sound security man would know, instantly, what was subversive and what was not, remarking at one point: 'We have followed the common practice of using the phrase "communist" throughout to include fascists.' The point is that *any* term would have been as good as any other — anarchist, situationist, rapist, or agronomist — provided that it signified to the proper people opinions and associations which, in current conditions, proper people disapprove.

There are two further points. First, liberal-minded opinion in Britain today is very properly angered by the loud and intrusive measures (*Berufsverbot,* etc.) of the West German authorities against political dissenters of the left. I am glad that this solidarity is being shown. But it is not always remembered that the *Berufsverbot* of 'positive vetting' goes on in the British public services every day, in ways that are certainly less intrusive and that are very certainly less loud. What goes on, in the screening of applicants, in the promotion of public servants and in their allocation to different departments, we do not know; nor do we know what criteria are employed; and we would not be told even if we (or the House of Commons) asked. All that we do know is that men and women are passed through screens which select, for the most privileged and influential positions, those whose records appear to be most 'moderate', conservative and orthodox. It is perhaps time that a Russell Tribunal sat in Whitehall, where — and this is my second point — it could take no evidence, since evidence would be, by definition, an 'official secret'.

This is to return once more to the John Buchan theme. The ruling group within the state in Britain has a kind of arrogance about it which may be historically unique. It has a settled habit of power, a composure of power, inherited from generations of rule, renewed by imperial authority, and refreshed perennially from the springs of the best public schools. It is a group which does not bother, or need to bother, to get itself elected. It knows what 'British interests' are, and defends these through every change of political weather. It decides whether you or I are subversive, and whether our actions should be watched. It does not have to justify its decisions in any public arena. It rules, unobtrusively, from within.

What it does is an 'official secret'. For example, do the security services simply invigilate 'subversives', and pass on information promptly to appropriate authorities, or do they also engage in provocations and 'dirty tricks'? A historian is well aware of the latter in the longer record. At one time, in the Napoleonic Wars, the main centre of underground English 'Jacobinism' was, with some difficulty, kept in being only by the unremitting efforts of several government spies, as a kind of honey-pot in London which might attract to it unwary reformers. In the next decades, the official papers in the Public Record Office are abundantly covered in the slime left behind by Oliver, Castles, and successive spies and provocateurs within the Chartist and Irish movements. In later decades the trail is less evident, because it has been more effectively obscured. Not only are matters of 'security' covered by a 30-year rule prohibiting disclosure, but even where the records are opened one may sometimes detect where the hand of a 'weeder' has been at work. (A 'weeder' is a scrupulous civil servant trained as an *anti*-historian, whose business it is to remove from the files obnoxious materials.)

The innocent might suppose that such practices will have been curbed by the rise of Labour to political influence, and (purportedly) to power. If any such innocents still exist, they should read and reflect upon Sir Harold Wilson's account of his handling of the national seamen's strike in 1966, in Chapter 4 of *The Labour Government, 1964–1970: a Personal Record.* The seamen's union, which for decades had been reduced to little more than a servile 'company' shop, had at length, in response to the pressures of its own membership, proclaimed a strike in furtherance of a series of demands for improved wages and conditions. As ship after ship tied up in British ports, the crews joined the strike with enthusiasm. And also with unusual militancy — partly because conditions of work were bad, partly because a long record of union torpor had at last been broken, but particularly because a national strike of seamen is one of the most difficult industrial encounters to organize, and once it has been launched the seamen *must* hold firm until they obtain the optimum settlement. The usual mechanisms for fobbing-off such crises — for example, a minor concession, on condition that the strike is called off, followed by some committee of inquiry, and the distant hope of further concessions — can never be acceptable to seamen. For once the ships are untied and have put to sea again, for a hundred disparate destinations, they cannot be abruptly recalled again to muscle the union's negotiations: to strike on the high seas, or to turn back to port, is mutiny. Thus in 1966 even the union's very moderate leaders acted — and, for a time, actually were — very tough. They must stand out for the maximum settlement, since it might be many years before they were in so strong a bargaining position again.

That was the seamen's side of the matter. The other side of the matter is so familiar that I scarcely need to rehearse it, since it is the background of 'national interests in danger' against which, for 15 years, *every* strike has been enacted. The livelihood of 'the nation' was endangered; the national economic crisis was acute; the pound was falling; the government's policies of wage restraint must not be breached. The Minister of Labour at that time, Mr Ray Gunter, was a well-known 'Red-baiter', who was eventually to find that even Harold Wilson's Labour Party was too red for him to continue as a member. But Wilson and Gunter acted smoothly together in setting in motion the familiar and grossly inequitable repertoire of power. A State of Emergency was declared. The armed services were called upon, but only for limited purposes ('I announced the use of RAF Transport Command planes for help with urgent export shipments'). The TUC and a Court of Inquiry were brought in to bully the seamen's leaders. Wilson broadcast to the nation on television. Finally, in the House of Commons, the Prime Minister placed full responsibility for the strike upon a 'tightly knit group of politically motivated men'. As he recounts in his reminiscences, 'I did not use the word "Communist", though no one in the House or in the press, which next morning headlined my words as a sensation, had any doubts whom I had in mind.'

'The fact was', his account continues, 'that the moderate members of the seamen's executive were virtually terrorised by a small group of professional Communists or near-Communists . . .' But there was one trouble with this story: as every informed member of the trade union movement knew, there was *not one single Communist* on the executive of the National Union of Seamen. (If the 'moderates' were terrorized by anyone, apart from Wilson and Gunter, they were terrorized by the militancy of their own members.) Hence, eight days later, Wilson was forced into an unusual predicament in which he raised, for a brief instant, the veil of political lies and half-truths which is normally held between the public and the state within the state. 'From various sources we began to receive undeniable evidence of what was going on,' he tells us. (These sources may have been as 'various' as MI this or that, the Special Branch, and the Economic League.) Addressing the House once more, he itemized the (pathetically small) resources of Bert Ramelson, the Communist Party's industrial organizer: 'He has three full-time officials on his staff' — i.e. rather fewer than the staff of a firm making bicycle-clips, and very much fewer than the Merseyside Special Branch. More than this, he was able to report in detail upon the travels of militant members of the seamen's union, where they had been, whom they had visited, at which flats they had stayed overnight, and who had visited them there. It added up to a chilling James Bond scenario; or, if one was even moderately informed, to the normal lobbying accompanying any industrial dispute.

There was, however, one very curious episode within this drama, which is well to remember lest we fall into the error of assuming that 'the state' always operates as a well-oiled and synchronized ruling-class conspiracy. The Leader of the Opposition, Mr Edward Heath, saw through Wilson's rhetoric, and thought that Wilson and Gunter had mishandled the situation and provoked the seamen into stubbornness. Knowing that there were no Communists on the seamen's executive, he pressed Wilson to disclose his evidence and substantiate his charges. Wilson complied by arranging for Heath a highly secret meeting, 'on Privy Counsellor terms', to which meeting he brought not only the 'senior people responsible for these matters' but also *one of the operators "in the field"*. Despite all these remarkable favours, Heath, to his credit, remained unconvinced. But Wilson pursued his cloak-and-dagger script to the bitter end. Unprecedented measures were taken to split the seamen's executive, Wilson personally bullied their general secretary (giving him 'a sealed envelope' with information from the 'operators in the field'), and the strike was smashed.

I have run through this narrative because, while it should be familiar, it is not: people have short memories, and official mythologies seek to make them shorter. We are rarely allowed as much information as to the operation of the state as we have in this episode, since few senior politicians have as large and loose a mouth as Sir Harold Wilson. We will note only three points. The first is that it should not be assumed that Tories are always more active in their capitulation to the state within the state than Labour ministers. A certain kind of Labour politician may have a malice against 'militants' and, above all, a deeply engrained reflex of deference towards the 'real' guardians of British interests (whether in the Treasury or in the security services) which a certain kind of Tory — who meets these operators as class equals — need not always have.

Second, this episode illustrates not only how information is gathered upon subversives, but how it may be *put to use*. In 'normal' conditions of industrial and social peace, it is very rarely necessary for the 'operators in the field' to disclose their operations. And this leads to a certain complacency in the public. After all, if all that these people are doing is observing and invigilating us, but putting all this information to no use (unless against terrorists, spies, etc.), then let them have their fun — and let them have the most advanced, computerized data bank as well. What harm is there in that? But the point about the seamen's strike is that it demonstrates that we remain safe from intervention, blackmail and state-suborned calumny only so long as we remain good and quiet. The state within the state only becomes, briefly, visible during a State of Emergency; and a State of Emergency is a moment when any group of people with economic or social power stand up vigorously for their own rights. When the immediate crisis is over, the pall of invisibility settles down once more.

Third, I have recited this episode because, in its general outlines, it is now so familiar. The national crisis — the State of Emergency — the deployment of armed forces — the attempts to induce panic on the national media — the identification of some out-group as a 'threat to security' — all these are becoming part of the *normal* repertoire of power. Of course, there are historical precedents for all these things; but never before, since 1816, has government been able to employ this repertoire without inflaming the nerves of outrage and resistance in a minority — a minority which, by patient agitation and political education, has often been able to influence the majority, and, in the long run, secure some reversal of the pretentions of power. What is new, in the last two decades, is the dulling of the nerve of resistance and of outrage. Familiarity has bred contempt — not contempt for the state and for the specious alarms and rationalizations of power, but contempt for any possible alternative. And in this moment a new danger appears. For once the libertarian responses of the British people have been brought under sedation, then the reasons for the invisibility of the state within the state begin to lose their force. And so we see the evidence, in the present decade, of the police, the army, the security services, the quasi-official and the pseudo-private agencies of control, becoming *more* public, engaging in active 'public relations', lobbying for new curbs on civil rights and for 'simplified' legal process, and attempting to familiarize the public with their intrusive presence. And in face of this new danger, the ancient historical nerve begins to throb once more.

5.5

Accumulation, Legitimation and the State: the Ideas of Claus Offe and Jürgen Habermas

DAVID HELD AND JOEL KRIEGER

I Claus Offe

From the late sixties, debate amongst Marxists began to focus on the state, and particularly on its relation to the capitalist mode of production.

Invigorating the debate in Marxist circles about state, bureaucracy and class, Claus Offe has challenged — and attempted to recast — the terms of reference of both Miliband and Poulantzas. For Offe, the state is neither simply a 'capitalist state' as Poulantzas contends (a state determined by class power) nor 'a state in capitalist society' as Miliband argues (a state which preserves political power free from immediate class interests). Starting from a conception of contemporary capitalism which stresses its internal differentiation into four sectors (the competitive and oligopolistic private sectors, the residual labour sector, and the state sector), Offe maintains that the most significant feature of the state is the way it is enmeshed in the contradictions of capitalism. Hence, the state is faced with contradictory tasks. On the one hand, the state must sustain the process of accumulation and the private appropriation of resources; on the other hand, it must preserve belief in itself as the impartial arbiter of class interests, thereby legitimating its power (see Offe, 1972, 1974).

Source I: From David Held and Joel Krieger 'Theories of the state: some competing claims' in S. Bornstein *et al.*(eds) *The State in Capitalist Europe* (1983) London, Allen & Unwin.

The institutional separation of state and economy means that the state is dependent upon the flow of resources from the organization of profitable production, through taxation and finance from capital markets. Since in the main the resources from the accumulation process are 'beyond its power to *organize*', there is an 'institutional *self-interest* of the state' and an interest of those with state power to safeguard the vitality of the capitalist economy (see Offe and Ronge, 1975). With this argument, Offe differentiates himself from Miliband and Poulantzas. As Offe puts it, the institutional self-interest of the state 'does not result from alliance of a particular government with particular classes also interested in accumulation, nor does it result from any political power of the capitalist class which "puts pressure" on the incumbents of state power to pursue its class interest' (Offe and Ronge, 1975, p. 140). For its own sake, the state is interested in sustaining accumulation.

Political power is determined, then, in a dual way: by formal rules of democratic and representative government which fix the institutional form of access to power and by the material content of the accumulation process which sets the boundaries of successful policies. Given that governments require electoral victory and the financial wherewithal to implement policy, they are forced increasingly to intervene to manage economic crisis. The growing pressure for intervention is contradicted, however, by capitalists' concern for freedom of investment and their obstinate resistance to state efforts to control productive processes (seen, for example, in efforts by business to avoid 'excessive regulation').

  · The state, therefore, faces contradictory imperatives: it must maintain the accumulation process without either undermining *private* accumulation or the belief in the market as a fair distributor of scarce resources. Intervention into the economy is unavoidable and yet the exercise of political control over the economy risks challenging the traditional basis of the legitimacy of the whole social order — the belief that collective goals can be properly realized only by private individuals acting in competitive isolation and pursuing their sectoral aims with minimal state interference. The state, then, must intervene but conceal its purpose. Thus, Offe defines the capitalist state '(a) by its exclusion from accumulation, (b) by its necessary function for accumulation, (c) by its dependence upon accumulation, and (d) by its function to conceal and deny (a), (b) and (c) (Offe, 1975, p. 144).

He argues that if these analytical propositions are valid, then 'it is hard to imagine that any state in capitalist society could succeed to perform the functions that are part of this definition simultaneously and successfully for any length of time' (Offe, 1975, p. 144). To investigate this hypothesis, he focuses on the nature of state administration and, in particular, on its capacity for rational administration. The problems of administration are especially severe, Offe suggests, since many of the policies undertaken by contemporary governments do not simply complement market activities but actually replace them. Accordingly, Offe argues in an interesting parallel to the corporatist view, that the state selectively favours those groups whose acquiescence and support are crucial to the untroubled continuity of the existing order: oligopoly capital and organized labour. The state helps to defray the costs of production for capital (by providing cheap energy for heavy users through the pricing policies of nationalized industries, for example) and provides a range of benefits for organized labour (for instance, by tacitly supporting high wage demands and enhanced wage differentials and relativities). In a recent article Offe contends, furthermore, that the representatives of these 'strategic groups' increasingly step in to resolve threats to political stability through a highly informal, extra-parliamentary negotiation process (1979, p. 9).

Starting from a critique of Weber's basic assumption that the main reason for the expansion of bureaucratic forms of organization in modern capitalist societies is their technical superiority, Offe attempts to demonstrate that no method of state administration can be 'adequate for solving the specific problem of the capitalist state'. These he characterizes as the 'establish[ment] of a balance between its *required functions*' which result from a certain state of the accumulation process on the one side and its '*internal structure*' on the other side (Offe, 1975, p. 140). Offe argues that the 'three "logics" of policy production' which are available to the capitalist state — based in turn on bureaucratic rules, purposive action, and consensus formation — necessarily undermine its operation once the burgeoning demands from the economic sphere impel the state decisively into market-replacing activities (Offe, 1975, p. 136). For Offe, each logic of policy production encounters a particular dynamic of failure: bureaucratic policy production cannot escape its dependence upon fixed hierarchical rules and therefore cannot respond flexibly to externally determined policy objectives; policy production governed by purposive action fails for lack of clear-cut, uncontroversial, and operational goals transmitted from the environment; the consensus mode of policy production fails because it generates conflict by inviting 'more demands and interests to articulate themselves than can be *satisfied*' by the capitalist state, bound as it is by considerations of accumulation (Offe, 1975, p. 140). Modern states are hamstrung by a bureaucracy which operates by invariant rules and procedures and by too limited goals or with overly narrow and strict jurisdictional areas of responsibility which limit the flexibility and, in a word, the rationality of administrative responses to externally formulated demands.

Offe's writings on the internal workings of bureaucracy within capitalist states are important: he has offered significant insights about the limitations of rule-bound administration in promoting aims which are beyond its jurisdictional competence. When, for example, national railways consider the elimination of an 'unprofitable' service, by what rules — and from what rational stance — can they evaluate the complex consequences of the decision for the pursuit of leisure activities, investment in local industry, employment, settlement patterns, tourism, etc? Moreover, Offe's emphasis on the way capitalist states are pushed into providing a range of services which directly benefit the best organized sectors of the working class, surmounts some of the limitations of Poulantzas' account of the state as functionally interlocked to the needs of capital. As Offe and Ronge argue provocatively, the state 'does not defend the interests of one class, but the *common* interests of all members of a *capitalist class society'* (Offe and Ronge, p. 139).

But Offe may skew his understanding of state power and administrative capacity, in assuming that because of the logic of policy production, state administration cannot successfully execute policies with political ramifications. This argument, which recalls Weber's specific analysis of the limitations of bureaucratic initiative and the necessity for parliamentary direction in Germany, underestimates the capacity of state administrators to be effective agents of *political* strategy. In an essay on the politics of French planning, Peter Hall argues that there is an implicit intelligence in a state seemingly divided against itself and torn by competing pressures.

> A state faced with multiple tasks and well-defined conflicts of interest among the social classes it governs, or the groups within these, may find it necessary to maintain a degree of deliberate malintegration among its various policy-making arms so that each can mobilize consent among its particular constituencies by pursuing policies which, even if never fully implemented, appear to address the needs of these groups. In many cases the pursuit of incompatible policies renders all of

them ineffective, but this strategy prevents any one group from claiming that the state has come down on the side of its opponents (Hall, 1981).

Offe's tendency to explain the success and failure of state policy by reference to functional imperatives (accumulation and legitimation) encourages him to ignore the strategic intelligence which government and state agencies often display.

II   Jürgen Habermas

Habermas elaborates upon the discussion of legitimacy in an interesting manner (1976, 1979). He explores, in particular, the way 'advanced' (or, as he sometimes calls it, 'late' or 'organized') capitalism is susceptible to 'legitimation crisis' — the withdrawal from the existing order of the support or loyalty of the mass of the population as their motivational commitment to its normative basis is broken. It is his contention that the seeds of fundamental social change — the overcoming of capitalism's underlying class contradiction — can be uncovered in this and other related crisis tendencies.

Habermas first provides an analysis of liberal capitalism which follows Marx closely. He explicates the organizational principle of this type of society — the principle which circumscribes the 'possibility spaces' of the system — as the *relationship of wage labour and capital*. The fundamental contradiction of capitalism is formulated as that between social production and private appropriation, i.e. social production for the enhancement of particular interests. But, as Habermas stresses, a number of questions have to be posed about the contemporary significance of Marx's views. Have events in the last hundred years altered the mode in which the fundamental contradiction of capitalism affects society's dynamic? Has the logic of crisis changed from the path of crisis growth, unstable accumulation, to something fundamentally different? If so, are there consequences for patterns of social struggle? [...]

The model of advanced capitalism Habermas uses follows many well-known recent studies. He begins by delineating three basic

Source II: From David Held 'Crisis tendencies, legitimation and the state', in John B. Thompson and David Held (eds) *Habermas: Critical Debates* (1982) London, Macmillan.

subsystems, the economic, the political-administrative and the socio-cultural. The economic subsystem is itself understood in terms of three sectors: a public sector and two distinct types of private sector. The public sector, i.e. industries such as armaments, is oriented towards state production and consumption. Within the private sector a distinction is made between a sector which is still oriented towards market competition and an oligopolistic sector which is much freer of market constraints. Advanced capitalism, it is claimed, is characterized by capital concentration and the spread of oligopolistic structures.

Habermas contends that crises specific to the current development of capitalism can arise at different points. These he lists as follows:

Point of origin (subsystems)	System crisis	Identity crisis
Economic	Economic crisis	—
Political	Rationality crisis	Legitimation crisis
Socio-cultural	—	Motivation crisis

His argument is that late-capitalist societies are endangered from at least one of four possible crisis tendencies. It is a consequence of the fundamental contradiction of capitalist society (social production versus private appropriation) that, other factors being equal, there is either: an economic crisis because the 'requisite quantity' of consumable values is not produced; or a rationality crisis because the 'requisite quantity' of rational decisions is not forthcoming; or a legitimation crisis because the 'requisite quantity' of 'generalized motivations' is not generated; or a motivational crisis because the 'requisite quantity' of 'action-motivating meaning' is not created. The expression 'the requisite quantity' refers to the extent and quality of the respective subsystem's products: 'value, administrative decision, legitimation and meaning' (1976, p. 49).

The reconstruction of developmental tendencies in capitalism is pursued in each of these dimensions of possible crisis. For each sphere, theorems concerning the nature of crisis are discussed, theories which purport to explain crisis are evaluated, and possible strategies of crisis avoidance are considered. 'Each individual crisis argument, if it proves correct, is a sufficient explanation of a possible case of crisis.' But in the explanation of actual cases of crises, Habermas stresses, 'several arguments can supplement one another'. [. . .] What is presented is a typology of crisis tendencies, a logic of their development and, ultimately, a postulation that the [capitalist] system can only be preserved at the cost of individual autonomy, i.e. with the coming of a totally administered world in which dissent is successfully repressed and crises are defused. Since Habermas regards legitimation and motivation crises as the distinctive or central types of crisis facing advanced capitalist societies, I should like to give a brief *résumé* of them.

Increased state activity in economic and other social realms is one of the major characteristics of contemporary capitalism. In the interests of avoiding economic crisis, government and the state shoulder an increasing share of the costs of production. But the state's decisions are not based merely on economic considerations. While on the one hand, the state has the task of sustaining the accumulation process, on the other it must maintain a certain level of 'mass loyalty'. In order for the system to function, there must be a general compliance with the laws, rules, etc. Although this compliance can be secured to a limited extent by coercion, societies claiming to operate according to the principles of bourgeois democracy depend more on the existence of a widespread belief that the system adheres to the principles of equality, justice and freedom. Thus the capitalist state must act to support the accumulation process and at the same time act, if it is to protect its image as fair and just, to conceal what it is doing. If mass loyalty is threatened, a tendency towards a legitimation crisis is established.

As the administrative system expands in late capitalism into areas traditionally assigned to the private sphere, there is a progressive demystification of the nature-like process of social fate. The state's very intervention in the economy, education, etc. draws attention to issues of choice, planning and control. The 'hand of the state' is more visible and intelligible than 'the invisible hand' of liberal capitalism. More and more areas of life are seen by the general population as politicized, i.e. as falling within its (via the government's) potential control. This development, in turn, stimulates ever greater demands on the state, for example for participation and consultation over decisions. If the administrative system cannot fulfil these demands within the potentially legiti-mizable alternatives available to it, while at the same time avoiding economic crisis, that is, 'if governmental crisis management fails . . . the penalty . . . is withdrawal of legitimation' [1976, p. 69]. The underlying cause of the legitimation crisis is, Habermas states rather bluntly, the contradiction between class interests: 'in the final analysis . . . *class structure* is the source of the legitimation deficit' [1976, p. 73]. The state must secure the loyalty of one class while systematically acting to the advantage of another. As the state's activity expands and its role in controlling social reality becomes more transparent, there is a greater danger that this asymmetrical relation will be exposed. Such exposure would only increase the demands on the system. The state can ignore these demands only at the peril of further demonstrating its non-democratic nature.

So far the argument establishes only that the advanced capitalist state might experience legitimation problems. Is there any reason to expect that it will be confronted by a legitimation crisis? It can be maintained that since the Second World War, Western capitalism has been able to buy its way out of its legitimation difficulties (through fiscal policy, the provision of services, etc.). While demand upon the state may outstrip its ability to deliver the goods, thus creating a crisis, it is not necessary that this occurs. In order to complete his argument, therefore, and to show — as he sceks to — that 'social identity' crises are the central form of crises confronting advanced capitalism, Habermas must demonstrate that needs and expectations are being produced (on the part of at least a section of the population) which will 'tax the state's legitimizing mechanisms beyond their capacity'.

Habermas's position, in essence, is that the general development of late capitalism, and in particular the increasing incursion of the state into formerly private realms, has significantly altered the patterns of motivation formation. The continuation of this tendency will lead, he contends, to a dislocation of existing demands and commitments. Habermas analyses these issues, not under the heading 'legitimation crisis', . . . but under the heading 'motivation crisis'. 'I speak of a motivation crisis when the socio-cultural system changes in such a way that its output becomes dysfunctional for the state and for the system of social labour' [1976, p. 75]. This crisis will result in demands that the state cannot meet.

The discussion of the motivation crisis is complex. The two major patterns of motivation generated by the socio-cultural system in late capitalist societies are, according to Habermas, civil and familial-vocational privatism. Civil privatism engenders in the individual an interest in the output of the political system (steering and maintenance performances) but at a level demanding little participation. Familial-vocational privatism promotes a family-oriented behavioural pattern centred on leisure and consumption on the one hand, and a career interest oriented towards status competition on the other. Both patterns are necessary for the maintenance of the system under its present institutions. Habermas argues that these motivational bases are being systematically eroded in such a way that crisis tendencies can be discerned. This argument involves two theses: (1) that the traditions which produce these motivations are being eroded; and (2) that the logic of development of normative structures prevents a functionally equivalent replacement of eroded structures.

The motivational patterns of late capitalism are produced, Habermas suggests, by a mixture of traditional pre-capitalist elements (e.g. the old civic ethic, religious tradition) and bourgeois elements (e.g. possessive individualism and utilitarianism). Given this overlay of traditions, thesis (1) can itself be analysed into two parts: (a) that the pre-bourgeois components of motivational patterns are being eroded; and (b) that the core aspects of bourgeois ideology are likewise being undermined by social developments. Habermas acknowledges that these theses can only be offered tentatively.

The process of erosion of traditional (pre-bourgeois) world-views is argued to be an effect of the general process of rationalization. This process results in, among other things, a loss of an interpretation of the totality of life and the increasing subjectivizing and relativizing of morality. With regard to thesis (1b), that the core elements of bourgeois ideology are being undermined, Habermas examines three phenomena: achievement ideology, possessive individualism, and the orientation towards exchange value. The idea of endless competitiveness and achievement-seeking is being destroyed gradually as people lose faith in the market's capacity to distribute scarce values fairly — as the state's very intervention brings issues of distribution to the fore and, for example, the increasing level of education arouses aspirations that cannot be coordinated with occupational opportunity. Possessive individualism, the belief that collective goals can only be realized by private individuals acting in competitive isolation, is being undermined as the development of the state, with its contradictory functions, is (ever more) forced into socializing the costs and goals of urban life. Additionally, the orientation to exchange value is weakening as larger segments of the population — for instance, welfare clients, students, the criminal and sick, the unemployable — no longer reproduce their lives through labour for exchange value (wages), thus 'weakening the socialization effects of the market'.

The second thesis — that the logic of development of normative structures prevents a functionally equivalent replacement of eroded traditions — also has two parts. They are (a) that the remaining residues of tradition in bourgeois ideology cannot generate elements to replace those of destroyed privatism, but (b) that the remaining structures of bourgeois ideology are still relevant for motivation formation. With regard to (a), Habermas looks at three elements of the contemporary dominant cultural formation: scientism, post-auratic or post-representational art, and universalistic morality. He contends that in each of these areas the logic of development is such that the normative structures no longer promote the reproduction of privatism and that they could only do so again at the cost of a regression in social development, i.e. increased authoritarianism which suppresses conflict. In each of these areas the changing normative structures embody marked concerns with universality and critique. It is these developing concerns which undermine privatism and which are potentially threatening to the inequalities of the economic and political system. [. . .]

On this basis, [Habermas] argues, individuals will increasingly be produced whose motivational norms will be such as to demand a rational justification of social realities. If such a justification cannot be provided by the system's legitimizing mechanisms on the one hand, or bought off via distribution of value on the other, a motivation crisis is the likely outcome — the system will not find sufficient motivation for its maintenance.

Habermas's conclusion, then, is that, given its logic of crisis tendencies, organized capitalism cannot maintain its present form. If Habermas's argument is correct, then capitalism will either evolve into a kind of 'Brave New World' or it will have to overcome its underlying class contradiction. To do the latter would mean the adoption of a new principle of organization. Such a principle would involve a universalistic morality embedded in a system of participatory democracy . . . What exact institutional form the new social formation might take Habermas does not say; nor does he say, in any detail, how the new social formation might evolve.

References

Habermas, Jürgen (1976) *Legitimation Crisis,* London, Heinemann.
Habermas, Jürgen (1979) *Communication and the Evolution of Society,* London, Heinemann.
Hall, Peter (1981) 'Economic planning and the state: the evolution of economic challenge and political response in France' in G. Esping-Andersen, and R. Friedland (eds) *Political Power and Social Theory,* Vol. III, Greenwich, Connecticut, Jai Press.

Offe, Claus (1972) 'Political authority and class structure', *International Journal of Sociology,* Vol. 2, No. 1.

Offe, Claus (1974) 'Structural problems of the capitalist state', *German Political Studies,* Vol. 1.

Offe, Claus (1975) 'The theory of the capitalist state and the problem of policy formation', in L. Lindberg *et al.* (eds) *Stress and Contradiction in Modern Capitalism,* Lexington, Massachusetts, Lexington Books.

Offe, Claus (1979) 'The state, ungovernability and the search for the "non-political"', presented at the conference on 'The Individual and the State', University of Toronto, Centre for International Studies, 3 February.

Offe, Claus and Ronge, V. (1975) 'Theses on the theory of the state', *New German Critique,* No. 6.

For important further reading, see Claus Offe (1983) *Contradictions of the Welfare State,* London, Hutchinson, and Jürgen Habermas (1981) *Theorie des kommunikativen Handelns,* 2 Vols, Frankfurt, Suhrkamp, and forthcoming in English (1984) Cambridge, Massachusetts, MIT Press.

Part 6
Nation-States in the World Context

Introduction

LAURENCE HARRIS

The theory of the state has often suffered from a neglect of the international context. The new theses, concepts and historical applications of theories of the state since the 1960s have invariably focused upon its connection with a purely domestic structure of social, economic and political relations. External factors can easily be assumed under the definitional view that the state has a responsibility for the territorial integrity of 'its' society. Thus, the pursuits of wars, diplomacy, treaties and alliances, and policies regarding migration, the exchange rate and balance of payments are factors at the very centre of the state's existence, but, on this view, once recognized they do not need to be examined explicitly. A domestic bias, whether rationalized in those terms or not, does foreclose the possibility of developing a state theory that can account for the complexities of modern states and their variety. Nevertheless, two perspectives on the international dimensions of states are found in the literature, although it is a literature that rarely impinges upon the theory of the state as an explicit issue.

One tradition is that of international relations. Each state is seen as having its own integrity and relating to other integral states, so that an important issue is the nature of each state's policy regarding war and defence, the balance of payments, and political and economic alliances. A distinct tradition is that which goes in the opposite direction, arguing from the existence of an international system — an international economy or international political system — to the nature of the individual state. The chapters in Part 6 are concerned with the latter tradition, although the interaction of the external system with the internal dynamic behind states is recognized and emphasized in each chapter.

The most uncompromising theory which starts from the existence of a world system is that of Wallerstein. Arguing that a unified capitalist economy, structured around a world market,

501

pervades the whole world, Wallerstein's approach implies that states are subordinate to the forces generated by that world system. An extreme interpretation of this approach is that the study of the relations between states and their particular societies is invalid. Another radical implication is that the lines of division in the modern world between socialist and capitalist systems for example are more apparent than real. In Chapter 6.1 Peter Worsley takes issue with the latter implication of the world system approach and with its general obliteration of economic and political variations and historical developments.

Against Wallerstein, Worsley argues the merits of seeing the world in terms of competing and interrelated systems. He discusses whether there is greater validity to the notion of three world systems — advanced capitalist, advanced socialist and the Third World — with types of states appropriate to the distinct socio-economic characteristics of each. Mandel, in Chapter 6.2 sets out a theory of the manner by which advanced capitalist societies are related to each other in a hierarchy and by which Third World societies are subordinated to them. He employs a theory of imperialism derived from Lenin, but modified and illustrated by modern developments. The underlying perspective is one of an essentially international economic system, capitalism, extending and developing its international structure over time and determining to a significant extent the position and role of nation-states.

The simplest conception of the constraints upon a nation-state that arise from capitalism's international expansion is that of a colonial or client state subordinated to an imperial power, but Mandel examines a variety of more complex possibilities: the rivalry between imperialist states that Lenin identified, the rise of a single hegemonic imperialist state, or the growth of cooperation between advanced capitalist states based on a harmony of economic interests. His arguments postulate a very direct connection between the state and the economic base, and are related to the effect on nation-states of the growth of multinational corporations and the effect of the rise of institutions such as the EEC (or, he could add, the IMF or World Bank) which have elements of state power but are supra-national.

The direct connection that Mandel posits between the international economy and the state points toward a concentration upon states' economic policies whereas, employing a similar framework, Lenin's startling result was the implication that inter-imperialist wars were inevitable. The nuclear arms race of the post-Second World War decades could not be explained by the straightforward application of that theory even if it were correct for its time, for the modern growth of genocidal weapons involves a symbiotic rivalry between socialist and capitalist states, whereas Lenin's theory concerned only the motive forces behind capitalist states' militarism. The chapter by Fred Halliday which concludes Part 6 is concerned with explaining the nuclear arms race and has implications for our understanding of the state's location in an international system, in this case an international system of military and geopolitical rivalry.

It consists of excerpts from a wide-ranging text principally concerned with explaining the phenomenon of nuclear terror and it is written as polemic in the best sense of the word, as an attempt to persuade people to a point of view with a bearing on political action. Nevertheless, throughout it is unavoidably concerned with a problem that must be central to any understanding of the state, the special character of the great powers' states and the dynamic that drives the exercise of their power on the world scene. Halliday is responding to an argument put forward by E. P. Thompson. While Thompson argues that the nuclear arms race has its own dynamic (which he characterizes as 'exterminism') such that the characters of the Soviet and American states are similar ('isomorphic'). Halliday criticizes his conceptual framework because it ignores the political dynamic, its historical development and its origins in the differences in the two states (partly in terms of their relationship to Third World states).

It is a simple matter to draw links between Halliday's view of the American state's concern for hegemony over the Third World and the economic motive force that Ernest Mandel's Chapter, 6.2, on imperialism discusses, while the importance Halliday attaches to the difference between the USA and USSR echoes Peter Worsley's view and, in a different way, the arguments that Rakovski put forward against the convergence thesis in Part 4. One problem which Halliday touches but does not examine fully is the relationship between individual states, whether great powers or not, and supra-national bodies with some elements of state power. In the present context, the connection between the USA and USSR on the one hand, and NATO and the Warsaw Pact on the other, is left as an open question in the theory of the state; it is a problem which has acute practical implications in the era where disagreements between the partners in each alliance have impinged upon the military and geopolitical strategies of the two major powers.

6.1

One World or Three? A Critique of the World-system Theory of Immanuel Wallerstein

PETER WORSLEY

Our thinking about the process of development has been fundamentally changed in recent years by the emergence of world-system theory, notably in the writings of André Gunder Frank, Immanuel Wallerstein and Samir Amin. It is with the thought of the first two, and primarily Wallerstein, that I shall be concerned here. All of us stand deeply in their debt, not only for the clarity with which they have presented their theoretical frameworks, but also for the serious documentation they have adduced from the historical record. One has only to contrast, for example, the impressionistic account of the 'creation of the world' that I sketched in the first chapter of my book, *The Third World*, in 1964, to see what a step forward their work represents in terms of theoretical rigour and empirical research.[1]

World-system theory was initially generated in reaction to 'dualistic' notions which informed most of the development theory of the period following World War II. The most important theoretical statement of the dualist approach was Arthur Lewis' *The Theory of Economic Growth* (Allen & Unwin, London, 1955), for which he has been awarded a Nobel Prize. But in terms of its influence upon government policy, the Economic Commission for Latin America (ECLA) achieved much more than did Lewis' abortive venture into planning in Africa and elsewhere. The basic assumption was that the economies of the backward countries

Source: From R. Miliband and J. Saville *Socialist Register, 1980* (1980) (eds) London, Merlin Press.

could be divided into a modern and a traditional sector respectively. The task of 'modernization' then consists, it was argued, in shifting resources from the latter to the former; the strategy advocated that of import-substitution.

The debate that followed was a highly political encounter, the riposte of the world-system theorists being aimed, on the one hand, at this advocacy of capitalist modernization, and on the other, at another set of 'dualists', the Communist Parties which were advocating a policy of allying with the 'national' bourgeoisies against both the reactionary, allegedly 'feudal' landowning oligarchies at home and their new allies, the foreign multinational corporations abroad. As against both ECLA and the Communists, the world-system critique argued that there were not two distinct economic sectors, but that both were merely parts of a wider whole: the world capitalist economic system. The landowners, then, were not 'feudal', but an agro-exporting bourgeoisie, and had been for centuries. Nor were the industrial bourgeoisie any more 'national' or progressive. They would never provide principled opposition to foreign capital because they themselves were only junior partners in an alliance with foreign multinational corporations. Between them, they controlled the state, which acted as the bridge between foreign and local capital, mobilized capital and controlled labour. In this alliance, it was the multinational corporation which was predominant. Being capital-intensive, the industrial sector, under their aegis, would be unable to absorb the growing population, much of it displaced from the countryside by the penetration of capitalism into agriculture. Those who did find employment would be subjected to intensified exploitation, while those who resisted could expect the ultimate in repression to be unleashed against them — state terror.[2]

In wider historical terms, world-system theorists carried out detailed analyses of the process by which capitalism had implanted itself across the globe: its growth and maturation in Europe, and its subsequent expansion abroad. From the sixteenth century onwards, they argued, the world had become a *system*. From thenceforth, what happened to the silver mines of Peru and Mexico, the textile industry in India, or the gold mines in South Africa would have direct and fateful consequences for Madrid and Lancashire, and even for Poland and Portugal — and *vice versa*. Whole states would be destroyed; others invented; pre-existing polities fused together and their economies similarly transformed. Burma was to become, in Furnivall's phrase, a 'factory without chimneys'; Java a 'vast coffee estate';[3] Egypt a cotton plantation.

So convincing seemed this model, especially since its prophecies seemed to have been borne out by events, that it came to dominate the thinking of an entire generation seeking for an intellectual alternative to the then dominant functionalist, diffusionist and evolutionist schools of 'modernization' theory largely developed in the USA, and a political alternative to capitalist growth-strategies and Communist dogma respectively. Here, the turning-point — which Foster-Carter has termed a 'classic paradigm-shift'[4] — was the devastating critique by Frank of *The Sociology of Development and the Underdevelopment of Sociology,* published in 1967.[5]

True, there were those who asked how we could speak of a capitalist *world*-system, when the expansion of Europe only began in the sixteenth century and was not finally completed until the nineteenth. To them, Wallerstein replied that a 'world-system' doesn't have to be *world-wide* at all; merely to operate at a level 'larger than any juridically-defined political unit'.[6] In his first volume (there are three more to come), he was attempting the initial task of charting the emergence and maturation of capitalism within the core of this system, Western Europe, and the subsequent extension of its trading activity across the globe during the mercantilist phase of capitalism in the sixteenth century.

But there were also those who felt uneasy about the notion that the world had become *capitalist* so early. They noted the persistence of pre-capitalist relations in colonial zones, and the use of the term 'capitalist' to describe what many would have simply called 'trade'. Nor did the colonies seem particularly capitalist in terms of the ways in which goods were produced or in terms of their political institutions. Moving to the present, it seemed difficult to reconcile the notion of a single world-system — which, for shorthand, I shall dub the 'monistic' approach — with the notion that there is not just one world, but three — or more.

Hence when people were asked how they reconciled these two different models, they were often taken aback. Until recently, the question was not often asked. Most of us operated not only with both monistic and 'pluralistic' models at one and the same time, but with *more than one version of the pluralist model.* I wish to argue here that this is a perfectly defensible heuristic procedure, not mere eclecticism or sloppy-minded empiricism, and a far more adequate response to the complexity of the real world than that provided by world-system theory. Like Foster-Carter, however, I have no desire whatsoever to engage in 'sectarian' denunciations of world-system theorists, in so far as I share with them certain fundamental assumptions: that all countries now form part of a world international order in which a handful of those countries which industrialized early have the capacity to keep the rest 'dependent'.

World-system theorists themselves, equally, do not simply insist that there is a world-system, *tout court*. But they start from the assumption that the world is the only meaningful framework within which the history of any particular country or group can be understood, and as Herbert Spencer classically observed in the nineteenth century, what distinguishes a system from a mere assemblage or congeries is not simply that a system is made up of parts, but that the relations between the parts *are themselves systematic* in such a way that changes in one part have effects on the other parts of the system. (We will take up later the question of the *degree* of systematicity, or, to put it another way, the degree of autonomy of the parts.)

So, the system theorists say, we must abandon the view that the world is composed of so many nation-states, each with 'separate parallel histories', for 'societies' are merely 'parts of a whole reflecting that whole' and it is this whole — 'one capitalist economic system with different sectors performing different functions' — that must therefore be taken as the basic logical and historical-sociological framework within which the 'society' can then be located. 'A state', he rightly observes, 'no more has a mode of production than does a firm. The concept "mode of production" describes an *economy*, the boundaries of which are . . . an empirical question.' In the case of the capitalist mode of production, its boundaries are world-wide.[7] 'To understand the internal class-contradiction and political struggles of a particular state, we must first situate it in the world-economy. And that economy is 'a single capitalist world-economy, which had emerged historically since the sixteenth century and which still exists today'.[8]

The parts within this whole, then, are determined by an international division of labour which allots 'tasks' as between the industrialized 'core' countries and those on the periphery: an international division of labour which is not just a functional division, but also a relationship of exploitation.

The core countries are those which began by successfully developing 'a complex variety of economic activities — mass-market industries . . . international and local commerce in the hands of an indigenous bourgeoisie, and relatively advanced forms of agriculture . . . with a high component of yeoman-owned land'. The peripheral countries became monocultural economies, spe-cializing in cash crops produced by coerced labour; and the semi-peripheral countries were those that went downhill, *de*industrializing and losing their former core status. In these latter, the forms of labour are typically intermediate between 'the freedom of the lease system and the coercion of slavery and serfdom . . . for the most part, sharecropping'.[9]

Now pluralists equally accept that the three or more worlds they identify are not economically, politically or culturally sealed off from each other, but form part of an over-arching world-order. But this world-order is not a capitalist world-order. Within it, there is a capitalist *sector*, which is still the most powerful sector. Within that capitalist sector, there are two distinct sub-sectors: the developed, industrial countries and the dependent, agrarian ones. But the world is no longer a capitalist world, whatever may have been the case in the past. Rather, the capitalist 'world', like the other 'worlds', has *another* major system alternative and rival, Communism. Hence the system as a whole is *neither capitalist nor Communist*, but a system of oppositions based on two major polarities: developed versus under-developed, and capitalist versus Communist. The world is constituted by the alliances and antagonisms between these sets of countries. Each set has as its main unit 'the country' (nation-state), though each country is especially influenced by the most powerful members of the set, the superpowers, and, because of 'unequal development' between its component zones, is not internally homogeneous either. Hence these cross-cutting pairs of polarities result logically in four boxes — four 'worlds', not three. Much of the confusion in the literature comes from trying to squeeze four types of country into three boxes and from the equally mystifying 'linear' procedure of merely listing countries according to indicators of levels of development.[10]

For world-system theory, there is only *one* world, divided into three components (completely different from the three 'worlds' discussed above): the core, peripheral, and semi-peripheral countries. Communist societies, though they have special characteristics of their own which set them off from capitalist countries, are not a set of countries *different in kind* from capitalist ones. Hence the Communist 'world', in this model, is decomposed, and its component countries also treated variously as core, peripheral, or semi-peripheral.

The growth of the world-system

The differences between monists and pluralists, then, arise at all levels and at all points: over the conceptualization of the whole; over the conceptualization of the parts; and over the nature of the relationship between the parts and the whole.

The point of departure is the assumption on the part of the monists that the world-system is a *capitalist* world-system. For myself, *per contra*, though I accept that the world did indeed . . . come into being as a single social system only during the period beginning with European mercantilist expansion and ending with modern imperialism, it did so as a system in which production for the market was conducted on the basis of non-capitalist relations, for the hallmark of mercantilist colonialism was the establishment of a mode of production in which forms of coerced labour persisted or were introduced which depended upon the direct use of force, and in particular upon the power of the state, which intervened directly in both constructing and operating the economy.

I would have liked to have called this the 'colonial' mode of production, had this term not been pre-empted (indeed invented) by Alavi and used in a different sense.[11] Alavi calls the initial, 'political' phase of colonialism that I am describing 'pre-capitalist'. Since this is a negative or residual designation — and to avoid confusion — I will call it, rather, 'mercantilist'. It is later displaced, at points in time that varied from the late eighteenth century for India to the Independence period for Latin America — by a dependent capitalism that he labels the 'colonial' mode of production. In his discussion of India, Alavi shows clearly the centrality of the political coercion of labour in the 'mercantilist' phase:

> the social relations of production were reconstituted on the basis of ownership of the land that was *conferred . . . under the authority of the colonial state,* the state of the metropolitan bourgeoisie. The landlords no longer exercised direct coercive force over the peasant. Their class power was now articulated through, and by, the colonial state.[12]

'The landlord became landowner' (p. 24) and the conformity of the producer was ensured by one of the East India Company's servants, 'a man with a cane who would watch over the weaver and beat him "to quicken his deliveries".'

Panikkar painted a similar picture for Java, twenty years ago:

> It was a silent but far-reaching revolution that the plantation-system introduced . . . Previously the Dutch had only been

merchants buying the spices and rice . . . and selling them at a profit. True, they used their powers to establish a monopoly, but beyond this the trading activities did not interfere with the life of the people. But the change over into a plantation economy involved the actual exploitation of labour, a control of the economic activity of the population and an effective supervision . . . in fact 'estate management' over a whole country. The island of Java became a plantation of the Dutch United East India Company . . . The relations between the sovereign [the Company PW] . . . and its subjects were in substance those of planter and coolie, in which the former was not merely the employer of labour, but also the authority vested with the rights of life and death . . . A whole people was . . . converted by the exercise of sovereignty into a nation of estate coolies, with their own natural aristocracy reduced to the position of foremen and superintendents (Panikkar, *loc. cit.*).

After this initial period of colonial transformation through the exercise of the direct political power of the East India Company, for example, the Industrial Revolution in Europe stimulated a second-stage transformation of the colonies. Now, Alavi emphasizes, 'the peasant was . . . driven to work for the landowner', not by 'direct [i.e. "extra-economic" PW] coercion', but by economic necessity — the threat of starvation.[13] By the late eighteenth century, then, the 'freedom' of the dispossessed — *capitalist* relations — was being substituted for the political compulsions of the mercantilist phase. Nevertheless, the new phase of capitalism was still 'colonial', he insists, in that 'the colonial economy . . . is only completed via the imperialist centre' and because it has been thenceforward 'distorted', since 'surplus value is realized only by and through the imperialist capital accumulation'.[14]

Today, the dependent economies originally implanted by political force can continue to work according to the logic of the world capitalist market, because they have become capitalist in their internal constitution; not merely because they are articulated to a world capitalist market. Yet political force is still needed because the dichotomy between the capitalism of the centre and the capitalism of the periphery creates new contradictions. The first of these is that the world was not simply integrated by imperialism. It was divided at the same time, between several major imperialist powers. The second was the resistance and counter-attack provoked in the colonized countries. And the third was the decisive breach in a capitalist world-system that had only very recently become established: the Bolshevik seizure of power in 1917.

Today, despite increasing differences between socialist states, then, the 'principal contradiction' that has developed since then has been the polarization of the world as between two different kinds of social system, the capitalist and the socialist respectively. World-system theorists, however, discount this difference as subsidiary, if not an illusion. For them, the fundamental divisions are those of core, periphery and semi-periphery. To my mind, this simply ignores the qualitative differences not only in the way Communist countries organize their economies, but also the distinctive features of the entire political and cultural life of those societies.

The discounting of these differences of social system is not peculiar to world-system theorists. Various *non*-Marxist 'Third Worldists', for example, in a spirit of 'a plague on both your houses', most explicitly and militantly expressed during the Bandung era of 'non-alignment', contrast their backwardness with the technological and economic levels obtaining in *both* the capitalist *and* the Communist industrialized societies.

For Wallerstein, Russia possesses a productive system in which 'private ownership is irrelevant',[15] a negative formulation which he amplifies elsewhere more positively: the Communist state is merely a 'collective capitalist firm so long as it remains a participant in the market of the capitalist world-economy' (*ibid,* pp. 68—9). Since there can only be *one* world-system at global level, and since existentially that system is a capitalist one, 'there are today no socialist systems in the world-economy' (*ibid,* p. 35), and the USSR is merely a 'core power in a *capitalist* world-economy' (*ibid,* p. 33, Wallerstein's italics).

This treatment of what to me is *the* central division in the world derives from a methodological assumption that capitalism is a system in which 'production is for exchange, that is . . . determined by its profitability on a market'.[16] In my view, this mistakenly locates the defining properties of capitalism in exchange and not in the relations that govern the way commodities are produced: in trade rather than in production.[17] A 'capitalist' system for Wallerstein is merely one in which the producer receives less than he produces. All then, are 'objectively proletarian', even peasants: 'Africans working on the land in the rural areas should be thought of as "peasants" who are members of the "working class", that is who sell their labour-power even when they are technically self-employed cash-crop farmers'. (*CWE,* p. 176).

Slaves, too, are 'proletarians'. In the literal, etymological sense the proletariat are those who have nothing but their children. Historically, they didn't even necessarily labour much, but were supported by state handouts — the *panes* that were coupled with *circenses.* But the term has come to be used to refer to those who produce (labour) but own no means of production. Because they work for those who do own these means they 'yield part of the value they have created to others'. Of course, there are variations in the amount yielded — all or part — and the forms which the surplus takes. 'Proletarian', in this sense, simply means any exploited producer, Wallerstein distinguishes eight varieties of proletarians, only one of which meets the classical model, and instances the wage-worker, the 'petty producer' (or 'middle peasant'), the tenant farmer, the share-cropper, the peon and the slave.

Rather than 'clarify' the phenomenon of exploitation (p. 290), what he acknowledges to be 'great differences between the various forms of labour' — the modes of social control entailed; the legitimating ideologies; the relative extent of reliance on force, persuasion, etc. — are reduced to a lowest common property: exploitation-in-general. The analogue, at system level, would be simply to treat capitalism, feudalism, slavery, etc. as variants of class society. Undoubtedly they are, but the analytical problems we face require going beyond this level of abstraction to the specific properties of each *type* of social relationship and institution.

Finally, I consider the model over-deterministic. It rightly emphasizes the impressive historical power of capitalism, which swept all existing political and economic competitors before it. But at the level of conceptualization, it depends upon 'the teleological assertion . . . that things at a certain place and time *had to be* a certain way *in order to* bring about later states of development . . . [that Wallerstein's] model of the world capitalist economy required and predicts'.[18] And at the level of implications for social action, it is a picture of a world *so* determined by capitalism, and particularly by those who control the core capitalist states, that it leads logically to fatalism and resignation, for it becomes difficult to see how any part of such a tightly-knit system can possibly break away. Indeed, movements which purport to do so, or already to have done so, are, we are told, either deluding themselves or those who believe in them, or both. But I say 'logically' because there is, happily, a contradiction between this 'managerialist perspective' and the 'metaphysical pathos' implicit in it, on the one hand, and the recognition that since the parts always stand in conflictful relationships, exploited classes and countries have always struggled to improve their position *vis-à-vis* the core countries and at times even tried to break out of the system altogether. Frank and Wallerstein not only recognize this, but laud it. Nevertheless, the model they use does not accord with their political stance.

For it is a model which emphasizes the capacity of the ruling classes to manipulate the system, and others in it, as they wish, whilst underplaying resistance to their domination. 'The system', at times, is as endowed with a logic, power and even quasi-personality as it is in that other major variant of Marxist system-theory, Althusserianism.[19] But systems do not take decisions. Ruling classes do. They try to run the system in their own interests. In this, overall, they succeed — by definition, otherwise they wouldn't continue to rule. But those they rule also try to maximize their interests. Such models therefore underestimate agency, especially resistance to domination. In the colonial context, they also underestimate the role of the 'collaborators' — those who possess or develop *local* political power and who use it actively to assist the colonizers, firstly, in establishing colonial institutions and then in participating in their operation as junior partners. [. . .]

The world today

As Marx was fond of quoting, 'the owl of Minerva only flies at dusk'. For no sooner were . . . accounts of the completion of capitalist mastery of the globe written, than the first major defection from that system occurred, in 1917, together with the first major stirrings within the colonized world of a new kind of future-oriented rejection of imperialism in China and India. Hence after the white-hot experience of those few years which saw the establishment of a Bolshevik regime in Russia, and the new growth of nationalism in the colonies, Lenin, whose *Imperialism,* written in 1916, had charted the irresistible expansion and ultimate hegemony of capitalism as a world-system, was, within a few years, predicting that world revolution would triumph, not in the heartlands of imperialism, as Marxists had hitherto asserted, but in what we now call the Third World.

Since that time, one-third of humanity has come to constitute a world-alternative to capitalism, dedicated, indeed, to 'burying' capitalism. Hence for most of us, the distinction between 'capitalism' and 'Communism' is the first pluralist distinction with which we commonly operate. The second is the distinction between the core countries of the capitalist world and the exploited segment of that world. The assumptions underlying these two polarities, however, are quite different, implicit rather than explicit, and sometimes contradictory. Further, they cross-cut each other.

What is usually taken for granted is not so much the mere number of 'worlds' identified as the nature of the underlying rationale which generates the typology itself as well as the component worlds. The first dichotomy has as its main criterion differences in 'social system' or 'ideology'; the second, differences in levels or kinds of technological development (e.g. in Marxist versions, 'levels of development of the productive forces'). These are usually measured in terms of production, productivity, output, etc, using 'indicators' such as GNP per head, income, etc.

In the former, the differences of social system usually identified — and rightly so — are those between capitalist and socialist (or Communist, according to taste) societies respectively. For Pierre Jalée, for instance, the world is 'sliced into two' in this way. But those who think in terms of technology/production divide the world into 'agrarian' and 'industrialized' or into 'rich' and 'poor', rather than capitalist and Communist. Note that Marxists are to be found in both camps, Jalée adhering to the ideological model; Frank and Wallerstein to models in which level and form of development (underdeveloped/developed) is more significant than social system or ideology.

Technology/output models are also characteristic of circles far removed politically from Frank and Wallerstein, notably the 'aid lobby', which embraces a wide liberal spectrum of Christians, non-Marxist socialists, pacifists and humanists who see differences between capitalist and socialist countries as insignificant in comparison with their respective statuses as either developed or underdeveloped countries. These are not, we should note, what are often called, for shorthand, 'class' models — based on differences between capitalism and socialism.

The most important specimen of this class of theory, surprisingly, is the Chinese world-model, which sees the First World as constituted by the superpowers; the Second World by a set of technologically developed intermediate countries; and the large Third World (which includes China) — the majority of mankind — the backward countries. This model thereby conflates the USA *and* the USSR together (though pride of place in the hierarchy of enemies of mankind is now given to the latter); puts Hungary and

Switzerland in the same bed; and makes no distinction between Haiti and Cuba. All this, of course, has implications for policy: China finds it perfectly acceptable to ally herself with Mrs Bandaranaike, with General Zia or with Chancellor Schmidt, or with 'feudal' or military allies, whilst at the same time directing its fiercest fire at the largest and pioneer Communist power.

To explain the apparent paradox of Chinese 'convergence' with technological (non-class) models, we have to turn to the ways in which they are located within wider systems of values. For the aid lobby, the implications are, firstly, that what is needed is 'aid' or 'development'; ideology and social system are secondary, if not irrelevant, or even barriers to growth; secondly, that the poorest and/or the non-aligned need/deserve it most. The Chinese, of course, don't accept *that*. Though they see themselves as a poor country, potentially leading the mass of humanity, the Third World, against the two super-imperialisms (First and Second Worlds), to do this they have to defend and promote socialism, of which their country is the only uncorrupted exemplar.

Yet socialism, as Wallerstein rightly insists, is based upon the nation-state. As a world economic system, on the other hand, socialism, he claims, does not exist. Yet he never examines the considerable degree of interdependence and trade within COME-CON, or the pattern of aid to countries like Cuba and Vietnam. If he did, there would seem no logical reason, according to his own criteria, for refusing the Communist trade bloc the title of a 'world system'. Nor — because his model is one in which 'the economic' is abstracted and given causal priority — does he consider the persisting political and military dependence of the Communist world, China apart, on the USSR.

This refusal of the status of world-system to the Communist world is, in fact perfectly consistent with his neo-Trotskyist world-view. Capitalism is, for him, a system of production for profit on the market; socialism, in principle, a system of production collectively organized, at world level, for the satisfaction of human wants. This is an implicit criticism of those socialists who think that internationalism (and equality) have to be deferred until the effective majority of nation-states go socialist, and the 'forces of production' then become fully developed. As against that scenario, pragmatists reply that socialism can only be developed within nation-states at present, and that even if this falls short of the ideal, it is the only practicable 'transition'. To that riposte the world-system theorists retort that the 'transition' will be permanent if *inter*national economic planning between socialist states does not begin, however cautiously, now.

However, basically all can agree that the current reality is not internationalism; not even 'socialism in one country' — true when there was only *one* socialist state, but not now, when there are many 'socialisms in one country'. Hence the distinguishing feature of all these socialist states today is their fierce nationalism, however much it may be discounted in the formal ideology of 'proletarian *inter*nationalism', but as characteristic of socialist states today as it was of the capitalist countries during their internal consolidation and mobilization for development, whether from the absolutist period onwards, or in the nation-building of Third World countries today.

State socialism, in the absence of world revolution, is, then, national socialism, oriented, internally, to consolidation and mobilization for development, and, externally, to the defence of the nation, not to cooperation with other like-minded countries to coordinate their economies through collective decision making.

Unequal development has left them, too, with a heritage of disparities, commonly culturally consolidated as national and ethnic superiority and inferiority, which make for potential conflicts, especially between advanced and backward countries, above all, between the superpowers and the rest. Hence, not only do socialist states not 'converge' with capitalist ones; they increasingly — 'polycentrically' — diverge from each other.[21]

In the development of the USSR, that country, endowed with abundant human and natural resources, was able to opt for a policy of largely autarkic development. Such an option is impossible for the smaller Communist states that have emerged subsequently. Hence only China has had a similar endowment which permitted her to found her economic development, too, on 13 years of virtual autarky, and only China has had the resources to stand up to the Soviet Union. The rest, especially micro-countries with a legacy of monocultural economies like Cuba, are forced into a new dependence, as the Chinese rightly point out, on the Communist superpower, as are those countries where newly-victorious Marxist regimes have inherited a devastated economy (Angola, Mozambique, Vietnam, Cambodia). Since the establishment of Communist power has everywhere been *both* a struggle to establish a new kind of social system *and* a *national* liberation struggle, nationalism is at flash-point in precisely those countries that have just — proudly and paid in blood — established their Communist regimes. It is between them that actual war has broken out.

In the last resort, then, the socialist state is not only a state, but a nation-state. Like *any* state, it resorts to force in defence of its interests if necessary. The phenomenon unthinkable to the pioneers of Marxism — of actual war between socialist states — was naturally delayed until after World War II, before when a plurality of socialist states to have war between them did not exist, but the first near miss did not take long — Yugoslavia's defiance of the Cominform, followed by actual invasion of Hungary and Czechoslovakia (leaving aside 'internal war' in East Germany and Poland). Socialist countries, living in a world-system of nation-states, have, therefore, to distinguish, politically, between their friends and their enemies (and those in between), and geopolitically, between those zones on their borders, remote countries and intermediate zones. It is this logic that informs Chinese foreign policy, and which explains their formal convergence with technologistic models of the world.

The two modes of 'slicing' the world, then, ideological and technological, can be diagrammatically and ideal-typically represented as follows (only the more important or typical countries being shown in Table 6.1.1):

Table 6.1.1

	Superpower	*Developed*	*Underdeveloped*
Communist	USSR	Eastern Europe, North Korea	China
			Vietnam, Cuba, Mozambique, Angola
Capitalist	USA	EEC and other Western European countries, Japan, Australia, South Africa	Rest of capitalist world

Ideological models read across the rows, treating all Communist and capitalist countries as falling into one or other of two great opposed 'camps'. Technical-economic models read down the columns, separating industrialized countries, whether capitalist or Communist, from agrarian. (China is separated by dots from the rest of the Third World, for those who wish to distinguish her for either sheer size or ideological heterodoxy.) But since both polarities reflect real properties of the world, all models in actual use inevitably combine elements of both. Analytically, two bipolar models, in any case, cross-cut each other so as to yield not *three* worlds, but four. This was not so serious when only two countries, China and Cuba, awkwardly aligned themselves with the 'non-aligned' capitalist Third World. Now that there are many under-developed Communist countries, that box becomes more import-ant. Now we have both industrialized Communist states and underdeveloped ones. I have already mentioned the dire con-sequences of trying to squeeze four worlds into three boxes. Four, because Communist countries, merely by virtue of being Com-munist, are not thereby necessarily either industrialized or agrarian, though historically, nearly all (East Germany and Czechoslovakia apart) began as agrarian societies, and backward ones at that. Leaving aside the capitalist 'newly-industrializing countries' (NICs), it has been the historic role and achievement of Communism to have carried out the industrialization which capitalism had previously refused and continues to refuse to the majority of Third World countries. The whole of Eastern Europe (except Albania), plus North Korea, is now industrialized, as UN agencies now recognize. But the newer Communisms remain agrarian and underdeveloped. [...]

Hence the two cross-cutting axes in the above diagram generate four logical *and real* boxes: capitalist-industrial; capitalist-dependent (underdeveloped/agrarian); Communist-industrialized; and Com-munist-agrarian.

The use of such categories, of course, implies a rejection of any model of the world-system which postulates merely one dominant world-system, one 'world'. Lest anyone object that such taxonomies are mere scholasticism, I would remind them that the world is complex, and that schematically forcing simplicity upon it 'by *fiat*' is dangerous, for ideas are real in their consequences and bad ones can lead to ineffective and mistaken behaviour in the real world, as the above discussion of Chinese foreign policy shows. Most inhabitants of the globe recognize that these are *not* mere academic abstractions but real differences in the nature of the world around them, the stuff of their lives, and therefore find the categories meaningful. To them, differences between capitalism and socialism or between developed and underdeveloped are not just verbal games, but significant realities. For those who, like refugees and migrants, have actually lived under more than one of these systems, say, the three million who fled the German Democratic Republic or the twelve million migrant workers from the peripheral

Mediterranean countries working in Western Europe, the proposition that they are living within a world-system is something they would readily recognize and endorse. But they have also moved because the differences between the four worlds were real to them.

The Turkish migrant is experiencing the logic of the capitalist world: the difference between development and underdevelopment — as have millions who constitute 'cheap labour' and have sought out its opposite — capital — either by going where the capital is — to 'runaway' zones and richer countries — or who have been sought out by capital in their own countries. The East German refugees, too, were reacting to the pull of superior development. But they were reacting even more to the second polarity: differences of social system.

At the risk, therefore, of boring Turkish migrants and East German refugees, and because world-system theory accords so much more importance to level of development rather than differences of social system, we now need to explain the nature of the parts of the world system: their *internal* constitution.

The First World consists of those advanced capitalist countries (with a few thoroughly capitalistic satellites closely dependent upon their markets for the export of primary products: Australia, New Zealand, Canada, in part, Denmark), in all of which the fundamental institutions of private ownership of the means of production and the operation of the economy according to the logic of market competition persist, but are now combined with heavy state intervention in the economy; in the political sphere, with parliamentary and institutional pluralism (separation of powers and legitimate opposition); and socially, with a developed welfare state, all of which qualify the primary ideology and practice of competitive possessive individualism.

The Second World cannot be treated simply as a component or set of components of the capitalist world-system. 'Genotypically, stratification in Soviet society is significantly different from stratification in the West', because it is 'subject to political regulation' in which the central goal of the leadership is 'a future Communist society' . . . characterized by a high level of social welfare, and indeed eventually by private affluence, while still under the undisputed dominance of the Party'.[22] Many labels have been used to describe the specificity of these social systems (and, I insist, *social* systems, not just economic): 'socialist', 'Communist', 'state socialist', 'state Communist', 'deformed workers' states', 'social imperialism', and so on. (I restrict myself to Marxist usages since it is with Marxist theoreticians that we are here debating.) Now it does matter what label we use, for labelling implies not only a cognitive statement, but also an evaluative one about the nature of the social system in question. Such statements are also 'real in their consequences'. But even those who use different labels can probably agree on at least certain central characteristics of those societies.

Economically, the means of production are not privately owned, and the economy is planned. Politically, they are run by an all-powerful Party, entry to which is determined not by ascription or wealth, but by meritocratic performance. Conformity to the official ideology and value-system is of course, a *sine qua non* in that performance, and its role becomes ever more important as monopoly of the means of opinion-formation and communication increasingly replaces terror as the decisive instrumentality of social control.

Both these worlds, as the Chinese insist, are dominated by a superpower — with decreasing effectiveness.

The Third World consists of a subset of underdeveloped capitalist countries, which, in Robin Jenkins' mordant formula, are 'owned, run and underdeveloped by the First World'.[23] The main political forms in these countries have been variants of demagogic populism, on the one hand, and repressive authoritarian right-wing regimes on the other, both strongly monocentric. Culturally, apart from such important trans-societal, but not universal 'world'-religions such as Islam, Christianity, Buddhism and Hinduism, they only share a common experience of imperialism and the pervasive influence of capitalist consumerist values.

The Second World, then, is distinct in *kind* from the First World. It is not, *pace* world-system theory, simply a part of the capitalist world-system, but a social system of a different order which constitutes a rival and an alternative to capitalism. Of course, this social system is no longer a disciplined bloc, as it was under Stalin. It is now 'polycentric', and the two largest Communist powers are at each others' throats. The smaller ones, as we have seen, depend heavily upon the USSR, but also resist the pressures coming both from that superpower and the pressures of their fellow-Communist regimes.

The most fundamental differences, however, exist between the two social systems. The antagonisms between nation-states are either epiphenomenal 'spin-offs' of these more fundamental conflicts, or historical legacies of unequal development. The 'principal contradiction', then, should not be obscured either because of *rapprochement* or because Communist powers can have capitalist allies. That the Soviet Union once allied itself with the leading capitalist countries against the Nazi invasion (and the obverse — that the capitalist powers allied themselves with, to them, unspeakable Communists) does not make either any the less Communist or capitalist. [. . .]

In world-system theory, it is the universal processes that are emphasized, and rightly so. Nor do differences of social system pass unnoticed. But they occupy a quite different place within their models. Whether a country is capitalist or Communist, for them, is not of first importance. What is important is whether or not they are core, peripheral or semi-peripheral countries: the position they are allotted in a 'hierarchy of occupational tasks' (*MWS*, p. 350).

Thus Wallerstein, as we have seen, follows the earlier Marxist and later Trotskyist tradition of dismissing 'socialism in one country' as a 'logical and actual impossibility', since socialism can only, in this view, be instituted on the basis of egalitarian, collectivistic political and economic decision making *between* countries, which would eventually necessitate world-government. But, Wallerstein observes 'world-government does not exist' (*ibid*, p. 348); therefore, logically, neither does socialism. There are not even 'socialist economies', only 'socialist movements controlling certain state machineries'. Hence, the claim that they are socialist 'needs to be treated with circumspection' (p. 351). 'It is', he declares, 'merely a variant of classic mercantilism' (*CWE*, p. 90); the Communist state merely, as we saw above, a 'collective capitalist firm' because 'it remains a participant in the market of the capitalist world-economy' (*ibid*, pp. 68—9).

This theory shares the common view that whatever it is, it isn't socialism, or the cognate view that it may have begun as such, but went wrong somewhere along the line. In my view, this is an idealist, stipulative defining-away of the problems of socialist construction, for the fact of the matter is that these countries are organized on quite different lines from capitalist societies in every institutional sphere and it is these internal arrangements that constitute their distinctive character. The crucial defining property is that they are 'command economies', based on collectivistic production and oriented to an ethic of 'social' distribution, an alternative world-system in which both the ends and the politically monistic means are based on an interpretation of *Marxism,* not of *laissez-faire* economic theory or bourgeois-democratic constitutional theory. Hence the notion that they are not 'really' *pure*

Marxist states ('deformed') and that the human costs of using these means — including twenty-five million dead — cannot be charged against socialism, constitutes both a philosophical sophism and a political evasion, an evasion that commonly takes the form of the argument that 'socialism (like Christianity) hasn't even been tried yet'. These are, however, states constituted precisely upon a 'reading' — not the only one possible — of Marx. [. . .]

Capitalism, like any other social system, is faced with trying to impose its cultural logic on the whole range of institutions inherited from the past. It need not do so absolutely, making everything anew, only at decisive points. Nor is it always *able* to uproot or transform everything: it has to come to terms with deeply-entrenched structures and values, 'reworking' the old so as to be at least minimally consistent with the requirements of the new. These include not only the socio-cultural legacy inherited from the *immediate* past, since societies typically embody a number of coexistent and conflicting modes of production and institutions which persist across whole epochs: 'Rather than presenting . . . a cumulative chronology, in which one phase succeeds and super-sedes the next . . . the course towards capitalism reveals a *remanence* of the legacy of one mode of production within an epoch *dominated* by another . . .'[24]

In the colonies, equally, modern colonial capitalism was stamped with the legacy not only of the immediate past epoch — that of mercantilist capitalism — but of the precolonial heritages that preceded it.

What is produced and who gets what, then, are culturally and not just economically determined. The crassest forms of reduction-ist materialism, we might note, are not those of Marxists, but of non-Marxists technological determinists and anthropological 'materialists'. And some Marxists have, at last, become aware of the concept of culture.

The myth of the 'nightwatchman' state has now been definitively exploded by Foster's analysis of the crucial role played by the state in England's Industrial Revolution. Moreover, despite his retention of 'base/superstructure' language, he has also demonstrated that the Industrial Revolution entailed, certainly economic and political class struggle, but also total confrontation of class *cultures* in every sphere of life, from schools to friendly societies, pubs and churches:[25] the enclosure of the land through parliamentary legislation; the dispossession of those who worked it; the making of a working class; the deportation of their leaders to England's Siberia, Australia, when they resisted; the counter-terror and espionage visited upon trade unions and popular organizations; in general, the removal of a proto-revolutionary threat in England that saw cotton operatives drilling nightly on the moors outside the mill-towns, and in which there were more troops quartered on the population than were used to defeat Napoleon in the Peninsular War; the mounting of a concerted campaign to undermine the independent political and social institutions built up by the working class, from churches to pubs; and the provision of charitable relief for some at least. In all this, the state played a central role. Within 30 years the threat of revolution had been removed.

Nevertheless, it is not ever thus: the extent and manner of state intervention have still to be taken as problematic, as matters for empirical historical investigation, for ruling classes are not often or always obliged to mount that kind of cultural counter-offensive. These relationships between polity, economy and the rest of the social order varied from epoch to epoch, just as they vary from society to society. They cannot be reduced to some schematic formula about '*the* role of *the* state' under capitalism, when, as we have seen, 'capitalism' underwent successive transformations. What proved distinctive about capitalism in the end, however, was its built-in drive toward infinity, (a drive which is today evoking the counter-philosophy of 'limits to growth'). This dynamic is equally typical of state socialism, devoted as it is to the raising of living-standards as its primary goal, a contrast most vividly seen when contrasted with those societies which possess what Sahlins had called 'Zen economies' or those he labels the 'original affluent societies',[26] those peoples who produce individually and appropriate socially.

Notes

1. Weidenfeld & Nicolson, London (revised 1967).
2. A good account of the debate is provided by Philip J. O'Brien (1975) 'A critique of Latin American theories of dependency', in Ivar Oxaal, Tony Barnett and David Booth (eds) *Beyond the Sociology of Development: economy and society in Latin America and Africa,* London, Routledge & Kegan Paul, pp. 7—27. See also the article 'André Gunder Frank: an introduction and appreciation', by David Booth, in the same volume (pp. 50—85).
3. K. M. Panikkar, (1954) *Asia and Western Dominance: a survey of the Vasco da Gama epoch of Asian history 1498—1945,* London, Allen & Unwin, p. 88.

4. Aidan Foster-Carter, 'Marxism versus dependency theory? a polemic', *Occasional Papers in Sociology,* No. 8, Leeds University, p. 13.

5. Originally in *Catalyst,* University of Buffalo; republished (1969) in *Latin America: Underdevelopment or Revolution,* New York, Monthly Review Press, pp. 21—94.

6. *The Modern World-System: capitalist agriculture and the origins of the European world-economy in the sixteenth century* (1974) New York, Academic Press, p. 15 (hereinafter '*MWS*').

7. Immanuel Wallerstein, (1979) *The Capitalist World-Economy* (hereinafter '*CWE*'), Cambridge University Press, p. 220, (Wallerstein's italics). This is not the second volume in Wallerstein's tetralogy, but a separate volume of collected essays.

8. *CWE,* pp. 68 and 53.

9. *Op. cit,* p. 38.

10. I discuss some typical instances in my (1979) 'How Many Worlds?' *Third World Quarterly,* Vol. 1, No. 2, pp. 100—7.

11. 'India and the colonial mode of production', (1975) *Socialist Register* 1975, (eds), R. Miliband and John Saville, London, Merlin Press, pp. 160—97.

12. 'The structure of colonial social formations', (for publication); my italics.

13. 'The structure of colonial social formations', pp. 21, 22.

14. 'India and the colonial mode of production', p. 192.

15. *CWE,* p. 34.

16. *CWE,* p. 159. Though elsewhere in *CWE* capitalism is characterized not in terms of the market, but as a system oriented to 'endless accumulation' (p. 272); 'the only mode of production in which the *maximization* of surplus creation is rewarded *per se*' (p. 285, his italics).

17. A line of criticism first developed by Ernesto Laclau (1977) in his 'Feudalism and capitalism in Latin America', *New Left Review,* 67, pp. 19—38, and by Robert Brenner (1977) in his 'The origins of capitalist development: a critique of neo-Smithian Marxism', *New Left Review,* 104, pp. 25—92. My intellectual debt to both of them will be obvious in these pages.

18. Theda Skocpol, 'Wallerstein's world capitalist system: a theoretical and historical critique', *American Journal of Sociology,* Vol. 32, No. 5, p. 1088 (my italics).

19. On which see the definitive philippic by E. P. Thompson (1978) *The Poverty of Theory,* London, Merlin, pp. 193—397. The resort to 'system-maintenance' arguments, and *ad hoc* 'repairs' where the historical evidence does not support the model; and the replacement of one inadequate form of 'outmoded theoretical category' by another (i.e. 'system' in its functionalist version) are noted by Skocpol (pp. 1088—9), since 'national system' has merely been displaced by 'world-system'.

20. 'The pillage of the Third World' (1968) New York, *Monthly Review Press,* Ch. 2.
21. See the incisive critique of 'convergence' theory by John H. Goldthorpe (1964) 'Social stratification in industrial society', in *The Development of Industrial Societies,* Sociological Review Monograph, No. 8, Keele, pp. 97−122.
22. John H. Goldthorpe, *op. cit.,* pp. 110, 112, 113.
23. *Exploitation: the world power-structure and the inequality of nations* (1970) London, Macgibbon and Kee, p. 18.
24. Anderson, *Lineages,* p. 421.
25. *Class Struggle in the Industrial Revolution: early industrial capitalism in three English towns* (1974) London, Weidenfeld & Nicolson.
26. Marshall Sahlins, (1972) *Stone Age Economics,* Chicago, Aldine.

6.2
The Nation-state and Imperialism

ERNEST MANDEL

Capital by its very nature tolerates no geographical limits to its expansion. Its historical ascent led to the levelling of regional boundaries and the formation of large national markets, which laid the foundation for the creation of the modern nation-state. Hardly had capital penetrated into the sphere of production, however, before its expansion brushed aside these national limits as well. It sought to create a genuine world market for all its commodities instead of only for the luxury goods which were traded internationally in the pre-capitalist age. The cheap mass production made possible by capitalist large industry was the most important weapon in this process, but it was not the only one. The state, as the servant of the bourgeoisie, had to use political and often military force to remove the obstacles which pre-capitalist classes and states represented to the unrestricted expansion of the capitalist export of commodities. Even the most 'liberal' and 'pure' bourgeois states of the age of freely competitive capitalism never dispensed with this use of coercion to capture international markets: it is enough to recall the examples of the opium wars conducted by British capitalism in China and the English campaigns of conquest and consolidation in India, the expansionary war of the USA in Mexico, France's war in Algeria, and so on.

The relation between the national and international expansion of capital thus determined a combined structure from the start, and this was reflected in the contradictory attitudes of the bourgeoisie when it came to the use of force on the international plane. In the final analysis, this relation was an expression of the law of uneven and combined development which is inherent in the capitalist mode of production. Capital innately tends to combine

Source: From E. Mandel, *Late Capitalism* (1975) London, New Left Books.

international expansion with the formation and consolidation of national markets. Depending on the development of productive forces and social conditions, therefore, world-wide capitalist relations of exchange bind together capitalist, semi-capitalist and pre-capitalist relations of production in an organic unity.

In the imperialist, monopoly capitalist phase of development of the capitalist mode of production, a new dimension was added both to the relationship between national and international expansion and to the relationship between capitalist laws of development and the deliberate use of state coercion for economic purposes. The *concentration* of capital on a national level — accelerated by the second technological revolution and the consequent substantial increase in the accumulation of capital needed for effective competition in the growth sectors of that time — increasingly led to the *centralization* of capital. This meant a radical reduction in the number of 'different capitals' competing with one another, until entire branches of industry were dominated by a handful of trusts, companies and monopolies, and common price agreements altered the economic behaviour of these monopolies. The resultant tendency for competition and hence also the expansion of the home market to be narrowed down then tended to generate overcapitalization, increasing export of capital and a growing capitalist interest not only in *periodic* gunboat expeditions to ensure a free path for commodity exports, but *permanent* military occupation and control of new fields of investment for capital exports. The universal division of the world by the big imperialist powers, itself a result of the contraction of capitalist competition on the domestic market, led to an intensification of international capitalist competition on the world market, to inter-imperialist rivalry and to the tendency for the world market to be redistributed periodically, including by means of armed force — in a word, by imperialist wars.

With the outbreak of the general structural crisis of capitalism in the twentieth century, however, a vast zone was subtracted from the capitalist world market by the victory of the October Revolution in Russia. The secular tendency was thereafter towards a further restriction of the geographical sphere of capital accumulation, which had come to the end of its victorious march around the globe with the incorporation of China at the close of the nineteenth century. International competition now increasingly rebounded from foreign markets back into the home countries of imperialism. These now gradually started to change from subjects into objects of the international competition of capital, as became clear especially during and after the Second World War. Simultaneously the coercive power of the bourgeois state intervened ever more directly in the economy, both to ensure the smooth collection of monopoly surplus-profits abroad and to guarantee conditions for smooth capital accumulation at home. This step marked the beginning of the late capitalist era.

[In the late capitalist era, capital has become internationalized in new forms. Since the Second World War in particular, the multinational corporation has characterized what Mandel calls 'the international centralization of capital'. These corporations organize production on an international level, an international division of labour, as well as trading across international boundaries. But since multinational corporations are not confined to the economy of a particular nation-state, their existence raises the problem of how they relate to nation-states — Eds' comment.]

Three variant types of relationship between the bourgeois 'nation-state' and the international centralization of capital must be distinguished here. The international centralization of capital may be accompanied by the international extension of the power of *one single state*. This tendency was already observable in the First World War, and in the course of the Second World War and its aftermath it found spectacular expression in the world-wide political and military hegemony of US imperialism. It basically corresponds to the first of the two major forms of the international centralization of capital: decisive control over an increasing share of the international apparatus of production by the owners of a single national class of capitalists, with foreign capitalists participating at most as *junior partners* The increasing international power of a single imperialist state is congruent with the growing international supremacy of a single national group of capital owners in the total field of international capital.

The international centralization of capital may also be accompanied by a gradual dismantling of the power of the various bourgeois national states and the rise of a *new, federal,* supranational *bourgeois state power*. This variant, which seems at least possible, if not even probable, for the West European EEC area, corresponds to the second major form of the international centralization of capital: the international fusion of capital without the predominance of any particular group of national capitalists. Just as no kind of hegemony is tolerated in these really multinational companies, the state form corresponding to this form of capital cannot in the long run involve the supremacy of a single bourgeois nation-state over others, nor a loose confederation of sovereign nation-states. It must rather take the form of a supra-national federal state characterized by the transfer of crucial sovereign rights.

It would certainly be a grave mistake to treat purely economic forces as absolute in this respect and to divorce them from the overall historical context. It is not only the immediate economic interests of capital-owners — or of the decisive group of capitalists in each phase of the capitalist mode of production — that the bourgeois state functions to safeguard. To perform this role effectively, in fact, it must also extend its activity to all the spheres of the superstructure, a task which presents great difficulties if it is undertaken without careful consideration of the national and cultural peculiarities of each particular nationality. In the late capitalist epoch, the direct or indirect economic functions of the bourgeois state apparatus are pushed so far into the foreground — by the constraint to gain increasing control over all the phases of the processes of production and reproduction — that under certain conditions monopoly capital may undoubtedly consider a certain division of labour between a supra-national federal state and cultural activity by nation-states a lesser evil. It should not be forgotten that in the United States, for example, all questions concerning education, religion and culture have — ever since the foundation of the Union — remained in the hands of the individual states rather than those of the federal government. Moreover, regulation of educational and cultural questions in various languages is by no means impossible (witness the cantonal system of the Swiss Federation).

The overwhelming compulsion towards the creation of a supra-national imperialist state in Western Europe — if the international centralization of capital were in fact to take the predominant form of capital fusion on a European level without the hegemony of any one national bourgeois class — springs precisely from the immediate economic function of the state in late capitalism. Economic programming within the nation-state is incompatible in the long run with multinational fusion of capital. The first will either force back the second, especially in periods of crisis or recession, or the second will have to create an international form of programming congruent with itself.

The choice between these two alternatives will ultimately come to a head over the issue of anti-cyclical economic policy, for a successful struggle against crises and recessions, in harmony with the interests of multinational companies, cannot be conducted on a national level; it can only be international. Since the instruments of anti-cyclical policy consist of monetary, credit, budgetary, tax, and tariff devices, such a policy must ultimately have at its disposal a uniform international currency, and a uniform international line on credit, budgeting and taxes (a common international trade policy is already a reality in the EEC). But it is impossible in the long run to have a common currency, a common budget, a common system of taxes and a common public works programme without a federal government with sovereignty in matters of taxation and finance, and with an executive power of represssion to enforce its authority — in other words, without a common state. It should also be said that big multinational companies also create a multinational capital market which in any case makes the survival of national currencies, national credit policies and national budgets and taxes more and more problematic.

The third possible variant of the relationship between the international centralization of capital and the development of the late capitalist state is that of a relative *indifference* of the former to the latter. The example of big British, Canadian and some Dutch companies, in particular, is often cited in this connection. It is customary to emphasize that these companies have international-ized their activities to such an extent, and produce and realize surplus-value in so many countries, that they have become largely indifferent to the development of the economic and social conjuncture of their mother country.

Without denying the existence of this variant, we may, however, regard it as basically no more than an intermediate between the two main variants outlined above. For on closer analysis we must distinguish between two different cases in the operations of these 'state-indifferent' companies. There is the case in which they operate in countries where national state power is itself so weak that it offers no resistance to the quest for additional profits by expatriate concerns: this is ultimately only true of, say, semi-colonial countries controlled by British capital. Or there is the case in which they operate in countries where the national state power that intervenes in the economy is independent of them. With further intensification of international competition and the cen-tralization of capital, the countries in the first group will tend to become increasingly liable to use what state power they have at their disposal to defend their own interests from possible com-petitors. In the countries of the second group, however, the position of 'state-indifferent' companies is liable to become increasingly threatened by those corporations that enjoy the real support of the local state apparatus. It is then only a question of time before such companies abandon their attitude of indifference to the state and seek to dominate either their home state or the local state within whose frontiers the bulk of their operations takes place. If they fail, these once 'indifferent' companies may have to pay a high price for having underestimated the role of the state in the epoch of late capitalism; they will ultimately fall to their competitors.

Thus the only significant conclusion that can be drawn from a consideration of this third variant is that even without international-ization of capital-ownership, the increasing internationalization of the production of surplus-value can lead to the 'denationalization' of a big company. In other words, if a company such as Philips or British Petroleum were to transfer a major part of its activities to North America, it would be more interested in the economic conjuncture of Canada or the USA than that of Britain or Europe, and would therefore have to make more use of the North American than the British state apparatus to pursue its economic interests, and might ultimately itself become a part of the US bourgeoisie, perhaps via its amalgamation with 'purely' North American concerns. There is no space here to investigate the probability of such a 'migration', beyond establishing its theoretical possibility. But any such evolution only leads us back by a detour to the first two variants.

All those writers who, like Charles Levinson, regard the multi-national companies as sovereign colossi overriding the power of the late capitalist state, tacitly assume a notion which was extremely popular in the 1950s and '60s, namely that big capital no longer needs to reckon with any serious difficulties in sales or realization, or with major social crises, and that even in times of so-called 'bad business' their investment activity proceeds unscathed. In other words, they simply presuppose that there is no further need for the state to intervene in the economy in order to master acute cyclical and structural crises, or great eruptions of the class struggle. The recession in West Germany in 1966−7; the French revolt of May 1968; the 'hot autumn' in Italy in 1969−70; the US recession of 1969−71; and the worldwide recession in all the imperialist countries in 1974−5, have shown the unrealism of this assumption. In fact, the one certain prediction that can now be made is that multinational companies will not only need a state, but a state which is actually stronger than the 'classical' nation-state, to enable them, at least in part, to overcome the economic and social contradictions which periodically threaten their gigantic capitals.

These three variants of the possible relationship between the international centralization of capital and the late bourgeois state provide three possible models for the international structure of the metropolitan political system of imperialism in the coming years and decades.

1. The model of *super-imperialism*. In this model a single imperialist power possesses such hegemony that the other imperialist powers lose any real independence of it and sink to the status of semi-colonial small powers. In the long run such a process cannot rest solely on the military supremacy of the super-imperialist power — a predominance which could only be possessed by US imperialism — but must drive towards direct ownership and control of the most important production sites and concentrations of capital, banks and other financial institutions elsewhere. Without such direct control, in other words, without the immediate power to dispose of capital, there is nothing to ensure that in the long run the law of uneven development will not again so change the economic relationship of forces between the major capitalist states that the military supremacy of the foremost imperialist power is itself undermined.

The advocates of the notion of 'super-imperialism' accordingly see the major US international companies as the real — potential or virtual — rulers of the world market. They doubt the ability of the big European and Japanese companies to provide effective competition to their US counterparts in the long run, because the latter are deemed to be too technologically backward, possess too little capital strength, or lack 'managerial skills'. Alternatively, they doubt the political will of European or Japanese companies, even if perhaps capable of 'purely economic' competition, to resist US competition, when such obstruction might deal a fatal blow to the military and political centre of contemporary world imperialism and hence in the final resort to themselves. In this respect, Poulantzas's contention that we ourselves have been misled by 'territorial' statistics into underestimating the supremacy of American capital (including European-based US corporations) is typical, but it has no foundation. Our arguments on this score have always been based on the competition between various international corporations *owned* by different (US, European or Japanese) groups of national capitalists. Philips, Fiat, ICI, Siemens or Rhône-Poulenc are owned by European capitalists, just as Mitsubishi, Hitachi, Matsushita or Sony are owned by their Japanese counterparts, and General Motors, Exxon, General Electric or US Steel are owned by American capitalists.

2. The model of *ultra-imperialism*. In this model the international fusion of capital has advanced so far that all critical differences of economic interest between the capital owners of the different nationalities disappear. All major capitalists have spread their capital ownership, production of surplus-value, realization of surplus-value and capital accumulation (new investments) so evenly over different countries and parts of the world that they have become completely indifferent to the particular conjuncture, the particular course of the class struggle and the 'national' peculiarities of political development in any particular country. Incidentally, it is obvious that such a complete internationalization of the world economy would also mean the general disappearance of national economic cycles. In this eventuality, all that would remain would be competition between big multinational companies; there would no longer be any inter-imperialist competition proper — in other words, competition would finally be freed from its starting point in the nation-state. Naturally in such a case the imperialist state would not 'wither away'; all that would vanish is its role as an instrument of inter-imperialist competition. Its role as the central weapon for the defence of the common interests of all the imperialist owners of capital from the threat of economic crises, the insurgency of the proletariat within the imperialist countries, the revolt of the colonial peoples, and the power of non-imperialist states abroad, would be more pronounced than ever before. Only this state would no longer be an imperialist nation-state but a supra-national imperialist 'world state'. Many advocates of the thesis of the growing 'indifference' of multinational companies towards the power of the bourgeois state come very close to this notion of a nascent 'ultra-imperialism'; this is especially so in the case of Levinson.

3. The model of continuing *inter-imperialist competition,* taking new historical forms. In this model, although the international fusion of capital has proceeded far enough to replace a larger number of independent big imperialist powers with a smaller number of imperialist superpowers, the counteracting force of the uneven development of capital prevents the formation of an actual global community of interest for capital. *Capital fusion is achieved on a continental level, but thereby intercontinental imperialist competition is all the more intensified.* The novelty of this latter-day inter-imperialist competition, by comparison with the classical imperialism of Lenin's analysis, lies in the first instance in the fact that only three world powers confront each other in the inter-

national imperialist economy, namely US imperialism (which has largely pocketed Canada and Australia), Japanese imperialism and West European imperialism. The further development of Japanese imperialism, in the direction of either independence or fusion with the big US companies, would here probably decide the final outcome of this competitive struggle. Secondly, of course, there is the fact that in the present socio-political world conjuncture, which is basically unpropitious to capital, global inter-imperialist world wars have become extremely unlikely, if not impossible. This does not, of course, exclude either local inter-imperialist wars (by proxy, so to speak), new colonial wars of pillage, or counter-revolutionary wars against national liberation movements — let alone the danger of a nuclear world war against the bureaucratized workers' states.

The last of the three models set out above is thus by far the most probable, at least in the visible future. In the final analysis, the respective realization of each of these models depends on the predominant form taken by the international centralization of capital, however important may also be the temporarily auto-nomous weight of military or political forces.

Super-imperialism can only be realized if the monopoly capital of the hegemonic imperialist power acquires a decisive degree of *capital ownership* within its most important potential competitors. Hitherto US imperialism has failed to achieve this in either Western Europe or in Japan. The financial capital of these countries is largely independent of its US counterpart. US banks play only a marginal role in their economies. Although US ownership of industrial capital is of greater import, and especially in so-called growth sectors is sometimes well above the average, its current share can be estimated at little more than 10—15 per cent of total capital investments. Nor is any tendency evident for this share to grow uninterruptedly; it seems rather to be levelling out. So far, therefore, it emphatically cannot be said that the West European or Japanese states have sunk to the status of semi-colonies. They pursue independent policies in trade, foreign and military affairs, even if this independence is exercised within the framework of a common alliance against common class enemies. It should be noted that this alliance fully accords with the common interests of all capitalist classes and by no means only with the particular interest of US imperialism. Indeed, it may be added that since the beginning of the 1950s the relationship of forces between US imperialism and its West European and Japanese counterparts has continuously altered to the disadvantage of the former and the advantage of the latter.

Evolution of Economic Relationship of Forces
USA — Western Europe — Japan

Percentage of Total Capitalist World Industrial Output

	1953	1963	1970
USA	52	44	40.5
EEC	16	21.1	22
UK	10	6.4	5
Japan	2	5.3	9.5

Percentage of Total Capitalist World Exports

	1953	1963	1970
USA	21	17	15.5
EEC	19.3	27.8	32
UK	9.7	8.7	7
Japan	1.7	4	7

Percentage of Total Capitalist World Gold and Foreign Reserves

	1953	1963	1970
USA	43	25	8.3
EEC	11.5	29.5	37.0
UK	5	4.3	3.5
Japan	1.5	3.0	11.2

Percentage of Total Capitalist World Foreign Investment

	1960	1971
USA	59.1	52.0
UK	24.5	14.5
France	4.7	5.8
W. Germany	1.1	4.4
Japan	0.1	2.7
Switzerland		4.1
Canada		3.6
Netherlands		2.2
Sweden		2.1
Belgium		2.0
Italy		2.0

Developments in this field, however, have by no means yet reached their conclusion. The intensification of international capital competition has been gathering momentum for a number of years, and sooner or later must lead to a new and qualitatively higher stage of the international centralization of capital. The number of important international companies is today estimated at approximately 800. Perlmutter has predicted that by about 1985 the capitalist world economy will be dominated by some 300 such companies. In a somewhat impressionistic work, Lattes foresees some 60 multinational companies sharing the world market between them. Will these be solely US companies, or US companies on the one hand, and European and Japanese, or European, Nippo-European and Nippo-American companies on the other? The answer to this question will doubtless settle the probability or improbability of the model of super-imperialism. In the end everything will depend on which of the two major forms of the international centralization of capital ultimately triumph, in the event of a further postponement of the proletarian revolution in the metropolitan countries.

It is plain that the so-called multinational companies of the USA enter this new phase of intensified competitive struggle with two critical advantages over their rivals: they at present possess on average much greater capital resources (three or four times that of their most important competitors) and a much more powerful state at their disposal. Their West European and Japanese counterparts will only be able to survive if they in turn undergo a rapid process of international mergers, attain a scale of capital ownership and productive capacity equal to that of their largest US rivals and, at least in Western Europe, establish a federal state on an equal political and military footing with the USA. The fate of the EEC in the next and next-but-one recessions will thus probably decide the possibility or impossibility of an independent West European superpower — and therewith the chances of realization of a US super-imperialism.

For the ultra-imperialist model to become a reality there must first be a much greater degree of international centralization of capital than appears to be in prospect today. Above all, it presupposes the massive participation of large European and Japanese shareholders in the running of the most important US companies, which implies a reduction in native US ownership of these companies to relative minority holdings. Today this seems even more unlikely than a parallel reduction in the ownership pattern of large European and Japanese companies.

It is certainly true that the rapid extension of European and Japanese exports to the American market — which today plays the same central role on the world market as the British domestic market once did in the epoch 1780—1880 — is accompanied by a tendency towards wider European and Japanese capital investment in the United States. Although this movement is not yet anything like as important as US capital investment in Western Europe, it nonetheless cannot be discounted as insignificant. Besides direct investments of European firms in the USA, some notable absorptions of US companies by European corporations should also be mentioned. British Petroleum has acquired *de facto* control over Standard Oil of Ohio, and a big stake in Alaskan oil. Fiat now possesses similar control over the road-building equipment division of Allis Chambers. Olivetti has bought up Underwood. It is also true that the World Bank and other international organizations have promoted common projects linking many of the most important industrial giants of the world. In addition, conscious efforts have been made by lobbies inspired by 'Atlantic' ideology to achieve an increasingly close community of interest and interlocking of capital between Europe and North America. But the merciless dictates of competition outweigh political insight or notions of world citizenship in the conduct of the imperialist bourgeoisies. *The main tendency of the intensifying international competitive struggle today is not for big capital to merge on a world scale, but for several imperialist formations to harden in their mutual antagonism.*

The model of continuing inter-imperialist rivalry consequently seems the most probable and realistic of the three, even with the proviso that an international fusion of capital must be achieved with some speed in Western Europe and Japan to safeguard the independence of the imperialist classes of these zones from US imperialism. In the final analysis, the greater probability of this third model is linked to the question of whether the second major form of international centralization will effectively counter the first — in other words, *whether the international centralization of capital in the coming decades will take the form of a combination of US-dominated companies on the one hand, and internationally fused, multinational companies on the other.*

It is true that up to now, direct capital interpenetration inside the EEC has advanced rather slowly. Between 1961 and 1969, there were a total of 257 fusions between firms from several EEC member countries, as against 820 fusions between firms of member countries and firms of third countries, and 1861 fusions between firms of the same country. Juridical and organizational difficulties — which correspond in the final analysis to the absence of a West European federal state — have played an important role in slowing down capital interpenetration within the EEC. In these circumstances, cooperation between firms of different European countries has developed more rapidly than outright fusion. Examples are Unidata, the computer consortium created by Philips (Netherlands), Siemens (West Germany) and CII (France); and Eurodif and Urenco for the construction of enriched uranium plants, the fuel for light nuclear reactors.

The more the rhythm of growth of the international imperialist economy slows down, the more acute will become the social contradictions within the most important capitalist states. The fiercer the international competition of capital, the more these social contradictions will be further sharpened, and with them the attempts of each individual imperialist class to resolve its particular contradictions and difficulties at the expense both of its own workers and its rivals — in other words, to export them to the countries of their competitors. The outcome of the intensifying class struggles of the coming years will in turn co-determine the rhythms and forms of the international centralization of capital. The more the class struggle swings upwards from campaigns over the distribution of the national income to attacks on the control of the means of production and assaults on capitalist relations of production, the more independent will be the stance of the working class towards *all* variants of the international centralization of capital, the more will it avoid the road of any policy of the 'lesser evil', and, in Western Europe, the less bemused it will be in the conflicts between US hegemony, projects for an 'Atlantic Community', a European federal state as a new imperialist superpower or a continuation of the plethora of small European states; and the more confidently and vigorously it will assert its own standpoint — for the United Socialist States of Europe!

In conditions of decelerated economic growth and intensified international competition, any temporary solution to the problem of the international centralization of capital can only be achieved at the expense of the working class. For every such solution is in the end determined by a sudden increase in the average rate of profit in the monopoly sector, and in the coming years an increase of this kind can only be secured by raising the rate of surplus-value, in other words, by intensified exploitation of the working class. The fact that the West European working class, and later the North American and Japanese proletariats, will resist such an intensification of exploitation can be seen from the practical experience of the past four years.

Above all, a more savage attack on real wages can be expected in the USA itself. American industry could sustain its substantial wage differential for decades because of its lead in productivity. Today this lead is disappearing in many branches of production. In the period from 1950 to 1965, the average productivity of labour in the USA grew by 2.6 per cent a year against 4 per cent in Western Europe and 6.8 per cent in Japan. In the period from 1965 to 1969 these figures were respectively 1.7 per cent, 4.5 per cent and 10.6 per cent. In 1973—4, labour productivity stopped growing altogether in the USA. In these circumstances, US capital has an urgent interest in reducing wage differentials. Thus in 1968 output per employee in the steel industry was the same in the USA, Belgium and Japan, whereas wage-costs per hour in the USA were twice as high as in Belgium and four times as high as in Japan.

The international centralization of capital must be understood as capital's attempt to break through the historical barriers of the nation-state, just as national (and tomorrow perhaps supra-national) economic programming represents an attempt partially to overcome the barriers of private ownership and private appropriation for the further development of the forces of production.

6.3
The Sources of the New Cold War

FRED HALLIDAY

In the course of his essay 'Notes on exterminism', Edward Thompson remarks that it is 'now beside the point' to investigate the historical responsibility of the main protagonists for the current arms race. 'To argue from origins,' he writes, 'is to take refuge from reality in moralism'. It is the great merit of Thompson's argument to bring home to every reader, forcefully and unforgettably, the urgency of political action now to fight against the danger of nuclear extermination. The injunction to dispense with investigation of origins derives its legitimacy in part from this overriding call to a sense of immediate priority. Rejection of historical inquiry, however, also involves something more than this. For it underlies many of the very analytic themes upon which the category of exterminism rests — in particular, the view that the arms race now under way is essentially irrational, impermeable to the normal methods of historical investigation and the political judgments which may follow from this.

Yet it is precisely here that a problem arises: for the validity or otherwise of some of the main themes of the argument for exterminism must depend upon judgments about post-war world history. In this sense, far from being irrelevant, historical investigation may have a central place in our understanding of the present world crisis and in our framing of political programmes designed to check and overcome it. Thompson is right to warn us that such an investigation could become purely moralistic — an ascription of blame to one side, of innocence to another. But it *need* not be moralistic: it can rather be a study — as calm and measured as we can make it — of the responsibility, distributed and differentiated,

Source: From 'Exterminism and cold war' in E. Thompson *et al.* (eds) *New Left Review* (1982) London, Verso, pp. 289–329.

of the two major world powers, as well as of other historical forces at work, in the emergence of the exceptionally perilous international situation in which we now live. In this perspective, the case for exterminism can be examined, confirmed or challenged, by an inquiry that seeks to use an analysis of recent international politics to inform the present direction of the peace movement. In the face of the possible end of modern history as we know it, the pertinence of historical investigation is particularly strong.

There are three themes in Thompson's essay which we should address:

(1) that the nuclear arms race has acquired an autonomous dynamic in both domestic and international politics, one that is out of control, inertial, and irrational;

(2) that it is this dynamic, the logic of exterminism, which constitutes or structures world politics by establishing itself as the field of force of all state-to-state relations;

(3) that distinctions between the USSR and the USA are secondary compared to their common involvement in this exterminist logic, which generates an isomorphism of the two societies, born of their shared commitment to the nuclear arms race. Certain political conclusions are evident once these theses obtain explanatory force.

What follows here is an unashamed search for origins: our purpose will be precisely to see how far historical evidence bears out the themes of the case for exterminism. We must all accept that the world is threatened with annihilation and that it is an ethical and political imperative for every socialist to fight this possibility with all their might. But this is not the same thing as saying that this threat *constitutes* the overall structure of world politics today, or that the arms race defines the very nature of the societies of the major powers. In reply to Thompson, we will argue three alternative theses, matching the three arguments for exterminism set out above:

(1) that whilst nuclear weapons introduce entirely new possibilities of civilizational destruction, their manufacture is no more inertial, escaping any human social or political control, than other state policies have been in the past or present — but reflects identifiable processes of conscious agency and decision;

(2) that the deepest structures of international politics are constituted by the conflicts between and within social

systems — conflicts that are profoundly shaped, but not displaced, by the nuclear arms race;

(3) that despite a common participation in the arms race, the Soviet Union and the United States are fundamentally asymmetrical societies, governed by different histories and political priorities, and with quite distinct responsibilities for the current escalation of tension in world politics.

The recent past is not 'the irrational outcome of a collision of wills': nor, on the other hand, is it — any more than any other period of world history — the product of 'a single causative historical logic'. It is rather the product of the convergence of a *plurality* of historical processes, each involving deliberate human action and calculation, which have in their combination yielded us the dangers of the new cold war.

The category of cold war itself recurs in two key passages of Thompson's essay. On the first occasion he writes: 'What is known as the "cold war" is the central human fracture, the absolute pole of power, the fulcrum upon which power turns, in the world'. Later he remarks: 'No doubt we will have one day a comprehensive analysis of the origins of the cold war, in which the motives of the agents appear as rational. But that cold war passed, long ago, into a self-generating condition of cold war-ism (exterminism).' The general direction of the essay, it might be said, is to suggest that the cold war can now be equated with the nuclear arms race, in a single complex — exterminism — that has become the over-arching principle of world politics. In his discussion of arms production and its economic dimensions, Thompson later intro-duces a further element into his argument by identifying all major military expenditure with exterminism. We therefore have a fourfold equation: military expenditure = nuclear arms race = cold war = central fracture in world affairs. Yet forceful as it is, this equation is questionable: the four elements cannot be so easily elided.

First of all, the overwhelming bulk of military expenditure is today on conventional, not nuclear, armaments: this is not a trivial point, since much of the power of the argument for exterminism lies in its claim that the nuclear component, as a pervasively irrational and annihilatory force, has become the dominant principle of modern social and economic organization. Yet in both Russia and the USA, most arms expenditure is for those con-ventional purposes which are still regarded as comparatively rational in intent and non-exterminist in effect. Secondly, for all their death-dealing potential, it is difficult to describe the confrontation of the two major nuclear weapons systems as the central fracture in world affairs. It would be more accurate, we would argue, to say that they at once dramatize and endow with infinitely greater risk a conflict whose bases lie elsewhere — above all in the conflict between capitalist and post-capitalist worlds. This constitutive conflict is in its turn overdetermined by at least four others: the contrast between parliamentary democracies and authoritarian bureaucracies, the struggle between imperialist states and their former colonies, the contradictions internally dividing each type of society, and finally the rivalry between different powers within capitalist and post-capitalist worlds alike. The confrontation of capitalist and post-capitalist systems became a *global* conflict for the first time in 1945. It was a peculiar and largely accidental fate that this globalization coincided historically with the first production and use of nuclear weapons by one side. It is perfectly possible to imagine a — far direr — history in which the atomic bomb, if it had emerged a few years earlier, would have coincided rather with *inter-capitalist* military conflict, in the hands of Hitler as much as of Roosevelt. (Just as it is also possible, not only to imagine but to hope, and struggle for, a time when there is no longer a coincidence between the break beyond capitalism and the entrenchment of an authoritarian post-revolutionary bureaucracy.) The analytic task presented to us by the history that has unfolded since 1945 is first and foremost to trace out the connections between globalized social conflict — in all the complexity of its several dimensions — on the one hand, and the nuclear arms race on the other, rather than to elide these two distinct processes into a single logic.

It is also debatable whether the term 'cold war' is best used as a description of the whole of this period, since the social and political conflicts criss-crossing on an international scale have known periods of markedly greater and lesser intensity — phases that have had important and varied consequences for the arms race itself. The term 'cold war' was originally used to designate one, particularly acute, period of Soviet—US confrontation, distinct from hot war, but also from periods of greater collaboration, such as the wartime alliance or the detente of the early seventies. The first cold war lasted from 1947 to 1954. In this sense cold war is a phase or mode of globalized social conflict, rather than simply coextensive with it. Seen in this light, the cold war of the late seventies, and the increased levels of military expenditure associated with it, mark a new phase of international conflict: rather than confirming an inexorable and irrational process, we shall argue that the renewed incidence of cold war today raises questions of historical explanation as to why world politics deteriorated when and as they did. Any such explanation would have to give great emphasis to the nuclear arms race: but it could not reduce the new cold war to that race, nor could it treat the arms race itself as an independent variable determining all other political developments. It is in the interaction of nuclear arms race with globalized social conflict that the roots of the new cold war lie.

The late 1970s and early 1980s have been marked by a drastic heightening in the pitch of world politics, a much greater emphasis upon the need for military preparedness on all sides, more violent ideological campaigns against the respective evils of opposing camps. These changes have coincided with renewed calls for unity within American and Soviet blocs alike and official intolerance of dissent. In other respects this new cold war differs from the first: US—Soviet negotiations on arms limitation do continue, in contrast to the complete break in substantive diplomatic communications of the earlier period; the predominance of the USA *vis-à-vis* the USSR and *vis-à-vis* its capitalist allies is greatly reduced; the two major post-capitalist countries are divided; the Third World plays a much more prominent role. Yet, despite these differences, the two cold wars have common features and contain common risks of war.

The election of Reagan in November 1980 marks the full maturing of a new cold war, but the shift in world politics predates that. By 1978, half way through the Carter Administration, the main elements of a new cold war were already in place; while the tensions of this period have their root in the attempt by the USA in the early seventies to use SALT talks and trade as a means of controlling Soviet foreign and defence policy, and in the rebuffs which this attempt encountered — on the battlefields of Indochina and Angola, and in the continued enhancement of Soviet military capacity within the framework of the SALT-I agreement. In essence, the new cold war is a response by the USA and its allies to the failure of detente as a means of waging globalized social conflict to their own advantage. Neither side abandoned its commitment to this conflict; the Russians have essentially pursued the same military and foreign policies as before, with somewhat improved means for doing so. It is this Soviet refusal to alter traditional policies which, from the mid-1970s onwards, produced a change of posture in the West and the ultimate abandonment of detente. The deterioration in East—West relations was therefore neither irrational nor inevitable: it was not irrational in that it reflected responses by conscious political agents in the United States to what they saw as a challenge to capitalist power, and it was not inevitable in that this new cold war has been the product not of one inertial process but of several convergent developments in international politics, whose origins are distinct from each other and were not pre-programmed to coincide chronologically. It is the combination of these forces which explains the genesis of the new cold war with its accompanying intensification of the arms race.

Within the context of the 1970s, there are five processes which appear to have played a major causal role in precipitating the new cold war. Whilst they have operated on different timescales and exercised different forms of influence, it is their combination and mutual reinforcement which essentially accounts for the termination of detente. These five causal determinants are:

(1) the erosion of the US nuclear superiority by the USSR;
(2) a new wave of Third World revolutions;
(3) the rise of a new militarism in the USA;
(4) the political involution of post-revolutionary states;
(5) the sharpening of inter-capitalist contradictions . . .

The leading theme of new cold war advocates in the West has been the need to redress the shift in the East—West military balance. Allegedly, the USSR has drawn ahead and the West has to catch up: to 're-arm', 'rebuild our defences', 'restore the balance' and so forth. At one level, this argument is simply a myth: the West has not disarmed, so it cannot *re*-arm, and the Soviet Union has not attained superiority, in either the nuclear or the conventional fields. Yet as with all ideology this apparent set of falsehoods conceals certain real changes, to which the rhetorical calls to re-arm provide an encoded guide. For the past decade has seen a substantial improvement in the USSR's military potential, one that has reduced or — in certain limited fields — ended the overwhelming superiority which the West once enjoyed. What is now being called for is a new drive for superiority, an attempt to regain the margins of earlier decades under the guise of redressing an imbalance supposedly in the Soviet Union's favour. [. . .]

The contest between the two blocs has never been fought out in direct confrontation in the industrialized world since 1945. It has always been mediated through political and military conflicts in the Third World. It is here that during the 1970s an important shift in the correlation of international forces took place. The twin assumptions of the Western conception of detente proved in effect to be mistaken. The Third World could not be stabilized, and the USSR could not be dissuaded from providing assistance to unwelcome movements or states within it. Although often presented in a fused form, as a Soviet threat itself responsible for unpalatable changes in the Third World, the actual pattern of events has typically involved quite distinct elements: an autonomous maturing of social tensions in Third World countries, followed by a subsequent, separate, Soviet response to these. [...]

If the two immediately dynamic determinants of the present international crisis lie in the historical processes just discussed, these cannot on their own account for its full configuration. For the new cold war to emerge, the proximate causes in the arms race and in the Third World had to be complemented by reinforcing conditions within the Great Powers themselves. In fact, developments in both the USA and the USSR independently provided such a concomitance in the past decade. The third major determinant of the new cold war must be located within the world's major capitalist state. Whatever the importance of the reduction in Western nuclear superiority or the advance of Third World revolutions in this period, these needed translation into American domestic politics in order to produce the changes that culminated in the Reagan Presidency. Here, once again, no single synchronized logic was at work. For the forces within US society which eventually triumphed with the electoral victory of Reagan in 1980, and are now bidding to change the political economy of American capitalism, have been largely independent of wider movements in the outside world, just as their gradual ascent long *predates* the international convulsions of the late seventies.

Internal political changes in the USA, autonomously engendered within its continental economy and society, have thus had a formative impact on the turn towards a new cold war in the last few years. Developments within Europe and Japan provided no adequate counter-weight to the trend towards a new belligerence in Washington. But the ability of the Western powers to mobilize popular support and credibility for a confrontation with the USSR required certain objective preconditions within the adversary camp. The fact that the depiction of Soviet policy by Reagan and Haig is false does not mean that the USSR and other post-revolutionary states have played no part in generating the new cold war. For if US denunciations of Soviet military 'superiority' or 'violations' of detente in the Third World are ideological, there have been several respects in which the evolution of the USSR — not to speak of China — over the past decade or more has indeed contributed to the present dangerous international situation. [. . .]

The fifth component of the contemporary phase of cold war, however, is qualitatively new. Inter-capitalist contradictions have re-emerged to play a major role in the world politics of the seventies and eighties.

These contradictions are not so much *active determinants* of the new cold war (like the relative decline of Western nuclear superiority or the new wave of Third World revolutions), or *positive or negative conditions* of it (like the rise of the new militarism in the USA, or the involution of the USSR, respectively), as what can be termed its *complicating context.* The contradictions themselves are complex ones. They involve not only a revival of traditional inter-imperialist tensions, in new forms and within new limits, but also conflicts between industrial and less industrial — that is, imperial and former colonial — states within a common capitalist world, and finally antagonisms between the former colonial states themselves. The emergence of this skein of contradictions is still very recent; and the consequences of each of them for the future of world peace remain hard to foresee. But there can be little doubt that, so far, their net effect has been to increase rather than decrease the dangers inherent in the build-up of the new cold war. [. . .]

All-round confrontation with the USSR serves to create conditions of quasi-emergency in which the USA can reassert its suzerainty over the other advanced capitalist countries. [. . .] Such, we would argue, have been the main developments that have given rise to the new cold war. If unchecked, their momentum could lead towards a Third World War, that would realize the exterminist potential of the present arms race. With this, we return to the question posed at the outset of this chapter namely, the relevance of historical investigation to the political orientation and practical action of the peace movement, in a context of gathering dangers of nuclear annihilation.

A historical analysis suggests, as we have seen, that it is not the arms race alone which constitutes the basis of the contemporary international crisis, or indeed provides the over-arching unity of the post-war world. The stockpiling of nuclear weapons has always interrelated with other constitutive dimensions of world history since 1945, of which the most important so far has been the globalized social conflict of capitalist and post-capitalist states. International politics form an arena of social forces that are, albeit diverse, quite identifiable and, as much as any historical agencies, intelligible. Even the arms race itself is not a wholly inertial process. However instinctively difficult to do, it is necessary to distinguish between the horrendous *effects* of a nuclear war, which would be beyond reason for all those engaged in it, and the *causes* that could potentially generate one, which are rationally discoverable. Edward Thompson rightly abjures explanation of the present danger in terms of a 'single causative historical logic'. But his own presentation of the relentless thrust of exterminism itself tends at times to suggest such a logic — in which exterminism becomes a modern version of the doomsday machine, both source and consequence of an annihilationist demiurge. The reason, surely, is that the alternative he proposes to us is a misleading one — either a 'single historical logic' or a 'messy inertia'. If these are the only possibilities, the latter can all too easily become another, inverted variant of the former. In reality, human history and agency, individual or collective, typically form a world intermediate between the two, where rational intention and control are thwarted or deflected by antagonistic conflicts of interest, pressures of unconscious desires, or constraints of natural necessity, without ever being finally cancelled by them. The current critical condition of world politics contains the danger of nuclear war. But this danger is less a result of the inertial push of exterminism, than the consequence of a combination of international and national conflicts, within which competition in nuclear weapons — manipulated and managed for conscious purposes — forms the most incendiary component.

Does this component dictate the crystallization of essentially similar political formations in the two great powers, mediated by the reciprocity of their antagonism? The foregoing historical analysis lends little support to the thesis of an isomorphism of the USSR and USA, or of post-capitalist and capitalist societies generally. Nor is the oft-repeated claim that centrally planned economies and war economies are effectively equivalent, a persuasive one: it has to be asked under what conditions these were created, what purposes central control fulfils, what the mode of reproduction or internationalization of these systems is. It would be as relevant to compare a monastery to a regiment on the grounds that both involve pledges of obedience, male exclusivity and a sense of corporate identity. In the case of the USA and USSR such a comparison is particularly inapposite, given the totally different experiences of modern war that these two societies have had. The USA is, indeed, a vivid example of how centrally planned economic organization is not necessary for high levels of militarization. If we look at the historical character of the Soviet Union and the United States as societies, or at the respective roles they play in the world at large, there is not so much an isomorphism as an asymmetry of internal structure and international consequence.

The record of the past decade is, in this respect, clear enough. The two world powers do not have an equal responsibility for the current cold war, or for the arms race that is accompanying it. The deterioration in the international climate in the latter part of the 1970s has been essentially precipitated by changes in the global posture of one state, namely the USA. No such change can be detected in the USSR: it has not engaged in a sudden expansion of its military forces, it has not seen a quite new leadership emerge after a ferocious internal political debate, and it has not introduced new conditions into US—Soviet negotiations, let alone abandoned the explicit pursuit of detente. This is not to say, as we have stressed, that the USSR bears no responsibility for bringing the present crisis upon us. In a longer term sense its political involution has helped to render it possible at all. But this responsibility is different in kind from that of the USA. Lest this judgment appear unduly one-sided, it should be noted that such an interpretation is one with which the American protagonists of the new cold war effectively agree. Their argument is that the USA has had to change policy in the face of the continuity of Soviet designs, a continuity which it had earlier been hoped the USA could rupture by the enticements of detente. All the issues around which the new cold war is mobilized are issues upon which the USSR has maintained constant positions through the nearly two decades of the Brezhnev epoch: steady increase in military capability, cautious support for Third World revolutions, persistence of bureaucratic dictatorship. The new cold war is a response to this consistency, an expression of the refusal of the capitalist world to accept it.

Part 7
Future Directions for the State

Introduction

DAVID HELD

Since its inception, political and social theory has been concerned to examine the state as it is and as it might be. The chapters in Part 7 embrace both these concerns. From different perspectives they reflect upon the nature of the state, inquire into the justification of its character and form, and suggest alternative futures. Chapters 7.1 and 7.2 develop their ideas from an engagement with the liberal and liberal-democratic traditions, while Chapters 7.3 and 7.4 draw their inspiration from Marxism. Together, they reveal a provocative array of political aspirations.

In *Anarchy, State and Utopia*, Robert Nozick sets out a number of arguments concerning what he calls the 'minimal state' or the 'framework for utopia'. He seeks to establish that 'no more extensive state could be morally justified' because it would 'violate the rights of individuals' not to be forced to do certain things. In the extract included here, Nozick develops an argument which stands independently of others in his book but which converges with their result. Individuals are extraordinarily diverse. There is no one community which will serve as an ideal for all people; a wide range of conceptions of utopia exist. The question is: How can such radically different aspirations be accommodated? How can individuals and groups make progress toward their chosen ends? According to Nozick, we must get away from the idea that utopia represents a single conception of the best of all social and political arrangements. Rather, a society or nation in which utopian experimentation can be tried should itself be thought of as utopia. Utopia is a framework for utopias where people are 'at liberty to join together voluntarily to pursue and attempt to realize their own vision of the good life in the ideal community but where no one can *impose* his own utopian vision upon others'. To put the point another way, utopia is the framework for liberty and experimentation — it is the 'minimal state'.

The framework, Nozick argues, is 'libertarian and *laissez-faire*'. While it is not always clear precisely what Nozick means by this, it would not be misleading to point out that his views are broadly compatible with those of right-wing liberals like Milton Friedman and Friedrich Hayek. Only individuals can judge what they want and, therefore, the less the state interferes in their lives the better for them. The 'minimal state' is thus inconsistent with 'planning in detail' and with the active redistribution of resources, 'forcing some to aid others'. The state steps beyond its legitimate bounds when it becomes an instrument to promote equality, whether of opportunity or of result. What then is the proper role of the state? It appears that it should only, in Nozick's opinion, be a 'protective agency' against force, theft, fraud and the violation of contracts.

An alternative position is put forward in Chapter 7.2, from Macpherson's *The Life and Times of Liberal Democracy*. Macpherson makes the challenging claim that only a radically democratic society can sustain liberty in the contemporary world and thus far greater collective participation by citizens in the running of their lives is essential. Four models or theoretical accounts of liberal democracy are distinguished in the book itself. Model (1), advocated by Jeremy Bentham and James Mill, justifies democratic government on the grounds that people cannot trust their governors: democracy is a necessity to protect the governed from oppression by the state. A stronger moral case for democracy is set out in model (2) by John Stuart Mill, portraying democracy as a means for moral self-development and an essential basis for liberty. Advocates of model (3) include Joseph Schumpeter; they make a weaker normative case for democracy and see in it above all an efficient means for the authorization and coordination of decisions inevitably made by competing élites. The selection from Macpherson reproduced here is his account of model (4) or 'participatory democracy'. This model takes as its inspiration some of the arguments put forward by John Stuart Mill, but gives them a more radical twist by maintaining that liberty and individual development can only be fully achieved with the direct and continuous involvement of citizens in the regulation of society and state. (An expansion of these points can be found in the Introduction to this volume, pp. 23ff.).

In densely populated complex societies is it feasible, Macpherson asks, to consider extending the realm of democracy from periodic involvement in elections to participation in decision making in all spheres of life? The problems posed by the coordination of large-scale communities are considerable. It is hard to imagine any political system in which all citizens could be involved in face-to-face discussions every time a public issue arises. However, it does not follow from considerations such as this that society and the system of government cannot be transformed. Macpherson argues for transformation based upon a system combining competitive parties and organizations of direct democracy. There will, for as far as one can see, always be issues around which parties might form and only competition between political parties guarantees a minimum responsiveness of those in government to people at all levels below. The party system itself — like the management of workplaces and the local community — should be reorganized around less hierarchical principles, making administrators and managers more accountable to the personnel of the organizations they represent. Of course, the obstacles to the realization of 'participatory democracy' are, Macpherson points out, formidable.

In Marxian writings it has frequently been maintained that the state can only be radically transformed when a high level of industrialization has been reached, freeing people from the burden of endless hours of work. In some of Marx's and Engels' best known writings they elaborated a conception of history based upon the idea of successive stages of development — distinguished by different 'modes of production' — the dynamic of which is provided by the economic 'base', particularly the forces of production. The advance of production to a high level is a necessary condition of socialism (the first phase of political emancipation) in which the state, in the hands of the working classes and their allies, can transform social and economic relations while defending the revolution against remnants of the bourgeois order. The planned expansion of the forces of production under socialism is itself vital for the establishment of Communist society (the second phase) in which the very separation of state and society can be abolished: the state will 'wither away' leaving a system of self-government linked to collectively shared duties and work. Thus not only is a 'mature' industrial system a condition of the emancipation of people from the productive process and the division of labour but also of political liberation. Applying this framework of analysis, Rudolf Bahro, in chapter 7.3, argues that the existence of repressive regimes in those socialist societies already created is due above all to their 'industrial under-development' in a world economy dominated by older, 'more mature' capitalist countries. The possibility of 'harmony and freedom' in 'actually existing socialist societies' is stunted by their 'forced march into the modern era'. In such circumstances, the state can do nothing else but initiate a 'civilizing role'; it must become 'the taskmaster of society in its technical and social modernization'. Hence the subjection of Soviet society to a bureaucratic state machine can be seen, contends Bahro, as a necessary step to further transformations. A similar fate is the inevitable future of underdeveloped societies today.

But what of the Soviet Union now that the 'hardest work', as Bahro puts it, is over? In his account, a 'bureaucratic superstructure' persists because the Soviet Union is caught in a vicious circle constituted by the pressures of competition with the capitalist West on the one hand, and the self-perpetuating qualities of an ossified bureaucracy on the other. This circle can only be broken by a vital new Communist (i.e. neo-Leninist) movement generating a vigorous 'system of social self-organization from below'. The abolition of the gulf between mental and manual labour in politics and economics through the installation of direct democracy — a vision elaborated by Bahro at some length in *The Alternative in Eastern Europe* — should, Bahro concludes, be the central objective.

In the final extract, Poulantzas takes issue with the kind of position defended by Bahro. The development of Stalinism and a repressive state in Russia is not just due to the peculiarities of a 'backward' economy, but can be traced to problems in Lenin's thought and practice. The whole notion that the institutions of representative democracy can be simply swept away by organizations of rank-and-file democracy is erroneous. Poulantzas affirms Rosa Luxemburg's view that 'without general elections, without unrestricted freedom of press and assembly, without a free struggle of opinion, life dies out in every public institution'. Lenin mistakes the nature of representative democracy when he labels it simply as bourgeois. Underlying this typical Leninist view, Poulantzas maintains, is a fundamental distrust of the idea of competing power centres in society. Moreover, it was because of distrust of this kind that Lenin ultimately undermined the autonomy of the soviets.

Poulantzas argues that the whole relation between socialist thought and democratic institutions needs to be rethought in the light, not only of the reality of East European socialism, but also of the moral bankruptcy of the social democratic vision of reform. Social democratic politics has led to the adulation of 'social engineering', proliferating policies to make relatively minor adjustments in social and economic arrangements. The state has, accordingly, grown in size and power, undermining the vision that social democratic politics might have once had. But what then is the way forward? Institutions of direct democracy or self-management cannot simply replace the state; for they leave a coordination vacuum readily filled by bureaucracy. Poulantzas emphasizes two sets of changes which he believes, similarly to Macpherson, are vital for the transformation of the state in West and East into forms of 'socialist pluralism'. The state must be democratized by making parliament, state bureaucracies and political parties more open and accountable, while new forms of struggle at the local level (through factory-based politics, the women's movement, ecological groups) must ensure that society, as well as the state, is democratized. But how these processes interrelate Poulantzas does not say, stressing instead that there are 'no easy recipes'.

7.1
A Framework for Utopia

ROBERT NOZICK

The model

[. . .] That it is impossible simultaneously and continually to realize all social and political goods is a regrettable fact about the human condition, worth investigating and bemoaning. Our subject here, however, is the best of all possible worlds. For whom? The best of all possible worlds for me will not be that for you. The world, of all those I can imagine, which I would most prefer to live in, will not be precisely the one you would choose. Utopia, though, must be, in some restricted sense, the best for all of us; the best world imaginable, for each of us. In what sense can this be?

Imagine a possible world in which to live; this world need not contain everyone else now alive, and it may contain beings who have never actually lived. Every rational creature in this world you have imagined will have the same rights of imagining a possible world for himself to live in (in which all other rational inhabitants have the same imagining rights, and so on) as you have. The other inhabitants of the world you have imagined may choose to stay in the world which has been created for them (they have been created for) or they may choose to leave it and inhabit a world of their own imagining. If they choose to leave your world and live in another, your world is without them. You may choose to abandon your imagined world, now without its emigrants. This process goes on; worlds are created, people leave them, create new worlds, and so on.

Will the process go on indefinitely? Are all such worlds ephemeral or are there some stable worlds in which all of the original population will choose to remain? If this process does

Source: From *Anarchy, State and Utopia* (1974) Basic Books and Basil Blackwell, pp. 297—334.

result in some stable worlds, what interesting general conditions does each of them satisfy?

If there are stable worlds, each of them satisfies one very desirable description by virtue of the way the worlds have been set up; namely, *none* of the inhabitants of the world can *imagine* an alternative world they would rather live in, which (they believe) would continue to exist if all of its rational inhabitants had the same rights of imagining and emigrating. This description is so very attractive that it is of great interest to see what other features are common to all such stable worlds. So that we continually do not have to repeat long descriptions, let us call a world which all rational inhabitants may leave for any other world they can imagine (in which all the rational inhabitants may leave for any other world they can imagine in which . . .) an *association*; and let us call a world in which some rational inhabitants are not permitted to emigrate to some of the associations they can imagine, an *east-berlin*. Thus our original attractive description says that no member of a stable association can imagine another association, which (he believes) would be stable, that he would rather be a member of.

What are such stable associations like? Here I can offer only some intuitive and overly simple arguments. You will not be able to set up an association in which you are the absolute monarch, exploiting all the other rational inhabitants. For then they would be better off in an association without you, and, at the very least, they all would choose to inhabit that one containing all of them minus you, rather than remain in your creation. No stable association is such that everyone (but one) in it jointly would leave for their own association; for this would contradict the assumption that the original association was stable. This reasoning applies as well to two or three or *n* persons whom everyone else in an association would be better off without. Thus we have as a condition of stable associations: if *A* is a set of persons in a stable association then there is no proper subset *S* of *A* such that each member of *S* is better off in an association consisting only of members of *S*, than he is in *A*. For if there were such a subset *S*, its members would secede from *A*, establishing their own association.
[. . .]

The model projected onto our world

In *our* actual world, what corresponds to the model of possible worlds is a wide and diverse range of communities which people can enter if they are admitted, leave if they wish to, shape according to their wishes; a society in which utopian experimentation can be tried, different styles of life can be lived, and alternative visions of the good can be individually or jointly pursued. The details and some of the virtues of such an arrangement, which we shall call the *framework*, will emerge as we proceed. There are important differences between the model and the model's projection onto the actual world. The problems with the operation of the framework in the actual world stem from the divergencies between our earthbound actual life and the possible-worlds model we have been discussing, raising the question of whether even if the realization of the model itself would be ideal, the realization of its pale projection *is* the best we can do here.

1. Unlike the model, we cannot create all the people whose existence we desire. So that even if there were a possible maximally mutually valuing association containing you, its other members actually may not exist; and the other persons among whom you actually live will not constitute your best fan club. Also there may be a particular kind of community you wish to live in, yet not enough other actual people (can be persuaded to) wish to live in such a community so as to give it a viable population. In the model, for a diverse range of non-exploitative communities, there are always enough other persons who wish to live in one.

2. Unlike the model, in the actual world communities *impinge* upon one another, creating problems of foreign relations and self-defence and necessitating modes of adjudicating and resolving disputes between the communities. (In the model, one association impinges upon another only by drawing away some of its members.)

3. In the actual world, there are information costs in finding out what other communities there are, and what they are like, and moving and travel costs in going from one community to another.

4. Furthermore, in the actual world, some communities may try to keep some of their members ignorant of the nature of other alternative communities they might join, to try to prevent them from freely leaving their own community to join another. This raises the problem of how freedom of movement is to be institutionalized and enforced when there are some who will wish to restrict it.

Given the formidable differences between the actual world and the model of possible worlds, of what relevance is that fantasy to it? One should not be too quick, here or elsewhere, with such fantasies. For they reveal much about our condition. One cannot know how satisfied we shall be with what we achieve among our feasible alternatives without knowing how far they diverge from our fantasied wishes: and it is only by bringing such wishes, and their force, into the picture that we shall understand people's efforts toward expanding the range of their currently feasible alternatives. [...]

The framework

Utopia is the focus of so many different strands of aspiration that there must be many theoretical paths leading to it. Let us sketch some of these alternate, mutually supporting, theoretical routes.

The first route begins with the fact that people are different. They differ in temperament, interests, intellectual ability, aspirations, natural bent, spiritual quests, and the kind of life they wish to lead. They diverge in the values they have and have different weightings for the values they share. (They wish to live in different climates — some in mountains, plains, deserts, seashores, cities, towns.) There is no reason to think that there is *one* community which will serve as ideal for all people and much reason to think that there is not. [...]

Wittgenstein, Elizabeth Taylor, Bertrand Russell, Thomas Merton, Yogi Berra, Allen Ginsburg, Harry Wolfson, Thoreau, Casey Stengel, The Lubavitcher Rebbe, Picasso, Moses, Einstein, Hugh Heffner, Socrates, Henry Ford, Lenny Bruce, Baba Ram Dass, Gandhi, Sir Edmund Hillary, Raymond Lubitz, Buddha, Frank Sinatra, Columbus, Freud, Norman Mailer, Ayn Rand, Baron Rothschild, Ted Williams, Thomas Edison, H. L. Mencken, Thomas Jefferson, Ralph Ellison, Bobby Fischer, Emma Goldman, Peter Kropotkin, you, and your parents. Is there really *one* kind of life which is best for each of these people? Imagine all of them living in any utopia you've ever seen described in detail. Try to describe the society which would be best for all of these persons to live in. Would it be agricultural or urban? Of great material luxury or of austerity with basic needs satisfied? What would relations between the sexes be like? Would there be any institution similar to marriage? Would it be monogamous? Would children be raised by their parents? Would there be private property? Would there be a serene secure life or one with adventures, challenges, dangers, and opportunities for heroism? Would there be one, many, any religion? How important would it be in people's lives? Would people view their life as importantly centred about private concerns or about public action and issues of public policy? Would they be single-mindedly devoted to particular kinds of accomplishments and work or jacks-of-all-trades and pleasures or would they concentrate on full and satisfying leisure activities? Would children be raised permissively, strictly? What would their education concentrate upon? Will sports be important in people's lives (as spectators, participants)? Will art? Will sensual pleasures or intellectual activities predominate? Or what? . . .

The idea that there is one best composite answer to all of these questions, one best society for *everyone* to live in, seems to me to be an incredible one. (And the idea that, if there is one, we now know enough to describe it is even more incredible.) . . .

Utopian authors, each very confident of the virtues of his own vision and of its singular correctness, have differed among themselves (no less than the people listed above differ) in the institutions and kinds of life they present for emulation. Though the picture of an ideal society that each presents is much too simple (even for the component communities to be discussed below), we should take the fact of the differences seriously. No utopian author has everyone in his society leading exactly the same life, allocating exactly the same amount of time to exactly the same activities. *Why not?* Don't the reasons also count against just one kind of community?

The conclusion to draw is that there will not be *one* kind of community existing and one kind of life led in utopia. Utopia will consist of utopias, of many different and divergent communities in which people lead different kinds of lives under different institutions. Some kinds of communities will be more attractive to most than others; communities will wax and wane. People will leave some for others or spend their whole lives in one. Utopia is a framework for utopias, a place where people are at liberty to join together voluntarily to pursue and attempt to realize their own vision of the good life in the ideal community but where no one can *impose* his own utopian vision upon others[1] . . . Half of the truth I wish to put forth is that utopia is meta-utopia: the environment in which utopian experiments may be tried out; the environment in which people are free to do their own thing; the environment which must, to a great extent, be realized first if more particular utopian visions are to be realized stably.

If, as we noted at the beginning of this chapter, not all goods can be realized simultaneously, then trade-offs will have to be made. The second theoretical route notes that there is little reason to believe that one unique system of trade-offs will command universal assent. Different communities, each with a slightly different mix, will provide a range from which each individual can choose that community which best approximates *his* balance among competing values . . .

Design devices and filter devices

The third theoretical route to the framework for utopia is based on the fact that people are complex, as are the webs of possible relationships among them. Suppose (falsely) that the earlier arguments are mistaken and that *one* kind of society *is* best for all. How are we to find out what this society is like? Two methods suggest themselves, which we shall call design devices and filter devices.

Design devices construct something (or its description) by some procedure which does not essentially involve constructing descriptions of others of its type. The result of the process is one object. In the case of societies, the result of the design process is a description of one society, obtained by people (or a person) sitting down and thinking about what the best society is. After deciding, they set about to pattern everything on this one model.

Given the enormous complexity of man, his many desires, aspirations, impulses, talents, mistakes, loves, sillinesses, given the *thickness* of his intertwined and interrelated levels, facets, relationships (compare the thinness of the social scientists' description of man to that of the novelists), and given the complexity of interpersonal institutions and relationships, and the complexity of coordination of the actions of many people, it is enormously unlikely that, even if there were one ideal pattern for society, it could be arrived at in this *a priori* (relative to current knowledge) fashion. And even supposing that some great genius *did* come along with the blueprint, who could have confidence that it would work out well?

Sitting down at this late stage in history to dream up a description of the perfect society is not of course the same as starting from scratch. We have available to us partial knowledge of the results of application of devices other than design devices, including partial application of the filter device to be described below. It is helpful to imagine cavemen sitting together to think up what, for all time, will be the best possible society and then setting out to institute it. Do none of the reasons that make you smile at this apply to us?

Filter devices involve a process which eliminates (filters out) many from a large set of alternatives. The two key determinants of the end result(s) are the particular nature of the filtering out process (and what qualities it selects against) and the particular nature of the set of alternatives it operates upon (and how this set is generated). Filtering processes are especially appropriate for designers having limited knowledge who do not know precisely the nature of a desired end product. For it enables them to utilize their knowledge of specific conditions they don't want violated in judiciously building a filter to reject the violators . . . Generally, it seems, less knowledge (including knowledge of what is desirable) will be required to produce an appropriate filter, even one that converges uniquely upon a particular kind of product, than would be necessary to construct only the product(s) from scratch. [. . .]

A filtering process for specifying a society which might come to mind is one in which the people planning out the ideal society consider many different kinds of societies and criticize some, eliminate some, modify the descriptions of others, until they come to the one they consider best. This no doubt is how any design team would work, and so it should not be assumed that design devices exclude filtering features. (Nor need filter devices exclude design aspects, especially in the generating process.) But one cannot determine in advance which people will come up with the best ideas, and all ideas must be tried out (and not merely simulated on a computer) to see how they will work. And some ideas will come only as we are (*post facto*) trying to describe what patterns have evolved from the spontaneous coordination of the actions of many people.

If the ideas must actually be tried out, there must be many communities trying out different patterns. The filtering process, the process of eliminating communities, that our framework involves is very simple: people try out living in various communities, and they leave or slightly modify the ones they don't like (find defective). Some communities will be abandoned, others will struggle along, others will split, others will flourish, gain members, and be duplicated elsewhere. Each community must win and hold the voluntary adherence of its members. No pattern is *imposed* on everyone, and the result will be one pattern if and only if everyone voluntarily chooses to live in accordance with that pattern of community.[2]

The design device comes in at the stage of generating specific communities to be lived in and tried out. Any group of people may devise a pattern and attempt to persuade others to participate in the adventure of a community in that pattern. Visionaries and crackpots, maniacs and saints, monks and libertines, capitalists and Communists and participatory democrats, proponents of phalanxes (Fourier), palaces of labour (Flora Tristan), villages of unity and cooperation (Owen), mutualist communities (Proudhon), time stores (Josiah Warren), Bruderhof,[3] kibbutzim,[4] kundalini yoga ashrams, and so forth, may all have their try at building their vision and setting an alluring example. It should not be thought that every pattern tried will be explicitly designed *de novo*. Some will be planned modifications, however slight, of others already existing (when it is seen where they rub), and the details of many will be built up spontaneously in communities that leave some leeway. As communities become more attractive for their inhabitants, patterns previously adopted as the best available will be rejected. And as the communities which people live in improve (according to their lights), ideas for new communities often will improve as well. [. . .]

The framework as utopian common ground

The use of a filter device dependent upon people's individual decisions to live in or leave particular communities is especially appropriate. For the ultimate purpose of utopian construction is to get communities that people will want to live in and will choose voluntarily to live in. Or at least this must be a side effect of successful utopian construction. The filtering process proposed will achieve this. Furthermore, a filtering device dependent upon people's decisions has certain advantages over one which operates mechanically, given our inability to formulate explicitly principles which adequately handle, in advance, all of the complex, multifarious situations which arise. We often state *prima facie* principles without thinking that we can mark off in advance all of the exceptions to the principle. But though we cannot describe in advance all of the exceptions to the principle, we do think that very often we will be able to recognize that a particular situation we are presented with *is* an exception. [. . .]

We have argued that even if there is one kind of community that is best for each and every person, the framework set out is the best means for finding out the nature of that community. Many more arguments can and should be offered for the view that, even if there is one kind of society that is best for everyone, the operation of the framework (1) is best for anyone's coming up with a picture of what the society is like, (2) is best for anyone's becoming convinced that the picture is indeed one of the best society, (3) is best for large numbers of people's becoming so convinced, and (4) is the best way to stabilize such a society with people living securely and enduringly under that particular pattern. I cannot offer these other arguments here . . . However, I do wish to note that the arguments for the framework offered and mentioned here are even more potent when we drop the (false) assumption that there is *one* kind of society best for everyone, and so stop misconstruing the problem as one of which one type of community every individual person should live in.

The framework has two advantages over every other kind of description of utopia: first, it will be acceptable to almost every utopian at some future point in time, whatever his particular vision; and second, it is compatible with the realization of almost all particular utopian visions, though it does not guarantee the realization or universal triumph of any particular utopian vision.[5] Any utopian will agree that our framework is an appropriate one for a society of good men. [. . .] For each thinks his own particular vision would be realized under it.

Those with different utopian visions who believe the framework is an appropriate *path* to their vision (as well as being permissible after their vision is realized) might well cooperate in attempting to realize the framework, even given mutual knowledge of their different predictions and predilections. Their different hopes conflict only if they involve universal realization of one particular pattern. We may distinguish three utopian positions: *imperialistic* utopianism, which countenances the forcing of everyone into one pattern of community; *missionary* utopianism, which hopes to persuade or convince everyone to live in one particular kind of community, but will not force them to do so; and *existential* utopianism, which hopes that a particular pattern of community will exist (will be viable), though not necessarily universally, so that those who wish to do so may live in accordance with it. Existential utopians can wholeheartedly support the framework. With full knowledge of their differences, adherents of diverse visions may cooperate in realizing the framework. Missionary utopians, though their aspirations are universal, will join them in supporting the framework, viewing fully voluntary adherence to their preferred pattern as crucial. They will not, however, especially admire the framework's additional virtue of allowing the simultaneous realization of many diverse possibilities. Imperialistic utopians, on the other hand, will oppose the framework so long as some others do not agree with them. (Well, you can't satisfy everybody; especially if there are those who will be dissatisfied unless not everybody is satisfied.) Since any particular community may be established within the framework, it is compatible with all particular utopian visions, while guaranteeing none. Utopians should view this as an enormous virtue; for their particular view would not fare as well under utopian schemes other than their own.

Community and nation

The operation of the framework has many of the virtues, and few of the defects, people find in the libertarian vision. For though there is great liberty to choose among communities, many particular communities internally may have many restrictions unjustifiable on libertarian grounds: that is, restrictions which libertarians would condemn if they were enforced by a central state apparatus. For example, paternalistic intervention into people's lives, restrictions on the range of books which may circulate in the community, limitations on the kinds of sexual behaviour, and so on. But this is merely another way of pointing out that in a free society people may contract into various restrictions which the government may not legitimately impose upon them. Though the framework is libertarian and *laissez-faire, individual communities within it need not be,* and perhaps no community within it will choose to be so. Thus, the characteristics of the framework need not pervade the individual communities. In *this laissez-faire* system it could turn out that, though they are permitted, there are no actually functioning 'capitalist' institutions; or that some communities have them and others don't or some communities have some of them, or what you will.[6]

In previous chapters, we have spoken of a person's opting out of particular provisions of certain arrangements. Why now do we say that various restrictions may be imposed in a particular community? Mustn't the community allow its members to opt out of these restrictions? No; founders and members of a small Communist community may, quite properly, refuse to allow anyone to opt out of equal sharing, even though it would be possible to arrange this. It is not a general principle that every community or group must allow internal opting out when that is feasible. For sometimes such internal opting out would itself change the character of the group from that desired. Herein lies an interesting theoretical problem. A nation or protective agency may not compel redistribution between one community and another, yet a community such as a kibbutz may redistribute within itself (or give to another community or to outside individuals). Such a community needn't offer its members an opportunity to opt out of these arrangements while remaining a member of the community. Yet . . . a nation should offer this opportunity; people have a right to so opt out of a nation's requirements. Wherein lies the difference between a community and a nation that makes the difference in the legitimacy of imposing a certain pattern upon all of its members?

A person will swallow the imperfections of a package P (which may be a protective arrangement, a consumer good, a community) that is desirable on the whole rather than purchase a different package (a completely different package, or P with some changes), when no more desirable attainable different package is worth to him its greater costs over P, including the costs of inducing enough others to participate in making the alternative package. One assumes that the cost calculation for nations is such as to permit internal opting out. But this is not the whole story for two reasons. First, it may be feasible in individual communities also to arrange internal opting out at little administrative cost (which he may be willing to pay), yet this needn't always be done. Second, nations differ from other packages in that the individual himself isn't to bear the administrative costs of opting out of some otherwise compulsory provision. The other people must pay for finely designing their compulsory arrangements so that they don't apply to those who wish to opt out. Nor is the difference merely a matter of there being many alternative kinds of communities while there are many fewer nations. Even if almost everyone wished to live in a Communist community, so that there weren't any viable non-Communist communities, no particular community need also (though it is to be hoped that one would) allow a resident individual to opt out of their sharing arrangement. The recalcitrant individual has no alternative but to conform. Still, the others do not force him to conform, and his rights are not violated. He has no right that the others cooperate in making his non-conformity feasible.

The difference seems to me to reside in the difference between a face-to-face community and a nation. In a nation, one knows that there are non-conforming individuals, but one need not be directly confronted by these individuals or by the fact of their non-conformity. Even if one finds it offensive that others do not conform, even if the knowledge that there exist non-conformists rankles and makes one very unhappy, this does not constitute being harmed by the others or having one's rights violated, whereas in a face-to-face community one cannot avoid being directly confronted with what one finds to be offensive. How one lives in one's immediate environment is affected.

This distinction between a face-to-face community and one that is not generally runs parallel to another distinction. A face-to-face community can exist on land jointly owned by its members, whereas the land of a nation is not so held. The community will be entitled then, as a body, to determine what regulations are to be obeyed on its land; whereas the citizens of a nation do not jointly own its land and so cannot in this way regulate its use. If *all* the separate individuals who own land coordinate their actions in imposing a common regulation (for example, no one may reside on this land who does not contribute n per cent of his income to the poor), the same *effect* will be achieved as if the nation had passed legislation requiring this. But since unanimity is only as strong as its weakest link, even with the use of secondary boycotts (which are perfectly legitimate), it would be impossible to maintain such a unanimous coalition in the face of the blandishments to some to defect.

But some face-to-face communities will not be situated on jointly held land. May the majority of the voters in a small village pass an ordinance against things that they find offensive being done on the *public* streets? May they legislate against nudity or fornication or sadism (on consenting masochists) or hand-holding by racially mixed couples on the streets? Any private owner can regulate his premises as he chooses. But what of the public thoroughfares, where people cannot easily avoid sights they find offensive? Must the vast majority cloister themselves against the offensive minority? If the majority may determine the limits on detectable behaviour in public, may they, in addition to requiring that no-one appear in public without wearing clothing, also require that no one appear in public without wearing a badge certifying that he has contributed n per cent of his income to the needy during the year, on the grounds that they find it offensive to look at someone not wearing this badge (not having contributed)? And whence this emergent right of the majority to decide? Or are there to be no 'public' place or ways? . . . Since I do not see my way clearly through these issues, I raise them here only to leave them. [. . .]

Total communities

Under the framework, there will be groups and communities covering all aspects of life, though limited in membership. (Not everyone, I assume, will choose to join one big commune or federation of communes.) Some things about some aspects of life extend to everyone; for example, everyone has various rights that may not be violated, various boundaries that may not be crossed without another's consent. Some people will find this covering of all aspects of some person's lives and some aspects of all person's lives to be insufficient. These people will desire a doubly total relationship that covers all people and all aspects of their lives, for example, all people in all their behaviour (none is excluded in principle) showing certain feelings of love, affection, willingness to help others; all being engaged together in some common and important task.

Consider the members of a basketball team, all caught up in playing basketball well. (Ignore the fact that they are trying to win, though is it an accident that such feelings often arise when some unite *against* others?) They do not play primarily for money. They have a preliminary *joint* goal, and each subordinates himself to achieving this common goal, scoring fewer points himself than he otherwise might. If all are tied together by joint participation in an activity toward a common goal that each ranks as his most important goal, then fraternal feeling will flourish. They will be united and unselfish; *they* will be *one*. But basketball players, of course, do not have a common highest goal; they have separate families and lives. Still we might imagine a society in which all work together to achieve a common highest goal. Under the framework, any group of persons can so coalesce, form a movement, and so forth. But the structure itself is diverse; it does not itself provide or guarantee that there will be any common goal that all pursue jointly. It is borne in upon one, in contemplating such an issue, how appropriate it is to speak of 'individualism' and (the word coined in opposition to it) 'socialism'. It goes without saying that any persons may attempt to unite kindred spirits, but, whatever their hopes and longings, none have the right to impose their vision of unity upon the rest. [. . .]

Utopian means and ends

. . . [I do not] assume that all problems about the framework are solved. Let us mention a few here. There will be problems about the role, if any, to be played by some central authority (or protective association); how will this authority be selected, and how will it be ensured that the authority does, and does only, what it is supposed to do? The major role, as I see it, would be to enforce the operation of the framework — for example, to prevent some communities from invading and seizing others, their persons or assets. Furthermore, it will adjudicate in some reasonable fashion conflicts between communities which cannot be settled by peaceful means. What the best form of such a central authority is I would not wish to investigate here. It seems desirable that one not be fixed permanently but that room be left for improvements of detail. I ignore here the difficult and important problems of the controls on a central authority powerful enough to perform its appropriate functions, because I have nothing special to add to the standard literature on federations, confederations, decentralization of power, checks and balances, and so on.

One persistent strand in utopian thinking . . . is the feeling that there is some set of principles obvious enough to be accepted by all men of good will, precise enough to give unambiguous guidance in particular situations, clear enough so that all will realize its dictates, and complete enough to cover all problems which actually will arise. Since I do not assume that there are such principles, I do not assume that the political realm will wither away. The messiness of the details of a political apparatus and the details of how *it* is to be controlled and limited do not fit easily into one's hopes for a sleek, simple utopian scheme.

Apart from the conflict between communities, there will be other tasks for a central apparatus or agency, for example, enforcing an individual's right to leave a community. But problems arise if an individual can plausibly be viewed as *owing* something to the other members of a community he wishes to leave: for example, he has been educated at their expense on the explicit agreement that he would use his acquired skills and knowledge in the home community. Or, he has acquired certain family obligations that he will abandon by shifting communities. Or, without such ties, he wishes to leave. What may he take out with him? Or, he wishes to leave after he's committed some punishable offence for which the community wishes to punish him. Clearly the principles will be complicated ones . . . I mention these problems to indicate a fraction of the thinking that needs to be done on the details of a framework and to make clear that I do not think its nature can be settled finally now either. [. . .]

How utopia works out

'Well, what exactly will it all turn out to be like? In what directions will people flower? How large will the communities be? Will there be some large cities? How will economies of scale operate to fix the size of the communities? Will all of the communities be geographical, or will there be many important secondary associations, and so on? Will most communities follow particular (though diverse) utopian visions, or will many communities themselves be open, animated by no such particular vision?'

I do not know, and you should not be interested in my guesses about what would occur under the framework in the near future. As for the long run, I would not attempt to guess.

'So is this all it comes to: Utopia is a free society?' Utopia is *not* just a society in which the framework is realized. For who could believe that ten minutes after the framework was established, we would have utopia? Things would be no different than now. It is what grows spontaneously from the individual choices of many people over a long period of time that will be worth speaking eloquently about . . . Only a fool, or a prophet, would try to prophesy the range and limits and characters of the communities after, for example, 150 years of the operation of this framework.

Aspiring to neither role, let me close by emphasizing the dual nature of the conception of utopia being presented here. There is the framework of utopia, and there are the particular communities within the framework. Almost all of the literature on utopia is, according to our conception, concerned with the character of the particular communities within the framework. The fact that I have not propounded some particular description of a constituent community does *not* mean that (I think) doing so is unimportant, or less important, or uninteresting. How could that be? We *live* in particular communities. It is here that one's non-imperialistic vision of the ideal or good society is to be propounded and realized. Allowing us to do that is what the framework is *for*. Without such visions impelling and animating the creation of particular communities with particular desired characteristics, the framework will lack life. Conjoined with many persons' particular visions, the framework enables us to get the best of all possible worlds.

The position expounded here totally rejects planning in detail, in advance, one community in which everyone is to live yet sympathizes with voluntary utopian experimentation and provides it with the background in which it can flower; does this position fall within the utopian or the anti-utopian camp? My difficulty in answering this question encourages me to think the framework captures the virtues and advantages of each position. (If instead it blunders into combining the errors, defects, and mistakes of both of them, the filtering process of free and open discussion will make this clear.)

Utopia and the minimal state

The framework for utopia that we have described is equivalent to the minimal state. [. . .] The only morally legitimate state, the only morally tolerable one, we now see is the one that best realizes the utopian aspirations of untold dreamers and visionaries. It preserves what we all can keep from the utopian tradition and opens the rest of that tradition to our individual aspirations . . .

The minimal state treats us as inviolate individuals, who may not be used in certain ways by others as means or tools or instruments or resources; it treats us as persons having individual rights with the dignity this constitutes. Treating us with respect by respecting our rights, it allows us, individually or with whom we choose, to choose our life and to realize our ends and our conception of ourselves, in so far as we can, aided by the voluntary cooperation of other individuals possessing the same dignity. How *dare* any state or group of individuals do more. Or less.

Notes

1. Some theories underlying such impositions are discussed by J. L. Talmon in *The Origins of Totalitarian Democracy*, New York, Norton, 1970 and *Political Messianism*, New York, Praeger, 1961.
2. An illuminating discussion of the operation and virtues of a similar filter system is found in F. A. Hayek, *The Constitution of Liberty*, Chicago, University of Chicago Press, 1960, Chs 2 and 3. Some utopian endeavours have fit this, to some extent. '[The nondoctrinaire character of the origins of the Jewish communal settlements in Palestine] also determined their development in all essentials. New forms and new intermediate forms were constantly branching off — in complete freedom. Each one grew out of the particular social and spiritual needs as these came to light — in complete freedom, and each one acquired, even in the initial stages, its own ideology — in complete freedom, each struggling to propagate itself and spread and establish its proper sphere — all in complete freedom. The champions of the various forms each had his say, the pros and cons of each individual form were frankly and fiercely debated . . . The various forms and intermediate forms that arose in this way at different times and in different situations represented different kinds of social structure . . . different forms corresponded to different human types and . . . just as new forms branched off from the original Kvuza, so new types branched off from the original Chaluz type, each with its

special mode of being and each demanding its particular sort of realization . . .' Martin Buber, *Paths in Utopia,* New York, Macmillan, 1950, pp. 145—6. [. . .]

3. See Benjamin Zablocki, *The Joyful Community,* Baltimore, Penguin, 1971.

4. For a recent account see Haim Barkai, 'The Kibbutz: an Experiment in Micro-socialism', in Irving Howe and Carl Gershman (eds) *Israel, the Arabs, and the Middle East,* New Yorks, Bantam Books, 1972.

5. I say *almost* every utopia and *almost* all particular utopian visions because it is unacceptable to, and incompatible with, 'utopians' of force and dominance.

6. It is strange that many young people 'in tune with' nature and hoping to 'go with the flow' and not force things against their natural bent should be attracted to statist views and socialism, and are antagonistic to equilibrium and invisible-hand processes.

7.2
Participatory Democracy

C. B. MACPHERSON

The rise of the idea

To call participatory democracy a model at all, let alone a model
of liberal democracy, is perhaps to yield too much to a liking for
symmetry . . . It began as a slogan of the 'new left' student
movements of the 1960s. It spread into the working class in the
1960s and '70s, no doubt as an offshoot of the growing job
dissatisfaction among both blue- and white-collar workers and the
more widespread feeling of alienation, which then became such
fashionable subjects for sociologists, management experts, government commissions of inquiry, and popular journalists. One
manifestation of this new spirit was the rise of movements for
workers' control in industry. In the same decades, the idea that
there should be substantial citizen participation in *government*
decision making spread so widely that national governments began
enrolling themselves, at least verbally, under the participatory
banner, and some even initiated programmes embodying extensive
citizen participation.[1] It appears that the hope of a more participatory society and system of government has come to stay. [. . .]

The problem of size

It is not much use simply celebrating the democratic quality of life
and of decision making (that is, of government) that can be had in
contemporary communes or New England town meetings or that
was had in ancient city-states. There may be a lot to learn about
the quality of democracy by examining these face-to-face societies,

Source: Abridged from *The Life and Times of Liberal Democracy* by C. B.
Macpherson. © Oxford University Press 1977. By permission of Oxford University
Press.

but that will not show us how a participatory democracy could operate in a modern nation of twenty million or two hundred million people. It seems clear that, at the national level, there will have to be some kind of representative system, not completely direct democracy.

The idea that recent and expected advances in computer technology and telecommunications will make it possible to achieve direct democracy at the required million-fold level is attractive not only to technologists but also to social theorists and political philosophers.[2] But it does not pay enough attention to an inescapable requirement of any decision-making process: somebody must formulate the questions.

No doubt something could be done with two-way television to draw more people into more active political discussion. And no doubt it is technically feasible to put in every living-room — or, to cover the whole population, beside every bed — a computer console with yes/no buttons, or buttons for agree/disagree/don't know, or for strongly approve/mildly approve/don't care/mildly disapprove/strongly disapprove, or for preferential multiple choices. But it seems inevitable that some government body would have to decide what questions would be asked: this could scarcely be left to private bodies.

There might indeed be a provision that some stated number of citizens have the right to propose questions which must then be put electronically to the whole electorate. But even with such a provision, most of the questions that would need to be asked in our present complex societies could scarcely be formulated by citizen groups specifically enough for the answers to give a government a clear directive. Nor can the ordinary citizen be expected to respond to the sort of questions that would be required to give a clear directive. The questions would have to be as intricate as, for instance, 'what per cent unemployment rate would you accept in order to reduce the rate of inflation by x per cent?', or 'what increase in the rate of (a) income tax, (b) sales and excise taxes, (c) other taxes (specify which), would you accept in order to increase by blank per cent (fill in [punch in] the blank), the level of (1) old age pensions, (2) health services, (3) other social services (specify which), (4) any other benefits (specify which)?' Thus even if there were provision for such a scheme of popular initiative, governments would still have to make a lot of the real decisions.

Moreover, unless there were, somewhere in the system, a body whose duty was to reconcile inconsistent demands presented by the buttons, the system would soon break down. If such a system were to be attempted in anything like our present society there would almost certainly be inconsistent demands. People — the same people — would, for instance, very likely demand a reduction of unemployment at the same time as they were demanding a reduction of inflation, or an increase in government expenditures along with a decrease in taxes. And of course different people — people with opposed interests, such as the presently privileged and the unprivileged — would also present incompatible demands. The computer could easily deal with the latter incompatibilities by ascertaining the majority position, but it could not sort out the former. To avoid the need for a body to adjust such incompatible demands to each other, the questions would have to be framed in a way that would require of each voter a degree of sophistication impossible to expect.

Nor would the situation be any better in any foreseeable future society. It is true that the sort of questions just mentioned, which are about the distribution of economic costs and economic benefits among different sections of the population, may be expected to become less acute in the measure that material scarcity becomes less pressing. But even if they were to disappear as internal problems in the economically most advanced societies, they would reappear there as external problems: for instance, how much and what kind of aid should the advanced countries afford to the underdeveloped ones? Moreover, another range of questions would arise internally, having to do not with distribution, but with production in the broadest sense, that is, with the uses to be made of the society's whole stock of energy and resources, and the encouragement or discouragement of further economic growth and population growth. And beyond that there would be such questions as the extent to which the society should promote or should keep its hands off the cultural and educational pursuits of the people.

Such questions, even in the most favourable circumstances imaginable, will require repeated reformulation. And questions of this sort do not readily lend themselves to formulation by popular initiative. Their formulation would have to be entrusted to a governmental body.

It might still be argued that, even if it is impossible to leave the formulation of all policy questions to popular initiative, at least the very broadest sort of policy could be left to it. Granted that the many hundreds of policy decisions that are now made every year by governments and legislatures would still have to be made by them, it might be urged that those decisions should be required to conform to the results of referenda on the very broadest questions. But it is difficult to see how most of the broadest questions could be left to formulation by popular initiative. Popular initiative could certainly formulate clear questions on certain single issues, for instance, capital punishment or legalization of marijuana or of abortion on demand — issues on which the response required is simply yes or no. But for the reasons given above, popular initiative could not formulate adequate questions on the great interrelated issues of overall social and economic policy. That would have to be left to some organ of government. And unless that organ were either an elected body or responsible to an elected body, and thus at some remove responsible to the electorate, such a system of continual referenda would not really be democratic: worse, by giving the appearance of being democratic, the system would conceal the real location of power and would thus enable 'democratic' governments to be more autocratic that they are now. We cannot do without elected politicians. We must rely, though we need not rely exclusively, on indirect democracy. The problem is to make the elected politicians responsible. The electronic console beside every bed cannot do that. Electronic technology, then, cannot give us direct democracy.

So the problem of participatory democracy on a mass scale seems intractable. It *is* intractable if we simply try to draw mechanical blueprints of the proposed political system without paying attention to the changes in society, and in people's consciousness of themselves, which a little thought will show must precede or accompany the attainment of anything like participatory democracy. I want to suggest now that the central problem is not how a participatory democracy would operate but how we could move towards it.

A vicious circle and possible loopholes

I begin with a general proposition: the main problem about participatory democracy is not how to run it but how to reach it. For it seems likely that if we can reach it, or reach any substantial instalment of it, our way along the road to reaching it will have made us capable of running it, or at least less incapable than we now are.

Having announced this proposition, I must immediately qualify it. The failures so far to reach really participatory democracy in countries where that has been a conscious goal, for instance Czechoslovakia in the years up to 1968 and many of the Third World countries, demand some reservations about such a proposition. For in both those cases, a good deal of the road had already been travelled: I mean the road away from capitalist class division and bourgeois ideology towards, in the one case, a Marxist humanism and, in the other, a Rousseauan concept of a society embodying a general will, and in both cases towards a stronger sense of community than we have. And, of course, the whole of the road had there been travelled away from that mirror image of the oligopolistic capitalist market system: I mean the oligopolistic competition of political parties which prevails with us, which is not only not very participatory, but is recommended, by most current liberal-democratic theorists, as quintessentially non-participatory.

So there are still difficulties in reaching participatory democracy, even when much of the road has been travelled, i.e. when some of the obvious prerequisite changes in society and ideology *have* taken place. However, the roads they have travelled in such countries as I have just mentioned are significantly different from the road we would have to travel to come near to participatory democracy. For I assume that our road in the Western liberal democracies is not likely to be via Communist revolution; nor, obviously, will it be via revolutions of national independence beset by all the problems of underdevelopment and low productivity that have faced the Third World countries.

It therefore seems worth enquiring what road it may be possible for any of the Western liberal democracies to travel, and whether, or to what extent, moving along that road could make us capable of operating a system substantially more participatory than our present one. This becomes the question: What roadblocks have to be removed, i.e. what changes in our present society and the now prevailing ideology are prerequisite or co-requisite conditions for reaching a participatory democracy? [. . .]

One is a change in people's consciousness (or unconsciousness), from seeing themselves and acting as essentially consumers to seeing themselves and acting as exerters and enjoyers of the exertion and development of their own capacities. This is requisite not only to the emergence but also to the operation of a participatory democracy. For the latter self-image brings with it a sense of community which the former does not. One can acquire and consume by oneself, for one's own satisfaction or to show one's superiority to others: this does not require or foster a sense of community; whereas the enjoyment and development of one's capacities is to be done for the most part in conjunction with others, in some relation of community. And it will not be doubted that the operation of a participatory democracy would require a stronger sense of community than now prevails.

The other prerequisite is a great reduction of the present social and economic inequality, since that inequality, as I have argued, requires a non-participatory party system to hold the society together. And as long as inequality is accepted, the non-participatory political system is likely also to be accepted by all those in all classes who prefer stability to the prospect of complete social breakdown.

Now if these two changes in society — the replacement of the image of man as consumer, and a great reduction of social and economic inequality — are prerequisites of participatory democracy, we seem to be caught in a vicious circle. For it is unlikely that either of these prerequisite changes could be effected without a great deal more democratic participation than there is now. The reduction of social and economic inequality is unlikely without strong democratic action. And it would seem, whether we follow Mill or Marx, that only through actual involvement in joint political action can people transcend their consciousness of themselves as consumers and appropriators. Hence the vicious circle: we cannot achieve more democratic participation without a prior change in social inequality and in consciousness, but we cannot achieve the changes in social inequality and consciousness without a prior increase in democratic participation.

Is there any way out? I think there may be, though in our affluent capitalist societies it is unlikely to follow the pattern proposed or expected in the nineteenth century either by Marx or by Mill . . . But there is one insight common to both of them that we might well follow. Both assumed that changes in the two factors which abstractly seem to be prerequisites of each other — the amount of political participation on the one hand, and the prevailing inequality and the image of man as infinite consumer and appropriator on the other — would come stage by stage and reciprocally, an incomplete change in one leading to some change in the other, leading to more change in the first, and so on. Even Marx's scenario, including as it did revolutionary change at one point, called for this reciprocal incremental change both before and after the revolution. We also may surely assume, in looking at our vicious circle, that we needn't expect one of the changes to be complete before the other can begin.

So we may look for loopholes anywhere in the circle, that is, for changes already visible or in prospect either in the amount of democratic participation or in social inequality or consumer consciousness. If we find changes which are not only already perceptible but which are attributable to forces or circumstances which are likely to go on operating with cumulative effect, then we can have some hope of a breakthrough. And if the changes are of a sort that encourages reciprocal changes in the other factors, so much the better.

Are there any loopholes which come up to these specifications? Let us start from the assumption least favourable to our search, the assumption that most of us are, willy-nilly, maximizing calculators of our own benefit, making a cost/benefit analysis of everything, however vaguely we make it; and that most of us consciously or unconsciously see ourselves as essentially infinite consumers. From these assumptions the vicious circle appears to follow directly: most people will support, or not do much to change, a system which produces affluence, which continually increases the Gross National Product, and which also produces political apathy. This makes a pretty strong vicious circle. But there are now some visible loopholes. I shall draw attention to three of them.

1. More and more people, in the capacity we have attributed to them all, namely as cost/benefit calculators, are reconsidering the cost/benefit ratio of our society's worship of expansion of the GNP. They still see the benefits of economic growth, but they are now beginning to see some costs they hadn't counted before. The most obvious of these are the costs of air, water, and earth pollution. These are costs largely in terms of the quality of life. Is it too much to suggest that this awareness of quality is a first step away from being satisfied with quantity, and so a first step away from seeing ourselves as infinite consumers, towards valuing our ability to exert our energies and capacities in a decent environment? Perhaps it is too much. But at any rate the growing consciousness of these costs weakens the unthinking acceptance of the GNP as the criterion of social good.

Other costs of economic growth, notably the extravagant depletion of natural resources and the likelihood of irreversible ecological damage, are also increasingly being noticed. Awareness of the costs of economic growth takes people beyond sheer consumer consciousness. It can be expected to set up some consciousness of a public interest that is not looked after either by the private interest of each consumer or by the competition of political élites.

2. There is an increasing awareness of the costs of political apathy, and, closely related to this, a growing awareness, within the industrial working class, of the inadequacy of traditional and routine forms of industrial action. It is coming to be seen that citizens' and workers' non-participation, or low participation, or participation only in routine channels, allows the concentration of

corporate power to dominate our neighbourhoods, our jobs, our security, and the quality of life at work and at home. Two examples of this new awareness may be given.

(a) The one that is most evident, at least in North American cities, which have hitherto been notoriously careless of human values, is the rise of neighbourhood and community movements and associations formed to exert pressure to preserve or enhance those values against the operations of what may be called the urban commercial-political complex. [. . .]

(b) Less noticeable, but probably in the long run more important, are the movements for democratic participation in decision making at the workplace. These movements have not yet made decisive strides in any of the capitalist democracies, but pressure for some degrees of workers' control at the shopfloor level and even at the level of the firm is increasing. [. . .]

3. There is a growing doubt about the ability of corporate capitalism, however much aided and managed by the liberal state, to meet consumer expectations in the old way, i.e. with the present degree of inequality. There is a real basis for this doubt: the basis is the existence of a contradiction within capitalism, the results of which cannot be indefinitely avoided.

Capitalism reproduces inequality and consumer consciousness, and must do so to go on operating. But its increasing ability to produce goods and leisure has as its obverse its increasing need to spread them more widely. If people can't buy the goods, no profit can be made by producing them. This dilemma can be staved off for quite a time by keeping up cold war and colonial wars: as long as the public will support these, then the public is, as consumers, buying by proxy all that can be profitably produced, and is wasting it satisfactorily. This has been going on for a long time now, but there is at least a prospect that it will not be indefinitely supported as normal. If it is not supported, then the system will either have to spread real goods more widely, which will reduce social inequality; or it will break down, and so be unable to continue to reproduce inequality and consumer consciousness. [. . .]

So we have three weak points in the vicious circle — the increasing awareness of the costs of economic growth, the increasing awareness of the costs of political apathy, the increasing doubts about the ability of corporate capitalism to meet consumer expectations while reproducing inequality. And each of these may be said to be contributing, in ways we have seen, to the possible attainment of the prerequisite conditions for participatory democracy: together, they conduce to a decline in consumer consciousness, a reduction of class inequality, and an increase in present political participation. The prospects for a more democratic society are thus not entirely bleak. The move towards it will both require and encourage an increasing measure of participation. And this now seems to be within the realm of the possible.

Before leaving this discussion of the possibility of moving to a participatory democracy, I must emphasize that I have been looking only for possible, even barely possible, ways ahead. I have not attempted to assess whether the chances of winning through are better or worse than 50/50. And when one thinks of the forces opposed to such a change, one might hesitate to put the chances as high as 50/50. One need only think of the power of multinational corporations; of the probability of the increasing penetration into home affairs of secret intelligence agencies such as the American CIA, which have been allowed or required by their governments to include in 'intelligence' such activities as organizing invasions of some smaller countries and assisting in the overthrow of disliked governments of others; and of the increasing use of political terrorism by outraged minorities of right and left, with the excuse they give governments of moving into the practices of the police state, and even getting a large measure of popular support for the police state. Against such forces can only be put the fact that liberal-democratic governments are reluctant to use open force on a large scale, except for very short periods, against any widely supported popular movements at home: understandably so, for by the time a government feels the need to do this it may well be unable to count on the army and the police. [. . .]

I do not know of enough empirical evidence to enable one to judge the relative strength of the forces in our present society making for, and those making against, a move to a more participatory democracy. So my exploration of possible forces making for it is not to be taken as a prophecy, but only as a glimpse of possibilities.

Models of participatory democracy

Let me turn finally to the question of how a participatory democracy might be run if we did achieve the prerequisites. How participatory could it be, given that at any level beyond the neighbourhood it would have to be an indirect or representative system rather than face-to-face direct democracy?

Model (4A): an abstract first approximation

If one looks at the question first in general terms, setting aside for the present both the weight of tradition and the actual circumstances that might prevail in any country when the prerequisites had been sufficiently met, the simplest model that could properly be called a participatory democracy would be a pyramidal system with direct democracy at the base and delegate democracy at every level above that. Thus one would start with direct democracy at the neighbourhood or factory level — actual face-to-face discussion and decision by consensus or majority, and election of delegates who would make up a council at the next more inclusive level, say a city borough or ward or a township. The delegates would have to be sufficiently instructed by and accountable to those who elected them to make decisions at the council level reasonably democratic. So it would go on up to the top level, which would be a national council for matters of national concern, and local and regional councils for matters of less than national concern. At whatever level beyond the smallest primary one the final decisions on different matters were made, the issues would certainly have to be formulated by a committee of the council. Thus at whatever level the reference up stopped, it would stop in effect with a small committee of that level's council. This may seem a far cry from democratic control. But I think it is the best we can do. What is needed, at every stage, to make the system democratic, is that the decision makers and issue formulators elected from below be held responsible to those below by being subject to re-election or even recall.

Now such a system, no matter how clearly responsibilities are set out on paper, even if the paper is a formal national constitution, is no guarantee of effective democratic participation or control: the Soviet Union's 'democratic centralism', which was just such a scheme, cannot be said to have provided the democratic control that had been intended. The question is whether such failure is inherent in the nature of a pyramidal councils system. I think it is not. I suggest that we can identify the sets of circumstances in which the system won't work as intended, that is, won't provide adequate responsibility to those below, won't be actively democratic. Three such sets of circumstances are evident.

1. A pyramidal system will not provide real responsibility of the government to all the levels below in an immediately post-revolutionary situation; at least it will not do so if the threat of counter-revolution, with or without foreign intervention, is present. For in that case, democratic control, with all its delays, has to give way to central authority. That was the lesson of the immediate aftermath of the 1917 Bolshevik Revolution. A further lesson, to be drawn from the subsequent Soviet experience, is that, if a revolution bites off more than it can chew democratically, it will chew it undemocratically.

Now since we do not seem likely, in the Western liberal democracies, to try to move to full democracy by way of a Bolshevik revolution, this does not appear to be a difficulty for us. But we must notice that the threat of counter-revolution is present not only after a Bolshevik revolution but also after a parliamentary revolution, i.e. a constitutional, electoral, takeover of power by a party or popular front pledged to a radical reform leading to the replacement of capitalism. That this threat may be real, and be fatal to a constitutional revolutionary regime which tries to proceed democratically, is evident in the example of the counter-revolutionary overthrow of the Allende regime in Chile in 1973, after three years in office. We have to ask, therefore, whether the Chilean sequence could be repeated in any of the more advanced Western liberal democracies. Could it happen in, say, Italy or France? If it could, the chances of participatory democracy in any such country would be slim.

There is no certainty that it could not happen there. We cannot rely on there being a longer habit of constitutionalism in Western Europe than in Latin America: indeed, in those European liberal democracies which are most likely to be in this situation in the forseeable future (e.g. Italy and France), the tradition of constitutionalism cannot be said to be much older or firmer than in Chile. We should, however, notice that Allende's popular front coalition was in control of only a part of the executive power (the presidency, but not the *contraloria,* which had power to rule on the legality of any executive action), and was in control of none of the legislative (including taxing) power. If a similar government elsewhere came into office with a stronger base it could proceed democratically without the same risk of being overthrown by counter-revolution.

2. Another circumstance in which a responsible pyramidal councils system would not work would be a reappearance of an underlying class division and opposition. For, as we have seen, such division requires that the political system, in order to hold the society

together, be able to perform the function of continual compromise between class interests, and that function makes it impossible to have clear and strong lines of responsibility from the upper elected levels downwards.

But this also is not as great a problem for us as it might seem. For if my earlier analysis is right, we shall not have reached the possibility of installing such a responsible system until we have greatly reduced the present social and economic inequalities. It is true that this will be possible only in the measure that the capital/labour relation that prevails in our society has been fundamentally changed, for capitalist relations produce and reproduce opposed classes. No amount of welfare-state redistribution of income will by itself change that relation. Nor will any amount of workers' participation or workers' control at the shop-floor level or the plant level: that is a promising breakthrough point, but it will not do the whole job. A fully democratic society requires democratic political control over the uses to which the amassed capital and the remaining natural resources of the society are put. It probably does not matter whether this takes the form of social ownership of all capital, or a social control of it so thorough as to be virtually the same as ownership. But more welfare-state redistribution of the national income is not enough: no matter how much it might reduce class inequalities of income it would not touch class inequalities of power.

3. A third circumstance in which the pyramidal council system would not work is, of course, if the people at the base were apathetic. Such a system could not have been reached except by a people who had thrown off their political apathy. But might not apathy grow again? There can be no guarantee that it would not. But at least the main factor which I have argued creates and sustains apathy in our present system would by hypothesis be absent or at least greatly modified — I mean the class structure which discourages the participation of those in the lower strata by rendering it relatively ineffective, and which more generally discourages participation by requiring such a blurring of issues that governments cannot be held seriously responsible to the electorate.

To sum up the discussion so far of the prospects of a pyramidal councils system as a model of participatory democracy, we may say that in the measure that the prerequisite conditions for transition to a participatory system had been achieved in any Western country, the most obvious impediments to a pyramidal councils scheme being genuinely democratic would not be present. A pyramidal system might work. Or other impediments might emerge to prevent it being fully democratic. It is not worth pursuing these, for this simple model is too unrealistic. It can be nothing but a first approximation to a workable model, for it was reached by deliberately setting aside what must now be brought back into consideration — the weight of tradition and the actual circumstances that are likely to prevail in any Western nation at the time when the transition became possible.

The most important factor here is the existence of political parties. The simple model has no place for them. It envisages a no-party or one-party system. This was appropriate enough when such a model was put forward in the revolutionary circumstances of mid seventeenth-century England and early twentieth-century Russia. But it is not appropriate for late twentieth-century Western nations, for it seems unlikely that any of them will move to the threshold of participatory democracy by way of a one-party revolutionary takeover. It is much more likely that any such move will be made under the leadership of a popular front or a coalition of social-democratic and socialist parties. Those parties will not wither away, at least not for some years. Unless all of them but one are put down by force, several will still be around. The real question then is, whether there is some way of combining a pyramidal council structure with a competitive party system.

Model (4B): a second approximation

The combination of a pyramidal direct/indirect democratic machinery with a continuing party system seems essential. Nothing but a pyramidal system will incorporate any direct democracy into a nation-wide structure of government, and some significant amount of direct democracy is required for anything that can be called participatory democracy. At the same time, competitive political parties must be assumed to be in existence, parties whose claims cannot, consistently with anything that could be called a liberal democracy, be overridden.

Not only is the combination of pyramid and parties probably unavoidable: it may be positively desirable. For even in a non-class-divided society there would still be issues around which parties might form, or even might be needed to allow issues to be effectively proposed and debated: issues such as the overall allocation of resources, environmental and urban planning, population and immigration policies, foreign policy, military policy.[3] Now supposing that a competitive party system were either unavoidable, or actually desirable, in a non-exploitive, non-class-divided society, could it be combined with any kind of pyramidal direct/indirect democracy?

I think it could. For the main functions which the competitive party system has had to perform, and has performed, in class-divided societies up to now, i.e. the blurring of class opposition and the continual arranging of compromises or apparent com-promises between the demands of opposed classes, would no longer be required. And those are the features of the competitive party system which have made it up to now incompatible with any effective participatory democracy. With that function no longer required, the incompatibility disappears.

There are, in abstract theory, two possibilities of combining a pyramidal organization with competing parties. One, much the more difficult, and so unlikely as to deserve no attention here, would be to replace the existing Western parliamentary or congressional/presidential structure of government by a soviet-type structure, (which is conceivable even with two or more parties). The other, much less difficult, would be to keep the existing structure of government, and rely on the parties themselves to operate by pyramidal participation. It is true, as I said earlier, that all the many attempts made by democratic reform movements and parties to make their leaders, when they became the govern-ment, responsible to the rank-and-file, have failed. But the reason for those failures would no longer exist in the circumstances we are considering, or at least would not exist to anything like the same degree. The reason for those failures was that strict responsibility of the party leadership to the membership does not allow the room for manoeuvre and compromise which a govern-ment in a class-divided society must have in order to carry out its necessary function of mediating between opposed class interests in the whole society. No doubt, even in a non-class-divided society, there would still have to be some room for compromise. But the amount of room needed for compromise on the sort of issues that might then divide parties would not be of the same order of magnitude as the amount now required, and the element of deception or concealment required to carry on the continual blurring of class lines would not be present.

It thus appears that there is a real possibility of genuinely participatory parties, and that they could operate through a parliamentary or congressional structure to provide a substantial measure of participatory democracy. This I think is as far as it is now feasible to go by way of a blueprint.

Participatory democracy as liberal democracy?

One question remains: can this model of participatory democracy be called a model of liberal democracy? I think it can. It is clearly not dictatorial or totalitarian. The guarantee of this is not the existence of alternative parties, for it is conceivable that after some decades they might wither away, in conditions of greater plenty and widespread opportunity for citizen participation other than through political parties. In that case we should have moved to Model (4A). The guarantee is rather in the presumption that no version of Model (4) could come into existence or remain in existence without a strong and widespread sense of the value of that liberal-democratic ethical principle which was the heart of Model (2) — the equal right of every man and woman to the full development and use of his or her capabilities. And of course the very possibility of Model (4) requires also, as argued in the second section of this chapter, a downgrading or abandonment of market assumptions about the nature of man and society, a departure from the image of man as maximizing consumer, and a great reduction of the present economic and social inequality. Those changes would make possible a restoration, even a realization, of the central ethical principle of Model (2); and they would not, for the reason given earlier, logically deny to a Model (4) the description 'liberal'. As long as there remained a strong sense of the high value of the equal right of self-development, Model (4) would be in the best tradition of liberal democracy.

Notes

1. e.g. the Community Action Programs inaugurated by the United States federal government in 1964, which called for 'maximum feasible participation of residents of the areas and members of the groups served'. For a critical account of this, see 'Citizen participation in emerging social institutions' by Howard I. Kalodner (1975) in J. R. Pennock and J. W. Chapman (eds), *Participation in Politics*, New York.
2. See Michael Rossman (1972) *On Learning and Social Change*, New York, pp. 257—8; and Robert Paul Wolff (1970) *In Defense of Anarchism*, New York, pp. 34—7.
3. It is worth noticing that in Czechoslovakia, in the Spring and Summer of 1968 just before the overthrow of the reformist Communist Dubček

regime by the military intervention of the USSR, one of the widely canvassed proposals for enhancing the democratic quality of the political system was the introduction of a competitive party system, and that this had substantial public support and even some support within the ruling Communist Party. In a July public opinion poll 25 per cent of the CP members polled, and 58 per cent of non-party persons polled, wanted one or more new parties; in an August poll, in which the question was put ambiguously, the figures were 16 per cent and 35 per cent. (H. Gordon Skilling (1976) *Czechoslovakia's Interrupted Revolution,* Princeton University Press, pp. 550—1, 356—72.)

7.3
A Résumé of Premises

RUDOLPH BAHRO

Marx and Engels were convinced . . . that capitalism in its stage of free competition had essentially already brought about, or would bring about, the productive forces that provided the material conditions for universal emancipation, for the free development of all individuals. Once the exploiters were expropriated, they reckoned, the driving forces unleashed for a society now liberated from all former antagonisms would in a short time see to it that the sources of social wealth would flow abundantly enough for Communist organization to prevail in the relations of distribution, making any state regulation superfluous. The extent to which they overestimated the maturity of the productive forces is shown by the simple fact that a further one hundred years of rapid industrial progress has been made on the basis of this antagonistic formation, while in recent decades a second industrial revolution, this time a scientific one, has been carried through.

Disarmament would probably put the *richest* capitalist countries in a position to guarantee *today* the elementary requirements of free individuality for all, on the basis of the productivity now attained, but *only within their own frontiers.* And here we see the other and still more momentous aspect that forces us to speak of the immaturity of the productive forces in the nineteenth century: industrial progress has by-passed the overwhelming majority of the world's population. At the present time the problem might well consist in industrialism, taken from a global standpoint, having developed so disproportionately. Has it not in some regions already overstepped its useful limits and intensified a parasitism that is typical of capitalism to bring about an acute crisis in our

Source: From *The Alternative in Eastern Europe* (1981) London, New Left Books and Verso, pp. 123—38.

metabolism with nature? And is it not working, in a manner determined by its inner antagonistic mechanism of reproduction, to make the poverty of the rest of the world ever greater? This catastrophic drop in productivity and standard of living actually guarantees that the historically privileged nations will not disarm, so that in this way too emancipation is hindered (at least globally, not necessarily an emancipation within certain local limits, which cannot be genuine emancipation).

But the resources set free by disarmament would initially yield simply a sum of dead capital, as long as society did not reorganize them in a structurally different way. Let us assume that we have the necessary quantity of produced goods at our disposal. Let us further assume that the capitalist mode of production is abolished. It would then be finally clear that equal opportunity in the relations of *distribution* of material goods and possibilities of education is not a sufficient lever to produce free individuals on a mass level. *For social inequality is anchored in the division of labour, in the structures of technology and cooperation themselves.* In the whole of former world history only the agents of general labour were free, i.e. the privileged planners and politicians, thinkers, scientists and artists — in so far as the reflected self-consciousness that is subjectively decisive for freedom is only attained in relation to the totality of human objects. [. . .]

The bureaucratic informational superstructure of the modern apparatus of production gives the separation of mental and manual labour deeper roots than ever before, or more precisely, the separation between planning or command and execution. The same separation that the Chinese philosopher Meng-tse described nearly two and a half thousand years ago in the following terms: 'Some work with the mind and some with the bodily powers. Those who work with the mind rule others, and those who work with their powers are ruled by others. Those who are ruled carry others, and those who rule are carried by others.' This universal principle is certainly undermined by the fact that the 'carrying work' now involves a large number of compartmentalized intellectual operations as well, but this is by no means sufficient to break it down.

Even the richest peoples, therefore, if they could throw off the capitalist shell tomorrow, would still face a long struggle to take control of their technical and social apparatus from within, i.e. to divest the functions of regulation and administration bit by bit of their immanent character of domination. (The momentous anticipation of this goal was one of the essential inspirations of the French May revolt of 1968. It goes without saying, moreover, that

Marxism would not have played as great a role as it did in this movement's motivation, if Marx had not himself been aware of this problem of restructuring.)

In any case, Communism presupposes mature industrialism, although the question of what precisely constitutes maturity is, naturally, settled not just by technical criteria but rather by social movements. To this extent, even criticism of Marx and Engels' overestimation of the productive forces must be toned down. Given the present structure of industrial societies in both formations, the productive forces will never become mature, despite and precisely on account of their technical dynamic. Yet even today those countries that first set out on the industrial capitalist road are those materially closest to socialism. Nowhere is the *beginning* of the transformation more pressing than it is there. But it is also nowhere more hard. And neither the less developed nor the underdeveloped peoples can afford to wait for them.

Lenin was the first Marxist to recognize in the awakening of Asia, as a response to the destruction of its traditional social structure by modern imperialism, the perspectives that the popular masses of the colonial and semi-colonial countries would not remain in the role of passive objects of super-exploitation and absolute poverty. The Russian Revolution showed that these peoples could not escape their pariah role simply by political and military liberation struggles and revolutions. The specific task of these revolutions is the restructuring of the pre-capitalist countries for their own road to industrialization, the non-capitalist one that involves a different *social formation* from that of the European road. While Lenin did not have sufficient time to generalize all the consequences of this development, he did assert very clearly that the industrialization of the Soviet Union to the point of catching up with the developed capitalist countries would only create the *preconditions* of socialism. He could only hope, more as revolutionary than as historical materialist, that the political structure of the country, the character of the relations of domination, could be kept at the level of anticipation of 1917, if not without temporary compromises and retreats. [. . .]

The term 'non-capitalist' covers developments that display very different phenomenal forms according to the traditional milieu that is to be transformed. The singularity of the concept, on the other hand, indicates the common basic tendency that all these developments are dictated by the demand that produces them. In its very negativity it expresses the fact that it is still European and American *capitalist* industrialism, now joined also by the Japanese, that sets the rest of the world its problems, even if the balance of forces is gradually tilting against it. The state repression in the countries of actually existing socialism is in the last analysis a function of their industrial underdevelopment, or more exactly, of the task of actively overcoming this underdevelopment by an 'inorganic' restructuring, so as to preserve their national identity ('inorganic' in the sense that the Russian peasantry, for example, had simply no organic socio-economic inclination towards collectivization.) The pressure of a materially superior civilization can not be met by a minority regime that gives itself such a task without erecting a defensive 'iron curtain' both internally and against the outside world, and without comprehensive regimentation against any 'spontaneity'.

The industrial civilization that has changed European life beyond recognition in the last two centuries leaves other nations no alternative. Whether they had already reached the threshold of capitalism and industrialization in their own evolution, or whether it encountered them epochs removed from it — they must go through this crucible. If those too brusquely ejected from an earlier age have always turned time and again to the past, in search of the lost paradise, similar illusions today are assured of a rapid and bitter end. The 'guarantees of harmony and freedom', if they exist, can only be attained the other side of industrialism, which means by the social mastery of the material basis industrialism has created. And only those nations whose history, and the immensity of their demand, gives them the capacity to organize themselves for the forced march into the modern era, have a prospect of maintaining their identity and bringing the treasures of their cultural tradition into that global human culture that is already in the process of arising. Their traditional life is not mercilessly shattered only by the direct aggression of the rich countries, but even more so by the overall effect of their technical and scientific civilization. Even the genuine 'blessings of Western civilization', for example its achievements in hygiene and medicine, act initially in the agricultural countries to increase the spread of poverty, prolong the torment of the path of development, and deepen the feeling of despair, given their particular law of population.

In order to understand what has been happening in the most vital countries since 1917, not those of the 'Third' world, but more specifically those of a precapitalist 'Second' world, we must in the first place understand the civilizing role of the state that has been confirmed throughout world history. Marx and Engels in no way denied it, yet their concentration on bourgeois conditions gave the European labour movement too specific a concept of the state, one which sees only its function of domination, its relationship to the special interests of the economically ruling classes. When we look at history tectonically, this function is only the secondary one. Primarily, the state was *the* institution of civilization, of the original formation of the different social bodies. It arises with the earliest class antitheses, but it is not simply their derivative or product. Of course, the objective general interest whose instrument it formed was diverted straight away by the special interest of the minority who bore it. But this antagonism only became acute when the rulers foresook their general functions in pursuit of their own particular interests, and so provoked the rebellion of the oppressed. How far the overall relationship was justified, however, can be precisely measured by the historical gulf that today lies between the exploited industrial workers and engineers of the rich countries, and — let us say — the 'freemen' in the Indian tribes of Latin America.

The anti-state and anti-authoritarian ideology of many intellectuals in the West, though it is generally too unenlightened, does have its historical justification in countries that have already industrialized, where the material conditions for the demise of the state are maturing. But those people who are just in the process of organizing themselves for industrialization cannot abandon this instrument, and their state can be nothing other than bureaucratic.

The state as taskmaster of society in its technical and social modernization — this fundamental model can be found time and again since 1917, wherever pre-capitalist countries or their decisive minorities have organized themselves for active entry into the twentieth century. If, from this standpoint, the Soviet Union is identical not only with China, but also with Burma, Algeria or Guinea, and not only with Guinea, but recently also with Peru or Zaire, and not only Zaire, but even Iran . . . this only underlines the fundamental value of the state in this context. And we can conclude that the cause that has produced such a common feature in the most varied of historical milieus, while it certainly had to find a more or less favourable national soil, is in the last analysis not of an internal nature but rather an external one. In a way similar to how the advanced civilizations of the ancient world — the Babylonians, Egyptians, Chinese or Romans — started a ferment in the barbarian tribes on their borders, drew them into their own crises and forced them to form a state of their own, so modern capitalism and imperialism has borne the germs of dissolution into the stagnant hearths of earlier civilizations, destroyed their social balance and provoked their reorganization. It was international imperialism that shook the ground beneath the thrones of the Romanovs and Manchus, and which brought Asia,

Africa and Latin America to rise against it.

Russia had the good fortune — which was at the same time the reason for the prolonged self-deception as to the character of its revolution — that one class in the post-revolutionary society already stood on the ground of modern industrialism, even if this was for the most part that of the nineteenth century: textile factories, munitions, railways, mining and metallurgy. The small working class was the motor of the revolution and the pledge of its industrial possibilities. In completely pre-capitalist countries the traditional social structure, the traditional constellation of economic interests, does not enable a single class or group to assume the hegemony in such a reorganization. Tribal, caste and kinship relations, together with the political inheritance, provide an overwhelming tendency for any progressive orientation to be corrupted. Authorities rooted in the old relations are completely unsuited for initiatives that would inevitably lead to the destruction of these roots. The only alternative here is a bureaucracy, civilian or military, whose members are corruptible chiefly through their power over the process of transformation itself. The discipline of obedience to instructions, which can only be made effective with a despotism of some kind or other, is the surest guarantee that the progressive interests will carry the day, in the actions of individual officials who are personally rooted in the old structures by a thousand threads. Party centres such as Lenin and Mao Tse-tung were able to forge for their future bureaucracies, are up till now still unparalleled prototypes of a discipline not rooted only in terror, and which therefore proves extraordinarily fruitful.

It was also the influence of industrial capitalism that fostered a social basis of recruitment for this necessary state apparatus, or gave groupings that were already present their modern significance. As a rule, the combination of imperialism with local commercial and money-lending capitalists who become comprador elements holds back the development of a national industrial bourgeoisie for so long that, when the time comes for the political reorganization that introduces economic transformation, they are not sufficiently consolidated to become representative hegemonial classes. Where the bourgeoisie can still makes its influence decisively felt, as for example in India, the nation pays with the slowing down of industrialization and of the necessary reorganization in general. In the typical case it is generally a quite different social grouping which separates itself from the upper and middle strata of the old society, gets its education in the industrialized countries, undertakes agitation for liberation and national renewal, appears politically, ideologically and militarily at the head of the liberation struggle and finally, in a changed and expanded connection, creates the state machine for 'development' and forms its cadre: a national intelligentsia, and, when the crisis in their conditions of life comes to a head in such a way as to sufficiently mobilize the masses, a social-revolutionary intelligentsia.

The basis of this intelligentsia is not a specific socio-economic position of power — it grows into this only in the process of the post-revolutionary transformations — but rather the consensus of the popular masses, who can no longer go on living as before and are therefore waiting for a leadership. Precisely in the ideal case of a revolution of national liberation — i.e. if this succeeds in effectively out-manoeuvring the traditional powers and mastering the necessities of development of the productive forces — the basic structure of society on the non-capitalist road is anticipated in the relationship between the agitated masses and the intelligentsia as a grouping organized for political and military leadership. The intelligentsia as a bureaucratic officialdom will become the (hopefully effective) guardian and goad of the working masses, who have little to hope for in their own lifetimes on the long, hard road of renunciation that leads to an indigenous industrial base, and who will soon come to understand this. The antagonisms or 'contradictions among the people' at which the remoulded society toils are then perfected.

If everything that has been said so far on this theme is brought together, we can then give the following as historical roots for the subjection of Soviet society to a bureaucratic state machine.

1. The pressure of the technological superiority of the imperialist countries, enforced by their policy of military intervention and encirclement. This factor has in fact exerted a *deforming* effect from outside on the development of the political superstructure, and represents the deepest reason for the *excesses* of the Stalin terror. The constant external threat reinforced the pressure that already burdened the process of political self-management within the ruling party and created the specific fortress neurosis in which friend and foe could no longer be distinguished.

2. The semi-Asiatic past of Russia, with
   (a) the inherited fragmentation of its agricultural base;
   (b) the extremely heterogenous national composition of its colonialist multinational state;
   (c) the political traditions of Tsarist autocracy going back to the despotism of Baty Khan; and

(d) the psychology of the masses still trapped to a large extent in primary patriarchy.

Antonio Gramsci coined the concept of revolution-restoration to express the way that the political leap must always be followed by a settlement with the past, because the new social forces never immediately embrace the totality of economic relations and the productive forces that bear these, and are therefore constrained to compromise precisely for the sake of their own hegemony. The averting of political restoration and the defence of the state had to be paid for with important concessions to the old way of life and ideology. The people, including a working class for the most part newly recruited, were waiting for their *nachalniki* (bureaucrats).

3. The revolutionary situation itself. Even those formations renowned for their pluralist economic power structure stood at their beginning and end under the sign of an overwhelming state power. Periclean Athens fell between Solon, Pisistratos and his sons and Cleisthenes on the one hand, and Alexander on the other, republican Rome between the Tarquins and the Caesars, feudal particularism between Charlemagne and Louis XIV, capitalism of free competition between the military dictatorships of Cromwell and Bonaparte, and the state monopoly regime of the present. On the methods of primitive accumulation of capital (of *capital*, mark you!), Marx wrote: 'But they all employ the power of the state, the concentrated and organized force of society, to hasten, as in a hothouse, the process of transformation of the feudal mode of production into the capitalist mode, and to shorten the transition. Force is the midwife of every old society which is pregnant with a new one'. (This sentence is customarily quoted in connection with the political revolution.) 'It is itself an economic power.' In the first years of Soviet power, the Bolsheviks, in particular Preobrazhensky, openly discussed the implication of the 'primitive accumulation' of modern productive forces in Russia. And here we come on to the fourth decisive root of the preceptor role of the state power in the Soviet Union, a correct understanding of which is of extreme importance for a realistic perspective of further transformations.

4. The productive forces that had to be accumulated under the pressure of the capitalist environment, in order to create the preconditions of socialism, themselves bear an antagonistic character. If, as Marx maintains, the means of labour 'indicate the social relations within which men work' ('it is not what is made but how, and by what instruments of labour, that distinguishes different economic epochs'), how then can we base Communism on the

Taylorism we have today, on a kind of machinery that is for the most part that depicted in Marx's *Capital*? Even such a writer as Rostow is correct in rebutting this pretence, which has long been more hypocrisy than genuine illusion. Whether the role played by the level of the productive forces is made into something absolute or not, these certainly cannot be overrated. The slogan that labour is a cause for renown and honour is no better than the work ethic of Protestantism at covering up the underlying fact that industrial work, in the form so far prevailing, bears a compulsive character. This is precisely the reality that this slogan presupposes. Via a principle of reward according to work that is in no way taken from Marx, the Soviet state has fulfilled the most important double function of achieving labour discipline and combatting the egalitarian tendencies of the masses. This was the precondition for economic advance in the conditions inherited from the Russian past.

The kernel of the state economic policy was positive, in its rigorous centralization of the entire surplus product of the workers, and later and above all also of the peasants; yet the purpose was to accumulate more on this narrower basis than the capitalists whom it was seeking to overtake. From the standpoint of the working masses, this meant wage-labour in its most naked form, labour for the simple reproduction of their physical existence as producers. [. . .] All in all, the Soviet state, with the party as its core, was not the substitute for a working class too weak to exercise power, but rather the special substitute for an exploiting class.

But what explains the fact that *now*, when the hardest work in the Soviet Union is already over, when the material preconditions of socialism are at least achieved far above that minimum that Lenin once took to be necessary, the Stalinist superstructure still so obstinately persists?

Above all, the measure of accumulation needed for socialism is not determined within the system itself, but rather in so-called economic competition with capitalism. [. . .]

The relationship between people and leadership is institutionally the same as in the 1930s, where it functioned despite the terror in the direction of progress. But today this relationship proves increasingly ineffective. Here the inertia of the institutions plays a particularly ominous role, as it is anchored in the immediate vital interest of several million peoples, those who created the Stalin apparatus or were at least moulded by it, representing it right down to the tiniest kholkoz village. Every time contradictions come to a head, they tend spontaneously to regress to the same 'measures', campaigns and 'structural changes', in variations that are no longer even resourceful in their senile mechanism. In its present form, the Soviet system of government is locked in a vicious circle, consisting on the one hand of the dilemma of economic competition, on the other of the social and mental regression of the party, state and economic bureaucracy. This vicious circle must of course be broken, starting with this second element. The Party and the Soviet state can refer to their forceful economic achievements — but these belong to history. The party will lose its birthright if it is not in a position to renovate both itself and the state in a fundamental way, i.e. socially instead of just bureaucratically.

Does the solution lie simply in an immediate demolition of the state machine? [. . .] The abstract centralist form of the state, by which the administration of things is entoiled, will only become positively superfluous to the extent that a system of social self-organization grows up from below into this inorganic scaffolding. The state too must be *raised to a higher level*. But this implies that instead of working under the bureaucratic control of an ossified party *apparatus*, it works under the ideological supremacy of an organized Communist movement, which decisively prevents it from holding back the construction of this social self-management.

7.4
Towards a Democratic Socialism

NICOS POULANTZAS

The question of socialism and democracy, of the democratic road
to socialism, is today posed with reference to two historical
experiences, which in a way serve as examples of the twin limits or
dangers to be avoided: the traditional social-democratic experience,
as illustrated in a number of West European countries, and the
Eastern example of what is called 'real socialism'. Despite
everything that distinguishes these cases, despite everything that
opposes social democracy and Stalinism to each other as
theoretico-political currents, they nevertheless exhibit a fundamental complicity: both are marked by *statism* and profound
distrust of mass initiatives, in short by suspicion of democratic
demands. In France, many now like to speak of two traditions of
the working-class and popular movements: the statist and Jacobin
one, running from Lenin and the October Revolution to the Third
International and the Communist movement; and a second one
characterized by notions of self-management and direct, rank-and-
file democracy. It is then argued that the achievement of
democratic socialism requires a break with the former and
integration with the latter. In fact, however, this is a rather
perfunctory way of posing the question. Although there are indeed
two traditions, they do not coincide with the currents just
mentioned. Moreover, it would be a fundamental error to imagine
that mere integration with the current of self-management and
direct democracy is sufficient to avoid statism.

First of all, then, we must take yet another look at Lenin and the
October Revolution. Of course, Stalinism and the model of the
transition to socialism bequeathed by the Third International

Source: From *State, Power, Socialism* (1980) London, New Left Books and Verso,
pp. 251–65.

differ from Lenin's own thought and action. But they are not simply a deviation from the latter. Seeds of Stalinism were well and truly present in Lenin — and not only because of the peculiarities of Russia and the Tsarist state with which he had to grapple. The error of the Third International cannot be explained simply as an attempt to universalize in an aberrant manner a model of socialism that corresponded, in its purity, to the concrete situation of Tsarist Russia. At the same time, these seeds are not to be found in Marx himself. Lenin was the first to tackle the problem of the transition to socialism and the withering away of the state, concerning which Marx left only a few general observations on the close relationship between socialism and democracy.

What then was the exact import of the October Revolution for the withering away of the state? Out of the several problems relating to the seeds of the Third International in Lenin, one seems here to occupy a dominant position. For all Lenin's analyses and actions are traversed by the following *leitmotif*; the state must be entirely destroyed through frontal attack in a situation of *dual power*, to be replaced by a second power — soviets — which will no longer be a state in the proper sense of the term, since it will already have begun to wither away. What does Lenin mean by this destruction of the bourgeois state? Unlike Marx, he often reduces the institutions of representative democracy and political freedoms to a simple emanation of the bourgeoisie: representative democracy = bourgeois democracy = dictatorship of the bourgeoisie. They have to be completely uprooted and replaced by direct, rank-and-file democracy and mandated, recallable delegates — in other words, by the genuine proletarian democracy of soviets.

I am intentionally drawing a highly schematized picture: Lenin's principal thrust was not at first towards a variant of authoritarian statism. I say this not in order to leap to Lenin's defence, but to point up the simplistic and befogging character of that conception according to which developments in Soviet Russia resulted from Lenin's 'centralist' opposition to direct democracy — from a Leninism which is supposed to have carried within it the crushing of the Kronstadt sailors' revolt, in the way that a cloud carries the storm. Whether we like it or not, the original guiding thread of Lenin's thought was, in opposition to the parliamentarianism and dread of workers' councils characteristic of the social-democratic current, the sweeping replacement of 'formal' representative democracy by the 'real', direct democracy of workers' councils. (The term 'self-management' was not yet used in Lenin's time.) This leads me on to the real question. Was it not this very line (sweeping substitution of rank-and-file democracy for representative democracy) which principally accounted for what happened in Lenin's lifetime in the Soviet Union, and which gave rise to the centralizing and statist Lenin whose posterity is well enough known?

I said that I am posing the question. But as a matter of fact, it was already posed in Lenin's time and answered in a way that now seems dramatically premonitory. I am referring, of course, to Rosa Luxemburg, whom Lenin called an eagle of revolution. She also had the eye of an eagle. For it was she who made the first correct and fundamental critique of Lenin and the Bolshevik Revolution. It is decisive because it issues not from the ranks of social democracy, which did not want even to hear of direct democracy and workers' councils, but precisely from a convinced fighter who gave her life for council democracy, being executed at the moment when the German workers' councils were crushed by social democracy.

Now, Luxemburg reproaches Lenin not with neglect or contempt of direct, rank-and-file democracy, but rather with *the exact opposite* — that is to say, *exclusive* reliance on council democracy and complete elimination of representative democracy (through, among other things, dissolution of the Constituent Assembly — which had been elected under the Bolshevik government — in favour of the soviets alone). It is necessary to re-read *The Russian Revolution*, from which I shall quote just one passage. 'In place of the representative bodies created by general, popular elections, Lenin and Trotsky have laid down the soviets as the only true representation of the labouring masses. But with the repression of political life in the land as a whole, life in the soviets must also become more and more crippled. Without general elections, without unrestricted freedom of press and assembly, without a free struggle of opinion, life dies out in every public institution, becomes a mere semblance of life, in which only the bureaucracy remains as the active element.'[1]

This is certainly not the only question to be asked concerning Lenin. An important role in subsequent developments was played by the conception of the Party contained in *What is to be Done?*; by the notion of theory being brought to the working class from outside by professional revolutionaries, and so on. But the fundamental question is the one posed by Luxemburg. Even if we take into account Lenin's positions on a series of other problems, as well as the historical peculiarities of Russia, what ensued in Lenin's own lifetime and above all after his death (the single Party, bureaucratization of the Party, confusion of Party and state, statism, the end of the soviets themselves, etc.) was already inscribed in the situation criticized by Luxemburg.

Be that as it may, let us now look at the 'model' of revolution that was bequeathed by the Third International, having already been affected by Stalinism in certain ways. We find the same position with regard to representative democracy, only now it is combined with statism and contempt for direct, rank-and-file democracy — in short, the meaning of the entire council problematic is twisted out of shape. The resulting model is permeated by the instrumental conception of the state. The capitalist state is still considered as a mere object or instrument, capable of being manipulated by the bourgeoisie of which it is the emanation. According to this view of things, the state is not traversed by internal contradictions, but is a monolithic bloc without cracks of any kind. The struggles of the popular masses cannot pass through the state, any more than they can become, in opposition to the bourgeoisie, one of the constituent factors of the institutions of representative democracy. Class contradictions are located *between* the state and the popular masses standing outside the state. This remains true right up to the crisis of dual power, when the state is effectively dismantled through the centralization at national level of a parallel power, which becomes the real power (soviets). Thus:

(1) The struggle of the popular masses for state power is, in essence, a frontal struggle of manoeuvre or encirclement, taking place outside the fortress-state and principally aiming at the creation of a situation of dual power.

(2) While it would be hasty to identify this conception with an assault strategy concentrated in a precise moment or 'big day' (insurrection, political general strike, etc.) it quite clearly lacks the strategic vision of a *process* of transition to socialism — that is, of a long stage during which the masses will act to conquer power and transform the state apparatuses. It presents these changes as possible only in a situation of dual power, characterized by a highly precarious balance of forces between the state/bourgeoisie and the soviets/working class. The 'revolutionary situation' is itself reduced to a crisis of the state that cannot but involve its breakdown.

(3) The state is supposed to hold pure power — a quantifiable substance that has to be seized from it. 'To take' state power therefore means to occupy, during the interval of dual power, all the parts of the instrument-state: to take charge of the summit of its apparatuses, assuming the commanding positions within the state machinery and operating its

controls in such a way as to replace it by the second, soviet power. A citadel can be taken only if, during the dual power situation, ditches, ramparts and casements of its instrumental structure have already been captured and dismantled in favour of something else (soviets); and this something else (the second power) is supposed to lie entirely outside the fortified position of the state. This conception, then, is still marked by permanent scepticism as to the possibility of mass intervention within the state itself.

(4) How does the transformation of the state apparatus appear during the transition to socialism? It is first of all necessary to take state power, and then, after the fortress has been captured, to raze to the ground the entire state apparatus, replacing it by the second power (soviets) constituted as a state of a new type.

Here we can recognize a basic distrust of the institutions of representative democracy and of political freedoms. But if these are still regarded as creations and instruments of the bourgeoisie, the conception of soviets has in the meantime undergone significant changes. What is to replace the bourgeois state *en bloc* is no longer direct, rank-and-file democracy. The soviets are now not so much an anti-state as a *parallel state* — one copied from the instrumental model of the existing state, and possessing a proletarian character in so far as its summit is controlled/occupied by a 'single' revolutionary party which itself functions according to the model of the state. Distrust of the possibility of mass intervention within the bourgeois state has become distrust of the popular movement as such. This is called strengthening the state/soviets, the better to make it wither away in the future . . . *And so was Stalinist statism born.*

We can now see the deep complicity between this Stalinist kind of statism and that of traditional social democracy. For the latter is also characterized by basic distrust of direct, rank-and-file democracy and popular initiative. For it too, the popular masses stand in a relationship of externality to a state that possesses power and constitutes an essence. Here the state is a subject, bearing an intrinsic rationality that is incarnated by political élites and the very mechanism of representative democracy. Accordingly, occupation of the state involves replacing the top leaders by an enlightened left élite and, if necessary, making a few adjustments to the way in which the existing institutions function; it is left as understood that the state will thereby bring socialism to the popular masses from above. *This then is the techno-bureaucratic statism of the experts.*

Stalinist state-worship, social-democratic state-worship: this is indeed one of the traditions of the popular movement. But to escape from it through the other tradition of direct, rank-and-file democracy or self-management would really be too good to be true. We should not forget the case of Lenin himself and the seeds of statism contained in the original workers' councils experience. The basic dilemma from which we must extricate ourselves is the following: *either* maintain the existing state and stick exclusively to a modified form of representative democracy — a road that ends up in social-democratic statism and so-called liberal parliamentarianism; *or* base everything on direct, rank-and-file democracy or the movement for self-management — a path which, sooner or later, inevitably leads to statist despotism or the dictatorship of experts. The essential problem of the democratic road to socialism, of democratic socialism, must be posed in a different way: *how is it possible radically to transform the state in such a manner that the extension and deepening of political freedoms and the institutions of representative democracy* (which were also a conquest of the popular masses) *are combined with the unfurling of forms of direct democracy and the mushrooming of self-management bodies?*

Not only did the notion of dictatorship of the proletariat fail to pose this problem; it ended by obscuring it. For Marx, the dictatorship of the proletariat was a notion of applied strategy, serving at most as a signpost. It referred to the class nature of the state and to the necessity of its transformation in the transition to socialism and the process of withering away of the state. Now, although the object to which it referred is still real, the notion has come to play a precise historical role: it obscures the fundamental problem of combining a transformed representative democracy with direct, rank-and-file democracy. It is for these reasons, and not because the notion eventually became identified with Stalinist totalitarianism, that its abandonment is, in my opinion, justified. [. . .]

This then is the basic problem of democratic socialism. It does not concern only the so-called developed countries, for there is no strategic model exclusively adapted to these countries. In fact, there is no longer a question of building 'models' of any kind whatsoever. All that is involved is a set of signposts which, drawing on the lessons of the past, point out the traps to anyone wishing to avoid certain well-known destinations. The problem concerns every transition to socialism, even though it may present itself quite differently in various countries. This much we know already: socialism cannot be democratic here and of another kind over there. The concrete situation may of course differ, and the strategies undoubtedly have to be adapted to the country's specific features. But democratic socialism is the only kind possible.

With regard to this socialism, to the democratic road to socialism, the current situation in Europe presents a number of peculiarities: these concern at one and the same time the new social relations, the state form that is being established, and the precise character of the crisis of the state. For certain European countries, these particularities constitute so many chances — probably unique in world history — for the success of a democratic socialist experience, articulating transformed representative democracy and direct, rank-and-file democracy. This entails the elaboration of a new strategy with respect both to the capture of state power by the popular masses and their organizations, and to the transformations of the state designated by the term 'democratic road to socialism'.

Today less than ever is the state an ivory tower isolated from the popular masses. Their struggles constantly traverse the state, even when they are not physically present in its apparatuses. Dual power, in which frontal struggle is concentrated in a precise moment, is not the only situation that allows the popular masses to carry out an action in the sphere of the state. The democratic road to socialism is a long process, in which the struggle of the popular masses does not seek to create an effective dual power parallel and external to the state, but brings itself to bear on the internal contradictions of the state. To be sure, the seizure of power always presupposes a crisis of the state (such as exists today in certain European countries); but this crisis, which sharpens the very internal contradictions of the state, cannot be reduced to a breakdown of the latter. To take or capture state power is not simply to lay hands on part of the state machinery in order to replace it with a second power. Power is not a quantifiable substance held by the state that must be taken out of its hands, but rather a series of relations among the various social classes. In its ideal form, power is concentrated in the state, which is thus itself the condensation of a particular class relationship of forces. The state is neither a thing-instrument that may be taken away, nor a fortress that may be penetrated by means of a wooden horse, nor yet a safe that may be cracked by burglary: it is the heart of the exercise of political power.

For state power to be taken, a mass struggle must have unfolded in such a way as to modify the relationship of forces within the state apparatuses, themselves the strategic site of political struggle.

For a dual-power type of strategy, however, the decisive shift in the relationship of forces takes place not within the state but between the state and the masses outside. In the democratic road to socialism, the long process of taking power essentially consists in the spreading, development, reinforcement, coordination and direction of those diffuse centres of resistance which the masses always possess within the state network, in such a way that they become the real centres of power on the strategic terrain of the state. It is therefore not a question of a straight choice between frontal war of movement and war of position, because in Gramsci's use of the term, the latter always comprises encirclement of a fortress state.

I can already hear the question: have we then given in to traditional reformism? In order to answer this, we must examine how the question of reformism was posed by the Third International. As a matter of fact, it regarded every strategy other than that of dual power as reformist. The only radical break allowing the seizure of state power, the only meaningful break making it possible to escape from reformism was the break between the state (as a simple instrument of the bourgeoisie external to the masses) and a second power (the masses/soviets) lying wholly outside the state. By the way, this did not prevent the emergence of a reformism peculiar to the Third International — one bound up precisely with the instrumental conception of the state. Quite the contrary! You corner some loose parts of the state machinery and collect a few isolated bastions while *awaiting* a dual power situation. Then, as time passes, dual power goes by the board: all that remains is the instrument-state which you capture cog by cog or whose command posts you take over.

Now, reformism is an ever-latent danger, not a vice inherent in any strategy other than that of dual power — even if, in the case of a democratic road to socialism, the criterion of reformism is not as sharp as in the dual-power strategy, and even if (there is no point in denying it) the risks of social-democratization are thereby increased. At any event, to shift the relationship of forces within the state does not mean to win successive reforms in an unbroken chain, to conquer the state machinery piece by piece, or simply to occupy the positions of government. It denotes nothing other than a *stage of real breaks*, the climax of which — and there has to be one — is reached when the relationship of forces on the strategic terrain of the state swings over to the side of the popular masses.

This democratic road to socialism is therefore not simply a parliamentary or electoral road. Waiting for an electoral majority (in parliament or for a presidential candidate) can be only a moment, however important that may be; and its achievement is not necessarily the climax of breaks within the state. The shift in the relationship of forces within the state touches its apparatuses and mechanisms as a whole; it does not affect only parliament or, as is so often repeated nowadays, the ideological state apparatuses that are supposed to play the determining role in the 'contemporary' state. The process extends also, and above all, to the repressive state apparatuses that hold the monopoly of legitimate physical violence: especially the army and the police. But just as we should not forget the particular role of these apparatuses (as is frequently done by versions of the democratic road that are founded on a misinterpretation of some of Gramsci's theses), so we should not imagine that the strategy of modifying the relationship of forces within the state is valid only for the ideological apparatuses, and that the repressive apparatuses, completely isolated from popular struggle, can be taken only by frontal, external attack. In short, we cannot add together two strategies, retaining the dual-power perspective in relation to the repressive apparatuses. Obviously, a shift in the balance of forces within the repressive apparatuses poses special, and therefore formidable, problems. But as the case of Portugal showed with perfect clarity, these apparatuses are themselves traversed by the struggles of the popular masses.

Furthermore, the real alternative raised by the democratic road to socialism is indeed that of a struggle of the popular masses to modify the relationship of forces within the state, as opposed to a frontal, dual-power type of strategy. The choice is not, as is often thought, between a struggle 'within' the state apparatuses (that is, physically invested and inserted in their material space) and a struggle located at a certain physical distance from these apparatuses. *First,* because any struggle at a distance always has effects within the state: it is always there, even if only in a refracted manner and through intermediaries. *Second,* and most important, because struggle at a distance from the state apparatuses, whether within or beyond the limits of the physical space traced by the institutional *loci,* remains necessary at all times and in every case, since it reflects the autonomy of the struggles and organizations of the popular masses. It is not simply a matter of entering state institutions (parliament, economic and social councils, 'planning' bodies, etc.) in order to use their characteristic levers for a good purpose. In addition, struggle must always express itself in the development of popular movements, the mushrooming of demo-cratic organs at the base, and the rise of centres of self-management.

It should not be forgotten that the above points refer not only to transformations of the state, but also to the basic question of state power and power in general. The question of *who* is in power *to do what* cannot be isolated from these struggles for self-management or direct democracy. But if they are to modify the relations of power, such struggles or movements cannot tend towards centralization in a second power; they must rather seek to shift the relationship of forces on the terrain of the state itself. This then is the real alternative, and not the simple opposition between 'internal' and 'external' struggle. In the democratic road to socialism, these two forms of struggle must be combined. In other words, whether or not one becomes 'integrated' in the state apparatuses and plays the game of the existing power is not reducible to the choice between internal and external struggle. Such integration does not necessarily follow from a strategy of effecting changes on the terrain of the state. To think that it does is to imagine that political struggle can ever be located wholly outside the state.

This strategy of taking power leads on directly to the question of transformations of the state in a democratic road to socialism. Authoritarian statism can be avoided only by combining the transformation of representative democracy with the development of forms of direct, rank-and-file democracy or the movement for self-management. But this in turn raises fresh problems. In the dual-power strategy, which envisages straightforward replacement of the state apparatus with an apparatus of councils, taking state power is treated as a preliminary to its destruction/replacement. Transformation of the state apparatus does not really enter into the matter: first of all the existing state power is taken, and then another is put in its place. This view of things can no longer be accepted. If taking power denotes a shift in the relationship of forces within the state, and if it is recognized that this will involve a long process of change, then the seizure of state power will entail concomitant transformations of its apparatuses. It is true that the state retains a specific materiality: not only is a shift in the relationship of forces within the state insufficient to alter that materiality, but the relationship itself can crystallize in the state only to the extent that the apparatuses of the latter undergo transformation. In abandoning the dual-power strategy, we do not throw overboard, but pose in a different fashion, the question of the state's materiality as a specific apparatus.

In this context, I talked above of a *sweeping transformation* of the state apparatus during the transition to democratic socialism. Although this term certainly has a demonstrative value, it seems to indicate a general direction, before which — if I dare say so — stand two red lights. First, the expression 'sweeping transformation of the state apparatus in the democratic road to socialism' suggests that there is no longer a place for what has traditionally been called *smashing* or *destroying* that apparatus. The fact remains, however, that the term smashing, which Marx too used for indicative purposes, came in the end to designate a very precise historical phenomenon: namely, the eradication of any kind of representative democracy or 'formal' liberties in favour purely of direct, rank-and-file democracy and so-called real liberties. It is necessary to take sides. If we understand the democratic road to socialism and democratic socialism itself to involve, among other things, political (party) and ideological pluralism, recognition of the role of universal suffrage, and extension and deepening of all political freedoms including for opponents, then talk of smashing or destroying the state apparatus can be no more than a mere verbal trick. What is involved, through all the various transforma-tions, is a real permanence and continuity of the institutions of representative democracy — not as unfortunate relics to be tolerated for as long as necessary, but as an essential condition of democratic socialism.

Now we come to the second red light: the term 'sweeping transformation' accurately designates both the direction and the means of changes in the state apparatus. There can be no question of merely secondary adjustments (such as those envisaged by neo-liberal conceptions of a revived *de jure* state), nor of changes coming mainly from above (according to the vision of traditional social democracy or liberalized Stalinism). There can be no question of a statist transformation of the state apparatus. *Transformation of the state apparatus tending towards the wither-ing away of the state* can rest only on increased intervention of the popular masses in the state: certainly through their trade union and political forms of representation, but also through their own initiatives within the state itself. This will proceed by stages, but it cannot be confined to mere democratization of the state — whether in relation to parliament, political liberties, the role of parties, democratization of the union and political apparatuses themselves, or to decentralization.

This process should be accompanied with the development of new forms of direct, rank-and-file democracy, and the flowering of self-management networks and centres. Left to itself, the trans-formation of the state apparatus and the development of represen-tative democracy would be incapable of avoiding statism. But there is another side to the coin: a unilateral and univocal shift of the centre of gravity towards the self-management movement would likewise make it impossible, in the medium term, to avoid techno-bureaucratic statism and authoritarian confiscation of power by the experts. This could take the form of centralization in a second power, which quite simply replaces the mechanisms of representative democracy. [...]

As we see then, the task is really not to 'synthesize' or stick together the statist and self-management traditions of the popular movement, but rather to open up a *global perspective of the withering away of the state.* This comprises *two* articulated processes: transformation of the state and unfurling of direct, rank-and-file democracy. We know the consequences of the formal split between the two traditions that has arisen out of the disarticulation of these processes. However, while it alone is capable of leading to democratic socialism, this path has a reverse side: two dangers are lying in wait for it.

The first of these is the *reaction of the enemy*, in this case the bourgeoisie. Although old and well-known, this danger appears here in a particularly acute form. The classical reponse of the dual-power strategy was precisely destruction of the state apparatus — an attitude which in a certain sense remains valid, since truly profound breaks are required, rather than secondary modifications of the state apparatus. But it remains valid in one sense only. In so far as what is involved is no longer destruction of that apparatus and its replacement with a second power, but rather a long process of transformation, the enemy has greater possibilities of boycotting an experience of democratic socialism and of brutally intervening to cut it short. Clearly, the democratic road to socialism will not simply be a peaceful changeover.

It is possible to confront this danger through active reliance on a broad, popular movement. Let us be quite frank. As the decisive means to the realization of its goals and to the articulation of the two preventives against statism and the social-democratic impasse, the democratic road to socialism, unlike the 'vanguardist' dual-power strategy, presupposes the continuous support of a mass movement founded on broad popular alliances. If such a movement (what Gramsci called the active, as opposed to the passive, revolution) is not deployed and active, if the Left does not succeed in arousing one, then nothing will prevent social-democratization of the experience: however radical they may be, the various programmes will change little of relevance. A broad popular movement constitutes a guarantee against the reaction of the enemy, even though it is not sufficient and must always be linked to sweeping transformations of the state. That is the dual lesson we can draw from Chile: the ending of the Allende experience was due not only to the lack of such changes, but also to the fact that the intervention of the bourgeoisie (itself expressed in that lack) was made possible by the breakdown of alliances among the popular classes, particularly between the working class and the petty bourgeoisie. Even before the coup took place, this had broken the momentum of support for the Popular Unity government. In order to arouse this broad movement, the Left must equip itself with the necessary means, taking up especially new popular demands on fronts that used to be wrongly called 'secondary' (women's struggles, the ecological movement, and so on).

The second question concerns the *forms of articulation* of the two processes: transformations of the state and of representative democracy, and development of direct democracy and the movement for self-management. The new problems arise as soon as it is no longer a question of suppressing the one in favour of the other, whether through straightforward elimination or — which comes to the same thing — through integration of the one in the other (of, for example, self-management centres in the institutions of representative democracy); that is to say, as soon as it is no longer a question of assimilating the two processes. How is it possible to avoid being drawn into mere parallelism or juxtaposition, whereby each follows its own specific course? In what fields, concerning which decisions, and at what points in time should representative assemblies have precedence over the centres of direct democracy: parliament over factory committees, town councils over citizens' committees — or *vice versa*? Given that up to a point conflict will be inevitable, how should it be resolved without leading, slowly but surely, to an embryonic or fully fledged situation of *dual power*?

This time, dual power would involve two powers of the Left — a left government and a second power composed of popular organs. And, as we know from the case of Portugal, even when two forces of the Left are involved, the situation in no way resembles a free play of powers and counter-powers balancing one another for the greatest good of socialism and democracy. It rather quickly leads to open opposition, in which there is a risk that one will be eliminated in favour of the other. In one case (e.g. Portugal), the result is social-democratization, while in the other variant — elimination of representative democracy — it is not the withering of the state or the triumph of direct democracy that eventually emerges, but a new type of authoritarian dictatorship. But in either case, the state will always end up the winner. Of course, there is a strong chance that, even before dual power reaches that outcome, something else will happen — something that Portugal just managed to avoid — namely, the brutal, Fascist-type reaction of a bourgeoisie that can always be relied upon to stay in the game. Thus, open opposition between these two powers seriously threatens, after a first stage of real paralysis of the state, to be resolved by a third contender, the bourgeoisie, according to scenarios that are not difficult to imagine. I said third contender, but it will not have escaped the reader's notice that in all these cases (Fascist-type intervention, social-democratization, authoritarian dictatorship of experts on the ruins of direct democracy) this contender is in one form or another ultimately the same: the bourgeoisie.

What then is the solution, the answer to all that? I could, of course, point to the observations made above, to the numerous works, research projects and discussions under way more or less throughout Europe, as well as to the partial experiences now taking place at regional, municipal or self-management level. But these offer no easy recipe for a solution, since the answer to such questions does not yet exist — not even as a model theoretically guaranteed in some holy text or other. History has not yet given us a successful experience of the democratic road to socialism: what it has provided — and that is not insignificant — is some negative examples to avoid and some mistakes upon which to reflect. It can naturally always be argued, in the name of realism (either by proponents of the dictatorship of the proletariat or by the others, the orthodox neo-liberals), that if democratic socialism has never yet existed, this is because it is impossible. Maybe. We no longer share that belief in the millenium founded on a few iron laws concerning the inevitability of a democratic-socialist revolution; nor do we enjoy the support of a fatherland of democratic socialism. But one thing is certain: socialism will be democratic or it will not be at all. What is more, optimism about the democratic road to socialism should not lead us to consider it as a royal road, smooth and free of risk. Risks there are, although they are no longer quite where they used to be: at worst, we could be heading for camps and massacres as appointed victims. But to that I reply: if we weigh up the risks, that is in any case preferable to massacring other people only to end up ourselves beneath the blade of a Committee of Public Safety or some Dictator of the proletariat.

There is only one sure way of avoiding the risks of democratic socialism, and that is to keep quiet and march ahead under the tutelage and the rod of advanced liberal democracy. But that is another story.

Note

1.   Rosa Luxemburg (1961) *The Russian Revolution,* Ann Arbor, p. 71.

Index

615